Fodor's

PORTUGAL

WELCOME TO PORTUGAL

Don't be fooled by Portugal's size: this small country is packed with vibrant culture, history, and natural beauty. Nestled between Spain and the Atlantic Ocean, Portugal contains striking landscapes ripe for exploration, from the exceptional beaches of the Algarve to the lush vineyards of the Douro River Valley. Its mountainous interior is dotted with hilltop castles and villages. Whether marveling at azulejo-studded palaces near Lisbon or relaxing in a countryside *pousada* with a glass of port, you'll be charmed by the rich and varied experiences Portugal provides.

TOP REASONS TO GO

★ **Lisbon:** The capital city combines old-time charm with buzzing dining and nightlife.

★ **Castles:** An illustrious hilltop fortress crowns many Portuguese towns.

★ **Beaches:** Whether rock-strewn, stylish, or secluded, beaches abound for all tastes.

★ **Glorious food:** Fresh-caught seafood, well-seasoned stews, flavorful pastries.

★ **Douro River cruises:** Scenic boat trips wind past stunning valleys and vineyards.

★ **Port vineyards:** There's no better place to sample Portugal's most renowned drink.

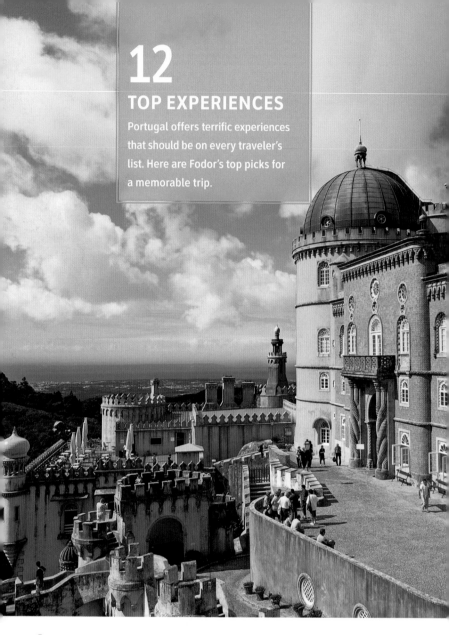

12
TOP EXPERIENCES

Portugal offers terrific experiences that should be on every traveler's list. Here are Fodor's top picks for a memorable trip.

1 Sintra

A UNESCO World Heritage Site, the town of Sintra teems with gorgeous palaces and gardens. The surrounding hills form a romantic backdrop for its historic charms. *(Ch. 3)*

2 Azulejos

Brightly colored ceramic tiles adorn numerous fountains, churches, and palaces, including the Queluz National Palace (pictured), throughout the country. *(Ch. 1)*

3 Port Wine Tasting

Near Porto, you can tour the caves that store Portugal's most famous drink. Top off the experience with generous tasting sessions. *(Ch. 1, 8)*

4 Pousadas

Spice up your trip with a stay in a *pousada*. These lodgings in restored castles, monasteries, and historic buildings meld luxury with regional charm. *(Ch. 4, 5, 7, 8)*

5 Porto

Porto is a travel destination in its own right, with Michelin-starred restaurants, restored historic sites, and breathtaking beaches. *(Ch. 8)*

6 Douro River Cruises

A cruise is a relaxing way to explore the eye-opening landscapes of the Douro River Valley, with its steeply terraced vineyards. *(Ch. 8)*

7 Évora

One of Portugal's best-preserved medieval towns, Évora has fortified walls and winding cobblestone lanes lined with Roman and Gothic architecture. *(Ch. 5)*

8 Lisbon

The vibrant capital encompasses cobblestoned streets, funicular railways, world-class museums, and top-notch dining, shopping, and nightlife scenes. *(Ch. 2)*

9 Beaches

Take your pick of beautiful beaches—from windswept surfing hubs to unspoiled, sheltered coves—on the long Atlantic coastline. *(Ch. 1, 3, 6)*

10 Fado

Don't miss a performance of this unique musical style at a fado house. Singers croon plaintive tunes to soulful Portuguese guitar accompaniment. *(Ch. 1, 7)*

11 Cafés and Pastelarias

You're never far from a café or pastry shop in Portugal. Be sure to take frequent breaks to savor coffee and delicious pastries like *pastel de nata*, an egg-custard tart. *(Ch. 1)*

12 Hilltop Villages

Fortified medieval walls, narrow streets, dramatic castles, and spectacular views of the countryside make these stunning settlements irresistible. *(Ch. 1, 4, 5)*

CONTENTS

1 EXPERIENCE PORTUGAL...... 13
What's Where 14
Need to Know 16
Portugal Today............. 18
Quintessential Portugal 20
Top Castles in Portugal 22
Portugal Like a Local.......... 23
If You Like................... 24
Flavors of Portugal 26
Portuguese Wine 28
Art, Architecture, and Azulejos.... 30
Golfing in Portugal 31
Great Itineraries 32
On The Calendar 39

2 LISBON...................... 45
Orientation and Planning....... 47
Exploring................... 56
Where to Eat 80
Where to Stay 93
Nightlife and Performing Arts ... 102
Sports and the Outdoors 109
Shopping 110

3 SIDE TRIPS FROM LISBON ... 117
Orientation and Planning...... 118
The Estoril Coast 124
Sintra and Queluz.......... 135
The Setúbal Peninsula....... 145

4 ESTREMADURA AND
THE RIBATEJO 157
Orientation and Planning...... 159
Estremadura 165
The Ribatejo 193

5 ÉVORA AND THE ALENTEJO.. 211
Orientation and Planning...... 212
Évora 216
Side Trips from Évora........ 227
Alto Alentejo 229
Baixo Alentejo 249

6 THE ALGARVE................ 263
Orientation and Planning...... 265
Faro and Nearby............ 271
The Eastern Algarve 279
The Central Algarve 283
Lagos and the Western Algarve.. 302

7 COIMBRA AND THE BEIRAS .. 313
Orientation and Planning...... 314
Coimbra 319
The Western Beiras.......... 329
The Eastern Beiras 350

8 PORTO AND THE NORTH 359
Orientation and Planning...... 361
Porto 366
The Coast and the Douro...... 385
The Minho and the Costa Verde . 397
Trás-os-Montes............. 412

PORTUGUESE
VOCABULARY 419

TRAVEL SMART PORTUGAL .. 425

INDEX 442

ABOUT OUR WRITERS 456

MAPS

Lisbon 48–49

Alfama 58

Baixa, Chiado, and Bairro Alto. . . . 64

The Modern City. 70

Alcântara and Belém. 76

Where to Eat in Lisbon 82–83

Where to Stay in Lisbon. 96–97

The Estoril Coast, Sintra,
and Queluz 127

The Setúbal Peninsula 147

Estremadura and the Ribatejo. . . 164

Évora 220

Side Trips from Évora
and Alto Alentejo 230

Baixo Alentejo 250

The Algarve 270

Faro. 272

Lagos 304

Coimbra 322

The Beiras. 330–331

Porto. 374

The Coast and the Douro,
the Minho and the Costa Verde,
and Trás-os-Montes. 386

ABOUT THIS GUIDE

Fodor's Recommendations
Everything in this guide is worth doing—we don't cover what isn't—but exceptional sights, hotels, and restaurants are recognized with additional accolades. Fodor'sChoice★ indicates our top recommendations. Care to nominate a new place? Visit Fodors.com/contact-us.

Trip Costs
We list prices wherever possible to help you budget well. Hotel and restaurant price categories from $ to $$$$ are noted alongside each recommendation. For hotels, we include the lowest cost of a standard double room in high season. For restaurants, we cite the average price of a main course at dinner or, if dinner isn't served, at lunch. For attractions, we always list adult admission fees; discounts are usually available for children, students, and senior citizens.

Hotels
Our local writers vet every hotel to recommend the best overnights in each price category, from budget to expensive. Unless otherwise specified, you can expect private bath, phone, and TV in your room. For expanded hotel reviews, facilities, and deals visit Fodors.com.

Top Picks	Hotels & Restaurants
★ Fodor'sChoice	🏨 Hotel
	🛏 Number of rooms
Listings	🍽 Meal plans
⊠ Address	✕ Restaurant
⊠ Branch address	⟲ Reservations
☎ Telephone	👔 Dress code
🖷 Fax	▭ No credit cards
⊕ Website	$ Price
✉ E-mail	
✉ Admission fee	**Other**
⊙ Open/closed times	⇨ See also
Ⓜ Subway	☞ Take note
⊹ Directions or Map coordinates	⚑ Golf facilities

Restaurants
Unless we state otherwise, restaurants are open for lunch and dinner daily. We mention dress code only when there's a specific requirement and reservations only when they're essential or not accepted.

Credit Cards
The hotels and restaurants in this guide typically accept credit cards. If not, we'll say so.

EUGENE FODOR

Hungarian-born Eugene Fodor (1905–91) began his travel career as an interpreter on a French cruise ship. The experience inspired him to write *On the Continent* (1936), the first guidebook to receive annual updates and discuss a country's way of life as well as its sights. Fodor later joined the U.S. Army and worked for the OSS in World War II. After the war, he kept up his intelligence work while expanding his guidebook series. During the Cold War, many guides were written by fellow agents who understood the value of insider information. Today's guides continue Fodor's legacy by providing travelers with timely coverage, insider tips, and cultural context.

EXPERIENCE
PORTUGAL

WHAT'S WHERE

Numbers refer to chapters.

2 Lisbon. One of Europe's smallest and sunniest capitals, Lisbon encompasses dramatic contrasts. The cobbled streets of Alfama complement Chiado's hip cafés and boutiques; out of 18th-century buildings skip stylish youths, and vibrant street art brightens walls while white sheets hang from windows to dry in the sun.

3 Side trips from Lisbon. The fairy-tale castles of Sintra are just a short train ride from Lisbon; windswept surf beaches lie nearby. Nearby at Cascais and Estoril, tourists can enjoy family-friendly beaches or try their luck at one of Europe's largest casinos. South of the River Tagus lie the dramatic mountains and pine forests of Serra da Arrabida, fresh local seafood at the seaside fishing town of Sesimbra, and endless white-sand beaches and dolphin-spotting boat trips on the Setúbal Peninsula.

4 Estremadura and the Ribatejo. This region to the north and east of Lisbon boasts several UNESCO World Heritage Sites, including the headquarters of the Knights Templar, the Convento de Cristo. The region is also the place to come for monster waves and sophisticated surf accommodations.

5 Évora and the Alentejo. In Évora, medieval walls encircle palatial buildings and a Roman temple: an architectural gem in one of Portugal's poorest regions. Thinly populated, the Alentejo is bracketed by spectacular but windy Atlantic beaches and the striking Guadiana Valley. Known as the "bread basket of Portugal," the Alentejo is also famed for its excellent wine: half the *vinho* in the country is produced here.

6 The Algarve. Sheltered by the Serra de Monchique and Serra de Caldeirão ranges to the north, the Algarve is Portugal's main holiday destination thanks to 3,000 hours of sunshine a year sweeping beaches, and ample facilities. Although famous for lively resorts, it is still possible to find unspoiled idylls away from the crowds.

7 Coimbra and the Beiras. The central Beiras region contains Portugal's most spectacular mountain range, the Serra da Estrela, ringed by towns that are home to superb Renaissance art. Just inland from the coast lies the university city of Coimbra, home to handsome historic buildings.

8 Porto and the North. The green Minho region is home to *vinho verde*, a distinctive young wine. Porto is a captivating mix of medieval and modern, its center a UNESCO World Heritage Site. Grapes for the port wine shipped from here come from the Douro Valley—part of ruggedly beautiful Trás-os-Montes.

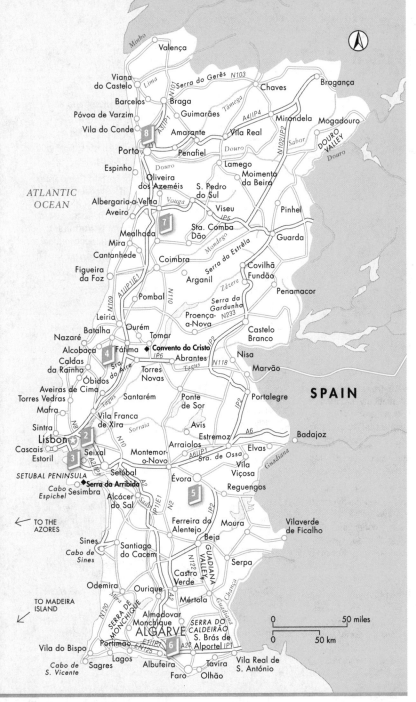

NEED TO KNOW

North Atlantic Ocean

PORTUGAL

Lisbon

AT A GLANCE

Capital: Lisbon

Population: 10,000,000

Currency: Euro

Money: ATMs are common

Language: Portuguese

Country Code: 351

Emergencies: ☏ 112

Driving: On the right

Electricity: 220-240V; electrical plugs have two round prongs

Time: Five hours ahead of New York

Documents: Up to 90 days with valid passport; Schengen rules apply

Mobile Phones: GSM (900 and 1800 bands)

Major Mobile Companies: Nós, TMN, Vodafone

WEBSITES

Portugal Government:
⊕ www.turismodeportugal.pt

Portugal Tourism:
⊕ www.visitportugal.com

Portugal Tips:
⊕ www.portugal.com

GETTING AROUND

✈ **Air Travel:** The major international airport is Lisbon; Faro and Porto have many intra-Europe flights.

🚌 **Bus Travel:** Comfortable express buses travel between main regions.

🚗 **Car Travel:** Rental cars are popular among tourists and generally a safe, reliable option, but driving in big cities such as Lisbon and Porto is not for the faint-hearted. Never leave valuables visible in the car.

🚆 **Train Travel:** The high-speed Alfa-Pendular train darts between the Algarve, Lisbon, and Porto. Slower regional and urban services travel within regions.

PLAN YOUR BUDGET

	HOTEL ROOM	MEAL	ATTRACTIONS
Low Budget	€100	€15	Jerónimos Monastery, €7
Mid Budget	€150	€25	Oceanarium, €14
High Budget	€300	€150	Yacht trip with dinner for two, €150

WAYS TO SAVE

Grab a takeaway. Take-out shops offer grilled meats like the famous piri-piri chicken, a great meal with fries or rice, a simple salad, and a glass of white wine.

Home away from home. There are plenty of lovely family-run guesthouses (called residenciais) throughout Portugal at a fraction of the price of a hotel.

Buy travel passes in advance. Buy rail, bus, and Metro tickets in advance online.

Party like a local. Join any local festivities, as most will feature traditional food, drink, music, and dancing.

Hassle Factor	Medium. There are some nonstop flights to Lisbon from some U.S. airports (New York, Miami), but more often you will have to connect elsewhere in Europe.
3 days	Explore the history and charm of Lisbon and its surrounding areas like Sintra.
1 week	Explore Lisbon, and then catch the high-speed Alfa-Pendular and spend a night either in the Algarve or in Porto.
2 weeks	After exploring the capital, head south to the Algarve, making sure you stop at a vineyard in the Alentejo. From the Algarve catch a cheap domestic flight all the way north to Porto and spend another few days there before returning to Lisbon.

WHEN TO GO

High Season: June through September is the busiest, hottest, and most expensive time to visit Portugal. While the north of the country remains cooler and quieter, Lisbon and the Algarve can be sweltering. Most Lisbon locals head south for the summer holidays.

Low Season: Winter in Portugal is growing in popularity due to the agreeable temperatures year-round and lower hotel prices. Off-season activities are still varied and plentiful, and while the beach may be off the menu, pleasant strolls and cozy evenings are definitely on it.

Value Season: Spring and autumn are both stunning seasons in which to visit Portugal. In April and October you may be lucky enough to enjoy a bracing dip in the pool or sea. Almond and orange blossoms perfume the air, key regions are quieter, and room prices have not yet peaked.

BIG EVENTS

February: Carnival fever sweeps the country in February, with one of the biggest parades in Torres Vedras. ⊕ www.carnavaldetorres.com

April: Lisbon hosts the Portugal Open tennis tournament at the end of April.

June: Porto explodes on June 23 (St. John the Baptist's Day). ⊕ www.portoturismo.pt

November: Festivities throughout the country celebrate São Martinho (St. Martin), with the focus on chestnuts and wine.

READ THIS

■ *The Food of Portugal,* Jean Anderson. All about Portuguese cuisine.

■ *Journey to Portugal: A Pursuit of Portugal's History and Culture,* José Saramago. The Nobel Prize–winner recalls a trip in 1979.

■ *Portugal and the Algarve: Now and Then,* Jenny Grainer. Memoirs of a long-time expat.

WATCH THIS

■ *Lisbon Story.* The fictional story of the capital city.

■ *Fados.* Explores the melancholic Portuguese music.

■ *Night Train to Lisbon.* Acclaimed intellectual thriller that explores Portugal's era of dictatorship.

EAT THIS

■ *Bacalhau á brás*: shredded codfish with egg and onion

■ *Paté de sardinha*: sardine pâté to spread on bread as a starter

■ *Pastel de nata*: a delicious custard tart

■ *Ensopado de borrego*: slow-roasted-lamb stew with bread

■ *Peixe grelhado*: grilled fish, found in abundance in restaurants along the coast

■ *Arroz de pato*: oven-baked, shredded duck with rice and chouriço on top

PORTUGAL TODAY

Portugal harkens back to a golden age. Some 500 years ago, Portugal was the richest country on Earth, and fascinating evidence of that storied past still abounds, from Vasco de Gama's old haunts to soaring castles and intricate medieval quarters. From the 14th century onward, Portugal's mariners plied far-flung sea routes, bringing back spices, gold, and a worldly outlook that's still evident today.

Unfortunately, Portugal is beset by economic problems and struggling to emerge from its worst economic depression since democracy arrived in the 1970s. Portugal's bailout by international creditors has ushered in a new era of austerity, and some of the country's youth are looking abroad for jobs even as young foreigners flock to Lisbon, where the lure of affordable rents, a buzzing creative scene, and lots of sunshine have made it a tech hub and major destination for startups.

Portuguese ingenuity and creativity are undiminished. While austerity has sparked violent street demonstrations in Greece and Spain, the Portuguese are more melancholy, singing folk songs in the streets. In sectors hit by globalization, such as textiles, firms are fighting back by specializing and increasing the value added to products. Portuguese winemakers are raising their international profile, applying new methods to a unique roster of native grape varieties. Portuguese chefs are finally catching up with their Spanish peers in applying new techniques to traditional dishes. And a fledgling new industry of renewable energy—produced by wind, sun, and even tides—is branding Portugal the new "west coast of Europe," California-style.

Today's Portugal

...is enjoying a renewed tourism boom. Despite fears that Portugal's EU bailout would send tourist numbers into a downward spin, tourism has surged. Hotel occupancy has been rising steadily since 2010, and in 2015, Portugal's visitor numbers topped 10 million for the first time. The Lisbon area is now a leading destination for corporate conferences, thanks to mild out-of-season weather, still-affordable facilities, and friendly locals. And with low-cost flights from northern Europe, Porto, too, with a similar combination of picturesque old and trendy new, is emerging as one of Europe's top urban break destinations.

...is proud of its traditions. Throughout the year, traditional *festas* are held up and

WHAT WE'RE TALKING ABOUT

Futebol (soccer) remains an obsession in Portugal: the three top-selling dailies are dedicated to it. Summer 2016 will go down in history as the year Portugal won the UEFA European Cup for the first time, and cities exploded into colorful celebrations. Today one footballer above all is a source of enormous national pride: Cristiano Ronaldo, captain of the Portuguese national team, currently plays in Madrid but is a hero to local fans. Foreign spectators may boo his on-field petulance, but here he appears in ads for everything from banks to hair gel. In 2016, Ronaldo opened the first of several boutique hotels on the island of Madeira.

Portugal's art scene has been shaken up by Joana Vasconcelos, who came to international attention with *The Bride*—a down the country on local saints' days or in line with ancient pagan traditions. Far from being staged for tourists' benefit, festivals are a central part of Portuguese life, and emigrants generally try to ensure that trips home coincide with the local festa. Youngsters these days have a renewed interest in their heritage, and are taking an active part in keeping festival traditions alive—although they also flock to a growing list of vibrant rock festivals.

…is great value. For all the inflationary impact of rising prosperity and entry into the eurozone, Portugal is one of Europe's best-value destinations. Especially in rural areas, you can eat delicious traditional food for as little as €6 for a main dish, a fraction of what you'd pay in a North American city—washed down with flavorful local wine that's often cheaper than bottled water. Portugal is dotted with comfortable bed-and-breakfast accommodations at affordable prices. And all forms of transport, even in the cities, remain amazingly cheap, with a one-way ride anywhere in the Lisbon metro system just €1.40 and a taxi in town as little as €5.

…is facing unprecedented economic and political challenges. As the eurozone faces an existential crisis exacerbated by the U.K.'s vote to leave the European Union, Portugal was one of four countries—and counting—to require a bailout from Europe. The government has slashed spending, cut welfare, and frozen major public works projects—like a high-speed train linking Lisbon to Madrid, which would have cut travel time from nine hours to less than three.

…is committed to a major expansion of renewable energy. Portugal has garnered global attention in recent years with a massive program of investment in renewables; it is now fourth in the European Union in terms of capacity relative to population. The EU is committed to getting 20% of energy from renewable sources by 2020, but Portugal has set more ambitious goals. More than half its electricity already comes from wind, solar, or hydro—saving $1.1 billion a year in oil imports. Despite tight financial conditions, it is also promoting wave-power projects, and rolling out a nationwide network of charging points for electric cars. In May 2016, Portugal made headlines worldwide when it ran entirely on renewable energy sources for four days straight.

chandelier made of thousands of tampons that represented the country at the 2005 Venice Biennale. In her installations, buildings or bridges have been made into artworks with crocheted aprons or colorful stuffed shapes. In 2010, *Marilyn,* a scaled-up shoe inspired by Monroe's heels but made from cooking pans, went for $780,000 at auction. Colorful street art abounds, livening up walls in Lisbon, Porto, and Coimbra. Even in smaller towns, you'll find thoughtful works with a social statement. Big-name Portuguese street artists include Pedro Campiche, Daniel Aime, and Angela Ferreira (Kruella D'Enfer), while works by Brazilian street-art superstars Os Gemeos can be spotted in the capital.

QUINTESSENTIAL PORTUGAL

Pastelarias

Only the staunchest dieter will not be tempted by Portugal's deliciously calorific cakes and pastries. The window displays are real cream-cake affairs, invariably wedged between trendy boutiques catering to fashionable beanpoles. Every region has its specialty sweet treat, known as *doces conventuais* (convent desserts), which usually originates from the local convent. And, yes, they really *are* a touch of heaven. In the Algarve, the Moorish influence is evident in marzipan and almond biscuits. Farther north, in Abrantes, the egg pastries known as *bolo de anjo* (angel cake—those nuns again) have a fluffy melt-in-your-mouth topping. If you are seeking true sublimity, however, bite into a warm *pastéis de nata,* straight from the oven. These custard tarts are made with flaky, light pastry, creamy egg custard, and are best eaten hot, with a sprinkling of cinnamon.

Feiras

The Portuguese love to party and there are countless annual celebrations and festas. Don't miss out when you're visiting, and be sure to check at the local tourist office for upcoming events. The country's fairs and festivals are far more than holidays, they are occasions in which to be immersed with passion and commitment. At saints' days, harvest festivals, pilgrimages, and *feiras* (fairs), you can expect everything from ceremonial pomp and religious processions to wild street parties and quaint traditions. St. John's in Porto (June 23) is a good example of the latter, with everyone hitting each other over the head with plastic hammers or leeks while enjoying a night of drinking, revelry, and dance until dawn in the city streets. In Lisbon, festivals of popular saints dominate the calendar for most of June, with locals gathering to feast on grilled sardines and sangria and dance to *pimba* pop music.

If you want to get a sense of contemporary Portuguese culture, and indulge in some of its pleasure, start by familiarizing yourself with the rituals of daily life. These are a few highlights—things you can take part in with relative ease.

Seafood

Few people understand the bounty of the sea more than the Portuguese. One singularly appetizing delicacy, called *bacalhau* (dried, salted cod), appears on the menu at virtually every restaurant, though it is definitely an acquired taste. There are reputedly 365 ways of preparing this curious delicacy, ranging from roasted with onions and potatoes to fish pie. The Portuguese love affair with seafood encompasses just about everything that swims in the sea, including limpets (normally braised with garlic). Grilled sardines are prevalent as well, but don't expect the canned variety you might be accustomed to (those can be found in any supermarket). The Portuguese prefer to serve them whole, head and all. During the summer, *caracóis* (snails) become the bar snack of choice, with locals gathering over huge bowls to share, and seemingly every bar displays a sign reading *"Há caraóis!"* (We have snails!).

Fado

The dramatic image of a black-shawled fado singer, head thrown back, eyes closed with emotion, has become an emblem of Portugal; the swelling, soulful song with the plaintive *guitarra* (Portuguese guitar) accompaniment embodies Portugal's romantic essence. Fado is so important that when the great *fadista* Amália Rodrigues died in 1999, the government declared three days of national mourning and awarded her a state funeral. When the singing begins in a fado house, talking ceases and a reverent silence descends on the tables. A world of immutable sadness appears, populated by the lost, the poor and oppressed, the abandoned and rejected. You should not miss an opportunity to witness this unique musical style.

TOP CASTLES IN PORTUGAL

It seems as if every Portuguese town with more than a handful of residents has its own castle. The Romans, Visigoths, Moors, Knights Templar, and Catholic kings all chose Portugal as home to their illustrious hilltop fortresses—and many of those castles still remain. Some have been transformed into luxury hotels, while others are mere ruins of the battlements they once were. Built over a millennium ago, they welcome tourists to walk along their ramparts and into their crumbling walls, on a ramble back in time.

The biggest string of Portuguese castles sit atop the low mountains that form a natural boundary with Spain: from Mertola in southern Alentejo, to Miranda do Douro and Bragança in the country's northeast corner. Others dot Portugal's main cities, from Lisbon to Porto.

Unlike in France or Germany, most of Portugal's castles are rustic and unrestored. Local tourist offices offer maps of walking trails around some castles and opening hours and admission charges for the few that you can enter. Be careful to stay within allocated boundaries, and keep children close. They'll love the fairytale setting, but some of the ramparts can be unsteady.

Recommended Castles

Castelo de Almourol: Legend has it that this impressive castle on an island in the Rio Tejo is haunted by the spirit of an ancient princess. With Celtic and Roman foundations, the fortress was rebuilt by the Knights Templar in 1171. The only way to visit is by boat, offering stunning views en route. ⇨ *Chapter 4, Estremadura and the Ribatejo*

Castelo de Marvão: This castle atop a mountain on the edge of the village of Marvão has perhaps the most spectacular setting of any in Portugal, with views of the São Mamede natural park and the border with Spain. The castle walls swell with revelers during Marvão's famed chestnut festival each November. ⇨ *Chapter 5, Évora and the Alentejo*

Castelo de São Jorge: Atop Lisbon's highest hill, this castle has offered the best views over Portugal's capital for more than 1,000 years. First built in the 6th century, the Castelo de São Jorge can singlehandedly tell Portugal's history, having been occupied by the Romans, Visigoths, Moors, Portuguese kings—and now by tourists from around the world. ⇨ *Chapter 2, Lisbon*

Castelo dos Mouros: All that's left of this 9th-century Moorish fortress is its outer walls, which offer one of Portugal's best rampart walks. Atop the castle walls there are excellent views of Sintra's other castle, the Palácio da Pena, and the Atlantic Ocean. ⇨ *Chapter 3, Side Trips from Lisbon*

Palácio da Pena: A UNESCO World Heritage Site, this otherworldly, pastel-color palace in Sintra is one of the best architectural expressions of over-the-top 19th-century Romanticism. It's a favorite among children, and those still young at heart. ⇨ *Chapter 3, Side Trips from Lisbon*

Pousada da Rainha Santa Isabel: One of the few fully restored castles in Portugal, this Estremoz fortress houses one of the country's finest pousadas. After driving out the Moors, Portugal's king chose this hilltop castle as his seat of power. It's named after his wife, Queen Santa Isabel, who lived and died here. *Chapter 5, Évora and the Alentejo*

PORTUGAL LIKE A LOCAL

If you want to get out and experience Portugal like a local, start with the following suggestions.

Drink your coffee neat. Milky coffee is all very well in the morning, but ordering it after a meal definitely marks you as a tourist. The standard local style is neat, or at most with a drop of milk (as a *pingado*), and perhaps with a packet of sugar stirred in. Decaf (*descafeinado*) is now widely available in cafés and restaurants.

Watch the big weekend soccer match. But not in the stadium—in your local bar or café. At any time during the week, one surefire way to get a conversation going is to ask about how Benfica is doing these days: at least a third of the country's population is said to support the club. To really get in tune with the locals, order an *imperial* (small draft beer).

Shop till you drop. Consumerism has swept this previously poverty-stricken country since the 1980s, and you'll find many families at the local megamall on weekends—though outdoor clothes markets remain popular, too. Larger shopping centers have cinemas, bowling alleys, ice rinks, and sometimes even roller coasters.

Choose your beach by its bar. In summer, the lure of the beach is stronger than the mall. A bar or café is invariably close at hand—as well as the lifeguard it is legally obliged to fund. Especially near cities, the kind of people on a beach is determined by the style of the bar that serves it, whether it's for techno-music fans or rents out kitesurfing equipment.

Patronize like-minded businesses. In a country with a history of empire and migration, the name of a business often points to a dramatic life story. Locals know that a hotel named "Pensão Luanda" means the owner was probably born in colonial Angola (and might never have set foot in Portugal before his and other white and mixed-race families were forced to take refuge here). Similarly, a name like "Café Zurich" is a sure sign the owner worked in Switzerland for a spell. Meanwhile, a grocer who migrated to Lisbon from the Beiras region will draw many clients with similar roots, who come to stock up on delicious cheese and sausages from back home.

Nibble local snacks with your beer. A common nibble in drinking dens is a plate of *tremoços* (soaked yellow lupin seeds), which bar staff occasionally hand you for free. Break the skin with your teeth and suck out the flesh; they're salty but strangely addictive. In Lisbon and the south of Portugal, locals might order a plateful of *caracóis*—snails cooked in an herb broth—to accompany their afternoon beer. They're smaller (and cheaper) than the ones you might have sampled in France, and skewering them with a wooden toothpick can be quite a challenge. A chewier snack is *orelha* (pig's ear), usually flavored with cilantro.

Adjust your hours. Touristy restaurants might start serving dinner at 7, but most Portuguese wouldn't dream of dining at that hour. During the week, 8:30 or 9 would be a more normal time for locals to gather, and on Friday or Saturday probably still later. As for going out dancing, don't even bother turning up at a nightclub before 2 am unless you're happy to be the only person on the dance floor.

IF YOU LIKE

Hilltop Villages

The hilltop villages of Portugal are especially beguiling, as they are often made of stone sculpted out of the rock face. Most of them date to Roman times, when they were garrison towns, but they later came in handy during the 17th-century War of Restoration against the Castilians. If you can manage an overnight stay, dusk is the best time of all to visit these castles. Visitors have left and the narrow streets take on a misty, otherworldly air.

Marvão. A small population of 1,000 inhabit this dramatic hilltop village in the Alto Alentejo, which is surrounded by the original 17th-century city walls. A castle founded by the Moors in AD 715 still reigns supreme.

Monsaraz. Another jewel in the Alentejo tiara, this tiny village is surrounded by fascinating Neolithic megaliths. Narrow lanes, lopsided cottages, and a handsome castle are here, together with stunning views of the surrounding olive groves, which are planted in straight lines along the ancient Roman roads.

Óbidos. Whitewashed houses bordering brilliantly colored bougainvillea make up this pretty medieval village, reputedly a wedding gift from Dom Dinis to his wife (beats a mere ring!). Óbidos has plenty of wining and dining choices and several places to stay.

Azulejos

Somehow, no matter how many catalogs you peruse and stores you tramp through, those tiles you end up decorating your bathroom or kitchen with at home just look so plain compared to Portugal's all-encompassing decorative *azulejos*. These colorful tiles are everywhere: houses, shops, monuments, and murals that brighten public spaces all over the country. Azulejos probably came to Portugal from Seville in the 15th century, made by Muslim craftsmen. They at first bore geometric designs, but have since gone through many stylistic revolutions.

Lisbon. The Museu Nacional do Azulejo traces the development of tile making from its Moorish roots. Don't miss the Cervejaria da Trindade, a vaulted beer hall on Rua Nova da Trindade that has stunning azulejos with figurative designs typical of the late 19th century, or the metro stations with their contemplative azulejo designs, including Colégio Militar and Camp Pequeno.

Porto. This is a fabulous city for azulejos, starting at the São Bento train station with its magnificent mural of battle scenes. Churches are literally smothered by tiles here, including the Igreja do Carmo and the Capela das Almas.

Sintra. One of the best places to see the early-16th-century geometric tiles is Sintra's magnificent Palácio Nacional da Pena. Throughout the historic property you'll find beautiful palaces and mansions adorned with azulejos.

Family Pursuits

The Portuguese adore children and welcome them everywhere, including at bars and restaurants where families drink and dine together. If your young ones grow tired of such grown-up pursuits, Portugal also has a healthy dose of sights and activities geared to children of all ages. This is a culture that revolves around family life throughout the day and well into the evening; bedtime is late here, with many children still up at midnight during the summer months.

Algarve. A major holiday destination, the Algarve offers plenty of choice, including water parks, zoos, boat trips, and horse riding. There are also miniature trains that chug around the resorts and, of course, the cheapest activities of all: making sand castles and splashing in the sea.

Churches and Castles. Children will love the fairy-tale quality of Portugal's magnificent churches and castles. Several stand out, including the Knights Templar Convento de Cristo, in Tomar, where kiddies can light a candle and wonder at its otherworldly *Da Vinci Code* feel. The castles at Sintra and Elvas are other winners.

Dinosaurs. For a real Jurassic Park experience check out the fascinating Parque Natural das Serras de Aire e Candeeiros, near Fátima, where you can follow in the footsteps of the dinosaurs. There are special children's tours available; otherwise, just follow the signs.

Beaches

The best-known area for beach holidays is, of course, the Algarve, with its relatively sheltered waters and oodles of tourist facilities. But for unspoiled coastal beauty or the right conditions for water sports, look elsewhere. Even the country's two largest cities have sandy beaches within easy reach, so you can balance sightseeing with sunbathing. If you're going to brave the relatively chilly waters, though, heed the color of the flag flying on the beach: if it's red, stay close to shore.

The Alentejo Coast. Some of Portugal's most stunning beaches are in its undeveloped southwest, protected from overbuilding by a long stretch of coastal national parkland. Towering cliffs give way to empty pristine coves. Until recently, facilities were limited to a couple of local cafés and a pensão, but a recent ecotourism project—a 345-km (215-mile) coastal hiking trail—is bringing more tourists. This area and the western Algarve to the south also draw water-sports enthusiasts, thanks to strong wind and waves.

Around Lisbon. The seemingly endless strands of the Caparica coast draw many of the capital's residents on warm weekends. Each stretch has its own restaurant or bar, with its specific atmosphere and clientele; in summer some later turn into nightclubs, rocking until dawn. Farther south, in the lee of the Serra da Arrábida, sandy beaches are lapped by warmer waters; across the Sado River is Troía's sweep of sands. And there's Guincho, a stunning cliffside beach less than an hour from the capital on public transport, which has often hosted the World Surf Championships.

Around Porto. South of Porto, the dunes around Espinho are topped by wooden decking that is great for lung-filling walks; to the city's north, Póvoa de Varzim is the gateway to the Costa Verde, named for the deep-green pine forests that line the coast.

Estremadura. Perhaps the most varied portion of Portugal's long western coast is in this region, around the fishing ports–cum-resorts of Peniche and Nazaré. The former has become a haven for fashionable international surfers since former Swedish surfing champ John Malmqvist opened Europe's first boutique surf lodge here in 2013, and the latter was made famous the same year when American surfer Garrett McNamara broke the world record for the surfing the biggest wave in the world—a 100-foot monster. Tourists who prefer a less death-defying experience can find excellent and affordable seafood just a few steps away from the beach.

FLAVORS OF PORTUGAL

Cuisine is one of the most integral parts of Portuguese culture. From the café culture to innovative restaurants to the markets and roadside stands found in every city, town, and small village, food (and drink) always seems to be on the mind of the Portuguese people.

Style

The heart of traditional Portuguese cuisine is all about simple yet flavorful home-style comfort food to be enjoyed leisurely with family and friends. Historically, the majority of the Portuguese population was poor farmers, and families depended on what they could grow, raise, or hunt. From these ingredients, families cooked up whatever could be used, with nothing going to waste. Today, much of this family-style cooking and serving remains ingrained in the cuisine, with an emphasis on simple local produce, grains, meats, and fish.

Common Ingredients

Though traditional Portuguese cuisine varies widely throughout each region, there are some general ingredients that you can find used extensively almost everywhere. Onions, garlic, and tomatoes are commonly used as a base, which is found in most stewed and braised fish dishes, such as *caldeirada* (rustic fish stew) and *arroz de marisco* or *tamboril* (shellfish or monkfish stewed with rice). With roasted foods, only roasted garlic and onions tend to be used. *Coentros* (fresh cilantro/coriander) is the favorite seasoning for almost every dish, whether it's stewed or roasted; other common seasonings include *louro* (bay leaf) and *oregãos* (oregano)—both grown and dried locally—and *pimentão doce* (paprika). Spicy food is not that common, but when the Portuguese want to add some spice, they use *piri-piri,* a small, red chili pepper that's also grown locally and can be found both fresh and ground up. Roasted chicken spiced up with piri-piri is a popular dish in the Algarve.

Regional and Seasonal Products

Central and southern Portugal are filled with acres of beautiful orange trees, and most cafés offer fresh-squeezed, naturally sweet orange juice that is delicious during the winter months. In summer, there's an excellent selection of ripe and juicy melons to choose from, such as your typical *meloa* (cantaloupe), *melancia* (watermelon), and *melão,* a general term for the other types of green, yellow, and white honeydew-style melons found in Portugal, which are generally the most flavorful. In the fall and early winter up north, wild mushrooms are plentiful. Hunting season is popular, with both local and gourmet restaurants offering fresh game, such as *veado* (venison), *codorniz* (quail), *perdiz* (partridge), *faisão* (pheasant), and *javali* (wild boar). *Coelho* (rabbit) and *pato* (duck) are generally farm raised and available year-round.

Specialties

Simple comfort food aside, the Portuguese also know how to make some excellent specialty artisanal food products, which you won't want to miss. The most famous are their delicious breads and pastries. Bread baking also originated from poor farming families having to make their own things, and with the historical abundance of windmills perched on nearly every hill and mountaintop, flour and cornmeal were easy commodities. There are numerous different types of bread from every region, some notable ones being *broa-de-milho,* a thick corn bread with a hard outer crust from Trás-os-Montes, and *pão alentejano,* a chewy and thick ciabatta-like bread from Alentejo, which is used in many of the local dishes.

Pastry making came about as a by-product from both the wine business and convents, when egg whites were used by winemakers for filtering wines, and by the convents and monasteries for pressing and starching their habits. Thus, there were tons of leftover egg yolks, and the friars and sisters used them along with sugar and cinnamon imported from the Portuguese colonies to start a business making little egg sweets. Nowadays, pastries are so popular you cannot walk down a street in Portugal without encountering at least a couple of cafés or *pastelerias.* With all these sweets, it's no surprise then that the Portuguese also have some excellent espresso to enjoy with them; two of the favorite national brands are Delta and Nicola.

If you don't have much of a sweet tooth, try some of Portugal's delicious seasoned *azeitonas* (olives), handmade cheeses (*queijo*), and charcuterie (*enchidos*), which come in all sorts of flavors and textures. Some of the most internationally famous Portuguese cheeses include the milky, soft *Queijo de Serpa* from southern Alentejo, *Serra de Estrela* from the mountains in the north, and *Azeitão* from the namesake town in the southerly region of Estremadura—all made from sheep's milk, pungent in aroma and flavor with an *amanteigado* ("smooth like butter") texture. For a harder and milder cheese, try *Nisa,* made with sheep's milk from the Alentejo, or *Pico,* made with raw cow's milk from the Azores. Charcuterie produced here includes a wide variety of *chouriço* (sausage) and *presunto* (Portuguese-style prosciutto), some favorites like *chouriço de porco preto* made from the local Iberian black pigs, as well as blood sausage (*morçela*) and a soft sausage called *alheira,* generally made from a mixture of pork, poultry, and bread.

Famous Dishes

■ *Açorda alentejana* (Alentejo), "bread soup" with garlic, olive oil, and cilantro.

■ *Ameijoas à Bulhão pato* (Estremadura), clams cooked with garlic, white wine, olive oil, and cilantro.

■ *Bacalhau á bras,* salt cod sautéed with onions, fried potato sticks, egg, and black olives.

■ *Bacalhau com natas,* salt cod with cream, gratin-style.

■ *Bifes de atum à madeirense* (Madeira), tuna steaks sautéed with garlic, bay leaf, and parsley.

■ *Bolo de Alfarroba* (Algarve), a sweet cake made from the local Alfarroba tree–seed pod.

■ *Chicharros recheados* (Azores), Azorean stuffed mackerel.

■ *Cozido à portuguesa,* hearty stew of beef, pork, sausage, cabbage, potatoes, and carrots.

■ *Francesinha* (Porto), sandwich of steak, sausage, and ham covered in melted cheese and spicy tomato sauce.

■ *Leitão à Bairrada* (Bairrada), roasted baby pig (not suckling) with spicy black-pepper sauce and oranges.

■ *Polvo à Lagareiro,* roasted octopus with garlic, onions, and potatoes.

■ *Rojões à minhota* (Minho), fried pieces of pork/pork fat with blood sausage, potatoes, and green olives.

PORTUGUESE WINE

Besides the well-known port and Madeira, Portugal produces many excellent wines, both high-end and ageworthy, as well as honest and straightforward youthful ones that you can buy inexpensively. If you're looking to try something different, Portugal has more than 300 different native grape varieties in use, which makes for an endless procession of delicious experiments. Portuguese wines also come in a wide variety of wine styles, including sparkling, still, rosé, dessert, and fortified wines. At mealtimes in restaurants it is common for house wine to be brought out in jugs. The white is often served *à pressão*—from a pressurized tap—and is lightly sparkling. Don't be afraid to try it—these table wines are usually astonishingly cheap and surprisingly pleasant.

Algarve and Alentejo

Algarve wine is largely red and is quite smooth, fruity, and full-bodied. Among the better producers are Quinta do Barranco Longo and Marques dos Vales Grace.

Alentejo wines and their producers are now among the best in Portugal—Esporão, Cortes de Cima, Malhadinha Nova, Redondo, Borba (with its lovely dark color and slightly metallic, astringent flavor), Monsaraz, and Vidigueira. The reds are rich in color and exhibit ripe fruits, the whites are pale yellow, citrusy, and fruity. These wines tend to be higher in alcohol than other regions and go well with rich Alentejo cuisine.

The Setúbal Peninsula and Moscatel de Setúbal

Wines produced on the Setúbal Peninsula are known abroad, mainly through the 150-year efforts of the house of José Maria da Fonseca, based in Azeitão. The Moscatel that Fonseca—together with the small vine growers who make up the local cooperative a few miles east of Azeitão in Palmela—produces is best known as a fortified dessert wine, aged with a mouthwatering taste of honey. If you find some that is 25 years old, you'll see that it has developed a licorice color; enjoy its sweet scent and taste. Besides Moscatel, José Maria da Fonseca produces many other wines—fine reds, rosés, and some clean, crisp whites, great with the local fresh seafood. Other notable producers on the peninsula include Quinta da Bacalhôa, Casa Ermelinda Freitas, and Pegões.

Bairrada and Dão

South of Porto is the coastal DOC region of Bairrada, producing some notable reds and sparkling reds, mainly from the local Baga grape. They have an intense color, with a delicious earthy nose and a smooth taste. They mellow with age and go well with stronger dishes such as game, roasts, and pungent cheeses. The sparkling reds (*espumante tintos*) are best with a popular local dish, *leitão à Bairrada*—roast baby pig served with a spicy black-pepper sauce. Notable Bairrada producers include Luis Pato and Quinta do Encontro.

Much of the wine here is red and matured in oak casks for at least 18 months before being bottled. When mature, the Dão wines have a dark, reddish-brown color, a "complex" nose, and a lasting, velvety taste, and go well with roast lamb and pork. Look for Quinta de Cabriz, Casa de Santar, and Vinhos Borges.

Vinho Verde (Minho)

This region to the north of Porto is Portugal's largest demarcated region. The name *vinho verde,* which translates to "green wine," refers not to the wine's color but to its youthful freshness from its particular production methods. Made from a mix of native white grapes, it is gently sparkling due to its high acidity, with a delicate, fruity flavor. Vinho verde goes well with any kind of seafood and can even age well while still maintaining its sprightliness. Vinho verde also comes in full sparkling, in white, rosé, and even red, which has an intense red color and flavor. Notable producers include Aveleda (Quinta da Aveleda, Casal Garcia, Follies), Quinta de Gomariz, Afros, and Soalheiro.

Douro and Port

The Douro DOC is home to port wine and some incredible red and white table wines. Reds are usually made from a blend of the native grape, Touriga Nacional, and are of a deep ruby color, very fruity with a bit of spice and a rounded taste. They go well with richer foods, a variety of meats, casseroles, and stews well flavored with herbs. The whites are dry, have a pale-yellow color with a full nose, and pair well with salads, appetizers, and chicken dishes. Some of the most respected producers of table wines in Douro are a group of five producers called the "Douro Boys"—Quinta do Vallado, Quinta do Vale Dona Maria, Quinta do Vale Meão, Quinta do Crasto, and Niepoort.

Port is a fortified wine that can only truly be labeled port if it's produced in this region under the strict regulations designed for the area. Port can be made from up to 48 different native Portuguese grape varieties, and can be divided into two major categories: ruby and tawny.

There has also been another recent addition to the port world—rosé port—introduced by the Croft house with its Croft Pink, currently marketed as an aperitif or for use in cocktails. Other notable producers include Taylor's, Sandeman, Ramos Pinto, Quevedo, and Niepoort.

Madeira

Madeira is a fortified and often blended wine produced on the Madeira Islands, and it's currently enjoying a surge in popularity on the international wine scene. It's produced in four distinct styles, named for their respective grape varieties: Boal and Malmsey (or Malvasia) styles are sweet and heavy, and make excellent dessert wines; Verdelho, not so sweet, is a nice alternative to sherry; and Sercial, dry and light, makes an excellent aperitif. Producers to look for are Blandy and Leacock.

ART, ARCHITECTURE, AND AZULEJOS

Portuguese artistic styles were inspired first by the excitement of the newly emerging nation and then by the baroque experimentation that wealth from the colonies made possible.

Painting came into its own in the 15th century with the completion of Nuno Gonçalves's Flemish-inspired polyptych of São Vicente (St. Vincent), which portrayed the princes and knights, monks and fishermen, court figures and ordinary people of imperial Portugal. It's on display in Lisbon's Museu de Arte Antiga. The work of the next great Portuguese painter, the 16th-century Vasco Fernandes (known as Grão Vasco, or the Great Vasco), has an expressive, realistic vigor. His masterpieces are on display in Viseu.

The elaborate decoration that is the hallmark of Manueline architecture is inspiring in its sheer novelty. Structures are supported by twisted stone columns and studded with emblems of seaborne exploration and conquest—particularly under Dom Manuel I (1495–1521)—with representations of anchors, seaweed, and rigging mingling with exotic animals.

Following the discovery of gold in Brazil at the end of the 17th century, churches in particular began to be embellished in a rococo style that employed *talha dourada* (polychrome and gilded carved wood) to stupendous effect. There are superb examples at the churches of São Francisco in Porto and Santo António in Lagos, and at the Convento de Jesus at Aveiro. For rococo at its most restrained, visit the royal palace at Queluz, near Lisbon.

In the 18th century, the sculptor Machado de Castro produced perhaps the greatest equestrian statue of his time, that of Dom José I in Lisbon's Praça do Comércio. Domingos António Sequeira (1768–1837) painted prominent historic and religious subjects. Portrait and landscape painting became popular in the 19th century; works by José Malhoa and Miguel Angelo Lupi can be seen in the Museu de José Malhoa in Caldas da Rainha. The Museu Soares dos Reis in Porto—named after the 19th-century sculptor of that name (1847–89)—was the country's first national museum. His pupil António Teixeira Lopes (1866–1942) achieved popular success and has a museum named after him in Vila Nova de Gaia, near Porto.

Of all Portugal's artistic images, its *azulejos* (painted ceramic tiles) are perhaps the best known. It is thought the Moors introduced these tiles to Iberia, and although many are blue, the term "azulejo" may not come from *azul,* the Portuguese word for that color, but rather from the Arabic *az-zulayj* (little stones). By the 17th century whole panels depicting religious or secular motifs were common, for example at the Fronteira palace on the outskirts of Lisbon.

Tiles in a wide variety of colors adorn many fountains, churches, and palaces. The Paço Real (Royal Palace) in Sintra is one remarkable example of their decorative effect, but there are delightful combinations on the nation's *quintas* or *solares* (country residences) with interesting examples in the Minho region in the north. There are also well-preserved works on display in several museums, including Lisbon's Museu Nacional do Azulejo and Museu de Arte Antiga and Coimbra's Museu Machado de Castro.

GOLFING IN PORTUGAL

Portugal has been attracting golfers from all over Europe since it was discovered that it had the perfect climate for winter golf, particularly on the Algarve's stunning coastline of sandy beaches. It was Sir Henry Cotton, winner of three Open Championships and the father of golf on the Algarve, who turned a marshy field near the old fishing village of Portimão into the famous Penina golf course in the mid-1960s, thereby putting Portugal on the world golfing map.

Although Portugal has always rated highly on the international golf map, it has really come into its own this past decade. The hosting of major tournaments, such as the World Cup in 2005 or the Portugal Masters held in the Algarve, has allowed an increasing number of players to discover this once well-kept secret. From the picturesque courses found on the Azores and Madeira islands in the Atlantic to the challenging courses in northern Portugal, no avid golfer will leave Portugal disappointed.

Some of the finest layouts in continental Europe are found in the Algarve, which holds the majority of Portugal's courses and continues to boom as a tourism market. There's also golf on the west coast around Lisbon. The five-star Penha Longa Resort has a 27-hole course designed by the famed Robert Trent Jones Jr. and is ranked among the best 30 courses in the world. There are two courses in the rather remote region of Beiras in the northern center of the country. Four fine 18-hole courses are on the island of Madeira, with a stunning new course designed by Nick Faldo on the way. Golfers will be able to enjoy views while watching wayward tee shots fly off the landscaped clifftops into the Atlantic Ocean.

Generally, winter weather is perfect for golf, particularly on the southern coast of the Algarve. January can be temperamental with rains, however. The northern courses suffer more in this regard in winter. In summer, high temperatures across the country are made more bearable by cool sea breezes. Motorized golf carts are available at most courses in Portugal, and major courses have caddies available on request. All courses are walkable.

Golf at the most popular courses is expensive, with fees varying with the seasons and running €85–€190. Greens fees are generally cheaper in the north, but if you shop around online, you can find some discounts for the Algarve. Also, calling and speaking to a golf receptionist (most speak English) might allow for additional last-minute bargains, as courses regularly announce promotions whenever bookings appear to have dwindled.

Recommended Courses

Millennium Course, Vilamoura, ⇨ *Chaper 6, The Algarve*

Ocean Course, Vale do Lobo, ⇨ *Chaper 6, The Algarve*

Oitavos Dunes, Cascais, ⇨ *Chapter 3, Side Trips from Lisbon*

Old Course, Vilamoura, ⇨ *Chaper 6, The Algarve*

Penha Longa, Sintra, ⇨ *Chapter 3, Side Trips from Lisbon*

Penina, Portimão, ⇨ *Chaper 6, The Algarve*

Quinta de Cima, Tavira, ⇨ *Chaper 6, The Algarve*

Royal Course, Vale do Lobo, ⇨ *Chaper 6, The Algarve*

Vale da Pinta, Carvoeiro, ⇨ *Chaper 6, The Algarve*

GREAT ITINERARIES

CLASSIC PORTUGAL

This classic itinerary hits all the highlights for your first trip to Portugal. You'll start in the Algarve, Portugal's southernmost region of gorgeous beaches, vibrant resorts, and secluded hill villages, and continue north via the country's major towns. Landscapes along the way include the picturesque coast and the arid plains of the south; vibrant Lisbon and its lush environs; and the rivers, valleys, forests, and mountains of the north.

Days 1–2: The Algarve

Faro makes an ideal base for exploring the most attractive resorts and villages in the Algarve. Don't miss lovely riverside Tavira, bustling Lagos, and gorgeous mountain-based Monchique. ⇨ *Chapter 6*

Day 3: Évora

On your way north, spend a day in Évora, one of Portugal's most charming and historic cities. Stroll the Cidade Velha (Old Town) maze of narrow streets and lunch on traditional Alentejo regional fare. Before continuing on to Lisbon, consider stopping at one of the area's cromlechs and dolmens—prehistoric stone monuments. ⇨ *Chapter 5*

Days 4–5: Lisbon

Don your walking shoes and range across the seven hills of the Portuguese capital. If your knees can't cope, hop on one of the vintage street trams that snake up and down the hills. You should plan on enjoying at least one meal by the river on a terrace and drinks at one of the many hilltop *quiosques* (refreshment kiosks) or esplanade bars—the views of the city are magnificent. Take in a fado show as well, and make time for the picturesque suburb of Belém, whose monastery and riverfront tower are UNESCO World Heritage sites. ⇨ *Chapter 2*

TIPS

■ August is the Algarve's hottest and busiest month. Sintra is best avoided on summer weekends, when it gets very crowded.

■ Drop into the Lisbon Welcome Centre and buy a Lisboa Card; it will save significant time and euros for travel and admission to museums and monuments.

■ Many monuments close on Monday, though some instead close Tuesday (the palace at Mafra, for instance) or Wednesday (Sintra's National Palace). Entrance to many museums and monuments is free the first Sunday of every month, while others offer free entrance until 2 pm every Sunday.

Day 6: Sintra

On the way out of Lisbon, stop for a day to see Sintra's roster of fairy-tale palaces, castles, and romantic gardens, which together make it another UNESCO World Heritage Site. The leafy Serra de Sintra range is a lovely place for walks, and you could easily spend an extra day or more here. ⇨ *Chapter 3*

Day 7: Mafra to Óbidos

After all that trudging, take it easy with a meandering drive through the fertile Estremadura region. On your way to the enchanting walled village of Óbidos, you'll pass Mafra, an otherwise unassuming town that is home to an ostentatious 18th-century palace, whose construction was financed by gold from Brazil. Famous for its cherry liquor and chocolate, Óbidos is a wonderful place to rest for a night after the hectic pace of touring Lisbon and its environs. You can even sleep in a castle-turned-pousada. ⇨ *Chapter 4*

Day 8: Coimbra

Coimbra, a delightful town abuzz with students, boasts heady architecture, a sophisticated shopping scene, and romantic squares and gardens. The place oozes history: Portugal's first king was born and buried here. It's a hilly city, so be prepared, but the center is reasonably compact and you should be able to cover all the main sights easily in a day. Kids will love the mini-monuments at Portugal dos Pequenitos (⊕ *www.portugaldospequenitos.pt*), where the entire country has been shrunk to child-size proportions. Don't miss the quirky *elevador*—a combination of funicular, elevator, and walkway—or fado, the most characteristic of Portugal's folk music. ⇨ *Chapter 7*

Days 9–10: Porto

Portugal's second city and gateway to the north, Porto has a beguiling air of faded grandeur, with its peeling buildings and medieval tangle of river-frontage streets. It's gaining in popularity as a city break destination, and has a lively nightlife scene as well as ample opportunities to sample port wine. Start by picking up a map at the tourist office and heading for the atmospheric Ribeira embankment, with its buildings strung with laundry and superb *tascas,* where you can tuck into fresh fish and admire the colorful lights of the impressive port lodges across the water. Some visitors might want to take a half-day boat trip up the River Douro, whose amazing terraced vineyards form another World Heritage Site. ⇨ *Chapter 8*

Day 10: Braga

The country's religious nerve center, Braga is an ecclesiastical heavyweight with a massive archbishop's palace at the center. A tiara of impressive religious buildings and sanctuaries encircle the town, including the extravagant Bom Jesus baroque pilgrim church, located 5 km (3 miles) to the east. Braga is a city for strolling. If you have the time, it's an easy day trip from Braga to medieval Guimarães with its lovely town center and magnificent palace of the dukes of Bragança. ⇨ *Chapter 8*

Day 11: Viana Do Castelo

A low-key Portuguese resort and the country's folkloric capital, this elegant seaside town has grandiose 16th-century buildings, superb restaurants, and sweeping beaches. Chug across the Rio Lima by ferry to the local strip of sand, stroll around the picturesque town center, and, if your timing permits, visit the bustling

Friday market to pick up a few hand-embroidered linens as gifts for the folks back home. ⇨ *Chapter 8*

BYWAYS AND BACKWATERS

This meandering tour of the northern rivers, valleys, and mountains steers clear of the hustle-bustle of cities and tourist crowds, allowing you to absorb the local life and culture—Portugal's mellow pleasures. This makes a great add-on to our classic itinerary, or is great for repeat visitors who want to see something new.

Day 1: Ponte de Lima

You can do this handsome town justice in a day. Its highlight is the ancient bridge with its 31 arches spanning the River of Oblivion, as it was known. Riverside promenades, mansions, elegant manor-house accommodations, museums, and churches are included in the attractions; pick up a map at the helpful tourist office. ⇨ *Chapter 8*

Day 2: Barcelos

If you like markets, you have come to the right place. Held every Thursday (just follow the shopping baskets), this is celebrated as one of Portugal's biggest and best. Despite the busloads of visitors, the market is essentially organized by locals for locals and chockablock with ceramics, baskets, toys, fresh produce, agricultural supplies, clothes, shoes, and household equipment. We recommend Barcelos as a day trip, because the market is so well attended that overnight accommodations are scarce. ⇨ *Chapter 8*

Days 3–4: Guimarães

After its reign as the European Capital of Culture in 2012, and the European Capital of Sports in 2013, the once-sleepy

TIPS
■ Winter is not the time for this trip. Northern Portugal can be cold and wet from December to February; spring (March to late May) is ideal, however, as much of the countryside is blanketed with a dazzle of wildflowers.
■ The driving conditions are relatively relaxing and easy in this region, mainly because of the relative lack of Portuguese drivers with their penchant for overtaking on blind corners.
■ One of the most delightful stretches of train track in the country runs from the Douro mainline at Livração to Amarante. There are up to nine trains a day on this narrow-gauge railroad, most with connections to Porto.

northern town of Guimarães is seeing a tourist boom, and deserves two days of your time. Stroll its charming historic quarter, often called the "birthplace of Portugal," because the country's first king was born here. The entire city was recently named a UNESCO World Heritage Site. ⇨ *Chapter 8*

Day 5: Bragança

Within the walls of the Cidadela (Citadel) is a superbly preserved medieval village. Wander the cobbles and gaze at neighboring Spain from the castle walls, then descend to the modern town. Parking is refreshingly easy in this town, with plenty of places by the bus station and even up in the citadel itself. Just follow the signs. ⇨ *Chapter 8*

Days 6–7: The Eastern Beiras

With fertile valleys, medieval villages, castles, and fortresses, this area is atmospheric and rugged with tucked-away

villages and towns like Fundão, Castelo Rodrigo, and Almeida. Every castle wall tells a story, while every abandoned house or tower harbors a ghost or two. Note that a car is essential for this part of the route as the bus coverage is patchy and sporadic. ⇨ *Chapter 7*

Day 8: Sortelha

It's not quite the land that time forgot, but Sortelha comes as close as anywhere in Portugal. Ancient walls, crumbling houses, cobbled streets, and simple back-to-basics accommodations all contribute to the stuck-in-a-time-warp atmosphere. Again, getting here by public transport is possible but problematic, as several of the bus lines operate only during school-term time. ⇨ *Chapter 7*

CASTLES, CROMLECHS, AND CORK

Lisbon residents increasingly see the wide-open spaces of the Alentejo as a refuge from city hustle, and life definitely moves at a slower pace here. Across mile after mile of rolling plains, sheep graze and black pigs root for acorns under cork oaks that are stripped of their bark every few years. The region bears the marks of ancient civilizations, and hilltop fortresses

regularly heave into view. There are more fairy-tale castles along the River Tagus, just to the west.

Day 1: Évora

The capital of the Upper Alentejo, the walled town of Évora is steeped in history. Lose yourself in the Cidade Velha, but be sure to see the main square, the Praça do Giraldo, and the impressive Roman temple to Diana.

Rota dos Vinhos do Alentejo. Wine buffs can pick up information on touring the region's wineries at the Rota dos Vinhos do Alentejo, which also has tastings. ⊠ *Praça Joaquim António de Aguiar, Praça Joaquim António de Aguiar No. 20–21, Apartado 2146, Valverde* ☎ *266/746498, 266/746609* ⊕ *www.vinhosdoalentejo.pt* ◷ *Closed Sun.*

Day 2: Arraiolos and Estremoz

Before leaving the Évora area, consider stopping off at a local cromlech or dolmen—prehistoric stone monuments. Then stop off in Arraiolos, famed for its handmade tapestries, before traveling on to Estremoz, the most important of the region's "marble towns" (Portugal is Europe's second-biggest producer, after Italy). ⇨ *Chapter 5*

Days 3–4: Portalegre

Base yourself in the Portalegre area for a couple of days. Though the charms of the town itself are fairly soon exhausted, many stimulating trips out are possible: to the stunning hilltop villages of Castelo de Vide and Marvão, with its ancient battlements; to the Parque Natural da Serra de São Mamede—a lovely area for walking; or to the former royal stud farm at Alter do Chão. ⇨ *Chapter 5*

Day 5: Abrantes

Head northwest toward the Tagus River, sighting the spectacular castle at Belver on your way. The flower-bedecked village of Sardoal makes for an enjoyable stop on the way to Abrantes—and yet another hilltop castle. ⇨ *Chapter 4*

Day 6: Constância and Almourol

The pretty little town of Constância, on the confluence of the Zêzere and Tagus Rivers, is a good base for canoeing and other outdoor pastimes, or just to picnic on the neat riverside parkland. A little farther on, the castle at Almourol on its own island in the Tagus is perhaps Portugal's most fairy-tale edifice.

Day 7: Santarém

If you don't need to head straight back to Lisbon to catch a flight, spend at least half a day in the regional capital of Santarém, with its impressive Gothic church and fine views over the plains that you have just traversed. ⇨ *Chapter 4*

SANCTUARY AND SOLITUDE

One of Portugal's best-kept secrets used to be its southwestern corner, where deserted beaches and cliffs are protected by Natural Park status. But a new ecotourism project—a 345-km (215-mile) hiking

TIPS

■ Avoid heading inland in high summer, when temperatures can be scorching (literally: wildfires are an annual threat). Spring is delightful, with wildflowers galore. Fall sees many food-related festivals taking place in both the Alentejo and the Ribatejo.

■ The driving conditions are relatively relaxing and easy in this region, with long-distance roads fairly flat and gently curving. As for public transport, the Alentejo is not well served by trains, but express and local bus services are reliable.

■ Both the Alentejo and Ribatejo are wine-producing regions (half of all Portuguese wine is produced in the Alentejo), and many vineyards are pleased to welcome visitors. The Portuguese tourist office can provide contact details.

trail called the Rota Vicentina (⊕ *www. rotavicentina.com*)—has sparked a sustainable-tourism boom. More ecolodges and facilities are popping up, but beaches remain pristine, and the fish and shellfish served at local restaurants are among the freshest and best to be found anywhere in the country. This area also boasts some of the country's best surfing spots.

Day 1: Arrábida and Setúbal

If you're starting out from Lisbon, don't miss the Serra de Arrábida, with its deep-green pine forests. The sheltered beaches on its southern flanks are bathed by warmer waters than those on the west coast of the peninsula. Overnight in the lovely seaside town of Sesimbra, where calm waters invite swimmers from April through November, and the cobbled streets of the historic center are lined with simple restaurants serving some of the best seafood in Portugal (the town's symbol is a swordfish, and it's motto is *Sesimbra é Peixe,* meaning "Sesimbra is Fish"). Half an hour away, the small city of Setúbal offers Gothic architecture, colorful street art, and dolphin-watching boat trips. ⇨ *Chapter 3*

Day 2: Alcácer do Sal

This ancient town is famed for its salt-making tradition, castle, and profusion of storks. The nearby Reserva Natural do Sado offers opportunities for walkers, or you could head for the beach at Comporta, which also has several excellent restaurants. ⇨ *Chapter 5*

Day 3: Vila Nova de Milfontes

Just to the south of the port city of Sines, the real wilderness begins: the Parque Natural do Sudoeste Alentejao e Costa Vicentina. Vila Nova de Milfontes is among the few towns along this bit of coast, which has stunning beaches at places such as Zambujeira do Mar. ⇨ *Chapter 5*

Day 4: Vila do Bispo

As you cross the border into the Algarve, smaller local roads continue to lead off the highway to an amazing variety of beaches, such as Arrifana. They lack fancy hotels and restaurants but are popular with water-sports enthusiasts. End your day at Vila do Bispo, a handy local base. ⇨ *Chapter 6*

Day 5: Sagres

Even nonsurfers will find plenty to enthuse at Portugal's southwestern corner. The views from the hilltop fort at Sagres and the lighthouse on Cape Saint Vincent are truly spectacular. From here you can head east for a spell at noisier, more sociable resorts such as Albufeira, or head north from there up the motorway to Lisbon. ⇨ *Chapter 6*

> **TIPS**
>
> ■ Public transport is limited and infrequent in Portugal's wild west, so for much of this itinerary you'll need your own wheels. Road surfaces are decent, but routes often narrow, so be patient to stay safe.
>
> ■ Facilities are limited in this less developed area, so if you want to stay in small *pensões* or even hunt for rooms in local houses, plan ahead or arrive early.
>
> ■ The Atlantic waters along this coast are never warm, but on hot summer days they're just what is needed after a spell of sunbathing. The water is often warmer toward the end of the summer, or even as late as October.
>
> ■ Make sure to sample fresh fish, grilled simply in a local restaurant.

ROMANTIC GETAWAY

With its huge variety of natural scenery and a swashbuckling history, Portugal is a wonderful place for the romantically inclined—whether lone daydreamers, honeymooners, or inseparable couples.

Day 1: Sintra

There's nowhere in Portugal more Romantic than Sintra. In the 19th century this royal retreat was Europe's first center of Romantic architecture; the pioneering approach to landscaping evident in its lush gardens also helps underpin its status as a UNESCO World Heritage Site. ⇨ *Chapter 3*

Day 2: Óbidos

This postcard-perfect hilltop village wows with charming flower-bedecked houses and stone battlements. A fairy-tale castle that is also a pousada completes the scene. ⇨ *Chapter 4*

Day 3: Alcobaça

Continue north for your first encounter with Pedro and Inês, star-crossed protagonists of one of history's great true-life love stories. The gorgeous 12th-century monastery at Alcobaça contains their tombs: placed so that on Judgment Day the first thing they would see on rising from the grave would be each other. ⇨ *Chapter 4*

Day 4: Tomar

Head northeast for Tomar, once the headquarters of the Knights Templar. Their remarkable Convento de Cristo is studded with over-the-top architectural features; the grounds afford wonderful views. ⇨ *Chapter 4*

Day 5: Coimbra

There are more links to Portugal's most famous love story at Coimbra, where Pedro and his lover dallied at the Quinta da Lágrimas (today a luxury hotel and spa with a renowned restaurant) and Inês was later shut up in the now ruined convent of Santa Clara-a-Velha. At night, try to get to a fado venue. Unlike the Lisbon fado, the local style here developed from medieval troubadour music and was traditionally sung by male students at the university, often to serenade lovers. ⇨ *Chapter 7*

Day 6: Penacova

Head up the River Mondego toward Penacova, a small town that affords breathtaking views. There are more thrills nearby in the form of opportunities to go hiking or kayaking. For something a little calmer, visit the medieval monastery at Lorveiro, a place that seems frozen in time. ⇨ *Chapter 7*

TIPS

■ Both Óbidos and Alcobaça are centers for the production of *ginjinha*, a liqueur made from the *ginja*, or sour cherry. In some bars, it may be served in edible chocolate cups.

■ History buffs won't want to miss Conimbriga, Portugal's largest Roman site, where you can spend a couple of hours wandering the ruins.

■ The west of Portugal can be notably chilly and damp between November and February, particularly in hilly or forested areas. Dress warmly and check in advance whether your lodgings have heat or a wood-burning fire.

Day 7: Buçaco

With its neo-Gothic touches and medieval decor, the former royal hunting lodge at Buçaco is a uniquely atmospheric place. Marked trails here lead into the cool green depths of a dense forest. ⇨ *Chapter 7*

ON THE CALENDAR

	Religious celebrations, called *festas* (feasts or festivals), *feiras* (fairs), and *romarias* (pilgrimages or processions), are held throughout the year. Some of the leading annual events are listed below. Verify specific dates with the people at the Portuguese tourism office, who can also send you a complete list of events.
January	**Cantar as Janeiras.** In many parts of Portugal it is still common to Cantar as Janeiras—sing January in. From January 1 to 6 groups of friends go door to door, proclaiming Jesus's birth and wishing their listeners a happy new year. This is often accompanied by traditional instruments. (Originally it was done in the hope householders might hand out Christmas leftovers.)
	Feira do Fumeiro. The Feira do Fumeiro, a celebration of smoked and cured sausages and hams in the village of Montalegre in Trás-os-Montes, is a major gastronomic event in northern Portugal and draws thousands of visitors in January every year. A similar event in the same region takes place in February in Vinhais, the self-proclaimed *capital do fumeiro*. ⊕ *www.fumeiro.org*.
February–March	**Carnaval** (*Carnival*). The final festival before Lent, Carnaval is held throughout the country, with processions of masked participants, parades of decorated vehicles, and displays of flowers. Nowadays it is influenced by the wilder Brazilian celebrations; the most genuinely Portuguese events are held in Ovar, Nazaré, Loulé, and Portimão, though there's a big one near Lisbon at Torres Novas. Some towns, including Loulé and the seaside town of Sesimbra, also hold Carnavals in August, when the weather is better suited to the skimpy samba costumes than chilly February.
	Feira do Queijo do Alentejo. Portugal's most prized cheese comes from Serpa, a charming walled city in Baixo Alentejo, which hosts the country's biggest cheese festival each February. There are cheese-making demonstrations, sheep shearing and milking, and street dances with choral performances.
March	**Essência do Vinho.** Portugal's biggest wine showcase is Essência do Vinho, with thousands flocking to the Palácio da Bolsa in Porto, the city's old stock exchange, to sample the products of vineyards around the country. Check the website for wine events throughout the country all year. ⊕ *www.essenciadovinho.com*.

March–April	**Semana Santa** (*Holy Week*). Festivities for Semana Santa are held in Braga, Ovar, Póvoa de Varzim, and other cities and major towns, with the most important events taking place on Monday, Thursday, and Good Friday. Easter also marks the start of the bullfighting season and—outside Lisbon's Campo Pequeno arena at any rate—protests by animal rights groups.
April	**Peixe em Lisboa.** Lisbon's biggest gastronomic event, Peixe em Lisboa, or Lisbon Fish and Flavors as it's called in English, features top Portuguese and foreign chefs, who set up food stalls and do cooking demonstrations and talks. It's usually held in the second week of April; check the website for specific dates and venues. ⊕ *www.peixemlisboa.com*.
	25 de Abril. The anniversary of the 1974 Carnation Revolution (actually an almost-bloodless coup) that brought down a dictatorship of four decades in Portugal is known simply as 25 de Abril. In Lisbon, official ceremonies mark the day, while nostalgic lefties parade down the Avenida da Liberdade.
May	**Caparica Primavera Surf Fest.** Across the River Tejo from Lisbon lie the white-sand beaches of Costa da Caparica. Here, surfers welcome the arrival of spring with this lively three-day festival of live music, DJs, and, of course, first-class wave riding. Usually held in early May, full dates and lineups are published on the website in the months leading up to the festival. ⊕ *www.caparica-primaverasurffest.pt*.
	Festas das Cruzes (*Festival of the Crosses*). Legend has it that, in the early 16th century, a peasant who insisted on working on the Day of the Holy Cross saw a perfumed, luminous cross appear on the ground where he was digging. Ever since, Barcelos has held the colorful Festas das Cruzes, with a large fair, concerts, an affecting procession, and a fireworks display on the Rio Cavado. There are smaller celebrations and a fair in Monsanto.
	Romaria de Fátima. During the Romaria de Fátima, thousands make the pilgrimage to the town from all over the world to commemorate the first apparition of the Virgin to the shepherd children on May 13, 1917. These are repeated monthly through October 13, the anniversary of the last vision.
	Millennium Estoril Open. Sponsored by Millennium Bank, this is Portugal's biggest and most famous tennis tournament, and takes place on the clay court at the Clube de Ténis

		do Estoril. The tournament usually draws one or two top international players, and some up-and-coming Iberian stars. It usually falls in the last week of April, or first week in May. Check the website for schedules and ticket info. ⊕ *www.millenniumestorilopen.com/en.*
		Rock in Rio Lisboa. Late May sees the start of the music festival season, with Rock in Rio Lisboa (the events were initially held in Rio de Janeiro before crossing the Atlantic to be held in Portugal and Spain) first off the blocks with its family-friendly layout and predominately mainstream fare. Portugal's growing number of rock fests are a great place to see your favorite bands—tickets are cheaper than for events in most of Europe and generally mud-free. ⊕ *rockinriolisboa.sapo.pt.*
	June	**Festa de São Gonçalo.** Amarante hosts the fertility-focused Festa de São Gonçalo, when St. Gonçalo (a locally born priest) is commemorated by the baking of phallus-shape cakes, which are then exchanged between unmarried men and women. Events also include a fair, folk dancing, and traditional singing.
		Festa de Santo António. This festival is the first of June's Festas Populares, and the biggest party of the year in Lisbon. On June 12, trestle tables are set up in the city's traditional neighborhoods (and some modern ones), colorful flags are strewn overhead, and grilled sardines and sangria are served. Throughout the month, there are free concerts and other events around town, and the streets of the Bairro Allto throng with revelers dancing to *pimba* (Portuguese pop music) through the night. ⊕ *www.festasdelisboa.com.*
		Festa de São João. This festival is especially colorful in Porto, where the whole city erupts with bonfires and barbecues and every corner has its own *cascatas* (arrangements with religious motifs). Locals roam the streets, hitting passersby on the head with, among other things, leeks and plastic hammers.
	June–July	**Festival de Sintra.** One of Portugal's longest-running annual cultural events, the Festival de Sintra in mid-May or early June includes classical music and ballet performances by international and Portuguese groups. Check the website for dates and ticket information. ⊕ *festivaldesintra.pt.*

July	**Festa do Colete Encarnado** (*Red Waistcoat*). The Ribatejo region's biggest festival, the Festa do Colete Encarnado in Vila Franca de Xira honors the *campinos* (cowboys) who guard the wild bulls in nearby pastures. Streets are cordoned off, and bulls are let loose as would-be bullfighters try their luck at dodging the beasts. It's a spectacle, but visitors should be cautious, as injuries occur every year.

Festival Estoril Lisboa. Formerly known as Festival de Música do Estoril, this music festival includes concerts by leading Portuguese and foreign artists in several towns along the Estoril Coast, with an emphasis on performers from Mediterranean countries. ⊕ *www.festorilisbon.com.*

Festa dos Tabuleiros. On the first Sunday of July every four years, Tomar hosts the spectacular Festa dos Tabuleiros in which young women march through town with trays on their heads piled absurdly high with bread and flowers. ⊕ *www.tabuleiros.org.*

NOS Alive. The biggest of Portugal's outdoor summer rock festivals, NOS Alive is held in Lisbon's riverside Algés district with a lineup that spans the musical spectrum, from indie rock to electronica. It's held over three days, and revelers can enjoy mud-free camping or buy day tickets and retreat to the comfort of a hotel bed at night. With impressive lineups each year, NOS Alive is often cited as one of Europe's best (and sunniest) music fests. ⊕ *nosalive.com/en.* |
| August | **Festas da Nossa Senhora da Agonia.** In mid-August every year, the Festas da Nossa Senhora da Agonia, at Viana do Castelo, is just one of myriad summer events in the Minho Province that feature processions, folk music and dancing, greasy pastries, and fireworks. Usually held a week later, the Festa da Nossa Senhora dos Remédios in Lamego is a similar party. ⊕ *www.vianafestas.com.*

Festas da Nossa Senhora da Boa Viagem. In the Festas da Nossa Senhora da Boa Viagem, at Peniche, locals organize processions on land and sea in honor of the patron saints they hope will keep fishermen safe. It's usually celebrated on the Sunday closest to August 20. The date is also marked at other fishing ports up and down the country, such as Ericeira, near Sintra. |

	Festival Sudoeste. Another of Portugal's major outdoor music events, Festival Sudoeste is held near the otherwise-sleepy town of Zambujeiro on the Alentejo coast during the first weekend of August. Expect three days of rock concerts and dance music, with top national and international names. Camping and local transport are included in the ticket, which you can buy online. ⊕ *www.meosudoeste.pt/en.*
September	**Festa das Vindimas de Palmela** (*Grape Harvest*). This festival in the historic town of Palmela, near Lisbon, has a symbolic treading of the grapes and a blessing of the harvest, accompanied by a parade of harvesters, wine tastings, the election of the Queen of the Wine, and fireworks. It is usually held in early September; check website for exact dates. ⊕ *www. festadasvindimas.org.*
	Queer Lisboa. In Lisbon, an active film festival season kicks off with Queer Lisboa, one of the leading gay and lesbian events of its kind in Europe. The months that follow see showcases and competitive events focusing on genres from documentaries to horror movies. ⊕ *queerlisboa.pt/en.*
October	**Feira de Outubro** (*October Fair*). In Vila Franca de Xira, a short distance from Lisbon, the Feira de Outubro has farming and agricultural activities, handicraft displays, bullfights, and a running of the bulls in the streets.
	Festival Nacional de Gastronomia (*National Gastronomy Festival*). This festival in Santarém consists of cooking contests, lectures, and the preparation (and consumption) of traditional regional dishes. ⊕ *www.festivalnacionalde-gastronomia.pt.*
November	**Festa de São Martinho.** On November 11, the Festa de São Martinho is celebrated above all by *magustos*—tastings of the first barrels of the year's new wine. Farmers and vintners gather around a fire to roast chestnuts and open the first vintage. Celebrations, sometimes called the Festa da Castanha or Festa do Castanheiro (chestnut festival), are held in villages across the country. The biggest and most famous one is in Marvão, in Alto Alentejo.
	Feira Nacional do Cavalo (*National Horse Fair*). This festival in Golegã, in the Ribatejo region, combines parades of saddle and bullfighting horses with riding competitions, handicrafts exhibitions, and wine tastings.

December–January	**Réveillon.** Portugal rings in the new year in grand style, traditionally with fireworks as the clock strikes midnight. The biggest and best displays are held in Madeira's largest town, Funchal, which is transformed into a vast fairground, with bands of strolling dancers and singers.
	Festa dos Rapazes. The remote Trás-os-Montes region unsurprisingly retains some of Portugal's most ancient pagan traditions. The Festa dos Rapazes in the villages around Bragança is one example; in the period between Christmas and the Noite dos Reis (the night of January 5) unmarried "boys" indulge in traditional high jinks, such as dressing up in straw costumes to scare children and girls. It's the biggest spectacle of the year in these parts.

LISBON

Updated by
Lucy Bryson

Affordable prices and an alluring combination of sunny skies, glorious architecture, deep-rooted traditions, and thoroughly modern flair have made Lisbon into a top destination for travelers. Record numbers of cruise ships are now docking at the revamped port, and Lisbon has gained a reputation as one of the best spots on the continent for live music—from rock to jazz and classical—with many events held in the city's numerous leafy green spaces. Famously built on seven hills, Lisbon's terra-cotta-roofed homes, turreted castles and cathedrals, and gleaming white basilicas appear to tumble down the cobbled slopes towards the glimmering River Tagus, as visitors traverse the city on antique, rattling streetcars, modern tuk tuks, and Segways.

Lisbon has embraced change without casting aside its much-loved heritage. Colorful murals on every corner make it one of the best cities in Europe to see street art, while white sheets flap from the windows of the tightly packed hillside homes of Moorish Alfama. Boutique hotels sit beside hole-in-the-wall bars where locals sip *ginjinha* and strong espresso as they nibble on the world's most irresistible custard tarts. The mournful sound of fado music still draws huge crowds of locals and visitors, even as hip bars and clubs move into formerly run-down areas of town. UNESCO World Heritage Sites sit proudly in the postcard-perfect suburb of Belém, the site from which Vasco da Gama and his fellow explorers set out during the much-celebrated Age of Discovery.

In its heyday in the 16th century, Lisbon was a pioneer of the first wave of globalization. Now, the empire is striking back, with Brazilians and people from the former Portuguese colonies in Africa enriching the city. The Brazilian influence is particularly evident—young locals are more likely to sip a caipirinha than a glass of port wine. The city is also a major draw for young entrepreneurs from across Europe, enticed by affordable rents, sunny skies, and a lively nightlife scene.

As Europe's sunniest capital—basking in an average of 2,799 hours of sunshine a year—Lisbon's clear-blue skies provide a gorgeous backdrop to the views that unfold from its many lofty vantage points, and the summer months see rooftop bars cropping up across the city, while locals and tourists alike sip coffee and sangria at esplanade bars, and the waterfront becomes an urban beach, complete with deck chairs and swimwear-clad sunseekers.

Counting some of Europe's finest galleries, museums and cultural centers, and a vast aquarium among its indoor attractions, Lisbon has

TOP REASONS TO GO

World Treasures. Lisbon's Mosteiro dos Jerónimos and Torre de Belém, both UNESCO World Heritage sites, are grand monuments reflecting Portugal's proud seafaring past.

City Sophistication. The Museu Colecção Berardo and Museu Gulbenkian are just two of the museums that make the city a cultural hub.

Victorian Style. Explore Lisbon on ancient trams that wind through narrow cobbled streets where washing flaps from the windows of pastel-color houses and sardines sizzle on the grill.

Beaches on the Doorstep. The deck chairs and sunbathing youths that line Lisbon's revitalized riverfront make the wide River Tagus feel like an urban beach, and it's just a short hop to the real thing, whether you're looking to sunbathe, swim, or surf.

Buzzing Nightlife. Lisbon has a reputation across Europe as a great place to hit the town, with bars and nightclubs often located in stunning riverside settings or atop high-rise buildings—all the better to admire the glorious views.

plenty to offer, even under rainy skies. An increasingly sophisticated dining scene is building on a growing appreciation for Portuguese food, with its abundant fresh fish, fruit and vegetables, and the astonishingly affordable wines that seem to accompany every meal. The relatively compact size of the city means it is possible to pack a lot into a short break, and visitors with the luxury of a longer stay can find fairy-tale mountain towns, rolling wine country, dolphin-filled bays, and long, white-sand beaches within less than an hour's reach. Despite the rising costs that have accompanied the tourism boom, prices for most goods and services are still lower than most other European countries. You can still find affordable places to eat and stay, and with distances between major sights fairly small, taxis are astonishingly cheap. All this means that Lisbon is not only a treasure chest of historical monuments, but also a place where you won't use up all your own hard-earned treasure.

ORIENTATION AND PLANNING

GETTING ORIENTED

Lisbon was built across seven hills on the north bank of the Tagus estuary, whose vast expanse ebbs and flows with the tides from the Atlantic Ocean. Nowadays, Lisbon sprawls over considerably more than seven hills: the city proper is 85 square km (33 square miles), though the metropolitan area is many times larger. The historic downtown is dominated by a castle perched on the highest of the seven hills. The part of town where business was historically transacted is a low-lying area that separates the hillier neighborhoods of Alfama and Chiado. The broad avenues of this modern grid start at the river and run northward.

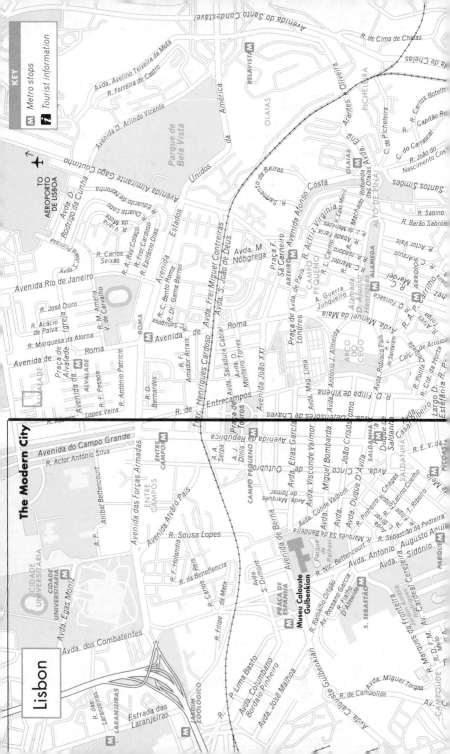

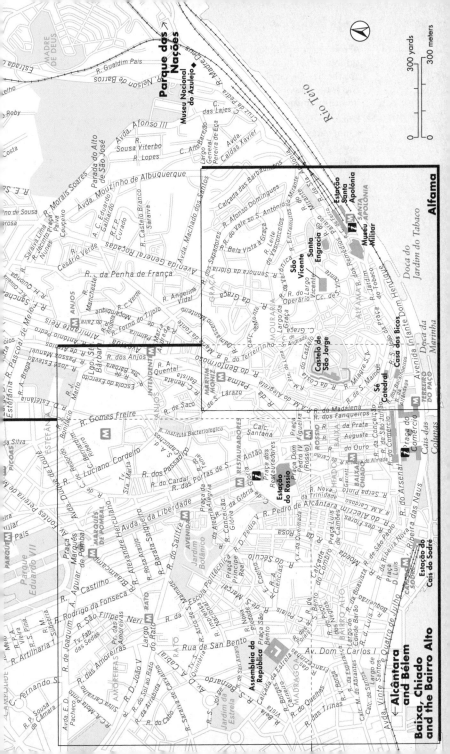

Alfama. East of the Baixa lies Alfama, the old Moorish quarter whose sinuous street plan survived the 1755 earthquake. In this part of town are the Sé (the city's cathedral) and, on the hill above, the Castelo de São Jorge (St. George's Castle). It's also the home of fado, the stirringly mournful musical style that has captivated audiences for centuries.

Baixa. The center of Lisbon stretches north from the spacious Praça do Comércio—one of Europe's largest riverside squares—to Praça Dom Pedro IV, universally known by its ancient name of Rossio, a smaller square lined with shops and cafés. The district in between is known as the Baixa (Lower Town), an attractive grid of parallel streets built after the 1755 earthquake and tidal wave.

Chiado and Bairro Alto. To the west of the Baixa is Chiado, the city's classy shopping district, and Bairro Alto (Upper Neighborhood), an area of intricate 18th-century streets, houses with peeling paint, and Gothic churches that's nowadays best known for its bars, restaurants, and hip stores.

The Modern City. The Modern City begins at Praça dos Restauradores, adjacent to Rossio. From here the main Avenida da Liberdade stretches northwest to the landmark Praça Marquês de Pombal, dominated by a column and a towering statue of the man himself. This busy traffic roundabout is bordered by the green expanse of the Parque Eduardo VII, named in honor of King Edward VII of Great Britain, who visited Lisbon in 1902.

São Bento. Downhill from the Bairro Alto, this maze of streets harbors cozy restaurants and, on the Rua de São Bento itself, some pricey antiques shops.

Lapa and Estrela. On another hill to the west of São Bento, foreign embassies cluster in the Lapa neighborhood, no doubt providing some of the customers in the posh restaurants and fine hotels found here.

Cais do Sodré and Santos. The riverside district of Cais do Sodré was long a seedy backwater mainly patronized by crews from passing ships, but is now increasingly a place for locals to eat out and go barhopping. Neighboring Santos is a favorite with young partiers, too.

Alcântara and Belém. Two km (1 mile) west of the Baixa, former docks in the Alcântara area have been overhauled and turned into hip places to drink, dine, and shop, while a former warehouse has become one of Lisbon's prime museums. Another 3 km (2 miles) west along the Rio Tejo is Belém, home to the Mosteiro dos Jerónimos, the famous monastery, as well as a royal palace and several of the city's best cultural centers.

Parque das Nações. Located about 5 km (3 miles) northeast of Lisbon's center is Parque das Nações, site of the World Exposition in 1998. This revitalized modern district on the banks of the Rio Tejo includes the spectacular Oceanário de Lisboa, an aquarium built for the Expo.

PLANNING

WHEN TO GO

It's best not to visit at the height of summer, when the city is hot and steamy and lodging is expensive and crowded. Winters are generally mild and usually accompanied by bright blue skies, and there are plenty of bargains to be had at hotels. For optimum Lisbon weather, visit on either side of summer, in May or late September through October. The city's major festivals are in June, when the Santos Populares (popular saints) festivals see days of riotous celebration dedicated to saints Anthony, John, and Peter.

PLANNING YOUR TIME

You'll want to give yourself a day at least exploring the *bairro* of Alfama, climbing up to the Castelo de São Jorge (Saint's George's castle) for an overview of the city; another in the monumental downtown area, Baixa, and in the neighboring fancy shopping district of Chiado, and perhaps also in the funkier shops of Bairro Alto. Another again could be spent in historic Belém, with its many museums and monuments. Note that many are closed Monday, and churches often close for a couple of hours at lunchtime. It's worth noting that Sunday is usually a good day for a cultural outing: many national museums offer free entry until 2 pm every Sunday, while others waive the entrance fee on the first Sunday of each month.

There are other attractions dotted around the modern city, and families will appreciate the child-friendly attractions of the Parque das Nações, the former Expo site. There's easily enough to do and see to fill a week—and it's well worth taking the time to see some of the surrounding area.

GETTING HERE AND AROUND

AIR TRAVEL

Lisbon's small, modern airport, sometimes known as Aeroporto de Portela, is 7 km (4½ miles) north of the center. Getting downtown is simple and inexpensive thanks to a new metro extension that goes via the Gare de Oriente rail station, and to the special Aerobus shuttles. Line 1, which departs every 20 minutes between 7 am and 11:20 pm, stops near major downtown hotels, at Praça Marquês de Pombal, Avenida da Liberdade, Rossio, Praça do Comércio, and Cais do Sodré train station. Line 2 departs every 40 minutes from 7:30 am to 11 pm, taking in key financial districts and Praça de Espanha, ending at Avenida José Malhoa.

Tickets from the driver cost €3.50, or you can buy them online for €3.15; these are valid for all local buses for the next 24 hours. Two 24-hour Aerobus tickets cost €5.50 (or €4.95 online). The cheaper (€1.80) city Bus 744 departs every 15–30 minutes between 5 am and 1:40 am from the main road in front of airport arrivals. At night, Bus 208 plies a route between Oriente station and Cais do Sodré that takes in the airport.

For a taxi, expect to pay €15–€25 to get downtown, plus a €1.60 surcharge per item of luggage in the trunk. To avoid hassle, a prepaid taxi voucher (from €16 for downtown in daytime) may be bought at the tourist desk in the airport: you'll pay a little more but won't be taken for an extra-long ride. Uber users will find it quick and easy to order a ride from the airport, and most drivers speak English.

Contact **General and flight information.** ✉ *Alameda das Comunidades Portugueses* ☎ *21/841–3500* ⊕ *www.ana.pt* Ⓜ *Aeroporto.*

BUS TRAVEL

Lisbon's main bus terminal is the Gare do Oriente, adjacent to Parque das Nações, also served by rail and metro. Most international and domestic express buses (mostly run by the Rede Expressos company) operate from the Sete Rios terminal, beside the metro and suburban train stations of the same name.

Bus Contact **Rede Expressos.** ✉ *Terminal Rodoviário de Sete Rios , Praça Marechal Humberto Delgado , Estrada das Laranjeiras, Sete Rios* ☎ *707/223344* ⊕ *www.rede-expressos.pt* Ⓜ *Jardim Zoológico.*

CAR TRAVEL

Heading in or out by car, there's rapid access to and from points south and east via the Ponte 25 de Abril bridge across the Rio Tejo (Tagus River), although in rush hour the 17-km-long (11-mile-long) Ponte Vasco da Gama is a better option. To and from Porto, the A1 is the fastest route.

Parking is difficult in the capital, so your rental car is best left in a lot while in town.

FERRY TRAVEL

Ferries across the Rio Tejo are run by Transtejo, from terminals at Belém, Cais do Sodré, and Terreiro do Paço. They offer unique views of Lisbon, and their top decks are a nice way to catch the sun. Prices (loaded onto a €0.50 electronic card) run €1.20–€2.70.

Ferry Contact **Transtejo.** ☎ *21/213500115* ⊕ *www.transtejo.pt.*

PUBLIC TRANSPORT

The best way to see central Lisbon is on foot; most points of interest are within the well-defined older quarters. However, the city's cobblestone sidewalks and steep climbs make walking tiring, even with comfortable shoes, so at some point you'll want to use the public-transportation system, if only to experience the old trams and *elevadores*: funicular railways and elevators linking high and low parts of the city. Like the buses, they are operated by the public transportation company, Carris.

For all these forms of transport, paying as you board means paying much more (€1.80 a ride for the bus, €2.85 the tram, €3.60 for the funicular, and €5 for the elevator), in cash. It's better to purchase a 7 Colinas or Viva Viagem travel card, both of which can also be used on the metro and ferries. Buy them at transport terminals and at the foot of the Elevador de Santa Justa.

Lisbon's modern metro system (station entrances are marked with a red "M") is cheap and speedy, though it misses many sights and gets crowded during rush hour and for big soccer matches. You can charge your Viva Viagem card with cash. For €1.40, you get one hour's access

2

to buses, trams, and the metro: choose the "Zapping" option to load larger amounts onto your card if you intend to make multiple journeys.

The Lisboa Card is a special pass that allows free travel on all public transportation (including trains to Sintra, Cascais, and Estoril) as well as free or discounted entry into 27 museums, monuments, and galleries. The cards are valid for 24 hours (€18.50), 48 hours (€31.50), or 72 hours (€39). It's sold at the airport (in well-signed kiosks), across from the Mosteiro dos Jerónimos, in the Lisbon Welcome Centre, at the tourist office in the Palácio Foz, and at major hotels and other places around the city. Cardholders get to skip the line at many attractions, too.

Carris's tourism unit, Yellow Bus Tour, operates a special Hills Tramcar Tour, tickets for which are €18: the tram rattles through the most scenic parts of old Lisbon. Yellow Bus Tour also runs two different hop-on, hop-off routes (€17) in open-top buses, starting at Praça da Figueira. The Tagus Tour circles downtown and stops at the Belém Tower and the Jerónimos Monastery; the Olisipo Tour heads east to the Military Museum, Ceramic Tile Museum, and Parque das Nações. These special trams and buses depart from Praça do Comércio, starting at about 10 am. There is also a minibus in Belém, shuttling between museums and other sites in that area. ■TIP➔ **Keep a close eye on your belongings when using public transportation, especially Tram 28, during busy times. Pickpockets ply their trade on crowded trains, buses, and trams.**

Carris Contacts Carris. ☎ *21/361–3000* ⊕ *www.carris.pt.* **Yellow Bus Tour.** ☎ *21/347–8030 tourist information* ⊕ *www.yellowbustours.com/en-GB/Lisbon/ Circuits.aspx.*

Metro Contact Metropolitano de Lisboa. ☎ *21/3500115* ⊕ *metro.transporteslisboa.pt.*

TAXI TRAVEL

Taxis in Lisbon are relatively cheap, and the airport is so close to the city center that many visitors make a beeline for a cab queue outside the terminal. To avoid any hassle over fares you can buy a prepaid voucher (which includes gratuity and luggage charges) from the tourist office booth in the arrivals hall. Expect to pay €10–€20 to most destinations in the city center and around €40 if you're headed for Estoril or Sintra. Uber is also very popular in Lisbon, and it's worth downloading the app even if you're not a regular user. Prices are at least a third cheaper than taxis on most journeys, and you won't have to fiddle around with cash.

Drivers use meters but can take out-of-towners for a ride, literally, by not taking the most direct route. If you book a cab from a hotel or restaurant, have someone speak to the driver so there are no "misunderstandings" about your destination. The meter starts at €3.25 during the day and €3.90 at night (9 pm–6 am) and on weekends. You pay what is on the meter. Supplementary charges are added for luggage (€1.60) and if you phone for a cab (€0.80). The meter isn't always used for long-distance journeys outside Lisbon, so it is often possible to agree a flat fare up front. Do this before you get in or load your luggage, and don't be afraid to bargain.

You may hail cruising vehicles, but it's sometimes difficult to get drivers' attention; there are taxi stands at most main squares. Contrary to the norm in many countries, when the green light is on it means the cab is already occupied. Tips—no more than 10%—for reliable drivers are appreciated.

Taxi Contacts Autocoope. ☎ *21/793–2756* ⊕ *autocoope.pai.pt.* **Retális.** ☎ *21/811–9000* ⊕ *www.retalis.pt.* **Teletáxis.** ☎ *21/811–1100* ⊕ *www.teletaxis.pt.*

TRAIN TRAVEL

International and long-distance trains arrive at Santa Apolónia station, to the east of Lisbon's center, after passing through Gare do Oriente, where commuter trains from south of the river, and fast trains from the Algarve also stop. Services to Sintra use Rossio station, a neo-Manueline building just off Rossio square itself. Trains along the Estoril Coast terminate at the waterfront Cais do Sodré station.

TOURS

Beware of unauthorized guides who approach you outside popular monuments and attractions: they're usually more concerned with "guiding" you to a particular shop or restaurant.

BUS TOURS

Many companies organize half-day group tours of Lisbon and its environs and full-day trips to more distant places of interest. Reservations can be made online, at Ask Me Lisboa kiosks, or through your hotel; some tours will pick you up at your door. A half-day tour of Lisbon starts at €35. As well as its city tram and bus tours, public transport company Carris also does a half-day tour of Sintra, Cascais, and the stunning coast between them. A full-day trip north to Obidos, perhaps also including Batalha, Alcobaça, Nazaré, and Fátima, will start at €70 for the ticket only, or €80 including lunch, as will a full day east to Évora and Monsaraz. Several of these companies also organize hop-on, hop-off tours of Lisbon, similar to those Carris offers, with open-top buses departing from the north side of Praça Marquês de Pombal. Cascais-based Guincho Aventours offers not only night tours of Lisbon but has off-road buggies for exploring the countryside outside the city, as well as bicycles for hire. Surfers of every ability can take trips, lessons included, out to the best breaks with Surf Bus.

Operators Cityrama Gray Line Portugal. ✉ *Av. João XXI Nº 78-E 1000-304, Areeiro* ☎ *21/319–1070, 21/352–2594* ⊕ *www.cityrama.pt.* **HIPPOtrip.** ✉ *Associação Naval de Lisboa, Doca de Santo Amaro, Alcântara* ☎ *21/192–2030* ⊕ *www.hippotrip.com.* **Rota Monumental.** ✉ *Rua Castelo Branco Saraiva 38* ☎ *916/306682* ⊕ *www.rotamonumental.com.*

PRIVATE GUIDES

For names of personal guides, contact Lisbon's main tourist office. An English-speaking guide for a half day starts at around €55, while a full day starts at around €95. For private wine-themed tours to Lisbon's hinterland, contact Have a Wine Day.

Contacts AGIC. ✉ *Rua Alexandre Herculano, 19, Sala 5, Liberdade* ☎ *931/108540* ⊕ *agic-portugal.com/english.* **Have a Wine Day.** ✉ *Largo de Santa Marinha 25, 2nd fl., Baixa* ☎ *916/470995* ⊕ *www.en.haveawineday.com.*

Lisbon Tour Guides. ✉ *Av. Brasilia, Belém* ⊕ *lisbontourguides.pt.* **We Hate Tourism Tours.** ✉ *LX Factory, Rua Rodrigues de Faria 103* ☎ *91/377–6598* ⊕ *www.wehatetourismtours.com.*

ADVENTURE TOURS

FAMILY **Guincho Aventours.** This enduringly popular tour company runs adventure tours in Lisbon's environs, including kayaking and quad biking, as well as family-friendly excursions such as dolphin-spotting boat trips. ✉ *Rua da Areia n.° 1306, Cascais* ☎ *21/486–9700* ⊕ *www.guincho-tours.net* ✆ *Tours from $40.*

Surf Bus. Surf Bus runs private and group trips to the best surf beaches surrounding Lisbon, including Guincho, Costa da Caparica, and Praia Grande. Full-day tours can take in farther-flung spots such as Ericeira or Peniche. Hotel pickup, lessons, and equipment are available. ✉ *Condomínio Alcântara Rio, Rua Cozinha Economica, No. 36, 2 Dto, Alcântara* ☎ *918/ 592002 (mobile)* ⊕ *www.surfbus.pt* ✆ *Half-day trips from €10 per person.*

WALKING TOURS

Walking tours of Lisbon require strong legs and sturdy shoes, but walkers are well rewarded with incredible views and unique insights into the city and its history. Visitors can take free (donations are encouraged) walking tours of Lisbon with Lisbon Chill-Out Free Tour, or pay around $15 for more personalized trips with outfits such as Inside Lisbon and Cool Tour LX. Lisbon Walker does tailor-made walks and also has the widest range of regular theme tours, such as Jewish Lisbon, African Lisbon, and even Lisbon: City of Spies. For most you don't need to book; just check the schedule and turn up at the meeting point by the tourist office on Praça do Comércio. Lisbon Explorer, by contrast, specializes in prearranged group and individual tours, often with special themes such as food and wine.

Contacts Cool Tour LX. ✉ *Av. Infante Santo 23, 5th fl.* ☎ *21/395–1624* ⊕ *www.cooltourlx.com.* **Inside Lisbon.** ✉ *Av. Forças Armadas, n.° 95, 1st fl.* ☎ *21/1914545* ⊕ *www.insidelisbon.com.* **Lisbon Chill-Out Free Tour.** ✉ *Praca Luis de Camoes, Baixa* ⊕ *lisbonfreetour.blogspot.pt* Ⓜ *Baixa-Chiado.* **Lisbon Explorer.** ☎ *21/362–9263, 96/825–3684* ⊕ *www.lisbonexplorer.com.* **Lisbon Walker.** ☎ *21/886–1840, 96/357–5635* ⊕ *www.lisbonwalker.com.*

VISITOR INFORMATION

Visitors' first port of call in downtown Lisbon should be the Ask Me Lisboa welcome center at Terreiro do Paço, where English-speakers offer advice on everything from public transport to booking wine tours and surf classes. There are pamphlets offering all manner of officially approved trips and tours, along with free Wi-Fi. You can also pick up a Lisboa Card here, which offers unlimited travel on public transport as well as discounted or free access to many major tourist attractions. The passes cost €11.50 for 24 hours, €17.50 for 48 hours, or €20.50 for 72 hours. There's also a branch at the airport that's open daily 7 am to midnight, and booths at key spots including Santa Apolónia (daily 8–1 and 2–4), Rossio (Praça D. Pedro IV, 10–1 and 2–6), and across from Mosteiro de Jerónimos in Belém (10–6).

Visitor Information Ask Me Lisboa. ✉ *Praça do Comércio (Terreiro do Paço),
Baixa* ☎ *21/031–2810, 21/845–0660 for airport branch* ⊕ *www.askmelisboa.
com* Ⓜ *Terreiro do Paço.* **Ask Me Palácio Foz.** ✉ *Palácio Foz, Praça dos Restauradores* ☎ *21/346–3314* ⊕ *www.askmelisboa.com/palacio_foz.*

EXPLORING

Although Baixa, or downtown, was Lisbon's government and business center for two centuries until the mid-20th century, the most ancient part of the city lies on the slopes of a hill to its east. Most visitors start their exploration there, in Alfama. All but the very fittest ride the antique Tram 28 *eléctrico* (streetcar) most of the way up to Saint George's Castle (or take Bus 737 or a taxi all the way up). The views from its ramparts afford a crash course in the city's topography. You can then wander downhill to absorb the atmosphere (and more views) in the winding streets below. There are several museums and other major sights in this area, so give yourself plenty of time.

On the slope to the west is the chic Chiado district, traditionally the city's intellectual center, with theaters, galleries, and literary cafés. A little farther uphill is the Bairro Alto. Originally founded by the Jesuits (whose church is among Lisbon's finest), it was long known for rather sinful pursuits and today is a great place for barhopping. Both neighborhoods are great places to shop.

Modern Lisbon, meanwhile, begins just north of Baixa. The city's tree-lined central axis, the Avenida da Liberdade, forges up to the Praça Marquês de Pombal roundabout, with a rather formal park beyond. Dotted around the area north of here are major museums and other sights.

West of Baixa, along the river, a onetime red-light area at Cais do Sodré, has been given a stylish overhaul to become a hot spot for boutique hotels and trendy gin bars, while former docklands such as Alcântara are now home to stylish restaurants and nightclubs. The city's hipster headquarters, at LX Factory, boasts a collection of trendy boutiques, cafés, and coworking spaces as well as a celebrated rooftop bar with magnificent views over the river. Farther west is historic Belém, arguably the most picturesque of Lisbon's neighborhoods, and home to two UNESCO monuments including a magnificent Manueline monastery that should be on every sightseer's agenda. It's also home to excellent cultural centers, and the most famous *pastéisde nata* (egg custard tart) in the country. On the city's eastern flank, the modern Parque das Nações has family-oriented attractions, including Europe's largest aquarium, and green spaces.

ALFAMA

In the Alfama district, narrow, twisting streets and soaring flights of steps wind up to an imposing castle on one of the city's highest hills. This is a grand place to get your bearings and take in supreme views. Because its foundation is dense bedrock, the district—a jumble of whitewashed

A BIT OF HISTORY

Lisbon's geographical location, sitting alongside the wide and natural harbor of the Tejo River, has made it strategically important as a trading seaport throughout the ages. The city was probably founded around 1200 BC by the Phoenicians, who traded from its port and called it Alis-Ubo. The Greeks came next, naming it Olisipo. But it wasn't until 205 BC that Lisbon prospered, when the Romans, calling it in their turn Felicitas Julia, linked it by road to the great Spanish cities of the Iberian Peninsula. The Visigoths followed in the 5th century and built the earliest fortifications on the site of the Castelo de São Jorge, but it was with the arrival of the Moors in AD 714 that Lisbon, then renamed Al-Ushbuna, came into its own. The city flourished as a trading center during the four centuries of Moorish rule, and the Alfama—Lisbon's oldest district—retains its intricate Arab-influenced layout. In 1147 the Christian army, led by Dom Afonso Henriques and with the assistance of northern Crusaders, took the city after a ruthless siege. To give thanks for the end of Moorish rule, Dom Afonso planned a cathedral on the site of a mosque, and the building was dedicated three years later. A little more than a century after that, in 1255, the rise of Lisbon was complete when the royal seat of power was transferred here from Coimbra by Afonso III, and Lisbon was declared capital of Portugal.

The next great period—that of *os descobrimentos* (the discoveries)—began with the 15th-century voyages led by the great Portuguese navigators to India, Africa, and Brazil. During this era, Vasco da Gama set sail for the Indies in 1497–99 and Brazil was discovered in 1500. The wealth realized by these expeditions was phenomenal: gold, jewels, ivory, porcelain, and spices helped finance grand buildings and impressive commercial activity. Late-Portuguese Gothic architecture—called Manueline (after the king Dom Manuel I)—assumed a rich, individualistic style, characterized by elaborate sculptural details, often with a maritime motif. The Torre de Belém and the Mosteiro dos Jerónimos (Belém's tower and monastery) are supreme examples of this period.

A dynastic coup led to a few decades of rule from Madrid, which ended in 1640. With the assumption of the throne by successive dukes of the house of Bragança, Lisbon became ever more prosperous, only to suffer calamity on November 1, 1755, when it was hit by the last of a series of earthquakes. Two-thirds of Lisbon was destroyed, and tremors were felt as far north as Scotland; 40,000 people in Lisbon died, and entire sections of the city were swept away by a tidal wave.

Under the direction of the prime minister, Sebastião José de Carvalho e Melo, later to be named Marquês de Pombal in reward for his efforts, Lisbon was rebuilt quickly and ruthlessly. The medieval quarters were leveled and replaced with broad boulevards; the commercial center, the Baixa, was laid out in a grid; and the great Praça do Comércio, the riverfront square, was planned. Essentially, downtown Lisbon has an elegant 18th-century layout that remains as pleasing today as it was intended to be 250 years ago.

Casa dos
Bicos **7**

Castelo de
São Jorge **1**

Galeria Filomena
Soares **11**

Lisbon Cathedral
(Sé de Lisboa) .. **6**

Miradouro de
Santa Luzia **4**

Mosteiro de
São Vicente **2**

Museu do Teatro
Romano **5**

Museu-Escola
de Artes
Decorativas **3**

Museu Militar **8**

Museu
Nacional do
Azulejo **10**

Panteão de Santa
Engrácia **9**

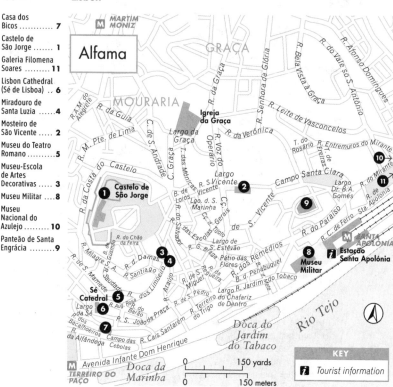

houses with flower-laden balconies and red-tile roofs—has mostly survived the wear and tear of the ages, including the great 1755 earthquake.

The timeless alleys and squares have a notoriously confusing layout, but the Alfama is relatively compact, and you'll keep circling back to the same buildings and streets. Once rather run-down, it now throngs with tourists as cool bars, boutique hotels, and restaurants are moving in.

GETTING HERE AND AROUND

The Alfama's streets and alleys are very steep, and its levels are connected by flights of stone steps, which means it's easier to tour the area from the top down. Take a taxi up to the castle or approach it by Tram 28 from Rua da Conceição in the Baixa or Bus 737 from Praça da Figueira. The large terrace next to the church of Santa Luzia, just below the castle, gives a glorious overview of the Alfama and the river. There are two metro stations on the southern edge of the neighborhood: Terreiro do Paço and Santa Apolónia.

TIMING

Allow two to three hours to walk the Alfama, perhaps more on a hot day, when you'll want to rest on the castle grounds or stop for drinks in a café. A visit to the Museu-Escola de Artes Decorativas will occupy at least an hour or two. It is closed Tuesday, while most other museums are closed Monday; churches generally close for a couple of hours in the middle of the day.

TOP ATTRACTIONS

FAMILY

Fodor's Choice

★

Castelo de São Jorge. Although St. George's Castle was constructed by the Moors, the site had previously been fortified by Romans and Visigoths. To your left as you pass through the main entrance is a statue of Dom Afonso Henriques, whose forces in 1147 besieged the castle and drove the Moors from Lisbon. The ramparts offer panoramic views of the city's layout as far as the towering Ponte 25 de Abril suspension bridge; be careful of the uneven footing. Remnants of a palace that was a residence of the kings of Portugal until the 16th century house a snack bar, a small museum showcasing archeological finds, and beyond them a stately restaurant, the Casa do Leão, offering dining with spectacular sunset views. From the *periscópio* (periscope) in the Torre de Ulísses, in the castle's keep, you can spy on visitors going about their business below. Beyond the keep, traces of pre-Roman and Moorish houses are visible thanks to recent archaeological digs, as well as the remains of a palace founded in the 15th century. The castle's outer walls encompass a small neighborhood, Castelo, the medieval church of Santa Cruz, restaurants, and souvenir shops. ⊠ *Rua de Santa Cruz do Castelo, Alfama* ☎ *21/880–0620* ⊕ *www.castelodesaojorge.pt* ⊠ *€8.50.*

Fodor's Choice

★

Galeria Filomena Soares. Housed in a large former warehouse not far from the Museu Nacional do Azulejo, this gallery is owned and bears the name of one of Europe's leading female art dealers. Her roster includes leading local and international artists, such as Ângela Ferreira and Shirin Neshat. ⊠ *Rua da Manutenção 80, Xabregas* ☎ *21/862–4122* ⊕ *www.gfilomenasoares.com.*

Museu-Escola de Artes Decorativas. In the 17th-century Azurara Palace, the Museum-School of Decorative Arts has objects that date to the 15th through 19th centuries. Look for brightly colored Arraiolos—traditional, hand-embroidered Portuguese carpets based on imported Arabic designs—as well as silver work, ceramics, paintings, and jewelry. With so many rich items to preserve, the museum has become a major center for restoration. Crafts such as bookbinding, carving, and cabinetmaking are all undertaken here by highly trained staff; you can view the restoration work by appointment. ⊠ *Largo das Portas do Sol 2, Alfama* ☎ *21/881–4600* ⊕ *www.fress.pt* ⊠ *€4* ☉ *Closed Tues.*

Fodor's Choice

★

Museu Nacional do Azulejo. A tile museum might not sound thrilling, but this magnificent museum dedicated to Lisbon's eye-catching azulejos is one of the Alfama's top tourist attractions—and with good reason. Housed in the16th-century Madre de Deus convent and cloister, displays range from individual glazed tiles to elaborate pictorial panels. The 118-foot *Panorama of Lisbon* (1730) is a detailed study of the city and waterfront and is reputedly the country's longest azulejo piece. The richly furnished convent church contains some sights of its own: of note are the gilt baroque decoration and lively azulejo works depicting the life of St. Anthony. There are also a little café-bar and a gift shop that sells tile reproductions. ⊠ *Rua da Madre de Deus 4, Madre de Deus* ☎ *21/810–0340* ⊕ *www.museudoazulejo.pt* ⊠ *€5 (free Sun. until 2 pm)* ☉ *Closed Mon.*

WORTH NOTING

Casa dos Bicos. This Italianate dwelling is one of Alfama's most distinctive buildings. It was built in 1523 for Bras de Albuquerque, the son of Afonso, who became the viceroy of India and who conquered Goa and Malacca. The name translates as "house of points," and it's not hard to see why—it has a striking facade studded with pointed white stones in diamond shapes. The top two floors were destroyed in the 1755 earthquake, and restoration did not begin until the early 1980s. Since 2012 the building has housed the José Saramago Foundation, a cultural institute set up in memory of the only Portuguese-language winner of the Nobel Prize in Literature, with two floors dedicated to his life and works. ⊠ *Rua dos Bacalhoeiros, Alfama* ☎ *21/880–2040* ⊕ *www.josesaramago.org* ⛶ *€3* ☉ *Closed Sun.* Ⓜ *Terreiro do Paço.*

Fodor'sChoice **Lisbon Cathedral (Sé de Lisboa).** Lisbon's austere Romanesque cathedral, ★ Sé (which stands for *Sedes Episcopalis*), was founded in 1150 to commemorate the defeat of the Moors three years earlier. To rub salt in the wound, the conquerors built the sanctuary on the spot where Moorish Lisbon's main mosque once stood. Note the fine rose window, and be sure to visit the 13th-century cloister and the treasure-filled sacristy, which, among other things, contains the relics of the martyr St. Vincent. According to legend, the relics were carried from the Algarve to Lisbon in a ship piloted by ravens; the saint became Lisbon's official patron. The cathedral was originally built in the Romanesque style of the time, but has undergone several rebuilds and refurbishments over the years, and today its rather eclectic architecture includes Gothic, baroque, and neoclassical adornments. ⊠ *Largo da Sé, Alfama* ☎ *21/887–6628* ⊕ *www.patrimoniocultural.pt/en/* ⛶ *Cathedral free, cloisters €2.50.*

Miradouro de Santa Luzia. Hop off Tram 28 at the Miradouro de Santa Luzia, a terrace-garden viewpoint that takes in the Alfama and the river. Here, and around the corner at Largo das Portas do Sol, there are a number of small café-bars with outside seats from which you can watch ships on the Rio Tejo. Artists here sell reasonably priced etchings of the scene. ⊠ *Miradouro de Santa Luzia, Alfama* ☎ *21/887–4859.*

Mosteiro de São Vicente. The Italianate facade of the twin-towered St. Vincent's Monastery heralds an airy church with a barrel-vault ceiling, the work of accomplished Italian architect Filippo Terzi (1520–97), finally completed in 1704. Its superbly tiled cloister depicts the fall of Lisbon to the Moors. The monastery also serves as the pantheon of the Bragança dynasty, who ruled Portugal from the restoration of independence from Spain in 1640 to the declaration of the Republic in 1910. It's worth the admission fee alone to climb up to the towers and rooftop terrace for a look over the Alfama, the dome of the nearby Santa Engrácia, and the river. ⊠ *Largo de São Vicente, Alfama* ☎ *21/888–5652* ⛶ *€5* ☉ *Closed Mon.*

FAMILY **Museu do Teatro Romano.** This small museum close to the cathedral displays some of the few visible traces of Roman Lisbon. The space was once a Roman amphitheater with capacity for 5,000 spectators, and was built by Emperor Augustus in the 1st century BC. It fell into disrepair during the Middle Ages, and lay buried and forgotten until reconstruction of the area began in the 18th century. Columns and other interesting artifacts are on display here, and multilingual touch-screen videos outline the history of the amphitheater and Lisbon's Roman history. ⊠ *Rua de São Mamede, nº 3 A, Alfama ⊹ Entrances are on Rua de São Mamede, and on the main road opposite the cathedral* ☎ *21/817–2450* ⊕ *www. museudelisboa.pt/equipamentos/ teatro-romano* ✆ *€1.50 (free Sun. after 2 pm)* ⊗ *Closed Mon.*

FEIRA DA LADRA FLEA MARKET

If you're in Alfama on a Tuesday or Saturday, make sure to take in the Feira da Ladra flea market, which takes place on Campo de Santa Clara, from dawn to early afternoon (it runs a bit later on Saturday). The quality of the wares on offer varies tremendously, but it's a fun place for people-watching.

Museu Militar. The spirit of heroism is palpable in the huge Corinthian-style barracks and arsenal complex of the Military Museum, which houses one of the largest artillery collections in the world. Visitors can ogle a 20-ton bronze cannon and admire Vasco de Gama's sword in a room dedicated to the explorer and his voyages of discovery. As you clatter through endless, echoing rooms of weapons, uniforms, and armor, you may be lucky enough to be followed—at a respectful distance—by a guide who, without speaking a word of English, can convey exactly how that bayonet was jabbed or that gruesome flail swung. In this beautifully ornate building there is also a collection of 18th- to 20th-century art. The museum is on the eastern edge of the Alfama, at the foot of the hill and opposite the Santa Apolónia station. ⊠ *Largo do Museu da Artilharia, Alfama* ☎ *21/884–2300* ⊕ *www.exercito.pt/sites/MusMilLisboa/Paginas/ default.aspx* ✆ *€3* ⊗ *Closed Mon.* Ⓜ *Santa Apolónia.*

Panteão de Santa Engrácia. The large domed edifice immediately behind and below São Vicente is the former church of Santa Engrácia. It took 285 years to build, hence the Portuguese phrase "a job like Santa Engrácia," meaning one that seems to take forever. Today the building doubles as Portugal's Panteão Nacional (National Pantheon), housing the tombs of Portugal's former presidents as well as cenotaphs dedicated to its most famous explorers and writers. A more recent arrival is fado diva Amália Rodrigues, whose tomb is invariably piled high with flowers from admirers. ⊠ *Campo de Santa Clara, Alfama* ☎ *21/885–4820* ✆ *€4* ⊗ *Closed Mon.* Ⓜ *Santa Apolónia.*

NEED A BREAK

For one of of Lisbon's loveliest views, take the Tram 28 all the way up to Graça and then walk to the miradouro in front of the local church, the Igreja da Graça, where a kiosk serves snacks and drinks until well past midnight. It's a particularly nice place to watch the sun set over the city.

EN ROUTE

On your way up to the Sé, note the small baroque church on the left: it was built on the birthplace of the man the Catholic Church calls St. Anthony of Padua, but whom Lisboetas just call "Santo António." On June 12, the eve of his saint's day, the church hosts mass weddings paid for by the city hall. Most of those present will then stay up much of the following night, celebrating along with the rest of town the most important of the month's Santos Populares festivals. Next door to the saint's church is the Museu Antoniano, with its curious collection of religious and secular items relating to him.

BAIXA

The earthquake of 1755, and the ensuing massive tidal wave and fires, killed thousands of people and reduced 18th-century Lisbon to rubble. But within a decade, frantic rebuilding under the direction of the king's minister, the Marquês de Pombal, had given the Baixa, or downtown, a neoclassical look. Full of shops, restaurants, and other commercial enterprises, it stretches from the riverfront Praça do Comércio to the square known as the Rossio. Pombal intended the various streets to house workshops for certain trades and crafts, something that's still reflected in street names such as Rua dos Sapateiros (Cobblers' Street) and Rua da Prata (Silversmiths' Street).

Near the neoclassical arch at the bottom of Rua Augusta you'll find street vendors selling jewelry. Northeast of Rossio, the Rua das Portas de Santo Antão has seafood restaurants, while the area also has three surviving ginjinha bars—cubbyholes where local characters throw down shots of cherry brandy. One is in Largo de São Domingos itself, another a few doors up Rua das Portas de Santo Antão, and the third 66 feet east along Rua Barros Queiroz.

GETTING HERE AND AROUND

Baixa is Lisbon's downtown, so the area is well served by public transport. Local metro stations include Terreiro do Paço, Baixa-Chiado, and Rossio; large numbers of buses also ply the north–south streets of its regular grid, though their stops are all at its northern and southern ends, on Rossio and on or near Praça do Comércio.

TIMING

You could walk the Baixa in a half hour, but multiply that by four to allow time to explore the sights and poke into shops. Then add an hour or more for people-watching or lingering in a café, enjoying the Rossio's satisfying chaos.

TOP ATTRACTIONS

Elevador de Santa Justa. Built in 1902 by Raul Mésnier, who studied under Eiffel, the Santa Justa Elevator, inside a Gothic-style tower, is one of Lisbon's more extraordinary structures. Queues are often frustratingly long in high season, but it's an enjoyable ride up to the top. After stepping outside the elevator compartment at the upper level, you can either take the walkway leading to the Largo do Carmo, or climb the staircase to the miradouro at the very top of the structure (147½ feet up) for views of the Baixa district and beyond. The return ticket sold on board includes access to the miradouro, but at €5 is poor value—a 24-hour Carris public transport card costs €6 and is valid on all Lisbon's lifts as well as buses, trams, and metro. There's a an extra €1.50 charge for access to the viewpoint when using the public transport card, but it's included in the price when using a Lisboa Card. ⊠ *Rua do Ouro, Baixa* ⊕ *carris.transporteslisboa. pt/en/elevators* 🎫 *€5 round-trip* Ⓜ *Baixa-Chiado.*

FAMILY
Fodor'sChoice
★

Praça do Comércio. Known to locals as the Terreiro do Paço, after the royal palace (the Paço) that once stood here, the Praça do Comércio is lined with 18th-century buildings now fronted by expansive esplanades and doing a roaring trade in light meals and drinks. Down by the river, steps and slopes—once used by occupants of the royal barges that docked here—lead up from the water, and sunbathers strip down to catch rays here during the summer months. The equestrian statue in the center is of Dom José I, king at the time of the earthquake and subsequent rebuilding. In 1908, amid unrest that led to the declaration of a republic, King Carlos and his eldest son, Luís Filipe, were assassinated as they rode through the square in a carriage. On the north side, the Arco Triunfal (Triumphal Arch) was the last structure to be completed, in 1873. ⊠ *Praça do Comércio, Baixa* Ⓜ *Terreiro do Paço.*

Arco da Rua Augusta. Capping the post-earthquake restoration of Lisbon's downtown, the Triumphal Arch offers a splendid viewpoint from which to admire the handsome buildings that were constructed in the wake of the devastating quake. Access is via an elevator and then up two narrow, winding flights of stairs. Once at the top, young visitors delight in ringing a giant bell, while the grown-ups can admire views over Praça do Comércio and the River Tejo in one direction, and peek at shoppers, street performers, and sightseers ambling along Rua Augusta in the other. The red-roofed houses and grand religious buildings that climb up the surrounding hillsides complete the scene. ⊠ *Rua Augusta 2, Baixa* 🎫 *€2.50* Ⓜ *Terreiro do Paço.*

Lisboa Story Centre. Enjoying a prime location on the Terre, this family-friendly interactive museum uses multimedia exhibits to bring Lisbon's fascinating history to life. The story is broken down into chapters, with a significant focus on the golden age of Portuguese maritime discoveries. A multilingual audio guide takes visitors through a series of exhibits. Midway through, a small cinema shows a short but dramatic reenactment of the 1755 earthquake and the fiery aftermath. Visitors can buy a ticket that gives access to the Story Centre and Rua Augusta Arch for a discounted price. ⊠ *Praço do Comércio 78-81, Baixa* ⊕ *www.lisboastorycentre.pt* 🎫 *€7* Ⓜ .

NEED A
BREAK

Café Martinho da Arcada. One of the original buildings on Praça do Comércio houses the Café Martinho da Arcada, a literary haunt since 1782, favored by modernist poet Fernando Pessoa. The main rooms contain an expensive restaurant; adjacent to it is a more modest café-bar. ⊠ *Praça do Comércio 3, Baixa* ☎ *21/887–9259* ⊕ *www.martinhodaarcada.pt.*

FAMILY
Fodor'sChoice
★

Rossio. The formal name for this grand public square is Praça Dom Pedro IV, but locals prefer to call it by its former name, Rossio. Built in the 13th century as Lisbon's main public space, it remains a bustling social hub and, traffic noise aside, it's still a grand public space where lively crowds gather to socialize among baroque fountains beneath a statue of Dom Pedro atop a towering column. Visitors can admire the dramatic wave-pattern cobblestones (famously reconstructed on the beach promenades of Rio de Janeiro) and soak up the sense of drama. The square was founded as the largest public space in the city, and has

Baixa ▼

Elevador de
Santa Justa **5**

Núcleo
Arqueologico da
Rua dos
Correeiros **4**

Praça do
Comércio **1**

Rossio **7**

**Chiado and
Bairro Alto** ▼

Convento do
Carmo **6**

Elevador da
Glória **9**

Igreja e
Museu de
São Roque **8**

Museu da
Farmácia **3**

Museu Nacional
de Arte
Contemporânea .**2**

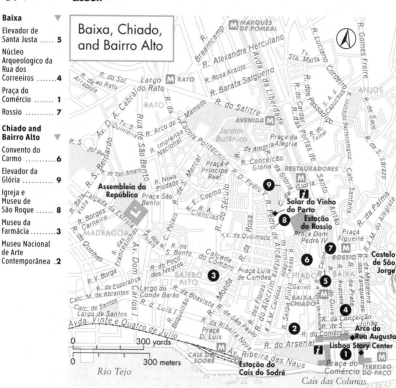

seen everything from bullfights and musical performances to public
executions. During the Portuguese Inquisition, it was the setting for
public autos-da-fé. The site of the gruesome procedures is now occupied
by the imposing 19th-century Teatro Nacional (National Theater). On
nearby Largo de São Domingos, where thousands were burned, there's
a memorial to Jewish victims of the Inquisition. Today, locals come
here to relax with a newspaper, have their boots polished by the shoe
shiners, or sip a *ginjinha* (traditional sour-cherry liqueur) at one of the
bars. Tourists come to sip somewhat overpriced coffees and snacks at
the café-bars that flank the square, and protestors come to loudly but
respectfully state their political case. Another suitably grand building
houses downtown's main train station, which is the starting point for
trips to Sintra. ⊠ *Praça Dom Pedro IV (Rossio), Baixa* Ⓜ *Rossio.*

WORTH NOTING

Fodor's Choice   **Núcleo Arqueologico da Rua dos Correeiros.** More than 2,500 years of his-
★   tory has been uncovered at this archaeological treasure trove hidden
beneath a bank on one of Lisbon's busiest shopping streets. The buried
network of tunnels occupies almost a whole block in Lisbon's historic
center, and was unearthed in the 1990s during excavation works carried out by Millennium BCP, the bank to whom the site belongs. The
digs revealed homes and artifacts from the Roman, Visigoth, Islamic,

medieval, and Pombaline periods, and much of the space appears to have been used as a major-scale Roman fish-salting factory. It was later used as a Christian burial ground, and there's even a well-preserved skeleton to be seen. Free guided visits (in English or Portuguese) lead visitors through underground walkways, catching a glimpse of how post-earthquake foundations were laid for the Pombaline buildings that still stand proud today. Free tours in English leave roughly every two hours, on the hour; arrive at least 30 minutes before to book your place, as space is (quite literally) limited. ⊠ *Rua dos Correeiros, n° 21, entrance on Rua Augusta, Baixa* ☎ *21/1131004* ⊕ *ind.millenniumbcp. pt/en/Institucional/fundacao/Pages/fundacao_NARC.aspx* ⊘ *Closed Sun.* Ⓜ *Baixa-Chiado or Terreiro do Paço.*

CHIADO AND BAIRRO ALTO

West of Baixa is the fashionable shopping district of Chiado. Although a calamitous 1988 fire destroyed much of the area, an ambitious rebuilding program restored some of the fin de siècle facades. A chic retail complex and hotel on the site of the old Armazéns do Chiado—once Lisbon's most celebrated department store—has given the district a modern focus. Along Rua Garrett and Rua do Carmo are some of Europe's best shoe stores as well as glittering jewelry shops, hip boutiques, and a host of delis and cafés.

Chiado's narrow, often cobbled streets lead to the Bairro Alto and often follow contours of the hills, which can make getting around confusing. Although the settlement of Bairro Alto dates to the 17th century, most of the buildings are from the 18th and 19th centuries and are an appealing mixture of small churches, warehouses, antiques and art galleries, artisans' shops, and town houses with wrought-iron balconies.

GETTING HERE AND AROUND

Chiado is served by the Baixa-Chiado metro station, with a series of escalators bearing passengers up under Rua Garrett to Largo do Chiado. Tram 28 rumbles through here, on its way between the Baixa and Estrela. Farther uphill, Bairro Alto can be reached by the Elevador de Santa Justa elevator or the Elevador da Glória funicular, which steams up from a standing start on Praça dos Restauradores, at the start of the Avenida da Liberdade, the city's modern central axis. Another approach to Bairro Alto is from Rato metro station, passing the Jardim Botânico and the Jardim do Príncipe Real on the way. Head this way for superchic shopping at the grand Embaixada gallery of upscale boutiques.

TIMING

Both Chiado and Bairro Alto are remarkably compact, and it takes little time to walk from one end to the other; an hour would cover it. But once you start diving off into the side streets and lingering in the shops, galleries, and bars, you'll find you can happily spend a morning or afternoon here (or a night in the case of the late-opening Bairro Alto). After midnight the streets get very busy, especially on weekends, when seemingly half of Lisbon comes here to eat, drink, and party.

TOP ATTRACTIONS

Igreja e Museu de São Roque. Designed by Filippo Terzi and completed in 1574, this church was one of the earliest Jesuit buildings in the world. While the exterior is somewhat plain and austere, the inside is dazzling, with abundant use of gold and marble. Eight side chapels have statuary and art dating to the early 17th century. The last chapel on the left before the altar is the extraordinary 18th-century Capela de São João Baptista (Chapel of St. John the Baptist): designed and built in Rome, with rare stones and mosaics that resemble oil paintings, the chapel was taken apart, shipped to Lisbon, and reassembled here in 1747. The museum adjoining the church displays a surprisingly engaging collection of clerical vestments and liturgical objects. There is also a stylish café with patio, serving light gourmet meals and snacks; they also do weekend brunches. ⊠ *Largo Trindade Coelho, Bairro Alto* ☎ *21/323–5421* ⊕ *www.museudesaoroque.com* ✉ *Church free, museum €2.50 (free Sun.)* Ⓜ *Baixa-Chiado or Restauradores (then Elevador da Glória).*

WORTH NOTING

Convento do Carmo. The Carmelite Convent—once Lisbon's largest—was all but ruined by the 1755 earthquake, and its skeletal remains are stark reminders of the quake's devastating impact. Its sacristy houses the **Museu Arqueológico do Carmo** (Archaeological Museum), a small collection of ceramic tiles, medieval tombs, ancient coins, and other city finds. The tree-shaded square outside—accessible via a walkway from the top of the Elevador da Santa Justa —is a great place to dawdle over a coffee. ⊠ *Largo do Carmo, Chiado* ☎ *21/347–8629* ⊕ *www.museuarqueologicodocarmo.pt* ✉ *€3.50* ⊘ *Closed Sun.* Ⓜ *Baixa-Chiado or Rossio (then Elevador de Santa Justa).*

FAMILY   **Elevador da Glória.** One of the finest approaches to the Bairro Alto is via this funicular railway inaugurated in 1888 on the western side of Avenida da Liberdade, near Praça dos Restauradores. It runs up the steep hill and takes only about a minute to reach the São Pedro de Alcântara Miradouro, a viewpoint that looks out over the castle and the Alfama. ⊠ *Calçada da Glória, Bairro Alto* ✉ *€3.60 round-trip (free with Viva Viagem card)* Ⓜ *Restauradores.*

Museu da Farmácia. The Museum of Pharmacy, within an old palace, covers more than 5,000 years of pharmaceutical history, from prehistoric cures to the fantastic world of fictive potions à la Harry Potter. Ancient objects related to pharmaceutical science and art—from Mesopotamian, Egyptian, Roman, and Incan civilizations—are on display in well-lighted showcases, as are those from Europe. Whole pharmacies have been transported here intact from other parts of Portugal, even a traditional 19th-century Chinese drugstore from Portugal's former territory of Macau. There's also a smart bar and restaurant called Pharmacia that serves lunch and dinner as well as afternoon *petiscos,* tasty Portuguese bar snacks. ⊠ *Rua Marechal Saldanha 1, Chiado* ☎ *21/340–0680* ⊕ *www.museudafarmacia.pt* ✉ *€5* ⊘ *Closed Sun.* Ⓜ *Baixa-Chiado.*

Museu Nacional de Arte Contemporânea. Also known as the Museu do Chiado, this museum—built on the site of a monastery—specializes in Portuguese art from 1850 to the present day, covering various movements: Romanticism, Naturalism, Surrealism, and Modernism. The museum also hosts temporary exhibitions of paintings, sculpture, and multimedia installations, as well as summer jazz concerts in its small walled garden. ⊠ *Rua Serpa Pinto 4, Chiado* ☎ *21/343–2148* ⊕ *www.museuartecontemporanea.pt* ◪ *€4.50 (free 1st Sun. of the month)* ⊘ *Closed Mon.* Ⓜ *Baixa-Chiado.*

NEED A BREAK

Santini Chiado. For some of the best ice cream in town, drop into Santini Chiado, the Lisbon branch of a family concern founded in 1949 in the nearby resort of Cascais. The *travesseiros* (egg pastries) and *tarte de amêndoa* (almond tart) are also worth trying, as is the self-proclaimed World's Best Chocolate Cake—a delicious frozen dessert created in conjunction with famous Lisbon bakery O Melhor Bolo do Chocolate no Mundo. ⊠ *Rua do Carmo 9, Chiado* ☎ *21/835929* ⊕ *www.santini.pt* Ⓜ *Baixa-Chiado.*

THE MODERN CITY

The attractions of 19th- to 21st-century Lisbon are as diverse as they are far-flung. Near the large square Praça dos Restauradores, north of Rossio, the southern reaches of the modern city echo some of the Baixa. With its 10 parallel rows of trees, and themed drink-and-snack kiosks, Avenida da Liberdade is a pleasant place in which to linger and an easy-to-find reference point if you get lost in the surrounding backstreets. North of the city's main park, Parque Eduardo VII, the modern city stretches into residential suburbs with only the occasional attraction.

GETTING HERE AND AROUND
Unlike the Baixa, this area cannot be covered easily on foot. You can reach all its sights by metro, in some cases by bus or, if time is short, by taxi.

TIMING
The attractions of the Modern City are scattered over a large area, so it makes sense to set your itinerary according to your mood, energy levels, and the weather. It's best to focus on one area if you have just one day—to see everything, allow two or three days. It could take three hours to do justice to the Gulbenkian alone—especially if you have lunch on the premises. The palace and its gardens justify another hour easily; add another for walking (or two if you eschew any travel by taxis or metro), and perhaps another hour for shopping and a coffee break on the Avenida da Liberdade.

TOP ATTRACTIONS

Fodor'sChoice ★ **Museu Calouste Gulbenkian.** Set in lovely gardens filled with leafy walkways, blooming flowers, and waddling ducks, the museum of the celebrated Calouste Gulbenkian Foundation houses treasures collected by Armenian oil magnate Calouste Gulbenkian. The collection is split in two: one part is devoted to Egyptian, Greek, Roman, Islamic, and Asian art, and the other to European acquisitions. The quality of the pieces is magnificent, and you should aim to spend at least two hours here. English-language notes are available throughout. Varied and interesting temporary exhibitions are also often staged in the Foundation's main building, and the summer months see live classical music performances on the grounds. A walk through the gardens leads to the foundation's Modern Collection: 9,000 pieces from the 20th and 21st centuries, including sculptures, paintings, and photography. Portuguese artists make up the bulk of the collection, along with some big-name international artists including British artist David Hockney and renowned sculptor Antony Gormley. ⊠ *Av. de Berna 45, Praça de Espanha* ☎ *21/782–3000* ⊕ *gulbenkian.pt/en* 🎫 *Museum (Founder's Collection plus Modern Collection), €10; temporary exhibitions vary (free Sun. from 2)* ⊘ *Closed Mon.* Ⓜ *São Sebastião or Praça de Espanha.*

FAMILY **Palácio dos Marqueses da Fronteira.** Built in the late 17th century, the Palace of the Marquises, often called the Palácio Fronteira, remains one of the capital's most beautiful houses, containing splendid reception rooms with 17th- and 18th-century tiles, contemporary furniture, and paintings. Note that visits to this still-family-owned property are limited to guided tours in the morning—the palace itself is usually closed to visitors in the afternoon. The grounds have a terraced walk, a topiary garden, a statuary, and fountains. Some of the city's finest azulejos adorn the fountains and terraces and depict hunting scenes, battles, and religious themes. The palace is tricky to reach by public transport, but a taxi from Jardim Zoológico metro stop, about a mile away, will be quick and inexpensive. ⊠ *Largo de São Domingo de Benfica 1, Benfica* ☎ *21/778–2023* 🎫 *Palace and gardens €7.50, gardens €3* ⊘ *Closed Sun. and afternoons* Ⓜ *Jardim Zoológico (then 20-min walk, taxi, or Bus 770).*

WORTH NOTING

Avenida da Liberdade. In the Restauradores neighborhood, Liberty Avenue was laid out in 1879 as an elegant rival to the Champs Élysées. It has since has lost some of its allure: many of the late-19th-century mansions and art-deco buildings that once graced it have been demolished; others have been turned into soulless office blocks. There are, however, still some high-class hotels on the lower and midlevel sections, mixed in with international fashion outlets and the odd theater. Vehicles roar down both sides. It's still worth a leisurely stroll up the 1½-km (1-mile) length of the avenue, from Praça dos Restauradores to the Parque Eduardo VII, at least once—if only to cool off with a drink in one of the *quiosque* (refreshment kiosks) beneath the trees. ⊠ *Restauradores* Ⓜ *Avenida.*

OFF THE BEATEN PATH

Aqueduto das Aguas Livres. Lisbon was formerly provided with clean drinking water by means of the Aqueduct of Free Waters (1729–48), built by Manuel da Maia and stretching for more than 18 km (11 miles) from the water source on the outskirts of the city. The most imposing section is the 35 arches that stride across the Alcântara river valley beyond the Amoreiras shopping complex: the largest of these is said to be the highest ogival (pointed) arch in the world. You can access this section from the Campolide neighborhood. Nearer the city center, another 14 arches run 200 feet along the Praça das Amoreiras, ending in the Mãe d'Agua, an internal reservoir capable of holding more than a million gallons of water. This extraordinary structure is open for visits, providing a chance to see the holding tank, lavish internal waterfall, and associated machinery. ⊠ *Praca das Amoreiras 10, Campolide* ☏ *21/810–0215* ⊕ *www.epal.pt/EPAL/en/homepage* ⬛ *€2* ⊘ *Closed weekends.*

Casa-Museu Medeiros e Almeida. One of central Lisbon's best-kept secrets, this museum displays just part of a staggeringly rich private collection of furniture, porcelain, clocks, paintings, gold, and jewelry. In all, some 2,000 pieces are on show on two floors of the lovely 19th-century mansion where the eponymous collector once lived. ⊠ *Rua Rosa Araújo 41, Avenida da Liberdade* ☏ *21/354–7892* ⊕ *www.casa-museumedeirosealmeida.pt* ⬛ *Visits €5, guided tours €6 (min. 6 people)* ⊘ *Closed Sun.* Ⓜ *Marquês de Pombal.*

Fundação Arpad Szenes–Vieira da Silva. This stylishly adapted former royal silk factory is dedicated to Portuguese modernist painter Helena Vieira da Silva (1908–92) and her Hungarian-born husband Arpad Szenes (1897–1985), both of whom worked mainly in Paris. The museum not only showcases works from its own collection, but often stages interesting exhibitions featuring pieces by the likes of Picasso, Chagal, and others from that time. Guided tours of the gallery may be booked from Tuesday to Sunday, between 10 am and 5 pm. ⊠ *Praça das Amoreiras 58, Rato* ☏ *21/388–0044* ⊕ *www.fasvs.pt* ⬛ *€5 (free 1st Sun. of the month)* ⊘ *Closed Mon.* Ⓜ *Rato.*

Galeria 111. You might spot works of the famed Portuguese painter Paula Rego at Galeria 111, one of Portugal's best-known galleries. ⊠ *Campo Grande 113, Alvalade* ☏ *21/797–7418* ⊕ *www.111.pt.*

FAMILY
Fodor's Choice
★

Jardim Zoológico. Families should set aside a full day to explore this deservedly popular and immaculately maintained zoo, which is home to more than 3,000 animals from more than 330 species. The grounds are huge, but visitors can leap aboard a cable car to whiz from one attraction to another. Those who don't have a head for heights can board a miniature train (not included in entrance price) that trundles around the gardens. Highlights include a "Tigers' Valley," a gorilla house, a petting zoo, and twice-daily animal shows (you have your pick of those that feature parrots, pelicans, dolphins, sea lions, reptiles, or lemurs). There are several cafés on the grounds, as well as picnic areas for those who prefer a packed lunch. ⊠ *Praça Marechal Humberto Delgado, Sete Rios* ☏ *21/723–2910* ⊕ *www.zoo.pt* ⬛ *€19* Ⓜ *Jardim Zoológico.*

Praça de Touros de Campo Pequeno. Built in 1892, Lisbon's circular, redbrick, Moorish-style bullring is an eye-opening site. Encompassing esplanades and an underground mall, the ring holds about 9,000 people who crowd in to watch Portuguese-style bullfights (in which the bull is never killed in the ring), in season (April–October). The arena is also used as a venue for concerts and other events. Tickets for all are sold from a booth in the new shopping mall under the building, which is open daily from 10 am to 11 pm. (On show nights only, the little ticket windows on either side of the bullring's main gate are also open.) ⊠ *Av. da República, Campo Pequeno* ☏ *21/782–0572 for ticket office* ⊕ *www.campopequeno.com* ⬛ *Bullfights from €16* Ⓜ *Campo Pequeno.*

Aqueduto das
Aguas Livres **7**

Avenida da
Liberdade **2**

Casa-Museu
Medeiros e
Almeida **3**

Fundação Arpad
Szenes—Vieira da
Silva **4**

Galeria III **12**

Jardim
Zoológico **11**

Museu Calouste
Gulbenkian **8**

Palácio dos
Marqueses da
Fronteira **10**

Parque
Eduardo VII **6**

Praça dos
Restauradores .. **1**

Praça Marquês de
Pombal **5**

Praça de
Touros de Campo
Pequeno **9**

The Modern City

KEY

🛈 *Tourist information*

CIDADE
UNIVERSITARIA

CIDADE
UNIVERSITARIA

A. P.
Anibal Bettencourt

0 — 300 yards
0 — 300 meters

Avda. Egas Moniz

Az. das Galhardas

Avda. dos Combatentes

R. das Laranjeiras

LARANJEIRAS

TO BENFICA

Estrada das Laranjeiras

Estrada de Benfica

JARDIM ZOOLÓGICO

Avenida das Forças Armadas

ENTRE CAMPOS

Avenida Alvaro Pais

R. F. Holandia

R. Sousa Lopes

R. da Beneficencia

R. Carlos Reis

R. Filipe da Mata

R. P. Lima Basto

Avda. Columbano Bordalo Pinheiro

Avda. José Malhoa

R. de Campolide

Avda. S. Dumont

PRAÇA DE ESPANHA

Avenida da Berna

Avda. Marquês Sá da Bandeira

Avda. Marquês de Tomar

Avda. E. Garcia

Avda. Conde Valbom

Avda. M. Bombarda

Avda. V. Valmor

R. Ramalho Ortigão

Av. Ressano Garcia

R. Fialho de Almeida

R. Nic. Bettencourt

Parque de Palhava

Avda. J. Crisostomo

Avda. Duque D'Avila

Cinco

Outubro

Avenida Calouste Gulbenkian

R. de Campolide

Avda. Miguel Torga

Centro de Arte Moderna

S. SEBASTIÃO

Avda. António Augusto Aguiar

Avda. Conde Valbom

R. Pinheiro Chagas

R. Sebastião da Pedreira

R. L. Bivar

Avda. Sidónio Pais

R. F. Folgueira

R. T. Ribeiro

R. Latino Coelho

Aqueduto das Aguas Livres

C. da Quintinha

R. D. C. de Mascarenhas

R. Arco do Carvalho

R. P. Sousa da Camara

CAMPOLIDE

Av. C. Fernando

R. Marques de fronteira

Jardim Amália Rodrigues

R. D. F. M. Melo

R. P. A. Vieira

R. Artilharia 1

R. S. Pina

R. M. Subserra

Av. Cardeal Cerejeira

PARQUE

PICOAS

Avda. Eng. Duarte Pacheco

R. José Gomes Ferreira

R. de Campo de Ourique

R. D. A. Mota Pinto

Silva Carvalho

R. das Amoreiras

R. de Joaquim A. Aguiar

R. Rodrigo da Fonseca

R. São Filipe Nery

R. Castilho

Av. Fontes Pereira de Melo

Avda. Duque de Loulé

R. de C. de Redondo

T.v. Sta. Marta

R. Pereira e Sousa

R. Correia Teles

R. de Infantaria 16

Ferreira Borges

AMOREIRAS

R. D. João V

R. do Sol ao Rato

R. da Arrabida

Pr. das Amoreiras

Largo do Rato

RATO

R. Braamcamp

R. Alexandre Herculano

R. Rosa Araújo

R. Barata Salgueiro

Avda. da Liberdade

MARQUÊS DE POMBAL

R. Luc. Cordeiro

R. Almeida e Sousa

R. Coelbo da Rocha

R. Saraiva de Carvalho

R. de Cabo

R. S. Jorge

R. D. Sequeira

Av. D'Quintinha

Av. D. A. Cabral

R. de Santo Amaro

R. Nova da Piedade

R. de S. Marcal

Rua de São Bento

R. Arco de Jesu

Escola Politecnica

R. Imprensa Nacional

Jardim Botânico

Praça Principe Real

R. D. Pedro V

R. da Conceição da Glória

Praça da Alegria

da Alegria

AVENIDA

R. do Salitre

R. do Passadiço

R. do Cardal

R. das Pratas

R. do Telhal

Basílica da Estrela

Praça da Estrela

Jardim da Estrela

Assembleia da República

Praça São Bento

R. E. Coelho

R. D. Pedro V

C. da Glória

RESTAURADORES

🛈

Praça dos Restauradores. This square, which is adjacent to Rossio train station, marks the beginning of modern Lisbon. Here the broad, tree-lined Avenida da Liberdade starts its northwesterly ascent. *Restauradores* means "restoration," and the square commemorates the 1640 uprising against Spanish rule that restored Portuguese independence after a 60-year hiatus; an obelisk (1886) commemorates the event. Note the elegant 18th-century Palácio Foz on the square's west side. Before World War I, it contained a casino; today it houses a national tourist office, the tourist police, and a shop selling reproductions from the country's state museums. The only building to rival the palace is the restored Éden building, just to the south. This art-deco masterpiece of Portuguese architect Cassiano Branco now contains the VIP Éden aparthotel. ⊠ *Avenida da Liberdade* Ⓜ *Restauradores.*

Praça Marquês de Pombal. Dominating the center of Marquês de Pombal Square is a statue of the marquis himself, the man responsible for the design of the "new" Lisbon that emerged from the ruins of the 1755 earthquake. On the statue's base are representations of both the earthquake and the tidal wave that engulfed the city; a female figure with outstretched arms signifies the joy at the emergence of the refashioned city. The square is effectively a large roundabout and a useful orientation point, since it stands at the northern end of Avenida da Liberdade with Parque Eduardo VII just behind, and the metro station here is an interchange between two lines. ⊠ *Avenida da Liberdade* Ⓜ *Marquês de Pombal.*

Parque Eduardo VII. Established at the beginning of the 20th century in the São Sebastião district, Lisbon's version of Central Park was named to honor the British monarch's 1902 visit here during his brief reign. It's a wonderful place to take a break, with small lakes, trickling waterfalls, statues, and colorful plants. On the park's west wide, the **Estufa Fria** is a beautifully kept, romantic oasis in the middle of the city: a sprawling 1930s greenhouse garden whose various habitats are arranged around a pretty pool. There are sweeping views from the avenue at the top of the park, where modernist towers topped by concrete wheat sheaves stand like sentinels. Just across the road, the landscaped Jardim Amália Rodrigues, named in honor of the fado diva, has a stylish café, the **Linha d'Água,** with wooden decking bordering a pretty pool. ⊠ *São Sebastião* 🎟 *Park free, Estufa Fria €3.10 (free Sun. until 2 pm)* Ⓜ *Parque or Marquês de Pombal.*

LAPA AND ESTRELA

Lapa is a quiet residential neighborhood with several chic eateries and one of Lisbon's most renowned *casas de fado,* Senhor Vinho. The Museu Nacional de Arte Antiga is at the foot of the district and is likely Portugal's most important art museum. Nearby is Madragoa, a small grid of streets where Lisbon's fishermen once lived and where you can still get a cheap fish dinner. Dominating the hilltop above Lapa is the Basílica de Estrela church, across from a pretty garden that takes its name.

PLANNER

GETTING HERE AND AROUND

The famous Tram 28 rumbles up from downtown to Estrela, with a stop at the Basilica. Rato metro station is a 5- to 10- minute walk away—but with its narrow lanes, one-way streets, and steep stairs, much of Lapa needs to be explored on foot.

TIMING

It's worth setting aside at least a day to explore these scenic parts of town; just be sure to wear comfortable shoes. The Basilica and nearby Jardim da Estrela merit an hour or so, and the café-bar, playground, and weekend craft markets at Jardim da Estrela may entice you to linger considerably longer. Leave 20 minutes or so for a downhill stroll past grand old buildings and narrow cobbled lanes to reach the Museu de Arte Antiga, which itself merits a couple of hours' contemplation, and allow another hour, plus around 15 minutes' walking time, if you plan to visit the Museu da Marioneta.

TOP ATTRACTIONS

Fodor's Choice ★ **Museu Nacional de Arte Antiga.** On route from the center of Lisbon to Belém is this impressive art museum, housed in a 17th-century palace once owned by the counts of Alvor. The museum has a beautifully displayed collection of Portuguese art, mainly from the 15th through 19th centuries.

The religious works of the Flemish-influenced Portuguese school stand out, especially Nuno Gonçalves's masterpiece, the *St. Vincent Panels.* Painted between 1467 and 1470, the altarpiece has six panels believed to show the patron saint of Lisbon receiving the homage of king, court, and citizens (although there are other theories). Sixty figures have been identified, including Henry the Navigator; the archbishop of Lisbon; and sundry dukes, fishermen, knights, and religious figures. In the top left corner of the two central panels is a figure purported to be Gonçalves himself.

The museum also boasts early Flemish works that influenced the Portuguese, and other European artists are well represented, such as Hieronymous Bosch, Hans Holbein, Brueghel the Younger, and Diego Velázquez. There are also extensive collections of French silver, Portuguese furniture and tapestries, Asian ceramics, and items fashioned from Goan ivory. Tram 15 from Praça do Comércio drops you at the foot of a steep flight of steps below the museum. ⊠ *Rua das Janelas Verdes, Lapa* ☎ *21/396-2825, 21/396-4151, 21/391-2800* ⊕ *www. museudearteantiga.pt* ☑ *€6 (free 1st Sun. of the month).*

WORTH NOTING

Basílica da Estrela. A standout on Lisbon's skyline, this gleaming white basilica was built in the baroque and neoclassical styles, and its location at the top of one of Lisbon's seven hills makes for dramatic views from its rococo *zimbório* (dome). It was built at the end of the 18th century under the command of Queen Maria I (whose tomb lies within the building) to fulfill a religious promise she made in praying (ultimately successfully) for a male heir. The interior is striking, too, with black-and-pink marble walls and floors, and a famously elaborate nativity scene. Displayed year-round, the scene comprises some 500 figures and was created by the scupltor Joaquim Machado de Castro. Just across the road is the leafy **Jardim da Estrela,** one of Lisbon's loveliest green spaces. Stroll the shaded paths and then pull up a chair in the café for a drink or a snack. Estrela is a short walk west of Largo do Rato, where the metro's yellow line terminates. You can also take the scenic route on Tram 28 from Praça Luís de Camões in the Chiado neighborhood; you'll pass through the São Bento district, dominated by Portugal's grand parliament building (yet another former monastery) on the way. ⊠ *Praça da Estrela, Lapa* ✉ *Basilica free, dome €4.50* ⊘ *Closed Mon. afternoon and Sun. morning* Ⓜ *Rato.*

Galeria Cristina Guerra. This gallery shows work by Portuguese heavyweights, including Julião Sarmento. ⊠ *Rua Santo António à Estrela 33, Estrela* ☎ *21/393–9559* ⊕ *www.cristinaguerra.com.*

FAMILY **Museu da Marioneta.** The intricate workmanship that went into the creation of the puppets on display at this museum is remarkable, and it's not just kids' stuff: during the Salazar regime, puppet shows were used to mock the pretensions and corruption of the politicians. The collection encompasses both Portuguese and foreign figurines. Puppet shows are often staged in the former chapel at varying times; check the website or phone for details. The Museu da Marioneta is in the old fishermen's district of Madragoa, not far from the Museu Nacional de Arte Antiga. ⊠ *Convento das Bernardas, Rua da Esperança 146, Madragoa* ☎ *21/394–2810* ⊕ *www. museudamarioneta.pt* ✉ *€5 (free Sun. until 2)* ⊘ *Closed Mon.*

ALCÂNTARA AND BELÉM

The old port district of Alcântara got a face-lift in the 1990s, and since then it has been a nightlife hub, as well as a great place to relax by the river on warm days. The inauguration in 2008 of the Museu do Oriente was a regeneration landmark, and the colorful LX Factory has transformed a derelict industrial site into a creative hub of coworking spaces, café-bars, and boutiques, while the revamped docks are now home to smart bars and restaurants.

Farther west, some of Lisbon's grandest monuments and museums are in the district of Belém (the Portuguese word for Bethlehem). It was from here that the country's great explorers set out during the period of the discoveries. The wealth brought back from the New World helped pay for many of the neighborhood's structures, some of which are the best examples of the uniquely Portuguese late-Gothic architecture known as Manueline. The area's historical attractions are complemented by the modern and contemporary art and performances showcased in Lisbon's largest cultural center.

GETTING HERE AND AROUND

Alcântara and Belém are easily reached by train from Cais do Sodré station. Trains leave every few minutes, but make sure you catch a local train rather than an express. Alternatively, several buses will get you here from Lisbon's center, and the 30-minute ride on Tram 15 (plied by both antique and modern models) from the Baixa district's Praça do Comércio is very scenic. Tram 15 also passes close by or stops right at several of the important sights.

TIMING

Set aside an hour or two for the Mosteiro dos Jerónimos, and a further couple of hours to see the waterfront tower and stop for a coffee or glass of wine at one of the many cafés and stalls in this picturesque area. This leaves an hour or two for one of the other museums and monuments—creative types should be sure to check out LX Factory. After that, you'll probably want to just flop into a chair at an Alcântara district bar or restaurant. Note that most of Belém's sights are closed Monday. As elsewhere, Sunday morning sees free or reduced admission at many attractions.

TOP ATTRACTIONS

FAMILY **Mosteiro dos Jerónimos.** This UNESCO World Heritage Site is a supreme
Fodor's Choice example of the Manueline style of building (named after King Dom
★ Manuel I), which represented a marked departure from earlier Gothic architecture. Much of it is characterized by elaborate sculptural details, often with a maritime motif. João de Castilho was responsible for the southern portal, which forms the main entrance to the church: the figure on the central pillar is Henry the Navigator. Inside, the spacious interior contrasts with the riot of decoration on the six nave columns and complex latticework ceiling. This is the resting place of both explorer Vasco da Gama and national poet Luís de Camões. Don't miss the Gothic- and Renaissance-style double cloister, also designed to stunning effect by Castilho. ⊠ *Praça do Império, Belém* ☎ *21/362–0034* ⊕ *www. mosteirojeronimos.pt* 🖾 *Church free, cloister €10 (free 1st Sun. of the month), €12 Discovery ticket includes Torre de Belém* ⊙ *Closed Mon.*

NEED A
BREAK

Antiga Confeitaria de Belém. For a real taste of Lisbon, stop at the Antiga Confeitaria de Belém, a bakery shop–café specializing in pastéis de nata—delicious, warm custard pastries sprinkled with cinnamon and powdered sugar. Although the sweet treats are ubiquitous in Portugal—most Lisboetas will admit to consuming at least one or two with coffee every day—the version here is the most celebrated. Made from a secret recipe since 1837, the legendary pastéis *de Belém* are so good that lines snake out of the door of this traditional blue-and-white-tiled establishment, and tourists and locals alike load up on packages to take home. ⊠ *Rua de Belém 84–92, Belém* ☎ *21/363–7423* ⊕ *www.pasteisdebelem.pt.*

FAMILY **Torre de Belém.** Another UNESCO World Heritage Site, the openwork
Fodor's Choice balconies and domed turrets of the fanciful Belém Tower make it per-
★ haps the country's purest Manueline structure. It was built between 1514 and 1520 on what was an island in the middle of the Rio Tagus, to defend the port entrance, and dedicated to St. Vincent, the patron saint of Lisbon. Today the chalk-white tower stands near the north bank—evidence of the river's changing course. Cross the wood gangway and walk inside to admire the cannons and descend to the former dungeons, before climbing the steep, narrow, winding staircase to the top of the tower for a bird's-eye view across the Tagus and over the city. ⊠ *Av. Brasília, Belém* ☎ *21/3620034* ⊕ *www.torrebelem.pt* 🖾 *€6 (free first Sun. of the month)* ⊙ *Closed Mon.*

WORTH NOTING

Champlimaud Centre for the Unknown. In a prime riverside location, this giant, curving medical research and clinical facility, completed in 2010 from a design by Pritzker Prize winner Charles Correa, has become a pilgrimage site for architecture buffs. Its Darwin's Café restaurant is open to the public and has stunning river views, not least from its charming esplanade café. ⊠ *Av. Brasília, Ala B, Belém* ☎ *21/048–0222 restaurant* ⊕ *www.darwincafe.com.*

Doca de Santa Amaro. The docks are alive with music in Alcântara, where late-night bars attract Lisbon's young—and young at heart. Here, in the lee of the huge Ponte 25 de Abril, the old wharves have been made over, and you can walk from here along the landscaped riverfront all the way to Belém (a 30-minute stroll). At Doca de Santo Amaro, known to locals simply as "Docas" (docks) a line of swanky restaurants and clubs now inhabit the shells of former warehouses. These establishments are often more fashionable than culinary, though, and the constant rumble of cars passing over the bridge combined with occasional low-level airplanes preparing to land may disrupt your dining experience. Either way, the people-watching and potential for late-night mirth are extraordinary. On the terrace in front of the marina, the party goes on until late into the night. During the day, the easiest way to get here is by train from Cais do Sodré station or on Tram 15; at night, take a taxi. ⊠ *Alcântara.*

FAMILY **Jardim Botânico da Ajuda.** Portugal's oldest botanical garden—laid out in 1768 by the Italian botanist Domenico Vandelli (1735–1816)—is an enjoyable place to spend an hour or so. You can stroll up here from the river at Belém, or take Tram 18 from Cais do Sodré station (it terminates near here). Ornate fountains and strolling peacocks create a sense of splendor, and many species of flora, labeled in Latin, can be viewed in several greenhouses covering 4 acres. The larger Jardim Botânico Tropical at the bottom of the hill, whose entrance is just opposite the Mostèrio dos Jerónimos, was created later and contains hundreds of species from the Azores, Madeira, and Portugal's former colonies. ⊠ *Calçada da Ajuda, Ajuda* ☎ *21/365–3137* ⊕ *www.jardim-botanicodajuda.com* ☑ *€2.*

LX Factory. A once-derelict industrial area has been transformed into a symbol of Lisbon's creative spirit, at this colorful collection of bars, boutiques, cafés, and coworking spaces. An organic-produce market is held here each Sunday, and a fantastic rooftop bar-restaurant offers laid-back drinking and dining with a first-class view over the river. ⊠ *Rua Rodrigues Faria, 103 Lisboa, Alcântara* ☎ *21/314–3399* ⊕ *www. lxfactory.com.*

Museu Berardo. Housed in the minimalist Belém Cultural Center, the Museu Berardo is a showcase for one of Europe's most important private collections of modern art. Works from this treasure trove—which ranges from Picasso through Warhol to Portugal's own Paula Rego—are regularly rotated through the galleries, and there are also excellent visiting exhibitions. The complex has a restaurant and several cafés. Its roof gardens feature an expansive terrace where cooling jets of water spray out from the ground; it's a fun place for kids to race around while their

Champalimaud Centre for the Unknown 1

Doca de Santa Amaro 10

Jardim Botânico da Ajuda 12

LX Factory 7

Mosteiro dos Jerónimos 5

Museu Berardo ...3

Museu de Marinha 4

Museu Nacional dos Coches (National Coach Museum) 11

Museu do Oriente 9

Padrão dos Descobrimentos ..6

Palacio da Ajuda 13

Ponte 25 de Abril 8

Torre de Belém 2

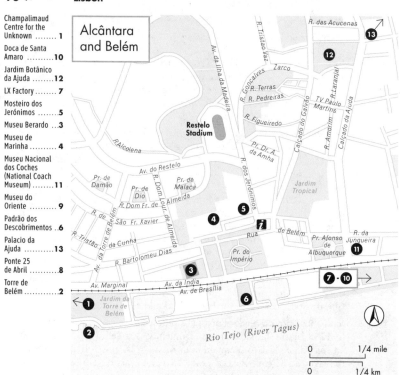

Alcântara and Belém

parents soak up the wonderful views of the Mosteiro dos Jerónimos and the Rio Tejo. ✉ *Praça do Império, Belém* ☎ *21/361–2400* ⊕ *en. museuberardo.pt* ✉ *Free.*

FAMILY **Museu de Marinha.** One of Lisbon's oldest museums (it was founded in 1853), the large, navy-run Maritime Museum showcases the importance of the seafaring tradition in Portugal. With its thousands of maps and maritime codes, navigational equipment, full-size and model ships, uniforms, and weapons, the museum appeals to visitors young and old. ✉ *Praça do Império, Belém* ☎ *21/097–7388* ⊕ *museu.marinha.pt* ✉ *€6.50* ⊗ *Closed Mon.*

Museu do Oriente. Housed in a former *bacalhau* (salted cod) cold store with impressive bas reliefs on its facade, the Museo do Oriente opened in 2008 and has become one of Lisbon's most important cultural institutions. Funded by the Fundação Oriente (a legacy of colonial Macau and its gaming revenues), this dockside giant seeks both to tell the story of the centuries-long Portuguese presence in Asia and to provide a showcase for Asian cultures. Highlights of the permanent collections include unique maps and charts from the golden age of Portuguese maritime exploration and stunning Chinese and Japanese painted screens. The museum hosts excellent, inexpensive concerts in its cozy auditorium, and organizes a plethora of cooking and crafts workshops. ✉ *Av.*

Brasília, Doca de Alcântara (Norte), Alcântara ☎ *21/358–5200* ⊕ *www. museudooriente.pt* ⌂ €6 *(free Fri. 6–10)* ⊙ *Closed Mon.*

FAMILY **Museu Nacional dos Coches (National Coach Museum).** In a former royal riding school with a gorgeous painted ceiling, the National Coach Museum has a dazzling collection of gloriously gilded horse-drawn carriages. The oldest on display was made for Philip II of Spain in the late 1500s; the most stunning are three conveyances created in Rome for King John V in 1716. The museum, Portugal's most visited, is right next door to the official residence of the president of the Republic, whose **Museu da Presidência** tells the story of the presidency, profiles the officeholders, and displays gifts they have received on state visits. The Coach Museum has recently moved across the road into a purpose-built structure designed by Brazilian Pritzker Prize winner Paulo Mendes da Rocha; it was inaugurated in May 2015. The sunny terrace of the bar and restaurant Cavalo Lusitano is a pleasant place for post-sightseeing snacks and drinks. ✉ *Av. da Índia n° 136, Belém* ☎ *21/049–2400* ⊕ *www.museudoscoches.pt* ⌂ €6 ⊙ *Closed Mon.*

FAMILY **Padrão dos Descobrimentos.** The white, monolithic Monument of the Discoveries was erected in 1960 to commemorate the 500th anniversary of the death of Prince Henry the Navigator. It was built on what was the departure point for many voyages of discovery, including those of Vasco da Gama for India and—during Spain's occupation of Portugal—of the Spanish Armada for England in 1588. Henry is at the prow of the monument, facing the water; lined up behind him are the Portuguese explorers of Brazil and Asia, as well as other national heroes. On the ground adjacent to the monument, an inlaid map shows the extent of the explorations undertaken by the 15th- and 16th-century Portuguese sailors. Walk inside and take the elevator to the top for river views. ✉ *Av. Brasília, Belém* ☎ *21/303–1950* ⊕ *www.padraodosdescobrimentos.pt* ⌂ €4 ⊙ *Closed Mon. Sept.–Mar.*

Palácio da Ajuda. In 1802 construction began on the Ajuda Palace, which was intended as a royal residence. Its last regal occupant (Queen Maria) died here in 1911, and the fixtures and fittings are preserved just as they were during royal occupancy. Today, the ornate neoclassical building functions as a museum. Visitors can take a peek at how Portuguese monarchs lived, as well as admire 18th- and 19th-century paintings, furniture, and tapestries. It is also used for official ceremonies and functions by the Presidency of the Republic, and one wing houses the government's Culture department. It's a 20-minute walk up Calçada da Ajuda from the Museu Nacional dos Coches, or, from downtown, Tram 18 stops outside the palace. ✉ *Largo da Ajuda, Ajuda* ☎ *21/363–7095, 21/362–0264* ⊕ *www.palacioajuda.pt* ⌂ €5 *(free 1st Sun. of the month)* ⊙ *Closed Wed.*

Ponte 25 de Abril. Lisbon's first suspension bridge across the Rio Tejo, linking the Alcântara and Almada districts, stands 230 feet above the water and stretches almost 2½ km (1½ miles). Reminiscent of San Francisco's Golden Gate Bridge, it's somewhat smaller but still a spectacular sight from any direction, although most gasps are reserved for the view from the top downward. Overlooking the bridge from a hill

Prince Henry the Navigator

The linkage of England and Portugal and the beginning of Portugal's Age of Discovery can be traced back to the 14th century, when England's John of Gaunt gave his daughter, Philippa of Lancaster, in marriage to King João I. The couple's third son, Infante Dom Henrique, is known widely today as Prince Henry the Navigator (1394–1460). By the end of his lifetime, this multidimensional soldier-scientist had conceptualized, funded, and inspired discoveries beyond the borders of the world that Europe knew. No matter how they assess later misuses of exploration and conquest, scholars today generally agree that the prince paved the way for explorers such as Vasco da Gama and Ferdinand Magellan.

Unusual for a royal family in those (or any) times, João and Philippa raised six intelligent, apparently happy children. Alternately contemplative and restlessly athletic, Henry persuaded his father to let the four boys earn their knighthoods in an invasion of Morocco and the capture of its fortress at Ceuta. If the prince had not led his 70 soldier-filled ships to victory, Portugal's Age of Discovery might have been very different.

At least three achievements secured Henry his place in the vanguard of explorers. In the Algarve, where he was governor, he founded a nearly legendary marine navigation school.

He also sent ships where none had gone before—especially around Cape Bojador, the "impassable wall" jutting out from West Africa at the end of the European-known Atlantic Ocean. And he required that expeditions chart the seas as they sailed. Charts made of Cape Bojador later led Vasco da Gama to sail around it, then past the Cape of Good Hope and on to India.

Seen through the prism of history, Prince Henry seems a royal contradiction. He earned his knighthood defeating infidels and was eventually named Grand Master of the Order of Christ, the successor in Portugal to the Knights Templar. But since he lived before the Inquisition began, he may have met some of the Latin-, Greek-, and Hebrew-speaking scholars who came to the royal court. Further, his ships engaged in Africa's lucrative slave trade, but he himself lived simply and, having given away his profits to fund further expeditions, died broke. The navigator-prince was not technically a navigator, and he rarely boarded a ship, but he pointed the way for generations of future explorers—such as yourself. In Lisbon, stop at breezy Belém on the Rio Tejo, where, at the prow of the ship-shape *Padrão dos Descobrimentos* (Monument to the Discoveries), Prince Henry stands, leading other Portuguese explorers and even King Afonso V.

on the south bank is the **Cristo Rei** (Christ the King) statue, which is smaller and stiffer than Rio's more famous Redeemer. The observation deck, from where you can actually look down on the bridge, is open daily. To get here, catch Bus 101 (on the hour and half hour) from the south-bank ferry station of Cacilhas. ⊠ *Ponte 25 de Abril, Alcântara.*

PARQUE DAS NAÇÕES

To prepare for the World Exposition in 1998, Lisbon's officials wisely kept in mind not only the immediate needs of the event, but also the future needs of the city. The result was the Parque das Nações, or Park of Nations, a revitalized district on the banks of the Rio Tejo, 5 km (3 miles) northeast of Lisbon's center. Before it became the Expo 98 site, empty warehouses and industrial waste filled the district, which was once a landing area for seaplanes. Today it has apartment buildings, office complexes, hotels, restaurants, bars, the Centro Vasco da Gama mall, and a modern casino, interspersed with landscaped parkland. It's also home to a marina; the MEO Arena, a venue for major cultural and sporting events; and the Feira Internacional Lisboa (FIL) convention center.

The centerpiece of the Parque das Nações is the popular Oceanário de Lisboa, an aquarium built for the Expo. Near it is the Pavilhão do Conhecimento: a hands-on science museum that is great fun for kids. The Pavilhão de Portugal, with its stunning concrete canopy, housed the host nation's contribution to the Expo; it was designed by multiple-prize-winning Porto architect Álvaro Siza Vieira, while the soaring Gare do Oriente train station is the work of Spain's Santiago Calatrava. From the cable car that soars over the area, the views are impressive. Beyond the Parque das Nações to its north, parkland continues along the river, affording close-up views of the waterbirds that thrive here. You can make the most of all the open space by renting bicycles at the Marina (€5 per hour or €15 per day; rent bikes at the Marina reception between 9 am and 6 pm).

GETTING HERE AND AROUND

The Parque das Nações may be on the eastern edge of Lisbon but is easy to reach by public transport. The metro stops at Oriente station here on the route between Alameda and the airport, an interchange with the green line that runs from Cais do Sodré via Baixa-Chiado and Rossio stations, downtown. Above ground is the elegant Gare do Oriente, designed by Spanish star architect Santiago Calatrava, where fast trains from Porto and the Algarve stop, as well as some express buses. Gare do Oriente is also just a seven-minute trip on a suburban train from Santo Apolónia, downtown, but services are rather irregular.

TIMING

You can spend anywhere from a couple of hours to all day (and all night) sightseeing, shopping, eating, and drinking here. Allot about two hours for the Oceanário de Lisboa and another hour for the Pavilhão do Conhecimento. Although the last metro train departs from Oriente station at 1 am, taxis wait at the Gare de Oriente until all hours.

TOP ATTRACTIONS

FAMILY

Fodor's Choice

★

Oceanário de Lisboa. Europe's largest indoor aquarium wows children and adults alike with a vast saltwater tank featuring a massive array of fish, including several types of shark. Along the way you pass through habitats representing the North Atlantic, Pacific, and Indian Oceans, where puffins and penguins dive into the water, sea otters roll and play, and tropical birds flit past you. You then descend to the bottom of the tank to watch rays float past gracefully and schools of silvery fish darting this way and that. To avoid the crowds, come during the week or early in the day. The Oceanário also hosts a range of activities outside normal opening hours, such as Saturday-morning concerts for kids under age three, against the lively backdrop of the central tank. Book online to skip the lines and get a 10% discount. ⊠ *Esplanada D. Carlos I (Doca dos Olivais), Parque das Nações* ☎ *21/891–7006* ⊕ *www.oceanario.pt/en* ⌹ *€16.50* Ⓜ *Oriente.*

WORTH NOTING

FAMILY **Pavilhão do Conhecimento.** The white, angular, structure designed by architect Carrilho de Graça for the Expo seems the perfect place to house the Knowledge Pavilion, or Living Science Centre, as it's also known. The permanent and temporary exhibits here are all related to math, science, and technology; most are also labeled in English (a manual is available for the few that aren't), and all are interactive. A café, free Wi-Fi, a media library, a gift shop, and a bookstore round out the offerings. The €20 family ticket is a good value. ⊠ *Alamada dos Oceanos, Lote 2.10.01, Parque das Nações* ☎ *21/891–7104* ⊕ *www. pavconhecimento.pt* ⌹ *€9* Ⓜ *Oriente.*

WHERE TO EAT

Lisbon's dining scene has evolved dramatically in recent years to include any number of high-end dining opportunities, but amid the international fare, Michelin-starred restaurants, and molecular gastronomy, the city's simplest and most traditional restaurants still do a roaring trade. Meals generally include three courses, a drink, and coffee. Many restaurants have an *ementa turistica* (tourist menu), a set-price meal, most often served at lunchtime. Note that you'll be charged a couple of euros if you eat any of the *couvert* items—typically appetizers such as bread and butter, olives, and the like—that are brought to your table without being ordered.

Lisbon's restaurants usually serve lunch from noon or 12:30 until 3 and dinner from 7:30 until 11; many establishments are closed Sunday or Monday. Inexpensive restaurants typically don't accept reservations. In the traditional *cervejarias* (beer-hall restaurants), which frequently have huge dining rooms, you'll probably have to wait for a table, but usually not more than 10 minutes. In the Bairro Alto, many of the reasonably priced *tascas* (taverns) are on the small side: if you can't grab a table, you're probably better off moving on to the next place. Throughout Lisbon, dress for meals is usually casual, but exceptions are noted below.

Prices in the reviews are the average cost of a main course at dinner or, if dinner isn't served, at lunch.

WHAT IT COSTS IN EUROS				
	$	$$	$$$	$$$$
AT DINNER	Under €16	€16–€20	€21–€25	over €25

Restaurant prices are per person for a main course at dinner.

ALFAMA

$$$
ECLECTIC

✕ **Bica do Sapato.** A favorite among fashionable locals, this riverfront restaurant is known for its stylish interior and furnishings: Knoll, Eero Saarinen, and Mies van der Rohe all feature. It serves modern Portuguese fare and nouvelle cuisine. The changing menu may include braised tuna with mashed sweet potato and spinach, or shoulder of lamb cooked at ultralow temperatures and served with roast tomato, yam, and *cremoso de nabiças* (turnip tops with cream). There are always a couple of vegetarian entrées, too. Desserts include eggy Portuguese classics but also *tarte de alfarroba* (carob tart) and homemade ice creams and sorbets. From September through June, they also do Sunday brunch (€27). Upstairs, a sushi bar (dinner only) offers a range of classic Japanese and fusion dishes. $ *Average main: €24* ⊠ *Av. Infante D. Henrique, Armazém B, Alfama* ☎ *21/881–0320* ⊕ *www.bicadosapato. com* ⊗ *No dinner Sun., no lunch Mon. No lunch at sushi bar* ✛ *G5.*

$$
PORTUGUESE
Fodor'sChoice
★

✕ **Memmo Alfama Wine Bar and Terrace.** The terrace bar and restaurant at the casual-chic Memmo Alfama boutique hotel is open to nonguests, and has some of the best views in the neighborhood, with tables and chairs arranged around a small infinity pool. Tapas-style small plates are what to order here, and the selection of Portuguese cheeses, served with a basket of breads and crispbreads, is a good place to start. $ *Average main: €20* ⊠ *Memmo Alfama Hotel, Travessa das Merceeiras 27, Alfama* ☎ *21/0495660* ⊕ *www.memmohotels.com/alfama/wine-bar-amp-outdoor-pool.html* ▭ *No credit cards* ✛ *F6.*

$
PORTUGUESE

✕ **Parreirinha de São Vicente.** In a row of eateries round the corner from the Feira da Ladra flea market, this place is so popular it has taken over two neighboring house numbers. The food here is well seasoned and mostly comes in portions large enough for two. The brothers who run the place are from the northern Beiras region, and many of the dishes here are meat-rich examples of its traditions, but there is plenty of seafood on the menu. On Sunday locals pile in for *chocos à setubalense* (Setubal-style fried battered cuttlefish). As for wine, the house red and slightly sparkling white come by the glass or jug; there are also pricier bottles. $ *Average main: €12* ⊠ *Calçada de São Vicente 54–58, Alfama* ☎ *21/886–8893* ▭ *No credit cards* ✛ *F5.*

$$
PORTUGUESE

✕ **Santo António de Alfama.** Up some steps from the Travessa do Terreiro do Trigo, you'll find this simple but sophisticated restaurant hung with black-and-white photos of famous artists. The mushrooms stuffed with Gorgonzola and deep-fried potato skins are tasty starters. Steak, fish, or duck accompanied by steamed vegetables are the most popular main dishes, but there are authentic Portuguese flavors such as *morcela com grelos* (blood sausage and turnip leaves, sautéed with potatoes); note

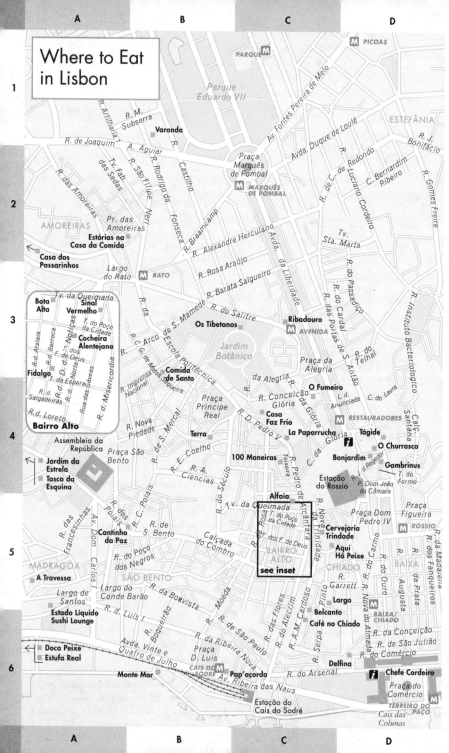

Where to Eat in Lisbon

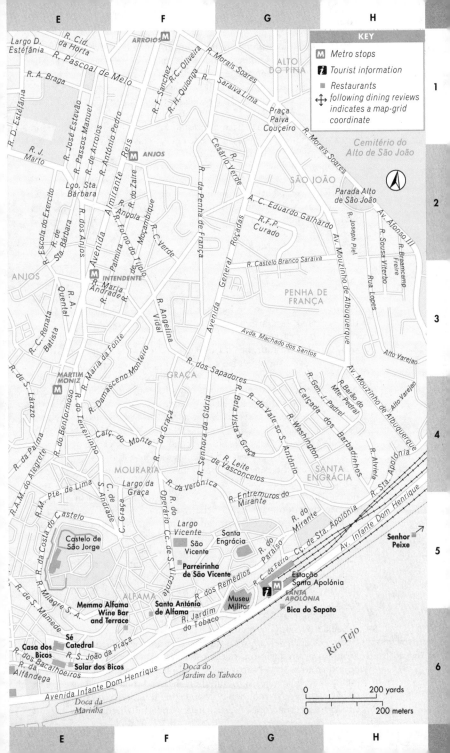

there's less choice at lunch than at dinner, when the kitchen also stays open till 2 am. In summer, good use is made of the large terrace. The motto here is "we don't have sardines or fado," and it's testament to the great food and atmosphere that it's consistently busy despite the absence of these tourist favorites. [$] *Average main: €19* ✉ *Beco de São Miguel 7, Alfama* ☎ *21/888–1328* 🌐 *www.siteantonio.com* ✣ *F6.*

$ PORTUGUESE 🍴 **Solar dos Bicos.** This charming restaurant with its stone arches and beautiful azulejos offers typical Portuguese cuisine at very reasonable prices. Seafood is the main attraction: grilled sole, grouper, sea bass, bream, or squid are all good options, or two diners could split a rich *caldeirada* (fish stew) or plate of mixed grilled fish with seasoned potatoes. There are plenty of no-nonsense meat dishes, too, like barbecued pork chops, which come with fries and salad. After-dinner selections include achingly sweet desserts and fresh fruit. [$] *Average main: €12* ✉ *Rua dos Bacalhoeiros 8A, Alfama* ☎ *21/886–9447* 🌐 *www.solardos-bicos.pt* 🕘 *Closed Mon.* ✣ *E6.*

BAIXA

$ PORTUGUESE 🍴 **Bonjardim.** In an alley between Praça dos Restauradores and Rua das Portas de Santo Antão, and known locally as "Rei dos Frangos" (King of Chickens), Bonjardim specializes in superbly cooked spit-roasted chicken, best eaten with fries, a salad, or creamed spinach, and spicy piri-piri. The restaurant and esplanade are crowded at peak times (8–10), but you shouldn't have to wait long, and watching the frenzied waiters is entertaining. An overflow dining room on the opposite side of the alley serves a similar menu but with more grilled meats and is similarly good value (each has a different rest day, so one is always open). They also do takeout. [$] *Average main: €9* ✉ *Travessa de Santo Antão 11 and 12, Baixa* ☎ *21/342–4389, 21/342–7424* ✣ *D4.*

$$ PORTUGUESE 🍴 **Chefe Cordeiro.** This slick but informal *taberna*—headed up by José Cordeiro, one of Portugal's best-known chefs—is the only gourmet option among the esplanade restaurants on Terreiro do Paço, as locals call Praça do Comércio. The stress is on the finest ingredients in top-notch traditional *petiscos* (snacks) and entrées, prepared in an open kitchen that dominates one of the two dining rooms. The *pastéis de bacalhau* (fried cod cakes) are good, and even the squeamish will be won over by the tender, well-seasoned *orelheira de porco fumada e cozida* (smoked, stewed pig's ear). Signature dishes include flavorful *arroz malandro* (rice stews): with beans or tomatoes as a side dish, or with lobster, or monkfish and prawns, as a main. Diners should note that the restaurant closes early by local standards (10:30 pm). [$] *Average main: €19* ✉ *Praça do Comércio 20/23, Baixa* ☎ *21/608–0090* 🕘 *Closed Sun. and Mon.* ✣ *D6.*

$$ PORTUGUESE Fodor's Choice ★ 🍴 **Delfina.** Occupying a corner of one of downtown's finest squares, Delfina offers a deliciously fresh take on traditional Portuguese dishes. From its prime location, the house restaurant at the chic AlmaLusa boutique hotel serves tapas-style small plates throughout the day and night, as well as more substantial lunches and dinners. Alongside fish dishes such as an exceptionally good seared tuna starter, there are some enticing vegetarian options, such as a wonderfully rich *açorda*—bread

stew seasoned with garlic, coriander, and cilantro. [$] *Average main: €17* ✉ *Praça do Município 21, Baixa* ☎ *21/269–7445* 🌐 *www.almalusahotels.com* 💳 *No credit cards* ✥ *D6.*

$$$$ SEAFOOD 🍴 **Gambrinus.** On a busy street that's full of fish restaurants, Gambrinus stands out from the competition, with more than 70 years of experience in serving the finest fish and shellfish. In a series of somber, dark-paneled dining rooms, and even sitting at the bar, you're led through the intricacies of the day's seafood specials by waiters who know their stuff. Prawns, lobster, and crab are always available; seasonal choices such as sea bream, sole, and sea bass are offered grilled or garnished with clam sauce. [$] *Average main: €32* ✉ *Rua das Portas de Santo Antão 23–25, Restauradores* ☎ *21/342–1466* 🌐 *www.gambrinuslisboa.com* ✥ *D4.*

$ PORTUGUESE FAMILY 🍴 **O Churrasco.** On a street lined with tourist traps, O Churrasco is more formal than most eateries and attracts many locals. They come for the piri-piri grilled chicken, and grilled meats and fish, but other dishes, such as the paella, are good, too. [$] *Average main: €15* ✉ *Rua das Portas de Santo Antão 83–85, Restauradores* ☎ *21/342–3059* ✥ *D4.*

CHIADO AND BAIRRO ALTO

$$ PORTUGUESE 🍴 **Alfaia.** In this traditional restaurant (it's one of the oldest in Lisbon) in the former stables of what was once a local nobleman's palace, courteous staff serve up Portuguese classics such as *arroz de galo* (chicken rice), *lulas grelhadas* (grilled squid), and açorda *de gambas* (with prawns). As is evident from the dining room decoration, wine is a big deal here; indeed, there are 600 for you to choose from. Note that if you just want a drink and a snack, the Alfaia Garrafeira wine and tapas bar across the road is an excellent place to stop. [$] *Average main: €17* ✉ *Travessa da Queimada 22, Bairro Alto* ☎ *21/346–1232* 🌐 *www.restaurantealfaia.com* 🕒 *No lunch Sun.* ✥ *C5.*

$$ PORTUGUESE-SEAFOOD Fodor's Choice ★ 🍴 **Aqui Há Peixe.** "There's fish here" is this restaurant's name, and make no mistake: it's one of the most fashionable places in town to eat seafood. At night this informal place attracts a youngish crowd clearly intent on hitting the Bairro Alto's bars later. Popular dishes here include fish stews and tuna steak sautéed with pink peppercorns; and locals also rave about the Brazilian-style *picanha,* the "rump cap" that clued-in carnivores consider to be the king of all beef cuts. There are cheaper lunchtime specials, rustled up from whatever was in the market in the morning. Desserts are homemade—and delicious. [$] *Average main: €19* ✉ *Rua da Trindade 18A, Chiado* ☎ *21/343–2154* 🌐 *www.aquihapeixe.pt* 🕒 *Closed Mon. No lunch weekends* [M] *Baixa-Chiado* ✥ *C5.*

$$$$ ECLECTIC Fodor's Choice ★ 🍴 **Belcanto.** José Avillez, one of Portugal's most renowned young chefs, is synonymous with fine dining in Lisbon, with several high-end establishments bearing his name. To see what all the fuss is about, visit Belcanto, which holds two Michelin stars. The inventive cuisine uses the latest techniques in playing on traditional themes. The à la carte list features signature Avillez dishes such as the heavenly *pombo à "Convento-de-Alcântara"* (stewed pigeon); and *raia Jackson Pollock*—skate presented to look just like one of the artist's paintings (a copy is provided for comparison). The olive trilogy (crunchy, spherified, and liquid) is a fun starter, while the petits fours are a divine ender. [$] *Average main:*

€45 ✉ Largo de São Carlos 10, Bairro Alto ☎ 21/342–0607 🌐 www.joseavillez.pt ⏲ Closed Sun. and Mon. ✍ Reservations essential ✥ C5.

$ PORTUGUESE 🍴 **Bota Alta.** This wood-paneled tavern is one of the Bairro Alto's oldest and most popular—lines form outside by 8 pm. There's little space between the tables, but this only enhances the buzz. Once you've secured a seat, choose from a menu strong on traditional Portuguese dishes—perhaps bacalhau *à bras* (shredded, with onions and matchstick fried potatoes in scrambled egg), *carne de porco à alentejana* (pork with clams), steaks in wine sauce, or grilled fish. Come hungry: portions are huge. The house wine comes in ceramic jugs and is both very affordable and very good. [$] *Average main: €13 ✉ Travessa da Queimada 37, Bairro Alto ☎ 21/342–7959 ⏲ Closed Sun. No lunch Sat. ✥ A3.*

$$ CAFÉ 🍴 **Café no Chiado.** There are some tasty fish and meat dishes on offer at this sophisticated yet friendly downtown café-restaurant: cod with sautéed chickpeas, cabbage, chouriço, and poached egg is a favorite on the menu, as are mini sirloin steaks with cream sauce, mustard, french fries, and creamed spinach. For dessert, the apple pie with crumble and ice cream is a good bet. The shaded esplanade is a pleasant place to absorb local atmosphere (including the antique trams rumbling past) away from the hustle of Rua Garrett, the area's main shopping drag. The wide selection of Portuguese and international newspapers adds to its laid-back attractions. Open daily from 10 am to 2 am, it's a good option for a late-night bite. [$] *Average main: €17 ✉ Largo do Picadeiro 10–12, Chiado ☎ 21/346–0501 🌐 www.cafenochiado.com ✥ C6.*

$$ INDIAN 🍴 **Cantinho da Paz.** This mom-and-pop establishment specializes in the cuisine of former Portuguese colony Goa—otherwise surprisingly hard to find in Lisbon. The spicy veal *balchão* and ginger-and-cardamom-flavored *xacuti* are particularly rich examples of Goa's unique mix of Portuguese and Indian influences, but there are also tasty seafood dishes. The English-speaking staff can guide you through the menu. Vegetarians take note: you may have been spoiled for choice in Indian restaurants back home, but there are slim pickings here. This place is on an alley off the Tram 28 route from Chiado to Estrela, but take a taxi if you're worried about getting lost. [$] *Average main: €16 ✉ Rua da Paz 4, off Rua dos Poiais de São Bento, Bairro Alto ☎ 21/390–1963 ⏲ Closed Sun. ✥ B5.*

$ PORTUGUESE 🍴 **Casa Faz Frio.** This convivial *adega* (tavern)—complete with wood beams, stone floors, and bunches of garlic suspended from the ceiling—may look a little faded. But it is now one of just two in Lisbon to boast *gabinetes*—paneled booths traditionally used for trysts but also handy for working lunches—and is a great place to sample rustic food on the cheap. There is a different bacalhau dish every day, and paella is always on the menu; other house specialties include grilled cuttlefish and *secretos,* lean meat from the belly of the *porco preto* pig. [$] *Average main: €12 ✉ Rua de Dom Pedro V 96–98, Bairro Alto ☎ 21/346–1860 💳 No credit cards ⏲ Closed Sun. ✥ C4.*

$$ PORTUGUESE 🍴 **Cervejaria Trindade.** The colorful azulejo wall tiles and vaulted ceiling of this former monastery hint at its long history, and it's popular with locals and tourists alike. A homey bar at the entrance will quench your thirst as you wait—you can also just come here for a drink and some

pataniscas (tasty cod fritters). Seafood feasts include crayfish, lobster, crab, and tiger prawns. You might start with *ameijoas à Bulhão Pato* (clams in a garlic-butter-and-cilantro sauce) before moving on to *bife de vazia à Trindade* (steak with a choice of three sauces) or *bacalhau à Santo Ofício* (baked cod with olive oil). It all tastes great with the house wine. $ *Average main: €17* ✉ *Rua Nova da Trindade 20, Bairro Alto* ☎ *21/342–3506* ⊕ *www.cervejariatrindade.pt* ✛ *C5.*

$ ✕ **Cocheira Alentejana.** The rustic decor really fits with the traditional
PORTUGUESE cooking from the rural Alentejo region here, in what is one of the area's coziest, friendliest, and best-value restaurants. Dig into regional dishes such as *migas com carne de porco* (pork with bread crumbs and garlic fried in olive oil), *sopa de cação* (dog fish soup), and seared tuna with port-wine sauce. Dishes may be flavored with locally used herbs such as *poejo* (pennyroyal) as well as the more internationally known *coentros* (cilantro). The wine list is dominated by Alentejo wines—widely considered to be some of the best in the country. It's enough to make you resolve to head off for the countryside the very next day. $ *Average main: €13* ✉ *Travessa do Poço da Cidade, Bairro Alto* ☎ *21/346–4868* ⊕ *cocheiraalentejana.pt* ⊘ *Closed Sun. No lunch Sat.* ✛ *A3.*

$ ✕ **Comida de Santo.** Excellent northeastern Brazilian food served in a
BRAZILIAN funky, brightly painted dining room to a suitably lively sound track keeps this tiny place buzzing until late at night. Come and enjoy classic Bahian dishes, such as fish soups, *feijoada* (black bean stew with sausage, pork, and dried beef), or *vatapá* (a spicy shrimp concoction thickened with ground peanuts). Sip a caipirinha and munch on manioc fries while you wait, and finish your meal with coconut-rich *manjar branco* or *pudim de aipim* (ground manioc, cooked with condensed milk). There are several unusual vegetarian options, such as pumpkin stuffed with palm heart and cheese. Comida de Santo is down a side street off Rua da Escola Politécnica; ring the bell for entrance. $ *Average main: €14* ✉ *Calçada Engenheiro Miguel Pais 39, Rato* ☎ *21/396–3339* ⊕ *www.comidadesanto.pt* ⊘ *Closed Tues. No lunch in Aug.* ⌑ *Reservations essential* ✛ *B3.*

$ ✕ **Fidalgo.** The local intelligentsia have made this low-key, comfortable
PORTUGUESE restaurant their refuge, though owner Eugenio Fidalgo has been welcoming every sort of patron for four decades now. He'll gladly help you with the Portuguese menu and the excellent, well-priced wine list. Try one of the specialties, such as bacalhau or octopus *à lagareiro* (baked in olive oil, with tiny potatoes), or the incredibly succulent *medalhões de javali* (wild boar cutlets). $ *Average main: €14* ✉ *Rua da Barroca 27, Bairro Alto* ☎ *21/342–2900* ⊕ *www.restaurantefidalgo.com* ⊘ *Closed Sun.* ✛ *A3.*

$$$$ ✕ **La Paparrucha.** Lisbon's only Argentine restaurant is known above all
ARGENTINE for the quality of its meat, but slick service and a great location also
FAMILY help attract well-heeled locals. Tables by the picture windows or on the large wooden deck out back (where you may smoke) afford sweeping views across central Lisbon; there's a heaping buffet of meats, mains, and salads at lunchtime on weekdays, as well as à la carte options and a kids' menu. Many starters are meat-free; then it's mainly steaks galore and *parilladas*—mixed grills. For dessert, the *panquecas de dulce*

de leite (pancakes with caramel) are a popular treat. [$] *Average main: €33* ✉ *Rua D. Pedro V 18–20, Bairro Alto* ☎ *21/342–5333* 🌐 *www.lapaparrucha.com* ✣ *C4.*

$$$$ MEDITERRANEAN Fodor's Choice ★

🍴 **Largo.** Founded by celebrated Porto chef Miguel Castro e Silva, this upscale restaurant was an immediate hit with the critics when it opened in 2009. And while Castro has moved on, the stylish restaurant retains the flair which won the hearts of Lisbon's fashionable foodies. The setting itself is a selling point: tables are set beneath ancient brick arches offset with modern features, including artfully lit tanks containing colorful jellyfish. The restaurant has maintained its reputation for high-quality, high-end contemporary cuisine, and some classic dishes remain. The wine list is both extensive and predictably expensive, and there's even a menu of premium gins. The lunch menu, which includes starter and main, is a good value at €18. [$] *Average main: €26* ✉ *Rua Serpa Pinto 10A, Chiado* ☎ *21/347–7225* 🌐 *www.largo.pt* ⏲ *Closed Sun.* ✣ *C5.*

$$$$ ECLECTIC Fodor's Choice ★

🍴 **100 Maneiras.** In a cozy, all-white space, Serbian-born Ljubomir Stanisic offers one of Lisbon's most stimulating tasting menus, changing every six weeks. Book a table at this 30-seat restaurant, sit back and enjoy nine creative, often playful starter-size dishes, like the *Estendal do Bairro* (neighborhood clothesline): bacalhau chips hung up like drying linens. Others might include sea urchin and crab crème brûlée; confit of pork shoulder with creamy beet polenta, clams, delicate pickles, and baby vegetables; and prawn head with lime and garlic mayo, prawn olive oil, and the North African spice mix *ras el hanout*. It's not cheap—€60 gets you the tasting menu, while an extra €35 includes the standard wine pairings and €60 more gets the deluxe pairings—but as a special-occasion restaurant it's hard to beat. Chef Ljubo also runs lively Bistro 100 Maneiras at nearby Largo de Trindade 9, whose globe-spanning menu includes Serbian dishes. The two venues share a phone; when reserving, make clear which you want. [$] *Average main: €60* ✉ *Rua do Teixeira 35, Bairro Alto* ☎ *21/099–0475, 91/030–7575* 🌐 *www.restaurante100maneiras.com* ⏲ *No lunch* ✍ *Reservations essential* ✣ *C4.*

$ PORTUGUESE

🍴 **Sinal Vermelho.** At this update of a traditional adega, the split-level dining room is traditionally tiled, and the food is thoroughly Portuguese. But the prints on the wall are modern, and the wine list wide ranging. The excellent fresh seafood dishes here include *chocos dourados à moda de Setúbal* (battered, deep-fried chunks of cuttlefish) and filetes de *peixe galo* (John Dory) served with tomato rice or açorda. The meat dishes are less inspiring, although in winter a hearty dish such as veal with chestnuts and mushrooms might appeal. [$] *Average main: €14* ✉ *Rua das Gáveas 89, Bairro Alto* ☎ *21/346–1252* ✣ *A3.*

$$$ PORTUGUESE

🍴 **Tágide.** In a fine old house that looks out over the Baixa and the Rio Tejo (reserve a table by the window), you can have one of Lisbon's great food experiences. The dining room lined with 18th-century tiles is a charming place to sample Portuguese fare, from both tasting and seasonal à la carte menus. The eight-course tasting menu is good value at €52. If you're going à la carte, you might start with a platter of cured meats from the Iberian black pig and move onto entrées like bacalhau with cured ham, spinach, and chickpea puree, or veal medallions with Azeitão cheese. Vegetarians are well served here with interesting dishes like chickpea curry with apple, spinach, and olive oil crispbreads. Among the desserts, the tiramisu with "drunken" pear (poached in port wine) stands out. On arrival at the restaurant, ring the bell to get in. The downstairs wine bar has similarly panoramic views and a more informal atmosphere. $ *Average main: €22 ⊠ Largo Academia Nacional de Belas Artes 18–20, Chiado ☎ 21/340–4010 ⊕ www.restaurantetagide. com ⊘ Closed Sun. ⚐ Reservations essential ✛ D4.*

$$ ✕ **Terra.** Countering the common local view that vegetarians must suffer
VEGETARIAN for their convictions, Terra offers a meatless buffet feast The cheaper
FAMILY lunchtime deal includes drink and dessert. At dinner, dishes change daily and include adaptations of Portuguese classics like seitan à alentejana (instead of pork) and feijoada *de batata doce* (with sweet potato). Around 80% of the dishes are vegan, and staff will point out those that are not. There are some good wines, including a kosher one from northeastern Portugal, and the delicious desserts include homemade brownies, ice cream, and, in summer, melon soup. The place is cozy rather than sophisticated, but the large, plant-filled back garden is a plus. $ *Average main: €16 ⊠ Rua da Palmeira 15, Bairro Alto ☎ 21/3421407 ⊕ www. restauranteterra.pt ⊘ Closed Mon. ✛ B4.*

THE MODERN CITY

$ ✕ **Casa dos Passarinhosdos.** This traditional restaurant has been welcom-
PORTUGUESE ing diners since 1923 and is not only efficient and friendly, but serves delicious food at extremely fair prices. At lunch, workers from the nearby Amoreiras office complex and mall come for the house specialties, which include a famous *naco na pedra* (steak cooked on a hot stone), *vitela barrosã* (tender veal from the north), grilled fish, and açorda de gambas. In the evening, Casa dos Passarinhos draws mainly locals, from its own solidly middle-class Campo de Ourique neighborhood and farther afield. The two dining rooms are decorated in appropriately rustic style. $ *Average main: €14 ⊠ Rua Silva Carvalho 195, Amoreiras ☎ 21/388–2346 ⊘ Closed Sun., and 2 wks in Aug. ✛ A2.*

$$$$ ✕ **Estórias na Casa da Comida.** This gourmands' haven near Jardim das
PORTUGUESE Amoreiras has been serving up high-end cuisine for over 35 years, and
Fodor's Choice has now been given a new lease on life by chef Duarte Lourenço and
★ sommelier Ricardo Morais. The long-standing foodie favorite was dramatically redesigned in 2014, wowing interior design aficionados with an artfully eclectic look that blends kitschy chaise longues and ornate mirrors with the cool whites and crisp blues of Lisbon's iconic azulejo tiles. A candlelit terrace provides a romantic setting for alfresco dining during the summer months. Guests can snack on a superior line of *petiscos* (light bites) in the bar area, go à la carte, or opt for the eight-course "Madness of the Chef" tasting menu. For €60, expect gourmet treats like juniper-smoked rabbit, and a fish cake made from gooseneck barnacles and crab. $ *Average main: €30 ⊠ Travessa das Amoreiras 1, Amoreiras ☎ 21/386–0889, 21/388–5376 ⊕ www.casadacomida.pt ⊘ Closed Sun. No lunch ⚐ Reservations essential ✛ A2.*

$
PORTUGUESE
✕ **O Fumeiro.** Two brothers from the Beiras region have been serving up hearty portions of traditional food in this picturesquely tiled space off Avenida da Liberdade for two decades. A plethora of fish stews cooked in traditional oval *cataplanas* is complemented by dishes featuring roast suckling pig, rabbit and hare, or bacalhau cooked in so many ways only a few are listed on the menu. Everything here is cooked from scratch, which means a longish wait if you want off-the-menu dishes like *chanfana* (kid marinated in red wine). $ *Average main: €12* ✉ *Rua Conceição da Glória 25, Avenida da Liberdade* ☎ *21/347–4203* ⊙ *Closed Sun.* ✛ *C4.*

$
VEGETARIAN
✕ **Os Tibetanos.** Delicious meat-free dishes such as mango and tofu curry, seitan steak, and spinach-filled Tibetan *momo* dumplings ensure that there's always a line for a table in this restaurant's dining room or pleasant garden. Daily specials cost less than €10, and fixed-price menus are excellent values. The savory pastries are legendary among vegetarian Lisboetas. Os Tibetanos is part of a Buddhist center: a small shop stocks books and crafts, incense, homeopathic medicines, and other natural products, while yoga and meditation classes take place upstairs. $ *Average main: €9* ✉ *Rua do Salitre 117, Avenida da Liberdade* ☎ *21/314–2038* ▭ *No credit cards* ⊙ *Closed Sun. No lunch on public holidays* ✛ *C3.*

$$$
SEAFOOD
✕ **Ribadouro.** One of Lisbon's best-known seafood spots, Ribadouro is a smarter-than-average beer hall that offers the works: take your pick from lobster, mantis shrimp, crayfish, tiger shrimp, whelks, oysters, and clams, or combine the lot in a vast seafood platter. The wares are displayed in glass counters and in enormous aquariums. Popular light dishes include *gambas ao alhinho* (prawns fried in garlic), while meatier mains include *bife do Ribadouro* (steak in a creamy wine-and-butter sauce). When crowds spill out of the nearby theaters, you may have to wait for a table; on weekends, try to arrive before 8 pm or, better still, reserve a table in advance. A large TV is usually tuned to local soccer games, with the sound down. $ *Average main: €23* ✉ *Av. da Liberdade 155, Avenida da Liberdade* ☎ *21/354–9411, 93/652–0721* ⊕ *www.cervejariaribadouro.pt* ✛ *C3.*

$$$$
PORTUGUESE
✕ **Varanda.** The main restaurant at the Ritz is rare among hotel eateries in staying consistently at the top of its game. Frenchman Pascal Meynard keeps a tight grip on the reins here, overseeing a seasonally changing *menu de degustação* (dinner only) and a wide choice of Portuguese and international dishes. These might include seafood *cataplana*, (slow-cooked cod served with celery and garlic fries) or, in colder months, veal mignon with truffles and pine nuts. Expert advice is on hand to help you select wines from the long list. Achingly sweet Portuguese desserts are available, as well as lighter sweets such as berries marinated with herbs. At lunch, you may order à la carte or dig into a buffet (€56) that many see as Lisbon's best. $ *Average main: €43* ✉ *Four Seasons Hotel Ritz Lisbon, Rua Rodrigo de Fonseca 88, Marquês de Pombal* ☎ *21/381–1400* ⊕ *www.fourseasons.com* ⌖ *Reservations essential* ✛ *B1.*

LAPA AND ESTRELA

$$$$ **BELGIAN** 🍴 **A Travessa.** Its lovely location in an 18th-century former convent (also home to the Museu da Marioneta) is just one of the trump cards of this Luso-Belgian restaurant. Meals begin with a selection of at least eight starters, including the restaurant's famous "black pork secrets" and scrambled egg with wild mushrooms. Fish and meat mains are superb, and come accompanied by a selection of separately plated sides such as spinach and turnip purees and oven-baked potatoes. The interior is inviting and, on warm days, you can sit at tables set out in the old convent's courtyard. Parking is a puzzle in the narrow streets of the old fishermen's neighborhood of Madragoa, but the restaurant has an arrangement with the Largo Vitorino Damásio car park in Santos (with transfer service, no fee). Call to be picked up in the restaurant's van. [$] *Average main: €30* ✉ *Travessa do Convento das Bernardas 12, off Rua das Trinas, Madragoa* ☎ *968/939125, 21/394–0800* 🌐 *www.atravessa.com* 🕒 *Closed Sun. No lunch Mon. and Sat.* ✍ *Reservations essential* ✥ *A5.*

2

$ **CAFÉ** **FAMILY** 🍴 **Jardim da Estrela.** This cozy café at the entrance to the garden of the same name is a top choice for families, thanks to a leafy terrace with waddling ducks and a miniature Tram 28, and a colorful interior complete with a games-filled kids' corner. The menu is filled with kid-friendly options such as supersize toasted sandwiches and homemade cakes; grown-ups can sip cider, sangria, or very reasonably priced jugs of wine while tucking into quiches, salads, soups, and pastries. Blankets are provided after dark during cooler months, and DJs sometimes spin tunes beneath trees strewn with fairy lights. [$] *Average main: €15* ✉ *Jardim da Estrela , close to the park entrance that faces the basilica, Lapa* ☎ *21/397–4276* 🌐 *www.ojardimdaestrela.com* 💳 *No credit cards* ✥ *A4.*

$$ **PORTUGUESE** 🍴 **Tasca da Esquina.** In this informal corner eatery, top-quality Portuguese produce is transformed into lip-smacking dishes for modern palates. There are a few entrées, but it's more common to order a battery of smaller dishes—diners can choose from the menu or opt for the "In the Hands of the Chef" surprise selections, which range from three to eight small plates. Daily specials are revealed on the website each morning, and might include *berbigão no tacho* (steamed cockles, seasoned with ginger as well as the traditional cilantro), *fígado de aves com pêra* (chicken liver with pear), *farinheira com favas* (traditional sausage with beans), or even gastronomically daring options such as pork testicles with foie gras. For dessert, chocolate mousse with walnut and *ginja* wild cherry is an excellent option. Space in the glass-walled dining space is at a premium, so it's best to book in advance. [$] *Average main: €17* ✉ *Rua Domingos Sequeira 41C, Campo de Ourique* ☎ *21/099–3939* 🌐 *www.tascadaesquina.com* 🕒 *Closed Sun. No lunch Mon.* ✍ *Reservations essential* ✥ *A4.*

CAIS DO SODRÉ AND SANTOS

$$$ JAPANESE 🍴 **Estado Líquido Sushi Lounge.** Scallop carpaccio with salmon, caviar, and a spicy sauce; a house maki featuring salmon, cream cheese, and sesame seeds; and soft-shell crab urumaki are among the popular dishes at this fashionable eatery in the nightlife hub of Santos. Wash them down with hot or cold sake—or a "Sakerinha," an adaptation of the Brazilian lime-and-sugar caipirinha—and perhaps finish with a velvety chocolate-and-rum mousse. The insistent, funky sound track suits the young crowd here, as do the low tables and lighting. [$] *Average main: €22* ✉ *Largo de Santos 5A, Santos* ☎ *21/397–2022* ⌚ *No lunch* ✥ *A5.*

$$$ SEAFOOD 🍴 **Monte Mar.** A city-smart sister to the celebrated formal dining restaurant in Cascais, Monte Mar Lisboa offers the same superior seafood with a suitably relaxed riverside ambience. Occupying one of the formerly disused warehouses along the revitalized docks, Monte Mar has a terrific view of the river, the 25 de Abril suspension bridge, and across to the Cristo Rei on the other side, while indoors it is all slick black and chrome. Service is attentive but not stuffy, and staff will bring out blankets for patrons dining alfresco if the temperatures dip. Spider crab, oysters, and deliciously fresh grilled sea bream and salmon are among the standouts of the seafood-focused menu. [$] *Average main: €23* ✉ *Rua da Cintura Armazem 65, Cais do Gás, Cais do Sodré* ☎ *21/322–0160* 🌐 *www.mmlisboa.pt/en/restaurant-monte-mar-lisboa* ⌚ *Closed Mon.* ✥ *B6.*

$$$ PORTUGUESE Fodor's Choice ★ 🍴 **Pap'açorda.** A onetime hipster favorite in the Bairro Alto, Pap'açorda has now moved to the laid-back-cool confines of the Time Out Mercado da Ribeira in Cais do Sodré, bringing its delicious dishes and its famously glitzy chandelier along for the ride. The menu still lists cutting-edge versions of Portuguese classics—grilled sole or John Dory; breaded veal cutlets; and a famous açorda, that bread-based stew rich in seafood (the luxury version contains lobster) and flavored with garlic and cilantro. The fried whitebait with tomato açorda makes for a great starter. For dessert, scrumptious chocolate mousse is spooned with panache from a giant bowl. The wine list has been extended, and one wall is entirely taken up with wine bottles. [$] *Average main: €21* ✉ *Mercado da Ribeira, Av. 24 de Julho, Mercado da Ribeira 1200-479, nº49 - 1º Andar, Cais do Sodré* ☎ *21/120–0479* 🌐 *papacorda.com* ⌚ *Closed Mon.* ✍ *Reservations essential* ✥ *B6.*

ALCÂNTARA

$$$ SEAFOOD 🍴 **Doca Peixe.** The display of the day's catch on ice at the entrance and the small aquarium clue you in to what's served at this well-regarded riverside spot.You might start with a tomato-and-mozzarella salad or prawns seared in cognac, then move on to sea bass with clams, or codfish baked in a cornbread crust served with turnip leaves. Meaty alternatives are limited but include steak with green pepper sauce and grilled pork fillet. [$] *Average main: €21* ✉ *Armazém 14, Doca de Santo Amaro, Alcântara* ☎ *21/397–3565* 🌐 *www.docapeixe.com* ✥ *A6.*

$$ PORTUGUESE 🍴 **Estufa Real.** Every Sunday starting at noon, a wonderful brunch buffet with lots of salads (€37 per person, half price for children under 11) is served inside the 18th-century "Royal Greenhouse" of the Ajuda Botanical Gardens. Surrounded by exotic trees and plants, you will be cordially welcomed with a glass of orange juice or sparkling wine on the house. On other days, the à la carte lunch menu varies according to the season, with Portuguese and international dishes which may include white sausage risotto, or lighter fare such as sauteed salmon tataki with grilled zucchini and a cold tomato jam. Prices are surprisingly accessible given the luxurious surrounds and high-quality ingredients. $ *Average main: €17* ✉ *Jardim Botânico da Ajuda, Calçada do Galvão, Calçada do Galvão, Ajuda* ☎ *21/361–9400* ⊕ *www.estufareal.com* ⊗ *Closed Sat. No dinner* ✛ *A6.*

PARQUE DAS NAÇÕES

$$ ✗ **Senhor Peixe.** At "Mr. Fish," seafood straight from the port of Setúbal
SEAFOOD is grilled over charcoal. Shellfish is sold by weight (some catches are much more expensive than others, so check the price list if you don't want to blow the budget) while house specialties in servings for one, two, or more people include dishes like lobster rice and fried cuttlefish. $ *Average main: €17* ✉ *Rua da Pimenta, Parque das Nações* ☎ *21/895–5892* ⊕ *senhorpeixe.pt* ⊗ *Closed Mon. No dinner Sun.* ✛ *H5.*

WHERE TO STAY

Lisbon has an excellent range of accommodations serving just about every market niche, from luxury pads in the historic downtown to workaday, business-oriented hotels in the modern Parque das Nações. Even in the city's hotels, consider inspecting a room before taking it: street noise can be a problem, and, conversely, quieter rooms at the back don't always have great views (or, indeed, any views). Also, some hotels charge the same rate for each of their rooms, so by checking out a couple you might be able to get a better room for the same price. This is especially true of the older hotels and inns, where no two rooms are exactly alike.

Lisbon is busy year-round, so it's best to secure a room in advance of your trip. Peak periods are Easter and June through September; budget *pensões* are particularly busy in summer. Despite the high year-round occupancy, substantial discounts—sometimes 30%–40%—abound from November through February. *Prices in the reviews are the lowest cost of a standard double room in high season. For expanded hotel reviews, visit Fodors.com.*

WHAT IT COSTS IN EUROS				
	$	$$	$$$	$$$$
FOR TWO PEOPLE	Under €140	€140–€200	€201–€260	over €260

Hotel prices are for a standard double room, including tax, in high season (off-season rates may be lower).

ALFAMA

$ HOTEL **Albergaria Senhora do Monte.** If you want expansive views of the castle and river, book a room on one of the upper floors of this modern hotel. **Pros:** amazing views; in quiet residential neighborhood with restaurants and stores nearby; free Wi-Fi. **Cons:** on a steep hill; limited facilities; small breakfast selection. [$] *Rooms from: €132* ✉ *Calçada do Monte 39, Alfama* ☎ *21/886–6002* *24 rooms, 4 suites* 🍴 *Breakfast* ✣ *F4.*

$$ HOTEL **Olissippo Castelo.** This small, elegant hotel pampers guests with luxurious linens, thick carpeting, elegant furnishings, comfy mattresses, and marble bathrooms. **Pros:** great views; quiet area; free Wi-Fi; babysitting can be arranged on request. **Cons:** up a steep hill; no pool. [$] *Rooms from: €180* ✉ *Rua Costa do Castelo 112–116, Alfama* ☎ *21/882–0190* 🌐 *www.olissippohotels.com* *20 rooms, 4 suites* 🍴 *Breakfast* ✣ *E5.*

$$$$ B&B/INN Fodor's Choice ★ **Solar do Castelo.** A member of the Historic Hotels of Europe, this boutique hideaway is located in an 18th-century mansion within the walls of Saint George's Castle. **Pros:** charm to spare; quiet location; free Wi-Fi and Internet terminal. **Cons:** up a steep cobbled road; some rooms only have showers; no restaurant. [$] *Rooms from: €290* ✉ *Rua das Cozinhas 2, Alfama* ☎ *21/880–6050* 🌐 *www.heritage.pt* *20 rooms* 🍴 *Breakfast* ✣ *E5.*

$ B&B/INN **Solar dos Mouros.** This pink, artistic town house has individually decorated rooms in a great location near the Castelo de São Jorge. **Pros:** close to the castle; lovely views; helpful staff. **Cons:** up a steep hill and with stairs to climb: no elevator; no parking; no facilities for the disabled. [$] *Rooms from: €129* ✉ *Rua do Milagre de Santo Antonio 6, Alfama* ☎ *21/885–4940* 🌐 *www.solardosmouros.com* *13 rooms* 🍴 *No meals* ✣ *E5.*

BAIXA

$$ HOTEL Fodor's Choice ★ **AlmaLusa.** This chic boutique hotel set in an artfully restored historic building has fantastic service, locally produced products, and luxe amenities. **Pros:** central location; historic building; great on-site restaurant; luxurious amenities and great service. **Cons:** no pool or gym; some rooms have poor views. [$] *Rooms from: €190* ✉ *Praça do Munícipio 21, Baixa* ☎ *21/269–7440* 🌐 *www.almalusahotels.com/hotel* *16 rooms, 12 suites* 🍴 *Breakfast* ✣ *C6.*

$$$ HOTEL **Altis Avenida.** In what was once a government building, this large boutique hotel from the Altis group offers glamour and comfort in a central location ideal for sightseeing. **Pros:** great views from restaurant; pets welcome; free Wi-Fi. **Cons:** most rooms lack private terraces; no on-site exercise facilities. [$] *Rooms from: €230* ✉ *Rua 1° de Dezembro 120, Restauradores* ☎ *21/044–0000* 🌐 *www.altisavenidahotel.com* *68 rooms, 2 suites* 🍴 *Breakfast* [M] *Restauradores* ✣ *D4.*

$$$ HOTEL **Avenida Palace.** Built in 1892, Lisbon's first luxury hotel combines regal elegance with modern comfort. **Pros:** elegant and luxurious; central yet tranquil; free Wi-Fi. **Cons:** some may find it overly formal; no restaurant or spa. [$] *Rooms from: €250* ✉ *Rua 1° de Dezembro 123, Restauradores* ☎ *21/321–8100* 🌐 *www.hotel-avenida-palace.pt* *64 rooms, 18 suites* 🍴 *Breakfast* [M] *Restauradores* ✣ *D4.*

$$$ HOTEL Fodor's Choice ★ **Internacional Design Hotel.** The rooms—designated S, M, L, XL—in this elegant hotel facing Rossio square are decorated with style and come equipped with a LCD Sony TVs, an espresso machine, and a Jacuzzi. **Pros:** well located for sightseeing; lots of amenities; marketed as gay-friendly. **Cons:** modern style may not be to every traveler's taste; not really family-oriented with just three extra beds available; no exercise facilities. [$] *Rooms from: €250* ✉ *Rua da Betesga 13, Baixa* ☎ *21/324090* 🌐 *www.idesignhotel.com* *55 rooms* 🍴 *Breakfast* [M] *Rossio* ✣ *D5.*

$$ HOTEL **Lisboa Tejo Hotel.** Just a few steps away from the busy Praça da Figueira, this three-star hotel is close to the city's shopping, sightseeing, and nightlife. **Pros:** central location; free Wi-Fi hot spot; 24-hour bar. **Cons:** basic facilities; noisy at night; rooms looking dated. [$] *Rooms from: €150* ✉ *Rua Condes de Monsanto 2, Baixa* ☎ *21/886–6182* 🌐 *lisboatejohotel.com* *51 rooms, 7 suites* 🍴 *Breakfast* [M] *Rossio* ✣ *D5.*

$ HOTEL **Mundial.** Steps from the Rossio and Restauradores squares, this large property looks uncompromisingly modern, but inside there's lots of good, old-fashioned charm combined with modern facilities. **Pros:** stunning views and great lounge bar on the rooftop; vehicle hire at hotel; free parking; free Wi-Fi; friendly staff. **Cons:** unattractive exterior; no pool; Praça Martim Moniz is still an up-and-coming square. [$] *Rooms from: €139* ✉ *Praça Martim Moniz 2, Baixa* ☎ *21/884–2000* 🌐 *www.hotel-mundial.pt* *347 rooms, 3 suites* 🍴 *Breakfast* [M] *Rossio* ✣ *D4.*

$ B&B/INN Fodor's Choice ★ **Residencial Florescente.** Rooms at this welcoming inn are on five azulejo-lined floors and vary in size (the smallest is very small); all are bright and cheerful and dotted with naïf paintings. **Pros:** friendly staff; great location; some superior rooms have a small living room. **Cons:** street noise at night; rooms in front catch less sunlight; no vehicle access after 11 am. [$] *Rooms from: €75* ✉ *Rua Portas de Santo Antão 99, Baixa* ☎ *21/342–6609* 🌐 *www.residencialflorescente.com* *68 rooms* 🍴 *Breakfast* [M] *Restauradores* ✣ *D3.*

CHIADO AND BAIRRO ALTO

$$$$ HOTEL Fodor's Choice ★ **Bairro Alto Hotel.** Lisbon's first contemporary boutique hotel offers sleek design and five-star luxury right in the heart of the city. **Pros:** cutting-edge design; terrace bar with stunning views; good service. **Cons:** some rooms are small; rooftop bar often packed with non-guests. [$] *Rooms from: €290* ✉ *Praça Luís de Camões 2, Bairro Alto* ☎ *21/340–8288* 🌐 *www.bairroaltohotel.com* *51 rooms, 4 suites* 🍴 *Breakfast* [M] *Baixa Chiado* ✣ *C5.*

$ B&B/INN FAMILY **Casa de São Mamede.** One of the first private houses to be built in Lisbon after the 18th-century earthquake has been transformed into a relaxed boutique guesthouse endowed with antique, country-style furniture; a tiled dining room; a grand staircase; and stained-glass windows. **Pros:** family-friendly; tranquil, yet bars and restaurants are close by; free Wi-Fi and business center. **Cons:** no parking; perhaps a little staid for younger travelers. [$] *Rooms from: €110* ✉ *Rua da Escola Politécnica 159, Rato* ☎ *21/396–3166* 🌐 *www.casadesaomamede.pt* *25 rooms, 1 suite* 🍴 *Breakfast* [M] *Rato* ✣ *A3.*

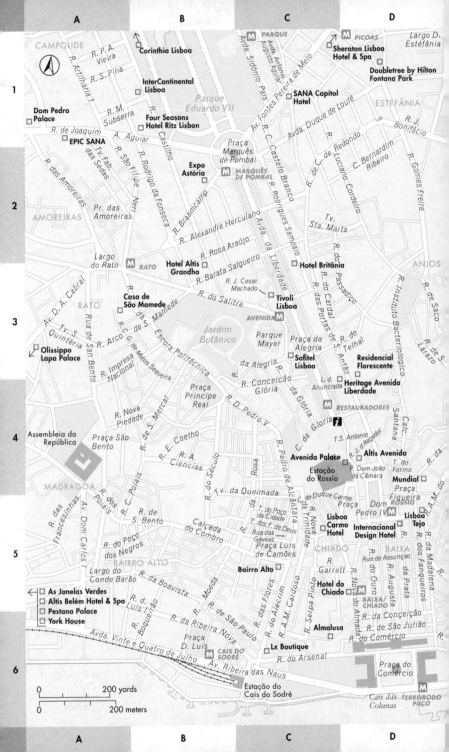

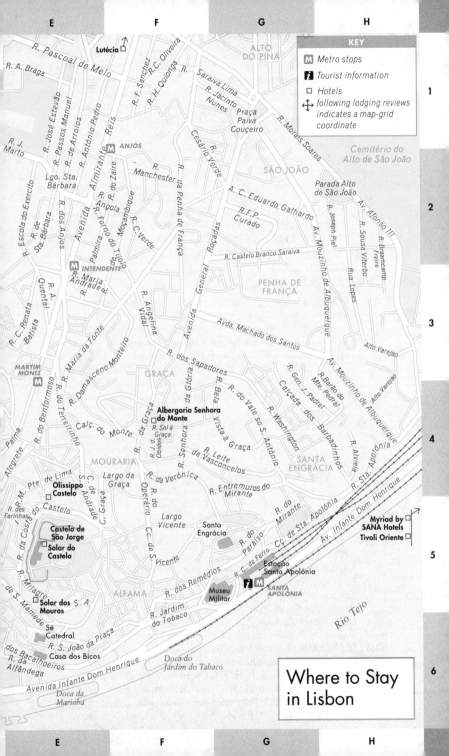

Where to Stay in Lisbon

$$$$ HOTEL 🏨 **Hotel do Chiado.** This boutique hotel occupies the sixth to eighth floors of the Grandes Armazéns do Chiado shopping complex, which was painstakingly restored by the famous Siza Vieira after being destroyed by a dramatic fire in 1998. **Pros:** fantastic central location and views; trendy café-bar with large terrace. **Cons:** breakfast not included in price. [$] *Rooms from: €297* ✉ *Rua Nova de Almada 114, Chiado* ☎ *21/325–6100, 21/325–6200* 🌐 *www.hoteldochiado.pt* 🛏 *38 rooms, 2 suites* 🍴 *Breakfast* [M] *Baixa-Chiado* ✣ *D5.*

$$$$ HOTEL Fodor's Choice ★ 🏨 **Lisboa Carmo Hotel.** This boutique charmer, located in the upscale, hilly Chiado neighborhood, features a historic setting and Lisbon city views, plus a team of "hotel tailors" who "fit" each guest with a unique experience. **Pros:** prime location for sightseeing and barhopping; chic decor; historic charm. **Cons:** some rooms are small; restaurant can be inconsistent. [$] *Rooms from: €350* ✉ *Rua da Oliveira ao Carmo, 1, 2, 3, Largo do Carmo, Chiado* ☎ *213/264710* 🌐 *www.lisboacarmohotel.com* 🛏 *45 rooms* 🍴 *No meals* ✣ *C5.*

THE MODERN CITY

$$ HOTEL 🏨 **Corinthia Lisboa.** An excellent option for visitors looking to stay close to the airport, Corinthia Lisboa offers five-star accommodations and impeccable service just a short hop from both the airport and the historic downtown. **Pros:** luxury amenities; excellent service; good pool and spa; excellent business facilities. **Cons:** it's a metro or cab ride to downtown nightlife and attractions; location is not scenic. [$] *Rooms from: €150* ✉ *Av. Columbano Bordalo Pinheiro 105, Saldanha* ☎ *21/723–6363* 🌐 *www.corinthia.com/hotels/Lisbon* 🛏 *518 rooms* 🍴 *Breakfast* 💳 *No credit cards* ✣ *B1.*

$$ HOTEL 🏨 **Dom Pedro Palace.** This is no historic palace, but rooms and suites at this smart modern high-rise have rich fabrics and polished-wood furniture, including executive desks and other amenities for the prosperous business travelers who favor the hotel. **Pros:** great views; close to shopping opportunities; ultra-efficient service. **Cons:** it's a 10-minute walk to nearest metro; neighborhood often choked with traffic; breakfast not included in room rate. [$] *Rooms from: €170* ✉ *Av. Engenheiro Duarte Pacheco 24, Amoreiras* ☎ *21/389–6600* 🌐 *www.dompedro.com* 🛏 *254 rooms, 8 suites* 🍴 *No meals* ✣ *A1.*

$$$ HOTEL 🏨 **DoubleTree by Hilton Fontana Park.** This contemporary hotel from Hilton's DoubleTree brand offers excellent service and amenities, including warm chocolate-chip cookies at check-in, 26-inch LCD TVs, a work area, and Wi-Fi. **Pros:** excellent service; good on-site restaurants; good amenities. **Cons:** a metro ride to the main sights; the contemporary design is not to everybody's taste. [$] *Rooms from: €260* ✉ *Rua Engenheiro Vieira da Silva, Saldanha* ☎ *21/041–0600* 🌐 *doubltree3.hilton.com* 🛏 *137 rooms, 2 suites* 🍴 *Breakfast* [M] *Saldanha* ✣ *D1.*

$$$$ HOTEL FAMILY 🏨 **EPIC SANA.** With an enormous spa, pool, and well-equipped gym that look out onto a beautiful botanical garden, this well-located hotel draws in the leisure crowd. **Pros:** great amenities; fabulous spa and rooftop pool; well located for shopping and out-of-town travel. **Cons:** far from historical sights; king-size beds leave little space in some guest rooms; lacks local flavor. [$] *Rooms from: €350* ✉ *Av. Engenheiro Duarte*

Pacheco 15, Marquês de Pombal ☎ *21/159–7300* ⊕ *www.lisboa.epic. sanahotels.com* ⇆ *291 rooms, 20 suites* ⦿ *No meals* ✛ *A1.*

$
HOTEL

🏨 **Expo Astória.** This slick, artsy hotel is housed in a fabulous art-deco building, and its funky, colorful decor should appeal to those who find high-rise hotels a little lacking in soul. **Pros:** good transport links; free Wi-Fi. **Cons:** noisy rooms; breakfast €10 extra. ⓢ *Rooms from: €125* ✉ *Rua Braancamp 10, Marquês de Pombal* ☎ *21/386–1317* ⊕ *www. expoastoria.pt* ⇆ *113 rooms* ⦿ *No meals* Ⓜ *Marquês de Pombal* ✛ *B2.*

$$$$
HOTEL
FAMILY
Fodor's Choice
★

🏨 **Four Seasons Hotel Ritz Lisbon.** The luxury starts the minute you step into the marbled reception area and continues through to the lounge bar, whose terrace overlooks Lisbon's central park. **Pros:** luxury accommodation; stunning views; outstanding restaurant, exercise facilities, and spa. **Cons:** expensive; parking not free; formal decor may feel stuffy to some guests. ⓢ *Rooms from: €490* ✉ *Rua Rodrigo da Fonseca 88, Marquês de Pombal* ☎ *21/381–1471* ⊕ *www.fourseasons.com/lisbon* ⇆ *262 rooms, 20 suites* ⦿ *Breakfast* Ⓜ *Marquês de Pombal* ✛ *B1.*

$$$
HOTEL

🏨 **Heritage Avenida Liberdade.** This style-conscious boutique hotel is located in an 18th-century town house styled by the Portuguese architect Miguel Cancio Martins, and has an excellent location right next to the Praça dos Restauradores. **Pros:** free Wi-Fi; 24-hour room service; striking decoration. **Cons:** some rooms a little boxy; pool rather small. ⓢ *Rooms from: €260* ✉ *Av. da Liberdade 28, Avenida da Liberdade* ☎ *21/340–4040* ⊕ *www.heritage.pt* ⇆ *42 rooms* ⦿ *Breakfast* Ⓜ *Restauradores* ✛ *C4.*

$$$$
HOTEL

🏨 **Hotel Altis Grandho.** Formerly known as Hotel Altis, this large, renovated, five-star hotel has been in business for over 40 years and has 300 rooms and suites with crisp, clean decor and fantastic city views. **Pros:** recently remodeled; good gym and pool; comfortable beds. **Cons:** chain hotel with little local flavor; some bathrooms are small; service not as attentive as some five-star hotels in Lisbon. ⓢ *Rooms from: €290* ✉ *Rua Castilho 11, Marquês de Pombal* ☎ *21/310–6000* ⊕ *www.altishotels. com* ⇆ *289 rooms, 11 suites* ⦿ *Breakfast* Ⓜ *Marquês de Pombal* ✛ *B2.*

$$$
HOTEL
Fodor's Choice
★

🏨 **Hotel Britânia.** Part of the Heritage Lisbon suite of boutique hotels housed in notable historic buildings, the art-deco touches throughout Hotel Britânia are the key selling point—from the original marble panels in the baths to the "porthole" windows in the facade, the columns and candelabra in the lobby, and the murals in the bar. **Pros:** unique art-deco building and period decor; spacious rooms; free afternoon teas. **Cons:** no restaurant; no exercise facilities. ⓢ *Rooms from: €210* ✉ *Rua Rodrigues Sampaio 17, Avenida da Liberdade* ☎ *21/315–5016* ⊕ *www. hotel-britania.com* ⇆ *32 rooms, 1 suite* ⦿ *Breakfast* Ⓜ *Avenida* ✛ *C2.*

$$$$
HOTEL

🏨 **InterContinental Lisboa.** Business travelers like this comfortable and upscale hotel for its location—right by Parque Eduardo VII—and facilities. **Pros:** excellent business facilities including 24-hour business center; smart bar and restaurant; good service. **Cons:** no in-house pool or spa; more of a business than vacation ambience. ⓢ *Rooms from: €290* ✉ *Rua Castilho 149, Marquês de Pombal* ☎ *21/381–8700* ⊕ *www. ihg.com/intercontinental/hotels/gb/en/lisbon/lisha/hoteldetail* ⇆ *314 rooms, 17 suites* ⦿ *Breakfast* Ⓜ *Marquês de Pombal* ✛ *B1.*

$ HOTEL **Lutécia.** Billing itself as a "smart design hotel," Lutecia has a bold decor, with rooms arranged on themed floors: expect to see giant, lip-shape cushions on the Kiss Me floor, and a more minimalist design in White Space. **Pros:** excellent service; most rooms have balconies. **Cons:** no exercise facilities; breakfast not included in room rate; decor will not appeal to everybody; far from center of town. [$] *Rooms from: €125* ✉ *Av. Frei Miguel Contreiras, Roma* ☎ *21/841–1300* 🌐 *www.luteciahotel.com* 🛏 *171 rooms, 4 suites* 🍴 *No meals* [M] *Roma* ✥ *F1.*

$$ HOTEL **SANA Capitol Hotel.** In a quiet backstreet near Praça Marquês de Pombal, this hotel offers exceptional location and comfort for its three-star ranking. **Pros:** well located near metro and Lisbon's central park; good service; modern, attractive decor. **Cons:** facilities limited; some taxi drivers may not know street. [$] *Rooms from: €140* ✉ *Rua Eça de Queiroz 24, Marquês de Pombal* ☎ *21/353–6811* 🌐 *www.capitol.sanahotels.com* 🛏 *58 rooms, 1 suite* 🍴 *Breakfast* [M] *Marquês de Pombal* ✥ *C1.*

$$$ HOTEL **Sheraton Lisboa Hotel & Spa.** Even those who eschew chain hotels will appreciate this Sheraton overlooking modern Lisbon; its many advantages include a huge reception area with a comfortable bar, a helpful staff, and guest rooms with many amenities. **Pros:** top-notch room amenities; choice of bars and restaurants; excellent free gym. **Cons:** pricey Internet and Wi-Fi access; spa and pool not free to guests; need to take transport to reach main sights. [$] *Rooms from: €240* ✉ *Rua Latino Coelho 1, Saldanha* ☎ *21/357–5757* 🌐 *www.sheratonlisboa.com* 🛏 *358 rooms, 11 suites* 🍴 *Breakfast* [M] *Picoas* ✥ *C1.*

$$$ HOTEL **Sofitel Lisboa.** Right in the middle of the Avenida da Liberdade and mere steps away from the metro, the handsome Sofitel has comfortably appointed rooms decorated in attractive colors. **Pros:** ultracomfortable rooms; free Wi-Fi and use of the business center. **Cons:** hotel often packed with conference participants; no pool and gym is rather small; as a chain hotel, it feels a little impersonal. [$] *Rooms from: €240* ✉ *Av. da Liberdade 127, Liberdade* ☎ *21/322–8300* 🌐 *www.sofitel-lisboa.com* 🛏 *151 rooms, 12 suites* 🍴 *Breakfast* [M] *Avenida* ✥ *C3.*

$$$ HOTEL **Tivoli Lisboa.** There's enough marble in the public areas to make you fear for the future supply of the stone, but grandness gives way to comfort in the rooms, which are characterized by stylish dark wood and well-equipped bathrooms. **Pros:** modern facilities; steps from metro; rooftop views are outstanding. **Cons:** free Internet access only in common areas; hotel often overrun by conferences. [$] *Rooms from: €240* ✉ *Av. da Liberdade 185, Liberdade* ☎ *21/319–8900* 🌐 *www.tivolihotels.com* 🛏 *306 rooms, 48 suites* 🍴 *Breakfast* [M] *Avenida* ✥ *C3.*

LAPA

$$$ B&B/INN Fodor's Choice ★ **As Janelas Verdes.** On the same street as the Museu de Arte Antiga and part of the Heritage Lisbon stable of historic hotels, this boutique spot in a late-18th-century mansion maintains fittings, furnishings, paintings, and tile work throughout that are in keeping with the building's historic character. **Pros:** elegant and peaceful; unique literary associations. **Cons:** just five parking spots; limited facilities; some distance from city center. [$] *Rooms from: €255* ✉ *Rua das Janelas Verdes 47, Lapa* ☎ *21/396–8143* 🌐 *www.asjanelasverdes.com* 🛏 *29 rooms* 🍴 *Breakfast* [M] *Cais do Sodré* ✥ *A5.*

$$$$ HOTEL Fodor's Choice ★ **Olissippo Lapa Palace.** Combining the elegance of a 19th-century manor house with the modern amenities of a luxury resort, the Olissippo Lapa Palace has spectacular gardens complete with lakes and waterfalls, along with an expansive swimming pool, children's plunge pool, and sundeck. **Pros:** luxury accommodations; historic charm; gorgeous gardens. **Cons:** location is not convenient for sightseeing. [$] *Rooms from: €390 ✉ Rua Pau de Bandeira 4, Lapa ☎ 21/395–0665, 21/394–9494 🌐 www.lapapalace.com 🛏 109 rooms 🍴 Breakfast ✥ A3.*

$$$ B&B/INN **York House.** While each guest room at York House is unique, all are spacious and have good-quality reproduction furniture—including four-poster beds—and beautiful rugs, which also adorn the tiled corridors. **Pros:** authentic period charm; handy for one of Lisbon's top art museums; good restaurant. **Cons:** steep climb up steps from main street; long walk or cab ride from most tourist attractions and nightlife. [$] *Rooms from: €220 ✉ Rua das Janelas Verdes 32, 1°, Lapa ☎ 21/396–2435 🌐 www.yorkhouselisboa.com 🛏 32 rooms 🍴 Breakfast ✥ A5.*

CAIS DO SODRÉ AND SANTOS

$$$ HOTEL Fodor's Choice ★ **Lx Boutique.** This chic boutique hotel with themed rooms boasts a hip location in one of Lisbon's hottest new neighborhoods for drinking and dining. **Pros:** well located for sightseeing; excellent amenities; boutique flair. **Cons:** rooms rather small; no exercise facilities; just four parking spots (fee). [$] *Rooms from: €225 ✉ Rua do Alecrim 12, Cais do Sodré ☎ 21/347–4394 🌐 www.lxboutiquehotel.com 🛏 60 rooms, 1 suite 🍴 No meals [M] Cais do Sodré ✥ C6.*

BELÉM

$$$$ HOTEL Fodor's Choice ★ **Altis Belém Hotel & Spa.** The decor at this elegant riverside hotel harks back to Portugal's Age of Discovery, but that's not to say it's stuck in the past—the overall feel is light and modern. **Pros:** lovely riverside location; convenient for Belém monuments and museums; excellent spa. **Cons:** far from downtown sights; must cross rail tracks to reach public transport. [$] *Rooms from: €425 ✉ Doca do Bom Sucesso, Belém ☎ 21/040–0200 🌐 www.altisbelemhotel.com 🛏 45 rooms, 5 suites 🍴 Breakfast ✥ A5.*

$$ HOTEL **Jerónimos 8.** Just around the corner from the famous monastery of the same name, Jerónimos 8 harmoniously blends past and present. **Pros:** near top Belém sights; pleasant sundeck. **Cons:** no exercise facilities; a half-hour streetcar or 15-minute taxi ride from downtown. [$] *Rooms from: €160 ✉ Rua dos Jerónimos 8, Belém ☎ 21/360–0900 🌐 www.jeronimos8.com 🛏 61 rooms, 4 suites 🍴 Breakfast ✥ A5.*

$$$$ HOTEL FAMILY Fodor's Choice ★ **Pestana Palace.** This hotel's palatial main building, the former home of the Marquis of Valle Flôr, is a National Monument that harbors a collection of fine 19th-century art. **Pros:** unique historic property in stunning grounds; outstanding facilities; well-equipped business center. **Cons:** some distance to major sights and attractions; outdoor pool area busy in summer; can be packed with conference goers. [$] *Rooms from: €275 ✉ Rua Jau 54, Ajuda ☎ 21/361–5600, 21/040–1711 for reservations 🌐 www.pestana.com/en/hotel/pestana-palace 🛏 176 rooms, 17 suites 🍴 Breakfast ✥ A5.*

PARQUE DAS NAÇÕES

$$$$ HOTEL Fodor's Choice ★ **Myriad by SANA Hotels.** The Myriad's guest rooms—serenely decorated in white with dashes of red and black—all have jaw-dropping views of the river and Parque das Nações, and cocoon swings from which to contemplate them. **Pros:** unparalleled views and serene riverside location; stylish decor; close to the Oceanário and other family attractions favorites. **Cons:** far from historical sights; metro/rail station a 15-minute walk away; no outdoor pool. [$] *Rooms from: €320* ✉ *Rua do Cais das Naus, Parque das Nações* ☎ *21/110–7600* 🌐 *myriad.pt* 🛏 *176 rooms, 10 suites* 🍴 *No meals* [M] *Oriente* ✥ *H5.*

$$$$ HOTEL **Tivoli Oriente.** This large, four-star hotel is well located for the airport, long-distance trains and buses, and sights such as the Oceanário. **Pros:** short distance to airport; excellent spa. **Cons:** far from downtown sights. [$] *Rooms from: €290* ✉ *Av. Dom João II, Parcela 1.14, Lote 03, Parque das Nações* ☎ *21/891–5100* 🌐 *tivolihotels.com* 🛏 *262 rooms, 17 suites* 🍴 *No meals* [M] *Oriente* ✥ *H5.*

NIGHTLIFE AND PERFORMING ARTS

Lisbon has a thriving arts-and-nightlife scene, and there are listings of concerts, plays, and films in the monthly *Agenda Cultural,* available from the tourist office and in many museums and theaters. Also, the Friday editions of both the *Diário de Notícias* and *O Independente* newspapers have separate magazines with entertainment listings. The weekly Portuguese-language magazine *Time Out Lisboa* is still more comprehensive. An English version (*Time Out Lisboa: Lisbon for Visitors*) is published each spring and autumn, and available at newsstands all year.

It's best to buy tickets to musical and theatrical performances at the box office or online. Agencies accepting international cards include Ticketline (🌐 *ticketline.sapo.pt/en*), where tickets can usually be picked up at the venue, stored as an electronic ticket, or printed out (hotels are usually happy to help).

NIGHTLIFE

Newcomers to Lisbon often hit the bars around 9 pm and head home at midnight thinking that the bar scene is rather quiet. In fact, Lisbon bars don't get going until after midnight, clubs even later. On weekends, lively groups spill out of bars and stand shoulder to shoulder in the streets, especially in the lively Bairro Alto and the revamped Cais do Sodré. Many places are rather quiet from Sunday through Wednesday although, in the summer high season, bars fill every night of the week with holidaymakers who don't need to rise early the next day.

Some dance clubs charge a cover of €15 (more on weekends), which includes one drink; if you come early you may get in free. Clubs are open from about 10 or 11 pm (but only start filling up well after midnight) until 4 or 5 am; a few stay open until 8 am. Be aware that some unscrupulous door staff will try to overcharge out-of-towners; if the price seems way over the odds, walk away.

FADO

Fado is a haunting music that emerged in Lisbon from hotly disputed roots: African, Brazilian, and Moorish are among the contenders. A lone singer—male or female—is accompanied by a Spanish guitar and the 12-string Portuguese guitar, a closer relative of the lute. Today most *casas de fado* (fado houses) are in the Bairro Alto or Alfama.

They serve traditional Portuguese food (it's rarely anything special), and the singing starts at 9 or 10 and may continue until 2 am. Reservations for dinner are essential, but if you want to go along later just to listen, most establishments will let you do so if you buy drinks, usually around €10 minimum. Whenever you do arrive, fado etiquette is strict on one point: when the singing starts, all chatter must stop. *Silêncio, canta-se fado!*

For a less boisterous evening out, visit a café-bar or a *casa de fado*, where professional or amateur performers sing the city's world-renowned, beautifully mournful style of music.

Lisbon has a well-established gay and lesbian scene, concentrated primarily in and around the Bairro Alto and the neighboring Príncipe Real area, on the way to Rato.

ALFAMA

BARS

Wine Bar do Castelo. This is a great place to flop down after visiting the Castelo de São Jorge: it has a good selection of wines to sample, plus authentic Portuguese snacks. ⊠ *Rua Bartolomeu de Gusmão 11–13, Castelo* ☎ *21/887–9093* ⊕ *www.winebardocastelo.blogspot.pt.*

DANCE CLUBS

Lux. The most famous club in Lisbon is east of the city center. It's dotted with designer furniture and has two dance floors favored by big-name local and foreign DJs—plus a rooftop terrace with great river views. The club attracts a young, stylish crowd who come to dance until dawn. ⊠ *Armazém A, Av. Infante D. Henrique, Santa Apolónia* ☎ *21/882–0890* ⊕ *www.luxfragil.com* ⊟ *From €15.*

FADO CLUBS

Fodor's Choice ★ **Baiuca.** At the family-run Baiuca, the quality of both food and singing varies, but a great atmosphere is guaranteed. It's a *fado vadio* (literally, "vagabond fado") spot, which means enthusiasm alone will get you onto the stage. Nights often end with local amateurs literally lining up outside, raring to perform (you can just drop in after dinner if you order a few drinks). ⊠ *Rua de São Miguel 20, Alfama* ☎ *21/886–7284.*

Clube de Fado. Locals and tourists flock to this spot to hear established performers, such as owner Mário Pacheco, and rising singing stars. Dinners here are pricey, but music fans arriving from around 10:30 pm can skip the food and concentrate on the fado. ⊠ *Rua S. João de Praça 86–94, Alfama* ☎ *21/885–2704* ⊕ *www.clube-de-fado.com.*

Fodor'sChoice
★
Mesa de Frades. All the rage among local fado lovers, this place is housed in a tiny, azulejo-lined former chapel. Food quality varies, but the music and atmosphere are always top rate; in any case, you can slip in at the end of the night, order a drink or two, and enjoy the show. ⊠ *Rua dos Remédios 139A, Alfama* ☎ *91/702–9436.*

Museu do Fado. Prominent fadistas perform most nights in the restaurant attached to the city-run Museu do Fado. Since this is a popular spot, reservations are essential here. ⊠ *Largo do Chafariz de Dentro 1, Alfama* ☎ *21/882–3470* ⊕ *www.museudofado.pt.*

Fodor'sChoice
★
Parreirinha d'Alfama. This little club is owned by fado legend Argentina Santos. She doesn't sing very often herself these days, but she sits by the door most nights and the place hires many other highly rated singers. Food plays second fiddle to the music, but you could do worse than enjoy fresh grilled fish and a bottle of wine as the singers work their magic. ⊠ *Beco do Espírito Santo 1, Alfama* ☎ *21/886–8209* ⊕ *www. parreirinhadealfama.com.*

LIVE MUSIC
Onda Jazz. This established jazz venue often hosts performers from Africa and other places around the world. ⊠ *Arco de Jesus 7, Alfama* ☎ *21/888–3242, 92/697–7352.*

BAIXA
Baixa has traditionally been better known for sightseeing and shopping than nightlife, but the esplanades that have sprung up around Praça do Comércio in the past couple of years have changed the area's vibe. There are now plenty of chic cocktail lounges to be found among the traditional ginjinha joints, making it a good starting point for a night's barhopping. There are a couple of late-opening clubs here, too.

DANCE CLUBS
Ministerium. This slick, modern club takes its name from the government departments that once dominated Lisbon's riverside square. On Saturday, a well-heeled crowd dances to electronica and house music. ⊠ *Praça do Comércio, Ala Nascente 72-73, Baixa* ☎ *21/888–8454* ⊕ *www.ministerium.pt* ☉ *Closed Sun.–Fri.*

CHIADO AND BAIRRO ALTO
Bairro Alto, long the center of Lisbon's nightlife, is the best place for barhopping. Most bars here are fairly small, but many have DJs every night and stay open until 2 am or so. There's a street-party vibe on weekends, when revelers take their drinks outdoors. A number of bars have a predominately gay clientele but invariably welcome all.

BARS
Bairru's Bodega. This is one of several wine bars that have sprung up to meet the growing curiosity of foreign visitors about Portugal's vinhos, which are sold here by the glass or bottle. Along with regional cheeses, hams, and sausages, you can sample homemade ginjinha and other liqueurs—all to an exclusively Portuguese sound track. ⊠ *Rua da Barroca 3, Bairro Alto* ☎ *21/346–9060* ⊕ *www.bairrusbodega.com.*

Cinco Lounge. Expertly run by a young British couple, this cocktail bar on the edge of the Príncipe Real neighborhood has a modern vibe. ☒ *Rua Ruben Leitão 17A, Bairro Alto* ☎ *21/342–4033* ⊕ *www.cincolounge.com.*

Fodor'sChoice **Garrafeira Alfaia.** This cozy wine bar has tasty snacks such as meat *cro-*
★ *quetes* and *bacalhau à brás* to accompany wines from a vast range of Portuguese vineyards. ☒ *Diário de Notícias 125, Bairro Alto* ☎ *21/343–3079* ⊕ *www.garrafeiraalfaia.com.*

Maria Caxuxa. This unique, DJ-driven venue in a former bakery (complete with giant kneading machine) is often packed with young media types. Its toasted sandwiches are perfect for late-night munchies, while the famous shots of strong spirits can ramp up a night on the town. ☒ *Rua da Barroca 6–12, Bairro Alto* ⊗ *Closed Sun.*

Park. On warm evenings (and quite a few cooler ones) this esplanade on the roof of a multilevel parking lot heaves with bright young things drinking in the stunning views and well-mixed cocktails. Live music and excellent local DJs provide the sound track. Weather permitting, it's open from 1 pm to 2 am, serving light meals until 6. ☒ *Calçada do Combro 58, Bairro Alto.*

Fodor'sChoice **Pavilhão Chinês.** For a quiet drink in an intriguing setting, you can't beat
★ this spot. It's filled to the brim with fascinating junk collected over the years—from old toys to statues—and it has two snooker tables. ☒ *Rua Dom Pedro V 89, Bairro Alto* ☎ *21/342–4729* ⊕ *barpavilhaochines. blogspot.pt.*

Fodor'sChoice **Solar do Vinho do Porto.** The most refined place in Bairro Alto to start off
★ your evening (or perhaps end it) is the relaxed Solar do Vinho do Porto. It's in a formidable old building where you can sink into an armchair and sample port wines from a list of several hundred. You can also buy bottles to take away. ☒ *Rua de São Pedro de Alcântara 45, Bairro Alto* ☎ *21/347–5707.*

DANCE CLUBS

Silk. On the edge of the Bairro Alto, Silk has a terrace with arguably the best view of any Lisbon club. In theory, entry is for members only, but if you are staying at a top-end hotel or dining at a gourmet restaurant, staff can often get you on the guest list for a night. They also do executive lunches. ☒ *Rua da Misericórdia 14, 6th fl., Chiado* ☎ *91/796–1934* ⊕ *www.silk-club.com.*

GAY AND LESBIAN CLUBS

Finalmente. Finalmente has been in business for over 40 years, attracting a high-camp crowd for drag shows in the early hours. Today, it has one of the best sound systems in town, and is open every night of the week. ☒ *Rua da Palmeira 38, Principe Real* ☎ *21/347–9923* ⊕ *www. finalmenteclub.com.*

Portas Largas. A mixed crowd spill out into the street from this tiled tavern with barn doors, which often has live Brazilian music. Sangria and caipirinha are the house drinks. Things get crowded after midnight. ☒ *Rua da Atalaia 105, Bairro Alto* ☎ *21/346–6379* ⊗ *Closed Mon.*

Fodor's Choice
★ **Purex.** Known for its trendy music and cocktails, this little place is run by a lesbian couple but is extremely diverse and welcoming. It gets packed on Friday and Saturday nights. ⊠ *Rua das Salgadeiras 28, Bairro Alto* ☎ *21/342–1942* ⊙ *Closed Mon.*

Fodor's Choice
★ **Trumps.** The city's longest-serving gay disco (at 35 years and counting) may only open on weekends but it remains lively—and hetero-friendly. ⊠ *Rua da Imprensa Nacional 104B, Principe Real* ☎ *21/395–1135* ⊕ *www.trumps.pt* ⊙ *Closed Sun.–Thurs.*

THE MODERN CITY

LIVE MUSIC

Hot Clube de Portugal. The city's best jazz joint since the 1950s moved to larger premises a few years ago after a fire gutted its historic basement home. Its program, which starts at 10 pm, includes leading local and foreign names. ⊠ *Praça da Alegria 47–49, Liberdade* ☎ *21/361–9740* ⊕ *www.hcp.pt* ⊙ *Closed Sun. and Mon.*

LAPA

FADO CLUBS

Fodor's Choice
★ **Senhor Vinho.** This Lisbon institution attracts some of Portugal's most accomplished fado singers. It also serves better food than many casas de fado, and is one of the few touristic spots that still attracts local fado fans. The name literally means "Mister Wine," and as expected, there are some good bottles to choose from. A voucher on the website gets you a 10% discount on dinner. ⊠ *Rua do Meio à Lapa 18, Lapa* ☎ *21/397–2681* ⊕ *www.srvinho.com.*

CAIS DO SODRÉ AND SANTOS

Once a seedy red-light district, Rua Nova de Carvalho and the surrounding area are now home to some of Lisbon's hippest bars. Farther west, you'll find large designer bars along Avenida 24 de Julho and in the Santos neighborhood, where some places can stay open until 5 or 6 am.

BARS

K Urban Beach. This slick venue right on the river draws a rich, hip, young crowd. It has a pool, restaurant, and sushi bar as well as a lively dance floor. ⊠ *Cais da Viscondessa, Rua da Cintura do Porto, Santos* ☎ *21/3932931* ⊕ *www.grupo-k.pt.*

Fodor's Choice
★ **Lounge.** This hip joint is where twenty- and thirtysomething crowds chat—or shout—to the pumping sound of dance music; there are regular live music events—think funky Brazilian or African sounds, not fado. It gets packed on weekends. ⊠ *Rua da Moeda 1, Cais do Sodré* ☎ *21/397–0071* ⊕ *www.loungelisboa.com.pt.*

Meninos do Rio. Beyond the railway tracks (round the back of Cais do Sodré station) is this riverside bar with a restaurant and sushi bar attached. It's a terrific place to hang out in summer amid the palm trees. ⊠ *Rua Cintura do Porto, Armazém 255, Santos* ☎ *21/324–2910* ⊕ *meninosdorio.com/.*

Fodor's Choice
★ **Pensão Amor.** There's no hipper place in Lisbon than the "Love Guesthouse," housed in a former brothel whose decor recalls its decadent past. Its warren of rooms house a café, erotic bookshop, bar, and dance floor.

There's another entrance on buzzing Rua Nova de Carvalho. ⊠ *Rua do Alecrim 19, Cais do Sodré* ☎ *21/314–3399* ⊕ *www.pensaoamor.pt.*

Sol e Pesca. This former fishing-tackle shop is now a trendy late-opening bar—with much of the original decoration—serving canned delicacies (mostly involving fish) and inexpensive draft beer. ⊠ *Rua Nova do Carvalho 44, Cais do Sodré* ☎ *21/346–7203* ⊕ *www.solepesca.com* ⊘ *Closed Sun. and Mon.*

LIVE MUSIC

Fodor's Choice
★

MusicBox. In a once-seedy, now-happening area, MusicBox regularly provides a stage for local and visiting rock bands, and hosts DJ nights and other live events. ⊠ *Rua Nova do Carvalho 15, Cais do Sodré* ☎ *21/347–3188* ⊕ *musicboxlisboa.com.*

ALCÂNTARA

Along the riverbank, under the bridge in Alcântara, the Doca do Santo Amaro has terrace bars and restaurants converted from old warehouses. There are dance clubs in this district that can stay open until 6 am.

BARS

Doca de Santo. In the main Doca de Santo Amaro development is this restaurant-bar with a palm-lined esplanade. It's a great place to start the night. ⊠ *Doca de Santo Amaro, Armazém CP, Alcântara* ☎ *21/396– 3522* ⊕ *www.grupodocadesanto.com.pt.*

Fodor's Choice
★

Rio Maravilha. Occupying a space that was once a tea-break room for factory workers, Rio Maravilha is now a place for Lisbon's hardworking creative types to eat, drink, and be merry. The Brazil-themed decor is colorful, the ambience relaxed, and the menu—created by celebrated local chef Diogo Noronha—is good, but it's the views over the river and 25 de Abril suspension bridge that steal the show. It's open until late on weekends, and there are regular DJ sets and live music. ⊠ *LX Factory, Rua Rodrigo Faria 103, 4th fl., Alcântara* ☎ *966/029229.*

PARQUE DAS NAÇÕES

BARS

Peter Café Sport. If you can't make it to transatlantic yachtie favorite "Peter's bar" on Faial Island in the Azores, you can visit its Lisbon replica. Situated in front of the Garcia da Horta gardens in the former site of the Expo 98 World's Fair, at the eastern edge of town, it's known for its gin-tonics and simple but tasty snacks such as toasted ham-and-cheese sandwiches. ⊠ *Rua da Pimenta, Parque das Nações* ☎ *21/895–0060* ⊕ *www.petercafesport.com.*

CASINO

Casino Lisboa. In addition to 22 gaming tables and 1,000 machines, the gleaming black Casino Lisboa has gourmet restaurants and a fun rotating bar that often stages free live jazz and blues. There are also paying shows by middle-of-the-road performers in a large, comfortable auditorium. ⊠ *Alameda dos Oceanos Lote 1.03.01, Parque das Nações* ☎ *21/892–9000* ⊕ *www.casinolisboa.pt.*

PERFORMING ARTS

FILM

You can usually find the latest Hollywood releases playing around town. ■TIP→ **Films are generally shown in their original language with Portuguese subtitles.** The exceptions are children's cartoons, which are normally dubbed but often have at least one original-version screening.

Cinemateca Portuguesa. Portugal's national film theater is the place to catch key Portuguese films and art-house reruns. More obscure non-Portuguese movies might have subtitles in English, French, or Spanish rather than Portuguese. There are regular children's screenings, although these are usually in Portuguese. ⊠ *Rua Barata Salgueiro 39, Marquês de Pombal* ☎ *21/359–6200, 21/359–6262 for ticket office* ⊕ *www.cinemateca.pt.*

Fodor's Choice **Medeia Monumental.** This cinema in the Monumental mall has four
★ screens. Expect a mixture of art films, commerical releases, and classics. ⊠ *Edifício Monumental, Av. Praia de Vitória 72, Saldanha* ☎ *21/314–2223* ⊕ *www.medeiafilmes.com.*

FAMILY **UCI El Corte Inglés Lisboa.** The latest in screen technology and extra-comfy seats are among the draws at this cinema underneath Lisbon's largest department store. Cheap-ticket night here is Wednesday. ⊠ *Av. António Augusto de Aguiar 31, São Sebastião* ☎ *707/232221 for ticket office* ⊕ *www.ucicinemas.pt.*

OPERA

Fodor's Choice **Teatro Nacional de São Carlos.** Opera season here runs September through
★ July. Guided visits around this lavishly decorated 18th-century theater may be booked in advance, for any weekday. ⊠ *Rua Serpa Pinto 9, Baixa* ☎ *21/325–3000* ⊕ *tnsc.pt.*

PERFORMING ARTS VENUES

Classical music concerts are staged from about October through June by the Fundação Calouste Gulbenkian. The Orquestra Metropolitana de Lisboa performs a regular program at various city venues, with many concerts free. Big-name American and British bands, as well as superstar Brazilian singers, often play in Lisbon's large concert halls and stadiums, and the summer months see major rock festivals across the city, as well as free live jazz in the city's parks and green spaces.

Coliseu dos Recreios. This circular concert hall is a Lisbon cultural landmark. It hosts international performers and musicals as well as some of the best Portuguese stars. ⊠ *Rua das Portas de Santo Antão 96, Restauradores* ☎ *21/324–0580* ⊕ *www.coliseulisboa.com.*

Culturgest. This convention center mounts a major concert and exhibition program, often of cutting-edge contemporary art. ⊠ *Caixa Geral de Depósitos, Rua Arco do Cego 1, Campo Pequeno* ☎ *21/790–5155* ⊕ *www.culturgest.pt.*

MEO Arena. The country's biggest indoor arena is the main venue for rock concerts. It also hosts large-scale classical concerts, dance performances, and sporting events. ⊠ *Rossio dos Olivais, Lote 2.13.01A, Parque das Nações* ☎ *21/891–8409* ⊕ *arena.meo.pt.*

THEATER

Chapitô. A good way to hurdle the language barrier is to see a show at this theater, where contemporary clowning and physical theater, often with a mix of languages, is the order of the day. There's also a bustling esplanade, a pleasant restaurant with fine views of the city and river, and a downstairs bar with a mix of live music and DJs. ⊠ *Costa do Castelo 1–7, Castelo* ☎ *21/885–5550* ⊕ *www.chapito.org.*

Teatro Nacional Dona Maria II. Although Lisbon's principal theater stages plays primarily in Portuguese, there are occasional foreign-language productions. Performances run August through June. ⊠ *Praça Dom Pedro IV (Rossio), Baixa* ☎ *800/213250 (toll-free), 21/325–0835 for ticket office* ⊕ *www.teatro-dmaria.pt.*

SPORTS AND THE OUTDOORS

HEALTH AND FITNESS

Clube VII. A €35 day pass at this well-equipped fitness center gives you access to the chlorine-free pool, gym, fitness clases, and squash and tennis courts (the latter for up to two hours). A racket may be hired for €5 an hour, and balls are on sale for the same price. ⊠ *Parque Eduardo VII, Marquês de Pombal* ☎ *21/384–8300* ⊕ *www.clubevii.com.*

SOCCER

Soccer is by far Portugal's most popular sport, and Lisbon has three teams, which play at least weekly during the September–May season. Although you can buy tickets on the day of a game at the stadiums, it's best to get them in advance from the ABEP booth in the Praça dos Restauradores.

Arrive at matches early; there's usually a full program of entertainment first, including children's soccer, marching bands, and fireworks. Before every Benfica home game the club's emblem, an eagle, swoops around the stadium. ■TIP→ **Be wary of pickpockets in soccer stadium crowds.**

FAMILY
Fodor'sChoice
★
Estádio da Luz. Benfica, Lisbon's most famous soccer team, plays in the northwest part of the city. Their stadium holds 65,000 spectators, is the biggest in Portugal, and is one of the biggest in Europe. Inside is a small museum that is open daily. It costs €10, and a stadium visit also costs €10 (€4 for kids); if you combine them it's €15. ⊠ *Av. General Norton Matos, Benfica* ☎ *707/200100* ⊕ *www.slbenfica.pt* Ⓜ *Alto dos Moinhos.*

SHOPPING

Shopping in Lisbon is less about multinational chains and more about locally owned shops. Instead of the same-old mass-produced goods, you'll find ceramics and lace made by Portuguese craftspeople, foodstuffs and wine that impart the nation's flavor, and clothes by established local designers.

Family-owned stores are still common in Lisbon, especially in Baixa, where a grid of streets from the Rossio to the Rio Tejo has many small shops selling jewelry, shoes, clothing, and foodstuffs. Trendy Bairro Alto is another district full of little crafts shops with stylish, contemporary ceramics, wooden sculpture, linen, and clothing; some open only in the afternoon and stay open—sometimes with their own resident DJ—until after the restaurants and bars around them have begun filling up.

Bairro Alto is also one of the shopping hubs of Lisbon's flourishing fashion scene. The brightly lighted modern shops of local designers stand in stark contrast to the area's 16th-century layout and dark, narrow streets. The Principe Real area is home to one of the best spots in the city for boutique browsing at the grand Embaixada gallery. Many antiques stores can be found on a single long street that changes its name four times as it runs southward from Largo do Rato: Rua Escola Politécnica, Rua Dom Pedro V, Rua da Misericórdia, and Rua do Alecrim. Look on the nearby Rua de São Bento for more stores. There's also a cluster of antiques shops on Rua Augusto Rosa, between the Baixa and Alfama districts.

Chiado, Lisbon's smartest shopping district, has a small shopping complex as well as many stores with considerable cachet, particularly on and around Rua Garrett. And Praça de Londres and Avenida de Roma—both in the Modern City—form one long run of haute-couture stores and fashion outlets. International luxury brands are also increasingly found on the city's downtown axis, Avenida da Liberdade.

Several excellent shops in Baixa sell chocolates, marzipan, dried and crystallized fruits, pastries, and regional cheeses and wines—especially varieties of port, one of Portugal's major exports. Baixa is also a good place to look for jewelry. What is now called Rua Aurea was once Rua do Ouro (Gold Street), named for the goldsmiths' shops installed on it under Pombal's 18th-century city plan. The trade has flourished here ever since.

ALFAMA

CERAMICS

Loja dos Descobrimentos. You can often see artists at work in this shop specializing in hand-painted tiles. What's more, they ship worldwide, and you can even order online so there's no need to haul any breakables home in your bags. ✉ *Rua dos Bacalhoeiros 12A, Alfama* ☎ *21/886–5563* ⊕ *www.loja-descobrimentos.com.*

CRAFTS AND SOUVENIRS

Fodor'sChoice
★
Arte da Terra. Opposite the Sé in the old cathedral stables, Arta da Terra uses old stone mangers as display cases for handiwork, traditional and modern, from around the country. As well as linen, felt hats, wool blankets, embroidery, and toys, you can pick up fado and folk CDs and an amazing range of representations of Santo António, the city's favorite saint. ⊠ *Rua Augusto Rosa 40, Alfama* ☎ *21/274–5975* ⊕ *www. aartedaterra.pt/en.*

FOOD AND WINE

Fodor'sChoice
★
Conserveira de Lisboa. There's a feast for the eyes at this shop, whose walls are lined with colorful tins of sardines and other seafood, as well as fruit preserves and other delicacies. Staff serve from behind an antique wooden counter. ⊠ *Rua dos Bacalhoeiros 34, Alfama* ☎ *21/886–4009* ⊕ *www.conserveiradelisboa.pt.*

MARKETS

Fodor'sChoice
★
Feira da Ladra. One of Lisbon's main shopping attractions is this flea market held on Tuesday morning and all day Saturday. It's fun, and you never know what sort of treasure you'll come across. Just be sure to watch your wallet. ⊠ *Campo de Santa Clara, Alfama.*

BAIXA

ANTIQUES

M. Murteira Antiguidades. Several centuries are represented at this shop near the cathedral. It carries furniture, painting, sculpture, and religious art from the 17th and 18th centuries as well as 20th-century artwork. ⊠ *Rua Augusto Rosa 19–21, Baixa* ☎ *21/886–3851* ⊙ *Closed Mon.*

CLOTHING

A Outra Face da Lua. This place is about as unconventional as Lisbon shopping gets. Prepare to be completely engaged by the eclectic mix of vintage clothes, items made using recycled materials, unique accessories, music, gadgets, temporary tattoos—you name it, really. Plus there's a tearoom and bistro. There's now another outlet around the corner at Rua dos Douradores 119. ⊠ *Rua da Assunção 22, Baixa* ☎ *21/347–1570* ⊕ *www.aoutrafacedalua.com.*

CRAFTS AND SOUVENIRS

Casa de Bordados da Madeira. For fine embroidered goods from the island of Madeira, stop by Bordados da Madeira. They also sell traditional ceramics from around Portugal. ⊠ *Rua 1° de Dezembro 135–139, Baixa* ☎ *21/342–5974* ⊕ *bordadosmadeira.pt/en* ⊙ *Closed Sun.*

FOOD AND WINE

Fodor'sChoice
★
GN Cellar`. This branch of a long-established Baixa wine merchant is geared to foreign visitors, with clearly presented wares, knowledgeable English-speaking staff, and an efficient shipping service. It's open daily 10–9; you can also order online. The original store, known also for its selection of whiskies, is at Rua Santa Justa 18. ⊠ *Rua da Conceição 20-26, Baixa* ☎ *21/885–2395* ⊕ *www.gncellar.com.*

Manuel Tavares. Just off the Rossio, this charming shop, which opened in 1860, stocks cheeses, preserves, vintage port, wine, and other fine Portuguese products. ⊠ *Rua da Betesga 1A, Baixa* ☎ *21/342–4209* ⊕ *www.manueltavares.com.*

Queijaria Nacional. This store is a showcase for Portugal's wealth of cheeses and other fine products which complement them. You can sample the wares while staff explain their origins. ⊠ *Rua da Conceição 8, Baixa* ☎ *91/208–2450.*

JEWELRY

Fodor'sChoice **W.A. Sarmento.** One of the city's oldest goldsmiths (since 1870), Sar-
★ mento produces characteristic Portuguese gold- and silver-filigree work. ⊠ *Rua Aurea 251, Baixa* ☎ *21/342–6774.*

MUSIC

Discoteca Amália. Come here to shop for soulful music by Amália Rodrigues and other leading fadistas. The store's well-stocked vintage van is also usually stationed on Rua do Carmo, blaring out fado. ⊠ *Rua Áurea 272, Baixa* ☎ *21/324–0939.*

CHIADO AND BAIRRO ALTO

ANTIQUES

J. Andrade Antiguidades. Museum curators are among the regulars poring over the unusual objects, paintings, sculptures, and furniture to be found in this store, run by two brothers since 1985. ⊠ *Rua da Escola Politécnica 39, Bairro Alto* ☎ *21/342–4964* ⊕ *www.jandrade-antigu-idades.com.*

Solar. One of Lisbon's best-known antiques shops, Solar specializes in azulejo panels and also stocks 16th- to 18th-century Portuguese furniture and paintings. ⊠ *Rua Dom Pedro V 68–70, Bairro Alto* ☎ *21/346–5522* ⊕ *solar.com.pt.*

ART GALLERIES

Galeria Graça Brandão. This gallery focuses on contemporary works from Portuguese and Brazilian artists. ⊠ *Rua dos Caetanos 26, Bairro Alto* ☎ *21/346–9183* ⊕ *www.galeriagracabrandao.com.*

Galeria Novo Século. If you're looking for contemporary Portuguese art that has yet to catch the eye of critics or collectors, try this gallery. ⊠ *Rua do Século 23A, Bairro Alto* ☎ *21/342–7712.*

CERAMICS

Fodor'sChoice **Fábrica Sant'Anna.** Founded in the 1700s, this store sells wonderful hand-
★ painted ceramics and tiles based on antique patterns. Many think that the pieces sold here are Lisbon's finest. There's another showroom on the way to Belém at Calçada da Boa-Hora 96; it's right next to the factory, which may also be visited during the week. ⊠ *Rua do Alecrim 95, Chiado* ☎ *21/342–2537* ⊕ *www.fabrica-santanna.com.*

Vista Alegre. Portugal's most famous porcelain producer, Vista Alegre, established its factory in 1824. A visit to the flagship store is a must even though you can buy perfect reproductions of their original table services and ornaments at dozens of shops. There are seven other

Vista Alegre–owned stores in Lisbon, including at the Colombo and Amoreiras malls. ⊠ *Largo do Chiado 20–23, Chiado* ☎ *21/346–1401* ⊕ *vistaalegre.com/pt.*

CLOTHING

A Fábrica dos Chapéus. The young proprietor of this funky store stocks a huge range of hats—more than 1,000—and also makes exclusive designs to order. For other accessories, head across the street to its sister store, A Fábrica do Acessório. ⊠ *Rua da Rosa 130, Bairro Alto* ☎ *21/308–6880* ⊕ *www.afabricadoschapeus.com.*

Cantê. Exclusivity is guaranteed at this bikini store: they sell only their own inventive designs, and stock no more than eight of each model. ⊠ *Rua Garrett n. 19, Chiado* ☎ *21/302–6618* ⊕ *www.cantelisboa.com.*

Lena Aires. Stylish, figure-hugging dresses and sweaters in bright colors, made from Portuguese materials, are the norm from this renowned designer. ⊠ *Rua da Atalaia 96, Bairro Alto* ☎ *21/346–1815.*

Fodor'sChoice ★ **Storytailors.** For some fairy-tale shopping, browse the racks here filled with fantastical frocks, capes, and more. Madonna is whispered to be among the celeb customers to have done so. ⊠ *Calçada do Ferragial 8, Chiado* ☎ *21/343–2306* ⊕ *www.storytailors.pt.*

CRAFTS AND SOUVENIRS

Fodor'sChoice ★ **A Vida Portuguesa.** Out of what was once the storeroom of an old perfumery, A Vida Portuguesa (The Portuguese Life) sells vintage Portuguese brands—from toys to toiletries—all of them stylishly packaged. Look out for items bearing the store's logo: a black swallow of the type that can often be seen swooping over Lisbon. ⊠ *Rua Anchieta 11, Chiado* ☎ *21/346–5073* ⊕ *www.avidaportuguesa.com.*

Cork & Co. Portugal is the world's leading producer of cork, but the treated bark of the cork oak isn't just good for bottle stoppers. This store turns cork into an astonishing variety of stylish artifacts, from handbags to umbrellas. ⊠ *Rua das Salgadeiras 10, Bairro Alto* ☎ *21/609–0231* ⊕ *www.corkandcompany.pt.*

Fabrica Features. Above a Benetton store, Fabrica Features sells design items made in Portugal and elsewhere and often has art on display. The views from this top-floor store are great, too. ⊠ *Rua Garrett 83, 4th fl., Chiado* ☎ *21/325–6764* ⊕ *fabrica-features-lisboa.blogspot.pt.*

FOOD AND WINE

Casa Pereira. Step into this charming old store (its owner started work behind the counter here in 1945) to buy exotic coffees, teas, and chocolates. ⊠ *Rua Garrett 38, Chiado* ☎ *21/342–6694.*

LEATHER GOODS

Fodor'sChoice ★ **Luvaria Ulissest.** Visit this art nouveau–style shop for gloves in the finest of kid and other leathers, in a variety of colors. ⊠ *Rua do Carmo 87, Chiado* ☎ *21/342–0295* ⊕ *www.luvariaulisses.com.*

MUU. The softest of cow's leather (hence the name) is used in the stylish but affordable, Portuguese-made handbags sold here. ⊠ *Rua da Misericórdia 102, Chiado* ☎ *21/347–2293* ⊕ *www.muuhandbags.com.*

MALLS

Embaixada. Shopping doesn't get any more stylish than at this grand 18th-century embassy building, which has been transformed into a gallery of superchic boutiques. Highlights include Latidid swimwear, smart shoes from Armando Cabral, and stylish, immaculately crafted home furnishings at Boa Safra. ✉ *Embaixada, Praça do Príncipe Real 26, Bairro Alto* ☎ *965/309154.*

Freeport Outlet Alcochete. This designer-outlet center on the south bank of the Tagus is said to be Europe's largest, with hundreds of big-name labels sold at discount prices. It's a 15-minute drive over the Ponte Vasco da Gama pontoon bridge. Buses 431, 432, and 437 will take you here directly from the Gare do Oriente station, or you can catch Freeport's shuttle service at 10 am or 1 pm from Praça Marquês do Pombal (returning at 4:30 or 7). The €10 ticket sold at the Cityrama kiosk here also gets you a 10% discount in participating stores—and a free drink when you're shopped out. Freeport is open Sunday through Thursday 10–10 and until 11 pm on Friday and Saturday. ✉ *Av. Euro 2004, Alcochete* ☎ *21/234-3500* ⊕ *www.freeport.pt.*

Grandes Armazéns do Chiado. Behind the restored facade of what was once the city's main department store is this stylish complex designed by acclaimed Portuguese architect Álvaro Siza Vieira. Anchor store Fnac and others are open daily 10–10; restaurants in the top-floor food court are open daily 10 am–11 pm. ✉ *Main entrance on Rua do Carmo, Chiado* ☎ *21/321-0600* ⊕ *www.armazensdochiado.com* Ⓜ *Baixa-Chiado.*

MARKETS

Mercado da Ribeira. Half of this domed building opposite Cais do Sodré train station has been transformed into a trendy collection of bars and restaurant concessions, but the other half remains a traditional working market. The vendors are entertainment in themselves. The market is open Monday through Saturday 6–2 for fresh produce of all kinds and weekdays 3–7 for florists. Every Sunday 9–1 the first floor is taken over by the Feira de Coleccionismo (Collectors' Market). ✉ *Av. 24 de Julho, Cais do Sodré* ☎ *21/346-2966.*

MUSIC

Fodor's Choice ★ **Fnac.** For books, computer products, and chart hits and music from Portugal and around the world, head to this store inside the Armazéns do Chiado shopping center. There's a branch out at the Colombo mall, too. ✉ *Armazéns do Chiado, lj. 4.07, Rua do Carmo 2, Chiado* ☎ *21/322-1800* ⊕ *www.fnac.pt.*

THE MODERN CITY

CERAMICS

Fodor's Choice ★ **Viúva Lamego.** The prices at Lisbon's largest purveyor of vintage tiles and pottery are competitive. It is possible to arrange a visit to the factory, out at Sintra. ✉ *Largo do Intendente 25, Intendente* ☎ *21/885-2408* ⊕ *www.viuvalamego.com.*

CLOTHING

Fodor'sChoice **Fly London.** Despite the name, this is the flagship store of one of Portu-
★ gal's most successful footwear brands, known for its funky yet comfortable styles. ✉ *Av. da Liberdade 230, Liberdade* ☎ *21/316–1169, 91/059–4564* ⊕ *www.flylondon.com.*

DEPARTMENT STORE

Fodor'sChoice **El Corte Inglés.** Lisbon's largest department store, part of a major Span-
★ ish chain, sells fashion and household articles and has excellent service. Be sure to check out the high-quality supermarket here, a favorite among locals. ✉ *Av. António Augusto de Aguiar 31, São Sebastião* ☎ *21/371–1700, 707/200026 for customer service* ⊕ *www.elcorteingles.pt* Ⓜ *São Sebastião.*

MALLS

Amoreiras Shopping Center. This mall west of Praça Marquês de Pombal has a multitude of shops selling clothes, shoes, food, crystal, ceramics, and jewelry. It also has a hairdresser, restaurants, and seven movie screens. It's open daily 10 am–11 pm. ✉ *Av. Eng. Duarte Pacheco, Amoreiras* ☎ *21/381–0240* ⊕ *www.amoreiras.com.*

Centro Colombo. One of the largest malls on the Iberian Peninsula, Colombo has more than 400 stores and restaurants, and a multiscreen cinema. The Colégio Militar–Luz metro station has an exit right inside the complex, which is open daily 9 am–midnight. ✉ *Av. Lusíada, Benfica* ☎ *21/711–3600* ⊕ *www.colombo.pt* Ⓜ *Colégio Militar-Luz.*

Centro Vasco da Gama. Suburbanites shop or catch a movie at this complex, which is open daily 9 am–midnight. An excursion here teams well with a visit to the Oceanário de Lisboa. ✉ *Av. D. João II, Parque das Nações* ☎ *21/893–0601* ⊕ *www.centrovascodagama.pt/en* Ⓜ *Oriente.*

MARKETS

Mercado 31 de Janeiro. You'll find all kinds of fresh produce here, Tuesday through Saturday 7–2. It's near the Picoas metro stop and the Sheraton hotel. ✉ *Rua Eng. Vieira da Silva, Saldanha* ☎ *21/354–0988* ⊕ *www.cm-lisboa.pt/pt/equipamentos/equipamento/info/mercado-31-de-janeiro* Ⓜ *Picoas.*

SÃO BENTO

ANTIQUES

Antiguidades Doll's. This store sells not only antique dolls but also Portuguese furniture and Indo-Portuguese art. Note that on Saturday the store is open 10:30–3 only (and not at all on Sunday). ✉ *Rua de São Bento 250–254, São Bento* ☎ *21/397815.*

BELÉM

ART GALLERIES

Galeria Arte Periférica. This gallery and arts store at the Centro Cultural de Belém is a good source of contemporary art, particularly by younger artists. ⊠ *Centro Cultural de Belém, loja 3, Belém* ☎ *21/361–7100* ⊕ *www.arteperiferica.pt.*

FOOD AND WINE

Coisas do Arco do Vinho. Next to the Centro Cultural de Belém, Coisas do Arco do Vinho sells prizewinning wines. The owners, wine connoisseurs, can give you expert advice. ⊠ *Rua Bartolomeu Dias, Lojas 7–8, Belém* ☎ *21/364–2031* ⊕ *www.coisasdoarcodovinho.pt.*

SIDE TRIPS
FROM LISBON

Updated by
Lucy Bryson

The capital's backyard is rich in possibilities. A succession of attractive coastal resorts and camera-ready towns lie within a 50-km (31-mile) stretch north and south of the Rio Tejo (Tagus River); more than mere suburbs, each is endowed with unique attributes and attractions. You'll find impressive palaces in Sintra, upscale entertainment in Cascais and Estoril, glorious beaches in Guincho and Costa da Caparica, a vine-covered countryside in the Setúbal Peninsula, and some of the best places to dine on delicious fresh seafood in Setúbal and Sesimbra.

Vacationers are nothing new here. The early Christian kings adopted the lush hills and valleys of Sintra as a summer retreat and designed estates that survive today. Similarly, Lisbon's 18th- and 19th-century nobility developed small resorts along the Estoril Coast; the amenities and ocean views are still greatly sought-after. For swimming, modern lisboetas look a little farther afield—south across the Rio Tejo to the beaches and resorts of the Costa da Caparica and the southern Setúbal Peninsula. But whichever direction you travel and whatever your interests, you'll be delighted with all that's available within an hour of Lisbon.

ORIENTATION AND PLANNING

GETTING ORIENTED

To the west of Lisbon, the Estoril Coast is a series of small beaches and rocky coves, the most popular being found around the towns of Estoril and Cascais. Farther north, the Atlantic makes itself felt in the wind-swept beaches and capes beyond Guincho and up to the lighthouse at Cabo da Roca—the westernmost point in Europe. A few miles inland, the Sintra hills are crisscrossed by winding roads marked by old monastic buildings, estates, gardens, and market villages.

To the south, across the Rio Tejo, the contrast of the Setúbal Peninsula couldn't be more pronounced. The beaches of the Costa da Caparica combine to form a 20-km (12-mile) sweep of sand, backed by the fertile wine-producing countryside where the hilltop town of Palmela looks toward the peaks of the Serra da Arrábida.

The Estoril Coast. Just a short, scenic train ride from Lisbon along the Tejo River toward the Atlantic sits the area known as the Portuguese Riviera. Expect luxury hotels, high-end boutiques, championship golf courses, and high-rolling nightlife.

TOP REASONS TO GO

Lovers' destination. Sintra—a UNESCO World Heritage Site—has gorgeous palaces and gardens, and a landscape that inspires poetry. The combination makes it ripe for romantics.

Endless beaches. All along the Estoril Coast and from Costa da Caparica to Cabo Espichel and around Arrabida, beautiful beaches await. If lively ones are your style, head to Cascais and Caparica; tranquil alternatives are hidden among the cliffs around Guincho, Cabo da Roca, and Cabo Espichel.

Divine wine. The Setúbal Peninsula is home to Moscatel de Setúbal (a much-admired fortified wine) and to several well-known wine producers, including JM Fonseca, Quinta da Bacalhoa, and João Pires (J.P. Vinhos). North of the Tejo are other historical wine regions, most notably Colares, near Sintra.

Fabulous seafood. *Marisqueiras* (seafood restaurants) are an essential component of Portuguese culture, and this region has some renowned ones. The selection is particularly broad in Sesimbra and Setúbal.

Sintra and Queluz. Near the Serra de Sintra, Queluz and Sintra are studded with palaces, gardens, and luxury *quintas*. A winding drive along the mountain to the rugged cliffs of Cabo da Roca, Azoia, and Guincho reveals the area's natural beauty.

The Setúbal Peninsula. Across the Rio Tejo just south of Lisbon, this peninsula is lined with unique beaches that stretch from lively Costa da Caparica to the mountainous Serra da Arrábida. Dine on delicious seafood in Cacilhas, Sesimbra, and Setúbal; then go inland to experience Azeitão's wine-rich farmlands and Palmela's fairy-tale hilltop castle.

PLANNING

WHEN TO GO

If you're planning to visit in summer, particularly July and August, you *must* reserve a hotel room in advance. If you can, travel to the coastal areas in spring or early fall: the crowds are much thinner, and it could be warm enough for a brisk swim in May and October.

Most of the region's festivals are held in summer. In São Pedro de Sintra, the Festa de São Pedro (St. Peter's Day) celebration is on June 29; there are summer music and arts festivals in Sintra, Cascais, and Queluz; September in Palmela sees the Festa das Vindimas (Grape Harvest Festival); the Feira de Santiago (St. James Fair) takes place in Setúbal at the end of July. Year-round markets include those in São Pedro de Sintra (second and fourth Sunday of every month) and Vila Nogueira de Azeitão (first Sunday of every month).

PLANNING YOUR TIME

With a car you can cover the main sights north and south of the Rio Tejo in two days, although this gives you little time to linger. A week wouldn't be too long to spend, particularly if you plan to soak up the sun at a resort or take an in-depth look at Sintra, whose beautiful surroundings alone can fill two or three days.

All the main towns and most of the sights are accessible by train or bus from Lisbon, so you can see the entire region on day trips from the capital. This is a particularly good way to explore the resorts on the Estoril Coast and the beaches of the Costa da Caparica, south across the Rio Tejo. The palace at Queluz also makes a good day trip; it is 20 minutes northwest of Lisbon by train. Using the capital as your base, a realistic time frame for visiting the major sights is four days: one each for the Estoril Coast, Queluz and Sintra, Caparica, and Setúbal.

GETTING HERE AND AROUND

BOAT AND FERRY TRAVEL

Transtejo ferries cross the river to Cacilhas (7 am–9 pm) from Fluvial terminal, adjacent to Praça do Comércio; the journey takes under 10 minutes. For information on car ferries from Cais do Sodré, check with the Lisbon tourist office. From Setúbal, Atlantic Ferries provides 24-hour service for car and foot passengers via ferry and catamaran across to the Tróia Peninsula; the ferry journey takes about 25 minutes, the catamaran takes 15, and the return journey from Tróia is free.

Ferry Information Atlantic Ferries. ☎ *265/235101* ⊕ *www.atlanticferries.pt.* **Transtejo.** ☎ *213/224000* ⊕ *www.transtejo.pt.*

BUS TRAVEL

Although the best way to reach Sintra and most of the towns on the Estoril Coast is by train from Lisbon, there are some useful bus connections between towns. Tickets are cheap (less than €3.50 for most journeys), and departures are generally every hour (less frequent on weekends); local tourist offices have timetables. Try to arrive at least 15 minutes before your bus departs.

At Cascais, the bus terminal outside the train station has regular summer service to Guincho (15 minutes) and Sintra (30 minutes on Bus 417, one hour's scenic route on Bus 403). From the terminal outside the Sintra train station, there is regular year-round service to Cascais and Estoril (Bus 418, 30 minutes). The most useful Sintra service, however, is the circular SCOTTurb Bus 434 (every 20–30 minutes, daily 9–6; €4.05 ticket, valid all day), which connects Sintra station, the town center (there's a stop outside the tourist office), Castelo dos Mouros, and the Pena Palace.

Buses to Caparica (45 minutes) depart from the TST terminal at Praça de Espanha (next to the metro station of the same name) in Lisbon, traveling over the 25 de Abril bridge. Regular buses to Caparica also leave from the quayside bus terminal at Cacilhas, the town immediately across the Rio Tejo from Lisbon, which you can reach by ferry from the ferry terminal, next to Cais do Sodré metro and rail station. Bus departures on both routes are as frequent as every 15 minutes in summer, and services run from 7 am until well after midnight, but can be very crowded.

Express buses to Setúbal (50 minutes) leave every hour (every half hour during peak commuter times on weekday mornings) from the TST terminal at Lisbon's Praça de Espanha; a local service also calls at Vila Nogueira de Azeitão (45 minutes) before traveling on to Setúbal (one hour). At Setúbal bus station you can connect with local services north to Palmela (20 minutes) and southwest to Sesimbra (30 minutes) via Vila Nogueira de Azeitão (20 minutes). On weekdays, eight buses daily (five on weekends) make the 30-minute trip from the Sesimbra bus station to the southwestern Cabo Espichel.

Bus Contacts Rede Expressos. ✉ *Praça Marechal Humberto Delgado - Estrada das Laranjeiras, Lisbon* ☎ *707/223344 for inquiries and phone sales (€0.25 per min)* ⊕ *www.rede-expressos.pt.* **TST (Transportes Sul do Tejo).** ✉ *Rua Marcos de Portugal, Almada* ☎ *211/126200, 707/508509 for info (fixed-rate number)* ⊕ *www.tsuldotejo.pt.*

CAR TRAVEL

Fast highways connect Lisbon with Estoril (A5/IC15) and Setúbal (A2/IP1), and the quality of other roads in the region is generally good. Take care on hilly and coastal routes, though, and, if possible, avoid driving out of Lisbon at the start of a weekend or public holiday or back in at the end. Both Rio Tejo bridges—especially the Ponte 25 de Abril but also the dramatic Ponte Vasco da Gama (the longest bridge in Europe)—can be very slow. Parking can be problematic, too, particularly in summer along the Estoril Coast. When you do park, avoid leaving valuables visible in the car. It's wise to clear out the trunk as well.

Lisbon is the initial point of arrival for almost all the destinations covered here; from the city, it's easy to take public transportation or drive to all the surrounding towns. Driving south from Peniche-Óbidos, you can take the N8/IC1, rather than the main highway, if you prefer to see Sintra before Lisbon. If you're traveling north from the Algarve, you reach the city of Setúbal and its sandy peninsula before arriving in Lisbon.

Car Rental Contacts Avis. ✉ *Tamariz Esplanade, Estoril* ☎ *214/668569* ⊕ *www.avis.com* ✉ *Av. Luisa Todi 96, Setúbal* ☎ *265/538710.* **Europcar.** ✉ *Estrada Marginal, Centro Comércial Cisne, Bloco B, Lojas 4 and 5, Cascais* ☎ *214/864438, 219/407790* ⊕ *www.europcar.pt.* **Hertz.** ✉ *Av. Luisa Todi 277, Setúbal* ☎ *219/426300* ⊕ *www.hertz.com.*

TAXI TRAVEL

If you don't have your own car, it can be worth taking a taxi to the towns around Lisbon. Cabs are relatively inexpensive, and you can usually agree on a fixed price that will include the round trip to an attraction (the driver will wait while you complete your tour). Tourist offices can give you an idea of what fares are reasonable for local trips; Sintra should cost roughly €60, Queluz should be €25, and Estoril €40 one-way. Prices will be higher on weekends and public holidays.

Taxi Contacts Central taxi lines. ☎ *214/660101, 914/659500 (mobile)* ⊕ *www.taxiscascais.com.*

TRAIN TRAVEL

Electric Comboios de Portugal (CP) commuter trains travel the entire Estoril Coast, with departures every 15–30 minutes from the waterfront Cais do Sodré station in Lisbon, west of the Praça do Comércio. The scenic trip to Estoril takes about 30 minutes, and four more stops along the seashore bring you to Cascais, at the end of the line. A one-way ticket to either costs €2.15; service operates daily 5:30 am–2:30 am. Trains from Lisbon's Rossio station, between Praça dos Restauradores and the Rossio, run every 15 minutes to Queluz (20 minutes) and on to Sintra (40 minutes total). The service operates between 6 am and 2:40 am, and one-way tickets cost €1.95 to Queluz, €2.70 to Sintra, loaded onto a €0.50 Viva Viagem card, which can be charged with larger amounts if you wish to make multiple journeys.

Fertagus trains from Lisbon's Roma–Areeiro, Sete Rios, and Entrecampos and Campolide stations cross the Rio Tejo via the Ponte 25 de Abril. Passengers on the double-decker railcars benefit from pleasant views, air-conditioning, and background music during the seven-minute crossing. Taxis at stations across the river can take you on to Cacilhas, or you can carry on to Setúbal, a journey of around an hour. Trains run between 5:30 am and 1:25 am (last train to Setúbal is at 12:43 am). First and last trains in other other direction are slightly earlier. From June through September a narrow-gauge railway runs for 8 km (5 miles) along the Costa da Caparica from the town of Caparica, on the Setúbal Peninsula. It makes 20 stops at beaches along the way, and a one-way ticket to the end of the line costs €4.50. The "mini train" opens up stretches of coastline that are otherwise inaccessible without a car, and even makes a call at a nudist beach.

Train Contacts CP (Comboios de Portugal). ☎ 707/210220 ⊕ www.cp.pt/passageiros. **Fertagus.** ☎ 707/127127 ⊕ www.fertagus.pt/ing.

RESTAURANTS

Restaurants on the coast tend to stick to seafood, whereas those farther inland may specialize more in grilled meats. Inexpensive restaurants don't generally take reservations, but it's advisable to reserve for the pricier ones. Dress for meals is usually casual, but people do dress up for dining at the Casino de Estoril or more expensive restaurants—namely those in luxury hotels.

City dwellers make a point of crossing the Rio Tejo to the suburb of Cacilhas for platefuls of *arroz de marisco* (rice with shellfish) or *linguado* (sole). One of Caparica's summer delights is the smell of grilled sardines wafting from restaurants and beachside stalls. Seafood is also the specialty along the Estoril Coast—even the inland villages here and on the Setúbal Peninsula are close enough to the sea to be assured a steady supply of fish.

In Sintra, *queijadas* (sweet cheese tarts) are a specialty; in the Azeitão region of the Setúbal Peninsula locals swear by the *queijo fresco,* a delicious white cheese made either of goat's or sheep's milk. Lisbon's environs also produce good wines. From Colares comes a light, smooth red, a fine accompaniment to a hearty lunch; Palmela, the demarcated wine-growing district of Setúbal, produces distinctive amber-color wines of recognized quality; and the Fonseca winery produces a splendid dessert wine called Moscatel de Setúbal. *Prices in the reviews are the average cost of a main course at dinner or, if dinner is not served, at lunch.*

HOTELS

Accommodations are more limited once the bright lights of Lisbon have been left behind. But the options, both old and new, are truly diverse. Historic lodgings are understandably popular, and *pousadas*—inns, often in converted buildings, that generally have superior facilities—are the top pick for many travelers. The three in this region are at Queluz, Setúbal, and Palmela. Modern alternatives may not have the same cultural cred, but they compensate by having up-to-date amenities and, in some cases, an eco-friendly outlook. No matter what you choose, advance booking is essential in summer. Out of season, many places offer substantial discounts. *Prices in the reviews are the lowest cost of a standard double room in high season. For expanded hotel reviews, visit Fodors.com.*

WHAT IT COSTS IN EUROS				
	$	$$	$$$	$$$$
Restaurants	under €16	€16–€20	€21–€25	over €25
Hotels	under €140	€140–€200	€201–€260	over €260

Restaurant prices are per person for a main course at dinner. Hotel prices are for a standard double room, including tax, in high season (off-season rates may be lower).

VISITOR AND TOUR INFORMATION

Lisbon's tourist offices (AskMe Lisboa) can provide information on a vast range of trips and tours in Lisbon's outskirts, from surf trips to winery visits, as well as more standard sightseeing tours by bus. The main branch is located at Terreiro do Paço (also known as Praça do Comercio) downtown and is open daily 9–8. Staff here can book trips and will also offer to sell you the Lisboa Card, valid for periods of 24, 48, or 72 hours (€18.50–€39); the card's benefits include free rail travel to Sintra and along the Estoril Coast, as well as discounted access to many of the region's tourist attractions. The Lisbon office of Turismo de Portugal (the Portuguese national tourist board, located between the Campo Pequeno and Entrecampos metro stations) also has information on the city's environs. Local tourist offices are usually open June through September, daily 9–1 and 2–6, sometimes later in resort areas. Hours are greatly reduced after peak season, and most offices are closed Sunday.

Most travel agents and large hotels in Lisbon can reserve you a place on a guided tour. Sightseeing bus operators Cityrama and Gray Line organize half- and full-day excursions to destinations like Sintra, Queluz, and Estoril. Tours typically cost €55–€85, depending on the distance and duration. For guided tours of the Sintra area, ask at the tourist information center, which has current schedules and can sell tickets. Half-day tours typically encompass visits to all the principal sights and some include wine tasting in Colares. While they each operate their own tours, they are owned by the same company and operate from the same terminal.

National Visitor Information AskMe Lisboa. ✉ *Terreiro do Paço, Baixa* ☎ *210/312810* ⊕ *www.askmelisboa.com.*

Tour Contacts Cityrama. ⊠ *Av. João XXI 78-E, Campo Pequeno* ☎ *213/191090* ⊕ *www.cityrama.pt.* **Gray Line Tours.** ⊠ *Av. João XXI 78 E, Campo Pequeno* ☎ *213/191090* ⊕ *www.grayline.com.*

THE ESTORIL COAST

The Estoril Coast extends for 32 km (20 miles) west of Lisbon, taking in the major towns of Estoril and Cascais as well as smaller settlements that are part suburb, part beach town. Proximity to the capital coupled with coastal charms make this a coveted residential area. Some fancifully refer to it as the Portuguese Riviera, and certainly the casino at Estoril and the luxurious seaside villas and hotels lend the area cachet.

Popularity, however, has a price. In summer, be prepared for crowds. Water pollution is also a long-standing problem. The quality of the water varies greatly from beach to beach, and although ongoing work is slowly rectifying the situation, you should avoid swimming in an area unless the water has been declared safe. Several beaches have been granted Blue Flag status, which means they meet the sringent sand- and water-quality criteria of the Foundation for Environmental Education (⊕ *www.blueflag.global*).

GETTING HERE AND AROUND

Unless you intend to tour the wider region, it's better to travel by train from Lisbon rather than drive. This section has been arranged accordingly, with coverage of Estoril first, followed by Cascais, which marks the end of the train line; from here, it's a short walk to the Boca do Inferno and a brief bus ride to the magnificent beach at Guincho. If you drive, leave Lisbon via the Avenida/Estrada Marginal (follow signs for Cascais and Estoril) and take the scenic coastal route (N6) or the faster Auto-Estrada da Oeste (A5/IC15).

TIMING

The best time to visit the Estoril Coast is in the spring (late April–May) and fall (late September–late October) when it's a lot less crowded but usually warm enough to go to the beaches. During the summer months, especially late July and all of August, the area is packed with tourists and locals, both on the beaches and in the cities.

ESTORIL

26 km (16 miles) west of Lisbon.

Having long ago established its reputation as an affluent enclave, Estoril is still the place to go for glitz and glamour. In the 19th century, it was favored by the European aristocracy, who wintered here in the comfort and seclusion of mansions and gardens. In the 20th century, it became popular among international stars and was a top playground for Europe's rich and famous. Although the town has elegant hotels, restaurants, and sports facilities, reminders of its genteel history are now few. It presents its best face right in the center, where today's jet set descends on the casino, at the top of the formal gardens of the Parque do Estoril.

GREAT ITINERARIES

3

IF YOU HAVE 2 DAYS

Public transportation is preferable if you're just hitting the main sights, but hiring a car is a good way to get a little off the beaten track and pack a lot of experiences into a short time. Start in Lisbon and drive to **Estoril**, where you can soak up the atmosphere in the gardens and on the seafront promenade. From here, it's only a short distance to **Cascais**, the perfect place for an alfresco lunch. Afterward, explore the little cove beaches and the **Boca do Inferno**. The next day, it's less than an hour's ride north to **Sintra**, where before lunch you'll have time to see its palace and climb to the **Castelo dos Mouros**. After lunch, return to Lisbon, stopping in **Queluz** to see the Palácio Nacional. For dinner, you might cross the Rio Tejo from Lisbon to **Cacilhas** for seafood.

IF YOU HAVE 4 DAYS

From Lisbon, head for **Queluz** and its Palácio Nacional. In the afternoon, make the short drive to **Sintra**, where you can spend the rest of the day seeing the sights

in and around the town. Consider having dinner in the adjacent village of **São Pedro de Sintra**. Head out early the next day to the extraordinary **Palácio Nacional de Pena**. To contrast this haughty palace with a more humble sight, travel west to the **Convento dos Capuchos** before continuing to the headland of **Cabo da Roca**. Wind south to the wonderful beach at **Guincho** to catch the late-afternoon sun and have a bite to eat. Stick to the coastal road as it heads east toward **Cascais**, where you can spend the night.

On the third day, drive back into Lisbon through **Estoril**. Cross the Rio Tejo via the mighty Ponte 25 de Abril, and detour for lunch at either **Cacilhas** or **Costa da Caparica**. It's then only an hour's drive to two attractive pousadas, one at **Palmela**, the other 10 km (6 miles) down the road in **Setúbal**. On the fourth morning drive through the **Serra da Arrábida**, stopping for lunch at an esplanade restaurant in **Sesimbra**. From here, you can return to Lisbon in around 90 minutes.

Across the busy main road, on the beachfront Tamariz esplanade, are alfresco restaurants and an open-air seawater swimming pool. The best and longest local beach is at Monte Estoril, which adjoins Estoril's beach; here you'll find restrooms and beach chairs for rent, as well as plenty of shops and snack bars.

Estoril is also very sports oriented. More than a magnet for golfers, it hosts major sailing, windsurfing, tennis, and equestrian events, as well as motor races at the old Formula 1 track.

GETTING HERE AND AROUND

The best way to arrive is via the CP urban train (Linha de Cascais ⇨ *see Train Travel, above*) departing from the Cais do Sodré station in Lisbon that runs directly to Estoril. You can also off at the previous station, São João do Estoril, and walk 2 km (1 mile) along the seafront promenade path; the route offers excellent views. The drive by car will take 25 minutes from Lisbon, either by the A2 highway or the scenic Avenida Marginal running along the coast. Just avoid driving on

Marginal to or from Estoril during the afternoon on summer weekends, as the traffic is horrendous.

ESSENTIALS

Visitor Information Cascais and Estoril Tourism. ✉ *Largo Cidade Vitória* ☎ *912/034214* 🌐 *www.visitcascais.com.*

EXPLORING

Espaço Memória dos Exílios. Inaugurated in 1999 and located above the post office in a striking 1942 Modernist building, this museum focuses on Estoril's community of aristocratic exiles, who fled here from northern Europe during World War II, but its collection of memorabilia relates broadly to Portugal's mid-20th-century history. The exhibit consists mostly of black-and-white photos with captions in Portuguese, and there's also an exhibit devoted to the Nazi persecution of the Jews. ✉ *Av. Marginal 7152-A* ☎ *214/825022* 🌐 *www.cm-cascais.pt/equipamento/espaco-memoria-dos-exilios* 🎟 *Free* ⏲ *Closed weekends.*

Estoril Casino. The glitzy Estoril Casino is said to have inspired Ian Fleming to write the James Bond adventure *Casino Royale,* and while it might not harbor international spies these days, it retains a glamorous allure. In addition to gambling salons, the casino is one of the largest in Europe and has a nightclub, bars, and restaurants. Tour groups often make an evening of it here, with dinner and a floor show, but it's a pricey night out. Most visitors are content to feed one of the 700 slot machines in the main complex and then check out the other entertainment options: art exhibits, movies, nightly cabaret performances, concerts, and ballets (in summer). To enter the gaming rooms you must pay a small fee (slots are free) and show your passport to prove that you're at least 21. Reservations are essential for the restaurant and floor show. Drink and show packages are available. ✉ *Parque do Estoril* ☎ *214/667700* 🌐 *www.casino-estoril.pt* 🎟 *€4 to enter gaming rooms, slot machines free.*

WHERE TO EAT

$$$ SEAFOOD 🍴 **A Choupana.** Just east of town, this restaurant, with English-speaking staff, has views of Cascais Bay from its picture windows and is a reliably good place to eat. The cuisine is primarily Italian, but there are good Portuguese dishes too—try the *cataplana,* a tangy, typically Portuguese dish of clams and pork. And it's one of relatively few places to offer vegetarian dishes that go beyond a basic salad and soup of the day. Here, there's a vast array of salads and dishes such as eggplant carpaccio with slivers of Parmesan cheese. Live piano recitals accompany dinner on Friday and Saturday nights. [$] *Average main: €25* ✉ *Estrada Marginal 5579* ☎ *214/664123* 🌐 *www.choupanagordinni.com.*

$$ ECLECTIC 🍴 **Cimas.** You're in for a good meal in these baronial surroundings of burnished wood, heavy drapes, and oak beams that have played host to royalty, high-ranking politicians, and other celebrities. The menu is an international hybrid: choose from game in season, fresh fish, chicken curry, even Indonesian *saté* (skewered, charcoal-broiled meats served with a peanut sauce). [$] *Average main: €20* ✉ *Av. Marginal* ☎ *214/681254* 🌐 *www.cimas.com.pt* ⏲ *Closed Sun.*

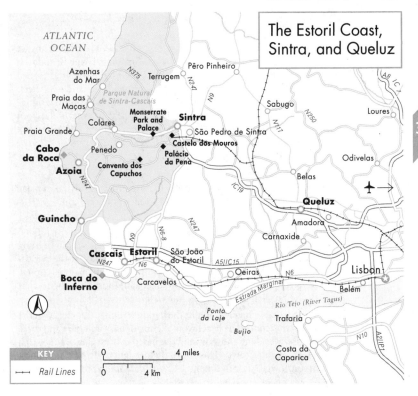

The Estoril Coast, Sintra, and Queluz

WHERE TO STAY

$ ⊞ **Amazonia Hotel.** This four-star boutique aparthotel sits on a hill just
HOTEL far enough off the main drag so that it's hidden from the noise and
FAMILY crowds but still convenient walking distance to all the attractions,
including Estoril Casino and Praia do Tamariz. **Pros:** near enough to
downtown but still private and tranquil; beautiful ocean views from
top-floor rooms. **Cons:** steep hill up to hotel. 🛒 *Rooms from: €105*
✉ *Rua Engenheiro Álvaro Pedro de Sousa 175, Cascais* ☎ 214/680424
⊕ *www.amazoniahoteis.com/estoril* ⇆ *28 rooms* ❙⊘❙ *Breakfast.*

$$ ⊞ **Estoril Eden Apartamentos Suites Hotel.** If you are looking for self-
HOTEL catering accommodations, the comfortable studios and suites in this
FAMILY modern apartment hotel are reasonably sized and equipped with cable
TV, fold-out beds, and a basic kitchenette. **Pros:** great ocean views;
convenient location right in front of beach; very pleasant staff. **Cons:**
outside of city; have to take the train or walk a long way to get here; fur-
niture is a bit dated and run-down. 🛒 *Rooms from: €150* ✉ *Av. Sabóia*
☎ 214/667601 ⊕ *www.hotelestorileden.pt* ⇆ *162 units* ❙⊘❙ *Breakfast.*

$$ ⊞ **Hotel Inglaterra.** Displaying the splendor of an early-20th-century
HOTEL Portuguese colonial mansion, the hilltop Hotel Inglaterra offers classy
ambience. **Pros:** convenient central location within walking distance of
the beach; very helpful staff; free Wi-Fi. **Cons:** some rooms are rather
small; no parking; some areas beginning to look a little run-down.

Ⓢ *Rooms from: €200* ✉ *Rua do Porto 1* ☎ *214/684461* ⊕ *www.hotel-inglaterra.com.pt* ⊅ *55 rooms* ⦿ *Breakfast.*

$$
HOTEL
Fodor's Choice
★

❄ **Palácio Estoril Golf and Spa Hotel.** This luxurious 1930s-era hotel hosted exiled European aristocrats as they waited out World War II; today it draws golfers, thanks to good-value packages with the splendid Estoril Golf Club, as well as travelers interested in fine dining and spa visits. **Pros:** impeccable old-world service; excellent dining; beautiful surroundings. **Cons:** the old-fashioned style will not appeal to everybody; pool area can be very crowded in summer. Ⓢ *Rooms from: €180* ✉ *Parque do Estoril, Rua do Parque* ☎ *214/680000* ⊕ *www.palacioestorilhotel.com* ⊅ *129 rooms, 32 suites* ⦿ *Breakfast.*

NIGHTLIFE

At night, the casino is a big draw; other barhopping typically takes place within the hotels. Most places are open from 10 pm to 3 am.

Piano & Co. Owned by well-known Portuguese singer and actor Vitor Espadinha, this spacious late-night venue (10 pm–4 am most nights) attracts a mixed-age crowd for regular live music. The walls are hung with images of old-school greats like Sinatra, but many of the performances are from young local talent—check the Facebook page for up-to-date listings. A separate bar area is popular with those wanting to chat without the musical backdrop. ✉ *Rua de Olivença 6* ☎ *216/040066.*

Tamariz Beach Club. Hugely popular during the summer (it's closed in the off-season), this enormous beachfront nightspot has eight bars and three dance floors. Resident and visiting DJs play the latest dance tunes to a young, fashionable crowd. This is strictly for night owls, as things don't get busy until well after midnight. ✉ *Praia da Tamariz* ☎ *919/573899.*

SPORTS AND THE OUTDOORS

GOLF

The superb golf courses near Lisbon attract players from far and wide. Most are the creations of renowned designers, and the climate means that you can play year-round. Many hotels offer golf privileges to guests; some even have their own courses. Package deals abound. For more information about most major golf courses in this area, check the Estoril Golf Coast website (⊕ *www.estorilgolfcoast.com/en*).

Fodor's Choice
★

Clube de Golfe do Estoril. A Heritage Golf Course, the Clube de Golfe do Estoril has an immaculately maintained 18-hole championship course, with some challenging holes. Guests of the Hotel Palácio receive special rates and privileges. The welcoming clubhouse serves good Portuguese dishes and a good range of drinks, all of which can be enjoyed overlooking the 18th hole and out to sea. ✉ *Av. da República* ☎ *214/680176* ⊕ *www.clubegolfestoril.com* ⛳ *18 holes €80* ⚑ *18 holes, 5810 yds, par 69* ⛳ *Reservations essential.*

Estoril Sol. Estoril Sol, on the Estoril–Sintra road, 7 km (4½ miles) north of Estoril, has a scenic 9-hole course, which can be repeated, with different tees, for those wishing to play an 18-hole game. ✉ *Quinta do Outeiro, Linhó* ✛ *Head north on EN9 toward Sintra, then turn left and follow signs to Lagoa Azul* ☎ *219/240331* ⊕ *www.portugalgolfe.com* ⛳ *€26 for 18 holes, €18 for 9 holes* ⚑ *9 holes, 3946 yds, par 62* ⛳ *Reservations essential.*

SHOPPING

FAMILY

Fodor's Choice

★

Feira do Artesanato. Each summer (late June–early September), Estoril hosts a huge open-air arts-and-crafts fair near the casino. Vendors sell local art, crafts, fashion, and food and drink every evening until midnight. With live music, dancing, and kid-friendly shows, it's a major event on Estoril's cultural calendar. ⊠ *Av. Amaral Estoril* ☎ *214/678210.*

Galeria do Casino Estoril. The Galeria do Casino Estoril holds three big art exhibitions during the year. In spring, talented young artists from Portuguese art schools are featured; naive art is the theme in summer; in October, Portuguese and international artists grab the spotlight. During the year there are also eight individual exhibitions. All the works— paintings, bronzes, ceramics, drawings, and sculptures, including marble pieces by Portugal's most famous sculptor, João Cutileiro—are for sale. ⊠ *Casino Estoril, Largo José Teodoro dos Santos* ☎ *214/667700 (ask for art gallery)* ⊕ *www.casino-estoril.pt.*

Mercado de Carcavelos. The Mercado de Carcavelos, in the nearby town of Carcavelos, 7 km (4½ miles) southeast of Estoril, has a busy market that sells food, clothes, and crafts; you can reach it by local train. ⊠ *Rua do Mercado, Parede.*

CASCAIS AND BOCA DO INFERNO

3 km (2 miles) west of Estoril.

Once a mere fishing village, the town of Cascais—with three small, sandy bays—is now a heavily developed resort packed with shops, restaurants, and hotels. Despite the masses of people, though, Cascais has retained some of its small-town character. This is most visible around the harbor, with its fishing boats and yachts, and in the old streets and squares off Largo 5 de Outubro, where you'll find lace shops, cafés, and eateries. The beaches are attractive, too; however, the water is very cold, and pollution can be a problem.

GETTING HERE AND AROUND

The CP urban train departing from Cais do Sodré (Linha de Cascais) in Lisbon arrives close to downtown Cascais (⇨ *see Train Travel, above*). To visit the surrounding area, an urban bus line (SCOTTurb) provides connections to Sintra, Estoril, and Oeiras. Motorists can make the 25-minute drive from Lisbon, either on the A2 highway or the more scenic Avenida Marginal, which runs along the coast and provides an easier way to travel to outer interest points such as Boca do Inferno. Just be advised that afternoon traffic on the latter is bad during summer weekends.

Bus Contacts Cascais bus terminal. ⊠ *Av. Costa Pinto 74, on lower level of Cascais Villa mall, Cascais* ☎ *214/836357.* **SCOTTurb.** ⊠ *R. de S. Francisco, nº 660, Alcabideche* ☎ *214/699100* ⊕ *www.scotturb.com.*

Taxi Contacts Taxis Cascais. ⊠ *Av. Júlio Dantas 769, Cascais* ☎ *214/659500, 214/660101* ⊕ *site.taxiscascais.com.*

EXPLORING

Fodor's Choice **Boca do Inferno** (*Mouth of Hell*). The most visited attraction in the area
★ around Cascais is the forbiddingly named "'Mouth of Hell," one of several natural grottoes in the rugged coastline. Located just 2 km (1 mile) west of town, it is best appreciated at high tide or in stormy weather, when the waves are thrust high onto the surrounding cliffs. You can walk along the fenced paths to the viewing platforms above the grotto and peer into the abyss. A path leads down to secluded spots on the rocks below, where fishermen cast their lines. Afterward, shop for lace, leather items, and other handicrafts at roadside stalls, or linger in one of the nearby cafés. ⊠ *Cascais.*

FAMILY **Museu do Mar** (*Sea Museum*). For an understanding of development in Cascais, visit this modern, single-story museum. Here, the town's former role as a fishing village is traced through model boats and fishing gear, period clothing, analysis of local fish, paintings, and old photographs. ⊠ *Rua Júlio Pereira de Melho, Cascais* ☎ *214/815906* ⊕ *www. cm-cascais.pt/museumar* 🖃 *Free* 🕙 *Closed Mon.*

Museu dos Condes Castro Guimarães (*Counts of Castro Guimarães Museum*). One of Cascais's 19th-century town houses serves as the museum's home with displays of 18th- and 19th-century paintings, ceramics, and furniture, as well as artifacts from nearby archaeological excavations. ⊠ *Av. Rei Humberto II de Itália, Cascais* ☎ *214/825401* ⊕ *www.cm-cascais.pt/mccg* 🖃 *€3* 🕙 *Closed Mon.*

FAMILY **Parque do Marechal Carmona.** The most relaxing spot in Cascais, apart from the beach, is this municipal park, which has a shallow lake, a café, a small zoo, plus tables and chairs under the trees for picnickers. ⊠ *Av. da Republica, Cascais* ⊕ *www.cm-cascais.pt/equipamento/ parque-marechal-carmona.*

NEED A BREAK **Santini Cascais.** In the heart of old-town Cascais, Santini Cascais is Portugal's most famous ice cream parlor and has what many people consider to be the best Italian-style gelato in the world. In 1949, Italian immigrant Attilio Santini opened his shop, serving hand-crafted gelato made from fresh, 100% natural ingredients. His business rapidly grew in popularity and throughout the years has been visited by important social and political figures, and even European royalty. Santini currently produces frozen treats in 31 flavors. Try classics like chocolate, strawberry, pistachio, and hazelnut or newer options like caramelized red berries. One seasonal favorite is blood-orange sherbet, made from imported Sicilian blood oranges. Branches have now opened across Lisbon and in Porto, but Santini Cascais is where it all began. ⊠ *Av. Valbom 28F, Cascais* ☎ *214/833709* ⊕ *www. santini.pt.*

WHERE TO EAT

$$$$ ✕ **Beira Mar.** One of several well-established restaurants behind the fish
SEAFOOD market, the Beira Mar has won a string of awards for the quality of its fish and seafood. An impressive glass display shows off the best of the day's catch, although (as always) you can end up paying top dollar for

dinner if you're not careful, because it's sold by weight. Make sure you know the price first, or stick to dishes with fixed prices—the rice with clams and steaks cut from swordfish or tuna are invariably good. Vegetarians aren't entirely overlooked; there's a good fresh vegetable risotto here. [$] *Average main: €27* ✉ *Rua das Flores 6, Cascais* ☎ *214/827380* 🌐 *www.restaurantebeiramar.pt* 🕒 *Closed Tues.*

$ FAST FOOD 🍴 **Dom Manolo.** The surroundings aren't sophisticated in this Spanish-owned grill-restaurant, but for down-to-earth fare it's a good choice. The waiters charge back and forth delivering excellent spit-roasted chicken (*frango* in Portuguese) and grilled fish to a largely local clientele. Whatever your main dish, order potatoes or fries on the side; avoid the poor, overpriced salads and factory-made desserts. [$] *Average main: €13* ✉ *Av. Marginal 13, Cascais* ☎ *214/831126* 💳 *No credit cards.*

$$$$ SEAFOOD Fodor's Choice ★ 🍴 **Monte Mar.** Superior seafood and steaks come with equally impressive sea views at this highly regarded, formal restaurant in Cascais that has been known to attract everyone from rock stars to visiting politicians (Bill Clinton, former New York City Mayor Rudolph Giuliani, and Bryan Adams have all been spotted here). Sitting right at the edge of the ocean, Monte Mar is famous for its shellfish, its cataplanas (seafood stews), as well as its excellent grilled fish. Reservations are recommended. [$] *Average main: €35* ✉ *Av. Nossa Senhora do Cabo, Guincho, Cascais* ☎ *214/869270* 🌐 *www.montemarrestaurante.com* 🕒 *Closed Mon.*

$ PORTUGUESE FAMILY Fodor's Choice ★ 🍴 **O Pereira.** Popular it may be, but this restaurant remains simple, with checked cotton tablecloths and very simple decor. The menu includes very cheap—and very good—dishes from every region in Portugal. The owner's cooking attracts many customers, so get there early: 12:30 for lunch and 7:30 for dinner. During summer, competition for the outdoor tables is fierce, and the interior is packed with locals all year round. [$] *Average main: €13* ✉ *Travessa Bela Vista 42, Cascais* ☎ *214/831215* 🌐 *restaurantepereira.pai.pt* 💳 *No credit cards* 🕒 *Closed Thurs.*

$ SEAFOOD FAMILY Fodor's Choice ★ 🍴 **O Pescador.** Fresh seafood fills the menu at this folksy restaurant, a favorite since 1964, where a cluttered ceiling and maritime-related artifacts distract the eye. Sole is one specialty; *bacalhau* (salt cod) is another—it's often baked here, either with cream or port wine and onions. There are usually one or two vegetarian options, such as a salad with tofu and asparagus, but it's really all about the seafood and the famously well-stocked wine cellar. [$] *Average main: €13* ✉ *Rua das Flores 10, Cascais* ☎ *214/832054* 🌐 *www.restaurantepescador.com* 🕒 *Closed Mon.*

$$ PIZZA FAMILY 🍴 **Pizza Itália.** There are plenty of other pizza joints in Cascais, but Pizza Itália is probably the best of the bunch. In its indoor dining rooms or on its sunny terrace you can choose from a range of authentic thin-crust pizzas and fresh homemade pasta dishes. [$] *Average main: €16* ✉ *R. Marques Leal Pancada 16-A, Cascais* ☎ *214/830151* 🕒 *Closed Wed. No lunch Thurs.*

WHERE TO STAY

$$$
HOTEL
Fodor's Choice
★

[ ] **The Albatroz Hotel.** On a rocky outcrop above the crashing waves, this gorgeous hotel was once the summer residence of the dukes of Loulé. **Pros:** fantastic central-seaside location; superior views; wonderful ambience. **Cons:** pool overlooking the ocean is pretty small; adjacent beach is also small and gets crowded quickly. $ *Rooms from: €245* ⊠ *Rua Frederico Arouca 100, Cascais* ☏ *214/847380* ⊕ *www.thealbatrozcollection.com* ⤳ *40 rooms* ⍥ *Breakfast.*

$$
HOTEL

[ ] **Albatroz Villa Cascais.** If Portugal's 18th-century writer Maria Amália de Carvalho could return today to her house on the harbor at Cascais Bay, she would surely check in and open up her laptop. **Pros:** food central location; friendly staff; excellent breakfast included. **Cons:** some rooms somewhat dark; less luxurious than five-star rating suggests. $ *Rooms from: €180* ⊠ *Rua Fernandes Thomaz 1, Cascais* ☏ *214/863410* ⊕ *www.thealbatrozcollection.com/villacascais* ⤳ *11 rooms* ⍥ *Breakfast.*

$$$$
HOTEL
FAMILY
Fodor's Choice
★

[ ] **Hotel Cascais Miragem.** Perfectly integrated into the landscape, this luxurious hotel is built in steps up the side of the hill above the sea. **Pros:** near train station and city center; excellent breakfast included in room rate; top-notch service. **Cons:** rooms lack individuality; some noise from main road nearby; paid parking. $ *Rooms from: €270* ⊠ *Av. Marginal 8554, Cascais* ☏ *210/060600* ⊕ *www.cascaismiragem.com* ⤳ *200 rooms* ⍥ *Breakfast.*

$
B&B/INN
Fodor's Choice
★

[ ] **Pérgola House.** Set back from the road amid gardens, this intimate town house has been in the hands of the same family for more than 100 years. **Pros:** lovely historic building and flower-filled garden; extensive breakfast; excellent central location. **Cons:** old-fashioned style not for everyone; books up very quickly; difficult parking. $ *Rooms from: €140* ⊠ *Av. de Valbom 13, Cascais* ☏ *214/840040* ⊕ *www.pergolahouse.pt* ⤳ *6 rooms* ⍥ *Breakfast.*

NIGHTLIFE

Cascais has plenty of bars on and around the central pedestrian street (Rua Frederico Arouca) and in Largo Luís de Camões. The marina is also a lively place to barhop, with a wide choice of places that stay open until around 2 am.

Chequers. The bar at Chequers restaurant is a popular spot to drink and dance the night away among a mixed crowd of locals and out-of-towners. ⊠ *Largo Luís de Camões 7, Cascais* ☏ *214/830926.*

Forte Dom Rodrigo. You can hear fado, the mournful Portuguese folk music, as you dine at Forte Dom Rodrigo. It's one of the most famous *casas de fado* in the region, owned by popular *fadisto* Rodrigo Ferreira. It opens at 7 pm; closing time depends on the performances. ⊠ *Rua Madressilvas 8, Cascais* ☏ *936/634192.*

John Bull. On hot summer nights, customers of the English-style pub-restaurant John Bull spill out into the square. ⊠ *Largo Luís de Camões 8, Cascais* ☏ *214/833319.*

SPORTS AND THE OUTDOORS
FISHING

FAMILY **Cascais Fishing.** This small company offers personlized fishing trips—including big-game fishing and night fishing—aboard an eight-foot Cheetah Marine catamaran. ⊠ *Marina de Cascais, Cascais* ☎ *918/917711* ⊕ *www.cascaisfishing.com* ⌲ *From €500.*

FAMILY **Marlin Boat Tours.** A wide program includes bike tours and surf trips as well as half- and full-day deep-sea-fishing tours, which include a Portuguese picnic lunch and drinks. ⊠ *Marina de Cascais, Cascais* ☎ *919/275509* ⊕ *www.marlinboattours.com* ⌲ *From €25.*

GOLF

Fodor'sChoice **Oitavos Dunes.** American architect Arthur Hills built this fine golf course
★ among pine woods and reforested dunes in an area of great natural beauty. The course is consistently rated as one of the top 100 in the world. It lies within the Sintra-Cascais Natural Park, and Hills made the most of three distinct landscape forms: umbrella pine forest, dunes, and the open coastal transition area. Every hole has a view of the Atlantic Ocean and the Sintra Hills. This was the first course in Europe to be recognized as a Golf Certified Signature Sanctuary, which is awarded by American Audubon International. A handicap certificate is required to play here. Golf and hotel packages include a stay at the luxurious Oitavos Hotel. ⊠ *25 Quinta da Marinha, Cascais* ☎ *214/860600* ⊕ *www.oitavosdunes. com* ⌲ *€90 weekdays, €150 weekends* ⅃ *18 holes, 6893 yds, par 71.*

SCUBA DIVING

Cascais Dive Center. Scuba course are available through the PADI-accredited Cascais Dive Center. Other services include specialized dive trips. ⊠ *Marina de Cascais, Loja 42a, Cascais* ☎ *969/913021* ⊕ *www.cascaisdive.com.*

SHOPPING

Cascais is arguably the best shopping area on the Estoril Coast, with pedestrian streets lined with stores and small market stalls. For smart fashions, gifts, and handmade jewelry, browse around Rua Frederico Arouca. Markets are held north of town at Rua Mercado (off Avenida 25 de Abril) on Wednesday and Saturday; you'll find produce such as fruit, vegetables, cheese, bread, and flowers.

Casa da Guia. Housed in a grand old building, Casa da Guia is a pretty outdoor shopping center that sits on a cliff right on the ocean at the far end of Cascais after Boca do Inferno. The shops are all high-end, brand-name boutiques, and there are several restaurants, bars, bakeries, and delis with large outdoor terraces scattered throughout the property. ⊠ *Av. Nossa Senhora do Cabo N° 101, Cascais* ☎ *214/843215, 214/818207* ⊕ *www.casadaguia.com.*

Cascais Villa. Cascais Villa is on the Marginal (coastal road) into Cascais from Lisbon. The shopping center has a cinema, restaurants, and shops carrying internationally known brands. ⊠ *Av. Dom Pedro I, Cascais* ☎ *214/828250.*

Ceramicarte. Fátima and Luís Soares present their carefully executed, modern ceramic designs alongside more traditional jugs and plates at Ceramicarte. There's also a small selection of tapestries and artworks.

The store is near the main Catholic church in the old town. ⊠ *Largo da Assunção 3–4, Cascais* ☎ *214/840170* ⊕ *www.ceramicarte.pt.*

Fnac. In the Cascais shopping mall on the road between Cascais and Sintra, the book-computer-record shop Fnac sells English-language books as well as tickets to cultural events. ⊠ *N9, Alcabideche, Cascais* ☎ *214/699000* ⊕ *www.fnac.pt.*

Torres. For typical Portuguese handmade jewelry such as filigree, go to Torres, which has its own designers and trademark brand. ⊠ *Cascais Shopping, Estrada Nacional Nº 9, Loja 8/9, Cascais* ☎ *214/603008* ⊕ *www.torres.pt.*

Vista Alegre Atlantis. For fine Portuguese porcelain visit Vista Alegre Atlantis. ⊠ *Cascais Shopping, Estrada Nacional 9, Lojas 0055/56, Cascais* ☎ *214/692397* ⊕ *vistaalegre.com.*

GUINCHO

9 km (5½ miles) north of Boca do Inferno.

The wide beach at Guincho is one of the most famous—and most visited—in the country. Atlantic waves pound the sand even on the calmest of days, providing perfect conditions for windsurfing (the annual world championships are often held here). The undertow is notorious, but the cool summer winds offer a refreshing break from the stuffier beaches on the Cascais line. Whether you go into the water or not, be sure to savor some fresh fish at one of the restaurant terraces overlooking the beach.

GETTING HERE AND AROUND

You can get to Guincho by bus both from Cascais and Sintra (Buses 405 and 415). SCOTTurb buses leave Cascais's train station every two hours (7:45 am–5:45 pm, journey time 25 minutes). Driving will take 5–10 minutes from Cascais, 20 minutes from Sintra, and 35 minutes from Lisbon (on the highway).

Contacts SCOTTurb. ⊠ *R. de S. Francisco, Nº 660, Adroana, Alcabideche* ☎ *214/699125* ⊕ *www.scotturb.com.*

BEACHES

Fodor'sChoice ★ **Praia do Guincho** (*Guincho Beach*). Cars often line either side of the road behind Guincho Beach on weekends, and surfers can always be seen braving its waves, irrespective of the season or prevailing weather conditions. The surf can be trying and the undertow dangerous: even accomplished swimmers have had to summon Guincho's lifeguards—it's not an activity for the fainthearted. If you prefer something more sedate, this beach—with the Serra da Sintra serving as a backdrop—is an ideal spot to watch the sunset. The Fortaleza do Guincho and Estalagem Muchaxo are the obvious choices for those seeking accommodation close by. **Amenities:** food and drink; parking (no fee); showers; toilets. **Best for:** sunset; surfing; swimming; windsurfing. ⊠ *N247.*

WHERE TO EAT AND STAY

$$$$ ✕ **João Padeiro.** "John the Baker," undoubtedly the most eclectic res-
PORTUGUESE   taurant in this area, was named after the owner who opened a small restaurant in Cascais 40 years ago that catered to local fishermen. The

place became so famous that it attracted Portuguese royalty. In 2001, John opened this establishment in what was once an indoor swimming pool—though he did keep the outdoor pool—in an isolated part of the Guincho beach. Now, under an elaborate wooden ceiling and surrounded by modern art and photographs of past guests, you can enjoy fabulous seafood dishes, including the famous Cascais Dover sole. [$] *Average main: €26* ✉ *Estrada do Guincho, Cascais* ☎ *214/857141* ⏲ *No dinner Sun. and during important football (soccer) matches.*

$ HOTEL **Estalagem Muchaxo.** Don't expect grandeur in this 17th-century fortress-turned-hotel in the rocks above Guincho Beach—much of the building is rustic, with stone floors, and wood furniture—but the views are simply spectacular. **Pros:** prime beachfront location; friendly staff; views of both the mountains and ocean. **Cons:** rooms are plain and rather run-down; parking is difficult during beach season; breakfast options are limited. [$] *Rooms from: €75* ✉ *Praia do Guincho, Cascais* ☎ *214/870221* 🌐 *www.muchaxo.com* 🛏 *60 rooms* 🍴 *Breakfast.*

$$$ HOTEL Fodor's Choice ★ **Fortaleza do Guincho.** Standing on the cliffs facing the ocean, this historic fort turned hotel (part of the Relais & Chateaux stable) may look cold and stiff from the outside, but upon entering you'll find all the luxury of an old-world palace, maintaining the association's high standards. **Pros:** beautifully designed; gorgeous location; Michelin-starred restaurant. **Cons:** standard rooms are quite small with a small window; bathtubs aren't that large; no pool. [$] *Rooms from: €235* ✉ *Estrada do Guincho, Cascais* ☎ *214/870491* 🌐 *www.fortalezadoguincho.pt* 🛏 *30 rooms* 🍴 *Breakfast.*

SPORTS AND THE OUTDOORS

Guincho Wind Factory. Call ahead for lessons in kite surfing, windsurfing, and regular surfing from Guincho Wind Factory, where you can also buy or rent on boards, leashes, and appropriate clothing. You can either meet at the shop in Cascais or on the beach itself. Guincho Wind Factory also operates a small guesthouse catering to a sporty young crowd. ✉ *Rua da Torre 1412, Cascais* ☎ *214/868332, 932/301378* 🌐 *www.guinchowindfactory.com.*

SINTRA AND QUELUZ

The town of Sintra—a UNESCO World Heritage Site—is the jewel in this region's proverbial crown. Fortified by Moors, popularized by palace-building royals, and beloved by Romantic writers, it has a storied past that manifests itself in stunning architecture. Moreover, it is blessed by natural beauty: the woods and valleys on the northern slopes of the Serra de Sintra are picturesque and provide the area with its own microclimate (it can be cool and misty in Sintra when Lisbon is sunny and warm). To the west, the Atlantic exerts its influence at windswept beaches and capes, including Cabo da Roca—the westernmost point in Europe. In the other direction, the town of Queluz, halfway between Lisbon and Sintra, is dominated by a magnificent baroque palace set in gardens dotted with statuary.

GETTING HERE AND AROUND
Sintra is a good base for exploring the countryside. The best way to reach it via public transport is the urban train—Linha de Sintra—which departs from Lisbon on a regular basis; it takes about 15 minutes to get to Queluz from Lisbon and about 40 minutes to get to Sintra. Sintra can also be reached by regular year-round bus service from Cascais and Estoril (one hour). Buses serve much of the surrounding area as well, including Cabo da Roca; tickets are cheap, particularly when purchased in advance (less than €3.50 for most journeys). Regional operator SCOTTurb has one-day passes, plus a combined pass that covers train travel to and from Lisbon.

By car, it takes 25 minutes to get to Sintra from Lisbon and 15 minutes from Cascais or Estoril. Avoid driving during rush hour on weekdays (5:30–7:30 pm); otherwise it may take twice as long.

SAFETY AND PRECAUTIONS
Keep an eye on your belongings if you choose the Linha de Sintra, especially when it is very crowded.

SINTRA

30 km (18 miles) northwest of Lisbon; 13 km (8 miles) north of Estoril.

Fodor's Choice ★ History buffs, architecture enthusiasts, literature lovers, hopeless romantics, and even hikers all fall under Sintra's seductive spell. The lush northern slopes of the Serra de Sintra (Sintra Mountains) have been inhabited since prehistoric times, although the Moors were the first to build a castle on the peaks. Later Sintra became the summer residence of Portuguese kings and aristocrats, and its late-medieval palace is the greatest expression of royal wealth and power of the time. In the 18th and 19th centuries, English travelers, poets, and writers—including an enthusiastic Lord Byron—were drawn by the region's beauty. The poet Robert Southey described Sintra as "the most blessed spot on the whole inhabitable globe." Its historic importance has been recognized by UNESCO, which designated it a World Heritage Site in 1995.

GETTING HERE AND AROUND
Trains from Lisbon's Rossio station, between Praça dos Restauradores and Rossio square, run every 15 minutes to Queluz and on to Sintra (40 minutes total). The service operates from 6 am to 2:40 am, and one-way tickets cost €1.95 to Queluz-Belas, €2.15 to Sintra. Both fares can be loaded onto the same €0.50 Viva Viagem card. Sintra's small train station gets packed during the peak summer season (July–early September), and queues at the ticket information desk are huge. Look for friendly young volunteers wearing yellow "Can I help?" T-shirts—these helpful folk will do their best to assist with everything from directions to finding a place to store extra bags.

Once in town, the nearest attractions are within walking distance. Several marked trails (ideal for escaping the summer crowds) also let you enjoy the countryside. If you'd rather not tackle steep hills, you can opt for a horse-drawn carriage ride, a guided tour (arranged through the tourist office), or a tour by taxi. Another option is taking SCOTTurb's

Bus 434, which loops around the key attractions; all-day tickets allow you to hop on and off as long as you don't backtrack. Note that the bus gets extremely busy on summer afternoons, so arrive early for a more comfortable trip.

Contacts CP (Comboios de Portugal). ☎ 707/210220 ⊕ www.cp.pt.

TOURS

Eléctrico de Sintra. From Wednesday through Sunday an antique red streetcar makes the 45-minute scenic journey from the center of Sintra through the countryside and down the mountain to the Praia das Maçãs on the sea. Seafood restaurants line the beach at the last stop. The trip costs €3 one way. During the summer season there are six hourly trams (the first at 10:20 am, the last at 5 pm); service is reduced in the winter. ⊠ *Rua General Alves Roçadas.*

Sintratur. Sintratur offers old-fashioned horse-and-carriage rides in and around the town. A short tour costs €30 for up to four people; longer trips run €60–€100 and go as far afield as Pena Palace and Monserrate. ⊠ *Av. Heliodoro Salgado 16* ☎ *219/241238* ⊕ *www.sintratur.com.*

Turis Tuk by TurisLua. Following Lisbon's lead, the town has now adopted tuk tuks for sightseeing. Turis Tuk's distinctive red tuk tuks zip around Sintra and beyond, saving tourists' legs as they visit the hilltop palaces, castles, and other key sights. ⊠ *2A Volta Duche* ☎ *219/243881* ⊕ *www. turislua.pt* 🖅 *Tours from €40.*

VISITOR INFORMATION

The main local tourist office, Ask Me Sintra, has details on opening hours and prices, on walking trails in the countryside, and on tour companies. It also houses an art gallery (the Galeria do Museu Municipal) specializing in works associated with Sintra. There's another office in the train station.

Contacts AskMe Sintra. ⊠ *Praça da República 23* ☎ *219/231157* ⊕ *www. cm-sintra.pt.*

EXPLORING

There are various ways to get to Palácio da Pena, Castelo dos Mouros, and Convento dos Capuchos. You can take a local bus or a horse-drawn carriage, sign up for a tour, or make the long, steep, but pleasant walk up from the center of Sintra (about 1½ hours). It's possible to drive, but there's limited parking once you get there. However you choose to arrive, note that the walk back down to Sintra is delightful: the route is through shaded woods with viewpoints under the cork trees.

TOP ATTRACTIONS

FAMILY **Castelo dos Mouros** (*Moorish Castle*). The battlemented ruins of this 9th-century castle still give a fine impression of the fortress that finally fell to Christian forces led by Dom Afonso Henriques in 1147. It's visible from various points in Sintra itself, but for a closer look follow the steps that lead up to the ruins from the back of the town center (40 minutes going up, 25 minutes coming down). Alternately, you can catch the SCOTTurb's Bus 434 or rent a horse-drawn carriage or tuk tuk in town. Panoramic views from the serrated walls explain why the

Moors chose the site. ⊠ *Estrada da Pena* ☎ *219/237300* ⊕ *www.parquesdesintra.pt* 📧 *€8.*

FAMILY
Fodor's Choice
★

Monserrate Park and Palace. This estate, 4 km (2½ miles) west of Sintra, was laid out by Scottish gardeners in the mid-19th century at the behest of a wealthy Englishman, Sir Francis Cook. The centerpiece is the Moorish-style, three-dome **Palácio de Monserrate.** The original palace was built by the Portuguese viceroy of India, and was later home to

VISITOR TIP

If you're planning to visit multiple attractions in Sintra, consider buying a *bilhete combinado* (combination ticket), which is valid for 30 days and costs around €36 per person or €90 for a family (two adults plus two children). ☎ *219/237300* ⊕ *www.parquesdesintra.pt*

Gothic novelist William Beckford. A regular ticket allows you to visit the park and part of the palace, and there are guided 1½-hour tours available at various times throughout the day. The gardens, with their streams, waterfalls, and Etruscan tombs, are famed for an array of tree and plant species, though labels are lacking. ⊠ *Estrada da Monserrate* ☎ *219/237300* ⊕ *www.parquesdesintra.pt* 📧 *€8.*

FAMILY
Fodor's Choice
★

Palácio da Pena. This Disney-like castle is a glorious conglomeration of turrets and domes awash in pastels. In 1503 the Monastery of Nossa Senhora da Pena was constructed here, but it fell into ruins after religious orders were expelled from Portugal in 1832. Seven years later the ruins were purchased by Maria II's consort, Ferdinand of Saxe-Coburg. Inspired by the Bavarian castles of his homeland, Ferdinand commissioned a German architect, Baron Eschwege, to build the castle of his fantasies, in styles that range from Arabian to Victorian. Work was finished in 1885, by which time he was Fernando II. The surrounding park is filled with trees and flowers from every corner of the Portuguese empire, as well as hidden temples, grottoes, and Valley of the Lakes, where black swans sit regally. Portugal's last monarchs used the Pena Palace as a summer home, the last of whom—Queen Amália—went into exile in England after the Republic was proclaimed on October 5, 1910. Inside is an ostentatious and often bizarre collection of Victorian and Edwardian furniture, ornaments, and paintings. Placards explain each room. Visitors can walk along high castle walls, peek into turrets, and finally reward themselves with a drink and a snack at one of two on-site cafés. A path beyond an enormous statue (thought to be Baron Eschwege, cast as a medieval knight) on a nearby crag leads to the **Cruz Alta**, a 16th-century stone cross 1,782 feet above sea level, with stupendous views. ⊠ *Estrada da Pena* ☎ *219/105340, 219/237300 for advance booking* ⊕ *www.parquesdesintra.pt* 📧 *€8.*

FAMILY
Fodor's Choice
★

Palácio Nacional de Sintra (*Sintra Palace*). The conical twin white chimneys of Sintra Palace are the town's most recognizable landmarks. There has probably been a palace here since Moorish times, although the current structure—also known as the Paço Real—dates to the late 14th century. It is the only surviving royal palace in Portugal from the Middle Ages, and displays a combination of Moorish, Gothic, and Manueline architecture. Bilingual descriptions in each room let you enjoy them at your own pace. The chapel has Mozarabic (Moorish-influenced) azulejos from the 15th and 16th centuries. The ceiling of the Sala das Armas is painted with the coats of arms of 72 noble families, and the grand Sala dos Cisnes has a remarkable ceiling of painted swans. The Sala das Pegas (magpies) figures in a well-known tale about Dom João I (1385–1433) and his dalliance with a lady-in-waiting. The king had the room painted with as many magpies as there were chattering court ladies, thus satirizing the gossips as loose-tongued birds. ✉ *Largo Rainha D. Amélia* ☎ *219/237300* 🌐 *www.parquesdesintra.pt* 🎟 *€10.*

Fodor's Choice ★ **Quinta da Regaleira.** A five-minute walk along the main road past the tourist office takes you to one of Sintra's most intriguing privately owned mansions. Quinta da Regaleira was built in the early 20th century for a Brazilian mining magnate with a keen interest in freemasonry and the Knights Templar (who made their 11th-century headquarters on this site). The estate includes gardens where almost everything—statues, water features, grottoes, lookout towers—is linked to one or the other of his pet subjects. Spookiest of all is the 100-foot-deep Poço do Iniciático (Initiation Well)—an inverted underground "tower."✉ *Rua Barbosa do Bocage 5* ☎ *219/106650* 🌐 *www.regaleira.pt* 🎟 *€6, guided tours €10.*

WORTH NOTING

Convento dos Capuchos. The plain main entrance to this extraordinarily austere convent, 13 km (8 miles) southwest of Sintra, sets the tone for the severity of the ascetic living conditions within. From 1560 until 1834, when it was abandoned, seven monks—never any more, never any less—prayed in the tiny chapel hewn out of the rock and inhabited the bare cells, which were lined with cork in attempt to maintain a modicum of warmth. Impure thoughts meant a spell in the Penitents' Cell, an excruciatingly small space. Guides for the 45-minute tour bring the history of the place to life with surprising zest and humor. No vehicles are allowed close to the convent, so the peace is disturbed only by birdsong. ✉ *Convento dos Capuchos, Colares* ☎ *219/237300* 🌐 *www.parquesdesintra.pt* 🎟 *€7.*

Museu Arqueológico de São Miguel de Odrinhas (*São Miguel de Odrinhas Archaeological Museum*). If your stay is longer than a day or so, then this museum is worth a visit. The displays include locally found ancient and medieval objects. ✉ *Av. Professor Dr. D. Fernando da Almeida-Odrinhas* ☎ *219/609520* 🌐 *museuarqueologicodeodrinhas.cm-sintra.pt.*

WHERE TO EAT

$ PORTUGUESE FAMILY 🍴 **Adega do Saloio.** Families fill this popular restaurant on weekends, drawn by the juicy steaks being cooked over the open fire as you walk in. The dining room is festooned with garlands of onions and garlic. House wine is served in brown clay jugs, and little plates of smoked ham, cheese, and black olives decorate the tables to whet the appetite. It's fun just watching the waiters bustling about with skewers of grilled meat and fish. The *espetada à Madeira* (beef and laurel leaves on a skewer) that drips its juices as it's hung in front of you on the table is quite a spectacle. [$] *Average main: €15* ✉ *Rua Álvaro Reis 49, Chão de Meninos* ☎ *219/231422.*

$$$ ✕ **Café Paris.** This chic bistro occupies a plum spot in front of the Palacio
ECLECTIC   Nacional and has been attracting a well-heeled crowd since the 1920s.
There's a covered area for outdoor dining, while the candelabra, ceiling
frescoes, and chandeliers of the interior are in keeping with the general
sense of opulence. There's a daily set lunch menu that's a good value.
Two enduringly popular choices among the á la carte options are the
house steak with herbs and cheese, and cod with a corn crust served
with olive tapenade. $ *Average main: €24* ⌧ *Praça da República 32–36*
☎ *21/232275* ⊕ *www.screstauracao.com/en/venues/Cafe-Paris/29.*

$ ✕ **Cantinho de São Pedro.** Imaginative Portuguese cuisine is served at
PORTUGUESE   this busy, rustic restaurant in a small courtyard of artisans' workshops,
just off the main square. Locals consider the food well worth the wait
for a table. Try the trout with almonds and cream, or look for the
fresh shellfish on the list of *pratos do dia* (dishes of the day). $ *Average main: €15* ⌧ *Praça Dom Fernando II 18* ☎ *219/230267* ⊕ *www.
cantinhosaopedro.com.*

$$ ✕ **Incomúm by Luis Santos.** Located between Sintra's train station and the
ECLECTIC   historic center, this restaurant is always busy, and with good reason—it
Fodor'sChoice   serves high-end cuisine in a relaxed setting at astonishingly fair prices.
★   While á la carte options are reasonably priced, it's the set lunches (weekdays noon–3 pm) that are really excellent value: for less than €10 diners can enjoy a glass of house wine, *couvert* of olives and home-baked
breads, soup or salad, a meat or fish main course, and a dessert. This
goes way beyond the standard *menu executivo* fare: the soup might
be cream of chestnut; the main might be chicken with goat cheese and
sweet potato; and the dessert might be a rich chocolate-orange mousse.
There's also a five-course tasting menu. There are two entrances and
two dining spaces; the small front room with a few tables and chairs
spilling out onto the sidewalk is the more casual. $ *Average main: €16*
⌧ *Rua Doutor Alfredo Costa 22* ☎ *219/243719* ⊕ *incomumbyluissan-
tos.pt* ⊘ *No lunch Sat.*

$ ✕ **Loja do Vinho.** This rustic spot opposite the Royal Palace was one
DELI   of the first wineshops to open in Sintra, and today the wine cellar has
been transformed into a cozy drinking and dining space for up to 30
people. It's a very sociable spot for a light lunch or afternoon snack.
Friendly staff serve small plates of cured meats, cheeses, and marinated
olives, as well as heartier salads and sandwiches. There's an aboveground space, complete with tables and chairs on the pavement, which
is a pleasant option on warmer days. $ *Average main: €9* ⌧ *Praça da
República 3* ☎ *219/244410* ⊕ *www.screstauracao.com/en/venues/Loja-
do-vinho/148* ⊘ *No dinner.*

$ ✕ **Neptuno.** Praia das Maçãs is a popular place to go for seafood res-
SEAFOOD   taurants on the beach. One of the best is Neptuno, a glassed-in eatery
practically on the sand. Hanging on the walls are photos of boats, big
catches, and the sea. Try *peixe a bulhão pato* (fish with garlic, olive oil,
and coriander) and seafood-rich arroz de marisco. $ *Average main: €10*
⌧ *Praia das Maçãs* ☎ *219/291222* ⊘ *Closed Tues.*

$ ✕ **Páteo do Garrett.** Arches divide three rooms where long tables are cov-
PORTUGUESE   ered in yellow tablecloths that match the chair cushions and curtains.
Bacalhau *à garrette* (cooked with onions, garlic, peppers, and olive oil

and garnished with coriander and boiled egg) is a good choice. Join the guests on the terrace who pose for pictures with views of the twin chimneys of the Paço Real, the church tower, and the distant beach. $ *Average main: €12* ⊠ *Rua Maria Eugénia Navarro* 🕾 *219/243380* ⊕ *www.pateodogarrett.com* ⊘ *Closed Wed. No dinner Nov.–Mar.*

$$ ✕**Tacho Real.** Locals climb a steep hill to this restaurant for traditional
PORTUGUESE   dishes cooked with panache, such as bacalhau *à brás* (with eggs, onions, and sliced potato), steaks, and game in season. The dessert cart allows you to choose from a selection of house-made cakes and tarts. On warm days the small terrace is delightful, and there is often live guitar music welcoming you at the door. $ *Average main: €18* ⊠ *Rua do Ferraria 4* 🕾 *219/235277* ⊘ *Closed Wed.*

WHERE TO STAY

$ 🏨**Casa Miradouro.** The Belgian owners of this candy-stripe 1890s house
B&B/INN   at the edge of Sintra have a keen eye for style and comfort. **Pros:** all
Fodor's Choice   rooms have views; in-room double-glaze windows and heating an
★   unusual winter bonus in this category; special deals in winter. **Cons:** requires very early booking; no phone or TV in rooms. $ *Rooms from: €90* ⊠ *Rua Sotto Mayor 55* 🕾 *914/292203* ⊕ *www.casa-miradouro. com* ⊘ *Closed 2 wks in Jan.* 🛏 *8 rooms* ⫴ *Breakfast.*

$$ 🏨**Lawrence's Hotel.** When this 18th-century inn, the oldest on the penin-
B&B/INN   sula, reopened in 1999, the U.S. secretary of state and the Netherlands'
Fodor's Choice   Queen Beatrix were among the first guests. **Pros:** old-world luxury; cozy
★   hotel; excellent restaurant. **Cons:** no pool, gym, or garden; some rooms are small. $ *Rooms from: €190* ⊠ *Rua Consiglieri Pedroso 38–40* 🕾 *219/105500* ⊕ *www.lawrenceshotel.com* 🛏 *16 rooms* ⫴ *Breakfast.*

$$$ 🏨**Penha Longa Resort.** Hidden among the rolling green hills and val-
RESORT   leys in the Sintra-Cascais nature reserve, halfway between Cascais and
FAMILY   Sintra, sits a five-star dream resort operated by Ritz-Carlton. **Pros:** spa-
Fodor's Choice   cious rooms and gorgeous views; excellent restaurants; fantastic kids'
★   facilities. **Cons:** everything is pricey; 10-minute cab ride into town. $ *Rooms from: €240* ⊠ *Estrada da Lagoa Azul* 🕾 *219/249011* ⊕ *www. penhalonga.com* 🛏 *221 rooms* ⫴ *Breakfast.*

$$$ 🏨**Tivoli Hotel Palácio de Seteais.** Built in the 18th century as a home for
HOTEL   the Dutch consul to Portugal, this suitably grand hotel is surrounded by
Fodor's Choice   pristine grounds 1 km (½ mile) from the center of Sintra. **Pros:** unique
★   palace ambience; beautiful location and views; excellent room ameni- ties. **Cons:** very expensive; no spa or gym. $ *Rooms from: €260* ⊠ *Rua Barbosa do Bocage 8* 🕾 *219/233200* ⊕ *www.tivolihotels.com/pt/hoteis/ sintra/tivoli-palacio-de-seteais/o-hotel.aspx* 🛏 *31 rooms* ⫴ *Breakfast.*

$ 🏨**Villa das Rosas.** A 15-minute stroll or short drive from the historic
B&B/INN   center of Sintra, this beautifully restored 19th-century estate has 10 rooms spread over a series of buildings within the carefully maintained garden, where guests can relax around a pool shaded by fruit trees. **Pros:** quiet location; lovely historic building and gardens; helpful staff. **Cons:** a walk or drive to Sintra's main attractions; no gym or spa. $ *Rooms from: €110* ⊠ *Rua António Cunha 2-4* 🕾 *219/100860* ⊕ *www.villadas- rosas.com* 🛏 *10 rooms* ⫴ *Breakfast.*

SPORTS AND THE OUTDOORS

GOLF

Fodor's Choice ★ **Penha Longa Golf Courses.** With magnificent ocean views, the Sintra Hills, and Estoril and Cascais in the foreground, architect Robert Trent Jones Jr. had a wonderful setting in which to create one of Portugal's most memorable courses. The Atlantic Course has great sweeping changes in elevation and often tight fairways that put a premium on driving accuracy. With the elevation often come strong breezes that add another dimension to what is in any case a demanding layout. Lower-handicap players will savor the challenge, but there is plenty of enjoyment here for all abilities. A handicap certificate is required. ⊠ *Estrada do Lagoa Azul* ☎ *219/249031* ⊕ *www.penhalonga.com* ☒ *€97 weekdays, €130 weekends* ⚐ *18 holes, 6878 yds, par 72* ⚑ *Reservations essential.*

PERFORMING ARTS

FESTIVALS

Festival de Sintra. Sintra's music and dance festival takes place during early summer (usually May or June) at the Centro Cultural Olga Cadaval as well as in the many palaces and gardens around Sintra and Queluz: Palácio Nacional de Sintra, Pena Palace, Quinta da Regaleira, Quinta da Piedade, Palácio de Seteais, and Queluz Palace. The Gulbenkian Symphony Orchestra and the Gulbenkian Ballet company as well as other international groups perform at the Olga Cadaval Cultural Center. The gardens of the Seteais Palace are well-known for their open-air ballet and classical music performances. Tickets can be bought online or at AskMe Sintra and AskMe Lisboa tourist-information offices. ⊠ *Praça Dr. Francisco Sá Carneiro* ☎ *219/107110* ⊕ *www.festivaldesintra.pt.*

SHOPPING

Sintra is a noted center for antiques, curios, and ceramics, although you'll need to choose carefully: prices are on the high side, and there's a fair amount of poor-quality merchandise for sale given the area's touristy environment. Keep an eye out for special in-store displays of hand-painted ceramics, many of them reproductions of 15th- to 18th-century designs, signed by the artists. Most stores in the historical center are open by 9 or 10 am, close for lunch (1–2 pm), and reopen until 7 pm. As you walk into town from the train station, you'll see people selling all manner of handicrafts, jewelry, and the like. Some of it is mass-produced tat, but some sellers have genuinely interesting wares.

Casa Alegria. Casa Alegria sells hand-painted tiles and can also reproduce pictures or drawings you supply. ⊠ *Escandinhas Felix Nunes 5* ☎ *219/234726.*

Henrique Teixeira. Henrique Teixeira sells antiques: 17th- and 18th-century tiles, sculptures, and bronze pieces. ⊠ *Rua Onsiglieri Pedroso 2* ☎ *219/231043.*

Pêro Pinheiro. The small town of Pêro Pinheiro is known for its marble, and several shops here sell stacks of cachepots, plaques, and other garden objects. The town is on the N9, 9 km (5½ miles) northeast of Sintra. ⊠ *Sintra.*

Violeta. For hand-embroidered linen tablecloths, bedspreads, towels, and sheets, visit Violeta. ⊠ *Rua das Padarias 19* ☎ *21/923–4095.*

AZOIA AND CABO DA ROCA

15 km (9 miles) west of Sintra; 20 km (12 miles) northwest of Cascais.

Fodor's Choice ★ Azoia is a quaint village in the district of Leira that has maintained a genuine rural charm. Surrounded by flora typical of the Serra de Sintra but perched on the edge of the Atlantic, it is an ideal place for countryside strolls. A stone's throw away is Cabo da Roca—mainland Europe's westernmost point. A lighthouse, originally built in 1772, sits dramatically atop the cape's jutting cliffs.

North of Cabo da Roca, the natural parkland extends through the villages of Praia Grande, Praia das Maçãs, and Azenhas do Mar. The first two have good beaches, and all have seafood restaurants. On the way down, the pretty open market with fresh fruit and vegetable stands along the side of a fork in the road makes a nice place to shop with the locals.

GETTING HERE AND AROUND

SCOTTurb Bus 403 will take you to Cabo da Roca from Cascais or Sintra with regular departures from outside either town's train station. The journey takes about 30–40 minutes.

The drive will take 20 minutes from both Sintra and Cascais and 40 minutes from Lisbon.

Contacts SCOTTurb. ☎ *214/699125* 🌐 *www.scotturb.com.*

EXPLORING

Cabo da Roca. Between enchanting, culturally rich Sintra and the beach resort of Cascais you'll discover a totally different face of Lisbon's environs in this protected natural park. The windswept Cabo da Roca and its lighthouse mark continental Europe's westernmost point and are the main reason that most people make the journey. As with many such places, stalls are laden with gimmicky souvenirs; an information desk and gift shop sells a certificate that verifies your visit. Even without the certificate, though, the memory of this desolate granite landscape will linger. The cliffs tumble to a frothing sea below, and on the cape a simple cross bears an inscription by Portuguese national poet Luís de Camões. ✉ *Colares.*

WHERE TO EAT

$$ PORTUGUESE Fodor's Choice ★ 🍴 **A Casa de Luis.** This typical restaurant in the heart of Azoia is fashioned right out of owner Joaquim Luis Da Silva's family home. The walls and ceiling are decorated with hanging *presuntos* (cured ham) and old-fashioned knickknacks. All diners start the meal with several little *entradas* of the hanging ham, local cheeses, olives, and fresh bread. The restaurant serves excellent grilled fish and meats with tableside service by Senhor Luis himself. The *polvo á lagareiro* (grilled octopus with garlic) and *robalo grelhado* (grilled sea bass) are absolutely delicious. For meat, try the *espetada mista de carne* (mixed grilled meat skewers). [$] *Average main: €19* ✉ *Rua Corredouras 2, Azoia* ☎ *219/292721* ⏲ *Closed Wed.*

$ CAFÉ 🍴 **Moinho Dom Quixote.** On the outskirts of Azoia, this bar and patio is built out of an old-fashioned windmill on a cliff overlooking the ocean with the mountain as the backdrop. The menu is made up of simple fare like salads, burgers, and lasagna, but the setting is lovely and the drinks menu extensive. The inside bar and lounge are decorated in colorful Mexican style with hanging lanterns, a fireplace, and tables and chairs made from petrified wood. The outdoor seating area has a staggered patio down the cliff with either café tables and chairs or stone benches and tables blended throughout a beautiful garden of pines, flowering cacti, and shrubs. While drinking in the fabulous views, enjoy a *café com natas* in winter or a Mexican-inspired frozen cocktail in summer. [$] *Average main: €10* ✉ *Rua do Campo da Bola-Azoia, Azoia* ☎ *219/292523* 💳 *No credit cards.*

QUELUZ

15 km (9 miles) east of Sintra; 15 km (9 miles) northwest of Lisbon.

Halfway between Lisbon and Sintra, the otherwise rather unremarkable town of Queluz is dominated by its magnificent palace and gardens, located in the plaza of the town's center. Across from the palace stand the rebuilt Royal Guard's quarters, which have been turned into a lovely pousada. Unlike its metropolitan surroundings, the rest of the town's buildings still mimic the 18th-century style of the palace, which gives you the unique feeling that you're stepping back in time once you cross the bridge into the area.

GETTING HERE AND AROUND

Queluz is just off N249/IC19, and the drive from Lisbon takes about 20 minutes, making this a good half-day option or a fine stop on the way to or from Sintra. It's also easy to take the train from Lisbon (15 minutes): get off at the Queluz-Belas stop, turn left outside the station, and follow the signs for the 1-km (½-mile) walk to the palace.

Contacts CP (Comboios de Portugal). ☎ *808/208208* 🌐 *www.cp.pt.*

EXPLORING

Fodor's Choice ★ **Palácio Nacional de Queluz** (*Queluz National Palace*). This palace was inspired, in part, by the palace at Versailles. The salmon-pink rococo edifice was ordered as a royal summer residence by Dom Pedro III in 1747. Architect Mateus Vicente de Oliveira took five years to make the place habitable; Frenchman Jean-Baptiste Robillon spent 40 more executing a detailed baroque plan that also comprised imported trees and statues, and azulejo-lined canals and fountains. You can tour the apartments and elegant staterooms, including the frescoed Music Salon, the Hall of Ambassadors, and the mirrored Throne Room with its crystal chandeliers and gilt trim. Some are now used for concerts and state visits, while the old kitchens have been converted into an ordinary café and a fancy restaurant with an imposing open fireplace and a vast oak table. ✉ *Largo do Palácio* ☎ *219/237300* 🌐 *www.parquesdesintra.pt* 🎫 *€10 palace and gardens, €5 gardens only; Happy Hour ticket €8 (daily 3:30–6:30 pm).*

WHERE TO STAY

$$ B&B/INN 🏨 **Pousada Palácio de Queluz.** The Royal Guard quarters beneath the clock tower opposite the palace have undergone a stunning transformation at this grand hotel, which is now owned by Pestana's Pousadas de

Portugal portfolio. **Pros:** excellent restaurant and service; great location; ambience, ambience, ambience. **Cons:** not suitable for children; lacking in activities. $ *Rooms from: €145* ✉ *IC19* ☎ *214/356158* ⊕ *www.pousadas.pt* ⇱ *26 rooms* ⦿ *Breakfast.*

SPORTS AND THE OUTDOORS

GOLF

Belas. Architect Rocky Roquemore built this tough but interesting layout in rolling countryside close to Lisbon and the Castle of Queluz. Perhaps not the easiest golf course to walk—a golf cart is a must during the heat of summer—it is a serious test and will be better appreciated by lower-handicap players. The handicap limit here is 28 for men and 36 for women. ✉ *Estrada Nacional, Belas* ☎ *219/626640* ⊕ *www.belasgolf.com* ⧉ *€80 weekdays, €95 weekends* ⅃ *18 holes, 6977 yds, par 72* ⚑ *Reservations essential.*

THE SETÚBAL PENINSULA

The Setúbal Peninsula, south of the Rio Tejo, is popular for its beaches in Costa da Caparica, Sesimbra, Arrábida, Tróia, and everywhere in between. These provide the cleanest ocean swimming closest to Lisbon. Other highlights include the delicious local seafood, pastries, and regional wines; the historic castles of Palmela and Sesimbra and the fort in Setúbal; plus the scenic mountain range—the Serra da Arrábida—that separates the port from the peninsula's southernmost beaches and fishing villages.

GETTING HERE AND AROUND

If you're intent on spending the day at a beach or simply touring the town of Setúbal, traveling by public transportation from Lisbon via bus or train is easiest. If you want to see most of the sights covered in this section, however—and particularly if you want to tour the southern coastal and mountainous region—you should rent a car. Connections between the Setúbal Peninsula and Lisbon are via the capital's two bridges. Returning on the impressive suspension bridge, the Ponte 25 de Abril, you're guaranteed terrific views of Lisbon.

▮TIP→ **Avoid crossing the Ponte 25 de Abril when coming from Lisbon during evening rush hour as well as early afternoon on weekends in summer because the traffic can be horrendous. When returning to Lisbon via the bridge, avoid crossing early evening on Sunday and late afternoon–early evening in summer.**

Contacts Rede Expressos. ✉ *Praça Marechal Humberto Delgado–Estrada das Laranjeiras, Lisbon* ☎ *213/581472* ⊕ *www.rede-expressos.pt.* **TST (Transportes Sul do Tejo).** ✉ *Rua Marcos de Portugal–Laranjeiro, Almada* ☎ *211/126200* ⊕ *www.tsuldotejo.pt.*

SAFETY AND PRECAUTIONS

The city of Almada, where Cacilhas is located, is not the best place to be after dark, so take the ferry directly there and stay in the immediate area. Be careful in Costa da Caparica and Setúbal at night during the busy summer tourist season, too.

COSTA DA CAPARICA

14 km (8½ miles) southwest of Lisbon

Costa da Caparica is a 20-km (12-mile) stretch of beach on the northwestern coast of the Setúbal Peninsula. White sand and a laid-back holiday vibe make it Lisbon's answer to the Algarve, and it's often packed with locals on summer weekends. The coastal strip centers on the lively resort of Caparica itself, at the north end of the beach, less than an hour from the capital.

GETTING HERE AND AROUND

Costa da Caparica is served by several TST bus lines that will get you to and from Lisbon (158, 159, 161, and 190), Almada (124, 127, and 135), and Cacilhas (106, 124, 125, 126, and 127). The drive from Lisbon takes around 25 minutes. Take the minor N377, a slower, more scenic route than the main IC20 route (off the A2/IP1).

From June through September, a small narrow-gauge train departs from Caparica and travels along an 8-km (5-mile) coastal route, making stops along the way; a one-way ticket to the end of the line costs €5.

BEACHES

FAMILY **Costa da Caparica Beach.** When lisboetas want to go to the beach, more often than not their preferred spot is the Costa da Caparica, which is packed in summer. Formerly a fishing village, the town itself is rather lacking in charm these days, but the beachfront is lively with surf schools, cafés, and bars catering to a relaxed, sandy-footed clientele. You may be able to avoid the crowds by heading south toward the less accessible dunes and coves at the end of the peninsula. Each beach is different: the areas nearest Caparica are family oriented, whereas the more southerly ones tend to attract a younger crowd (there are some nudist beaches, too). The Mélia Aldeia dos Capuchos Hotel offers some seclusion without being too far from the action. Beach erosion is a problem in winter (March through October is the best time to visit). **Amenities:** food and drink; lifeguards; parking (fee); showers; toilets; water sports. **Best for:** partiers; sunset; swimming; walking. ✉ *Costa da Caparica.*

WHERE TO EAT AND STAY

$$ ECLECTIC 🍴 **Borda D' Água.** Whether you drive to Praia da Morena or catch the small train at Caparica, stop at this restaurant—a glassed-in wooden cabana built in the sand dunes. The laid-back beach vibe is enticing, with colorful pillows, hammocks, and weathered wooden tables; and a caipirinha will add to the holiday vibe as you study the menu of suitably unpretentious fare such as salads, sweet crêpes, and hamburgers, as well as daily fish specials, served with boiled potatoes and vegetables. [$] *Average main: €18* ✉ *Praia da Morena* ☎ *212/975213* 🌐 *www.bordadagua.com.pt* 🕒 *Closed Dec.–mid-Jan.*

$$ HOTEL FAMILY 🏨 **Mélia Aldeia dos Capuchos.** Opened in 2007, this luxury resort—with a mix of regular hotel rooms and apartments—stands above Costa da Caparica beach in the historic village of Aldeia dos Capuchos. **Pros:** away from crowds; free shuttle to Caparica; excellent fitness center. **Cons:** rooms aren't very soundproof; furniture a bit cramped in smaller rooms. [$] *Rooms from: €145* ✉ *Largo Aldeia dos Capuchos* ☎ *212/909000* 🌐 *www.aldeiadoscapuchos.pt* 🛏 *180 rooms* 🍽 *Breakfast.*

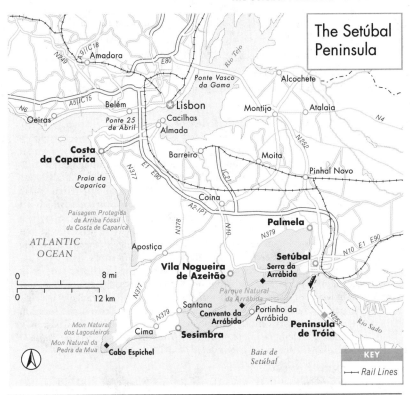

The Setúbal Peninsula

ATLANTIC OCEAN

KEY

⊢—⊢ Rail Lines

PALMELA

38 km (24 miles) southeast of Lisbon.

The small town of Palmela lies in the center of a prosperous wine-growing area, and every September the community holds a good-natured Festa das Vindimas (Grape Harvest Festival) which draws inhabitants from their whitewashed houses onto the cobbled streets. The village is dominated by the remains of a 12th-century castle that was captured from the Moors and enlarged by successive kings. In the 15th century the monastery and church of Sant'Iago were built within the castle walls. The structures were damaged in the 1755 earthquake and lay abandoned for many years. After extensive restoration, a pousada was opened in the monastic buildings. From this height, on a clear day, you can see Lisbon.

GETTING HERE AND AROUND

Public transportation to Palmela includes bus lines (TST) that will take you to and from Lisbon (565), Setúbal (413, 767, and 768, the latter two also calling at Azeitão), as well as the urban line train (Fertagus) between Lisbon and Setúbal. Driving will take 10 minutes from Setúbal or Azeitão and 30 minutes from Lisbon.

Bus Contacts **Palmela bus station.** ✉ *Largo do Chafariz D. Maria I* ☎ *212/350078.*

Train Contacts **Fertagus.** ☎ *707/127127* 🌐 *www.fertagus.pt.*

VISITOR INFORMATION
Contacts **Palmela Town Hall.** ✉ *Largo do Município* ☎ *212/336600.*

WHERE TO EAT AND STAY

$ CAFÉ FAMILY 🍴 **O Gaiteiro.** This casa de chá (teahouse) in the valley of Serra de Louro, down the road from Palmela, is a picturesque place to relax with a drink. There are two distinctly different cafés on the property: a winter one on the lower end among the pines with cozy seating, and a summer one perched on a small cliff with glassed-in walls and a balcony that faces the rolling hills. The latter (which also has a pool that you're welcome to swim in) serves one of area's best *café com natas,* which is a tall snifter filled with equal parts coffee and sweet whipped cream, then dusted with cinnamon. If you get this you likely won't need dessert, but the ice-cream sundaes are tempting, too. [$] *Average main: €12* ✉ *Quinta da Fonte Seca-Barris* ☎ *212/350109* 💳 *No credit cards.*

$$ B&B/INN Fodor's Choice ★ 🏨 **Pousada Castelo Palmela.** One of several grand, historic properties snapped up by Pestana's boutique offshoot Pousadas de Portugal, this building on a hill at the eastern end of the Arrábida range was originally a medieval fortress and later a monastery. **Pros:** castle location right in the city center; incredible views; unique ambience. **Cons:** now part of a chain; no pool. [$] *Rooms from: €150* ✉ *Castelo de Palmela* ☎ *212/351226* 🌐 *www.pousadas.pt* 🛏 *28 rooms* 🍽 *Breakfast.*

SHOPPING

Espaço Fortuna. Just down the road from Palmela is Espaço Fortuna, a wonderful little "quinta" in the country which has a shop selling hand-painted ceramics and azulejos along with a small selection of gourmet food and wine. On the top floor is the Cheiro a Lume café with an outdoor terrace, which is a great place to take a post-shopping coffee break and savor some local sweets. The café also has a restaurant down below, serving gourmet regional cuisine Tuesday through Sunday (no dinner). ✉ *Quinta do Anjo, Estrada Nacional 379* ☎ *212/871068* 🌐 *www.espacofortuna.com.*

SETÚBAL

10 km (6 miles) south of Palmela; 50 km (31 miles) southeast of Lisbon.

A colorful sister city to polished, cosmopolitan Lisbon, Setúbal lacks the tourist hordes of the capital but has plenty to offer the visitor. Along with its famous fresh fish and seafood—notably *choco frito* (fried cuttlefish)—the city has a lively cultural scene and is the starting point for dolphin-spotting trips out into the Sado Estuary.

At the mouth of the Rio Sado, Setúbal is the country's third-largest port and one of its oldest cities. A significant industrial town in Roman times, it became one again during Portugal's Age of Discovery and took off during the 19th century. Although parts of the city are industrial and unattractive, the center remains an attractive blend of medieval and modern. You could profitably spend a day here, strolling cobbled pedestrian streets that open onto pretty café-lined squares and lingering in sites like the handsome Igreja de Jesus. Start at the tourist office, which is built atop Roman ruins discovered during a construction project; inside, you'll be standing above and peering down through the glass floor into a 5th-century fish-processing room. Near the port, an agreeable clutter of boats and warehouses is fronted by gardens, where you can stock up for a picnic at a huge indoor fish-and-produce market (Tuesday–Sunday 7–2).

GETTING HERE AND AROUND

Setúbal can be reached by bus from most of the locations in the Setúbal Peninsula and Lisbon. It's also the last stop of the Fertagus urban train, which has an hourly departure to and from Lisbon. The drive from Lisbon takes 35 minutes, and it's 10 minutes from either Palmela or Azeitão. If you're heading directly for Setúbal, take the northern route across the Rio Tejo via the Ponte Vasco da Gama, from which the fast A12 highway cuts south and avoids the bottleneck over the Ponte 25 de Abril.

Bus Contacts Setúbal bus station. ⊠ *Av. 5 de Outubro 44* ☎ *265/525051.*

Train Contacts Fertagus. ☎ *707/127127* ⊕ *www.fertagus.pt.*

VISITOR INFORMATION

Contacts Visit Setúbal. ⊠ *Casa da Baía, Av. Luísa Todi 468* ☎ *265/545010* ⊕ *www.visitsetubal.com.pt.*

EXPLORING

Convento de Arrábida. From Portinho da Arrábida, the lower, coastal road hugs the shore nearly all the way to Setúbal; the upper road leads to this ramshackle, white-walled, 16th-century monastery built into the hills of the Serra da Arrábida. The views from here are glorious, but you'll have to contact the tourist office in Setúbal in advance to arrange a visit. ⊠ *Setúbal.*

Igreja de Jesus (*Church of Jesus*). This 15th-century Church of Jesus, perhaps Portugal's earliest example of Manueline architecture, was built with local marble and later tiled with simple but affecting 17th-century azulejos. The architect was Diogo de Boitaca, whose work here predates his contribution to Lisbon's Mosteiro dos Jerónimos (Jerónimos Monastery). Six extraordinary twisted pillars support the vault; climb the narrow stairs to the balcony for a closer look at the details, which would soon become the very hallmark of Manueline style. Outside, you can still admire the original, although badly worn, main doorway and deplore the addition of a concrete expanse that makes the church square look like a roller-skating rink.

The church's original monastic buildings and Gothic cloister—on Rua Balneário Paula Borba—house the **Museu de Setúbal,** a museum with a fascinating collection of 15th- and 16th-century Portuguese paintings, several by the so-called Master of Setúbal. Other attractions include azulejos, local archaeological finds, and a coin collection. ⊠ *Praça Miguel Bombarda* ☎ *265/537890* ⊕ *www.visitsetubal.com.pt* ⊠ *Free (€1 suggested donation)* ☉ *Closed Mon.*

Fodor's Choice ★ **Portinho da Arrábida.** The main road through the Parque Natural da Arrábida is the N10, which you can leave at Vila Nogueira de Azeitão to travel south toward the small fishing village of Portinho da Arrábida, at the foot of the mountain range. The village is a popular destination for lisboetas, who appreciate the good local beaches, which are famous for their wonderfully clear blue-green waters and white sands that create a dramatic contrast with the green, pine-covered hills. In high summer, when the number of visitors makes parking nearly impossible, leave your car above the village and make the steep walk down to the water, where you'll find several modest seafood restaurants that overlook the port. ✉ *N10.*

Serra da Arrábidaú. Occupying the entire southern coast of the Setúbal Peninsula is the Parque Natural da Arrábida, dominated by the Serra da Arrábida—a 5,000-foot-high mountain range whose wild crags fall steeply to the sea. There's profuse plant life at these heights, particularly in spring, when the rocks are carpeted with wildflowers. The park is distinguished by a rich geological heritage and numerous species of mammals, birds, butterflies, and other insects. The park is a favorite destination for cyclists, horse riders, and hikers as well as adventure-sports enthusiasts. Setúbal's visitor information service can provide information on local groups and reputable guides. There are also some lovely hidden beaches for those prepared to put in the footwork. ✉ *Setúbal.*

WHERE TO EAT

$ PORTUGUESE FAMILY Fodor's Choice ★ 🍴 **Casa da Baía.** Delicious breakfasts, brunches, and afternoon teas with local-specialty cakes and pastries are served at this surprisingly affordable café. It's in an eye-catching blue-and-white building that also houses the Visit Setúbal information center and a small museum. You place your order at a small deli (well stocked with Moscatel and Península de Setúbal wines) and then take a seat inside, or head out to a vast outdoor space complete with comfy deck chairs and walls painted with colorful marine-themed artworks. Lunch dishes include some supersize toasties. There's a good selection of cocktails and local wines for those who fancy something stronger than tea or coffee. [$] *Average main: €10* ✉ *Av. Luísa Todi 468* ☎ *265/545010* 🌐 *www.mun-setubal.pt/pt/pagina/casa-da-baia/170.*

$ SPANISH 🍴 **El Toro.** This pretty little Spanish hacienda, right next to the bullfighting ring, is run by Spanish immigrant Alfonso Vasquez and his Portuguese wife, Zélia Marques. The food is regional Spanish, mixed with local Portuguese ingredients and prepared by Zélia herself in the open kitchen. It overlooks an enclosed outdoor terrace draped in flowering vines and hanging birdcages. The inside dining room is just as nice, with bright walls and colorful paintings. Try the *pontillitas* (fried baby squid) to start, followed by the *parrillada* (mixed grill of meat, chicken, and chorizo)—a half portion is big enough to feed two. Cap your meal with one of the couple's homemade liquors. The *alfarroba* (made from the sweet seed pod of the carob tree) is among the best. [$] *Average main: €13* ✉ *Rua António José Batista 111–115* ☎ *265/524995* 🕓 *Closed Wed.*

$ ✕ **Rebarca.** At the east end of Avenida Luisa Todi, Rebarca typifies the
SEAFOOD casual restaurants on "Choco Frito Row" that serve up inexpensive but
delicious fresh seafood—including the titular fried cuttlefish (it's similar
to a large, meaty fried squid). Some of the grilled favorites are *dourada*
(gilt-head bream), *robalo* (sea bass), and *peixe espada* (this literally
means swordfish but is actually scabbard fish). Enjoy a light seafood
lunch with a carafe of the local house white wine, which always has a
refreshingly light effervescence. $ *Average main: €14* ⊠ *Av. Luisa Todi
70* ☎ *265/221309* ⊘ *Closed Tues.*

SPORTS AND THE OUTDOORS

BOAT TOURS

FAMILY **Vertígem Azul.** The Sado Estuary is famous for its resident bottlenose
Fodor'sChoice dolphins, and several companies offer boat trips out from Setúbal to see
★ them at play. Vertígem Azul is easily the best of the bunch. Founded in
1998, the company takes an eco-friendly approach to all its water-based
activities, which also include bird-watching boat trips and evening wine
jaunts, accompanied by live music as the sun sets. Three-hour dolphin
observation trips leave Setúbal at 9:30 and 2:30 every day. ⊠ *Rua Praia
da Saúde 11* ☎ *265/238000* ⊕ *vertigemazul.com* ✉ *From €35.*

PENINSULA DE TRÓIA

20 mins from Setúbal by boat.

Across the estuary from Setúbal is the Peninsula de Tróia—a long spit
of land blessed with clean water and fine beaches on both the Sado and
the Atlantic side.

GETTING HERE AND AROUND

Car ferries and passenger catamarans to the peninsula run every 30–60
minutes (24 hours a day) from Setúbal's port and cost €6.55 (catamaran) and €3.25 (car ferry) per person. Catamaran passengers pay on
the way to Tróia but the return journey is free.

Contacts Atlantic Ferries. ⊠ *Doca do Comércio, Tróia* ☎ *265/235101* ⊕ *www.
atlanticferries.pt.*

VISITOR INFORMATION

Contacts Tróia Resort. ⊠ *Tróia–Carvalhal, Tróia* ☎ *265/105500* ⊕ *www.
troiaresort.net.*

EXPLORING

FAMILY **Peninsula de Tróiaú.** Sunseekers from Setúbal—and many from Lisbon—
make the trip to Tróia Peninsula when they want plenty of elbow room
on the beach. Here, soft white sands stretch for some 17 km (10½
miles), growing ever more secluded. Wooden walkways connect the
beaches with the docks and their resort, and while the first strands are
busy with sunseekers, beach bars, and stand-up paddlers, the remain-
der are incorporated into the Sado Nature Reserve, with its thick pine
forests and abundant wlldlife. Keep walking until you find your perfect
spot; there are plenty to choose from.

The peninsula was the site of a Roman town destroyed by a tidal wave
in the 5th century: you can visit its scant ruins, opposite the marina, if

you need a break from the beach scene. If you'd rather be out on the water, you can also take a boat tour from here to see bottlenose dolphins in the Sado estuary. ✉ *Peninsula de Tróia, Tróia.*

WHERE TO STAY

$$ RENTAL FAMILY **Aqualuz Suite Hotel Apartamentos Tróia Mar.** Facing the beach and Serra da Arrábida, Aqualuz is a three-tower complex that offers studio, one-, and two-bedroom apartments. **Pros:** a quick walk to beach; excellent views; ideal for families. **Cons:** gets very crowded in summer; paid parking; looking dated. [$] *Rooms from: €150* ✉ *Tróia–Carvalhal, Tróia* ☎ *265/499000* 🌐 *www.aqualuz.com* 🛏 *79 apartments* 🍴 *Breakfast.*

$$ HOTEL **Blue and Green Tróia Design Hotel.** With an eye-catching wave design, this large hotel sits directly opposite the marina and has a wealth of facilities as well as easy access to beaches and boat trips. **Pros:** on the beach and next to the shops and ferry marina; great mountain views; spacious rooms. **Cons:** in need of refurbishment; large, ostentatious hotel unlikely to appeal to nature lovers; fees apply for sauna and steam room. [$] *Rooms from: €160* ✉ *Marina de Tróia–Carvalhal, Tróia* ☎ *265/498000* 🌐 *www.troiadesignhotel.com* 🛏 *125 rooms* 🍴 *Breakfast.*

SPORTS AND THE OUTDOORS

Troia Golf. What Robert Trent Jones had in mind when he laid out Troia back in 1981 is sometimes hard to figure out. Built on a peninsula close to the sea, the course has a strategic layout requiring a great deal of thought and first-class shot making, but it might create too much of a test for the average player to find totally enjoyable. Nevertheless, it's ranked highly in several lists of the best courses in Europe. A lot of sand, maritime pines, and flora make for a very beautiful setting. The course is accessible by ferry from Setúbal, which is a much shorter journey than by road around the Sado Estuary. A handicap certificate is required. ✉ *Complexo Turistico de Troia, Carvalhal* ☎ *265/494112* 🌐 *www.troiagolf.com* 🎫 *€85 weekdays, €102 weekends* ⛳ *18 holes, 6911 yds, par 72* ✍ *Reservations essential.*

VILA NOGUEIRA DE AZEITÃO

14 km (8½ miles) west of Setúbal.

The region around the small town of Vila Nogueira de Azeitão, on the western side of the Serra da Arrábida, retains a disproportionately large number of fine manor houses and palaces. In earlier times, many of the country's noblemen maintained country estates here, deep in the heart of a wealthy wine-making region. Wines made here by the José Maria da Fonseca Company are some of the most popular in the country (and one of Portugal's major exports); the best known is the fortified dessert wine called Moscatel de Setúbal.

GETTING HERE AND AROUND

Azeitão can be reached by the TST buses, from Lisbon (754, 755), Setúbal (230, 754, 755, 767, 783), Palmela (767), and Sesimbra (208, 230). Driving from Palmela or Setúbal takes about 10–15 minutes. From Lisbon it will be about a 30-minute drive.

VISITOR INFORMATION

Contacts **Azeitão Town Hall.** ⊠ *Rua José Augusto Coelho 27* ☎ *212/180729.*

EXPLORING

José Maria da Fonseca Company. For a close look at the wine business, seek out the original headquarters of the José Maria da Fonseca Company; their manor house and cellars stand on the main road through town. The intriguing tours talk about the long history of the winery and allow you to see all stages of production, including a peek into their dark and mysterious prized Moscatel cellars, where 200-plus year-old bottles are still aging gracefully. The tour takes around 20–40 minutes, depending on the size of the group, and at the end you are brought to their wineshop, where select products and be tasted and bought. ⊠ *Rua José Augusto Coelho 11–13* ☎ *212/198940* ⊕ *www.jmf.pt* 🍷 *Free.*

NEED A BREAK

Fábrica de Tortas Azeitonense. Aside from great cheese and wine, visitors should be sure to sample the local sweet treat, *tortas de azeitão*, little rolled tortes filled with an egg-and-cinnamon custard. Fábrica de Tortas Azeitonense started making this regional delicacy along with other varieties of egg-custard pastries in 1995 and are now the best-known producers in the area. Their main factory and café shop is on the main road in town (N10), just before the roundabout headed toward Coina, on the right. Stop in after lunch to savor some delicious tortas with a Portuguese *café*, and then buy a box of them to enjoy later. ⊠ *N10, Km 17, Setúbal* ☎ *212/190418* ⊕ *www.tortasdeazeitao.com.*

Quinta da Bacalhoa. The jewel in the crown of this late-16th-century L-shape mansion is its box-hedged garden and striking azulejo-lined paths. Although the grand home here is a private residence, visitors can take tours of the gardens—bookings are necessary, and can be made online. Among the highlights are three pyramidal towers—including the so-called Casa do Fresco, which houses the country's oldest azulejo panel. Dating to 1565, it depicts the story of Susannah and the Elders. Scattered elsewhere are Moorish-influenced panels, fragrant groves of fruit trees, and enough restful spots to while away an afternoon. ⊠ *4 km (2½ miles) east of Vila Nogueira de Azeitão on N1* ☎ *212/198060* ⊕ *www.bacalhoa.com* 🍷 *Weekdays €4, Sat. €8* ☉ *Closed Sun.*

SHOPPING

Azulejos de Azeitão. Stop here if you're eager to get your hands on some of those decorative and distinctive Portuguese tiles. The company uses traditional European methods to sketch, fabricate, hand-paint, and glaze each of the tiles sold in the shop. Reproduction Portuguese styles and murals range from the 16th to the 19th century (Spanish, Islamic, Hispano-Moorish, French, Italian, English, and Dutch styles from similar periods are also available). Choose from premade selections or design your own to be made and framed. They ship to the United States. ⊠ *Rua dos Trabalhadores da Empresa Setubalense 15* ✛ *To get to the store from Azeitão, follow N10 to the split with N379 and bear right, staying on N10; the turnoff is the second left* ☎ *212/180013* ⊕ *www. azulejosdeazeitao.com* ☉ *Closed Mon.*

Mercado do Azeitão. Vila Nogueira de Azeitão's agricultural traditions are trumpeted on the first Sunday of every month, when a country market is held in the center of town. Apart from the locally produced wine, you can buy *queijo fresco* (light, soft cheese made from cow, sheep, or goat milk) and the renowned local *queijo de Azeitão,* a handmade D.O.P. (Designated Product of Origin) certified cheese made from sheep milk and cured for a period of 20–40 days. This short curing process gives the cheese a very soft and creamy *amanteigado* (butterlike) texture, and it should be served like butter. It's sold in small rounds of various sizes; slice the top rind off and spoon the spread on a big hunk of excellent fresh bread from one of the market's bakery stalls. ■ TIP→ **You can buy everything you need here to make the perfect picnic lunch.** ⊠ *Vila Nogueira de Azeitão.*

SESIMBRA

40 km (25 miles) south of Lisbon; 30 km (18 miles) southwest of Setúbal.

Sesimbra, a lively fishing village surrounded by mountains and isolated bays and coves, is a popular day trip for lisboetas. And, despite high-rise apartments that now mar the approaches to the town, its surviving narrow, central streets reflect a traditional past. Moreover, the long beach is lovely, if a little crowded in high summer, and the calm waters are perfect for swimming (the coveted Blue Flag was raised here in 2016). The waterfront is guarded by a 17th-century fortress and overlooked by outdoor restaurants serving fresh fish. A short walk along the coast to the west takes you to the main port, littered with nets, anchors, and coils of rope and packed with fishing boats—which unload their catches at entertaining auctions. You can also take a 40-minute walk to the hilltop remains of a Moorish castle northwest of town—the grounds have jaw-dropping views over the sea, beaches, and surrounding Serra da Arrabida.

GETTING HERE AND AROUND

Sesimbra can be reached by the TST buses from several locations in the Setúbal Peninsula, including Setúbal (230), Azeitão (208), and Cacilhas (203). Bus 207 will take you to and from Lisbon. The driving time from Lisbon and Setúbal is 35 minutes. Coming from Azeitão will take 20 minutes.

Contacts Sesimbra bus station. ⊠ *Av. da Liberdade* ☎ *212/233071.*

VISITOR INFORMATION

Contacts Sesimbra Tourist Office. ⊠ *Forteleza do Santiago, Rua da Forteleza* ☎ *212/288540* ⊕ *visitsesimbra.pt.*

EXPLORING

Cabo Espichel. This salt-encrusted headland—crowned by a whitewashed convent surrounded by 18th-century pilgrim rest houses—is the southwestern point of the Setúbal Peninsula, marked by a red-and-white lighthouse. It's a ruggedly beautiful spot, where the cliffs rise hundreds of feet out of the stormy Atlantic. To the north, unsullied beaches extend as far as Caparica, with only local roads and footpaths connecting them.

There are six buses a day here from Sesimbra, and a small café greets those who make the trip. ✉ *Cabo Espichel.*

Castelo de Sesimbra. Sitting high above the city is the Castelo de Sesimbra, which was conquered in 1165 by Dom Afonso Henriques but fell back into the hands of the Moors until 1200. The castle lost importance and fell into disrepair during the next several hundred years until Dom João IV ordered that it be adapted for the use of artillery in 1648. Classified as a National Monument, reconstruction was done to restore it to its previous glory after the great earthquake of 1755. Follow the signs on the road that splits off right before arriving in Sesimbra and it will take you straight up to the castle. Aside from the incredible views of the ocean and the city of Sesimbra below, there is a chapel, a small photo museum in the front tower, and a café with an outdoor patio, where you can enjoy an afternoon coffee or a *bagaço* (a clear Portuguese liquor) as the sun goes down. ✉ *Castelo de Sesimbra, Rua Nossa Senhora do Castelo 11.*

WHERE TO EAT

$ SEAFOOD Fodor's Choice ★

🍴 **Café Filipe.** Set in a line of sidewalk restaurants overlooking the waterfront, the Filipe is always busy with diners digging into the terrific grilled fish, cooked outside on a charcoal grill, or arroz de marisco. There's no nicer spot for lunch, and you may have to wait in line for a table—but it's worth it. [$] *Average main: €15* ✉ *Av. 25 de Abril* ☎ *212/231653* 🌐 *www.restaurantefilipe.com.*

$$$ SEAFOOD Fodor's Choice ★

🍴 **Praia Mar.** Though not right on the ocean, this is the best restaurant in the area for seafood lovers. The menu is extensive and offers a wide variety of mixed shellfish or grilled fish platters to share in every size and price range. Try regional favorites, such as *sapateira recheada* (whole stuffed stone crab), *santola* (spider crab), *lagosta* (spiny lobster), and langostines, which look a bit like crawfish but are much bigger and taste more like lobster. The shellfish comes broken down into smaller pieces, which you can easily crack open with the little hammer and board provided. You can sit indoors or take a seat on the covered esplanade. ■ TIP→ **The restaurant doesn't take reservations, so come early to avoid the line that forms very quickly.** [$] *Average main: €25* ✉ *Rua Afonso Henriques 16* ☎ *212/234176* 🌐 *www.praiamar.com.*

WHERE TO STAY

$ B&B/INN

🏨 **Casa da Terrina.** This cute 19th-century country house turned bed-and-breakfast is in the village of Quintola de Santana, a five-minute drive up the hill from Sesimbra beach. **Pros:** friendly staff; beautiful location; great homemade breakfast. **Cons:** minimal amenities; only two rooms have double beds; not close to the beach. [$] *Rooms from: €85* ✉ *Estrada Quintola de Santana, Quintola de Santana* ☎ *212/680264* 💳 *No credit cards* ⏲ *Closed late Oct.–Apr.* 🛏 *5 rooms* 🍴 *Breakfast.*

$ RENTAL Fodor's Choice ★

🏨 **Quinta do Miguel.** This gated farm in the small village of Aldeia do Meco—just 12 km (7 miles) northwest of Sesimbra—is perfect for a romantic getaway. **Pros:** minutes from the beach but hidden among the pretty forest; private and peaceful; nice staff. **Cons:** car is necessary; a bit difficult to find; not good if you don't want to be around animals. [$] *Rooms from: €130* ✉ *Rua Do Casalinho, Aldeia do Meco* ☎ *212/684607* 🌐 *www.quintadomiguel.com* 💳 *No credit cards* 🛏 *8 units* 🍴 *No meals.*

$$ HOTEL FAMILY **Sana Park Sesimbra.** This modern hotel is directly across from the beach and very centrally located, close to the best seafood restaurants and within easy walking distance of the town's fortress. **Pros:** right on main drag; excellent views of the beach; nice outdoor pool. **Cons:** paid parking; rooms get outside noise. [$] *Rooms from: €140* ✉ *Av. 25 de Abril* ☎ *212/289000* 🌐 *www.sesimbra.sanahotels.com* 🛏 *103 rooms* 🍴 *Breakfast.*

$$ HOTEL FAMILY **Sesimbra Hotel & Spa.** This hotel sits on a cliff just above the beachfront and is the only one in the area with a spa. **Pros:** great beachfront location; beautiful views of the ocean and surrounding hills; large rooms and lots of comfortable common areas. **Cons:** the building's lower floors are occupied by an apartment complex; 10-minute walk to the historic center. [$] *Rooms from: €150* ✉ *Praça da Califórnia* ☎ *212/289800* 🌐 *www.sesimbrahotelspa.com* 🛏 *100 rooms* 🍴 *Breakfast.*

SPORTS AND THE OUTDOORS

Sesimbra, a deep-sea-fishing center, is renowned for the huge swordfish that are landed in the area. It's also a top spot for diving, hang gliding, and other adventurous pursuits. The tourist information office at the beachfront can provide details and book lessons and excursions.

FISHING

Clube Naval de Sesimbra. The Clube Naval de Sesimbra offers coastal fishing trips most Saturdays. ✉ *Av. dos Naufragos 143* ☎ *212/233451* 🌐 *www.naval-sesimbra.pt.*

SCUBA DIVING

Nautilus-Sub. Established since the mid-1980s, this PADI-accredited school offers dives and courses at every level, including baptisms and children's dive classes. ✉ *Porto de Abrigo 1* 🌐 *www.nautilus-sub.com.*

ESTREMADURA
AND THE
RIBATEJO

Updated by
Alison Roberts
and Alexandre
Bezerra

Estremadura and the Ribatejo are the two historical provinces north and northeast of Lisbon. Estremadura, with its green rural valleys, is characterized by a mix of maritime activities and where old traditions and feelings combine harmoniously with modernity. Meanwhile, on the banks of the Tagus River, Ribatejo is a land of agriculture and livestock, known as the heart of Portuguese bullfighting and a bastion of the famous Lusitano horse.

Water shapes the character of these two provinces. Estremadura stretches itself out along the coast, extending north from Lisbon to include the onetime royal residence of Leiria, 119 kilometers (74 miles) from the capital. Closely tied to the sea, the narrow province is known for its fine beaches, coastal pine forests, and picturesque fishing villages. Some of these have evolved, for better or worse, into popular resorts. Fruits and vegetables grow in fertile coastal valleys, and livestock contentedly graze in rich pastures. But Estremadura hasn't always been so peaceful. During the Wars of Reconquest, which raged from the 8th through the 13th century, it was the scene of a series of bloody encounters between Christians and Moors. The province's name means "farthest from the Douro River," an indication of how far south of the Douro River the Christians had advanced against the Moors. In the aftermath of the wars, Portuguese sovereignty was secured with the defeat of the Spanish at Aljubarrota in 1385 and the turning back of Napoléon's forces in 1810 at Torres Vedras. The bloodshed left behind masterpieces of religious architecture—such as those at Alcobaça and Batalha—which commemorate Portuguese triumphs.

Over the centuries Romans, Visigoths, Moors, and Christians built and rebuilt various castles and fortifications to protect the strategic Tagus River (Rio Tejo). Fine examples of this are along the river at Belver, Abrantes, and Almourol. Spanning the banks of the Rio Nabão (a tributary of the Tagus), Tomar is dominated by the hilltop Convento de Cristo (Convent of Christ), built in the 12th century by the Knights Templar. In the brush-covered hills at the province's western edge lies Fátima, one of Christendom's most important pilgrimage sites. As it flows south approaching Lisbon (Lisboa), the Tagus expands, often overflowing its banks during the winter rains, and the landscape changes to one of rich meadows and pastures and broad, alluvial plains, where grains grow in abundance.

The Ribatejo region developed along both sides of the Tagus, and it is this waterway, born in the mountains of Spain, that has shaped and sustained the province. In the north, inhabitants tend groves of olive and fig trees in a peaceful landscape that has changed little since Roman times. Ribatejans are said to be more reserved than their fellow Portuguese—that is, until they step into the arena to test their mettle against

TOP REASONS TO GO

Soak up the pleasures of the Atlantic Coast. Forty unique beaches dot Estremadura's 100-km (60-mile) coastline, allowing for a variety of choices, including relaxing in the sun and sand, catching the waves, or watching the sunset.

Experience the Middle Ages. Cities like Mafra, Tomar, Alcobaça Batalha, and Leiria boast medieval monasteries and castles, and royal palaces that provide an incredible view of times past.

Savor the freshest seafood. The fishing towns of Ericeira, Peniche,

and Nazaré are some of the best places in the country for seafood lovers.

Admire Portugal's beautiful countryside. The landscape along the Tagus and Zêzere Rivers is a perfect venue to experience the culture of the Portuguese countryside.

Horseback riding with famous horses. The Ribatejo is home to the famous breed of Lusitano horses, used in dressage and bullfighting.

a ton or so of charging bull. This is bullfighting country, the heartland of one of Portugal's richest and most colorful traditions. On the vast plains along the east bank of the Tagus, you'll encounter men on horseback carrying long wooden prods and often wearing the traditional waistcoats and stocking caps of their trade. These are *campinos,* the Portuguese "cowboys," who tend the herds of bulls and horses bred and trained for arenas throughout the country.

ORIENTATION AND PLANNING

GETTING ORIENTED

The sea is never far from sight in coast-hugging Estremadura, especially in fishing towns like Nazaré and Peniche. The same holds true for the lively town of Ericeira, where surfing also reigns supreme with its big waves. Coastal valleys witnessed many bloody battles between rival groups, including the Moors, but from them came extraordinary monasteries, such as the ones in Batalha and Alcobaça, built to celebrate Portuguese victories.

The Tagus River flows through the Ribatejo, where vast plains spread out from the riverbanks. The region is dotted with monuments and fortifications that emulate the country's religious history, from the impressive Convento do Cristo of the Knights Templar in Tomar, a UNESCO World Heritage Site, to the most famous pilgrimage site, the sanctuary in Fátima.

Estremadura. North of Lisbon, this area, which borders the Atlantic, is a coastal paradise of endless beaches, spectacular cliffs, and pastoral coastal valleys. You can sample delicious seafood and wines, and see some of the most beautiful monasteries and picturesque castles in Portugal.

The Ribatejo. To the east of Lisbon, the Tagus River valley is filled with lush farmland, vineyards, and cork forests, and is rich in old-world tradition and country hospitality.

PLANNING

WHEN TO GO

To avoid the busloads of visitors who inundate major monuments and attractions during July and August, visit the popular ones such as Óbidos and Mafra in the early morning. ■ TIP→ **Throughout Portugal, all state-run museums and monuments have free admission on the first Sunday of the month.**

This also helps to beat the oppressive summer heat, particularly inland. The best time of year for touring is in early spring and from mid-September until late October. The climate during this period is pleasant, and attractions and restaurants aren't crowded. If throngs of people don't bother you, time your visit to Fátima to coincide with May 13, when between 500,000 and 1 million pilgrims overwhelm this otherwise sleepy country town. Less spectacular pilgrimages take place year-round.

GETTING HERE AND AROUND

AIR TRAVEL

Estremadura and the Ribatejo are served by Lisbon's Aeroporto Humberto Delgado, 7 km (4½ miles) north of the city.

No trains run directly between the airport and Estremadura and the Ribatejo, but you can catch trains to several towns in the region from Lisbon's Oriente or Santa Apolónia stations, or suburban Agualva-Cacém. Very few regional buses make stops at the airport; most start instead from Campo Grande station, a short taxi ride from the airport. If you are landing in Lisbon and traveling directly to this area, your best bet may be to rent a car.

Airport Contacts Lisbon Airport. ☏ *21/841–3500, 21/841–3700 for flight info* ⊕ *www.aeroportolisboa.pt/en/lis/home.*

BUS TRAVEL

There are few places, if any, in this region which aren't served by at least one bus daily. Express coaches, usually with free Wi-Fi, run by national operator Rede Expressos travel regularly between Lisbon's Sete Rios bus stations and the larger towns such as Santarém, Leiria, and Abrantes, while various regional companies ply those routes and others, many of them from Campo Grande station in Lisbon. If you have the time and patience, bus travel is an inexpensive way to get around. If you know some Portuguese, you can also get a schedule and fee information on regional operators by calling the bus stations or checking out the companies' websites; in the case of Rede Expressos, its English website makes it easy to buy tickets with a credit card or PayPal.

Bus Contacts Barraqueiro Oeste. ☏ *21/758–2212 for Campo Grande station in Lisbon, 261/334150 for Torres Vedras* ⊕ *www.barraqueiro-oeste.pt.* **Boa Viagem (Ribatejo).** ☏ *263/730500, 707/201371* ⊕ *www.boa-viagem.pt.* **Mafrense (Estremadura).** ☏ *21/758–2212 for Campo Grande station in Lisbon,*

261/816152 for Mafra, 707/201371 ⊕ www.mafrense.pt. **Rede Expressos.**
☎ 707/223344 ⊕ www.rede-expressos.pt. **Ribatejana (Ribatejo).** ☎ 21/758–
2212 for Campo Grande station in Lisbon, 707/201371 ⊕ www.ribatejana.pt.
Rodoviária do Oeste (Estremadura). ☎ 262/831067 for Caldas da Rainha,
707/200334 ⊕ www.rodoviariadooeste.pt. **Rodoviária do Tejo.** ☎ 249/810704
for Torres Novas, 707/200334 ⊕ www.rodotejo.pt.

CAR TRAVEL

It's easy to reach Estremadura and the Ribatejo from Lisbon, because
both provinces begin as extensions of the city's northern suburbs. There
are two principal access roads from the capital: the A1 (also called E80
and IP1), which is the Lisbon–Porto toll road, provides the best inland
access; the A8 (also called IC1) is the fastest route to the coast. From
Porto there's easy access via the A1.

The roads are generally good, and traffic is light, except for weekend
congestion along the coast. There are no confusing big cities in which
to get lost, although parking can be a problem in some of the towns.
Hotels don't usually charge for parking. Drive with extreme caution.
Affable as they are on foot, the Portuguese are among Europe's most
aggressive drivers.

Car Rental Contacts Avis. ☎ 244/827131 for Leiria, 243/306780 for Santarém,
808/202038 ⊕ www.avis.com. **Hertz.** ☎ 21/942–6300 for Lisbon, 241/379767
for Abrantes, 262/889530 for Caldas da Rainha, 21/942–6300 for Leiria,
243/350920 for Santarém, 249/310820 for Tomar, 261/327717 for Torres Vedras
⊕ www.hertz.pt.

TRAIN TRAVEL

Travel by train within central Portugal isn't for people in a hurry. Service
to many of the more remote destinations is infrequent—and in some
cases nonexistent. Even major attractions such as Nazaré and Mafra
have no direct rail links. Nevertheless, trains will take you to most of
the strategic bases for touring the towns in this chapter.

The main line between Lisbon (Santa Apolónia and Oriente stations)
and Porto provides reasonably frequent service to Vila Franca de Xira,
Santarém, Tomar, and Fátima. Towns in the western part of the region,
such as Torres Vedras, Caldas da Rainha, Óbidos, and Leiria, are served
on another line to Figueira da Foz from Lisbon's Santa Apolónia station,
via Entrecampos and Agualva-Cacém (which is also a stop on the Sintra
line that runs from Lisbon's Rossio station).

Train Contacts CP. ☎ 707/201280, 808/208208 from Portugal only ⊕ www.cp.pt.

RESTAURANTS

Between mid-June and mid-September, reservations are advised at
upscale restaurants. Most moderate or inexpensive establishments,
however, don't accept reservations. They also have informal dining
rooms, where you may occasionally find yourself sharing a table with
other diners. Dress is casual at all but the most luxurious places.

In Estremadura restaurants, the emphasis is on fish, including the ubiquitous *bacalhau* (dried salt cod) and *caldeirada* (a hearty fish stew). The
seaside resorts of Ericeira, Nazaré, and Peniche are famous for lobster.
In Santarém and other spots along the Rio Tejo, an *açorda* (bread soup)

made with *sável,* a river fish also known as shad, is popular, as are *enguias* (eels) prepared in a variety of ways. Pork is a key component in Ribatejo dishes, and roast lamb and kid are widely enjoyed. Perhaps the result of a sweets-making tradition developed by nuns in the region's once-numerous convents, dessert menus abound with colorful-sounding—although often cloyingly sweet and eggy—dishes such as *queijinhos do céu* (little cheeses from heaven). The straw-color white wines from the Ribatejo district of Bucelas are among the country's finest. *Prices in the reviews are the average cost of a main course at dinner or, if dinner isn't served, at lunch.*

HOTELS

Estremadura has plenty of good-quality lodgings, especially along the coast; the Ribatejo is less well endowed. In summer, you need reservations. Most establishments offer substantial off-season discounts. Accommodations are classed as hotels if they have the requisite facilities, or as *alojamento local* (local lodging) if they are more basic. In this region, only the towns of Óbidos and Ourém can boast *pousadas*—formerly state-run, now privately run inns in historical buildings. Reserving well in advance is essential for these accommodations. There are also a number of high-quality, government-approved private guesthouses. Look for signs reading "Turismo Rural" or "Turismo de Habitação." *Prices in the reviews are the lowest cost of a standard double room in high season. For expanded hotel reviews, visit Fodors.com.*

WHAT IT COSTS IN EUROS			
$	**$$**	**$$$**	**$$$$**
Restaurants	under €16	€16–€20	€21–€25	over €25
Hotels	under €140	€141–€200	€201–€260	over €260

Restaurant prices are per person for a main course at dinner. Hotel prices are for a standard double room, including tax, in high season (off-season rates may be lower).

TOUR OPTIONS

ORIENTATION TOURS

Few regularly scheduled sightseeing tours originate within the region, but many of the major attractions are covered by a wide selection of half-day, one-day, or short package tours from Lisbon. Carristur does a half-day Fátima tour from Lisbon for €65 (€59 online); it departs Praça do Comércio at 9:30 am daily from May to October, and Monday, Thursday, Friday, and Saturday from November through April. Other companies' tours tend to start from Praça Marques de Pombal. For Fátima, Dianatours has a €40 half-day trip departing Campo Grande, Tuesday through Saturday from April to October (except the 13th of the month) at 9 am. Their rival Rota Monumental offers a €62 full-day tour taking in Fátima, Nazaré, Óbidos, and Batalha, departing daily at 9 am, while Inside Lisbon does Fátima, Óbidos, and sights in between for €64. For still more of Estremadura, Cityrama has a three-day "Wonders of

GREAT ITINERARIES

Three days will give you a sense of the region, five days will allow you to include a visit to the shrine at Fátima and the Convent of Christ, and a full week will give you enough time to cover the major attractions as well as explore the countryside. With additional days you can easily extend your itinerary to include Évora and the Alentejo or head north to Coimbra and the Beiras. It's best to explore these regions by car, unless you have a great deal of time and patience: trains don't serve many of the most interesting towns, and bus travel is slow.

IF YOU HAVE 3 DAYS

Start with a visit to the imposing monastery and palace at **Mafra,** then head for the coast, with a stop at the resort and fishing village of **Ericeira.** Continue north along the shore to **Peniche,** with its imposing fortress. Head inland to spend the night in the enchanting walled city of **Óbidos.** The next morning continue north, stopping at ceramics shops in **Caldas da Rainha.** En route to **Nazaré,** tour the church and cloister at **Alcobaça.** On your third day head inland to the soaring,

multispired monastery church in **Batalha.** Return to Lisbon.

IF YOU HAVE 5 DAYS

Follow the three-day itinerary to **Batalha,** and then continue north to **Leiria** and its hilltop castle. Take N113 east to the A1 and drive down to **Fátima,** one of Christendom's most renowned destinations. The next morning, continue east on N113 to **Tomar,** an attractive town dominated by its hilltop convent. Later in the day, follow N110 south and then take N358-2, a scenic road that follows the Rio Zêzere, to its union with the Rio Tejo. Just west of their confluence, on an island in the Tejo, is the **Castelo de Almourol,** one of Portugal's finest castles. From here, follow N118 southwest along the Tejo, stopping in **Alpiarça** to visit the Casa dos Patudos, a large country house containing the art collection of its former owner, and in **Almeirim** to see the winery at the Quinta da Alorna. Spend the night in **Santarém,** an important farming and livestock center with many fine sights. The next day return to Lisbon with a drive along the Tejo on N118 through the region of marshy plains known as the Lezíria.

Portugal" tour whose first two days take in many of the province's top sights. Most tour companies can also do made-to-measure group tours.

For private half- and full-day tours, with or without a visit to or more one of the region's charming wineries, there's Have a Wine Day, also based in Lisbon.

Contacts Carristur. ☎ 96/629–8558 (mobile), 21/347–8030 ⊕ www.yellowbustours.com. **Cityrama Gray Line Portugal.** ✉ Parque Eduardo VII, Praça Marquês de Pombal, Marquês de Pombal ☎ 21/352–2594 for ticket kiosk, 800/208513 (free in Portugal), 21/319–1090 for reservations, 21/319–1091 for reservations ⊕ www.cityrama.pt. **Dianatours.** ☎ 21/799–8540, 93/681–4154 (mobile) ⊕ dianatours.pt. **Have a Wine Day.** ☎ 91/647–0995 (mobile) ⊕ www.en.haveawineday.com. **Inside Lisbon.** ☎ 96/8412612 (mobile), 646/257–4042 in the U.S., 21/191–4545 ⊕ www.insidelisbon.com. **Rota Monumental.** ☎ 91/630–6682 (24 hrs) ⊕ www.rotamonumental.com.

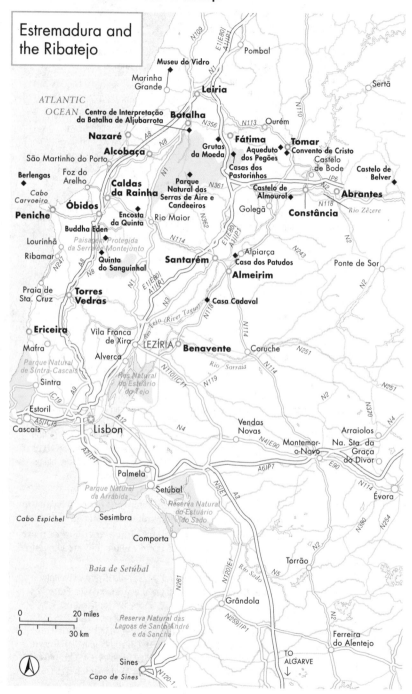

Estremadura and the Ribatejo

ATLANTIC
OCEAN

Museu do Vidro

Marinha
Grande

Leiria

Centro de Interpretação
da Batalha de Aljubarrota   **Batalha**

N356   N113   Ourém

Nazaré

Alcobaça   **Grutas**   **Fátima**   **Tomar**
            da Moeda   **Aqueduto**   **Convento de Cristo**
São Martinho do Porto   **dos Pegões**   Castelo
                        Casas dos   de Bode
Berlengas   Foz do   **Pastorinhos**   **Castelo de**
        Arelho   **Belver**
Cabo   **Caldas**   **Parque**   **Castelo de**
Carvoeiro   **da Rainha**   **Natural das**   **Almourol**   **Abrantes**
        Serras de Aire e   **Constância**
Óbidos   **Candeeiros**   Golegã
    Encosta   Rio Maior   Rio Zêzere
Peniche   **da Quinta**
        Buddha Eden
Lourinhã   Paisagem Protegida
        da Serra de Montejunto   Alpiarça
Ribamar   **Quinta**   **Santarém**   **Casa dos Patudos**   Ponte de Sor
        do Sanguinhal
                Almeirim
Praia de   **Torres**
Sta. Cruz   **Vedras**
                Casa Cadaval
Ericeira   Vila Franca
        de Xira
Mafra   **LEZÍRIA**   **Benavente**   Coruche
        Alverca   Rio Sorraia
Parque Natural
de Sintra-Cascais   Ros Natural
        do Estuário
Sintra   do Tejo
Estoril   Vendas   Arraiolos
Cascais   **Lisbon**   Novas   Montemor-   Na. Sta. da
                    o-Novo   Graça
                            do Divor
        Palmela   Évora
Parque Natural   Setúbal
da Arrábida   Reserva Natural
Cabo Espichel   Sesimbra   do Estuário
            do Sado
        Comporta

Baia de Setúbal

| 0 | | 20 miles |
| 0 | | 30 km |

Reserva Natural das
Lagoas de Santo André
e da Sancha

            Grândola

                        TO
                        ALGARVE
Sines   Ferreira
Capo de Sines   do Alentejo

ESTREMADURA

The narrow province surrounding Lisbon and extending north along the coast for approximately 160 km (100 miles) is known as Estremadura, referring to the extreme southern border of the land the Portuguese reconquered from the Moors. This is primarily a rural region, characterized by coastal fishing villages and small farming communities that produce mostly fruit and olives. A tour through the region includes visits to towns with some of Portugal's most outstanding architectural treasures, including Mafra, Alcobaça, Óbidos, Tomar, and Batalha.

ERICEIRA

11 km (7 miles) northwest of Mafra.

Ericeira, an old fishing town tucked into the rocky coast, is a popular seaside resort. Its core fans out from the sheer cliff, beneath which boats are hauled up onto a small, sheltered beach. The growth of summer tourism has caused a proliferation of bars, pubs, discos, pizzerias, and the like in the increasingly gentrified but still-attractive town center. But along the waterfront are a number of traditional seafood restaurants that are popular with both locals and visitors. Either end of the town has good sand for sunbathing; the south end is preferred by surfers, but about 2 km (1¼ miles) north of Ericeira is Ribeira d'Ilhas, one of Portugal's best surfing beaches. In 2009, Ericeira was declared Europe's first World Surfing Reserve by a global campaign to protect such destinations.

Perched atop the cliffs, the town's historic center is a beautiful place to walk around and explore, as it has completely maintained the traditional Portuguese coastal architecture that was popular in the 17th and 18th centuries when the fishing village really thrived. The buildings are all sandblasted white and framed with deep sea blues. The main fishing port in the center is also where the Portuguese royal family departed to exile in 1910 after the Republic was declared, not to return for a couple of generations.

GETTING HERE AND AROUND

There are several daily bus lines between Ericeira, Mafra, and Lisbon run by Mafrense. Driving from Lisbon is close to 45 minutes, and getting to Ericeira from Mafra takes 15 minutes.

ESSENTIALS

Bus Contact Bus Station. ☒ *Rua dos Bombeiros Voluntários / N247* ☎ *261/862717 for Mafrense* ⊕ *www.mafrense.pt.*

Visitor Information Ericeira. ☒ *Rua Eduardo Burnay 46* ☎ *261/863122* ⊕ *www.cm-mafra.pt/en/tourism.*

BEACHES

Ribeira d'Ilhas. One of Europe's best beaches for surfing—at pretty much any time of year—Ribeira d'Ilhas regularly hosts national and world championships. So when the surf is up on weekends, expect a crowd to gather. There's a large, modern restaurant with esplanade and disabled access. The beach is 2 km (1¼ miles) north of Ericeira, set in a picturesque gorge amid tall cane. The **Pocean Surf Academy** (☎ *91/217–5051* 🌐 *www.pocean.pt*) here will coach everyone from beginners to experts. **Amenities:** food and drink; parking; toilets; water sports. **Best for:** partiers; sunset; surfing. ✉ *Off N247.*

WHERE TO EAT

$$$ SEAFOOD 🍴 **Esplanada Furnas.** Perched on rocks overlooking the open Atlantic, on the site of a former shellfish nursery, this long-established but still fashionable restaurant offers some of the best seafood in the area. As you'd expect, the day's menu depends on the sea's bounty, but it might have *salmonete* (red mullet), *pregado* (turbot), *robalo* (sea bass), or *linguado* (sole). Alternatively, opt for a cataplana of fish stew for two, or even a juicy steak. Families tend to dominate on weekends, when both indoor and outdoor dining areas fill up; there's a more formal atmosphere at dinner during the week. If you're looking for something cheaper but still with good-quality seafood, sister restaurant Marisqueira Furnas—with more of a beer-hall atmosphere—is a few steps away. [$] *Average main: €23* ✉ *Rua das Furnas 2* ☎ *261/864870* 🌐 *www.restaurantefurnasericeira.com.*

$$ SEAFOOD 🍴 **Mar à Vista.** This revived Portuguese fisherman's tavern has a genuine feel—fishing nets and baskets hang from walls, and the loud service adds to its character. Seafood is the only option but it is renowned here, and many diners come for the *arroz de marisco* (shellfish and rice stew) or grilled fish. For afters, the options are limited to lemon sorbet and coffee. [$] *Average main: €19* ✉ *Rua Santo António 16* ☎ *261/862928* 💳 *No credit cards* ⏲ *Closed Wed., 2 wks in May, and 2 wks in Sept.* ✍ *Reservations essential.*

$$$ SEAFOOD 🍴 **Marisqueira Ribas.** This is your typical Portuguese marisqueira—large and noisy with family-style seating and the hammering and cracking of crab shells. Overlooking the harbor with indoor and outdoor tables, the restaurant greets you with beautiful murals of Ericeira's harbor and a huge display of fresh shellfish. Crabs and lobsters can be ordered individually, priced by the kilo or piled upon a large *mariscada* (mixed seafood platter) with clams, mussels, shrimp, and other native mollusks. The dish is served with warm, toasted bread and can be shared between two or more people. The heaps of empty shells piled on plates are testimony to the feasts that have taken place. [$] *Average main: €25* ✉ *Rua Mendes Leal 32* ☎ *261/865864* ⏲ *Closed Thurs., and 2 wks in Oct.*

$ PORTUGUESE-SEAFOOD 🍴 **O Gabriel.** This little family-run restaurant opposite the Vila Galé draws much of its custom from that and other local hotels, thanks to its fresh seafood and fish—the latter grilled over charcoal by the owner right out front. The two dozen seats in the white-tiled dining room are matched by a similar number on the sheltered terrace. In winter and spring, O Gabriel normally opens only for lunch (except for the odd weekend); in August, you'd do best to reserve. [$] *Average main: €10* ✉ *Praça dos Navegantes* ☎ *261/863 349, 91/961–6774 (mobile)* ⏲ *Closed Wed., Nov., and Sun.–Thurs. in Oct. and Dec.–May. No dinner in Oct. and Dec.–May.*

$$ SEAFOOD 🍴 **Viveiros do Atlântico.** Live seafood crawling around in a vivarium shaped like a blue-and-white fisherman's boat at the entrance gives you an idea of what to find on the menu. Pick out the fish or shellfish

of your choice to be prepared especially for you, such as a *sapateira recheada* (stuffed crab) brought to the table in its shell. Try the *cataplanas* (mixed seafood served in a copper steamer) or the mariscada, which is an excellent value. This large restaurant has ample parking and fantastic ocean views from all but a few tables—with the best to be had from the second-floor terrace (open June–September). $ *Average main: €20* ⊠ *N247 Km 46.5, Ribamar* ☎ *261/860300* ⊕ *www.vivatlantico. pt/index.php* ⊗ *Closed Mon., and Tues. Oct.–Apr., 2 wks in Jan., and 2 wks in Oct.*

WHERE TO STAY

$ 🏨 **Hotel Pedro O Pescador.** If you prefer your hotels on the small side, then you'll like this intimate, pastel-blue, family-run place near the beach. **Pros:** right on the main drag; minutes from beach; free Wi-Fi throughout. **Cons:** parking can be difficult; location and bar means it can be noisy at night in August; no phone in rooms. $ *Rooms from: €75* ⊠ *Rua Dr. Eduardo Burnay 22* ☎ *261/869121* ⊕ *www.hotelpedropescador.com* ⥲ *25 rooms* ❍ *Breakfast.*

HOTEL

$$ 🏨 **Hotel Vila Galé Ericeira.** This renowned, luxurious hotel overlooks the Atlantic, and half of the rooms have beautiful stone terraces with ocean views. **Pros:** great beach location; great for either couples or families; excellent value given amenities and facilities. **Cons:** the spa is inconveniently located under the outdoor patio; can get crowded with families and groups in summer. $ *Rooms from: €180* ⊠ *Largo dos Navegantes* ☎ *261/869900, 21/790–7600 for reservations* ⊕ *www. vilagale.com* ⥲ *210 rooms* ❍ *Breakfast.*

HOTEL
FAMILY

NEED A
BREAK

Pastelaria Fradinho. Just across from the Mostreiro Palacio Nacional de Mafra, the Pastelaria Fradinho is a welcome respite from the rigors of sightseeing. Light, cheerful, and adorned with tiles, the café is famed for its delicious homemade pastries including the little egg-and-almond tarts called, predictably, *fradinhos* (little friars). ⊠ *Praça da República 28–30, Mafra* ☎ *261/815738* ⊕ *www.pastelariapolonorte.com.*

TORRES VEDRAS

20 km (12 miles) northeast of Ericeira.

A bustling commercial center crowned with the ruins of a medieval castle, Torres Vedras is best known for its extensive fortifications—a system of trenches and fortresses erected by the Duke of Wellington in 1810 as part of a secret plan for the defense of Lisbon. It was here, at the Lines of Torres Vedras, that the surprised French army under Napoléon's Marshal Masséna was routed. You can see reconstructed remnants of the fortifications on a hill above town and throughout the area. The surrounding hills and countryside make for a picturesque drive to one of the several beaches on the coast at and around Santa Cruz, 20–30 minutes away.

CLOSE UP

Palácio Nacional de Mafra

The town of Mafra is one of the oldest in Portugal, with evidence of prehistoric settlements and remains of Roman and later Moorish occupation. Over the centuries the crown, church, and nobility have contested the ownership of the Mafra National Palace and Convent, which is 8 km (5 miles) southeast of Ericeira. From the 17th through 19th centuries this was a favorite residence for the Portuguese court. In 1711, after nearly three years of a childless union with his Hapsburg queen, Maria Anna, a despairing King João V vowed that should the queen bear him an heir, he would build a monastery dedicated to St. Anthony. In December of that same year, a girl—later to become queen of Spain—was born; João's eventual heir, José I, was born three years later. True to his word, King João V built an enormous monastery, which still looms above the small farming community of Mafra. The original project—entrusted to the Italian-trained German architect Johann Friedrich Ludwig, invariably known in Portugal as João Frederico Ludovice—was to be a modest facility that could house 13 friars. Construction began in 1717 and continued until 1755, with the final result being a rectangular complex containing a monastery large enough for hundreds of monks as well as an imposing basilica and a grandiose palace that has been compared to El Escorial outside Madrid, Spain. The numbers involved in the construction are mind-boggling: at times 50,000 workers toiled. There are 4,500 doors and windows, 300 cells, 880 halls and rooms, and 154 stairways. Perimeter walls that total some 19 km (12 miles) surround the park.

The highlight of any visit to the monument is the magnificent baroque library: the barrel-vaulted, two-tiered hall holds almost 40,000 volumes of mostly 16th- through 18th-century works and a number of ancient maps. Protection from insects is provided by bats, which slip into the room at night through tiny holes that were bored through stone under the windows for the purpose. The basilica contains 11 chapels and six organs—used simultaneously for splendid concerts at 4 pm on the first Sunday of every month except January and February—and was patterned after St. Peter's in the Vatican. The balcony of the connecting corridor overlooks the high altar and was a favorite meeting place for Dom João and Maria Anna, who had separate bedrooms. When you're in the gilded throne room, notice the life-size renditions of the seven virtues, as well as the impressive figure of Hercules, by Domingos Sequeira. On display in the games room is an early version of a pinball machine. Note the hard-planked beds in the monastery infirmary; the austere Franciscan monks who lived here did not use mattresses.

Guided visits may be booked in advance at an additional cost of €6 per person. ⊠ *Terreiro de Dom João V, Mafra* ☎ *261/817550, 261/817554 for guided visits, 261/817170 for Mafra visitor center* ⊕ *www.palacio-mafra.pt* ⊠ *€6 (free 1st Sun. of the month), organ concerts €3* ⊙ *Palace closed Tues.*

GETTING HERE AND AROUND

Torres Vedras can be reached from Lisbon by bus (Mafrense, Boa Viagem, Rede Expressos, and local operator Barraqueiro Oeste, which can also take you on to Lourinhã and Santa Cruz). Trains from Lisbon run on the regional line from Santa Apolónia or Entrecampos stations via Agualva-Cacém (on the Sintra line) that terminates in Figueira da Foz. Driving from Lisbon takes 30 minutes, from Mafra 20 minutes.

ESSENTIALS

Bus Contact Bus Station. ⊠ *Rua Dr. Ernesto Moreira, Peniche* ☎ *96/8903861 for Rodoviária do Tejo.*

Visitor Information Praia de Santa Cruz. ⊠ *Santa Cruz* ☎ *261/937524.* **Torres Vedras.** ⊠ *Rua 9 de Abril* ☎ *261/310483.*

EXPLORING

Castelo de Torres Vedras. Perched on top of a hill on the outer part of the city is the medieval castle. Built in the 12th century, it has been reinforced and reconstructed several times throughout the centuries, with the last repairs done in the 1980s. The cement recovered from the cisterns and various coins on display in the municipal museum in town attest to the presence of the Roman occupation here. The castle exhibits both Gothic and Manueline styles in its outside walls, and a medieval cemetery once existed where the church of Santa Maria stands. While exploring the towers, don't miss out on the incredible views of the city and surrounding valley and hills. ⊠ *Largo Coronel Morais Sarmento* 🈚 *Free* ⊘ *Closed Mon. and during Carnival.*

Museu Municipal Leonel Trindade. In the 16th-century Convento de Graça in the central square, the Municipal Museum has exhibits about the city's historical fortifications, as well as interesting archaeological finds from the castle grounds and all over the region. Audio guides to the city and to the Lines of Torres Vedras are available here. ⊠ *Convento de Nossa Senhora da Graça, Praça 25 de Abril* ☎ *261/310485* 🈚 *€2 (free Sun.)* ⊘ *Closed Mon., and Sun.–Tues. during Carnival.*

BEACHES

Praia da Mexilhoeira. Hedged in by rocky cliffs topped with the greenest of vegetation, this is one of the region's prettiest beaches. The strand is fairly narrow at high tide, but it rarely gets very crowded because it is served only by a simple café. Access to the beach is via a wooden walkway. The beach is signposted off the N247 north of Santa Cruz, where the beaches are broader but busier. **Amenities:** food and drink; lifeguards; parking (no fee). **Best for:** solitude; sunset; surfing; walking. ⊠ *Off N247, Póvoa de Penafirme.*

WHERE TO EAT AND STAY

$ ✕ **Trás d'Orelha.** Housed in a white-painted, airy building on the N9
PORTUGUESE highway a five-minute drive west of Torres Vedras, this restaurant lives up to its name, a Portuguese phrase meaning "it's really good." Among the best dishes are the *burras de porco preto* (slow-cooked cheek from the Iberian black pig), and game dishes such as *arroz de lebre* (rice with wild hare). For fish, try the *garoupa*, steamed or grilled, or in a cataplana big enough for two or three. In what is a prime

fruit-growing region, delicious desserts here include *pêra borrachona* ("drunken" pear, stewed in red wine) and figs in brandy. $ *Average main: €14* ⊠ *Casal de Sant'Anna 17 , Benfica , Ponte do Rol* ⊹ *N9 Hwy.* ☎ *261/326018, 96/301–0957 (mobile)* ⊕ *www.trasdorelha.com* ⊘ *Closed Mon., and 2 wks in Sept. No dinner Sun.*

$$$$
RESORT
Fodor'sChoice
★

Areias do Seixo. Opened in 2010 and set among the pine trees and dunes in front of Santa Cruz beach, this small and stylish eco-conscious hotel, 30 minutes from Ericeira, was built with a desire to harmoniously integrate with its surroundings, and all but one of the rooms have views of the ocean and dunes (the other has a private garden). **Pros:** stylish and luxurious accommodations; all rooms have fireplaces and private decks or patios; excellent restaurant with produce sourced from the property's garden. **Cons:** not cheap; not recommended for kids, unless they stay in the villas; beach at least a 10-minute walk and has no lifeguard. $ *Rooms from: €315* ⊠ *Praceta Do Atlântico, Mexilhoeira, Póvoa de Penafirme* ☎ *261/936340* ⊕ *www.areiasdoseixo.com* ⊘ *Closed 3 wks in Nov. and 3 wks in Dec.* ⇌ *14 rooms, 9 villas* ⎮◯⎮ *Breakfast.*

$
HOTEL
FAMILY

Ô Hotel Golf Mar. The idyllic location—on a rise overlooking an absolutely breathtaking view of the ocean, pounding waves, and the nearby cliffs, rolling hills, and lush green valley—is by far the best thing about this place near the town of Lourinhã, 16 km (10 miles) northwest of Torres Vedras. **Pros:** excellent location with panoramic views; wide variety of amenities; abundant activities for children. **Cons:** somewhat plain decoration despite recent overhaul; only superior rooms and suites have a/c; despite its name, the full-size golf course has closed. $ *Rooms from: €105* ⊠ *Praia do Porto Novo, Maceira* ☎ *261/980800* ⊕ *www. ohotelsandresorts.com* ⇌ *233 rooms* ⎮◯⎮ *Breakfast.*

GOLF

EN
ROUTE

Lourinhã, a town with a population of just 7,000, about halfway between Torres Vedras and Peniche, is famous in Portugal (and in certain circles abroad) for two things: its brandy and its dinosaurs. On the first count, the region is one of only three worldwide with an official denomination for the wine-based spirit (the others being the better-known Cognac and Armagnac, both in France). On the second, the local geology and ease of access to rocks in cliffs along the coast has meant astonishing quantities of important Jurassic-era fossils being found here. There is even a dinosaur named after the town: *Lourinhanosaurus.* Unsurprisingly, Lourinhã claimed the title "Land of the Dinosaurs," and the beasts now appear everywhere: as statues, on road signs, and even in the names of local businesses. It is worth stopping into the small museum (☎ *261/414003* ⊕ *www.museulourinha.org*)—open daily in July and August and Tuesday to Sunday the rest of the year—to see the amazing displays there.

PENICHE

32 km (20 miles) northwest of Torres Vedras.

In the lee of a rocky peninsula, Peniche is a major fishing-and-canning port that's also a popular summer resort known for its fine trimmed bilro lace. There are several beaches to choose from in the area as well as the beaches and fishing of the Berlengas archipelago, available to visit in the summer months. Besides Peniche being a major fishing port, locals and tourists know that this is one of the best places around to enjoy delicious fresh fish and seafood, especially sardines. Fans of lace will also want to track down fine examples in local shops of Peniche *renda de bilros*—a traditional craft that is now showcased in a well-appointed museum.

GETTING HERE AND AROUND

Peniche can be reached from Lisbon by express buses run by Rede Expressos and regional operator Rodoviária do Tejo, which along

> **GREAT DRIVES**
>
> For the most scenic drive to Peniche, return to the coast and follow N247 north for 43 km (27 miles) to Cabo Carvoeiro. About 3 km (2 miles) north of Torres Vedras is the archaeological site Castro do Zambujal, the remains of an Iron Age settlement of people who worked the copper mines that once existed here. Farther on, the jagged coast is interrupted by fine beaches at Ribamar, Santa Cruz, and Areia Branca.

with sister company Rodoviária do Oeste links it with other towns across Estremadura and the Ribatejo. Incoming buses stop first downtown (near the market) before continuing on to the out-of-town terminal; for outgoing Rede Expressos buses you may not board downtown unless you already have a ticket. Driving to Peniche takes 50 minutes from Lisbon, 15 minutes from Óbidos.

ESSENTIALS

Bus Contact Bus Station. ⊠ *Rua Dr. Ernesto Moreira* ☎ *96/8903861 for Rodoviária do Tejo.*

Visitor Information Peniche. ⊠ *Rua Alexandre Herculano* ☎ *262/789571* ⊕ *www.cm-peniche.pt.*

EXPLORING

Berlengas. The harbor at Peniche is the jumping-off point for excursions to the Berlenga archipelago—six islets that are part of a nature reserve and a favorite place for fishermen and divers. The islands are a nesting place and migratory route for many birds and marine life. Berlenga Grande, the largest of the group, is the site of a pretty lighthouse and the Forte de São João Baptista, a 17th-century fortress built to defend the area from pirates. There are trails around the island, including through caves. You can visit the islands by boat only from mid-May to mid-September; the largest boat company, **Viamar** (☎ *262/785646* ⊕ *www. viamar-berlenga.com*) operates round-trip on the Cabo Avelar Pessoa daily during the summer. The sea is often rough, so don't be alarmed by the rows of buckets under your seats. You can camp overnight on the main island or even stay in the fortress if you book ahead (although conditions are basic). The island has a restaurant and bar; there is also a small guesthouse and a visitor center, inaugurated in 2015. ⊠ *Boat departures, Ribeira Velha 2, Marina de Peniche* ⊕ *www.berlengas.eu* ⊠ *Boat €20 round-trip.*

Fortaleza de Peniche (*Museu Municipal*). The busy harbor is watched over by the sprawling 16th-century fort. At one time the fort's dungeons were full of French troops captured by the Duke of Wellington's forces. During Portugal's dictatorship, which ended in 1974, it was a prison for opponents of the regime. With the restoration of democracy, it came to house a Municipal Museum covering all of its eras. You can tour the former cells and take in a small archaeological exhibit. There are also some beautiful views of the ocean from its towers. For a good view of the fortress and the harbor, drive out to Cabo Carvoeiro; the narrow road winds around the peninsula, along the rugged shore, and past the lighthouse and bizarre rock formations. ⊠ *Campo da República* ☎ *262/780116* ⊴ *€1.60* ⊘ *Closed Mon.*

Igreja de São Leonardo. One of the area's most interesting churches is the Church of Saint Leonard in Atouguia da Baleia, a 10-minute drive inland. Dating back to the 12th century, it features Romanesque, Gothic, and Manueline architectural elements, and a ceiling depicting scenes from the Old Testament. Information on this and other local monuments is available at the village's Centro Interpretativo (closed Sunday and Monday), next to the Igreja de São José. ⊠ *Largo de São Leonardo, Atouguia da Baleia* ☎ *262/758644 for info center* ⊘ *Closed weekends.*

Museu das Rendas de Bilros. One of Peniche's most traditional products is *renda de bilros* (bobbin lace)—as is the case in many fishing centers, where making and repairing nets have long been essential skills. This small but well-organized museum downtown, inaugurated in 2016, displays every imaginable item relating to the craft—from antique instruments donated by locals, through elaborately decorated cushions and cloths, to modern fashion designs—with texts in English and multimedia displays. The skill is very much alive, with some 100 local craftsmen and -women involved in teaching enthusiasts young and old. Every July, the town hosts an international showcase attended by representatives from 30 or so countries. ⊠ *Rua Nossa Senhora da Conceição 1* ☎ *262/780100* ⊘ *Closed Mon.*

BEACHES

Praia da Areia Branca. The "white sand beach," 15 km (10 miles) south of Peniche, is composed of a broad, light sweep of sand backed by a small settlement that has taken its name from the beach, with plenty of stores and places to eat and drink. But if you want to get away from it all, there are cliff-top trails that are lovely for hiking. The waves here are suitable both for beginner and advanced surfers. **Amenities:** food and drink; lifeguards; parking (no fee); showers; toilets; water sports. **Best for:** sunset; surfing; swimming; walking. ⊠ *Alameda do Golfinho, Lourinhã.*

Praia do Baleal. This beach on a natural island that's now an artificially created peninsula has long been a surfer hangout thanks to its great waves—it's home to a well-reputed surf school. But Baleal is also popular with families, and there are plenty of sunshades for hire, and other facilities. Note that there are rocks in the water in some parts of the beach. **Amenities:** food and drink; lifeguards; parking (no fee); showers; toilets; water sports. **Best for:** partiers; sunset; surfing; swimming; windsurfing. ⊠ *Av. da Praia, Baleal.*

WHERE TO EAT AND STAY

$$$ SEAFOOD 🍴 **Nau dos Corvos.** On the cliffs at Cabo Carvoeiro with a dramatic view of the sea and the lighthouse, this restaurant specializes in traditionally prepared seafood dishes. There are also some fine meat dishes, such as duck magret with citrus sauce, plus pastas and risottos. Order the *arroz de tamboril com marisco* rice casserole; it is packed with monkfish and prawns and has a smattering of tangy cheese from the Azores—you won't regret it. [$] *Average main: €22* ✉ *Cabo Carvoeiro* ☎ *262/783168, 91/881–6515 (mobile)* 🌐 *www.naudoscorvos.pt.*

$ PORTUGUESE FAMILY Fodor's Choice ★ 🍴 **Tasca do Joel.** Tucked away on a side street far from the touristy seafront, this now not-so-little local tavern attracts diners from far and wide with delicious fresh fish and meat dishes cooked in its wood-burning oven. There are changing daily specials but regular dishes include bacalhau *à tasca* (fried codfish with onion and potato rings), confit of duck, grilled rabbit, and various *porco preto* (Iberian black pig) recipes. There's also a kids' menu with simpler fare. It's all fantastic value and all the better for being served in an informal ambience at long tables in two large rooms whose stone and white-painted walls are decorated with wine crates. There are more than a thousand wines on offer, including one produced by the owner. The attached wineshop hosts tastings. [$] *Average main: €12* ✉ *Rua do Lapadusso 73* ☎ *262 /782945* 🌐 *www.tascadojoel.pt* 🕒 *Closed Mon., and 2 wks in May–June. No dinner Sun.*

$ HOTEL FAMILY 🏨 **MH Atlântico Golfe.** Great for golfers but also anyone who loves waking up to a view, this hotel features balconies (some huge) that look over the links and the long beach at Praia da Consolação, just outside town. **Pros:** beachfront location; great views of the golf course and beach; lots of activities. **Cons:** on-street parking is free but garage is not; hotel style a bit dated despite regular refurbishments; tennis courts located at neighboring hotel. [$] *Rooms from: €95* ✉ *Complexo Turístico do Botado, Praia da Consolação, Atouguia da Baleia* ☎ *262/757700* 🌐 *www.mh-hotels.pt* 🛏 *96 rooms* 🍽 *Breakfast.*

SPORTS AND THE OUTDOORS

FISHING

The most commonly caught fish are sea bass, bream, and red mullet. A sports-fishing license (Licença de Pesca Desportiva) is needed, but if you go out with a tour company, they will arrange this.

Nautipesca. The charter-boat company Nautipesca offers deep-sea fishing excursions. Boats leave from the tourist pontoon on the Ribeira Velha, next to the marina, when conditions permit and when a minimum of 10 people are interested in heading out (or if you are willing to pay the equivalent). Per-person rates are €30 on weekdays, €35 on weekends. ✉ *Largo da Ribeira A-1* ☎ *91/758–8358.*

WATER PARK

FAMILY **Peniche Sportagua.** This large water-park complex delights with slides and separate adults' and children's swimming pools. There's a restaurant and snack bar on-site. Entrance rates are reduced after 3 pm and kids under five are free. ✉ *Av. Monsenhor Manuel Bastos* ☎ *262/789125* 🌐 *www.sportagua.com* 🎟 *€12 (€9.50 after 3 pm).*

WATER SPORTS

The clear waters and bizarre rock formations along Estremadura's coast make it a favorite with anglers, snorkelers, and scuba divers. A wet suit is recommended for diving and snorkeling, as the chilly waters don't invite you to linger long, even in summer.

Haliotis. This outfitter offers diving and snorkeling trips as well as dolphin watching around the Berlengas archipelago. ⊠ *Casal Ponte, Atouguia da Baleia* ☏ *262/781160* ⊕ *www.haliotis.pt.*

ÓBIDOS

20 km (12 miles) east of Peniche.

Fodor's Choice ★ The medieval village of Óbidos is a place to wander and wonder, both inside the city walls and out. Once a strategic seaport, Óbidos is now high and dry—and 10 km (6 miles) inland—owing to the silting of its harbor. On the approach to town, you can see bastions and crenellated walls standing like sentinels over the now-peaceful valley of the Ria Arnoia. It's hard to imagine fishing boats and trading vessels docking in places that are today filled by cottages and cultivated fields.

Óbidos has become known for its themed festivals, which draw visitors at various times of year.

GETTING HERE AND AROUND

Obidos can be reached by bus (Rede Expressos and regional operator Rodoviária do Oeste) from Lisbon. The regional train line from Lisbon's Santa Apolónia and Entrecampos stations (via Agualva-Cacém on the Sintra line) and Figueira da Foz stops in Óbidos as well. Driving from Lisbon takes 40 minutes, and coming from Peniche takes 15 minutes. *For Rede Expressos info, see Bus Travel, above.*

ESSENTIALS

Visitor Information Óbidos. ⊠ *Largo de São Pedro, Rua da Porta da Vila, outside town walls, at entrance to parking lot* ☏ *262/959231* ⊕ *www.obidos.pt.*

EXPLORING

As you enter town through the massive, arched gates, it seems as if you've been transported to Portugal in the Middle Ages, when the fortress was taken by Portugal from the Moors. The narrow Rua Direita, lined with boutiques and white, flower-bedecked houses, runs from the gates to the foot of the castle: you may want to shop for ceramics and clothing on this street. The rest of the town is crisscrossed by a labyrinth of stone footpaths, tiny squares, and decaying stairways. Each nook and cranny offers its own reward. Cars aren't permitted inside the walls except to unload luggage at hotels. Parking is provided outside town.

Away from the walled town, two pleasant marked walks enable you to see some rural history and Roman ruins or visit a bird observatory, respectively. It's a 1-km (½-mile) trek from the city gate through farmlands, a grove of poplar trees, and along the Arnoia River to the Eburobritium Roman ruins (established 1 BC to AD 5), where you can see ancient baths and a forum. Another walk is out to the free Lagoa de Óbidos observatories, from where you can spy aquatic birds and birds of prey. Maps of Óbidos are available at the tourist office in the parking lot at the gate into the city wall.

Fodor's Choice ★

Castelo de Óbidos. The outer walls of the fine medieval castle enclose the entire town, and it's great fun to walk their circumference, viewing the town and countryside from their heights. Extensively restored after suffering severe damage in the 1755 earthquake, the multitower complex has both Arabic and Manueline elements. Since 1952 most of the keep has been a pousada. ✉ *Óbidos.*

Igreja de Santa Maria. The 17th-century artist Josefa de Óbidos came to the town as a small child and lived here until her death in 1684. You can see some of her work in the azulejo-lined Church of Saint Mary, which was a Visigoth temple in the 8th century. The church is in a square off Rua Direita. Right next door is a small, charming museum dedicated to the work of local artist and theater designer Abílio de Mattos e Silva. ✉ *Óbidos.*

OFF THE BEATEN PATH

Buddha Eden. Just about the last thing you'd expect to find in rural Estremadura—about 10 minutes south of Óbidos—this landscaped "Garden of Peace" was inspired by the destruction in 2001 by the Afghanistan Taliban of the giant Buddhas of Bamiyan—one of which is reproduced here. Buddhas of various shapes and sizes dot the lawns and surrounding forest, as well as carved gates, dragons, and hundreds of figures from China's ancient Terracotta Army. There are also sculptures by leading contemporary artists. It all makes for a lovely place to stroll about and be inspired. There's a canteen serving decent Portuguese food (though if Asia fascinates you, **Supatra,** a five-minute drive away, may be more to your tastes) and a shop selling wines from the adjoining Quinta dos Loridos estate. Tastings (minimum six people) may be arranged on weekdays. To reach Buddha Eden from Óbidos, take the Carvalhal exit and follow the signs; it's off the A8. ✉ *Quinta dos Loridos, Bombarral* ☎ *262/605240, 91/300–5087 (mobile)* 🌐 *www.buddhaeden.com* 🎟 *€3.*

Quinta do Sanguinhal. This family-owned winemaker, founded in the late 19th century, is one of the companies best prepared to receive visitors (though you must still book in advance). You'll take in not only the winepresses and cellars but a magnificent antique distillery where *aguardentes* are still made. The tasting features seven wines, and you may also combine it with lunch. The place is south of Óbidos, not far from Buddha Eden. ✉ *Rua Principal, off N361, Sanguinhal* ☎ *262/609190, 91/449–3231* 🌐 *www.vinhos-sanguinhal.pt.*

WHERE TO EAT

$$$ PORTUGUESE Fodor's Choice ★

🍴 **A Nova Casa de Ramiro.** This longtime tourists' favorite just outside the town walls has been given a makeover, with the large dining room a blend of modern elegance and rustic chic. The fare remains reassuringly traditional, with dishes such as *arroz de pato* (rice with duck), fresh grilled fish, and various popular bacalhau options. There are some unusual desserts, such as local-fruit flambé and also tapas—great to enjoy with a glass of wine on the small terrace out front. [$] *Average main: €23* ✉ *Rua Porta do Vale* ☎ *262/958324* 🕒 *Closed Sun., and 1 wk in Sept.* ✍ *Reservations essential.*

Óbidos's Fun Festivals

CLOSE UP

Festival de Chocolate. Like a real-life Willy Wonka chocolate factory but even bigger, the outdoor feast that is the annual Festival de Chocolate attracts more than 200,000 people to Óbidos over almost four weeks in March and April. There are tons of activities to choose from, including chocolate workshops and demonstrations, cake design, chocolatherapy (think spa), body painting, and an annual chocolate sculpture contest done by locally known chefs with a new theme each year. Along with the many stands selling all kinds of delicious chocolate goodies, many local restaurants offer a chocolate-theme menu to indulge in. Avoid long ticket lines by buying online ahead of time. ✉ Óbidos ⊕ www.festivalchocolate.cm-obidos.pt ⌨ €6.

Festival Internacional Literário de Óbidos. The International Literature Festival, also known as "Folio," was launched in 2015 as part of a broader initiative to establish Óbidos as a Vila Literária (literary town). The focus was at first on Portuguese-language writers, but organizers have already branched out, with guests such as Salman Rushdie and V. S. Naipaul. This annual event is scheduled for late September or October. ✉ Óbidos ☎ 262/955500 ⊕ www.foliofestival.com ⌨ Free.

Mercado Medieval. Every July and August, the two-week Mercado Medieval enlivens the town. As well as the "Medieval Market" itself, each day there is a parade of people in medieval costumes around the city walls. You can rent costumes and take part, too. To buy some of the typical products of the region—ceramics,

cheeses, hams, and flowers—exchange your euros for replica torreões (the first coins struck in Portugal). Battles and court scenes are dramatized daily, and music animates the market all day up to midnight. As for a meal, consider a hunk of the wild boar being roasted on spits. ✉ Óbidos ⊕ www.mercadomedievalobidos.pt ⌨ €7 (free before 11 am).

Óbidos Vila Natal. From early December through New Year's, the Óbidos Vila Natal is the perfect miniature winter wonderland for children. This "Christmas Village" is built in the picturesque villa below the castle with everything covered in a light dusting of "snow." There's ice-skating (€4), an ice slide, the Carousel de Natal (€1.50), puppet shows, Christmas musicals, sing-alongs with Disney characters, and, of course, Santa Claus. There are also several organized games for all ages as well as a Christmas market selling traditional Portuguese Christmas sweets and other artisanal crafts. The Bar de Gelo (ice bar), which is open on weekends and holidays, is a popular "chill-out" spot for adults. ✉ Óbidos ⊕ www.obidosvilanatal.pt ⌨ €6.

Semana Internacional de Piano de Óbidos. The long-running Óbidos International Piano Festival offers two weeks of top-quality piano music as well as master classes for new talents. Concerts are staged in the compact Casa da Música, by the town's main gate, and given its—and the town's—small size you may well end up rubbing shoulders with a star performer during your stay. ✉ Óbidos ☎ 91/440-0702 ⊕ www.pianobidos.org ⌨ Concert €17, festival pass €110.

$ 🍴 **Alcaide.** From the upstairs dining room and terrace of this rustic
PORTUGUESE tavern, enjoy a lovely view of rooftops with the countryside beyond. This isn't a quiet hideaway—Alcaide draws many hungry sightseers, especially from May through October. The food, however, is always prepared and served with flair. *Filete de sardinha assada em broa* (fresh roast sardine on corn bread) is a tasty starter; also try the *requinte de bacalhau* (with cheese, chestnut, and apple stuffing) or the *tornedó com queijo da Serra* (steak with creamy rustic cheese). Desserts may include a traditional *toucinho do céu* ("heavenly" almond cake) and an English-style summer pudding with mixed berries. [$] *Average main: €15* ✉ *Rua Direita 60* ☎ *262/959220, 91/910–1795* 🌐 *www.restaurantealcaide.com* 🕒 *Closed Wed., and 2nd half Nov.*

$ 🍴 **Poço dos Sabores.** This rustic restaurant in the village of Usseira, 4 km
PORTUGUESE (2½ miles) south of Óbidos, has been serving hearty, mainly regional cuisine in its stone dining room for just over a decade. The menu changes every few months—barring favorites such as *arroz selvagem* (wild rice)—but any lamb or pork dish is a good option, as well as *polvo* (octopus) and, of course, bacalhau. This area has bountiful orchards, and apples, pears, and other fruit make a tasty appearance not only in desserts but also in some starters and mains. On some nights there's live fado music, too. [$] *Average main: €15* ✉ *Rua Principal 85-B, Usseira* ☎ *262/950086* 🕒 *Closed Mon. No dinner Sun. in July and Sept.*

$ 🍴 **Supatra.** This renowned Thai restaurant near Bombarral has perhaps
THAI the ideal location for fans of everything Asian: just down the road from the Buddha Eden garden. In a spacious former winery, smiling staff serve genuine Thai cuisine; expect chicken and pork satay, and salads featuring tropical fruit, but also specialties such as *tom yam* (hot-and-sour soup with mushrooms and shrimp), *pla lad prik* (sea bream in tamarind sauce), *gaeng kiaw wan kai* (green curry with chicken and coconut), and *kuai tiao phad thai kung sod* (stir-fried noodles with shrimp and peanut). For dessert, chestnut pudding is among the delicacies on offer. There's also a range of vegetarian dishes and a Sunday buffet lunch. Note: outside the peak months of July and August the restaurant is normally only open Friday through Sunday, so do phone ahead. [$] *Average main: €12* ✉ *Rua Poeta José Ferreira Ventura 73, Carvalhal, Bombarral* ☎ *262/842920, 91/826–1200 (mobile)* 🌐 *www.restaurantetailandessupatra.pt* 🕒 *Closed Mon., and Tues.–Thurs. Oct.–June. No dinner Sun.*

WHERE TO STAY

$ 🏨 **Casa das Senhoras Rainhas.** As its name suggests, this charming
B&B/INN "house" just inside the city walls pays tribute to the many queens associated with Óbidos over the centuries. **Pros:** great location; fine service; excellent food. **Cons:** parking is difficult; limited facilities. [$] *Rooms from: €119* ✉ *Rua Padre Nunes Tavares 6* ☎ *262/955360* 🌐 *www.senhorasrainhas.com* 🛏 *10 rooms* 🍽 *Breakfast.*

$ 🏨 **Casa d'Óbidos.** View the town's castle from this white manor house,
B&B/INN which dates to the 19th century and sits amid extensive lawns, gardens, and orchards, and provides guests with a swimming pool and amazing breakfast spread. **Pros:** great views of the city and castle; excellent breakfast; free Wi-Fi. **Cons:** outside the city; breakfast in the apartments

4

GINJA CHERRY LIQUEUR

One cannot visit Óbidos without trying its delicious cherry liqueur, *ginja*. Also known as *ginjinha de Óbidos*, it's made from the ginja sour cherry, whose origin is difficult to establish but is supposedly derived from the banks of the Caspian River and was gradually dispersed among the Mediterranean countries via trade routes. Thanks to the particular microclimate around the area of Óbidos, Portugal actually has the best wild ginja in Europe. As for the drink, it is thought to have originally started in the 17th century by a local friar who took a part of the large quantity of the fruit in the region and refined them into the liqueur that is known today.

The liqueur has a deep, dark red color with an intense flavor and aroma perfumed by the fermented cherries. It's produced and sold in two distinct varieties, the liqueur on its own or the liqueur with actual ginja cherries inside, sometimes flavored with vanilla or cinnamon. You can find numerous little shops and cafés in the walled village selling ginja as well as offering tastings. The best thing the locals recommend to have with ginja is chocolate, which they have cutely crafted into little chocolate cups in which to serve the liqueur. Or, you can enjoy it with a big slice of one of the shops' house-made chocolate cakes. The chocolate cups are also sold in packs of 6 and 12 to enjoy the ginja experience at home.

The two ginja producers in Óbidos are **FRUTÓBIDOS** (🌐 *www.frutobidos.pt*) and **OPPIDUM** (🌐 *www.ginjadeobidos.com*).

is self-service only. $ *Rooms from: €90* ✉ *Quinta de S. José, off N8/N114* ☎ *262/950924* 🌐 *www.casadobidos.com* ⏲ *Closed 2nd half of Nov.* 🛏 *6 rooms, 4 apartments* 🍴 *Breakfast.*

$ HOTEL 🏨 **Josefa d'Óbidos - Hotel.** This flower-bedecked inn is built into the hillside at the main gate. **Pros:** right in the city center; good value for money with free Wi-Fi throughout; friendly staff. **Cons:** can get noisy from outside traffic; often used by tour groups; some rooms a little humid. $ *Rooms from: €70* ✉ *Rua Dom João de Ornelas* ☎ *262/955010* 🌐 *www.josefadobidos.com* 🛏 *30 rooms* 🍴 *Breakfast.*

$ HOTEL Fodor'sChoice ★ 🏨 **The Literary Man Óbidos Hotel.** This 19th-century convent-turned-inn-turned-stylish hotel (inaugurated in its current form in 2015), near the main gate, has a bit of a split personality: a quarter of the rooms feature traditional wooden ceilings and floors and iron beds, while the rest are "eco-chic," employing recycled materials with contemporary flair. **Pros:** unusual and engaging literary theme; good value for money with free Wi-Fi throughout; central location. **Cons:** difficult parking; can get noisy from outside traffic. $ *Rooms from: €110* ✉ *Rua D. João d'Ornelas* ☎ *262/959217* 🌐 *www.theliteraryman.pt* 🛏 *30 rooms* 🍴 *Breakfast.*

$$$ HOTEL Fodor'sChoice ★ 🏨 **Pousada Castelo de Óbidos.** Sleep like medieval royalty—except for the electric lights and the relatively modern plumbing, the style of the Middle Ages prevails in this pousada, which occupies parts of the castle that Dom Dinis gave to his young bride, Isabel, in 1282. **Pros:** great location; incredible views of the castle and valley; fine service. **Cons:**

no elevator, so best rooms not suitable to those with limited mobility; must walk up a steep hill from parking to enter; pricey. $ *Rooms from: €220* ⊠ *Paço Real* ☎ *262/955080* ⊕ *www.pousadas.pt* ⟿ *17 rooms* ⫟ *Breakfast.*

$$$$
RESORT
FAMILY
Fodor'sChoice
★

🖼 **Praia d'El Rey Marriott Golf & Beach Resort.** This top-notch hotel, part of a sprawling luxury resort, is located 16 km (10 miles) west of the walled town of Óbidos and includes numerous amenities and activities. **Pros:** great location; ocean views; plenty of amenities and activities. **Cons:** food and drink are very expensive; far from any city; can get crowded in summer. $ *Rooms from: €403* ⊠ *Av. D. Inês de Castro 1* ☎ *262/905100* ⊕ *www.marriott.com/lisdr* ⟿ *177 rooms* ⫟ *Some meals.*

$$
HOTEL
Fodor'sChoice
★

🖼 **Rio do Prado.** "Eco-chic" is the phrase that best describes this award-winning hotel near the Óbidos Lagoon. **Pros:** unique setting and atmosphere; ecologically sensitive; restaurant serves delicious homemade food. **Cons:** few amenites; far from sights; no shade around pool. $ *Rooms from: €195* ⊠ *Rua das Poças, Arelho (Lagoa de Óbidos)* ☎ *262/959623* ⊕ *www.riodoprado.pt* ⟿ *17 rooms* ⫟ *Breakfast.*

SPORTS AND THE OUTDOORS

GO-KARTING

FAMILY
KIRO. This well-run go-kart track is a 15-minute drive south of Óbidos (if you take the A8, turn off at Exit 11 and then follow signs for "Kartódromo"). It also has a children's track for ages seven and up (or for those who can reach the pedals). Prices vary depending on the car, but the average is €20 per person for 15 minutes. Call ahead, because sometimes the track is rented for private races. It's open daily in July and August, and Thursday through Monday September through June. ⊠ *Quinta do Falcão, Bombarral* ☎ *262/609330, 93/612–4682 (mobile), 93/612–4681* ⊕ *www.kiro-karting.com* ☉ *Closed 1st 2 wks of Jan.*

GOLF

Fodor'sChoice
★
Praia d'El Rey Golf & Beach Resort. Less than an hour's drive from Lisbon's international airport, Praia d'El Rey is an excellent beachfront complex with one of the most picturesque golf courses in Europe. Undulating greens, natural sand-border areas, and bold, deep bunkers are the hallmarks of this Cabell Robinson design. The architect was at great pains to make the course friendly to women players by creating sensible women's tees that are placed far enough forward. The handicap limit here is 28 for men and women. Reservations must be made by email (*golf.reservations@preaia-del-rey.com*) but it is worth phoning ahead to ask about current promotions. ⊠ *Av. Dom Pedro Primeiro, Vale de Janelas* ☎ *262/099587* ⊕ *www.praia-del-rey.com* ⛳ *18 holes, 7110 yds, par 73. Greens fee €110 weekdays, €130 weekends (25% off Nov.–Jan.).*

SHOPPING

BOOKS

Livraria de Santiago. Óbidos has ambitions to become Portugal's prime literary town, with a high-profile international festival and bookshops springing up in the most unlikely places. The 18th-century Igreja de Santiago, by the castle keep, has been dramatically transformed, with bookshelves and wooden staircases whose curves echo its baroque interior. It stocks Portuguese literature and glossy coffee-table books. ✉ *Igreja de Santiago, Rua da Talhada* ☎ *262/103180.*

CERAMICS

Olaria S. Pedro. Óbidos is dotted with crafts shops, but the Olaria S. Pedro stands out, specializing as it does in ceramic works—many of them very large—by some of the wave of artists who are successfully updating this traditional form in Caldas da Rainha and other towns in the region. Sónia Borga, for example, mixes her own vibrant colors and often fires pieces several times to achieve just the striking result she wants. The shop also sells jewelry and Andalusia-style azulejos, and will ship any item. ✉ *Travessa de São Pedro 2–4* ☎ *93/386–7480* ⊕ *www.olariaobidos.com.*

CALDAS DA RAINHA

5 km (3 miles) north of Óbidos.

Caldas da Rainha (Queen's Baths), the hub of a large farming area, is best known for the fantastical, colorful ceramics produced in local factories and—for centuries before that—for its sulfur baths. In 1484 Queen Leonor, en route to Batalha, noticed people bathing in a malodorous pool. Having heard of the healing properties of the sulfurous water, the queen interrupted her journey for a soak and became convinced of the water's beneficial effects. She had a hospital built on the site and was reputedly so enthusiastic that she sold her jewels to help finance the project. There's a bronze statue of Leonor in front of the hospital. Major repairs to the hospital's thermal system are planned, meaning that treatments for rheumatism and respiratory diseases have been suspended.

GETTING HERE AND AROUND

Caldas da Rainha can be reached from Lisbon by buses run by Rede Expressos and local operator Rodoviária do Oeste, which serves other towns in the region from a smart downtown hub. The CP regional train line between Lisbon (Santa Apolónia and Entrecampos stations) and Figueira da Foz stops in Caldas da Rainha as well. Driving from Lisbon takes 50 minutes, from Óbidos 10 minutes.

ESSENTIALS

Bus Contact Bus Station. ✉ *Rua Coronel Soeira de Brito 35* ☎ *262/831067 for Rodoviária do Oeste.*

Visitor Information Caldas da Rainha. ✉ *Rua Provedor Frei Jorge de São Paulo 1* ☎ *262/240005* ⊕ *www.turismodocentro.pt.*

EXPLORING

Encosta da Quinta. One of the region's best small winemakers, Encosta da Quinta, outside of town, is known above all for a prizewinning organic red that goes by the earthy name of Humus. Call or email ahead to arrange a visit to the estate (parts of which date back to the 16th century) ending with a tasting with four organic wines—a combination of whites, rosés, or reds, according to visitors' preference—and regional cheeses. ✉ *Quinta do Paço, off Rua Principal de Alqueidão, Alvorninha* ☎ *91/727–6053* ⊕ *encostadaquinta.com.*

Museu da Cerâmica (*Ceramics Museum*). This museum in the Romantic-style former house of the Viscount of Sacavém contains works by the noted 19th-century artisan and artist Rafael Bordalo Pinheiro, as well as ceramics by his Caldas da Rainha contemporaries. Some of his most famous ceramic figurines, done in gaudy colors, are the fat peasant Zé Povinho, Ama das Caldas (the Caldas wet nurse), the civil guard, and John Bull. Other amusing figures include a pig's head on a platter and leaping frogs. There are a gift and bookshop and a cafeteria here as well. ✉ *Rua Dr. Ilídio Amado, Apartado 97* ☎ *262/840280* 🎟 *€3 (free 1st Sun. of the month)* 🕓 *Closed Mon.*

> **SHOPPING**
>
> The regions around Alcobaça and Leiria are well-known for their high-quality crystal and handblown glass. Traditional hand-painted ceramics are sold at shops and roadside stands throughout Estremadura. Caldas da Rainha, a large ceramics-manufacturing center, produces characteristic cabbage-leaf and vegetable-shape pieces. Traditional cable-stitch Portuguese fishermen's sweaters are for sale in towns all along the coast.

Museu José Malhoa. The expansive wooded park surrounding the town's spa contains a museum with works mostly by local José Malhoa (1854–1933), one of Portugal's most prominent Naturalist painters, as well as sculpture, drawings and ceramics from the 19th and 20th centuries. A handheld audio guide with English commentary is available. ✉ *Parque D. Carlos I* ☎ *262/831984* 🎟 *€3 (free 1st Sun. of the month)* 🕓 *Closed Mon.*

BEACHES

Praia da Foz do Arelho. Across the mouth of the Óbidos Lagoon, where it meets the sea, a large spit of sand juts out into the brackish tidal water. The broad expanse of sand here and the calmer waters of the lagoon make it popular with families with young kids, not least because the beaches here have been awarded the coveted Blue Flag (for water quality, safety, and access) several years running. As well as the public facilities, there are several lively esplanades along the promenade. **Amenites:** food and drink; lifeguards; parking (no fee); showers; toilets. **Best for:** partiers; sunset; swimming; windsurfing. ✉ *Foz do Arelho.*

WHERE TO EAT AND STAY

$ PORTUGUESE 🍴 **A Lareira.** With a name that is Portuguese for "fireplace," this elegant, spacious restaurant is nestled in pinewoods between Caldas da Rainha and the Foz do Arelho beach; it's a favorite with locals for special occasions. Try the salmon fillet with caviar sauce, the *tornedó de novilho* tenderloin with one of various sauces, or, for the more daring, the *ensopado de enguia* (eel stew). Seek assistance to get the best from the 300-strong wine list. Note that weekend meal prices are more expensive than the set menu option on weekdays (both lunch and dinner). [$] *Average main: €13* ✉ *Rua da Lareira 35, Alto do Nobre, Nadadouro* ☎ *262/823432* 🌐 *www.restaurantealareira.com.*

$$ ✕ **Sabores d'Itália.** Behind a vintage tiled facade is a widely acclaimed
ITALIAN   restaurant that is the place to go in Portugal for genuine Italian food.
Fodor's Choice   Everything—the pasta, bread, ice cream—is homemade and beautifully
★   presented and served by the owner, Norberto Marcelino, and his wife.
Veal medallions with port wine and truffles, and crab or scallop risotto
are among the mouthwatering main dishes on the menu, and desserts
include the ever-popular raspberry gratin with lemon sorbet, *sinfonia
de pêra rocha* (featuring a local pear variety), and fig crêpe with Mosca-
tel ice cream. They also provide for diners with food allergies. Wine
is served by the glass as well as by the bottle, with the extensive list
including several Italian wines as well as a vast selection of Portuguese,
from sparkling wines to an excellent organic red. Ⓢ *Average main: €18*
✉ *Praça 5 de Outubro 40* ☎ *262/845600* ⊕ *www.saboresditalia.com*
⊗ *Closed Mon. in Sept.–July.*

$ 🏠 **Casal da Eira Branca.** This rural retreat in Infantes, 7 km (4 miles)
B&B/INN   east of Caldas, is ideal for rest and recuperation, with its sprawling,
FAMILY   flower-filled garden and terraces with views. **Pros:** free Wi-Fi through-
out; cozy and friendly yet with an artsy feel; lots of outdoor activities.
Cons: far from sights; few amenities; no restaurant. Ⓢ *Rooms from:*
€65 ✉ *Rua Casal dos Pedreiros 3 , Infantes* ☎ *93/645–5837 (mobile),*
93/454–9185 (mobile) ⊕ *www.casaldaeirabranca.com* ⇋ *4 rooms, 3*
apartments ⧉ *Breakfast.*

$ 🏠 **Quinta da Foz.** This quiet base with a historical past allows for explo-
B&B/INN   ration of area towns such as Caldas da Rainha, 9 km (5½ miles) away,
Fodor's Choice   or the beach at Foz do Arelho, a 15-minute walk away. **Pros:** intriguing
★   historical atmosphere; near the beach; quiet and peaceful with a family
atmosphere. **Cons:** heating but no a/c; few modern amenities; Wi-Fi
signal elusive in some rooms. Ⓢ *Rooms from: €90* ✉ *Largo do Arraial,*
Foz do Arelho ☎ *262/979369, 91/755–7786* ⊕ *www.quintadafoz.co*
▭ *No credit cards* ⇋ *5 rooms* ⧉ *Breakfast.*

$$$ 🏠 **SANA Silver Coast Hotel.** Once a famous Victorian-era hotel, this long-
HOTEL   derelict grand building facing the park has been transformed by one
of Portugal's leading hotel chains into the only highly ranked hotel
between Lisbon and Leiria. **Pros:** great central location; free Wi-Fi and
Internet terminals; free covered parking. **Cons:** no pool; rooms at the
front can be noisy during the week. Ⓢ *Rooms from: €230* ✉ *Av. Dom
Manuel Figueira Freire da Câmara* ☎ *262/000600* ⊕ *www.silvercoast.
sanahotels.com* ⇋ *87 rooms* ⧉ *Some meals.*

SPORTS AND THE OUTDOORS

WATER SPORTS

Escola de Vela da Lagoa. The large wooden clubhouse with a sailing
school on the north bank of the Óbidos Lagoon near Foz do Arelho
has rentals by the hour: small sailboat €20, windsurfer €15–€22, canoe
€12, and catamaran €20–€30. A kitesurfing course costs €75 for two
hours of private lessons. The snack bar here serves hamburgers, salads,
shrimp and clams, sweet and savory crêpes, fresh fruit juices, milk
shakes, and cocktails. It's closed Tuesday to Thursday from October to
March. ✉ *Lagoa de Óbidos, 2½ km (1½ miles) after traffic circle at Foz,
Rua do Penedo Furado, Foz do Arelho* ☎ *262/978592, 96/256–8005*
⊕ *www.escoladeveladalagoa.com.*

SHOPPING

Caldas da Rainha is famous for its cabbage-leaf- and vegetable-shape ceramic pieces produced in several of the town's factories and workshops, which you can visit if you reserve ahead of time.

CERAMICS

Faianças Artísticas Bordallo Pinheiro. The shop at this factory, once overseen by famous artist Rafael Bordalo Pinheiro, has a good range of Caldas-style ceramics, many produced using vintage molds designed by the man himself. In recent years, leading contemporary artists—most notably Portugal's own Joana Vasconcelos—have worked with the company to produce new works, or to use old designs in unexpected ways. There are guided visits to Bordalo Pinheiro's former home, now a museum, on weekdays by appointment only. ⊠ *Rua Rafael Bordalo Pinheiro 53* ☎ *262/880568 for store, 262/839380 for museum* ⊕ *www. bordalopinheiro.com.*

NAZARÉ

24 km (15 miles) northwest of Caldas da Rainha.

Not so long ago you could mingle on the beach with black-stocking-capped fishermen and even help as the oxen hauled boats in from the crashing surf. But Nazaré is no longer a village and has long ceased to be quaint. The boats now motor comfortably into a safe, modern harbor, and the oxen have been put to pasture. The beachfront boulevard is lined with restaurants, bars, and souvenir shops, and in summer the broad, sandy beach is covered with a multicolor quilt of tents and awnings.

You can still catch an interesting piece of culture that has survived: the many *sete saias Nazarenas* or "seven skirts Nazarean women," who can be seen all around the town, dressed in colorful mismatching attire and, of course, wearing seven skirts. These women also sell crafts and souvenirs as well as dried, salted little fish (a local tradition) that they dry on wire racks along the boardwalk. They also have shops selling their particular style of clothing if you're adventurous enough to try them. It's said that the seven skirts represent, in religious terms, the seven virtues, the seven days of the week, the seven colors of the rainbow, the seven waves of the sea, and other biblical and magical attributes.

GETTING HERE AND AROUND

Nazaré can be reached by bus (Rede Expressos) from Lisbon. Driving from Lisbon takes one hour, and the drive from Alcobaça will take you close to 15 minutes. ■ TIP→ **For the most interesting route to Nazaré, head west from Caldas along the lagoon to the beach town of Foz do Arelho, then take the coast road 26 km (16 miles) north.**

ESSENTIALS

Bus Contact Bus Station. ⊠ *Av. do Município* ☎ *96/744–9868 for Rodoviária do Tejo.*

Visitor Information Nazaré. ⊠ *Mercado Municipal, Av. Vieira Guimarães* ☎ *262/561194* ⊕ *www.cm-nazare.pt.*

EXPLORING

Sítio da Nazaré. To find what's left of the Nazaré, once hailed by many as "the most picturesque fishing village in Portugal," either climb the precipitous trail or take the scenic funicular to the top of a 361-foot cliff to visit the settlement called Sítio (literally, "Place"). Clustered at the cliff's edge overlooking the beach is a small community of fishermen who live in tiny cottages and seem unaffected by all that's happening below. On this promontory stands the Igreja de Nossa Senhora da Nazaré, a predominately baroque church with a tiled and gilded interior that houses a figure of the Virgin Mary said to have been carved by Joseph himself in Nazareth—hence the town's name. ⊠ *Sítio*.

WHERE TO EAT AND STAY

$$
SEAFOOD
✕ **A Celeste.** Owner Celeste likes to personally greet guests—who lately have included record-breaking surfer U.S. Garreth McNamara—at the entrance to her seafood restaurant on the Atlantic seafront. Among popular dishes here are *espadarte à Celeste* (swordfish with cream-and-mushroom sauce) and squid or monkfish on the spit. This coast is famous for its caldeirada (a Portuguese version of bouillabaisse with nine kinds of fish). Perhaps the most spectacular dishes here are the *cataplana de peixe com camarão e amêijoas* for two (fish stew with shrimp and clams, served with a flourish) and the fish baked whole in salt. $ *Average main: €20* ⊠ *Av. República 54* 🕾 *262/551695.*

$
HOTEL
☷ **Hotel Mar Bravo.** This stylish boutique hotel is right over the road from the beach, just steps from both the sea and the center of town, and all rooms have a water view and almost all have balconies. **Pros:** romantic setting; great in-house restaurant right on the beach; good amenities including free Wi-Fi throughout. **Cons:** can get noisy from outside traffic; difficult parking. $ *Rooms from: €120* ⊠ *Praça Sousa Oliveira 71* 🕾 *262/569160* ⊕ *www.marbravo.com* ☾ *Closed Christmas wk* ⇱ *16 rooms* ⦿*Some meals.*

$
HOTEL
☷ **Hotel Oceano.** Balconies overlook the beach at this white, pleasantly appointed hotel that was given a full decorative revamp in early 2015. **Pros:** perfect location right on the main drag overlooking the beach; great beachfront restaurant; good value with a/c and free Wi-Fi in rooms. **Cons:** gets booked up super early in summer; very noisy at times; rooms without sea views of less interest. $ *Rooms from: €85* ⊠ *Av. da República 51* 🕾 *262/561161* ⊕ *www.adegaoceano.com* ⇱ *45 rooms* ⦿*Some meals.*

$
HOTEL
☷ **Hotel Praia.** Along with being only minutes away from the beach, this design hotel has a rooftop, glass-covered "indoor" pool and Jacuzzi with an infinity view of the ocean and surrounding city. **Pros:** great ocean view from the pool and rooftop terrace; short walk from beach; soundproof rooms. **Cons:** parking is not free unless booking is made directly with hotel; restaurant is pricey. $ *Rooms from: €140* ⊠ *Av. Vieira Guimarães N° 39* 🕾 *262/569200* ⊕ *www.hotelpraia.com* ⇱ *76 rooms, 4 duplex apartments* ⦿*Some meals.*

$
HOTEL
FAMILY
☷ **Miramar Hotel & Spa.** The sea and town views from this well-appointed hotel are fantastic: it's about 1 km (½ mile) *above* Nazaré, in the village of Pederneira. **Pros:** incredible views; great amenities; away from the city crowds. **Cons:** far from beach; no nightlife nearby. $ *Rooms*

from: €138 ✉ *Rua Abel da Silva, Pederneira* ☎ *262/550000* ⊕ *www. miramarnazarehotels.com* 🛏 *40 rooms* 🍽 *All meals.*

SHOPPING

The many shops and stands along the beachfront promenade have a good selection of traditional fishermen's sweaters as well as a wide array of caps and plaid shirts (the best are made of wool rather than acrylic blends). You'll find several shops that sell handcrafted ceramics and tiles in Sítio. It pays to shop around: prices vary widely, and bargaining is the order of the day.

BEACHES

Starting with Ericeira and extending north to São Pedro de Moel by Marinha Grande, there are a number of pleasant sandy beaches at convenient intervals along the coast. Some of the more popular stretches—with the customary range of facilities, hotels, and restaurants—are in Nazaré, Peniche, and Foz do Arelho. All beaches in Portugal are public.

4

SPA

Thalasso Nazaré. Overlooking the open Atlantic, this spa seeks to combine classic thalassotherapy treatments (using seawater) involving daunting-looking but highly relaxing hydrotherapy machines with the latest wellness and beauty therapies. Classic treatments (from €10) include Vichy shower with various massages, jet, Scottish, circular, and underwater showers; whirlpool, multijet, and seaweed baths; as well as seaweed and mud applications, and respiratory therapies. The area's waters have long been valued for their health-giving properties: the existence just offshore of the Nazaré Canyon—a huge submarine gorge—helps bring rich nutrients to the surface. The spa is an offshoot of the local Miramar Hotels group, so packages can be arranged. ✉ *Av. Manuel Remígio* ☎ *262/560450* ⊕ *www.thalassoportugal.com.*

ALCOBAÇA

10 km (6 miles) southeast of Nazaré; 20 km (12 miles) northeast of Caldas da Rainha.

Alcobaça is a town that still shows its old-world roots in its downtown architecture—pretty red-tile roofs and French chateau turrets. The town is in a picturesque valley between the towns of Nazaré and Batalha, and is known for its crystal as well as for its impressive church and monastery that date back to the 12th century.

GETTING HERE AND AROUND

Alcobaça can be reached from Lisbon and other cities by buses run by Rede Expressos and local operator Rodoviária do Tejo, which also links it with other towns in the region. Driving from Lisbon takes one hour, while the drive from Nazaré will take you close to 15 minutes. *For Rede Expressos info, see Bus Travel, above.*

ESSENTIALS

Visitor Information Alcobaça. ✉ *Rua 16 de Outubro, 7* ☎ *262/582377* ⊕ *www.turismodocentro.pt.* **São Martinho do Porto.** ✉ *Rua Vasco da Gama, 18, São Martinho do Porto* ☎ *262/989110* ⊕ *www.turismodocentro.pt.*

EXPLORING

Fodor's Choice **Mosteiro de Alcobaça.** Like the monastery at Mafra, the Mosteiro de
★ Alcobaça was built as the result of a kingly vow, this time in gratitude
for a battle won. In 1147, faced with stiff Muslim resistance during
the battle for Santarém, Portugal's first king, Afonso Henriques, promised to build a monastery dedicated to St. Bernard and the Cistercian
Order. The Portuguese were victorious, Santarém was captured from
the Moors, and shortly thereafter a site was selected. Construction
began in 1153 and was concluded in 1178. The church, the largest in
Portugal, is awe-inspiring. The unadorned, 350-foot-long structure of
massive granite blocks and cross-ribbed vaulting is a masterpiece of
understatement: there's good use of clean, flowing lines, with none of
the clutter of the later rococo and Manueline architecture. At opposite
ends of the transept, placed foot to foot some 30 paces apart, are the
delicately carved tombs of King Pedro I and Inês de Castro.

The graceful twin-tiered cloister at Alcobaça was added in the 14th and
16th centuries. The Kings Hall, just to the left of the main entrance, is
lined with a series of 18th-century azulejos illustrating the construction
of the monastery. ⊠ *Praça 25 de Abril* ☎ *262/505120* ⊕ *www.moste-
iroalcobaca.pt* ⊠ *€6 (free 1st Sun. of the month). Combined ticket €15
with Batalha monastery and Tomar convent.*

Museu Nacional do Vinho. Housed in an old winery just outside Alcobaça,
the National Wine Museum is the country's best showcase of antique
implements and presses, dating from the 17th to 21st centuries. Unless
you've booked a group visit ahead of time, you must opt for one of
the regular guided tours, which are on the hour from 10 to 5 (except
1 pm), in English and Portuguese, and conclude with a wine tasting.
Along with art displays and temporary exhibitions on wine and other
themes, it all makes for a pleasant couple of hours. The museum is on
the N8 heading north out of town. ⊠ *Rua de Leiria, Olival Fechado*
☎ *96/849–7832* ⊠ *€3.60* ⊗ *Closed Mon.*

São Martinho do Porto. The perfect horseshoe-shape bay here not only
makes this one of Portugal's prettiest beaches, but also ensures it
is lapped by calm waters that are ultrasafe for children. The ample
strand—patrolled by lifeguards so long as beach cafés are open—has
fine, yellow sand (cleaned daily) and areas with sunshades for rent.
Much of it is lined with well-preserved dunes; at its northern end, set
back from the promenade, are elegant old homes in the typical Caldas
style, restaurants, and many hotels. The beach is popular with local
families, so don't come in high summer if you dislike crowds; still,
it's almost always great for people-watching. Local companies also
offer boating and canoeing trips. São Martinho do Porto is served by
Rodoviário do Oeste buses from Caldas and Alcobaça. **Amenities:** food
and drink; lifeguards; parking (no fee); toilets; water sports. **Best for:**
sunset; swimming; walking. ⊠ *Av. Marginal, São Martinho do Porto.*

WHERE TO EAT AND STAY

$ ✕ **António Padeiro.** This restaurant in Alcobaça is best known for
PORTUGUESE   showcasing regional cuisine, with dishes such as chicken or partridge
na púcara (cooked in an clay pot)—many of which evolved in local

CLOSE UP

Pedro and Inês

The story of Pedro and Inês, one of the most bizarre love stories in Portuguese history, was immortalized by Luís de Camões in the epic poem *Os Lusiads.*

Pedro, son of King Afonso IV and heir to the throne, fell in love with the beautiful young Galician Inês de Castro, a lady-in-waiting to Pedro's Castilian wife, Constança. Fearful of the influence of Inês's family on his heir, the king banished her from the court. Upon the death of Constança, Pedro and Inês secretly married, and she lived in Coimbra, in a house later known as the Quinta das Lagrimas (House of Tears); two sons were born of this union. King Afonso, ever wary of foreign influence on Pedro, had Inês murdered. Subsequently, Pedro took the throne and had Inês's murderers pursued: two of the three were captured and executed, their hearts wrenched from their bodies. Pedro publicly proclaimed that he had been married to Inês and arranged an elaborate and macabre funeral for his wife. Before the procession, Inês's body, in royal garb, was enthroned beside him, and the courtiers were forced to kiss her lifeless hand. She was then placed in the tomb in Alcobaça that Pedro had designed, which lay, according to his wishes, opposite his own—so that on Judgment Day the lovers would ascend to heaven facing each other.

4

monasteries. Fans of bacalhau should try the house version: baked, with a crust of corn bread and *farinheira* sausage. There's a wide range of traditional eggy desserts as well as fresh fruit. It's all served in brisk but friendly fashion in a large downstairs space that's hung with local memorabilia and photos of the family that have run the place since 1938, although there are plans for a second dining room upstairs. [$] *Average main: €12* ✉ *Rua Dom Maur Cocheril 27* ☎ *262/582 295* 🌐 *www.antoniopadeiro.com* 🕒 *Closed Wed. Oct.–May.*

$ B&B/INN FAMILY 🏨 **Casa da Padeira.** This family-run guesthouse 5 km (3 miles) outside Alcobaça is named after a baker who fought the Spaniards with a wooden shovel—and pushed them into her oven—during the Battle of Aljubarrota in 1385. **Pros:** picturesque, peaceful location; playground for children; barbecue facilities. **Cons:** heating but no a/c in guest rooms; far from monastery; no elevator. [$] *Rooms from: €75* ✉ *N8, 19, Aljubarrota* ☎ *262/505240, 91/820–1972* 🌐 *www.casadapadeira.com* 🛏 *8 rooms, 5 apartments* 🍴 *Breakfast.*

$ B&B/INN 🏨 **Challet Fonte Nova.** This charming B&B, a five-minute walk from the monastery, has guest rooms in period style, while the more spacious lodgings in the new wing—including two suites with balconies—are more classically decorated. **Pros:** great location; romantic setting; toiletries by noted Portuguese brand Castelbel. **Cons:** no pool; no restaurant; Wi-Fi free but signal can be elusive. [$] *Rooms from: €120* ✉ *Rua da Fonte Nova 8* ☎ *262/598300* 🌐 *www.challetfontenova.pt* 🕒 *Closed 2 wks in Dec.* 🛏 *10 rooms* 🍴 *Breakfast.*

$ HOTEL 🏨 **Hotel Santa Maria.** With a perfect location facing the monastery, this hotel offers comfortable, if somewhat characterless lodging. **Pros:** great central location; air-conditioned, soundproof rooms; free Wi-Fi throughout. **Cons:** very limited facilities; lacks local character. $ *Rooms from: €57* ⊠ *Rua Dr. Francisco Zagalo 20–22* ☏ *262/590160* ⊕ *www. hotelsantamariaalcobaca.com* ⤳ *74 rooms* ⦿ *Breakfast.*

$ ⌖ **Quinta do Campo.** This imposing complex in the countryside between
B&B/INN   Alcobaça and Nazaré housed the country's first agricultural school—
founded in the 12th century by Cistercian monks at around the same
time as the monastery at Alcobaça; it is now a comfortable rural retreat.
Pros: lovely rural setting; plenty of outdoor activities; spacious acommodations. **Cons:** restaurant functions only in summer; few facilities;
far from sights. $ *Rooms from: €75* ⊠ *Rua Carlos O'Neill 20, Valado de Frades* ☏ *262/577135, 91/254–4151 (mobile)* ⊕ *www.aquintado-campo.com* ⤳ *8 rooms, 7 apartments* ⦿ *Breakfast* ▭ *No credit cards.*

SHOPPING

CERAMICS

Cristal Atlantis. The Atlantis outlet shop some 8 km (5 miles) north of
Alcobaça sells both first-rate crystal and secondhand items (good if you
don't want to pay high prices for the normal wares). There is a free
museum, and groups of five or more can visit the factory (40 minutes)
for €2.60 per person; you must book a day or two in advance, especially for an English-language tour (unless you are in luck and one is
already scheduled). Visits may be conducted Tuesday through Friday
at 10:30, 11:30, 2:30, and 3:30. ⊠ *Zona Industrial de Casal de Areia, Cós* ☏ *262/540269 for visitor center, 96/229–2668 (mobile)* ⊕ *www. vistaalegreatlantis.com* ⊙ *Closed weekends. Factory/museum closed 2 wks in Aug., and 1 wk in Dec.*

Spal. This factory store on the Nazaré road is a great place to buy
porcelain from this leading Portuguese manufacturer. Its outlet section
stocks discounted items with minimal defects. The staff here will box
and ship your purchases for you, too. ⊠ *Ponte da Torre, Valado dos Frades* ☏ *262/581751, 262/581339 for discounted items* ⊕ *www.spal. pt* ⊙ *Closed Sun.*

SPA

Your Hotel & Spa. The old Termas da Piedade resort, set between fruit
orchards and wooded hills off the N8-5 to Nazaré, is now a modern
hotel and spa with an impressive range of treatments (though the original thermal waters are no longer used). There's an indoor pool with
jets, Vichy shower, sauna, steam bath, and various relaxation beds.
Massages include straightforward antistress and lymphatic drainage as well as Reiki, ayurvedic, hot stone, reflexology, and shiatsu.
Then there's thalassotherapy, Balinese boreh, and seaweed wraps;
several types of peeling; and treatments involving wine or chocolate.
⊠ *Rua Manuel Rodrigues Serrazina, Fervença* ☏ *262/505376* ⊕ *www. yourhotelspa.com.*

BATALHA

18 km (11 miles) northeast of Alcobaça.

Batalha, which means "battle" in Portuguese, is the site of another of
the country's religious structures that memorialize a battle victory. The

monastery, classified as a UNESCO World Heritage Site, is surrounded by the small city center, with several other smaller, historical monuments scattered around the area.

Batalha is right in the Estremaduran countryside, with rolling hills, mountains, old windmills, pastures, and farming villages that create a fairy-tale-like view from higher points of the city. It's a great area to drive around and explore.

GETTING HERE AND AROUND

Batalha is served by the Rede Expressos buses from Lisbon to Leiria as well as other vicinities in between. Driving to Batalha from Lisbon takes 1 hour 10 minutes, 15 minutes if coming from Leiria. *For Rede Expressos info, see Bus Travel, above.*

ESSENTIALS

Visitor Information **Batalha.** ⊠ *Praça Mouzinho de Albuquerque* ☎ *244/765180* ⊕ *www.turismocentro.pt.*

EXPLORING

Centro de Interpretação da Batalha de Aljubarrota. On N8, 3 km (2 miles) south of Batalha's monastery, the Battle of Aljubarrota Interpretation Center is a project of the foundation of the same name, created to preserve and enhance understanding of the history surrounding the São Jorge battlefield. The main focus of the exhibition area (with labels in English) is on the 1385 military engagement that conclusively established Portugal's sovereignty, but it also documents conflicts with Spain from the early Middle Ages through the early 15th century. A multimedia show is screened at 11:30, 3, and 4:30 on weekends and holidays, but audio guides in various languages are always available; you may also book a guided tour in English in advance. If you plan on visiting the battlefield itself as well, set aside an hour and a half. ⊠ *Campo Militar de São Jorge, Av. Nuno Álvares Pereira 120, Calvaria de Cima* ☎ *244/480060, 244/480062 for guided tours* ⊕ *www.fundacao-aljubarrota.pt* 🖾 *€7* ☽ *Closed Mon.*

Fodor's Choice ★ **Mosteiro da Batalha.** The church monastery, dedicated to "Saint Mary of Victory," was built to commemorate a decisive Portuguese victory over the Spanish on August 14, 1385, in the Battle of Aljubarrota. In this engagement the Portuguese king, João de Avis, who had been crowned only seven days earlier, took on and routed a superior Spanish force. In so doing he maintained independence for Portugal, which was to last until 1580, when the crown finally passed into Spanish hands. The heroic statue of the mounted figure in the forecourt is that of Nuno Álvares Pereira, who, along with João de Avis, led the Portuguese army at Aljubarrota.

The monastery, a masterly combination of Gothic and Manueline styles, was built between 1388 and 1533. Some 15 architects were involved in the project, but the principal architect was Afonso Domingues, whose portrait, carved in stone, graces the wall in the chapter house. In the great hall lie the remains of two unknown Portuguese soldiers who died in World War I: one in France, the other in Africa. Entombed in the center of the Founder's Chapel, beneath the star-shape, vaulted ceiling, is João de Avis, lying hand in hand with his English queen, Philippa of

Lancaster. The tombs along the south and west walls are those of the couple's children, including Henry the Navigator. Perhaps the finest parts of the entire project are the Unfinished Chapels, seven chapels radiating off an octagonal rotunda, started by Dom Duarte in 1435 and left roofless owing to lack of funds. Note the intricately filigreed detail of the main doorway. ✉ *Largo Infante Dom Henrique* ☎ *244/765497* 🌐 *www.mosteirobatalha.pt* 🎟 *€6 (free 1st Sun. of the month); €15 combined ticket, includes Alcobaça monastery and Tomar convent.*

WHERE TO STAY

$$ HOTEL Fodor's Choice ★ 🏨 **Cooking and Nature–Emotional Hotel.** "Get connected with nature" is the slogan of this innovative hotel, set amid olive groves in the Parque Natural Serras de Aire de Candeeiros, 20 km (13 miles) south of Batalha. **Pros:** great for really getting away from it all; lively cooking workshops; friendly, enthusiastic staff. **Cons:** far from historic sights; pool rather small; no dinner on Sunday. [$] *Rooms from: €159* ✉ *Rua Asseguia das Lages 181, Alvados* ☎ *244/447000* 🌐 *www.cookinghotel.com* 🛏 *12 rooms* 🍴 *Breakfast.*

$ HOTEL 🏨 **Hotel Casa do Outeiro.** This cheerful little hotel in one of the quietest areas of Batalha offers a superb view of the historic monastery and valley below. **Pros:** great central location with beautiful views; homey feeling; rooms recently revamped. **Cons:** no restaurant; limited breakfast options. [$] *Rooms from: €69* ✉ *Largo Carvalho do Outeiro 4* ☎ *244/765806* 🌐 *www.hotelcasadoouteiro.com* 🛏 *23 rooms* 🍴 *Breakfast.*

$ HOTEL 🏨 **Hotel Mestre Afonso Domingues.** Named for the principal architect of the famous Batalha monastery, this pousada is full of modern comforts in a two-story white-stucco building. **Pros:** next to monastery; great service and value; free Wi-Fi throughout. **Cons:** can get noisy from outside traffic; restaurant is a bit pricey; limited facilities. [$] *Rooms from: €105* ✉ *Largo Mestre Afonso Domingues 6* ☎ *244/765260, 91/492–4723 (mobile)* 🌐 *www.hotel.mestreafonsodomingues.pt* 🛏 *22 rooms* 🍴 *Some meals.*

$ HOTEL 🏨 **Hotel Villa Batalha.** This smart, modern hotel is right on the edge of the old city, so guests can use it as a base to explore the historical monuments of Batalha, and also enjoy a round of golf on its private 6-hole pitch-and-putt course along the river. **Pros:** a wide variety of activities on offer; excellent spa; close to monastery. **Cons:** large size can feel a bit commercial; can get crowded from large group bookings and conferences. [$] *Rooms from: €103* ✉ *Rua Dom Duarte I 248* ☎ *244/240400* 🌐 *www.hotelvillabatalha.com* 🛏 *93 rooms* 🍴 *Some meals.*

OFF THE BEATEN PATH

Parque Natural das Serras de Aire e Candeeiros. This sparsely populated region straddles the border between Estremadura and the Ribatejo and is roughly midway between Lisbon and Coimbra. Within its 75,000 acres of scrublands and moors are small settlements, little changed in hundreds of years, where farmers barely eke out a living. In this rocky landscape, stones are the main building material for houses, windmills, and the miles of walls used to mark boundary lines. In the village of Minde, you can visit the Centro de Artes e Ofícios Roque Gameiro (on Rua Dr António da Silva Totta) to see women weaving the rough patchwork rugs for which this region is known. The park is well suited for leisurely hiking—with many well-marked trails—or cycling. If you're driving, the N362, which runs for approximately 45 km (28 miles) from Batalha in the north to Santarém in the south, is a good route. ✉ *Porto de Mós.*

LEIRIA

11 km (7 miles) north of Batalha.

Leiria is a pleasant, modern, industrial town at the confluence of the Rios Liz and Lena, overlooked by a wonderfully elegant medieval castle. The region is known for its handicrafts, particularly the fine handblown glassware from nearby Marinha Grande.

GETTING HERE AND AROUND

The best option to get here is by car. There are two alternative highways between Lisbon and Leiria (A1 and A8), each of which takes about 1 hour 15 minutes; from Batalha it's 15 minutes. It's also possible to take a Rede Expresso Bus from Lisbon to Leiria.

ESSENTIALS

Bus Contact Bus Station. ✉ *Av. Heróis de Angola* ☎ *244/811507* ⊕ *www.rodotejo.pt.*

Visitor Information Leiria. ✉ *Jardim Luís de Camões* ☎ *244/848770.*

EXPLORING

Castelo de Leiria. Leiria's castle, built in 1135 by Prince Afonso Henriques (later Portugal's first king), was an important link in the chain of defenses along the southern border of what was at the time the Kingdom of Portugal. When the Moors were driven from the region, the castle lost its significance and lay dormant until the early 14th century, when it was restored and modified and became the favorite residence of Dom Dinis and his queen, Isabel of Aragon. With these modifications the castle became more of a palace than a fortress and remains one of the loveliest structures of its kind in Portugal. Within the perimeter walls you'll encounter the ruins of a Gothic church, the castle keep, and—built into the section of the fortifications overlooking the town—the royal palace. There's also a small museum in the keep. Lined by eight arches, the balcony of the palace affords lovely views. ✉ *Largo de São Pedro* ☎ *244/839670* 🎫 *Castle and museum €2.10.*

Museu de Leiria. Housed in a former Augustinian monastery since November 2015, Leiria's main museum presents the city's development from pre-Roman times through the construction of the castle and the planting of the region's vast pine forests at the behest of medieval kings. Among prize items is the "Lapedo child"—a skeleton from the early Upper Paleolithic, excavated locally in 1998, which has fueled debate about the origins of modern humans. Your ticket includes a free audio guide in English and admission to the **Moinho do Papel,** a beautifully restored nearby watermill where you can see cereals being ground and paper made the traditional way. ✉ *Rua Tenente Valadim 4* ☎ *244/839677* 🎫 *€5.*

Museu do Vidro. Marinha Grande, just west of Leiria, is known for its fine-quality lead crystal, which has been produced in the region since the 17th century. The palatial 18th-century former home of William Stephens, the Englishman who re-established the Royal Glass Factory, now houses a museum showcasing glass and crystal from several periods and factories. There is a shop in the reception area. ✉ *Praça Guilherme Stephens, Marinha Grande* ☎ *244/573377* 🎟 *€1.50* 🕓 *Closed Mon.*

BEACHES

São Pedro do Moel. One of Portugal's most picturesque beaches is framed by steep cliffs and a fast-flowing stream. Strong tides can make the ocean here hazardous, but there are lifeguards in summer and a large swimming pool that's ideal for kids. The beach itself bustles with sporting activity, and at night the village bars are lively. Some local houses have an alpine look, thanks to the availability of pine from the forests that blanket the Leiria region—which also makes for lovely fresh air. **Amenities:** food and drink; lifeguards; parking (no fee); showers; toilets; water sports. **Best for:** sunset; surfing; swimming; walking. ✉ *São Pedro de Moel.*

WHERE TO EAT AND STAY

$$ PORTUGUESE

🍴 **Casinha Velha.** This restaurant is in an old house with rustic Portuguese furniture, 1 km (½ mile) from the center of town, on the same street as the more famous Tromba Rija. They bake their bread on the premises—including a delicious *pão chouriço*—and there's a series of tasty starters. The menu includes a noteworthy bacalhau *com natas* (codfish with cream) and *cabrito assado* (roasted kid); the latter isn't served on Wednesday and Friday. Leave some room for the mixed dessert platter or for the *brisa do Lis,* a local almond pudding. There is a pleasant downstairs bar where you may sip an aperitif if you must wait for a table. [$] *Average main: €19* ✉ *Rua Professores Portelas 23, Marrazes* ☎ *244/855355* 🌐 *www.casinhavelha.com* 🕓 *Closed Tues., 2 wks in Jan., and 2 wks in July. No dinner Sun.*

$ PORTUGUESE Fodor's Choice ★

🍴 **O Casarão.** About 5 km (3 miles) south of Leiria just off the N1, at the Azóia traffic circle, O Casarão occupies a large country house surrounded by gardens where you may take an apertif before your meal. The service and presentation are flawless without being pretentious, and the extensive menu includes several ancient recipes from nearby monasteries. Try the *ensopado de robalo com gambas* (sea bass stew with prawns) or, if there are two of you, split the *medalhões de noviho no espeta com gambas* (steak medallions, barbecued with prawns and bacon), which comes with beans and rice, *migas de nabiça* (fried bread crumbs and turnip tops) and açorda. There's a play area for children inside the restaurant, as well as free Wi-Fi. TIP→ **Leave room for one of the homemade desserts, such as leite creme.** [$] *Average main: €15* ✉ *Cruzamento de Azoia* ☎ *244/871080* 🕓 *Closed Mon.*

$$$ PORTUGUESE Fodor's Choice ★

🍴 **Tromba Rija.** One of Portugal's most famous restaurants, this one is 1 km (½ mile) from the city center off the N109 in Marrazes. Arched stone walls lend it a medieval atmosphere. From Friday dinner through Sunday lunch, guests serve themselves from a long table where some 35 regional appetizers are set out in clay pots. Mains include *secreto de porco preto* (a particularly succulent cut from the Iberian black pig) and baked bacalhau, and special dishes such as *lombo de porco recheado com ameixas* (pork loin stuffed with prunes) are available if you order ahead from the list on the website. During the week you remain seated and are served 20 starters and a choice of main dish; the all-in price does not include drinks. Be sure to make reservations or be prepared to wait. $ *Average main: €25 ⊠ Rua Professores Portela 22, Marrazes ☎ 244/852277 ⊕ www.trombarija.com ☉ Closed Mon. No dinner Sun. and holidays ⌕ Reservations essential.*

$

B&B/INN

FAMILY

▦ **Hotel Casa da Nora.** This pretty farmhouse turned cozy hotel is in beautiful countryside just a short drive outside of Leiria. **Pros:** friendly staff; great riverside location; perfect getaway for couples. **Cons:** no telephone in rooms; no elevator; out of town. $ *Rooms from: €89 ⊠ Largo José Marques da Cruz, 8, Cortes ☎ 244/891189, 91/970–3731 ⊕ www.casadanora.com ⤳ 14 rooms ⦿\ Breakfast.*

$

HOTEL

▦ **Hotel São Luís.** This simply furnished and decorated hotel in a quiet neighborhood overlooking the town is a five-minute walk from the center. **Pros:** great central location; very clean; free Wi-Fi in all rooms plus hotspot in lounge. **Cons:** outdoor parking only; noisy at night from outside traffic; breakfast lacking in variety. $ *Rooms from: €65 ⊠ Rua Henrique Sommer ☎ 244/848370 ⊕ www.saoluishotel.com ⤳ 54 rooms ⦿\ Breakfast.*

THE RIBATEJO

To the east of Estremadura, straddling both banks of the Rio Tejo, the Ribatejo is a placid, flat, fertile region known for its vegetables and vineyards. It's also famous for its horses and bulls; you may well see campinos in red waistcoats and green stocking caps moving bulls along with long wooden poles. As a consequence of its strategic location, the Ribatejo is home to a number of imposing castles as well as such diverse sights as the shrine at Fátima.

BENAVENTE

80 km southeast of Obidos.

Benavente is a small, country town in the heart of rural Ribatejo and of the Lezíria, which is Portuguese for the rich and fertile landscape stretching away from the banks of the Tagus River. The central location of Benavente is a great starting point for exploring the surrounding area, where there are several places for horseback riding, golf, wine tasting, and other outdoor activities. Benavente dates back to the 12th century, when Portuguese colonists settled on the southern bank of Tagus.

GETTING HERE AND AROUND

Benavente is served by Ribetajana Bus 901 and the faster 921 from Lisbon (Campo Grande), as well as the 903, which also links the town with Vila Franca de Xira. From Santarém there is the 902. By car it is 35 minutes away from Lisbon and 15 minutes from Vila Franca de Xira.

ESSENTIALS

Bus Contact Bus Station. ⊠ *Praça do Município* ☎ *263/516282 for Ribatejana* ⊕ *www.ribatejana.pt.*

Visitor Information **Benavente (Samora Correia).** ✉ *Palácio do Infantado, Praça da República 8, Samora Correia* ☎ *263/650510* 🌐 *www.turismolisboavaledotejo.pt.*

EXPLORING

Reserva Natural do Estuário do Tejo. This extensive natural reserve area lies along the banks of the Tejo River and has diverse fauna and flora, great bird-watching, and hiking through the Lezíria area. The **EVOA Visitor Centre** (☎ *92/6458963* 🌐 *www.evoa.pt*) at Lezíria Sul, run by the nearby **Companhia das Lezírias,** comprises large, comfortable hides for birding; guided tours are also organized from here. It's open March to October from 9 to 7 and November to February from 10 to 5. ✉ *Benavente* 🌐 *www.natural.pt/portal/en* 🎟 *€12 exhibition and birding tour* ⏲ *Visitor center closed Mon., and July.*

WHERE TO EAT AND STAY

$ PORTUGUESE 🍴 **A Coudelaria.** The restaurant at the equestrian complex of Portugal's largest agricultural holding, the Companhia das Lezírias, is noted for bacalhau and octopus dishes. On Saturday there is a hearty buffet (€18) and on Sunday, in two sittings at noon and after 2:30 pm, *cozido de carnes bravas à Ribatejana*—stew made with meat from local *touro bravo* bulls—is served. Note that, while lunch is served every day except Monday, dinner is available only if booked in advance. The complex also has a dozen bungalows arranged around a pool, if you want to stay over to make the most of the riding opportunities. The Coudelaria is clearly signposted, 2½ km (1½ miles) south of Porto Alto off the N118. [$] *Average main: €12.50* ✉ *Coudelaria da Companhia das Lezírias, N118, Km 19, Monte de Braço de Prata, Porto Alto* ☎ *263/654985* 🌐 *www.acoudelaria.com* ⏲ *Closed Mon., and Aug.* ✍ *Reservations essential.*

$ PORTUGUESE 🍴 **O Grilo.** On the outskirts of the historical center, this little local restaurant comprises a single airy dining room with an open kitchen at one end, so you can watch your meal being prepared. Service is friendly and the food is traditional fare that comes in inexpensive portions that are large enough for two. The cheap daily specials might include *sopa de cação* (dogfish soup), bacalhau *malandro* (fried with onion and potato rings), *migas com entrecosto* (pork ribs and bread stuffing), or *cozido à portuguesa* (a stew containing pork, beans, sausage, and vegetables). Save room for the *doce da casa,* made with cookies and cream. [$] *Average main: €9* ✉ *Largo do Jogo da Bola 6/7* ☎ *263/517199, 91/353–6071, 91/820–3467* ⏲ *Closed Sun., and 2nd half of Aug.*

$ HOTEL 🏨 **Benavente Vila Hotel.** This small boutique hotel on the main square in Benavente's historical center has clean rooms with a simple yet modern style that includes white linens accented with lime green. **Pros:** great views of the city and countryside; friendly staff; free Wi-Fi in rooms. **Cons:** no designated parking; rooms are a bit small. [$] *Rooms from: €65* ✉ *Praça Da República 39/40* ☎ *263/518210* 🌐 *www.benaventevilahotel.pt* 🛏 *20 rooms* 🍽 *Some meals.*

SPORTS AND THE OUTDOORS
GOLF

RibaGolfe. A 20-minute drive from Benavente, RibaGolfe has two 18-hole courses designed by architects Peter Townsend and Michael King of European Gold Design. They encompass more than 6,000 yards each and are set in beautiful sloping terrain lined with large cork-oak trees. The golf course also has a training center with a driving range, putting and pitching greens, and a practice bunker. ⊠ *Vargem Fresca, N119, Km 23, Infantado, Samora Correia* ☎ *263/930040, 96/171–8725, 263/930048 for restaurant* ⊕ *www.orizontegolf.com* ⊠ *€50 per round weekdays, €65 per round weekends* ⓧ *Ribagolfe I: 18 holes, 6707 m, par 72. Ribagolfe II: 18 holes, 6214 m, par 72. Greens fee €100 (9 holes €60)* ⚐ *Reservations essential.*

Santo Estêvão. This relatively plain but well-designed golf course 12 km (7½ miles) southeast of Benavente has facilities and service of a high standard. The course makes the most of existing landscape features on these rolling plains, with broad fairways and two pleasant lakes. The first few holes are straightforward, but by the 8th things have become rather more challenging on the greens. The 11th hole, a par 4, is generally seen as both the prettiest and the trickiest to play well. ⊠ *Vila Nova de Santo Estêvão, CCI 19* ☎ *263/949492* ⊕ *www.orizontegolf. com* ⓧ *18 holes, 6382 m, par 73. Greens fee: €90.*

HORSEBACK RIDING

Companhia das Lezírias. The largest agriculture, animal, and forest farmstead in Portugal covers about 44,500 acres. The area stretches across Ribatejo's Lezíria landscape, from Samora Correia all the way down toward the town of Alcochete, and includes the marshlands of Vila Franca de Xira and the Tejo Natural Estuary Reserve. The farmstead is filled with forests of cork oaks, stone pines, and eucalyptus trees, which the company harvests annually. Rice is also grown and sold under the "Belmonte" and "Bom Sucesso" labels, and the company does organic cattle farming and breeds prizewinning Lusitano stallions. For organized group activities, the company can arrange a number of radical sports, such as paintball, crossbow shooting, canoeing, and hot-air-balloon rides, as well as bird-watching and other tours of the area and of the production facilities, and wine tastings. But the best choice for tourists here is the excellent equestrian facilities, which offer lessons, guided riding excursions, and horse-drawn-carriage rides through the beautiful cork forests and Lezíria landscape. Riding tours include a half-day ride for €40, a full-day ride with picnic for €75, or longer tours around Sintra or Mafra, where you overnight in rustic lodgings; you must call or email ahead of time to arrange rides or lessons. The Companhia is based in Samora Correia, but its equestrian center (Coudelaria) is 2½ km (1½ miles) south of Porto Alto, clearly signposted off the N118. Its restaurant (listed separately) serves noted bacalhau and octopus dishes for lunch and, on Sunday, *cozido de carnes bravas à ribatejana*—stew made with meat from local *touro bravo* bulls. There are also a dozen bungalows and a pool, if you want to stay over. The company's winery, Adega Catapereiro, 2 km (1 mile) further south on the N118, has a shop attached. ⊠ *Coudelaria da Companhia das Lezírias, N118, Km 19,*

Monte de Braço de Prata, Porto Alto ☎ *96/152–3119, 92/672–9180 for equestrian center, 263/654985 for restaurant, 21/234–9016 for winery* ⊕ *www.cl.pt.*

EN
ROUTE

Casa Cadaval. If you're a fan of wine, stop by the prestigious Casa Cadaval on your way to Almeirim. This winery, on the Herdade de Muge estate, has belonged to the Alvares Pereira Melo (Cadaval) family since 1648. The winery produces red, white, and rosé wines under the Casa Cadaval, Marquesa de Cadaval, and Padre Pedro labels, using both native and international grape varieties, like Pinot Noir. The estate has a wine store with a tasting room, which is available for scheduled visits that can include a tour of the winery and stud farm; there's also a walk-in shop open to the public to purchase their wines. ⊠ *Rua Vasco da Gama, Muge* ☎ *243/588040* ⊕ *www.casacadaval.pt.*

ALMEIRIM

4 km (2½ miles) east of Santarém.

Almeirim, a pretty country town just across the river from Santarém, is surrounded by vineyards and cork-oak forests. Many people from nearby cities and all over Portugal come to this town dubbed the "capital of stone soup," which is a widely known local recipe that has cute story behind it.

GETTING HERE AND AROUND

Almeirim is served by the Ribatejana Bus 902 from Santarém and Vila Franca de Xira (via Benavente) and Rede Expressos from Lisbon. (The stop is at Travessa da Olaria 10A and tickets may be bought at Papelaria Fina at Rua 5 de Outubro 61.) By car, it is about 50–60 minutes away from Lisbon, 40 minutes from Vila Franca de Xira, and only 10 minutes from Santarém.

ESSENTIALS

Visitor Info Almeirim. ⊠ *Rua Dionísio Saraiva* ☎ *243/594107.*

EXPLORING

Quinta da Alorna. This 6,900-acre farm and winery encompasses a vineyard established in 1723 by the Marquês de Alorna, a viceroy of India. It is known particularly for its ripe, floral whites. There's a shop right outside the entrance where you can purchase the wines and other regional products such as honey, jams, olive oil, and sausages. There are no regular tours of the winery, but if you call a day or two ahead, they may be able to arrange a visit and tasting. ⊠ *N118, Km 73* ☎ *243/570700, 243/570706 for shop* ⊕ *www.alorna.pt.*

Quinta do Casal Branco. For the gastronome in you, spend a day wining and dining at this 1,630-acre estate; 346 acres are vineyards. The quinta has been owned by the same family for more than 200 years and used to be one of largest royal falconry grounds in the country. The winery produces red, white, rosé, and sparkling wines, as well as olive oil under numerous labels which include Capoeira, Terra de Lobos, "Q," their falcon tribute Falcoaria, and their flagship Casal Branco. They use native grape varieties such as Castelão for reds and Fernão Pires for whites, as well as international ones like Syrah, Merlot, Cabernet

LOCAL LEGENDS

Almeirim is visited mostly because it has a number of restaurants that serve a local delicacy called *sopa da pedra* (stone soup). A local legend says there was once a friar on a pilgrimage traveling through the area who was too proud to beg for food so he knocked on the doors of the houses and asked for only a pot "to make a delicious and filling … stone soup." Then he took a *pedra* (stone) and dropped it into a boiling pot of water. A little later, he tasted it and approached a housewife, saying, "it just needs a little seasoning." So, she came back with some salt, to which he said "maybe a little bit of sausage or if you also have some potatoes left over from the previous meal then maybe that would make it just a bit better." So she came back with all three and added them to the pot. Eventually, everyone in the village

came to contribute to the soup, with carrots, beans, meat, sausage, and other vegetables until it had indeed become a very hearty soup. At the end, the friar fished the stone out of the pot, washed it off, and tucked it into his pocket to save for the next meal. Today Almeirim's sopa da pedra recipe is judged as the best around, and it can easily be eaten as a meal on its own or as a starter to accompany other regional dishes if you have a healthy appetite. Some places still put a small (washed) stone at the bottom. ■ TIP➡ **You can find most of the sopa da pedra restaurants across from the bullfighting ring in the Largo da Praça de Touros.** Don't forget to pay a visit to the friar himself. There's a statue of him sitting in front of his soup, located just down the street from the bullfighting plaza on Rua de Coruche.

Sauvignon, and Petit Verdot. Call ahead for a guided tour of the cellar ending with a wine tasting, or for lunch or dinner in the small restaurant. You can also visit the stables with their Lusitano thoroughbreds. Or just stop by the quinta's shop, which sells its wines and olive oil, as well as homemade jams, cheeses, and traditional sausages. ⊠ *N118, Km 69, Benfica do Ribatejo* ☎ *243/592412* ⊕ *www.casalbranco.com.*

WHERE TO EAT AND STAY

$ ✕ **O Toucinho.** With four dining rooms (one of them set aside for smok-
PORTUGUESE   ers), this is Almeirim's most popular traditional restaurant, thanks to its
Fodor's Choice   excellent grilled meats—lamb and pork as well as steak—and of course
★   the sopa da pedra, which O Toucinho claims to have reinvented back in the 1960s. It is run by a former *forcado* (bullfighter)—as the bull's heads and bullfight posters will remind you. Enter from Rua de Macau and you can look into the kitchen where the rustic bread that comes fresh to your table is made all day long. Traditional desserts such as *arroz doce* and *pudim* are also cooked in a wood-burning oven. $ *Average main: €11* ⊠ *Rua de Timor 2* ☎ *243/592237* ⊕ *www.toucinho.com* ☾ *Closed Thurs., and 2 wks in Aug.*

$ ⌂ **Quinta da Gafaria.** This homestead midway between Santarém and
B&B/INN   Almeirim offers modern, tastefully decorated lodgings with plenty of
FAMILY   opportunities for contact with the farming and ranching operations.
Pros: free Wi-Fi; many activities. **Cons:** remote; few facilities. $ *Rooms*

from: €87 ⊠ *Almeirim* ☎ *96/173–6295* ⊕ *www.quintadagafaria.com* ⏎ *10 rooms, 2 apartments* ⦿ *Breakfast.*

**OFF THE
BEATEN
PATH**

Casa dos Patudos. Alpiarça is a pleasant little town 7 km (4 miles) northeast of Almeirim on the N118. Here you'll have the chance to see how a wealthy country gentleman lived at the beginning of the 20th century. The Casa dos Patudos, now a museum, was the estate of José Relvas, a diplomat and prosperous local farmer. This unusual three-story manor house with its zebra-stripe spire is surrounded by gardens and vineyards and is filled with an impressive assemblage of ceramics, paintings, and furnishings—including Portugal's foremost collection of Arraiolos carpets. ⊠ *Rua José Relvas, Alpiarça* ☎ *243/558321* ▣ *€2.50* ⊗ *Closed Mon.*

**EN
ROUTE**

Golegã. About 32 km (19 miles) northeast of Almeirim is the town of Golegã, one of Portugal's most notable horse-breeding centers. During the first two weeks of November, this is the site of the colorful **Feira Nacional do Cavalo** (National Horse Fair), the most important event of its kind in the country, staged for the past 250 years. It has riding displays, horse and trap competitions, and stalls that sell handicrafts. ⊠ *Largo Marquês de Pombal 25, Golegã* ☎ *249/979122 for horse fair, 91/789–5263 (mobile)* ⊕ *www.fnc.cm-golega.pt.*

SANTARÉM

7 km (4½ miles) northwest of Almeirim.

Present-day Santarém, high above the Tagus River, is an important farming and livestock center. It holds the largest agricultural fair in the country. Even with a tradition of bull breeding and bullfighting, Santarém curiously has what is considered the ugliest bullring on the Iberian Peninsula. Santarém also has bull farms and a working stud farm.

Some historians believe that Santarém's beginnings date to as early as 1200 BC and the age of Ulysses. Its strategic location led several kings to choose it as their residence, and the Cortes (Parliament) frequently met here. Thanks to its royal connections, Santarém is more richly endowed with monuments than other towns of its size. The Portuguese refer to it as their "Gothic capital."

GETTING HERE AND AROUND

Santarém is served by bus (Ribatejana via Vila Franca de Xira and Lisbon and Rede Expressos via Lisbon) and also by the Intercidades, Alfa Pendular, and Regional trains coming from Lisbon, Vila Franca de Xira, and many other stops to and from the north. By car, it's 45 minutes from Lisbon, 25 minutes from Vila Franca de Xira, and five minutes from Almeirim.

ESSENTIALS

Bus Station Bus Station. ⊠ *Av. Brasil 41* ☎ *243/333200 for Rodoviário do Tejo* ⊕ *www.rodotejo.pt.*

Visitor Information Santarém. ⊠ *Rua Capelo Ivens 63* ☎ *243/304437.*

CLOSE UP

Portugal's Oldest Food Festival

Festival Nacional de Gastronomia. From around mid-October through to early November, Santarém each year hosts the National Festival of Gastronomy, the longest-running in Portugal. It's held in the Casa do Campino, next to the bullfighting ring, where numerous restaurants from all over the country come to showcase the best gastronomy delights of their area and establishment. The festival includes competitions in various categories of cuisine—often with the opportunity for you to try the winners' wares—and you are guaranteed to eat well here. There is also plenty of handicrafts, folk music, and dancing. ✉ *Casa do Campino, Campo Infante da Câmara* ☎ *243/300900* 🌐 *www.festivalnacionaldegastronomia.pt* 🎟 *€2.*

4

EXPLORING

Igreja da Graça (*Graça Church*). The 14th-century Gothic church contains the gravestone of Pedro Álvares Cabral, the discoverer of Brazil. (There's also a tomb of the explorer in Belmonte, the town of his birth in northeastern Portugal, but no one is really sure just what—or who—is in which tomb.) Note the delicate rose window whose setting was carved from a single slab of stone. Guided visits to the church may be booked in advance. Santárem is often known as the Gothic capital of Portugal; the nearby **Igreja de Santa Clara** is another outstanding local example of this medieval architectural style. ✉ *Largo Pedro Álvares Cabral* ☎ *243/377297 for guided visits.*

Portas do Sol. Walk up to this lovely park within the ancient walls. From this vantage point you can look down on a sweeping bend in the river and beyond to the farmlands that stretch into the neighboring Alentejo. ✉ *Santarém.*

WHERE TO EAT AND STAY

$ PORTUGUESE 🍴 **Adiafa.** Excellent grilled meats and brisk service are the norm at this large typically Ribatejo restaurant by the bullring, decked out with suits-of-lights and other bullfight motifs. Non–meat eaters can try the *mangusto com bacalhau assado* (a garlickly bread-and-cabbage soup accompanying roasted codfish with fresh herbs) or, when available, fried *sável* (shad) from the River Tagus. In winter, a fire in the hearth may well welcome you. For dessert, ask for the *celestes Santa Clara* (almond cakes) or *arrepiados de Almoster* (almond meringues)—among many local sweets invented by medieval monks and nuns. [$] *Average main: €9* ✉ *Campo Emilio Infante da Câmara* ☎ *92/662–9314, 91/237–8869* 🌐 *restauranteadiafa.com* 🕒 *Closed Tues., last wk of Aug., and 1st wk of Sept.*

$ PORTUGUESE 🍴 **Taberna da Quinzena.** Photos of patrons vie for your attention with bullfight posters at this restaurant in a former house, now a rustic restaurant run by the great-grandson of the original owner, offering hearty traditional fare at low prices. Specialties include *toiro bravo* (wild bull), *entrecosto com arroz de feijoca* (spareribs with red beans and rice), and mangusto com bacalhau assado, but the menu is overhauled daily.

Taberna da Quinzena now has two other branches, one of them in the Santarém Hotel. Ⓢ *Average main: €7* ⊠ *Rua Pedro de Santarém 93* ☎ *243/322 804* ⊕ *www.quinzena.com* ▤ *No credit cards* ⊘ *Closed Sun., and 2nd half of Aug.*

$$ 🏠 **Quinta M.** Glamping has been slow to catch on in Portugal but these
B&B/INN gorgeous yurts in a lovely rural setting do the concept proud: beautifully decorated, with air-conditioning and Wi-Fi, and each boasting a private terrace. **Pros:** peaceful setting; friendly staff; unique accommodations. **Cons:** rather isolated; no restaurant. Ⓢ *Rooms from: €180* ⊠ *Casal da Avó, Várzea de baixo, Casével* ☎ *243/448206* ⊕ *www.quinta-m.com* ⇡ *5 yurts* ⑩ *Breakfast.*

$$$ 🏠 **Santarém Hotel.** Views, a nice on-site restaurant, and a large pool
HOTEL and fitness center are what you get at this contemporary hotel, where
FAMILY rooms overlook the plains or the town. **Pros:** right off the city center; free parking; excellent restaurant. **Cons:** hotel lacks local character; not cheap for what it offers. Ⓢ *Rooms from: €250* ⊠ *Av. Madre Andaluz* ☎ *243/330800* ⊕ *www.santaremhotel.net* ⇡ *105 rooms* ⑩ *Breakfast.*

CONSTÂNCIA

18½ km (11 miles) southeast of Tomar; 4 km (2½ miles) east of Castelo de Almourol.

Peaceful little Constância is at the confluence of the Zêzere and the Tagus. It's best known as the town where poet Luís de Camões was exiled in 1548, the unfortunate result of his romantic involvement with Catarina de Ataide, the "Natercia" of his poems and a lady-in-waiting to Queen Catarina. There's a bronze statue of the bard in a reflective pose at the riverbank. The town is surrounded by beautiful Ribatejan countryside and is a 10-minute drive to the famous Castelo de Almourol.

GETTING HERE AND AROUND
Bus services run by Rodoviária do Tejo links Constância with other towns in the region, but from Lisbon you should catch an express bus (Rede Expressos) to Torres Novas and change there. Driving from Lisbon takes about 1 hour 25 minutes, from Tomar about 30 minutes, and from Santarém about 40 minutes on A23 and A1.

ESSENTIALS
Visitor Information Constância. ⊠ *Av. das Forças Armadas* ☎ *249/730052.*

EXPLORING
Castelo de Almourol. For a close look at this storybook edifice on a craggy island in the Tagus River, take the 1½-km-long (1-mile-long) dirt road leading down to the water from the N3. The riverbank in this area is practically deserted, making it a wonderful picnic spot. From here, a small motorboat will ferry you across (€4 round-trip); for a more leisurely river cruise, board a larger vessel (€2.50) at the quay just downstream in the village of Tancos. The sight couldn't be more romantic: an ancient castle with crenellated walls and a lofty tower sits on a greenery-covered rock in the middle of a gently flowing river. The stuff of poetry and legends, Almourol was the setting for

Francisco de Morais's epic novel *Palmeirim da Inglaterra* (*Palmeirim of England*), about two knights fighting for a princess's favor. In 2015, a small museum was opened inside the keep. ✉ *Ilhota do Tejo, Almourol* ☎ *249/712094 for boat reservations, 96/262–5678 for boat reservations* 🌐 *www.cm-vnbarquinha.pt* 🎫 *€2.50* 🕒 *Closed Mon. Oct.–Apr.*

WHERE TO STAY

$ B&B/INN Fodor's Choice ★ 🏨 **Quinta de Santa Barbara.** Set on some 45 acres of farmland and pine forests overlooking the Tagus River, and just a short drive from town, this property with its several sprawling buildings, a few of which date to the 16th century, is the perfect place to immerse yourself in the Portuguese countryside. **Pros:** unique ambience; peaceful setting; lovely views poolside. **Cons:** no phone or TV in rooms; no elevator; restaurant not always open. [$] *Rooms from: €73* ✉ *Estrada da Quinta de Santa Bárbara,* ✣ *2 km (1 mile) east of Constância on N3; follow directions on sign at traffic circle to Refeitório Quinhentista* ☎ *249/739214, 96/603–9067* 🌐 *www.quinta-santabarbara.com* 🛏 *9 rooms* 🍴 *Breakfast.*

SPORTS AND THE OUTDOORS

GUIDED TOURS

gAventura. The English-speaking guides at this "nature and adventure" company based at a bar on the east bank of the Zêzere lead a wide variety of activities both on that river and on the Tagus, and in the surrounding forest, the Charneca Alentejana. The most popular are half-day excursions by canoe, but they also offer stand-up paddleboarding as well as BTT (mountain bike), horseback, and hiking expeditions. Food is not included unless you make arrangements beforehand, but you can always grab a bite at the riverside esplanade at gAventura's meeting point. Per-person rates range from €8 for biking and €10 for canoeing to €25 for horseback riding. The outfit also organizes multiday camping trips for children. ✉ *Av. das Forças Armadas, Parque de Campismo* ☎ *249/739972, 96/250–3986* 🌐 *www.gaventura.com.*

ABRANTES

16 km (10 miles) east of Constância.

Abrantes became one of the country's most populous and prosperous towns during the 16th century, when the Tagus River was navigable all the way to the sea. With the coming of the railroad and the development of better roads, the town's commercial importance waned. The breathtaking views of the valley from the top of the castle remain, however, and the historical center and friendly locals have also stayed true to tradition. A stroll through the narrow cobblestone streets is a perfect way to spend a lazy afternoon.

GETTING HERE AND AROUND

If you're already in the area, Abrantes is an easy 20-minute drive from Constância or 40-minute drive to Tomar. From Lisbon, it's about a 1½-hour drive. There are a few direct trains from Santa Apolónia and Oriente stations, taking at least one hour 30 minutes; you may have to change once or twice. By bus, the Rede Expressos and Rodoviária do Tejo leave daily from Sete Rios and Campo Grande depots, respectively.

4

ESSENTIALS

Bus Contact **Bus Station.** ✉ *Rua Vale do Aipo* ☎ *96/869–2113 for Rodoviária do Tejo.*

Visitor Information **Abrantes.** ✉ *Esplanada 1 de Maio* ☎ *241/362555* 🌐 *www.turismo.cm-abrantes.pt.*

EXPLORING

Castelo de Abrantes. Walk up through the maze of narrow, flower-lined streets to this 16th-century castle—still an impressive structure today. The garden between the twin fortifications, with its panoramic views, is a wonderful place to watch the sun set: the play of light on the river and the lengthening shadows along the olive groves provide a stirring setting for an evening picnic. The Gothic church within the castle walls, the Igreja de Santa Maria do Castelo, houses a museum that showcases sacred art from convents and monasteries around the region, as well as items from a large private collection of Iberian art from prehistoric to contemporary times. ✉ *Praça D. Francisco de Almeida* ☎ *241/371724 for museum* 🎫 *Free* 🕒 *Closed Mon.*

WHERE TO EAT AND STAY

$ PORTUGUESE 🍴 **Santa Isabel.** In this old town warren of stone-flagged rooms, authentic regional dishes are served with flair to well-heeled locals and the occasional foreign visitor. Specialties include *churrasquinho de porco preto com migas de alheira de caça* (grilled meats from the acorn-fed Iberian black pig, served with a bread-crumb-and-garlic-sausage mixture flavored with game sausage), *enguias fritas com açorda de ovas* (fried eels with fish-roe bread soup), and *arroz de lagosta* (lobster rice). Braver diners might try *cabidela de galo* (chicken cooked in blood). There's a good range of Portuguese wines to choose from to accompany your meal. On winter evenings a fire is lit in the grate, and there's often live piano music. [$] *Average main: €15* ✉ *Rua Sta. Isabel 12* ☎ *241/366230, 96/789–3970* 🌐 *www.restaurantesantaisabel.com* 🕒 *Closed Sun., and 3rd wk in July* ✍ *Reservations essential.*

$ B&B/INN 🏨 **Monte da Várzea.** This former farmstead 20 km (12½ miles) east of Abrantes is set in fertile land near the banks of the Tagus; its 12 houses—some traditionally decorated, others strikingly modern—afford a comfortable base to enjoy this peaceful setting. **Pros:** outdoor activities abound. **Cons:** remote location. [$] *Rooms from: €100* ✉ *Casa Branca, off N118, Alvega* ☎ *241/822284* 🌐 *www.montedavarzea.com* 🛏 *12 villas* 🍽 *Breakfast* 💳 *No credit cards.*

EN ROUTE

Castelo de Belver. This fairy-tale castle—the fortress of Belver—rests atop a cone-shape hill just over the border in the Alentejo, commanding a superb view of the Tagus River. It was built in the last years of the 12th century by the Knights Hospitallers under the command of King Sancho I. In 1194, this region was threatened by the Moorish forces who controlled the lands south of the river, except for Évora. The expected attack never took place, and the present structure is little changed from its original design. The walls of the keep, which stands in the center of the courtyard, are some 12 feet thick, and on the ground floor is a great cistern of unknown depth. According to local lore, an orange dropped into the well will later appear bobbing down the river. To drive here follow N244–3 through the pine-covered hills to Chão de Codes, then take N244 south toward Gavião. There are four trains a day to Belver from Abrantes (a 25-minute ride). ⊠ *Belver, Gavião, Portalegre* ☎ *241/639070 for Gavião municipality* 🖾 *€2* ⊗ *Closed Mon. and weekend mornings.*

TOMAR

24 km (15 miles) east of Fátima; 64 km (40 miles) northeast of Santarém.

Tomar is an attractive town laid out on both sides of the Rio Nabão, with the new and old parts linked by a graceful, arched stone bridge. The river flows through a lovely park with weeping willows and an old wooden waterwheel. The town is best known for being the former headquarters of the Order of the Knights Templar and home to their Convento do Cristo, which is a UNESCO World Heritage Site. The town also hosts the Festa dos Tabuleiros every four years in July (last in 2015). This ancient tradition is also the oldest festival in Portugal and consists of parades of girls carrying large *tabuleiros,* platters piled high with 30 loaves of bread fixed on rods, interspersed with flowers and topped with a crown. They wear these unusual headpieces in honor of the Holy Spirit, but the festival actually dates back to pagan times.

GETTING HERE AND AROUND

There's a train line between Lisbon (Santa Apolónia and Oriente stations) and Tomar with several daily departures that run through Vila Franca de Xira and Santarém. Taking the bus (Rede Expressos from Lisbon or other cities, or Rodoviária do Tejo from surrounding towns) is another possibility. Driving to Tomar takes 1 hour 15 minutes from Lisbon and close to 25 minutes from Santarém or Fátima.

ESSENTIALS

Bus Contact Bus Station. ⊠ *Av. Combatentes da Grande Guerra , Varzea Grande* ☎ *92/445–0001 for Rodoviária do Tejo* ⊕ *www.rodotejo.pt.*

Visitor Information Tomar. ⊠ *Av. Dr. Cândido Madureira* ☎ *249/329823.*

Trips along the Rio Zêzere on the large (40-passenger) motorboat São Cristóvão in summer depart from a dock at the Lago Azul hotel, upstream from the Castelo de Bode dam. Two-hour cruises (starting at 10 am or 5 pm) cost €15 per person; four-hour cruises including a buffet lunch with wine start at noon and cost €38. All cruises take place only when there are enough passengers—this is most likely to happen on weekends and national holidays. The Hotel dos Templários in Tomar handles reservations.

Contacts Barco São Cristóvão. ⊠ *Lago Azul, N348, Castanheira, Ferreira do Zêzere* ☎ *249/310100 for Hotel dos Templários* ⊕ *www.barcosaocristovao.com.*

EXPLORING

Aqueduto dos Pegões. Striding across the Ribeira dos Pegões valley, some 5 km (3 miles) northwest of Tomar, is a 5-km-long (3-mile-long) aqueduct, built in the 16th century to bring water to Tomar. It joins the walls of the Convent of Christ. ⊠ *Tomar.*

Fodors Choice   **Convento de Cristo.** Atop a hill rising from the Old Town is the remark-
★   able Convent of Christ. You can drive to the top of the hill or hike for
about 20 minutes along a path through the trees before reaching a formal garden lined with azulejo-covered benches. This was the Portuguese
headquarters of the Knights Templar, from 1160 until the order was
forced to disband in 1314. Identified by their white tunics emblazoned
with a crimson cross, the Templars were at the forefront of the Christian
armies in the Crusades and during the struggles against the Moors. King
Dinis in 1334 resurrected the order in Portugal under the banner of the
Knights of Christ and reestablished Tomar as its headquarters. In the
early 15th century, under Prince Henry the Navigator (who for a time
resided in the castle), the order flourished. The caravels of the Age of
Discovery even sailed under the order's crimson cross.

The oldest parts of the complex date to the 12th century, including the
towering castle keep and the fortresslike, 16-sided Charola, which—like
many Templar churches—is patterned after the Church of the Holy
Sepulchre in Jerusalem and has an octagonal oratory at its core. The
paintings and wooden statues in its interior, however, were added in
the 16th century. The complex's medieval nucleus acquired its Manueline church and cluster of magnificent cloisters during the next 500
years. To see what the Manueline style is all about, stroll through the
church's nave with its many examples of the twisted ropes, seaweed,
and nautical themes that typify the style, and be sure to look at the
chapter house window, one of the most photographed in Europe. Its
lichen-encrusted sculpture evokes the spirit of the great Age of Discovery. ⊠ *Tomar* ☎ *249/313481* ⊕ *www.conventocristo.pt* ✉ *€6 (free
1st Sun. of the month); €15 combined ticket, includes Alcobaça and
Batalha monasteries.*

Igreja de Santa Maria do Olival. Across the Rio Nabão is the 13th-century
Igreja de Santa Maria do Olival, where the bones of several Knights
Templar are interred, including those of Gualdim Pais, founder of the
order in Portugal. Popular belief—supported by some archaeological
evidence—has it that the church was once connected with the Convent
of Christ by a tunnel. ⊠ *Rua Aquiles de Mota Lima* ⊙ *Closed Mon.*

Museu Luso-Hebraico Abraham Zacuto–Sinagoga. In the Old Town, walk
along the narrow, flower-lined streets, particularly Rua Dr. Joaquim
Jacinto, which takes you to the heart of the Jewish Quarter and this former synagogue, now a modest museum. Built in the mid-15th century
for what was then a sizeable community, this is Portugal's oldest extant
synagogue, though there are only a handful of Jewish families living
in Tomar currently, so it's only used as a house of prayer when visiting
Jews make up the required numbers (at least 10 men). Inside, exhibits
chronicle the Jewish presence in the country, which all but ended in
1496, when Dom Manuel issued an edict ordering Jews to either leave
the country or convert to Christianity. Many, who became known as
Marranos, converted but secretly practiced Judaism. The building was
declared a national monument in 1921 and is open for visits. Call the
Tomar tourist office in advance to set up a free guided visit in English.
⊠ *Rua Dr. Joaquim Jacinto 73* ☎ *249/329823 for tourist office* ✉ *Free
(donations accepted)* ⊙ *Closed Mon.*

Roda do Mouchão. This enormous working wooden waterwheel—typical of those once used in the region for irrigation—stands in the Parque do Mouchão gardens by the Rio Nabão. The wheel is a replica but its design is thought to be of either Arabic or Roman origin. ✉ *Av. Marquês de Tomar.*

WHERE TO EAT AND STAY

$ ✕ **A Bela Vista.** The date on the *calçada* paving out front reads "1922,"
PORTUGUESE   which was when the Sousa family opened this attractive little restaurant next to the Ponte Velha, the old arched bridge. For summer dining there's a small, rustic terrace with views of the river and the Convent of Christ. Carrying on the family tradition, the kitchen turns out great quantities of hearty regional fare. Try the *fritada de gambas* (fried prawns, served with açorda bread soup), *filetes de pescada* (hake fillets in batter), *cabrito assado* (roast kid), *plumas de porco preto* (black pork cutlets), or *arroz de polvo* (octopus rice stew). For dessert, there's the local specialty, *fatia de Tomar*, made in-house with only egg yolks, sugar, and water. $ *Average main: €10* ✉ *Rua Marquês Pombal 6 Ponte Velha* ☎ *249/312870* ⊘ *Closed Tues. and 2 wks in Oct. No dinner Mon.*

$ ✕ **Chico Elias.** This charmingly rustic restaurant just outside Tomar owes
PORTUGUESE   its fame to chef Maria do Céu's creativity. At lunch on weekends deli-
Fodor'sChoice   cious hearty dishes such as cabrito assado and *cachola* (pork rib and
★   loin, served with cabbage) are available; to eat at other times or sample most other specialties you must call the day before, because the dishes take time to prepare in the wood-burning oven. To know what to order, click on the "Alguns Pratos" images on the Facebook page Restaurante Chico Elias; dishes include *feijoada de caracóis* (bean stew with snails), *coelho na abóbora* (rabbit in a pumpkin) and bacalhau *com porco* in a secret sauce. For dessert, there are fluffy fatias de Tomar and a delicious leite creme. $ *Average main: €15* ✉ *Rua Principal 70* ☎ *249/311067* ▭ *No credit cards* ⊘ *Closed Tues., 2 wks in July, and 2 wks in Sept.* ⌕ *Reservations essential.*

$ ▦ **Hotel dos Templários.** With its spacious grounds, reasonable rates, and
HOTEL   many amenities, this large, modern hotel in a tranquil park along the
Fodor'sChoice   Rio Nabão makes a good base for exploring the whole area. **Pros:** excel-
★   lent rooms; lots of amenities, including free Wi-Fi throughout; location and views are great. **Cons:** large size gives a somewhat impersonal feel; the spa and restaurant are a bit pricey; no covered parking. $ *Rooms from: €137* ✉ *Largo Candido dos Reis 1* ☎ *249/310100* ⊕ *www.hotel-ostemplarios.com* ⇆ *176 rooms* ⦿ *Some meals.*

EN
ROUTE From Tomar you can take N113 northwest to Ourem and visit its walled medieval castle, including its palace, church with crypt, and Gothic fountain built by King Afonso IV in the 15th century. To reach Castelo de Bode from Tomar, take EN110 south. Set between hills and forests with inviting sandy beaches and placid waters, the lake (Estala-gem Vale Manço) offers boating, fishing, and water sports.

FÁTIMA

20 km (12 miles) northwest of Torres Vedras; 16 km (10 miles) southeast of Batalha; 20 km (12 miles) southeast of Leiria.

On the western flanks of the Serra de Aire lies Fátima, an important Roman Catholic pilgrimage site that is, ironically, named after the daughter of Mohammed, the prophet of Islam. If you visit this sleepy little Portuguese town in between pilgrimages, it will be difficult to imagine the thousands of faithful who come from all corners of the world to make this religious affirmation, cramming the roads, squares, parks, and virtually every square foot of space. A few pilgrims go the last miles on their knees; many more complete their approach within the sanctuary that way.

GETTING HERE AND AROUND

The Rede Expressos and Rodoviária do Tejo bus lines can take you to Fátima from Lisbon or Leiria. Another option is driving, which will take close to one hour from Lisbon and 15 minutes from Leiria.

ESSENTIALS

Bus Contact Bus Station. ⊠ *Av. D. José Alves Correia Silva* ☎ *249/531611 for Rodovíaria do Tejo* ⊕ *www.rodotejo.pt.*

Visitor Information Fátima. ⊠ *Av. D. José Alves Correia da Silva 213* ☎ *249/531139* ⊕ *www.turismodocentro.pt.* **Santuário de Fátima.** ⊠ *Next to Capela das Aparições, Rua do Imaculado Coração de Maria* ☎ *249/539623 for sanctuary info service* ⊕ *www.fatima.pt.*

EXPLORING

Basílica da Santíssima Trindade. One of the largest Catholic churches in the world, seating some 8,500 worshipers, the Holy Trinity was consecrated in 2007 and raised to the state of basilica in 2012. Although it won prizes for engineering rather than architecture, its ample, curved form—designed by Greek architect Alexandros Tombazis—offers a pleasing contrast to its rather run-of-the-mill 1920s predecessor. Much of the iconography, including on the lavish main doors, was inspired by Byzantine and Orthodox motifs, and was produced by artists from Portugal and seven other countries. The Tall Cross crucifix outside the church is by the German artist Robert Schad. ⊠ *Rua João Paulo II* ☎ *249/539600 for sanctuary* ⊕ *www.santuario-fatima.pt* ⌦ *Free.*

Basílica de Nossa Senhora de Fátima. At the head of the huge esplanade is the large neoclassical basilica (built in the late 1920s), flanked on either side by a semicircular peristyle. ⊠ *Rua do Imaculado Coração de Maria* ☎ *249/539600 for sanctuary* ⊕ *www.santuario-fatima.pt* ⌦ *Free.*

Capela das Aparições (*Chapel of Apparitions*). This 20th-century chapel is built on the site where the appearances of the Virgin Mary are said to have taken place. A plinth with a statue of the Virgin marks the exact spot. Encrusted in her bejeweled, golden crown is the bullet extracted from the body of Pope John Paul II after the 1981 assassination attempt on him. Gifts, mostly gold jewelry and wax reproductions of body parts, are burned here as offerings to the Virgin in the hope of achieving a

Catholic Stories

It all began May 13, 1917, when three young shepherds—Lucia dos Santos and her cousins Francisco and Jacinta—reported seeing the Virgin Mary in a field at Cova de Iria, near the village. The Virgin promised to return on the 13th of each month for the next five months, and amid much controversy and skepticism, each time accompanied by increasingly larger crowds, the three children reported successive apparitions. This was during a period of anticlerical sentiment in Portugal, and after the sixth reputed apparition, in October, the children were arrested and interrogated. But they insisted the Virgin had spoken to them, revealing three secrets. Two of these, revealed by Lucia in 1941, were interpreted to

foretell the coming of World War II and the spread of communism and atheism. In a 1930 Pastoral Letter, the Bishop of Leiria declared the apparitions worthy of belief, thus approving the "Cult of Fátima."

In May 2000, Francisco and Jacinta were beatified in a ceremony held at Fátima by Pope John Paul II. The third secret, which was revealed after the beatification, was interpreted to have foretold an attempt on the life of the pope. On the 13th of each month, and especially in May and October, the faithful flock here to witness the passing of the statue of the Virgin through the throngs, to participate in candlelight processions, and to take part in solemn Masses.

miraculous cure. ⊠ *Santuário de Fátima, Cova da Iria* ☏ *249/539600 for sanctuary* ⊕ *www.santuario-fatima.pt* ⊠ *Free.*

Casas dos Pastorinhos. These are the cottages, in the nearby hamlet of Aljustrel, where the three shepherd children who saw the Virgin Mary were born. To reach them, from Fátima's Rotunda Sul (south roundabout) take the N360 to Aljustrel for just over 1 km (½ mile) and turn right onto Rua de Aljustrel (signposted "Museu"). At the next major junction, the two houses of the little shepherds are along the street to the left, along with the **Casa-Museu de Aljustrel,** a small house-museum. ⊠ *Rua dos Pastorinhos, Aljustrel* ☏ *249/532828* ⊙ *Closed Mon.*

FAMILY **Grutas da Moeda.** The hills to the south and west of Fátima are honeycombed with limestone caves. Legend has it that many years ago, a wealthy man carrying a bag of coins was traveling through the woods when he was attacked by a gang of thieves. Struggling from the attack, the man fell into one of the cave grottoes, still carrying the bag of coins. Through the cave, the lost coins were spread around, thus giving the Grutas da Moeda, 3 km (2 miles) from Fátima, their name, which means Coin Caves. Within about a 25-km (15-mile) radius of the town are four other major caverns—São Mamede, Alvados, Santo António, and Mira de Aire, the country's largest—equipped with lights and elevators. On a guided tour in any of these (ask for an English-speaking guide) you can see the subterranean world of limestone formations, underground rivers and lakes, and multicolor stalagmites and stalactites. At Mira d'Aire there's also an outdoor water park, open mid-June to mid-September;

joint tickets are available. ✉ *Largo das Grutas da Moeda, São Mamede* ☎ *244/703838* 🌐 *www.grutasmoeda.com* 🎟 *€6, visitor center €2.*

FAMILY **Museu de Cera** (*Wax Museum*). In the center of town, the wax museum has 30 tableaux depicting the events that took place in Fátima when the child shepherds first saw the apparitions in 1917, and subsequent developments. ✉ *Rua Jacinto Marto* ☎ *249/539300* 🌐 *www.mucefa.pt* 🎟 *€7.50.*

O Milagre de Fátima - Museu Interativo. A new high-tech rival to the nearby Museu de Cera and its waxworks, the Miracle of Fátima Interactive Museum also re-creates the events a century ago that resulted in the local Marian cult. Its use of multimedia technologies certainly helps generate a sense of wonder at the apparition of the Virgin and of the Angel of Portugal, and at what became known as the Miracle of the Sun. Visits are guided, with free time towards the end. The museum is under a small shopping mall near the new basilica. ✉ *Central Comercial Espaço Fatimae, Av. Dom José Alves Correia da Silva 123* ☎ *249/406881* 🌐 *www.omilagredefatima.com* 🎟 *€7.50.*

WHERE TO EAT

$ PORTUGUESE FAMILY 🍴 **O Crispim.** One of Fátima's longest-established restaurants, this place just outside the inner ring road is above all known for the quality of its grilled meat and fish. The vine-shaded esplanade is another big draw, creating a real family ambience. Leisurely lunches—either outside or in the wood-and-stone dining room—are made possible by the fact that the kitchen keeps going throughout the afternoon. Top dishes here include tender *vitela Mirandesa* steak and bacalhau *à lagareiro* (cod baked with onions, potatoes, and olives). If you fancy *codorniz* (quails) or other game, call the previous day to order. [$] *Average main: €14* ✉ *Rua São João Eudes 23* ☎ *249/532781, 91/542–6464* 🌐 *www.ocrispim.com* ⏲ *Closed Tues., 1st half of July, and Carnival wk. No dinner Mon.* ✍ *Reservations essential.*

$ PORTUGUESE 🍴 **Retiro dos Caçadores.** A big brick fireplace, wood paneling, and stone walls set the mood in this cozy hunter's lodge, where the food is simple, but portions are hearty and the quality is good. This is the best place in town for fresh game, especially codorniz and *coelho* (rabbit), which comes casserole-style, with rice or potatoes. [$] *Average main: €13* ✉ *Rua São João Deus 44* ☎ *249/531323* 🌐 *www.retirodoscacadores.com* ⏲ *Closed Wed.*

$$ PORTUGUESE 🍴 **Tia Alice.** Considered one of Portugal's best traditional restaurants, "Aunt Alice" is concealed in an inconspicuous old house with French windows, across from the parish church near the sanctuary. A flight of wooden stairs inside leads down to an intimate dining area with stone walls; there is now also an elegant flower-filled garden with some outdoor seating. The *arroz de pato* (duck rice) is among the many meat dishes worth trying, as is the bacalhau *gratinado* (baked salt cod with béchamel sauce), which serves two. After dinner, stop in at the little crafts shop at the top of the stairs; it sells hand-painted ceramics by various local artists, some of them just like those used in the restaurant. [$] *Average main: €19* ✉ *Rua do Adro 152* ☎ *249/531737, 249/533194,*

91/308–0334 ⊕ *www.tiaalice.com* ☉ *Closed Mon., and 1st 3 wks of July. No dinner Sun.* ⚿ *Reservations essential.*

WHERE TO STAY

$ 🏨 **Casa São Nuno.** This large rectory-style inn just a few minutes' walk
HOTEL from the sanctuary is run by the Carmelites but is open to visitors of all faiths. **Pros:** good value for money; hotel has its own chapel and private entrance to sanctuary; friendly service. **Cons:** attracts mostly older, religious clientele; not a good choice for nonreligious people or those seeking a romantic vacation; few amenities. ⓢ *Rooms from: €56* ⊠ *Av. Beato Nuno 271* ☎ *249/530230* ⊕ *www.casasaonuno.com* ☉ *Closed mid-Dec.–late Jan.* ⇴ *130 rooms* ⏐◯⏐ *Breakfast.*

$ 🏨 **Dom Gonçalo Hotel & Spa.** There is a pastoral view of gardens from
HOTEL every window of this elegant boutique hotel a 10-minute walk from the
FAMILY sanctuary, whose decoration and amenities make a striking contrast to
Fodor's Choice the austere style of many of its local rivals. **Pros:** bright, friendly service;
★ excellent value with unique spa facilities; free Wi-Fi throughout. **Cons:** not right by sanctuary; cheaper rooms on the small side. ⓢ *Rooms from: €71* ⊠ *Rua Jacinto Marto 100* ☎ *249/539330* ⊕ *www.hoteldg. com* ⇴ *71 rooms* ⏐◯⏐ *Breakfast.*

$ 🏨 **Hotel Lux Fátima.** This upscale hotel, just a couple of minutes' walk
HOTEL from the new basilica, stands out for its contemporary decor and all the amenities you'd expect in this category. **Pros:** central location; high-speed Internet via cable available; cable TV includes extra sport channels. **Cons:** no local character; no pool. ⓢ *Rooms from: €85* ⊠ *Av. Dom José Alves Correia da Silva, Lote 2, Urbanização das Azinheiras* ☎ *249/530690* ⊕ *www.luxhotels.pt* ⇴ *67 rooms* ⏐◯⏐ *Breakfast.*

$$ 🏨 **Hotel Santa Maria.** This recently renovated hotel is right in the center
HOTEL of Fátima and is a three-minute walk to the sanctuary. **Pros:** friendly staff; great value for money with free Wi-Fi throughout; free secure covered parking. **Cons:** no gym or pool; not a wide variety at breakfast; half- and full-board rates only available for groups. ⓢ *Rooms from: €170* ⊠ *Rua de Santo António* ☎ *249/530110* ⊕ *www.hotelstmaria. com* ⇴ *173 rooms* ⏐◯⏐ *Breakfast.*

ÉVORA AND
THE ALENTEJO

Updated by
Lauren Frayer

The Alentejo, which means "the land beyond the Rio Tejo" (Tagus River) in Portuguese, is a vast, sparsely populated area of heath and rolling hills punctuated with stands of cork and olive trees. Here you'll find a wide variety of attractions—from the rugged west-coast beaches to the Roman and medieval architecture of Évora, and the green northern foothills dotted with crumbling castles that form the frontier with Spain.

Portugal is the world's largest producer of cork, and much of it comes from the Alentejo. This industry is not for people in a hurry. It takes two decades before the trees can be harvested, and then their bark can be carefully stripped only once every nine years. The numbers painted on the trees indicate the year of the last harvest. Exhibits at several regional museums chronicle this delicate process and display associated tools and handicrafts.

The undulating fields of wheat and barley surrounding Beja and Évora, the rice paddies of Alcácer do Sal, and the vineyards of Borba and Reguengos de Monsaraz are representative of the region's role as Portugal's breadbasket. Traditions here are strong. Herdsmen tending sheep and goats wear the *pelico* (traditional sheepskin vest), and women in the fields wear broad-brim hats over kerchiefs and colorful patterned dresses over trousers. Dwellings are a dazzling white; more elegant houses have wrought-iron balconies and grillwork. The windows and doors of modest cottages and hilltop country *montes* (farmhouses) are trimmed with blue or yellow, and colorful flowers abound. The best time to visit the Alentejo is spring, when temperatures are pleasant and the fields are carpeted with wildflowers. Summer can be brutal, with the mercury frequently topping 37°C (100°F). As the Portuguese say, "In the Alentejo there is no shade but what comes from the sky."

ORIENTATION AND PLANNING

GETTING ORIENTED

This is the country's largest province, and it's divided roughly into two parts: the more mountainous Alto, or "upper," Alentejo north of Évora, and the flatter Baixo, or "lower," Alentejo that lies to the south. The area stretches from the rugged west-coast beaches all the way east to Spain, and from the Tejo in the north to the low mountains on the border of the Algarve, Portugal's southernmost province. Its central hub, Évora, is rich with traditional Portuguese architecture.

Évora. One of Portugal's best-preserved medieval towns, Évora's imposing outer walls give way to winding cobblestone lanes dotted with

TOP REASONS TO GO

Travel back in time. Wander amid megaliths erected 2,000 years before Stonehenge, Roman ruins, Moorish forts, and medieval monasteries in the province where Portugal's history is best preserved.

Wide-open spaces. With a third of Portugal's land area and only one-twentieth of its population, the Alentejo offers pristine open space even in one Europe's smallest countries. Stand atop a well-preserved medieval fortress and gaze out at undulating cork and wheat fields on every horizon. Even the more densely populated coastline has all of the Algarve's charm with a fraction of its tourists.

Traditional rural festivals. From Portuguese-style flamenco and bullfighting along the border with Spain, to autumn chestnut roasts in northern hill-town squares, and sardine festivals on the coast, every weekend offers another reason to celebrate in rural Alentejo.

Food and wine. Alentejano cuisine is considered Portugal's best, with centuries-old farming practices that were organic long before it was trendy. The highlight is *porco preto*, free-range black pigs that graze on acorns under Alentejo's ever-present cork trees.

architectural gems from the Romans, Visigoths, Moors, and the Middle Ages. It's also a lively university town, and a good base from which to explore the Alentejo.

Side Trips from Évora. Visit some of Portugal's best-kept secrets—rustic wineries, horse farms, medieval castles, Roman ruins, and prehistoric stone sculptures—all within day-tripping distance from Évora. Tapestries and carpets from the unassuming little village of Arraiolos are famous the world over.

Alto Alentejo. Portugal's most stunning walled fortresses and clifftop castles dot the province's northern half, along the frontier with its old archenemy, Spain. With the highest mountains in southern Portugal, this area has a more varied landscape than the flatter south, and is the country's best-kept secret for hiking and mountain biking.

Baixo Alentejo. This is Portugal's breadbasket, with undulating wheat fields, olive groves, and cork forests that stretch to golden dunes and dramatic cliffs over the Atlantic. A network of hiking trails along the coast attracts a new brand of environmentally minded tourists to this previously undiscovered corner of Europe.

PLANNING

WHEN TO GO

Spring comes early to this part of Portugal. Early April to mid-June is a wonderful time to tour, when the fields are full of colorful wildflowers. July and August are brutally hot, with temperatures in places such as Beja often reaching 37°C (100°F) or higher. By mid-September things cool off sufficiently to make touring this region a delight.

PLANNING YOUR TIME

You should allow 10 days to get a feel for the region, exploring Évora and visiting some outlying attractions such as Monsaraz, Castelo de Vide, and Mértola. This will also allow time for a day or two of sunbathing on a west-coast beach. If you skip the beach, you can cover the most interesting attractions at a comfortable pace in seven days. Three days will give you time to explore Évora and its surroundings along with one or two additional highlights.

GETTING HERE AND AROUND

AIR TRAVEL

You can fly into the Lisbon or Faro airports and then take ground transportation into the region. Évora is roughly 130 km (80 miles) from Lisbon and about 225 km (140 miles) from Faro.

Airport Contacts Faro Airport. ⊠ *Aeroporto de Faro, Faro* ☎ *289/800800* ⊕ *www.faro-airport.com.* **Lisbon Portela Airport.** ⊠ *Alameda Comunidades Portuguesas, Lisbon* ☎ *218/841–3500, 800/841–3700* ⊕ *www.lisbon-airport.com.*

BUS TRAVEL

There are few places in this region that aren't served by at least one bus daily. Express coaches run by several regional lines travel regularly between Lisbon and the larger towns such as Évora, Beja, and Estremoz. Because several companies leave for the Alentejo from different terminals in Lisbon, it's best to have a travel agent do your booking. Standard buses between Lisbon and Évora run at least once every hour between 6 am and 9:30 pm, and cost €12.

Bus Contacts Eva Transportes. ⊠ *Praça Marechal Humberto Delgado, Estrada das Laranjeiras, Av. República 5, Faro* ☎ *289/899700, 707/223344* ⊕ *www.eva-bus.com.* **Rede Expressos.** ⊠ *Terminal Rodoviário de Sete Rios, Praça Marechal Humberto Delgado, Estrada das Laranjeiras, Lisbon* ☎ *707/223344* ⊕ *www.rede-expressos.pt.* **TREVO (Transportes Rodoviários de Évora).** ⊠ *Estação Central de camionagem, Av. S. Sebastião, Valverde* ☎ *266/106923* ⊕ *www.trevo.com.pt.*

CAR TRAVEL

One of the best features of Alentejo is its seemingly untouched beaches and villages—which you'll need a car to reach. Driving will give you access to many out-of-the-way spots. A good network of modern toll roads crisscrossing the country, as well as very little traffic, make driving quick but expensive. A 1½-hour drive on the main A6 toll road from Lisbon to Évora costs about €10 for a standard sedan, and about €15 for an SUV. There are no confusing big cities in which to get lost, although parking can be a problem in some tight town centers, as in Évora.

The toll highway A6, which branches off A2 running south from Lisbon, takes you as far as the Spanish border at Elvas, where it links up with the highway from Madrid. This road provides easy access to Évora and Alto Alentejo. The A2 runs south to the Algarve, as does the non-toll IP1/E01. Farther inland and south of Évora, the IP2/E802 is the best access for Beja and southeastern Alentejo. The N521 runs

105 km (65 miles) from Cáceres, Spain, to the Portuguese border near Portalegre. To the south, the N433 runs from Seville, Spain, to Beja, 225 km (140 miles) away.

Car Rental Contacts **Algarve Car Hire.** ⊕ *www.carhire-algarve.com.* **Europcar Lisbon.** ⊠ *Lisbon Portela Airport, Lisbon* ☎ *21/8401176* ⊕ *www.europcar.com/ location/portugal/lisbon/lisbon-airport.* **Faro Car Hire.** ⊠ *Aeroporto de Faro, Apartado 488, Faro* ☎ *960/204709* ⊕ *www.farocar.com.* **Portugal-auto-rentals. com.** ⊠ *Edifício Fonte Nova Loja I, Rua da Fig. Foz, Pombal* ☎ *236/218999 from Portugal, 973/454–5732 from the U.S.* ⊕ *www.portugal-auto-rentals.com.*

TRAIN TRAVEL

During the economic crisis, the Portuguese government froze its plans for a high-speed rail network stretching across Alto Alentejo, which would have cut train travel time between Madrid and Lisbon from nine hours to as few as three. Spain has already built tracks on its side of the border, but it's unclear when Portugal will come up with the money to build its portion. Until then, train travel in the vast Alentejo is not for people in a great hurry. Service to the more remote destinations is infrequent—and in some cases nonexistent. A couple of towns, including Évora and Beja, are connected with Lisbon by several trains daily. The Intercidades train leaves from Lisbon's Oriente Station in the Parque da Nações to the Alentejo. You can also catch the Intercidades train at Lisbon's Entrecampos Station.

Train Stations **Beja CP Train Station.** ⊠ *Largo da Estação 17, Beja* ☎ *808/210220.* **Évora CP Train Station.** ⊠ *Largo da Estação, Valverde* ☎ *808/208208.*

RESTAURANTS

In the Alentejo, the country's granary, bread is a major part of most meals. It's the basis of a popular dish known as *açorda*, a thick, stick-to-your-ribs porridge to which various ingredients such as fish, meat, and eggs are added. Açorda *de marisco*—bread with eggs, seasonings, and assorted shellfish—is one of the more popular varieties. Another version, açorda *alentejana*, consists of a clear broth, olive oil, garlic, coriander (cilantro), slices of bread, and poached eggs. *Cação*, also called baby shark or dogfish, is a white-meat fish with a single bone down the back and is mostly served in a fish soup or as part of a porridge.

Pork from the Alentejo is the best in the country and often is combined with clams, onions, and tomatoes in the classic dish *carne de porco à alentejana.* One of Portugal's most renowned sheep's milk cheeses—tangy, but mellow when properly ripened—is made in the Serpa region. Alentejo wines—especially those from around Borba, Reguengos de Monsaraz, and Vidigueira—are regular prizewinners at national tasting contests.

Between mid-June and mid-September, reservations are advised at upscale restaurants. Many moderate or inexpensive establishments, however, don't accept reservations and have informal dining rooms where you share a table with other diners. Dress at all but the most luxurious restaurants is casual. *Prices in the reviews are the average cost of a main course at dinner or, if dinner isn't served, at lunch.*

HOTELS

The best accommodations in the Alentejo have long been considered the chain of government-run *pousadas,* hotels housed in historic properties like medieval convents or castles. But the pousadas' reign has been challenged recently by a new crop of private luxury hotels, such as the twin Hotel M'AR De AR properties in Évora. Since Portugal's economic crisis, the pousadas have recently begun lowering their rates to compete— good news for travelers. Still, some of the finest pousadas in the country are in the Alentejo, including one in the old Lóios convent in Évora and another in the castle at Estremoz. Many of the pousadas are small, some with as few as six rooms, so reserving well in advance is essential. There are also a number of high-quality, government-approved private guesthouses in the region. Look for signs that say "Turismo Rural" or "Turismo de Habitação." In summer, air-conditioning is absolutely necessary in Évora, where temperatures can soar to more than 44°C (110°F). *Prices in the reviews are the lowest price of a standard double room in high season. For expanded hotel reviews, visit Fodors.com.*

WHAT IT COSTS IN EUROS			
$	**$$**	**$$$**	**$$$$**
Restaurants	under €16	€16–€20	€21–€25	over €25
Hotels	under €141	€141–€200	€201–€260	over €260

Restaurant prices are per person for a main course at dinner. Hotel prices are for a standard double room, including tax, in high season (off-season rates may be lower).

VISITOR INFORMATION

The tourist office in Évora can schedule a variety of guided or unguided tours of megalithic sites, area wineries, and other attractions by bus, van, horse-drawn carriage, or foot. Many of the major sites are also covered by a wide selection of day tours from Lisbon.

Contacts Association of Tour Guides in Alentejo (*AGIA*). ✉ *Praça do Giraldo 73, Valverde* ☎ *963/702392* ⊕ *www.alentejoguides.com.* **Cityrama.** ✉ *Av. Joao XXI 78-E, Lisbon* ☎ *800/208513* ⊕ *www.cityrama.pt.* **RSI Sightseeing Tours.** ✉ *Edificio de Sta Catarina, Rua de Sta Catarina, loja 4, Valverde* ☎ *266/747871, 91/222–1444* ⊕ *www.rsi-viagens.com.*

ÉVORA

130 km (81 miles) southeast of Lisbon.

Dressed in traditional garb, shepherds and farmers with faces wizened by a lifetime in the baking sun stand around the fountain at Praça do Giraldo; a group of college girls dressed in jeans and T-shirts chats animatedly at a sidewalk café; a local businessman in coat and tie purposefully hurries by; and clusters of tourists, cameras in hand, capture the historic monuments on film—all this is part of a typical summer's day in Évora. The flourishing capital of the central Alentejo is also a

GREAT ITINERARIES

You can make convenient loops starting and finishing in Lisbon, or you can extend your travels by continuing south to the Algarve from Beja or Santiago do Cacém. You should allow 10 days to get a feel for the region, exploring Évora and visiting some outlying attractions such as Monsaraz, Castelo de Vide, and Mértola. This will also allow time for a day or two of sunbathing on a west-coast beach. If you skip the beach, you can cover the most interesting attractions at a comfortable pace in seven days. Three days will give you time to explore Évora and its surroundings along with one or two additional highlights.

IF YOU HAVE 3 DAYS

Be sure to include **Évora**, one of Portugal's most beautiful cities, in your first day of exploring. The following morning visit the rug-producing town of **Arraiolos** and then continue on to **Estremoz** and its imposing fortress, which doubles as a pousada. Head east past Borba and its marble quarries to **Vila Viçosa**, site of the Paço Ducal. Then continue south to visit

a winery or two in and around **Reguengos de Monsaraz**. In the morning visit the fortified hilltop town of **Monsaraz** before returning to Lisbon.

IF YOU HAVE 7 DAYS

After a day and night in **Évora**, head to the **Aqueduto da Agua da Prata** and the prehistoric sites just outside town, which include the **Cromlech and the Menhir of Almendres** and the **Dolmen of Zambujeiro**. On the way to your next overnight stop in **Estremoz**, take a break in **Arraiolos**. From Estremoz head east to the fortified town of **Elvas**, stopping en route at the Paço Ducal in **Vila Viçosa**. The following day continue to **Monsaraz**, with a stop along the way to do some wine tasting in **Reguengos de Monsaraz**. From Monsaraz head south to **Beja**, inspecting the Roman ruins at **São Cucufate** en route. The next day head west to **Santiago do Cacém** for more Roman ruins and a few hours at the beach. On your seventh day return to Lisbon, stopping along the way to see the castle at **Alcácer do Sal**.

university town with an astonishing variety of inspiring architecture, including pristine Roman ruins. Atop a small hill in the heart of a vast cork-, olive-, and grain-producing region, Évora stands out from provincial farm towns the world over: the entire inner city is a monument and was declared a UNESCO World Heritage Site in 1986.

GETTING HERE AND AROUND

Évora is, above all, a town for walking. Wherever you glance as you stroll the maze of narrow streets and alleys of the Cidade Velha (Old Town), amid arches and whitewashed houses, you'll come face to face with reminders of the town's rich architectural and cultural heritage. West of Praça do Giraldo, between Rua Serpa Pinto and Rua dos Mercadores you have the old Jewish quarter of narrow streets lined with medieval houses. A tourist bus (€2 for all-day ticket) sponsored by the city follows a blue line marked on the street through the historic center. To get on, just raise your hand anywhere along the blue line; you can get off whenever you wish. The area surrounding Évora is a rich agricultural region with scattered small villages and some of Portugal's earliest inhabited sites.

Cabs charge €1 per kilometer. Note that if you travel to another town from Évora, such as Beja, you'll have to pay for the taxi's return trip. To get a cab, head for one of the many taxi stands around town, such as the one in Praça do Giraldo (you can't hail them on the street) or call Radio Taxis Évora.

VISITOR INFORMATION

Walking tours of Évora are available through RSI and Mendes e Murteira, and both companies can also organize bus or van tours of the district's archaeological sites. AGIA offers 90-minute guided tours of Évora.

The Évora tourist office is helpful and can schedule tours or make phone calls to hotels or restaurants. The Alentejo wine route office is also open daily for tastings and can help schedule visits to local wineries.

ESSENTIALS

Carriage Tours Turalentejo. ⊠ *Rue Miguel Bombarda 37, Valverde* ☎ *266/702717, 266/705127* ⊕ *www.turalentejo.webnode.pt.*

Taxi Contact Auto Táxis Modelares Dianenses. ⊠ *R. António da Silveira 2* ☎ *968/035386.*

Tour Information Mendes e Murteira. ⊠ *Travessa do Harpa 9-A, Valverde* ☎ *266/746096, 917/236025* ⊕ *www.evora-mm.pt.*

Visitor Information Alentejo Regional Tourist Office. ⊠ *Praça da República 12, Apartado 335, Beja* ☎ *284/313540* ⊕ *www.visitalentejo.pt.* **Évora Tourist Office.** ⊠ *Praça do Giraldo 73, Valverde* ☎ *266/777071* ⊕ *www.visitalentejo. pt.* **Rotas dos Vinhos do Alentejo.** ⊠ *Praça Joaquim Antonio de Aguiar 20-21, Apartado 2146, Valverde* ☎ *266/746498* ⊕ *www.vinhosdoalentejo.pt.*

EXPLORING

Note that unless otherwise specified, few of the churches mentioned below have regular visiting hours. To view the interiors of the others you may have to sit in on a Mass (times for services are usually posted on church doors) and look around afterward.

TOP ATTRACTIONS

Fodor'sChoice **Igreja de São Francisco.** After the Sé, this is the most impressive of Évora's
★ churches. Its construction in the early 16th century, on the site of a former Gothic chapel, involved the greatest talents of the day, including Nicolas Chanterene, Oliver of Ghent, and the Arruda brothers, Francisco and Diogo. Magnificent architecture notwithstanding, the bizarre **Capela dos Ossos** (Chapel of Bones) is the main attraction. The translation of the chilling inscription over the entrance reads, "We, the bones that are here, await yours." The bones of some 5,000 skeletons dug up from cemeteries in the area line the ceilings and supporting columns. With a flair worthy of Charles Addams, a 16th-century Franciscan monk placed skulls jaw-to-cranium so they form arches across the ceiling; arm and leg bones are neatly stacked to shape the supporting

columns. ■TIP→ It costs €1 to take photos anywhere in the church or chapel. ⊠ *Praça 1 de Maio, Rua da República, Valverde* ☎ *266/704521* 🖰 *Church free, Chapel of Bones €2.*

NEED A
BREAK **Jardim Municipal (***Municipal Gardens***).** Off Rua 24 de Julho, a few steps from the Igreja de São Francisco, the Jardim Municipal is a pleasant place to rest after the rigors of sightseeing. The extensive and verdant gardens are landscaped with plants and trees from all over the world. ⊠ *Rua 24 de Julho, Valverde.*

Fodor'sChoice ★ **Igreja dos Lóios** (*Lóios Church or Igreja Sao Joao*). This small church next to the former Convento dos Lóios, which is now the Pousada dos Lóios, houses one of the most impressive displays of 18th-century *azulejos* (painted and glazed ceramic tiles) anywhere in Portugal. The sanctuary, dedicated to St. John the Evangelist, was founded in the 15th century by the Venetian-based Lóios Order. Its interior walls are covered with azulejos created by Oliveira Bernardes, the foremost master of this unique Portuguese art form. The blue-and-white tiles depict scenes from the life of the church's founder, Rodrigo de Melo, who, along with members of his family, is buried here. The bas-relief marble tombstones at the foot of the high altar are the only ones of their kind in Portugal. Note the two metal hatches on either side of the main aisle: one covers an ancient cistern, which belonged to the Moorish castle that predated the church (an underground spring still supplies the cistern with potable water), and beneath the other hatch lie the neatly stacked bones of hundreds of monks. This bizarre ossuary was uncovered in 1958 during restoration work. ■TIP→ **No photos are allowed.** ⊠ *Largo do Conde de Vila Flor, Valverde* ☎ *967/979763* 🖰 *Church €3; combined ticket €5, includes Cadaval Palace.*

Museu de Évora (*Évora Museum*). Newly renovated in 2015, this museum is in a stately late-17th-century baroque building between the Sé and the Largo do Conde de Vila Flor. The museum, once a palace that accommodated bishops, contains a rich collection of sculpture and paintings as well as interesting archaeological and architectural artifacts. Every summer, there's a program of film screenings and late night exhibits. The first-floor galleries, arranged around a pleasant garden, include several excellent carved pillars and a fine Manueline doorway. ⊠ *Largo do Conde de Vila Flor, Valverde* ☎ *266/730480* ⊕ *museudevora.imc-ip. pt* 🖰 *€3, family ticket €8 (free Sun. until 2)* ⊘ *Closed Mon.*

Fodor'sChoice ★ **Praça do Giraldo.** The arcade-lined square in the center of the old walled city is named after Évora's liberator, Gerald the Fearless. During Caesar's time, the square, marked by a large arch, was the Roman forum. In 1571 the arch was destroyed to make room for the fountain, a simple half sphere made of white Estremoz marble and designed by the Renaissance architect Afonso Álvares. Nowadays, it's a lovely spot to take in the scenery over coffee or cocktails at one of the many cafés with tables on the square. ⊠ *Valverde.*

5

Évora

R. da Mouraria

Largo
dos Duques
de Cadaval

R. do Colégio

R. José Elias Garcia

R. do Menino Jesus

R. de D. Isabel

Jardim
de Diana

Largo do
Colégio

Largo
do Conde
de Vila Flor

R. da Freiria de Cima

R. Gabriel Victor do
Monte Pereira

R. João de Deus

R. do Alfeirão

Largo
Alexandre
Herculano

R. do Conde da Serra
da Tourega

R. de Machede

R. 5 de Outubro

R. de Diogo Cão

R. de Serpa Pinto

Évora ◆
Tourist
Office

R. de Valdevinos

R. da Moeda

Largo da
Misericórdia

R. da
Misericórdia

Largo
dos
Mercadores

R. da
República

Largo de
Alvaro Velho

Cordovil ◆
Mansion

R. do Raimundo

R. Bernardo Matos

R. Romão Ramalho

Largo
da
Graça

R. das Três Senhoras

Largo da
Dr. Alves
Branco

Praça
1 de
Maio

Capela
dos Ossos

R. do Cicioso

R. da Rampa

R. Romão Ramalho

R. 24 de Julho

R. do Albarim

Jardim
Municipal

R. da República

Av. da Gulbenkian

Av. Marechal Carmona

Praça de
Touros

Igreja de
Misericórdia **7**

Igreja de
São Francisco **9**

Igreja dos Lóios **6**

Jardim de Diana **5**

Largo das Portas
de Moura **8**

Museu de Évora **11**

Palácio de
Dom Manuel **10**

Praça do Giraldo **2**

Rua 5 de Outubro **1**

Sé **3**

Templo Romano **4**

Universidade de Évora **12**

A BIT OF HISTORY

Although the region was inhabited some 4,000 years ago—as attested to by the dolmens and menhirs in the countryside—it was during the Roman epoch that the town called Liberalitas Julia in the province of Lusitania first achieved importance. A large part of present-day Évora is built on Roman foundations, of which the Temple of Diana, with its graceful Corinthian columns, is the most conspicuous reminder.

The Moors also made a great historical impact on the area. They arrived in 715 and remained more than 450 years. They were driven out in 1166, thanks in part to a clever ruse perpetrated by Geraldo Sem Pavor (Gerald the Fearless). Geraldo tricked Évora's Moorish ruler into leaving a strategic watchtower unguarded. With a small force, Geraldo seized the tower. To regain control of it, most of the Moorish troops left their posts at the city's main entrance,

allowing the bulk of Geraldo's forces to march in unopposed.

Toward the end of the 12th century Évora's fortunes increased as the town became the favored location for the courts of the Burgundy and Avis dynasties. It attracted many of the great minds and creative talents of Renaissance Portugal. Some of the more prominent residents at this time were Gil Vicente, the founder of Portuguese theater; the sculptor Nicolas Chanterene; and Gregorio Lopes, the painter known for his renderings of court life. Such a concentration of royal wealth and creativity superimposed upon the existing Moorish town was instrumental in the development of the delicate Manueline-Mudéjar (elaborate, Muslim-influenced) architectural style. You can see fine examples of this in the graceful lines of the Palácio de Dom Manuel and the turreted Ermida de São Bras.

NEED A BREAK

Café Arcada. Opposite the fountain on Praça do Giraldo, Café Arcada is an Évora institution. The large hall, divided into snack bar and restaurant sections, is decorated with photos of the big bands that played here in the 1940s. Tables on the square are just the place from which to watch the city on parade. ⊠ *Praca do Giraldo 7, Valverde* ☎ *266/741777.*

Rua 5 de Outubro. The narrow cobblestone pedestrian thoroughfare is lined with souvenir shops and whitewashed houses with wrought-iron balconies. It's one of the town's most attractive streets and connects the Praça do Giraldo and the cathedral. ⊠ *Rua 5 de Outubro, Valverde.*

Fodor's Choice ★ **Sé.** This transitional Gothic cathedral, declared a UNESCO World Heritage Site in 1988, was constructed in 1186 from huge granite blocks. It has been enhanced over the centuries with an octagonal, turreted dome above the transept; a blue-tile spire atop the north tower; a number of fine Manueline windows; and several Gothic rose windows. Two massive asymmetrical towers and battlement-ringed walls give the Sé a fortresslike appearance. At the entrance, Gothic arches are supported by marble columns bearing delicately sculpted statues of the apostles. With the exception of a fine baroque chapel, the granite interior is somber. The cloister, a 14th-century Gothic addition with Mudéjar vestiges, is one of the finest of its type in the country; it might look familiar to those who've visited a similar version at Lisbon's cathedral. Housed in the Sé's towers and chapter room is the **Museu de Arte Sacra da Sé** (Sacred Art Museum). Of particular interest is a 13th-century ivory Virgin of Paradise, whose body opens up to show exquisitely carved scenes of her life. ⊠ *Largo Marquês de Marialva, Valverde* ☎ *266/759330* ◪ *€4.50 cathedral, cloister, tower, and museum; €3.50 cathedral, cloister, and tower; €2.50 cathedral and cloister; €1.50 cathedral only.*

Fodor's Choice ★ **Templo Romano** (*Roman Temple*). The well-preserved ruins of the Roman Temple dominate Largo do Conde de Vila Flor. The edifice, considered one of the finest of its kind on the Iberian Peninsula, was probably built in the 1st and 2nd centuries AD. The temple, largely destroyed during the invasions of the barbarian tribes in the early 5th century, was later used for various purposes, including that of municipal slaughterhouse in the 14th century. It was restored to its present state in 1871. ⊠ *Largo do Conde de Vila Flor, Valverde.*

WORTH NOTING

Igreja de Misericórdia (*Mercy Church*). The interior of this 16th-century church is lined with large azulejo panels depicting scenes from the life of Christ; the unsigned 18th-century tiles are thought to be the work of António de Oliveira de Bernardes. ⊠ *Rua da Misericórdia, Valverde.*

Fodor's Choice ★ **Jardim de Diana** (*Diana Garden*). Opposite the Templo Romano, this restful, tree-lined park looks out over the aqueduct and the plains from the modest heights of what is sometimes grandiosely referred to as "Évora's Acropolis." You can take in nearly 2,000 years of Portuguese history from here. One sweeping glance encompasses the temple, the spires of the Gothic Sé, the Igreja dos Lóios, and the 20th-century pousada housed in the convent. A garden café at the corner of the park is a great spot to reflect on the architectural marvels before you, with a glass of port in hand. ⊠ *Largo do Conde de Vila Flor, Valverde.*

Largo das Portas de Moura. One of Évora's most beautiful squares is characterized by paired stone towers that guard one of the principal entrances to the walled old city. The spires of the Sé rise above the towers, and in the center of the square is an unusual Renaissance fountain. The large white-marble sphere, supported by a single column, bears a commemorative inscription in Latin dated 1556. Overlooking the fountain is the Cordovil Mansion, on whose terrace are several particularly attractive arches decorated in the Manueline-Mudéjar style. ⊠ *Bounded by Ruas D. Augusto Eduardo Nunes, Enrique da Fonseca, Mendes Esteves, de Machede, and Miguel Bombarda, a 5-min walk southeast of the Sé, Valverde.*

Palácio de Dom Manuel. At the entrance to the Jardim Municipal, only a part of this former royal palace remains. The existing wing was restored after a fire in 1916 and displays a row of paired, gracefully curved Manueline windows. On the building's south side there's a notable arcade of redbrick sawtooth arches. Currently used as an art gallery, the palace has witnessed a number of historic events since its construction in the late 15th century. It was here, for instance, in 1497, that Vasco da Gama received his commission to command the fleet that would discover the sea route to India. ⊠ *Jardim Municipal, Valverde* ☎ *266/777185* 📷 *Free.*

Universidade de Évora. From 1555 until its closure by the Marquis de Pombal in 1759, this university was a Jesuit college; in 1979, after a lapse of more than 200 years, Évora University resumed classes. Although enrollment is small, the college's presence enlivens this ancient city. It's worth a visit to the well-preserved buildings: the large courtyard is flanked on all sides by graceful buildings with double-tier, white-limestone, arched galleries in Italian Renaissance style. From the main entrance you'll see the imposing baroque facade of the gallery known as the Sala dos Actos (Hall of Acts), which is crowned with allegorical figures and coats of arms carved in white marble quarried in the region. Lining the gallery's interior are azulejo works depicting historical, mythological, and biblical themes. The university hosts a series of concerts, lectures, and other events open to the public, and often in English, courtesy of a growing international student population; check the website for listings. ⊠ *Rua do Colégio, Valverde* ☎ *266/740800* ⊕ *www.uevora.pt.*

> ### CERAMICS IN ALTO ALENTEJO
>
> The brightly colored, hand-painted plates, bowls, and figurines from the Alto Alentejo are popular throughout Portugal. The best selection of this distinctive type of folk art is in and around Estremoz, where the terra-cotta jugs and bowls are adorned with chips of marble from local quarries. Saturday morning the *rossio* (town square) is chock-full of vendors displaying their wares. Redondo and the village of São Pedro do Corval, near Reguengos de Monsaraz, are also good sources of this type of pottery, as is Évora. The village of Arraiolos, near Évora, is famous for its hand-embroidered wool rugs.

WHERE TO EAT

$ ⨯ **Adega do Alentejano.** Dine on hearty, simple food with in-the-know
PORTUGUESE locals at this pleasantly rustic Alentejo wine cellar. Walk through the
Fodor's Choice beaded curtain made of wine corks into a simple dining room with
★ red-and-white-checkered tablecloths, blue-and-white-tiled walls, and huge Roman-style clay wine jugs. The signature dish is tomato soup—a meal on its own—with soaked bread, a poached egg, and dried sausage served on the side. Black pork steaks are also a specialty. There's no English menu, but the helpful staff will guide you through the Portuguese version. Stick to the very reasonable local wine from the barrel, and you'll be agreeably surprised by the bill. 💲 *Average main: €10* ⊠ *Rua Gabriel Vito do Monte Pereira 21-A, Valverde* ☎ *266/744447* ➡ *No credit cards* 🕑 *Closed Sun.*

$ ⨯ **Cozinha de Santo Humberto.** One of Évora's oldest restaurants was
PORTUGUESE once a wine cellar. Try the *sopa de peixe alentejana* (a mixed fish soup) or the *carne de porco com ameijoas* (small pieces of pork sautéed with clams). Game dishes such as grouse, wild boar, and partridge are particularly good in season (Santo Humberto is, after all, the patron saint

of hunters). The list of Alentejo wines is excellent. $ Average main: €12 ⊠ Rua da Moeda 39, Valverde ☎ 266/701874 ⊘ Closed Thurs.

$ ✕ **Jardim do Cha.** A few minutes walk from the Sé, Jardim do Cha's
PORTUGUESE   leafy terrace provides a refuge from the tourist track and a comfortable place to contemplate history over a cup of herbal tea. The menu is modern Portuguese, with daily vegetarian specials. They also do fresh fruit smoothies. The café offers yoga and vegetarian cooking classes, and has opened a new retail outlet for organic products a short walk north, on Rua Cândido dos Reis. $ Average main: €12 ⊠ Rua Romão Ramalho n° 20, Valverde ☎ 266/702404.

$$$ ✕ **O Fialho.** The charming elderly owner, Amor Fialho, is the third gen-
PORTUGUESE   eration of Fialhos to operate this popular, traditional restaurant. Amor
Fodor's Choice   has handed off daily operations to his children, Helena and Rui Fialho,
★   but he's still present most evenings in the kitchen, and has been known to give foreign visitors a tour, pointing out photos of the former Spanish king's visit. The dining room, with a beamed ceiling and painted plates hung on its walls, is regularly packed on weekends, and reservations are essential. Fialho's renowned specialties are *borrego assado* (roasted lamb) and *perdiz de convento a cartuxa* (roast partridge with potatoes and carrots), made according to a recipe from a nearby monastery. There's a wide selection of Alentejo wines. $ Average main: €25 ⊠ Travessa das Mascarenhas 14, Valverde ☎ 266/703079 ⊕ www. restaurantefialho.pt ⊘ Closed Mon. ⌂ Reservations essential.

$$ ✕ **Tasquinha do Oliveira.** The charming husband-and-wife duo of Manuel
PORTUGUESE   and Carolina own and operate this tiny upscale dining room with huge taste. There are only 14 seats in the entire restaurant, creating the atmosphere of the Oliveiras' own family dining room. The tiny size makes reservations essential, and the restaurant is frequently booked solid on Friday and Saturday nights. Specialties include lamb, pork, and game dishes, served up by Carolina in the open kitchen, while Manuel runs the show outside. There are excellent Alentejo wines on offer. $ Average main: €18 ⊠ Rua Cándido dos Reis 45-A, Valverde ☎ 266/744841 ⊘ Closed Sun., and Aug. 1–15 ⌂ Reservations essential.

WHERE TO STAY

$ ⌂ **Évora Hotel.** On the route to Montemor-o-Novo, just outside town,
RESORT   you'll find this pleasant, sprawling establishment. **Pros:** self-contained
FAMILY   campus has ample space to relax or let the kids roam free; vegetarian restaurant is a rare find in meat-eating Alentejo. **Cons:** location outside the city center means it's a bit of a walk to the sights. $ Rooms from: €120 ⊠ Av. Túlio Espanca Apart. 93, Valverde ☎ 266/748800 ⊕ www. evorahotel.pt ⌿ 170 rooms, 1 suite ⦿ Breakfast.

$ ⌂ **Hotel Ibis.** Just outside the city gate, this international hotel chain is
HOTEL   a safe bet for those who want nothing more than comfortable, well-maintained rooms. **Pros:** cheery service; clean, comfortable rooms; affordable; one of the only places in town that allows pets. **Cons:** for the same price, you could stay in a charming guesthouse inside the medieval city walls. $ Rooms from: €60 ⊠ Quinta da Tapada, Urbanização da Muralha, Rua de Viana 18, Valverde ☎ 266/760700 ⊕ www.ibis.com ⌿ 87 rooms ⦿ Breakfast.

$$ 🖭**Hotel M'AR De AR Aqueduto.** The only five-star hotel inside Évora's
HOTEL   old city walls, this property's luxury is unmatched, with stark, mod-
Fodor'sChoice ern decor that echoes the city's medieval character. **Pros:** best hotel in
★   Évora; offers supreme luxury at a competitive price; free shuttle. **Cons:**
some visitors might find the modern style a bit stark or cold. $ *Rooms
from: €200* ⊠ *Rua Cândido dos Reis 72, Valverde* ☏ *266/740700,
266/739302* ⊕ *www.mardearhotels.com* ⇆ *70 rooms* ⦿ *Breakfast.*

$ 🖭**Mont'Sobro House.** If you like Portuguese handicrafts, you'll love
B&B/INN this impeccable guesthouse, run by the owners of one of Évora's most
renowned cork craft shops, Mont'Sobro. **Pros:** decorated in charming
antiques; hand-painted furniture and crafts on display; great location,
near the cathedral and Roman temple. **Cons:** some rooms are tiny, with
shared bathroom; reception only open until 9 pm; no parking. $ *Rooms
from: €45* ⊠ *Rua de Diogo Cão 1* ☏ *266/703710* ⊕ *www.montsobro.
com* ⇆ *6 rooms* ⦿ *No meals.*

$ 🖭**Pensão Policarpo.** The former home of a 17th-century nobleman, this
B&B/INN charming, family-run guesthouse offers one of the best values in Évora
Fodor'sChoice and is a great choice for families, with several different options for
★   rooms of different sizes and numbers of beds, and private parking out
back. **Pros:** family hospitality; local antiques; free bike storage. **Cons:**
only half of rooms have a/c and en-suite bathrooms; fee for secure park-
ing. $ *Rooms from: €60* ⊠ *Rua da Freiria de Baixo 16, Rua Conde da
Serra da Tourega, Valverde* ☏ *266/702424* ⊕ *www.pensaopolicarpo.
com* ⇆ *19 rooms* ⦿ *Breakfast.*

$$ 🖭**Pousada Convento Évora.** Also known as the Pousada de Loios, the for-
HOTEL   mer nuns' quarters and monks' cells in this luxurious convent-turned-
pousada have been polished off with modern conveniences, retaining
their old-world style but with no trace of monastic austerity. **Pros:** arguably Portugal's most famous and stately pousada; located in the heart
of Évora's historic center; free guided tours included. **Cons:** packed
mostly with fellow foreigners; small bathrooms and narrow hall-
ways. $ *Rooms from: €180* ⊠ *Largo do Conde de Vila Flor, Valverde*
☏ *266/730070* ⊕ *www.pousadas.pt* ⇆ *36 rooms, 1 suite* ⦿ *Breakfast.*

$ 🖭**Solar de Monfalim.** In a historic 16th-century nobleman's quarters
B&B/INN with a delightful arched gallery overlooking the street, this comfortable,
family-run guesthouse provides quiet, old-fashioned hospitality in the
heart of the old city. **Pros:** an architectural gem; charming, family-
oriented hospitality; in the heart of the old city. **Cons:** winding entry
staircase means no access for handicapped or disabled; no restaurant in
the guesthouse; no parking. $ *Rooms from: €80* ⊠ *Largo da Misericór-
dia 1, Valverde* ☏ *266/703529* ⊕ *www.solarmonfalim.com* ⇆ *26 rooms*
⦿ *Breakfast.*

NIGHTLIFE AND PERFORMING ARTS

NIGHTLIFE

Discoteca Praxis Club. The dance club Praxis Club has two dance floors,
one for house music and the other for chart favorites. Call ahead for
ladies' night specials, beer and wine tastings, and live music. ⊠ *Rua de
Valdevinos 21, Valverde* ☏ *266/708177.*

Hours Uncertain (Horas Incertas). As the name suggests, this trendy jazz club is open as late as its patrons want it to be. Frequent live jam sessions of jazz, bossa nova, and blues attract an international student crowd, as well as Portuguese locals. It's got an eclectic art nouveau decor, and a well-stocked bar. Check the website for events. ⊠ *Rua Serpa Pinto 141, Évora Monte* ☎ *266/092491* ⊕ *www.bar-horasincertas.com.*

PERFORMING ARTS

Festival Évora Clássica. Every July, the Casa Cadaval hosts the Festival Évora Clássica, during which nationally and internationally renowned classical musicians perform, including the Gulbenkian Orchestra. Performances are held at the Garcia de Resende Theater and the Palácio das 5 Quinas. Tickets cost €10–€20. ⊠ *Jardim do Paço, Praça Joaquim António de Aguiar, Valverde* ☎ *266/703112* ⊕ *www.cendrev.com.*

SPORTS AND THE OUTDOORS

JEEP AND BIKE TOURS

TurAventur. This company organizes jeep tours to megaliths and other sights, as well as bike tours in the surrounding countryside. ⊠ *Quinta de Serrado—Sr. dos Aflitos, Caminho Municipal 1182, Valverde* ☎ *266/743134* ⊕ *www.turaventur.com.*

HORSEBACK RIDING

Equeturi. The Equeturi horseback-riding center is about 2 km (1 mile) from Évora on the road to Montemor-o-Novo. It gives lessons and conducts escorted rides in the countryside. Reservations are advised. ⊠ *Quinta do Bacêlo, Valverde* ☎ *266/742884.*

SHOPPING

Rua 5 de Outubro is lined with shops selling regional handicrafts such as painted furniture, hand-painted ceramics, leather, cork, basketwork, ironwork, rugs, and quilted blankets.

ART GALLERY

João Cutileiro. Outside the city gate lies the workshop of Portugal's most internationally known sculptor, João Cutileiro. In 2016, he donated his estate to the city of Évora, but negotiations are still underway for a permanent exhibition space or museum. For now, and perhaps more interestingly, you can visit Cutileiro's own workshop, by appointment only. He works in the finest Alentejo and imported marble. Some of the pieces he's most famous for are female nudes, historical figures, and trees. To make an appointment, you must call noon–1 or 4–8, or send an email. ⊠ *Estrada de Viana 13, Valverde* ☎ *266/703972* ✎ *jc.ml@netvisao.pt.*

REGIONAL GIFTS

Mont'Sobro. This shop focuses solely on handmade cork products, and sells everything from cork photo frames and handbags to cork-lined umbrellas, and even a cork bikini. And if you really love cork, you can stay in the Mont'Sobro guesthouse, owned by the same family, and decorated in cork products. ⊠ *Rua 5 de Outubro 66, Valverde* ☎ *266/704609* ⊕ *www.montsobro.com.*

O Cesto Artesano. At the top of Rua 5 de Outubro, O Cesto Artesano specializes in local cork products and ceramics. ⊠ *Rua 5 de Outubro 57-A/77, Valverde* ☎ *266/703344* ⊕ *www.ocestoartesanato.com.*

SIDE TRIPS FROM ÉVORA

A trip through the countryside surrounding Évora will take you to some of the earliest-inhabited sites in Portugal, the country's carpet- and tapestry-making center, and to a stunning medieval castle in the lively town of Montemor-o-Novo. The area is also considered the capital of Iberian megaliths, with pastoral fields dotted with dolmens and menhirs (huge carved stones usually marking ancient graves or religious sites). While impressive, the megaliths are difficult to spot by car or to navigate by foot, and are better viewed as part of an organized tour (⇨ *see Tours, above, under Évora Essentials*). By foot or bicycle, it's rewarding to follow the path of Évora's ancient aqueduct, which crosses the city's medieval walls and juts out across rolling wheat fields and cork groves. A new system of trails along disused railways and ancient public footpaths delivers vast views of the countryside.

GUADALUPE

12½ km (8 miles) west of Évora.

The tiny village of Guadalupe takes its name from a 17th-century chapel that is dedicated to Nossa Senhora de Gaudalupe (Our Lady of Guadalupe). Henry the Navigator was known to attend Mass at this chapel. Nowadays this hamlet hosts a boisterous festival during the last 15 days of July, during which the town's population quadruples. The area is better known for its prehistoric relics. There's also a nighttime summer solstice festival each June.

GETTING HERE AND AROUND
Guadalupe is difficult for people to find, and is better seen as part of an organized megalithic tour rather than solo. However, if you do plan to drive, head northwest from Évora's center on the N114 for about 10 km (6 miles), and then turn left on a tiny road called Estrada do Norte, which takes you into the village of Guadalupe.

EXPLORING
Unless otherwise noted, all sites below are less than a 30-minute drive from Évora, and can be visited as part of a half-day excursion from the city. Évora's tourist office can provide maps and directions.

Aqueduto da Agua da Prata. The graceful arched Silver Water Aqueduct, which once carried water to Évora from the springs at Graça do Divor, is best seen along the road to Arraiolos (EN 144-4). You can also see a section of it within Évora, along the Rua do Cano in the city's northwest corner. Constructed in 1532 under the patronage of Dom João III, the aqueduct was designed by the famous architect Francisco de Arruda. Extensive parts of the system remain intact and can be seen from the road. Stop by Évora's tourist office for a map of the aqueduct and footpaths alongside it. ⊠ *Extends 18 km (11 miles) north of Évora, Valverde.*

Cromlech and the Menhir of Almendres. West of Évora in the tiny village of Guadalupe is the Menhir of Almendres, an 8-foot-tall Neolithic stone obelisk believed to have been used in fertility rites. Several hundred yards away is the cromlech, 95 granite monoliths arranged in an oval in the middle of a large field on a hill. The monoliths face the sunrise and are believed to have been the social, religious, and political center of the agro-pastoral, seminomadic population. The site is also believed to be linked to astral observations and predictions, fertility rites, and the worship of the mother goddess. ⊠ *15 km (9 miles) west of Évora.*

Dolmen of Zambujeiro. The 20-foot-high Dolmen of Zambujeiro is the largest of its kind on the Iberian Peninsula. This prehistoric monument is typical of those found throughout Neolithic Europe: several great stone slabs stand upright, supporting a flat stone that serves as a roof. These structures were designed as burial chambers. ⊠ *12 km (7 miles) southwest of Évora, Valverde ⊹ From N380 (the Évora–Alcaçovas road) take the turnoff to Valverde.*

MONTEMOR-O-NOVO

30 km (18 miles) northwest of Évora.

Driving east from the Portuguese capital, the first hilltop castle settlement you'll hit is also one of the most impressive. Montemor-e-Novo, or simply Montemor for short, has been a settlement from the time of the Romans, and its castle has been renovated and expanded by successive generations of Arab rulers, Christian monks, and Portuguese royals since then. Today the town is a prosperous agricultural hub with a surprisingly happening arts scene, and gastronomic festivals throughout the year. Montemor makes a pleasant half-day stop to or from Évora.

GETTING HERE AND AROUND

About 100 km (62 miles) east of Lisbon, Montemor is just past the point where the Portuguese capital's limits disappear into the countryside. It's an easy 90-minute drive from Lisbon, or about 30 minutes west of Alentejo's main city, Évora. Montemor is easily identified from afar by its hilltop castle, on a steep hill towering over clusters of houses hugging its sides.

ESSENTIALS

Taxi Contact Taxi Montemor. ☎ *266/892333, 266/892444.*

Train Station Estaçao Rodoviaria. ⊠ *Carreira de S. Francisco ☎ 266/892110.*

Visitor Information Montemor-o-Novo Tourist Office. ⊠ *Largo Calouste Gulbenkian ☎ 266/898103 ⊕ www.cm-montemornovo.pt.*

EXPLORING

Fodor's Choice ★ **Castelo de Montemor-o-Novo.** This huge complex towers over the city. The property includes an ancient gate to the city (Porta da Vila) that could be closed during possible times of attack or revolution, a Casa da Guarda (guard station), and a Torre do Relogio (clock tower). You can climb up onto the outer castle fortifications and walk around the complex for a 360-degree view of the town below and plains beyond. It's also a pleasant walk up to the castle through Montemor's winding, steep side streets lined with 17th-century manor houses and Manueline doorways. ✉ *Porta de Vila* 🎟 *Free.*

Convent of St. João de Deus. This former convent houses the municipal library, the town archives, and an art gallery with temporary exhibitions from local artists and on Montemor's history. In early March, the building is the hub of a citywide festival celebrating Montemor's patron saint, the 16th-century figure St. John of God. There's a crypt where the saint is said to have been born, and a nave covered with blue-and-white azulejo tiles depicting scenes from his life. ✉ *Terreiro de St. João de Deus* ☎ *266/898103* 🎟 *Free.*

Misericordia Church. This church has a splendid Manueline doorway, 17th-century altar pieces, and an 18th-century organ crafted in Italy. Near the front of the church, there rests a beautiful 15th-century Pietà sculpture carved from local marble. ✉ *Terreiro de St. João de Deus* ☎ *266/898410* 🌐 *www.scmmn.com* 🎟 *Free.*

5

WHERE TO EAT

$ CAFÉ 🍴 **Cafe Almansor.** Across the main square is an old-fashioned haunt for Montemor locals. Don't be put off by the slightly dark, dated art deco style inside. Café Almansor makes one of the best cups of coffee in town. This is also a popular local hangout, serving simple toasts and sandwiches. [$] *Average main: €3* ✉ *Praca de Republica 7* ☎ *266/892209* 💳 *No credit cards.*

$ CAFÉ Fodor's Choice ★ 🍴 **Sociedade Circulo Montemorense.** The best spot to sip a coffee or glass of wine in the sunshine is in the front garden of this social club in Montemor's main square. In pleasant weather you'll struggle to find a seat at this relaxed see-and-be-seen establishment—the town's most popular. Inside are banquet and game rooms for members, but the garden and bar are open to the public, with views of a charming park across the street. Food is simple lunch fare, including thick ham-and-cheese toasts, a variety of sandwiches, and occasionally soup. [$] *Average main: €5* ✉ *Praça de Republica, Rua Alvaro Castelões* ☎ *266/896063* 💳 *No credit cards.*

ALTO ALENTEJO

The Alto Alentejo (Upper Alentejo) is the hillier, rockier half of the great Alentejo Plain and has the region's highest mountain ranges—the Serra de São Mamede and the Serra de Ossa. Neither is very lofty, though, and the undulating fields, heaths, and cork plantations that make up most of the landscape leave the bigger impression. Quarries scar the landscape around Borba, Estremoz, and Vila Viçosa, but they produce Portugal's finest marble. (Portugal is second to Italy in marble exports.) Modern wine-making techniques have revolutionized production in Alto Alentejo's vineyards, and some of Europe's finest wines are now produced in areas such as Borba, Reguengos de Monsaraz, and Portalegre.

Side Trips from Évora and Alto Alentejo

Sertã

Castelo Branco

Parque Natural do Tejo Internacional

Rio Tejo, (River Tagus)

Castelo de Bode

Sardoal

Belver

Parque Natural da Serra de São Mamede

Santo António das Areias

Almourol Castle

Abrantes

Castelo de Vide

Marvão

SPAIN

Ponte de Sor

Portalegre

Coudelaria de Alter

Esperança

Monforte

Campo Maior

Estremoz

Borba

Elvas

TO LISBON

Évoramonte

SERRA DE OSSA

Vila Viçosa

Fort de Santa Luzia

Arraiolos

Montemor-o-Novo

Na. Sta. da Graça do Divor

Cromlech and Menhir of the Almendres

Aqueduto da Agua da Prata

Terena

Guadalupe

Dolmen of Zambujeiro

Évora see detail map

São Pedro do Corval

Menhir of Outeiro

Reguengos de Monsaraz

Monsaraz

Portel

Herdade do Esporão

Barragem do Alqueva

Moura

Rio Guadiana

0 — 20 miles
0 — 30 km

MONSARAZ

50 km (31 miles) southeast of Évora.

The entire fortified hilltop town of Monsaraz is a living museum of narrow stone streets lined with ancient white houses. The town's 150 or so permanent residents (mostly older people) live mainly off tourism, and because they do so graciously and unobtrusively, Monsaraz has managed to retain its essential character.

Old women clad in black sit in the doorways of their cottages and chat with neighbors, their ever-present knitting in hand. At the southern end of the walls stand the well-preserved towers of a formidable 13th-century castle. The view from atop the pentagonal tower sweeps across the plain to the west and to the east over the Rio Guadiana (Guadiana River) to Spain. Within the castle perimeter is an unusual arena with makeshift slate benches at either end of an oval field. Bullfights are held here several times a year and always in the second week of September (during the festival of Senhora Jesus dos Passos, the village's patron saint), but unlike in neighboring Spain, the bulls aren't killed here.

GETTING HERE AND AROUND
Approaching from any direction, you can't miss the tiny village perched on a hilltop surrounded by steep walls. Drive halfway up to the parking lot, then enter Monsaraz on foot through one of four arched entry gates. This is also where daily buses from Évora will drop you off; check with the tourist office for bus timetables.

ESSENTIALS
Visitor Information Monsaraz Tourist Office. ⊠ *Praça Dom Nuno Álavares Pereira* ☎ *266/550120* ⊕ *www.monsaraz.pt.*

EXPLORING
Barragem do Alqueva. If the valleys that you gaze at atop Monsaraz look flooded, that's because they are. In the late 1990s, Portugal and Spain jointly began work on a huge dam that created the 250-square-km (96-square-mile) Alqueva reservoir, Europe's largest lake. Most of the smaller lakes and flooded valleys you see from Monsaraz are part of the reservoir system. The project cost nearly €2 billion and aims to alleviate the dry Alentejo's chronic water shortages for decades to come. You can drive or walk across the dam, but one of the best ways to see the lake's expanse is by boat. Visit the **Amieira Marina** across the lake from Monsaraz in the town of Portel, where you can rent boats, book day trips on the lake, or have a meal at its beautiful panoramic restaurant. ⊠ *Amieira Marina, Amieira* ☎ *266/611173* ⊕ *www.amieiramarina.com.*

Fodor's Choice ★ **Herdade do Esporão.** This famed wine estate produces Esporão, one of Portugal's top labels. It's on a beautiful, sprawling property overlooking a lake that you won't believe is tucked away in the outskirts of this small Alentejo town. The winery's driveway cuts across miles of vineyards, up to the main house with an arched portico showcasing the vast property. The winery offers one-hour tours of its facilities at 11, 3, and 5 daily; otherwise you'll need to call ahead to make a booking. All tours end with a free glass of wine. You can also sample wines at the bar (you pay according to the number and type of wines tasted). Pair wines with sophisticated Portuguese cuisine in their elegant restaurant ($$; lunch only, reserve ahead). Chef Pedro Pena Bastos prepares dishes with wine, olive oil, and vinegar from the estate, which, along with other products, are also on sale at the shop. Restaurant guests can take a free tour. ⊠ *Herdade do Esporão, Apartado 31, Reguengos de Monsaraz* ✛ *From Reguengos, follow signs to Esporão/Zona Industrial and then signs for Turismo Rural* ☎ *266/509280* ⊕ *www.esporao.com.*

Menhir of Outeiro. The area around Monsaraz is dotted with megalithic monuments. This 18-foot-high menhir, 3 km (2 miles) north of town, is one of the tallest ever discovered. ⊠ *Monsaraz.*

Museu Monsaraz. This small museum, next to the parish church, displays religious artifacts, well-preserved frescoes, and the original town charter, signed by Dom Manuel in 1512. The former tribunal contains an interesting 15th-century fresco that depicts Christ presiding over figures of Truth and Deception. ⊠ *Largo Nuno Álvares Pereira* ☎ *266/508040* 🎟️ *€1.20.*

WHERE TO EAT AND STAY

$
PORTUGUESE
✕ **Casa do Forno.** At the entrance of this popular restaurant is a huge, rounded oven with an iron door, hence the name (*forno* is Portuguese for "oven"). Picture windows line the dining room and afford a spectacular view over the rolling plains. The Alentejan menu appropriately features roasts; one special dish worth trying is the *borrego assado no forno* (roast lamb prepared according to an ancient recipe of the nearby monastery). $ *Average main: €15* ⊠ *Travessa da Sonabre* ☎ *266/104008* ⊗ *Closed Tues.*

$
PORTUGUESE
✕ **Lumumba.** This little restaurant in one of the old village houses has a devoted clientele that hails from both sides of the Portuguese–Spanish border. The dining room is small, but there is a terrace for outside dining with views over the valley to distant mountains. The menu is classic Alentejo, with good lamb and kid roasts and casseroles. Although their main specialty is *ensopado de borrego* (lamb stew), the grilled fish dishes are also excellent, when available; try the *chocos grelhados* (grilled squid) or the *peixe espada grelhada* (charcoal-grilled swordfish). $ *Average main: €12* ⊠ *Rua Direita 12* ☎ *266/557121* ⊗ *Closed Mon.*

$
PORTUGUESE
✕ **O Gato.** O Gato is a bed and breakfast, pastry shop, and restaurant in a traditional Alentejan white-stucco building with blue awnings on the main street in Reguengos. Its a huge favorite with locals, serving traditional fare like lamb stew made with fresh herbs and spices. There's an extensive wine list $ *Average main: €11* ⊠ *Praça da Liberdade 11–13, Reguengos de Monsaraz* ☎ *266/502353* ⊕ *www.residencialogato.pt.*

$
PORTUGUESE
✕ **Restaurante Central.** A great place to stop for some authentic Alentejan cuisine on your way to Monsaraz or after a wine tasting, this restaurant has good-value daily specials, with a smaller bar-café offering tapas and good local wines, too. $ *Average main: €10* ⊠ *Largo da Fonte da Liberdade, Reguengos de Monsaraz* ☎ *266/502219* ⊗ *Closed Tues.*

$
B&B/INN
Fodor's Choice
★
🏨 **Casa Pinto.** This small, rustic guesthouse—a true romantic hideaway—occupies an old, restored whitewashed row house on the main street of the walled town. **Pros:** roof terrace offers best view in town; cozy and intimate; romantic setting; free Wi-Fi. **Cons:** rooms are on

the small side; no space for extra beds for children. [$] *Rooms from: €105* ✉ *Praça Dom Nuno Álavares Pereira 10* ☎ *266/557076* ⊕ *www. casapinto.pt* ⇌ *5 rooms* ❄ *Breakfast.*

$
RESORT
FAMILY
Fodor's Choice
★

▦ **Horta da Moura.** This ancient Moorish farm is now a sprawling rural hotel complex, with horses, an organic garden, and plenty of space to wander the countryside on foot or mountain bike. **Pros:** gorgeous rustic charm; lots of open space; friendly staff. **Cons:** inaccessible by public transport; few double rooms. [$] *Rooms from: €120* ✉ *Horta da Moura, Monsaraz, Apartado 64* ☎ *266/550100* ⊕ *www.hortadamoura.pt* ⇌ *4 double/single rooms, 21 suites (various sizes)* ❄ *Breakfast.*

SHOPPING

Reguengos de Monsaraz. This sleepy little Alentejo town is the center of a large wine-producing region and is also known for its handwoven rugs. The 19th-century neo-Gothic church here was built by the same Lisbon architect who built Lisbon's bullfight arena. ✉ *16 km (10 miles) west of Monsaraz, Reguengos de Monsaraz.*

Fodor's Choice
★

São Pedro do Corval. The tiny hamlet of São Pedro do Corval, 5 km (3 miles) northeast of Reguengos, is one of Portugal's major centers for inexpensive hand-painted pottery. There's a cluster of pottery workshops in the main square. You can watch them work, place custom orders, or buy premade ceramics. ✉ *São Pedro do Corval, Reguengos de Monsaraz.*

VILA VIÇOSA

60 (40 miles) northeast of Evora.

A quiet town with a moated castle, Vila Viçosa is in the heart of the fertile Borba Plain. It has been closely linked with Portuguese royalty since the 15th century, and court life in Vila Viçosa flourished in the late 16th and early 17th centuries, when the huge palace constructed by the fourth Duke of Bragança (Jaime) was the scene of great royal feasts, theater performances, and bullfights. Today Vila Viçosa is a pleasant, bustling town that remains affluent because of its ties to the region's wine industry and marble quarries. Most residents still live in the town center, and it's less touristy and untainted by the shopping malls and suburban sprawl that have cropped up on the edges of other provincial towns. The huge Praça da Republica, lined with orange trees and anchored by a castle on one end and a 17th-century church on the other, is one of the finest squares in all of Alentejo.

GETTING HERE AND AROUND

Vila Viçosa lies just past Borba, south of the highway that connects Évora with the Spanish border. Praça da Republica stretches across the town center, with the Paço Ducal and pousada about 300 meters to the northwest. Bus service from Évora is infrequent and slow, and Vila Viçosa is best reached by private car.

ESSENTIALS

Bus Station Belos Transportes. ✉ *Largo D. João IV* ☎ *266/769410.*

Taxi Contact Vila Viçosa. ✉ *Praça da Republica* ☎ *268/881101.*

5

Visitor Information **Vila Viçosa Tourist Office.** ⊠ *Praça da Republica 34* ☎ *268/889317* ⊕ *www.cm-vilavicosa.pt.*

EXPLORING

Marble Museum. This museum offers an interesting look at Alentejo's local marble industry, which has sustained Vila Viçosa and made it prosperous. It used to be housed inside the old train station—covered in intricate blue-and-white tiles and worth seeing in its own right—but recently moved to the site of a former quarry, near the road out of town toward Borba. There are free guided tours in Portuguese, Spanish, English, and French. ⊠ *Olival da Gradinha, Av. Duque D. Jaime* ☎ *268/889310* 🎫 *€2* ⊗ *Closed Mon.*

Museu dos Coches (*Coach Museum*). Renovated and reopened in 2015, this museum includes a collection of horse-drawn conveyances and antique automobiles. Even so, if you've seen or plan to see Lisbon's coach museum, you can skip this one; this is another branch of the same collection, which is interesting but isn't in the same league as the one in the capital. ⊠ *Terreiro do Paço* ☎ *268/980659* ⊕ *www.museu-doscoches.pt* 🎫 *€2* ⊗ *Closed Mon.*

Fodor's Choice ★ **Paço Ducal** (*Ducal Palace*). This opulent palace draws a great many visitors—and for good reason. Built of locally quarried marble, the palace's main wing extends for some 360 feet and overlooks the expansive Palace Square and the bronze equestrian statue of Dom João IV. At the north end of the square note the Porta do Nó (Knot Gate) with its massive stone shaped like ropes—an intriguing example of the Manueline style.

The palace's interior was extensively restored in the 1950s and contains all you'd expect to find: azulejos, Arraiolos rugs, frescoed ceilings, priceless collections of silver and gold objects, Chinese vases, Gobelin tapestries, and a long dining hall adorned with antlers and other hunting trophies. The enormous kitchen's spits are large enough to accommodate several oxen, and there's enough gleaming copper to keep a small army of servants busy polishing. Dom Carlos, the nation's penultimate king, spent his last night here before being assassinated in 1908; his rooms have been maintained as they were. Carlos was quite an accomplished painter, and many of his works (along with private photos of Portugal's last royal family) line the walls of the apartments.

The ground floor of the castle has displays of objects ranging from Paleolithic to 18th century and mainly Roman artifacts discovered during excavations. These include pieces from ancient Mediterranean civilizations—Egypt, Rome, Carthage, and also pre-Columbian. Also on view are coaches from the 17th to the 20th century. Hunting, rather than war, is the dominant theme of the armory that holds more than 2,000 objects. The treasury displays crucifixes from Vila Viçosa and those belonging to Dona Catarina de Bragança as well as more than 200 pieces of jewelry, paintings, crystal, and ceramics. The porcelain collection is made up of blue-and-white china from the 15th to 18th centuries. ⊠ *Terreiro do Paço, Terreiro do Paço* ☎ *268/980659* ⊕ *www.fcbraganca.pt* 🎫 *Palace €6; armory €3; treasury and porcelain collection €2.50 each; castle, archaeology museum, and game and hunting museum €3.*

The Allure of Azulejo

It's difficult to find an old building of any note in Portugal which isn't adorned somewhere or other with the predominantly blue-tone ceramic tiles called azulejos. The centuries-old marriage of glazed ornamental tiles and Portuguese architecture is a match made in heaven.

After the Gothic period, large buildings made entirely of undressed brick or stone became a rarity in Portuguese architecture. Most structures had extensive areas of flat plaster on their facades and interior walls that cried out for decoration. The compulsion to fill these empty architectural spaces produced the art of the fresco in Italy; in Portugal, it produced the art of the azulejo.

The medium is well suited to the deeply rooted Portuguese taste for intricate, ornate decoration. And, aesthetics aside, glazed tiling is ideally suited to the country's more practical needs. Durable, waterproof, and easily cleaned, the tile provides cool interiors during Portugal's hot summers and exterior protection from the dampness of Atlantic winters.

The term *azulejo* comes not from the word *azul* ("blue" in Portuguese), but from the Arabic word for tiles, *az-zulayj*. But despite the long presence of the Moors in Portugal, the Moorish influence on early Portuguese azulejos was actually introduced from Spain in the 15th century.

The very earliest tiles on Portuguese buildings were imported from Andalusia. They're usually geometric in design and were most frequently used to form panels of repeated patterns.

As Portugal's prosperity increased in the 16th century, the growing number of palaces, churches, and sumptuous mansions created a demand for more tile. Local production was small at first, and Holland and Italy were the main suppliers. The superb Dutch-made azulejos in the Paço Ducal in Vila Viçosa are famous examples from this period. The first Portuguese-made tiles had begun to appear in the last quarter of the 15th century, when a number of small factories were established, but three centuries were to pass before Portuguese tile making reached its peak.

The great figure in 18th-century Portuguese tile making is António de Oliveira Bernardes, who died in 1732. The school he established spawned the series of monumental panels depicting hunting scenes, landscapes, battles, and other historical motifs that grace many stately Portuguese homes and churches of the period. Some of the finest examples can be seen in the Alentejo—in buildings such as the university in Évora and the parish church in Alcácer do Sal—as well as at the Castelo de São Felipe in Setúbal. In Lisbon's Museu do Azulejo you can trace the development of tiles in Portugal from their beginnings to the present.

Portuguese tile making declined in quality in the 19th century, but a revival occurred in the 20th century, spearheaded by leading artists such as Almada Negreiros and Maria Keil. Today, some notable examples of tile use by contemporary artists can be seen in many of the capital's metro stations.

WHERE TO STAY

$$ HOTEL Fodor's Choice ★ **Pousada de D. João IV.** If you're hooked on Vila Viçosa's history, this luxury hotel, furnished with period reproductions, in a 500-year-old former convent next door to the palace has all the period atmosphere you'll need. **Pros:** a history buff's dream; period furnishings and half-restored frescoes on hallway walls. **Cons:** expensive. [$] *Rooms from: €160* ✉ *Convento das Chagas, Terreiro do Paço* ☎ *268/980742* 🌐 *www.pousadas.pt* 🛏 *34 rooms, 3 suites* 🍴 *Breakfast.*

$ B&B/INN FAMILY **Quinta do Colmeal.** About 3 km (2 miles) outside Vila Viçosa, this ancient Roman hermitage retains its historic touches—centuries-old olive, fig, almond, and orange groves—but has added modern amenities as well, transforming an old water cistern into a natural swimming pool, for example. **Pros:** romantic; rustic charm for a good price; warm, personal hospitality; good options for families or those who want to immerse themselves in nature. **Cons:** a bit of a walk from town. [$] *Rooms from: €80* ✉ *Estrada Vila Viçoso, Apartado 227* ☎ *919/569751, 627/050401* 🌐 *www.quintadocolmeal.net* 🛏 *3 cottages* 🍴 *Breakfast.*

ESTREMOZ

31 km (19 miles) northwest of Vila Viçosa.

Estremoz, which lies on the ancient road that connected Lisbon with Mérida, Spain, has been a site of strategic importance since Roman times, and the castle, which overlooks the town, was a crucial one of the Alentejo's many fortresses.

Today Estremoz is a bustling rural hub that's the seat of eastern Alentejo's growing arts scene, as well as a military garrison town complete with sword-wielding guards outside the cavalry regiment's headquarters across from the main park. Chock-full of history but not resting on its laurels, Estremoz is unfortunately often overlooked in favor of its more touristy sister city Évora, but it shouldn't be. Make Estremoz your base for exploring this half of the Alentejo and you won't be disappointed.

GETTING HERE AND AROUND

Estremoz lies about 45 km (30 miles) northeast of Évora along the nontoll road IP2. Most of the city lies within a low outer protective wall, with the castle, pousada, and some museums stop a central hill with another wall around it. Everything is within walking distance inside town.

TOUR INFORMATION

Rainha Santa Isabel, Viagens e Turismo Lda can arrange historical walking tours. Paladares e Aventuras can arrange mountain biking, 4X4 tours, horseback riding, and other adventure sports.

ESSENTIALS

Tour Guides **Paladares e Aventuras.** ✉ *Rua Francisco Manuel Cardoso 23 Arcos* ☎ *967/783169, 912/322911* 🌐 *www.paladareseaventuras.com.* **Rainha Santa Isabel, Viagens e Turismo Lda.** ✉ *Lg. Combatentes de Grande Guerra 9–10* ☎ *268/333228* 🌐 *www.rsiviagens.pt.*

Visitor Information **Estremoz Tourist Office.** ✉ *Casa de Estremoz, Rossio Marquês de Pombal* ☎ *268/339227* 🌐 *www.cm-estremoz.pt.*

EXPLORING

Irmas Flores Artesano. For authentic Estremoz crafts, head to this tiny workshop where you can watch local women molding clay and painting their ceramic creations in the back room. Besides ceramics, the adjacent shop also sells locally handmade blankets, fruit compote, and liqueurs. ⊠ *Largo da Republica 31-32* ☎ *268/324239, 268/323350.*

FAMILY **Living Science Museum (Centro Ciencia Viva).** Started centuries ago as a Catholic convent, this white stucco building became a science lab in the 20th century for the local university. Nowadays, it's a quirky little science museum—a great stop for families with children. The exhibits have a special emphasis on local geology, including displays of dinosaur fossils excavated nearby. Nearly everything is interactive. Check the website for workshops and special events. ⊠ *Espaço Ciência, Convento das Maltezas* ☎ *268/334285* ⊕ *www.ccvestremoz.uevora.pt* ☑ *€5.50, temporary exhibitions extra* ☉ *Closed Mon..*

Museu de Arte Sacra. Housed in a towering 17th-century convent next to the tourist office, it's worth a peek into this museum to see 17th- and 18th-century religious trinkets. You can also climb a blue-and-white-tiled stairway for an impressive view from the building's bell towers. ⊠ *Rossio Marquês de Pombal* ☎ *967/528298* ☑ *€1.*

Museu Municipal de Estremoz. This museum is housed in a lovely 17th-century almshouse across from the castle. Its displays chronicle the development of the region and range from Roman artifacts to contemporary pottery, including a collection of the brightly colored figurines for which Estremoz is famous. ⊠ *Largo D. Dinis* ☎ *268/339219* ⊕ *www.patrimoniocultural.pt/pt/museus-e-monumentos/rede-portuguesa/m/museu-municipal-de-estremoz* ☑ *€1.55* ☉ *Closed Mon.*

Rossio. The lower town of Estremoz, a maze of narrow streets and white houses, radiates from the Rossio, a huge, central square. Stands lining it sell the town's famous colorful pottery. In addition to the multicolor, hand-painted plates, pitchers, and dolls, note the earthenware jugs decorated with bits of local white marble. There's a weekly market here on Saturday mornings. ⊠ *Rossio Marquês de Pombal.*

Fodor'sChoice **Royal Palace.** The former Royal Palace, an impressive hilltop fortress ★ towering over the city that is now a luxury pousada, is the highlight of any visit to Estremoz. The palace was built in the 13th century by Portugal's King Dom Dinis. It's named after his wife, Queen Isabel of Aragon, who died here in 1336. An explosion in 1698 destroyed much of the medieval structure except the **Torre das Tres Coroas** (Tower of the Three Crowns), which you can still climb today for fantastic views of Estremoz and the surrounding countryside. The palace was restored after the ammunition blast and fire, and was converted into a pousada in 1970. The interior is like a museum, housing an impressive collection of 17th- and 18th-century artifacts and furniture. Across the street, Queen Isabel's personal chapel, **Capela de Santa Isabel,** a striking, richly decorated enclave lined with azulejos, is also open to visitors. ⊠ *Largo de D. Dinis* ☎ *268/332075* ⊕ *www.pousadas.pt* ☑ *Free admission to pousada lobby, tower, and chapel.*

NEED A BREAK

Café Alentejano. There are several refreshment stands and snack bars along the Rossio, but for more substantial fare try the Café Alentejano. From this popular 60-year-old art deco–style café and its first-floor restaurant, you can watch the goings-on in the square. Inexpensive accommodation can be found upstairs. ✉ *Rossio Marquês de Pombal 13–15* ☎ *268/337300, 268/337303, 967/286311.*

WHERE TO EAT

$ PORTUGUESE Fodor's Choice ★

🍴 **Adega do Isaias.** Hidden away on a narrow side street a few minutes' walk from the main square, this family-run restaurant is the best place in town for hearty, no-nonsense roasts and grilled meats. The front part of the former wine cellar is a rustic brick bar with a pork leg mounted on the counter, and a charcoal grill nestled in the front window alcove. Walk past the bar area across a sloping, concrete floor into a cozy dining room, lined with huge terra-cotta wine jugs. The furnishings are basic—benches at planked tables—and you can expect the service to be casual, at best. But the food will be great, and the place will probably be packed. Specialties include *burras* (pork chin), *migas* with wild asparagus, and *sopa de cacao,* or dogfish soup, a hearty dish made with a bony local fish which is sometimes also called baby shark. There's also a long list of Alentejo wines at very reasonable prices. [$] *Average main: €15* ✉ *Rua do Almeida 21* ☎ *268/322318* ⏲ *Closed Sun.*

$$$$ PORTUGUESE Fodor's Choice ★

🍴 **Gadanha.** If you'd like to grab a sandwich, cup of tea, or glass of wine between museum visits, there's no place better than Gadanha. You'll likely end up leaving with more than what you ate, as this deli also sells gift-wrapped gourmet treats like local ham, cheese, sweets, liqueurs, and chocolates. The café and shop are superb, and the restaurant ($$)—in an old barn annex, with exposed wood beams and an antique hearth—is even better. Specialties include lamb croquettes with mushroom mayonaise and platters of local Alentejan cheeses. You can dine on a smattering of *petiscos* (tapas) or settle in for the larger main courses. [$] *Average main: €30* ✉ *Largo Dragoes de Olivença 84-A* ☎ *268/333262, 965/171521* 🌐 *www.merceariagadanha.pt.*

$$$$ PORTUGUESE Fodor's Choice ★

🍴 **São Rosas.** The castle in the historic center of town also houses this gastronomic landmark, serving traditional cuisine in an upscale, white-tablecloth setting that caters to pousada guests and weekenders from Lisbon. When in season, wild asparagus, wild mushrooms, and truffles appear on the menu. Specialties include *tarte de perdiz* (partridge pie) and *sela de borrego* (baked lamb). For fish try the trout with *chouriço* (smoked sausage) and *poejos* (native herb) or the *sopa de cação* (dogfish soup). The tomato soup, soaked with bread and served with dried sausage on the side, is indeed a meal in itself. [$] *Average main: €30* ✉ *Largo D. Dinis 11* ☎ *268/333345.*

$ PORTUGUESE

🍴 **Zona Verde Restaurante.** This traditional restaurant is a favorite with locals, serving massive portions of Alentejo specialties like dogfish soup, borrego assado, and porco preto. Even half portions are huge, and a good value. [$] *Average main: €10* ✉ *Largo Dragoes de Olivença 86* ☎ *268/332008, 964/501676.*

WHERE TO STAY

$ HOTEL 🏨 **D. Dinis Low Cost Hostel.** Opened in spring 2012, this is more of a boutique design hotel than a hostel, although it is low-cost. **Pros:** free Wi-Fi throughout; free parking. **Cons:** funky decor isn't for everyone. [$] *Rooms from: €50* ✉ *Rua 31 de Janeiro 48* ☎ *268/333 929* 🌐 *www.ddinishostel.blogspot.com* 🛏 *8 rooms* 🍴 *Breakfast; No meals.*

$ B&B/INN FAMILY 🏨 **Monte dos Pensamentos.** Just over a mile outside Estremoz's historic quarter, this hotel is housed in an 18th-century manor house with sprawling gardens, a year-round heated outdoor swimming pool, and ample free parking. **Pros:** free Wi-Fi; hearty breakfast included; cozy common areas decorated beautifully in local antiques. **Cons:** outside the historic center; furnishings in cottages are modern and bland. [$] *Rooms from: €90* ✉ *N4, Estrada Estacao do Ameixial* ☎ *268/333166, 917/069699* 🌐 *www.montedospensamentos.com* 🛏 *9 rooms, 2 cottages* 🍴 *Breakfast.*

$$ HOTEL FAMILY 🏨 **Páteo dos Solares.** This modern boutique hotel is housed in a restored 19th-century manor near the old walls in the center of town, with a huge swimming pool and patio overlooking vineyards and farmland that slope down from the edges of Estremoz. **Pros:** sprawling property with modern facilities retains a historic feel; just steps from the town center; parking and breakfast included in room rate. **Cons:** tends to host weddings and corporate conferences. [$] *Rooms from: €150* ✉ *Rua Brito Capelo* ☎ *268/338400* 🌐 *www.pateosolares.com* 🛏 *40 rooms* 🍴 *Breakfast.*

$$ HOTEL Fodor's Choice ★ 🏨 **Pousada da Rainha Santa Isabel.** If there's one pousada in all of Portugal that you splurge on, this should be it; dubbed the "museum of all pousadas," this hotel evokes the feeling of staying in a medieval castle—because it is one. **Pros:** an architectural gem; a favorite for history buffs. **Cons:** besides a billiards room, no activities for children. [$] *Rooms from: €175* ✉ *Largo D. Dinis 1* ☎ *268/332075* 🌐 *www.pousadas.pt* 🛏 *33 rooms* 🍴 *Breakfast.*

ELVAS

40 km (25 miles) east of Estremoz; 15 km (9 miles) west of Spain.

Extensively fortified because of its proximity to the Spanish town of Badajoz, Elvas was from its founding an important bastion in warding off attacks from the east. Portugal's most formidable 17th-century fortifications are characterized by a series of walls, moats, and reinforced towers. The size of the complex can best be appreciated by driving around the periphery of the town. Inside you'll find a bustling, vibrant city with a stately town square, an impressive castle, an array of historic churches and museums, and almost no tourists.

GETTING HERE AND AROUND

Elvas lies on the Spanish frontier, just 15 km (9 miles) west of Badajoz. Praça da República lies at the center, with the castle at the town's northern end. The pedestrian Rua de Alcamim provides a lovely traffic-free entrance by foot from Elvas's southern walls. The bus station lies just outside the city walls, with service several times daily to Évora (check with the tourist office for updated timetable). Inside the city walls, there's a tourist bus that takes you to all the major sites; it costs €5, and runs 10–3 every day but Wednesday and Sunday.

ESSENTIALS

Bus Information Comboio Turistico. ⊠ *Praça da República* ☎ *268/622236.*

Tour Guides AGIA, Associacao de Guias Interpretes do Alentejo (Elvas). ☎ *933/259036* ⊕ *www.alentejoguides.com.*

Visitor Information Elvas Tourist Office. ⊠ *Praça da República* ☎ *268/622236* ⊕ *www.cm-elvas.pt/turismo.*

EXPLORING

Aqueduto da Amoreira. The 8-km (5-mile) Amoreira Aqueduct took more than a century to build and is still in use today. It was started in 1498 under the direction of one of the era's great architects, Francisco de Arruda—who also designed the Aqueduto da Agua da Prata north of Évora. The first drops of water didn't flow into the town fountain until 1622. Some parts of the impressive structure have five stories of arches; the total number of arches is 843. The aqueduct is best viewed from outside the city walls, on the road to/from Lisbon. ⊠ *Elvas.*

Castelo de Elvas. At this castle's battlements you'll have a sweeping view of Elvas and its fortifications. There's been a fortress here since Roman times, though this structure's oldest elements were built by the Moors and expanded by a handful of Portuguese monarchs. ⊠ *Parada do castelo* ☜ €2.

Fort de Santa Luzia. This impressive military fortress sits on a hill about 1½ km (1 mile) outside Elvas's city walls, and now houses a military museum. The fort's rectangular ramparts were first built in the 1640s during Portugal's centuries-long animosity with Spain, and the local governor's residence was at its center. Today the museum houses an array of artillery and weapons. ⊠ *Museu Militar de Elvas, Forte Sta. Luzia, Av. de São Domingos* ☎ *268/628357* ☜ *€2* ⊙ *Closed Mon.*

Igreja da Nossa Senhora da Assunção. The 16th-century Church of Our Lady of the Assumption at the head of the town square, the Praça da República, has an impressive triple-nave interior lined with 17th-century blue-and-yellow azulejos. The church was designed by Francisco de Arruda, architect of the Elvas aqueduct, but underwent subsequent modifications. It was a cathedral until the diocese was moved to Évora in the 18th century. ⊠ *Praça da República* ☜ *Free.*

Museu de Arte Contemporanea de Elvas (MACE). This modern art museum focuses on Portugal's 20th-century artists, and is definitely worth a visit if you're curious about modern aesthetics in otherwise traditional Alentejo. The well-organized exhibits feature about 300 works that rotate throughout the year. The baroque-style building itself is also exquisite, and used to be a hospital run by a religious order. Upstairs there's a chapel lined with azulejos, and a café with nice views of Elvas. ⊠ *Rua de Cadeia* ☎ *268/637150* ☜ *€2.*

Museu Fotografia. Housed in a 1930s movie theater, the municipal photography museum's permanent collection includes 19th-century cameras, black-and-white images from around Portugal, and an exhibit on the history of global photography. The highlight is often some of the temporary, visiting exhibitions. ✉ *Largo Luis de Camoes* ☎ *268/636470* 🌐 *www.museudefotografiaelvas.com.pt* 🎟 *€2.*

WHERE TO EAT AND STAY

$$$$ PORTUGUESE 🍴 **A Bolota Castanha.** People drive miles to dine at this well-known restaurant 16 km (10 miles) from Elvas in the town of Terrugem. The house takes pride in its *cozido de grão* (boiled dinner with pork, smoked sausages, cabbage, and chickpeas), but their menu also lists international dishes such as spinach with shrimp au gratin and delicious sorbets for dessert. Call ahead to book on weekends, as it's often booked solid with wedding parties. [$] *Average main: €30* ✉ *Quinta Janelas Verdes, Rua Madre Teresa, Terrugem* ☎ *268/656118* ⏲ *Closed Mon. No dinner Sun.*

$ PORTUGUESE 🍴 **A Coluna.** This simple, local restaurant serves Alentejo classics like bacalhau, grilled pork, and veal inside a welcoming white stucco dining room decorated with blue-and-white tiles. If you're brave, try the *cabrito* (baby goat), a local delicacy. The weekend tourist menu, offered at both lunch and dinner, is a great value at €12; it includes any starter, main course, and dessert off the menu. At lunch, the deal includes wine as well. [$] *Average main: €12* ✉ *Rua do Cabrito 11* ☎ *268/623728* 💳 *No credit cards* ⏲ *Closed Tues.*

$ HOTEL Fodor's Choice ★ 🏨 **Hotel São João de Deus.** Housed in a 17th-century convent and military hospital just inside the city's southwest walls, this is Elvas's most luxurious hotel for the price. **Pros:** historic; great value; free Wi-Fi and parking. **Cons:** some rooms are a bit small. [$] *Rooms from: €110* ✉ *Largo S. João Deus 1* ☎ *268/639220* 🌐 *www.hotelsaojoaodeus.com* 🛏 *56 rooms* 🍽 *Breakfast.*

$ B&B/INN 🏨 **Pousada de Santa Luzia.** Portugal's first pousada, opened in 1942, is in a two-story, Moorish-style building 12 km (7 miles) from one of the major border crossings between Spain and Portugal. **Pros:** splendid views of Spain; good restaurant; free Wi-Fi; huge bathtubs. **Cons:** less character than other pousadas. [$] *Rooms from: €120* ✉ *Av. de Badajoz* ☎ *268/637470* 🌐 *www.slhotel-elvas.pt* 🛏 *25 rooms* 🍽 *Breakfast.*

$ HOTEL FAMILY 🏨 **Quinta de Santo António.** About 8 km (5 miles) outside Elvas, this historic estate and beautiful hotel make for an restful overnight stop if you're driving between Elvas and the Portugal–Spain border. **Pros:** free Wi-Fi and parking; swimming pool. **Cons:** in the countryside; you'll need a car to get here. [$] *Rooms from: €85* ✉ *Estrada de Barbacena, Apartado 206* ☎ *268/636460* 🌐 *www.qsahotel.com* 🛏 *30 rooms* 🍽 *Breakfast.*

PORTALEGRE

60 km (40 miles) north of Elvas.

Portalegre is the gateway to the Alentejo's most mountainous region as well as to the Parque Natural da Serra de São Mamede. The town is at the foot of the Serra de São Mamede, where the parched plains of the south give way to a greener, more inviting landscape. Because it's a larger, more modern town, Portalegre lacks a bit of the charm of the whitewashed hamlets in the south of the province. But the city's vibrant spirit, buoyed by its large university, more than makes up for it. Unlike some of those deserted southern towns, Portalegre is alive with a diverse community and economy, and still has a university, Gothic cathedral, castle, and walled old town to explore.

It's a great base for outdoors lovers who want easy access to nearby mountains and villages. History buffs will enjoy exploring the remnants of its once-thriving textile industry—Portalegre retains a worldwide reputation for its handmade tapestries, which fetch high prices.

GETTING HERE AND AROUND

Portalegre is Alto Alentejo's largest hub, with good public transportation links. The tourist office can provide an updated bus schedule, with service several times daily to/from Évora. The city center is divided by the Jardim do Tarro, a public garden, with most historical points of interest to the south within easy walking distance, and residential areas to the north.

The tourist office also offers free guided walking tours at 9:30 on first Saturday of every month. Depending on the size and speed of the group, tours last up to 3½ hours and cover all major tourist sites in Portalegre, except for museums. The walk follows a circuit inside the city limits and isn't strenuous.

ESSENTIALS

Tour Guides Tempo Sem Fim. ⊠ *Rua 19 de Junho 40–42* ☎ *245/366076.*

Visitor Information Portalegre Tourist Office. ⊠ *Rua Guilherme Gomes Fernandes 22* ☎ *245/307445.*

EXPLORING

TOP ATTRACTIONS

Castelo de Portalegre. At the base of Portoalegre's sloping cobblestone streets stands the town's castle, which dates to the early 14th century. In the 1930s, the castle's walls were dissembled to open streets around it to traffic. Now a wooden structure, somewhat controversial in its design, links the castle's body with an adjacent tower, where you can climb up for splendid views of the cathedral and city. ⊠ *Rua Luis Barahona* ☎ *245/307540* 🆓 *Free.*

Fodor'sChoice
★
Coudelaria de Alter. If you're interested in horses, you must visit the Alter Stud Farm, 22 km (14 miles) southwest of Portalegre. It was founded by Dom João V in 1748 to furnish royalty with high-quality mounts. Dedicated to preserving and developing the beautiful Alter Real (Royal Alter) strain of the Lusitania breed, the farm has had a long, turbulent history. After years of foreign invasion and pillage, little remains of its original structures, but a huge modern equestrian complex now surrounds the older buildings. Fortunately, the equine bloodline, one of Europe's noblest, has been preserved, and you can watch these superb horses being trained and exercised on the farm. There are also three small but interesting museums here: one documents the history of the farm, one has a collection of horse-drawn carriages, and one has displays on the art of falconry (you can also watch the daily training sessions). Guided tours of the museums are available at 11 and 3. The town of Alter do Chão itself, with the battlements of a 14th-century castle

overlooking a square, is also worth a stroll. ⊠ *Coutada do Arneiro, Chão, Alter do Chão* ⊹ *Follow signs along a dusty track 3 km (2 miles) northwest of Alter do Chão* ☎ *245/610074/60* ⊕ *www.alterreal. pt* ⊠ *€7.50* ⊗ *Closed Mon.*

Fodor'sChoice
★

Mosteiro de S. Bernardo. Founded in 1518, the Monastery of Saint Bernard is a beautiful Renaissance property that includes a tiled church, cloisters with a central garden and fountain, and a mausoleum. The monastery closed after the last monk died in 1878, and since then the building has been used as a seminary, a high school, a municipal museum, and military barracks. It's now used by the National Guard, which opens the building to visitors during selected hours. ⊠ *Av. George Robinson* ☎ *245/307400* ⊠ *Free.*

Sé de Portalegre. About 400 meters north of the castle lies Portalegre's cathedral, a 16th-century church and the town's most prominent landmark. The 18th-century facade is highlighted with marble columns and wrought-iron balconies. Inside are early 17th-century azulejos depicting the Virgin Mary. ⊠ *Praça do Município* ☎ *245/330322* ⊠ *Free.*

NEED A BREAK

Pontofinal Paragrafo. The bohemian Pontofinal Paragrafo coffee shop and bookstore is a popular hangout for locals along the main street toward Portalegre's cathedral and castle. It draws a mix of students, bookworms, and wannabe poets. It's got a lovely atmosphere and serves an array of cakes, teas, wine, and cocktails. ⊠ *Rua Luiz de Camoes 43* ☎ *245/382041.*

WORTH NOTING

Casa-Museu José Regio. Roughly midway between the cathedral and the castle, the José Regio House and Museum, just off Avenida Poeta José Regio, was named for a local poet who died in 1969. He bequeathed his varied collection of religious and folk art to the museum, which is in his former home. ⊠ *Largo de Boa Vista* ☎ *245/307535* ⊠ *€2.10* ⊗ *Closed Mon.*

Museu de Tapeçaria Guy Fino. This wonderful museum holds a contemporary collection of the tapestries that made Portalegre world famous. The museum is named after Guy Fino, the founder of one of the city's textile factories. ⊠ *Rua da Figueira 9* ☎ *245/307530* ⊕ *www.mtportalegre.pt* ⊠ *€2.10* ⊗ *Closed Mon.*

Museu Municipal de Portalegre. The Museu Municipal, in a former seminary next to the cathedral, contains a wealth of religious art, including a gilded, 16th-century Spanish Pietà. ⊠ *Rua José Maria da Rosa* ☎ *245/307525* ⊠ *€2.10* ⊗ *Closed Mon.*

Parque Natural da Serra de São Mamede. This 80,000-acre nature park lies roughly 5 km (3 miles) northeast of Portalegre and extends north to the fortified town of Marvão and the spa town of Castelo de Vide, and south to the little hamlet of Esperança on the Spanish border. The sparsely inhabited park region is made up of small family plots, and sheepherding is the major occupation. The area is rich in wildlife, including many rare species of birds, as well as wild boars, deer, and wildcats. It's a pristine, quiet place for hiking, riding, or simply communing with nature, and you'll rarely spot another tourist for miles and miles. For hiking maps or information about activities, contact the park office. ✉ *Rua General Conde Jorge de Avilez 22* ☎ *245/909160, 245/203631* 🌐 *www.icnf.pt.*

WHERE TO EAT AND STAY

$$ PORTUGUESE 🍴 **O Abrigo.** On a quiet street around the corner from Portoalegre's cathedral you'll find this small, husband-and-wife-run restaurant. You enter the cork-lined dining area through a snack bar. One of the best dishes on the menu is the *migas alentejanas* (a tasty fried-pork-and-bread-crumbs concoction), served on a terra-cotta platter. [$] *Average main: €16* ✉ *Rua de Elvas 74* ☎ *245/331658* 💳 *No credit cards.*

$ PORTUGUESE Fodor's Choice ★ 🍴 **O Escondidinho.** It's worth the time it takes to find this lovely local restaurant, tucked away down a quiet street in Portalegre. Decorated with traditional tiles and brick archways, it's a charming local favorite that serves up amazing Alentejo dishes like migas, porco preto, and grilled fish. Half portions are huge and economical, and so are the ceramic pitchers of Alentejan red wine. Don't be surprised if you return twice in one weekend. [$] *Average main: €10* ✉ *Travessa das Cruzes 1* ☎ *245/202728* 💳 *No credit cards* 🕒 *Closed Sun.* ✍ *Reservations not accepted.*

$ HOTEL 🏨 **Pensao Novo.** This clean, simple guesthouse has 14 rooms in each of two downtown row houses. **Pros:** clean rooms; good value; big breakfast buffet included. **Cons:** front rooms are vulnerable to street noise; no restaurant. [$] *Rooms from: €45* ✉ *Rua 31 Janeiro 30* ☎ *245/331212, 245/330812* 🌐 *www.pensaonova.weebly.com* 🛏 *14 rooms* 🍽 *Breakfast.*

$ HOTEL Fodor's Choice ★ 🏨 **Quinta da Dourada.** This sprawling horse farm and vineyard is 7 km (4 miles) from Portalegre, but it feels like it's way out in the countryside, with 360-degree views of rolling hills, rows of grapevines, and forests—all from the swimming pool. **Pros:** rural retreat just a few minutes' drive from town; gorgeous swimming pool and gardens; kids are welcome. **Cons:** too far (and too steep a climb) to walk from town; no restaurant, but meals can be prepared upon request. [$] *Rooms from: €85* ✉ *Parque Natural Da Serra de S.Mamede-Ribeira de Niza* ☎ *937/218654, 245/203487* 🌐 *www.quintadadourada.pt* 💳 *No credit cards* 🛏 *2 double rooms, 4 apartments* 🍽 *Breakfast.*

$ HOTEL 🏨 **Rossio Hotel.** The decor in this sleek hotel in the historical center is modern and simple, dotted with low-energy LED lighting throughout. **Pros:** spa; free gym; free Wi-Fi; extra beds available for children; friendly service. **Cons:** off-street parking costs extra; there's a bar, but no restaurant. [$] *Rooms from: €85* ✉ *Rua 31 de Janeiro 6* ☎ *245/082218, 910/265268* 🌐 *www.rossiohotel.com* 🛏 *15 rooms, 3 suites* 🍽 *Breakfast.*

$ B&B/INN Fodor's Choice ★ 🏨 **Solar das Avencas.** This historic manor is traditional, old-world Portugal at its best, exquisitely adorned with local tapestries and chock-full of antiques. **Pros:** historic property with warm family hospitality; staying here offers a more authentic, historic experience than even some pousadas, at a fraction of the price. **Cons:** no central heating, but cozy fireplaces in bedrooms; no restaurant. [$] *Rooms from: €60* ✉ *Parque Miguel Bombarda 11* ☎ *245/201028* 💳 *No credit cards* 🛏 *5 rooms* 🍽 *Breakfast.*

MARVÃO

25 km (15 miles) northeast of Portalegre.

The views of the mountains as you approach the medieval fortress town of Marvão are spectacular, and the town's castle, atop a sheer rock cliff, commands a 360-degree panorama. The village, with some 120 mostly older inhabitants, is perched at 2,800 feet on top of a mountain, and laid out in several long rows of tidy, white-stone dwellings terraced into the hill.

The biggest event of the year here is the boisterous chestnut festival in early November, when marching bands take to the tiny streets and transform Marvão into a homemade wine-swigging, chestnut-roasting party. But be forewarned: parking is impossible, and hotels book up sometimes a year beforehand.

GETTING HERE AND AROUND

Marvão lies north of Portalegre and east of Castelo de Vide, in the Serra Mamede mountains overlooking Spain. For the most scenic approach from Portalegre, take N359 18 km (11 miles) to Marvão. The narrow but well-surfaced serpentine N359 rises to an elevation of 2,800 feet, past stands of birch and chestnut trees and small vegetable gardens bordered by ancient stone walls. At Portagem take note of the well-preserved Roman bridge.

The drive up to Marvão, hugging the side of the mountain, is breathtaking, but can also be hazardous in harsh weather. Although you can drive through the constricted streets, it's best to park in spaces outside the town walls and walk in as Marvão is best appreciated on foot.

ESSENTIALS

Visitor Information Marvão Tourist Office. ⊠ *Largo da Silveirinha* ☎ *245/993456* ⊕ *www.cm-marvao.pt.*

EXPLORING

Castelo de Marvão. You can climb the tower of Marvão's castle and trace the course of the massive Vauban-style stone walls (characterized by concentric lines of trenches and walls, a hallmark of the 17th-century French military engineer Vauban), adorned at intervals with bartizans, to enjoy breathtaking vistas from different angles. Given its strategic position, it's no surprise that Marvão has been a fortified settlement since Roman times or earlier. The present castle was built under Dom Dinis in the late 13th century and modified some four centuries later, during the reign of Dom João IV. The castle is open 24 hours, with no admission charge. ⊠ *Rua do Castelo* ⊠ *Free.*

Museu Municipal de Marvão. At the foot of the path leading to the town's castle is Marvão's municipal museum, in the 13th-century Church of Saint Mary. The small gallery contains a diverse collection of religious artifacts, azulejos, costumes, ancient maps, and weapons. ⊠ *Igreja de Santa Maria, Rua do Castelo* ☎ *245/909132* ⊠ *€1.90.*

Santo António das Areias. Scattered among the chestnut groves, 5 km (3 miles) northeast of Marvão, are some two dozen prehistoric dolmens. They're difficult to locate on your own, however, and it's best to ask the tourist office to organize a group with a guide. Some pieces of the dolmens and photos of them can also be found in the Museu Municipal. ✉ *Marvão.*

WHERE TO EAT AND STAY

$ PORTUGUESE 🍴 **Casa do Povo.** Nestled in a corner row house, this simple dining room serves up classic Alentejo dishes and local wines. The bar downstairs has a patio with good views for sundowners. The restaurant offers a €10 daily tourist menu, including soup, main course, dessert, and a drink. Any of Casa do Povo's soups are worth tasting, especially the dogfish soup with coriander. [$] *Average main: €10* ✉ *Travessa do Chabouco* ☎ *245/993160* ⊙ *No dinner Thurs.*

$ PORTUGUESE 🍴 **Varanda do Alentejo.** This boisterous bar and restaurant is a favorite among locals and out-of-town families, especially on Sunday. The cuisine is typical Alentejan, with specialties like migas with potato, grilled pork, and fish. The atmosphere is warm and friendly. [$] *Average main: €12* ✉ *Praça do Pelourinho 1-A, Rua das Protas da Vila 12* ☎ *245/909002* 🌐 *www.varandadoalentejo.com.*

$ B&B/INN 🏨 **Casa D. Dinis.** This Marvão house from the 17th century has stone arches and thick walls; original murals depicting scenes from the Alentejo adorn the rooms. **Pros:** cozy; no-frills family hospitality; terrace offers some of the best views in town; free Wi-Fi. **Cons:** some rooms are cramped and cold. [$] *Rooms from: €100* ✉ *Rua Dr. António Matos Magalhães 7* ☎ *245/909028, 245/909028* 🌐 *www.domdinis.pt* 🛏 *8 rooms* 🍽 *Breakfast.*

$ HOTEL 🏨 **Hotel El Rei Dom Manuel.** Five of its rooms in this 200-year-old inn inside the castle walls have fantastic cliffside views, and others range in size, with good options for families who need extra beds. **Pros:** historic building in quiet location; good views. **Cons:** decor is a bit dated. [$] *Rooms from: €90* ✉ *Largo da Olivença* ☎ *245/909150* 🌐 *www.turismarvao.pt* 🛏 *15 rooms* 🍽 *Breakfast.*

$$ HOTEL 🏨 **Pousada de Santa Maria.** In 1967 several old houses within the city walls were joined to create the Pousada de Santa Maria; the rooms are decorated with traditional Alentejo furnishings, and the restaurant, open to the public, serves some of the best regional dishes in the village. **Pros:** cozy atmosphere, especially in winter. **Cons:** lacks extraordinary features and grandiose charm of other pousadas. [$] *Rooms from: €150* ✉ *Santa Maria de Marvão* ☎ *245/993201, 245/993202* 🌐 *www.pousadas.pt* 🛏 *28 rooms, 3 suites* 🍽 *Breakfast.*

CASTELO DE VIDE

8 km (5 miles) west of Marvão.

A quiet hilltop town, Castelo de Vide is a picturesque place with pots of geraniums and dazzling flower beds throughout town. It's more lively than Marvão, with more options for restaurants, hotels, and sights, but still retains its rustic village feel. When Marvão holds its annual chestnut festival, drawing thousands of tourists from all over Portugal and Spain, Castelo de Vide holds a smaller, more intimate festival in its open-air market, complete with a pig roast and old men in felt hats sharing jugs of their homemade wine. You might be surprised to see a bagpiper strolling through the crowds during Castelo de Vide's festivals; the diverse town still celebrates some traditions from its ancient Gallic and Celtic ancestry.

There are steep cobbled streets that provide beautiful views of the white-washed town against a backdrop of olive groves and hills. As you walk along, notice the many houses with Gothic doorways in various designs. (The tourist brochures proclaim that Castelo de Vide has the largest number of Gothic doorways of any town in Portugal.) Castelo de Vide's history is as a spa town, renowned for its fresh mountain springs that feed a fountain in the main square today. The town had a sizeable Jewish community in the Middle Ages, and today has one of the oldest synagogues in Portugal.

GETTING HERE AND AROUND
An intriguing backcountry lane connects Marvão with Castelo de Vide. About halfway down the hill from Marvão, turn to the right toward Escusa (watch for the sign) and continue through the chestnut- and acacia-covered hills to Castelo de Vide. If you're traveling from Portalegre, take the N246 directly. At the town's main square is the Praça Dom Pedro V, with the castle to the west and a park to the east.

ESSENTIALS
Taxi Contact Castelo de Vide Taxi Service. ⊠ *Praça Dom Pedro V* ☎ *245/901271.*

Visitor Information Castelo de Vide Tourist Office. ⊠ *Praça Dom Pedro V* ☎ *245/908227* ⊕ *www.castelodevide.pt.*

EXPLORING
Castelo. You can venture into the tower in Castelo de Vide's castle and inside the well-preserved keep to the large Gothic hall, which has a picture window looking down on the town square and the church. ⊠ *Rua Direita do Castelo* 🎫 *Free.*

Mercado Franco. On the last Friday of every month this open-air market is held in Sitio do Canapé, next to the Municipal Market. You can find bargains in everything from T-shirts, shoes, jewelry, and electronic equipment. ⊠ *Sitio do Canapé.*

Praça Dom Pedro V. Castelo de Vide's large, baroque central square is bordered by the Igreja de Santa Maria (St. Mary's Church) and the town hall. An alleyway to the right of the church leads to the town symbol: a canopied 16th-century marble fountain. Another cobblestone lane leads from the fountain up to the Juderia (ancient Jewish quarter). The tourist office, on the north side of the square, often pipes classical music through speakers across the area, particularly around the holidays. ⊠ *Praça Dom Pedro V* ⊕ *www.castelodevide.pt.*

Fodor'sChoice **Sinagoga.** A Jewish community is believed to have existed in Castelo de
★ Vide since the 12th century, and reached its peak in the 15th century, bolstered by Jews fleeing the Inquisition in neighboring Spain. This tiny synagogue is believed to be from the late 13th century. There's a

small sign outside, but otherwise you might miss it—it looks exactly like all the other row houses. The synagogue was adapted from existing buildings, with two separate prayer rooms for men and women. Although its exact construction year is unknown, this is thought to be one of the oldest in all of Portugal. There are plans in the works for a comprehensive visitor center. ✉ *Rua da Judairia* 🎫 *Free.*

WHERE TO EAT AND STAY

$ BAKERY FAMILY 🍴 **Doces & Companhia.** This upscale coffee shop with friendly service serves light lunches like scones, cakes, baguettes, and sandwiches, and makes the perfect stop between sightseeing trips around town. The outdoor terrace in back offers superb views of the hillside across from Castelo de Vide. A kids' table with crayons and coloring books is downstairs. [$] *Average main: €7* ✉ *Praça Dom Pedro V 6* ☎ *245/901408* 🕒 *Closed Sun.*

$$ PORTUGUESE FAMILY Fodor's Choice ★ 🍴 **Restaurante D. Pedro V.** This is the best option for a traditional Alentejan meal in Castelo de Vide. Walk through the entryway bar into a lovely domed dining room decorated like an old wine cellar. Specialties include goat and lamb roasts and dogfish soup with local chestnuts. The €18 tourist menu (soup or starter, main course, dessert, and wine) is a good value. [$] *Average main: €16* ✉ *Praça Dom Pedro V* ☎ *245/901236* 🌐 *www.dpedrov.com.pt* 🕒 *Closed last 15 days of Jan.*

$ HOTEL Fodor's Choice ★ 🏨 **Casa Amarela.** The beautifully restored, bright-yellow 17th-century manor house on Castelo de Vide's main square features stone stairways to intricately decorated rooms with period antiques and spacious marble bathrooms. **Pros:** luxurious, intimate setting with views over Praça Dom Pedro V. **Cons:** outside rooms overlooking the square might get noisy in summer; no restaurant; no pool, but there's free access to pool at sister hotel, Casa do Parque, across town. [$] *Rooms from: €90* ✉ *Praça Dom Pedro V 11* ☎ *245/901250, 245/905878* 🌐 *www.casaamarelath.pt* 💳 *No credit cards* 🛏 *11 rooms* 🍽 *Breakfast.*

$ HOTEL 🏨 **Casa do Parque.** This charming, affordable guesthouse is a good option for those who want to absorb local atmosphere close to all the sights. **Pros:** quaint and clean; gorgeous swimming pool amid flowering trees. **Cons:** not very stately. [$] *Rooms from: €65* ✉ *Av. da Aramenha 37* ☎ *245/901250* 🌐 *www.casadoparque.net* 💳 *No credit cards* 🛏 *25 rooms* 🍽 *Breakfast.*

$ B&B/INN FAMILY Fodor's Choice ★ 🏨 **Vila Maria.** Named for its friendly owner, Maria Luisa, this historic guesthouse, decorated with antiques and local textiles, offers a great location on the edge of Castelo de Vide along with genuine personal charm. **Pros:** warm hospitality and care; free bikes and parking; delicious home cooking. **Cons:** limited space so not ideal for large groups; no dinner. [$] *Rooms from: €50* ✉ *Quinta do Patameiro, Bairro da Boavista* ☎ *960/100844* 🌐 *www.vilamaria-castelodevide.com* 🛏 *2 rooms, 1 apartment* 🍽 *Breakfast.*

BAIXO ALENTEJO

Extending south of Évora and from the rugged west-coast beaches east to the border with Spain, the Baixo Alentejo (Lower Alentejo) is a vast, mostly flat region of wheat fields, cork oaks, and olive trees. It rains very little here, and the summer months are particularly hot. Shepherds wearing broad-brim hats and sheepskin vests still tend their sheep in the fields. Gypsies still set up camp with makeshift tents, horse carts, and open fires. These scenes from a rapidly disappearing way of life contrast sharply with the modernization taking place in the region. A new system of hiking trails, linking old fishermen's and shepherds' paths, is drawing outdoors enthusiasts from all over the world.

ALVITO

40 km south of Evora.

Alvito is a typical, sleepy Alentejo town on a low hill above the Rio Odivelas. Noted for its fortresslike 13th-century parish church, the town also has a 15th-century castle converted into a pousada and a number of modest houses with graceful Manueline doorways and windows. The castle was built in 1482 by the Baron of Alvito, the first individual permitted to have his own castle. King Manuel I was born and died here.

GETTING HERE AND AROUND

Alvito lies south of Viana do Alentejo on the way to Beja, along the N257 and N258. There is no public transport in this remote, rural part of Portugal, and having your own car is essential for exploring the area. The small village of Alvito stretches just a few blocks out from the castle in all directions.

ESSENTIALS

Visitor Information **Alvito Tourist Office.** ✉ *Rua dos Lobos 13* ☎ *284/480808.*

WHERE TO EAT AND STAY

$ PORTUGUESE 🍴 **O Camões.** Roughly 7 km (4 miles) northwest of Alvito, the main attraction of this large, popular restaurant is its wood-burning oven in which delicious legs of lamb, pork, and other meats are cooked to perfection. They're first marinated in coriander, oregano, and aromatic herbs that grow in the region. Owner Sr. Camões is also well-known for his açorda dishes, the most popular being açorda *de cação* (with baby shark). The atmosphere is cozy and authentic, with brick domed walls, wood paneling, and a huge antique chandelier dangling overhead. [$] *Average main: €12* ✉ *Rua 5 de Outubro 13, Vila Nova da Baronia* ☎ *284/475209* 💳 *No credit cards* 🕒 *Closed Mon.*

$ PORTUGUESE Fodor's Choice ★ 🍴 **Taberna do Arrufa.** Enjoy divine traditional Alentejo cooking and local wine under a wood-beamed ceiling and a crystal chandelier, or under a cork tree on a stone terrace alfresco. You'll imbibe alongside six-foot clay jars, which locals have used to store wine since Roman times. Specialties include migas *com entrecosto* (bread crumbs with pork ribs), pork steaks with clam sauce, chickpea stew, and various fish and veggie

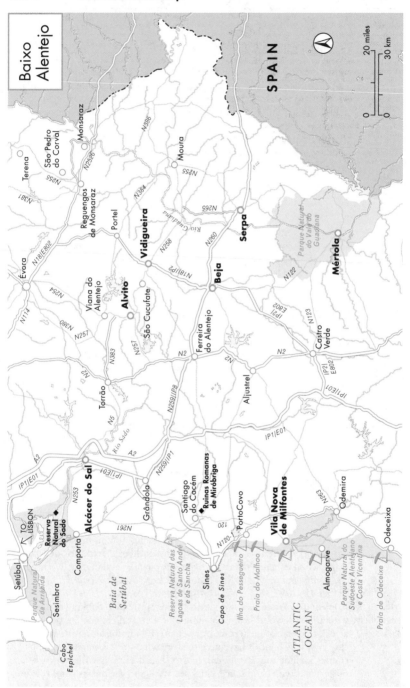

Baixo Alentejo

soups. If you're lucky, you might catch an impromptu performance of fado—the staff are known to join in. [$] *Average main: €12* ✉ *Travessa das Francas 3* ☎ *967/229487* ⏲ *Closed Tues.*

$ HOTEL FAMILY Fodor's Choice ★ 🏨 **Pousada do Castelo de Alvito.** The essential architectural elements of a castle, including crenellated battlements and massive round towers, a large garden, and a courtyard, have been retained in this pousada located within the walls of the fortress at the edge of the village. **Pros:** countryside setting makes the castle even more spectacular. **Cons:** this is a cozy retreat, but you'll be hard-pressed to find any nightlife. [$] *Rooms from: €120* ✉ *Largo do Castelo, Apartado 9* ☎ *284/480700* 🌐 *www.pousadas.pt* 🛏 *20 rooms, 1 suite* 🍴 *Breakfast.*

BEJA

36 km southeast of Alvito.

Midway between Spain and the sea is Beja, Baixo Alentejo's principal agricultural center that spreads itself across a small knoll. Much of the oldest part of town retains a significantly Arabic flavor—students of Portuguese even claim that the local dialect has Arabic characteristics—the legacy of more than 400 years of Moorish occupation.

Founded by Julius Caesar and known as Pax Julia, Beja is often overlooked in favor of its more popular and beautiful sister city, Évora, but that just means you'll have the town all to yourself to explore. It's also a classic example of an Alentejo town center that's been emptied of its residents, some of whom have moved to modern apartment complexes on the city's outskirts, and many others who've left altogether, seeking employment in Lisbon or Porto. Walking Beja's streets, it seems like the majority of the population is over 65—a sobering idea when it comes to the future here.

Many of the town's most interesting monuments were destroyed in the 19th century during the population's fury against the church's domination. In spite of that, Beja has an important, valuable heritage, and it can all be explored on foot.

GETTING HERE AND AROUND

Beja lies in the center of Baixo Alentejo, along the IP2 about halfway between Évora and the Algarve. The city's walkable center is bisected east to west by a public garden and three grand squares: Largo Dom Nuno Alvares Pereira, Largo dos Duques de Beja, and Praça da Republica.

ESSENTIALS

Visitor Information Beja Tourist Office. ✉ *Largo Dr. Lima Faleiro* ☎ *284/311913* 🌐 *www.cm-beja.pt.*

EXPLORING

Castelo de Beja. Beja's castle is an extensive system of fortifications whose crenellated walls and towers chronicle the history of the town from its Roman occupation through its 19th-century battles with the French. Once inside the central courtyard, climb up the castle's ramparts to the impressive 140-foot **Torre de Menagem,** a stone tower with gorgeous

An Affair to Remember

As the story goes, Mariana Alcoforado (1640–1723), a young Beja nun, fell in love with a French count named Chamilly, who was in the Alentejo fighting the Spaniards. When he went back to France, the nun waited longingly and in vain at the window for him to return. The affair was made public when five passionate love letters to the count, attributed to Mariana, were published in France in 1669 (the popular collection was known as the *Portuguese Letters*). The scandal brought a measure of lasting international literary fame to this provincial Alentejo town. But it's likely that it was actually another Frenchman who penned the infamous letters after hearing of the love story. Nevertheless, French nobles apparently began using the word *portugaise* as a synonym for a passionate love letter.

views of the surrounding countryside. The tourist office is also located inside the castle grounds. ⊠ *Largo Dr. Lima Faleiro* 🖾 *Free.*

Fodor'sChoice **Convento de Nossa Senhora da Conceição.** Facing a broad plaza in the
★ center of the oldest part of town, the Convent of Our Lady of the Conception was founded in 1459 by the parents of King Manuel I. Favored by the royal family, this Franciscan convent became one of the richest of the period. It now houses the **Museu Regional de Beja/Rainha Dona Leonor** (Regional Museum of Beja and its Queen Leonor), and if there's one museum you visit in Beja, this should be it. It's tough to decide which is more impressive, the exhibits inside or the building itself. You walk into an ornate, gold-encrusted chapel with saints' relics, and then proceed through the convent's old cloisters covered in azulejos from the 16th and 17th centuries. Some of them comprise panels depicting scenes from the life of St. John the Baptist, and there's also a section of Moorish tiles. At the far end of the second-floor gallery is the famous Mariana Window, named for the 17th-century nun Mariana Alcoforado, whose love affair with a French officer is the stuff of local legend. ⊠ *Largo da Conceição* 🕾 *284/323351* ⊕ *www.museuregionaldebeja.pt* 🖾 *€2 (free Sun. morning), includes admission to Museu Visigótico* ⊘ *Closed Mon.*

Igreja de Santa Maria (*St. Mary's Church*). This church across the square from the Convento de Nossa Senhora da Conceição was once a mosque, and can be easily recognized by its massive round pillars. It's a fine example of what's known as the "Gothic Alentejo" architecture style. Its Mudéjar arches and bell tower are similar to that of the famed Giralda Tower in Seville. ⊠ *Largo de Santa Maria* 🕾 *284/328438* 🖾 *Free.*

NEED A BREAK

Luiz da Rocha. This Beja institution was founded in 1893. The art deco–style main café on the ground floor serves great coffee and *conventuais*, sweets made according to recipes from local convents. In the pedestrian section of streets just outside the city walls, it's conveniently located next to a few hotels and offers better breakfasts, including the delicious *torradas* (simple white toast with butter). This is also a good local spot to have a sandwich between museum visits. Don't be surprised if you're the only tourist in there; the friendly barman may try his (rusty) English on you. ⊠ *Capitão João Francisco de Sousa 63* ☎ *284/323179* ⊕ *www.luizdarocha.com.*

Museu Visigótico (*The Visigoth Museum*). This museum is next to the Castelo de Beja in a 6th-century church—one of Portugal's oldest standing buildings. It houses an impressive collection of tombstones, weapons, and pottery that documents the Visigoth presence in the region. ⊠ *Largo de Santo Amaro* ☎ *284/321465* 🔖 *€2, includes admission to Convento da Conceição.*

Fodor's Choice ★ **Praça da República.** This stately square stretches across the western part of the city center, anchored at one end by the 16th-century Igreja de Misericordia, whose sprawling stone veranda used to be an open-air market. At one end is an ornate royal pillory from the 16th-century reign of Dom Manuel, restored in the 20th century. The square is also lined with lovely Manueline archways under residential buildings. Sadly, most of these buildings are in disrepair, as residents move to modern accommodation on the outskirts of town. But it's still worth visiting, in its charming decay, and patronizing one of the cafés still struggling along here. ⊠ *Praça da República.*

WHERE TO EAT

$ PORTUGUESE **✕ A Esquina.** Good local cooking—served with care in pleasant surroundings—is the attraction here. While the building isn't historic, the cuisine is authentic, and the service is warm, friendly, and genuine. There are few better places to try *lebre com feijão* (hare with beans) in season. The wine list is short, but there's usually a good selection of Serpa cheeses. The €15 tourist menu (soup or starter, main course, dessert, and glass of wine) is a good value. Ⓢ *Average main: €10* ⊠ *Rua Infante D. Henrique 26* ☎ *284/388851* ⊘ *Closed Sun.*

$ PORTUGUESE **✕ A Pipa.** This narrow little locals' favorite is a popular place for traditional Alentejan cuisine. The *prato del dia,* or daily menu specials, are a good value, with around €10 covering a starter or soup, main course, and dessert. This is a popular Plan B for diners who can't get in across the street at Adega Tipica 25 de Abril. Ⓢ *Average main: €10* ⊠ *Rua da Moeda 8* ☎ *284/327043, 968/115032* ⊘ *Closed Sun.*

$$ PORTUGUESE Fodor's Choice ★ **✕ Adega Tipica 25 Abril.** This rustic restaurant with red-and-white-check tablecloths and cork carvings adorning the walls serves typical Alentejan dishes, and it's the best value in town. The atmosphere is authentic, with long wooden tables for boisterous families and intimate little two-seaters tucked behind huge clay wine jugs. The porco preto is a specialty. The house wine—literally cheaper than the bottled water—is a wonderful value and complement to any meal. Ⓢ *Average main: €18* ⊠ *Rua da Moeda 23* ☎ *284/325960* ▭ *No credit cards* ⊘ *Closed Mon.*

$ PORTUGUESE **✕ Maria Papoila.** This restaurant's traditional Alentejan fare is a favorite with locals, and a good spot to grab a quick lunch between museums and sights. This restaurant is split into a dining area and a snack bar/takeout counter. The dining room has vaulted ceilings, and there's also an alfresco area beneath fruit trees in the inner courtyard. The *carne de porco à alentejana* (pork with clams) is recommended. Other specialties include snails and fondue. $ *Average main: €7* ⊠ *Rua Sousa Porto 43–45* ☎ *284/331724.*

$
PORTUGUESE

✕ **O Arbitro.** On the north side of town, behind the castle, sits this lively local favorite. The dining room is decorated in traditional blue-and-white azulejo tiles. Ask about the daily specials, which often include barbecued lamb chops, bean stew, or pork steaks. $ *Average main: €12* ⊠ *Rua Conselheiro Meneses 4* ☎ *284/389204.*

WHERE TO STAY

$
B&B/INN
Fodor's Choice
★

🖼 **Hotel Bejense.** Founded in 1889, this little inn along Beja's pedestrian shopping zone was the first public hotel in town, and it still retains its old stone doorway covered in vines and vibrant pink flowers. **Pros:** warm service; family-run establishment; good location; free Wi-Fi. **Cons:** no restaurant. $ *Rooms from: €55* ⊠ *Rua Capitão João Francisco de Sousa 57* ☎ *284/311570* ⊕ *www.hotelbejense.com* ⮐ *24 rooms* ⍾ *Breakfast.*

$
B&B/INN

🖼 **Hotel Santa Bárbara.** This elegant hotel has a cozy stone fireplace and a great location in Beja's pedestrian zone just outside the old city walls. **Pros:** good location; historic details inside; free Wi-Fi; kids under six stay free. **Cons:** front rooms with balconies can be a bit noisy; no restaurant. $ *Rooms from: €50* ⊠ *Rua de Mértola 56* ☎ *284/312280* ⊕ *www.hotelsantabarbara.pt* ⮐ *26 rooms* ⍾ *Breakfast.*

$$
HOTEL
FAMILY

🖼 **Pousada do Convento de São Francisco.** Surrounded by spacious gardens is a 13th-century convent that has been tastefully converted into a comfortable pousada, about a 10-minute walk from Beja's castle. **Pros:** elegant old-world style with modern swimming pool surrounded by palm trees; good option for children, with space to run around outside. **Cons:** more expensive; less historic detail than other pousadas. $ *Rooms from: €160* ⊠ *Largo Dom Nuno Álvares Pereira, Largo Dom Nuno Álvares Pereira* ☎ *284/313580* ⊕ *www.pousadas.pt* ⮐ *35 rooms* ⍾ *Breakfast.*

SERPA

27 km (17 miles) southeast of Beja.

In this sleepy agricultural town, men pass the time by gathering together in the compact Praça da República under the shadow of an ancient stone clock tower. One of the most authentic towns on the Alentejan Plain, Serpa's whitewashed medieval center is surrounded by rolling hills and vineyards, well off the tourist path but definitely worth a visit. In cubbyholes along narrow, cobbled streets, carpenters, shoemakers, basket weavers, and other craftsmen work in much the same manner as their forefathers.

Serpa's sleepy streets explode with life several times a year with festivals that draw visitors from across the Spanish border and around Europe, celebrating Serpa's local delicacies, including one of Portugal's most renowned sheep's milk cheeses.

GETTING HERE AND AROUND

Serpa lies along the IP8 east of Beja, and about equidistant to the Spanish border. It's best to park outside the old city walls near the impressive aqueduct, and navigate the town center by foot.

ESSENTIALS

Visitor Information Serpa Tourist Office. ⊠ *Rua dos Cavalos 19* ☎ *284/544727* ⊕ *www.cm-serpa.pt.*

> **TRADITIONAL MUSIC**
>
> If you're lucky, you may hear a group of Alentejo men, dressed in typical garb of sheepskin vest and trousers, singing medieval songs (*cante alentejano*), similar to Gregorian chants. These singers are famous all around Portugal.

EXPLORING

Aqueduto. This impressive structure from the 11th century used to ferry water to Serpa from wells in the countryside. In the 17th century, a wheel pump was added just outside the city's southern walls, and still stands there today. Follow the aqueduct's walls from the pump out across the city's west side. ⊠ *Rua dos Arcos.*

Fodor'sChoice
★ **Castelo de Serpa.** Serpa's 11th-century aqueduct forms an integral part of the walls of the 13th-century castle, from which there's a stunning view of town. The huge ruined sections of wall tottering precariously above the entrance are the result of explosions ordered by the Duke of Ossuna during the 18th-century War of the Spanish Succession. ⊠ *Alcáçova do Castelo* ☎ *284/540100* 🔁 *Free.*

Museu Arqueológico. This little gem of a museum located inside the castle walls reopened in spring 2016 after nearly a decade of renovations. Light-filled rooms display artifacts from Serpa dating from the Paleolithic to the Islamic period. The first floor covers the Prehistoric Period to the Iron Age, and the top floor houses artifacts from the Roman era, Late Antiquity, and the Moorish era. Artifacts include pottery, parts of marble and stone columns, coins, and jewelry. New features include video kiosks with content produced by a local Serpa filmmaker. ⊠ *Alcáçova do Castelo* ☎ *284/544663* ⊕ *www.cm-serpa.pt* 🔁 *Free* ☙ *Closed Mon.*

Museu do Relógio (*The Clock Museum*). Housed in a 16th-century convent, this quirky little museum displays a collection of thousands of clocks, with a permanent exhibition titled *400 Years of Clock-Making in Portugal*. There's also a workshop, where you can watch experts repairing old clocks, or bring in your own to be tinkered with. There's a sister museum in Évora, but this is the main branch. ⊠ *Convento do Mosteirinho, Rua do Assento* ☎ *284/543194* ⊕ *www.museudorelogio. com* 🔁 *€2* ☙ *Closed Mon.*

Fodor'sChoice
★ **Museu Etnográfico** (*Serpa's Ethnographic Museum*). Housed in the old market building, this small but well-appointed museum exhibits the tools of traditional local crafts, such as the production of cheese baskets and chairs, as well as ironwork and pottery. The permanent exhibition, *Earth Crafts*, provides an informative overview of how local industry has changed over the centuries. Free guided tours can be arranged if you call a day ahead. ⊠ *Largo do Corro* ☎ *284/549130* 🔁 *Free* ☙ *Closed Mon.*

WHERE TO EAT AND STAY

$ PORTUGUESE 🍴 **Cervejaria Lebrinha.** At the entrance of town near the Abade Correia da Serra (public gardens), this spacious *cervejaria* (beer house) is said to have been pouring the best beer in Portugal since 1957. Old pictures adorning the walls take you back in time to the way Serpa used to be. Wild asparagus with eggs is a good choice for a starter, and then try the grilled carne de porco preto, which is always a tasty choice. As in most cervejarias, the atmosphere is casual, and the service is fast and good. On festival days, when tourists crowd the city center, this is the place to escape the crowds and hang with locals instead. [$] *Average main: €8* ✉ *Rua Calvário 6-8* ☎ *284/549311* 🕒 *Closed Tues., and Sept. 1–15.*

$$ PORTUGUESE Fodor's Choice ★ 🍴 **Molhó Bico.** Hands down, this restaurant in a restored wine cellar near Praça da República serves the best food in Serpa, and perhaps even all of Alentejo. Huge wine barrels sit at the entrance to a traditional dining room with domed ceilings, tile floors, and antique farm implements hanging on the walls. Rotating exhibits with works by local painters also adorn the rustic walls. In winter, the specialty is grilled pork; in summer, try the gazpacho, followed by the fried fish. The Serpa cheese and the Alentejo wines are good at any time of year. Keep an ear out for some cante alentejano at this restaurant. [$] *Average main: €20* ✉ *Rua Quente 1* ☎ *284/549264* 🌐 *www.molhobicoserpa.com* 🕒 *Closed Wed.*

$ B&B/INN FAMILY 🏨 **Bética Hotel.** About a 20-minute drive northwest of Serpa, the Bética Hotel, housed in a big manor house on a cobblestone street, offers old Alentejo details and modern amenities. **Pros:** charm and convenience; great location to explore authentic Alentejan village; free bicyles and Wi-Fi. **Cons:** extra charge for pets; bar, but no restaurant. [$] *Rooms from: €75* ✉ *Rua Do Outeiro* ☎ *284/858714* 🌐 *www.beticahotelrural.com* 🛏 *14 rooms* 🍽 *Breakfast* 💳 *No credit cards.*

$ B&B/INN Fodor's Choice ★ 🏨 **Cantar do Grilo.** About a 15-minute drive from Serpa, this eco-house just outside the boundaries of the Vale do Guadiana natural park is modern, but with traditional Alentejo details like whitewashed facades, wood beams, tile floors, and stone fireplaces, and rooms that surround a communal patio and swimming pool. **Pros:** free Wi-Fi and parking; best views in southern Portugal; barbecue facilities. **Cons:** isolated (although that's the point), so you need your own car; two-night minimum stay. [$] *Rooms from: €90* ✉ *Vale de Milhanos, Correia da Mó, Apt. 668* ☎ *284/595415, 962/051066* 🌐 *www.cantardogrilo.com* 🛏 *4 rooms* 🍽 *Breakfast.*

$ B&B/INN Fodor's Choice ★ 🏨 **Casa de Serpa.** Its labyrinth of passageways, whitewashed walls, vaulted ceilings, and interior open courtyard reflect the Arabic influence in this 200-year-old manor house near the Igreja do Salvador. **Pros:** charming style; friendly management; good location. **Cons:** no restaurant. [$] *Rooms from: €65* ✉ *Largo do Salvador 28* ☎ *284/549238, 963/560624* 🌐 *www.casadeserpa.com* 🛏 *6 rooms* 🍽 *Breakfast.*

MÉRTOLA

56 km (35 miles) south of Serpa.

The ancient walled-in town of Mértola is on a hill overlooking the Rio Guadiana and its Roman quay. Mértola has seen several archaeological excavations in recent years. The artifacts from these digs are all part of the Museu Arqueológico (Archaeology Museum), which has branches—each with displays from different periods—in several locations around town. At any one of them you can buy a combined ticket for €5 that covers the entrance to all the town's museums.

GETTING HERE AND AROUND
Mértola lies inside the protected Parque Natural do Vale do Guadiana, about equidistant from Spain and the Algarve. Follow the N122 road into town and park below the hilltop village, which is best explored on foot. The natural park office can give you helpful maps and advice on how to explore one of Portugal's least touristed—and most spectacular—national parks.

ESSENTIALS
Visitor Information Mértola Tourist Office. ✉ *Rua da Igreja 31* ☎ *286/610109* ⊕ *www.cm-mertola.pt.* **Parque Natural do Vale do Guadiana.** ✉ *Rua Dr. Afonso Costa* ☎ *286/611084* ⊕ *www.natural.pt.*

EXPLORING
Castelo de Mértola. Built in 1292, this castle contains carved stone from the Roman, Moorish, and Christian periods. The courtyard has a very deep cistern in the center. From the castle's **Torre de Menagem,** you can look down on archaeological digs along the sides of the fortress, and out over the river and rolling hills toward Spain. ✉ *Castelo* ⊠ *€2, includes entrance to castle and several museums.*

Convento de São Francisco. This 400-year-old convent on a hill overlooking Mértola had fallen into ruin before a Dutch family stumbled upon it and bought it in the 1980s. The convent building is now open to the public on Sunday, and all 100 acres of surrounding land are a biological garden of local plants and flowers maintained without pesticides. There's also a water museum displaying a complex and sophisticated irrigation system designed in Moorish times. The convent hosts environmental projects and an artist-in-residence, with rotating exhibitions. You can even rent a room in the convent or a cottage on the grounds. ✉ *Convento de São Francisco* ☎ *286/612119* ⊕ *www.conventomertola. com* ⊠ *Free.*

Igreja Matriz. Rising from the slopes above the river are the 12 white towers of Mértola's 12th-century house of worship, built on the ruins of a Roman structure. It was once a mosque and retains many of its original Islamic features, including a *mihrab* (a prayer niche that indicates the direction of Mecca). ✉ *Rua da Igreja* ☎ ⊠ *Free* ⊙ *Closed Mon.*

Largo Luis de Camoes. This charming square lined with citrus trees lies at the heart of town. The town hall sits on the square's western end, with the **Torre do Relogio,** an impressive clock tower built in the late 16th century, on the opposite side. ✉ *Largo Luis de Camoes.*

Fodor'sChoice ★ **Museus de Mértola.** One ticket gains you admission to a handful of fine museums all within walking distance of one another on the town's hilltop, which together make a wonderful afternoon of sightseeing. The **Núcleo Islamico** has impressive displays of jewels, metal items, and a collection of ceramics from the 9th to 13th centuries, when Mértola was ruled by the Moors. The **Casa Romano** is a restored, Roman-era house in the basement of the city hall. You can walk through the house's foundations and view a small collection of pottery and kitchen tools excavated nearby. The nearby **Museu de Arte Sacra** has religious statues and carvings from the 16th through 18th centuries, borrowed from Mértola's various churches. The museum group's oldest collection is housed in the **Museu Visigótico–Basílica Paleocristã** and includes funery stones and other artifacts excavated from the site of the town's paleo-Christian basilica and nearby cemetery. ✉ *Praça Luís de Camões* ☎ *286/610100* 🌐 *museus.cm-mertola.pt* 🎟 *€2.*

WHERE TO STAY

$ B&B/INN Fodor's Choice ★ 🏨 **Casa da Tia Amália.** This renovated Mértola manor is just across the river from town and offers stunning views of the city at sunset. **Pros:** warm, family-run hospitality; free Wi-Fi; great views of Mértola. **Cons:** breakfast costs extra. [$] *Rooms from: €45* ✉ *Estrada dos Celeiros 16* ☎ *965/052379, 918/794579, 966/023305* 🌐 *www.casadatiaamalia.com* 🛏 *6 rooms* 🍴 *No meals.*

$ B&B/INN 🏨 **Residencial Beira Rio.** Some guest rooms in this former mill have balconies overlooking the Rio Guadiana; others face town. **Pros:** wonderful views from terrace; free Wi-Fi. **Cons:** rooms without balconies can be a bit cramped or noisy; no restaurant. [$] *Rooms from: €50* ✉ *Rua Dr. Afonso Costa 108* ☎ *962/683069, 913/402033* 🌐 *www.beirario.pt* 🛏 *24 rooms* 🍴 *Breakfast.*

VILA NOVA DE MILFONTES

162 km (101 miles) northwest of Mértola.

This small resort town is at the broad mouth of the Rio Mira, which is lined on both sides by sandy beaches. Overlooking the sea is an ivy-covered, late-16th-century fortress that protected Milfontes from the Algerian pirates who regularly terrorized the Portuguese coast. It was built on ancient Moorish foundations, because it was believed that the spirits there would ward off the pirates. Now the fortress is up for sale, as a result of Portugal's economic crisis. But Vila Nova de Milfontes is surviving in part with help from a new tourist draw, the Rota Vicentina hiking coast trail, which passes through here.

WHEN TO GO

Vila Nova de Milfontes is more historic and less touristy than many beach towns farther south in the Algarve, but it fills with Portuguese vacationers during the August school holidays. It's best to visit any time except then, when reservations can be difficult.

GETTING HERE AND AROUND

Vila Nova de Milfontes lies about halfway between the Setúbal Peninsula and the Algarve, along the N390/N393, and buses make the trip daily from both Lisbon and Faro. The tourist office can provide updated bus timetables. The town center lies north of the Rio Mira, but its beaches stretch to both sides of the river.

ESSENTIALS

Visitor Information Rota Vicentina. ⊕ *www.rotavicentina.com.* **Vila Nova de Milfontes Tourist Office.** ⊠ *Rua António Mantas* ☎ *283/996599* ⊕ *www.guia. vnmilfontes.info.*

BEACHES

The calm waters of the Franquia River beach, extending from the castle all the way to the Farol beach, are good for water sports and families with children. There are several scenic beaches between Porto Covo and Vila Nova de Milfontes. Rock formations stud Ilha do Pessegueiro beach, which is across from a tiny rocky island with a ruined fort, accessible by boat. The Aivados beach attracts fishermen, nudists, and surfers. The long Malhão beach is very popular and backed with dunes and fragrant scrubland. There are good access points and plenty of parking.

Farol Beach. Only a five-minute walk from the center of Vila Nova de Milfontes, this is the closest beach to town, named for the lighthouse at the peninsula's tip. It tends to fill up quickly on weekends in summer, and is lined with a seasonal beach bars. Dogs are prohibited. Keep in mind that the river and ocean currents mixing here can be strong during winter months, so children should be closely supervised while swimming. **Amenities:** food and drink; lifeguards; parking. **Best for:** sunset. ⊠ *Vila Nova de Milfontes.*

Furnas Beach (*Praia Das Furnas*). The Praia Das Furnas lies just south of Vila Nova da Milfontes, on the south banks of the Mira River. The southeast current makes it popular with surfers, but the current is calm enough for children to swim here, too. Because it's across the river, the beach is quieter in the busy summer months. You're likely to see hikers, as the Rota Vicentina trail passes through here. You can take a ferry across the Mira River (€3 round-trip; departs hourly) from Vila Nova. If you drive, there's a parking lot and snack bar just behind the dunes. **Amenities:** food and drink; lifeguards; parking. **Best for:** surfing; swimming. ⊠ *Vila Nova de Milfontes.*

Fodor's Choice ★ **Malhão Beach** (*Praia Do Malhão*). One of the longest beaches in the Vila Nova de Milfontes area, Malhão is popular with surfers, campers, and fishermen—as well as a small colony of nudists on the beach's northern end. It's about 5 km (3 miles) north of Vila Nova de Milfontes, inside the coastal national park (where construction is prohibited) so there's lots of empty space for beachgoers. You'll need your own transport to get here, along an unpaved road that branches off the main Vila Nova de Milfontes–Porto Covo road. The sheer size of these vast sand dunes ensures a sense that you have the place to yourself. **Amenities:** lifeguards. **Best for:** surfing. ⊠ *5 km (3 miles) north of Vila Nova de Milfontes, on the road to Porto Covo.*

WHERE TO EAT AND STAY

$$
SEAFOOD ✕ **Restaurante Marisqueira O Pescador.** Locals fondly refer to this bustling, air-conditioned *marisqueira* (seafood restaurant) as *"o Moura"* (Moura's place, a reference to the owner's name). Moura and his wife started off as fish sellers in the nearby market, so you know the seafood quality will be good. Try the monkfish with rice or seafood combo stew. Although meals are quite affordable here, as at any seafood house, large

lobsters can claim a price as high as €60. $ *Average main: €18* ⊠ *Rua da Praça 18* ☎ *283/996338* ☉ *Closed Tues.*

$$$$
SEAFOOD
Fodor's Choice
★

✕ **Tasca do Celso.** This wonderful spot serves up some of the best seafood and traditional Portuguese dishes on the entire coastline. The rustic dining room has old-fashioned Alentejan farm tools hanging on the walls, and opens up to the airy kitchen on one side and a small shop on the other that sells gourmet treats and local wine. The restaurant's name comes from owner José Ramos Cardoso, who as a boy was nicknamed "Celso" after his father, a well-known Vila Nova de Milfontes local. Specialties include shrimp sautéed in garlic, clams with coriander, grilled fish or veal with roasted tomatoes—but you can't go wrong with anything on the menu. $ *Average main: €26* ⊠ *Rua dos Aviadores* ☎ *283/996753, 968/175726* ⊕ *www.tascadocelso.com* ☉ *Closed Mon. in winter.*

$
HOTEL
FAMILY

🏠 **Casa da Eira.** Steps from the beach and the town center, this hotel is a favorite among the surfers, cyclists, kayakers, and hikers making their way along the Rota Vicentina. **Pros:** apartments have kitchenettes for self-catering; great value for families. **Cons:** no restaurant. $ *Rooms from: €50* ⊠ *Rua Eira da Pedra, Lote 7, Apartado 123* ☎ *961/339241, 283/997001* ☞ *6 rooms, 7 apartments* ⏸ *Breakfast.*

$
RESORT
FAMILY

🏠 **Duna Parque.** A 10-minute walk from town and a five-minute walk from the beach, this two-story complex features several apartments and semidetached villas, all of which have living-room areas, kitchens, and open fireplaces. **Pros:** plenty of space for families; good option for longer stays. **Cons:** lack of sidewalks means it's not advisable for children to walk to the beach alone. $ *Rooms from: €65* ⊠ *Eira da Pedra* ☎ *283/990072, 283/996459* ⊕ *www.dunaparque.com* ☞ *45 units* ⏸ *Breakfast.*

$
HOTEL

🏠 **HS Milfontes Beach.** Recently taken over by the Duna Parque local chain, the Hotel Social Milfontes Beach is just as it sounds—the most popular place in town, especially for big groups of twentysomethings who are lured by the best location in town, and a well-stocked bar. **Pros:** best view in town. **Cons:** bar is popular and thus noisy at night. $ *Rooms from: €110* ⊠ *Av. Marginal* ☎ *283/990074, 283/990070* ⊕ *www.dunaparquegroup.com/hs-milfontes-beach* ☞ *28 rooms, 1 apartment, 2 dormitories* ⏸ *Breakfast.*

ALCÁCER DO SAL

70 km east of Évora.

Salt production here has nearly disappeared, but it was because of this mineral that Alcácer do Sal became one of Portugal's first inhabited sites. Parts of the castle foundations are around 5,000 years old. The Greeks were here, and later the Romans, who established the town of Salatia Urbs Imperatoria—a key intersection in their system of Lusitanian roads. During the Moorish occupation, under the name of Alcácer de Salatia, this became one of the most important Muslim strongholds in all of Iberia. In the 16th century Alcácer prospered as a major producer of salt, and a brisk trade was conducted with the northern European countries, which used it to preserve herring. The hilltop castle is the town's most prominent attraction. Red-tile-roof buildings descend from the castle to the riverbank in long horizontal rows.

GETTING HERE AND AROUND

Alcácer do Sal lies upstream from the mouth of the Sado River, a quick drive south from Lisbon on the main north–south highway, the A2. Most of the town lies on the river's northern bank, and there's ample parking in the center. The tourist office can arrange half- or full-day boat trips or guided walks along the Sado River.

ESSENTIALS

Tours Rotas do Sal. ⊠ *Estação dos Caminhos de Ferro 2, Apartado 152* ☎ *967/066072, 962/375950* ⊕ *www.rotasdosal.pt.*

Visitor Information Alcácer do Sal. ⊠ *Praça Pedro Nunes 1* ☎ *265/610040* ⊕ *www.cm-alcacerdosal.pt.*

EXPLORING

FodorśChoice **Cripta Arqueológica do Castelo.** This stunning underground fortress dis-
★ plays archaeological relics from 2,600 years of settlement here. In the mid-1990s, archaeologists discovered traces of an Iron Age settlement from the 6th century BC, underneath the town's castle. Structures are believed to have existed here from Roman times, with later castles being built one on top of another through Moorish and medieval times. The current castle and adjacent church are from the 13th century. ⊠ *Castelo de Alcácer do Sal, in basement of Pousada de Dom Alfonso II* ☎ *265/612058* 🄳 *Free.*

Reserva Natural do Sado. The marshlands and the estuary of the Rio Sado that extend to the west of Alcácer form this vast nature reserve. The riverbanks are lined with salt pans and rice paddies, and the sprawling park gives shelter to wildlife such as dolphins, otters, white storks, and egrets. From the beach town of Comporta, Route N261 runs south along the coast through a mostly deserted stretch of dunes and pine trees with some undeveloped sandy beaches. ⊠ *Alcácer do Sal.*

WHERE TO EAT AND STAY

$$ ✕ **A Descoberta.** On the banks of the Sado River, this restaurant was
SEAFOOD named Hortelã da Ribeira, for the wild mint (*hortelã*) that grows nearby. It's now renamed and under new management, but don't be surprised if locals still refer to it by its old name. Specialties include local river fish cooked in Alentejo herbs, as well as *arroz de tamboril* (rice with monkfish), *chocos* (squid), and *ameijoas* (clams). An interesting feature in the restaurant is its walls adorned with animal-motif tiles hand-painted by the local villagers. Sit in the rustic dining room, or outside on the terrace in summer. Ⓢ *Average main: €20* ⊠ *Av. João Soares Branco 15* ☎ *265/612244* ▭ *No credit cards* ☉ *Closed Mon. No dinner Sun.*

$ ✕ **Porto Santana.** This restaurant is located just over the old bridge,
PORTUGUESE across the Rio Sado. You can take your lunch outside with a view of the river. Dinner is served indoors as at night the outdoor area becomes a bar. The specialty here is sopa de cação. Ⓢ *Average main: €15* ⊠ *Rua Senhora Santana* ☎ *265/613454, 265/622517* ☉ *Closed Tues., and Jan. No dinner Mon.*

$ HOTEL FAMILY Fodor's Choice ★ **Herdade da Barrosinha.** This whitewashed, one-story Alentejo country house is on a huge farm estate surrounded by cork and pine trees, about 3 km (2 miles) outside Alcácer do Sal. Red-and-white-striped curtains and bedcovers elegantly match the red-clay-tile floors, while bathrooms are decorated in blue-and-white Alcobaça tiles. **Pros:** rustic farm with space for children; breakfast included. **Cons:** too far to walk into town. [$] *Rooms from: €85* ✉ *Estrada Nacional 5, Barrosinha* ☎ *265/623142, 265/612833* 🌐 *www.herdadedabarrosinha.pt* 🛏 *17 rooms* 🍴 *Breakfast.*

$$ HOTEL Fodor's Choice ★ **Pousada de Dom Afonso II.** In the ancient castle that overlooks the Rio Sado, this very attractive pousada has comfortable and tastefully appointed guest rooms with elegant wooden furniture, blue sofa chairs, and Oriental rugs to match. **Pros:** beautiful, well-preserved medieval architecture makes the lobby alone worth a visit, regardless of whether you can afford to stay here. **Cons:** a bit expensive. [$] *Rooms from: €150* ✉ *Castelo de Alcácer* ☎ *265/613070* 🌐 *www.pousadas.pt* 🛏 *33 rooms, 2 suites* 🍴 *Breakfast.*

THE ALGARVE

Updated by
Liz Humphreys

The Algarve is deservedly popular, with millions of annual vacationers thronging here to enjoy sandy beaches, superb golf, and all the other enticements of seaside resorts. A mere 40 km (25 miles) from top to bottom, Portugal's southernmost province is bordered by the Atlantic to the south and west, the Serra de Monchique (Monchique Mountains) and the Serra de Caldeirão (Caldeirão Mountains) to the north, and the Rio Guadiana (Guadiana River) to the east. Its coast is cooled by sea breezes in summer, and the province as a whole is much warmer than the rest of the country in winter. The vegetation is far more luxuriant, too; originally irrigated by the Moors, the land supports a profusion of fruits, nuts, and vegetables. Proximity to the ocean, meanwhile, has allowed the fishing industry to flourish. And the region's 300 days of sunshine per year helps lure in tourists year-round.

During the past two decades, tourism has flourished, and parts of the once-pristine, 240-km (149-mile) coastline are now traffic-clogged and overbuilt. Even where development is heaviest, construction generally takes the form of landscaped villas and apartment complexes, which are often made of local materials and blend well with the scenery. And there are still small, undeveloped fishing villages and secluded beaches, particularly in the west. The west is also home to extraordinary rock formations and idyllic grottoes. In the east, a series of isolated sandbar islands and sweeping beaches balances the crowded excesses of the middle.

To see the Algarve at its best, though, you may have to abandon the shore for a drive inland. Here, rural Portugal still survives in tradition-steeped hill villages, market towns, and agricultural landscapes, which, although only a few miles from the coast, seem a world away in attitude.

ORIENTATION AND PLANNING

ORIENTATION

GETTING ORIENTED

For touring purposes, the province can conveniently be divided into four sections, starting with Faro—the Algarve's capital—and the nearby beaches and inland towns. The second section encompasses the region east to the border town of Vila Real de Santo António, from which you can cross into Spain. The most built-up part of the coast, and the section with the most to offer vacationers, runs from Faro west to Portimão. The fourth section covers Lagos, the principal town of the western Algarve, and extends to Sagres and Cabo São Vicente.

Even if you plan to stay at one resort for several days, make an effort to see both the eastern and western ends of the province plus an inland town or two; each has a distinct character. Motorists can see the entire region in a week, albeit at a fairly brisk pace. Two main roads run the width of the Algarve—the N125 and the A22 (Via do Infante). The former is toll-free, whereas tolls were introduced on the latter in 2011.

Buses are the primary means of public transport. Slow and old, they tend to bump along, stopping at every corner. Bus information is accurate and they generally leave on time. Trains are another way of traveling from A to B, though not as straightforward as buses. While bus stations tend to be in the heart of villages, towns, and cities, train stations can often be quite a distance away from the destination they purport to serve, so an additional taxi or bus ride may be required.

Faro and Nearby. Known as the capital of the Algarve, Faro is a cosmopolitan city. Home to a pretty marina, the region's only international airport, and several universities, it has a trendy, vibrant feel; the surrounding villages are authentically quaint.

The Eastern Algarve. Largely unaffected by mass tourism, the low-key eastern Algarve remains true to its regional roots, both in terms of architecture and attitude. Warm seawater and beautiful beaches give it added appeal.

The Central Algarve. The central Algarve is where it all happens: the region's wealthiest area, it's where younger crowds get their kicks and jet-setters relax. In summer, expect busy beaches and bustling bars and restaurants, plus a plethora of beautiful people.

Lagos and the Western Algarve. Famous for its waves and wilderness, the western Algarve is laid-back and cool. A surfer's paradise, its unspoiled beauty and invigorating breezes inspired Henry the Navigator's expeditions.

PLANNING

WHEN TO GO

The Algarvian spring, with its rolling carpets of wildflowers and characteristic almond and orange blossoms, is delightful. Late in the season, you can just about take a dip in the ocean, and there's plenty of space to

TOP REASONS TO GO

Fun in the sun. One of Europe's sunniest places, the Algarve guarantees great weather pretty much year-round—though August often sees temperatures in the high 90s and pockets of heavy traffic, especially around the most popular beaches.

Fun in the shade. Adrenaline junkies are now flocking to the region in winter when comfortable temperatures and bright skies make it an ideal destination for active pursuits like skydiving.

Glitz and glamour. During peak season, the Algarve rivals Europe's glitziest hot spots. Jet-setters travel from far and wide to attend what are fast becoming world-renowned events.

Green tee. Golf is a four-season game here. Its 37 acclaimed courses—designed by the likes of Henry Cotton, Frank Pennink, and Rocky Roquemore—include some of the continent's best.

Festivals galore. From city-size *festas* to the hundreds of smaller, rural village affairs, you can be sure that somewhere, at some point, there will be something going on to suit your tastes.

Fantastic food and drink. Rapidly making a name for itself on the international gastronomy scene, the Algarve is home to award-winning restaurants and appealing vineyards.

lay out your beach blanket. Summer (July and August) is high season, when lodging is at a premium, prices are at their highest, and crowds are at their thickest. But summer also brings warmer seas, piercing blue skies, and golden sands at the foot of glowing ocher-red cliffs. Autumn in the Algarve is stunning, with fresh clear days and little rain. The beaches are emptier and the pace of life more relaxed. Accommodation prices start to drop and parking can be found with ease. Winter is mild, so it's the perfect time to visit if you don't mind limiting your swimming to heated hotel pools. On land—or in the air—opportunities for mountain biking and skydiving are also plentiful.

GETTING HERE AND AROUND

AIR TRAVEL

TAP Air Portugal has regular daily service from Lisbon to Faro (45 minutes); Ryanair has regular daily service from Porto to Faro (90 minutes). All international and domestic airlines use Faro Airport, which is 6 km (4 miles) west of town. It's easy to find your way into Faro: after around 4 km (2½ miles), signs along the road from the airport direct you right into town.

Public buses run frequently between the airport and Faro city, with tickets costing about €2.20 per person. A taxi from the terminal building to the center of Faro costs around €10, slightly more on weekends. (There's also a small extra charge for baggage.) Ask the staff at the airport tourist office for a list of prices for rides to other destinations in the region. Always make sure that you agree on a price with the taxi driver before setting off.

Airline Contact TAP Air Portugal. ☎ *707/205700* ⊕ *www.flytap.com.* **Ryanair.** ☎ *871/246–0002* ⊕ *www.ryanair.com.*

Airport Contact Faro Airport. ☎ *289/800800* ⊕ *www.ana.pt.*

BUS TRAVEL

Various companies run daily express buses between Lisbon and Lagos, Portimão, Faro, Tavira, and Vila Real de Santo António. Allow 3½–4½ hours' travel time for all these destinations. Some luxury coaches have restrooms, TVs, and food service. Buy tickets online, over the phone, or at ticket offices near the bus terminals. In summer, reserve a seat at least 24 hours in advance.

The main form of public transport within the Algarve is the bus, and the primary company in the region is Eva, with some buses in the western Algarve run by Frota Azul. Every town and village has its own stop; however, you may have to walk from the main road to the more isolated beach areas. Individual tickets are relatively inexpensive, although a bus ride always costs more than the comparable train journey. Alternatively, you can purchase a tourist pass (€29.10 for three days, €36.25 for seven) that covers unlimited bus trips to some 16 popular destinations across the Algarve, both inland and along the coast. Most ticket offices have someone who speaks at least a little English. The booklet *Guia Horário,* which costs €3 and is available at main terminals, lists every bus service, with timetables and information in English.

■ TIP→ **Some local services are infrequent or don't run on Sunday or national holidays.**

Bus Contacts Eva Buses. ☎ *289/580611, 289/580614* ⊕ *www.eva-bus.com.* **Frota Azul Algarve.** ☎ *282/400610* ⊕ *www.frotazul-algarve.pt.*

CAR TRAVEL

To reach the Algarve from Lisbon—an easy 240-km (150-mile) drive south—cross the Ponte 25 de Abril and take the toll road to Setúbal. Beyond here, the main A2 motorway runs directly south, via Alcácer do Sal, Grândola, Aljustrel, and Castro Verde, eventually joining the A22 (Via do Infante), the Algarve's main east–west motorway, near Guia, north of Albufeira. To reach Portimão, Lagos, and the western Algarve, turn right; go straight to reach Albufeira; and turn left for Faro and the eastern Algarve. Driving the full stretch of the A22 will cost about €8.50 in tolls. Unless you have an electronic transponder in your rental vehicle, you can set up payment for the tolls online or by SMS, or have it deducted from your credit card by the rental car company. The drive from Lisbon to Faro, Lagos, or Albufeira takes about three hours, longer in summer, on weekends, and on holidays.

In the east, a suspension bridge crosses the Rio Guadiana between Ayamonte in Spain and Vila Real de Santo António in Portugal. The secondary east–west road, the N125, extends 165 km (102 miles) from the Spanish border all the way west to Sagres. It runs parallel to the coast and the A22, but slightly inland, with clearly marked turnoffs to the beach towns. Be very careful on this route, as it's one of Portugal's most hazardous. In summer expect traffic jams in several places along it.

Car Rental Contacts Auto Jardim. ⊠ *Head office, Av. da Liberdade, Edificio Brisa, Albufeira* ☏ *289/580500, 808/200613* ⊕ *www.auto-jardim.com.*

TAXI TRAVEL

If you intend to take a cab from Faro Airport there will be plenty of vehicles waiting outside the arrivals area, day and night. Fares to key destinations are pre-established, and rates should be regulated by ANTRAL, a national entity. Nevertheless, always establish the price before you set off to avoid unpleasant surprises. Luggage is extra. In Faro, you can call for taxis or hail them on the street; €4–€5 will get you across town (traffic permitting).

Taxi Contact ANTRAL taxis. ☏ *707/277277* ⊕ *www.antral.pt.*

TRAIN TRAVEL

The quickest, most comfortable way to travel to and from this region by rail is aboard the Alfa-Pendular—a high-speed train that connects southern Portugal with Lisbon, Coimbra, Porto, and Braga. The trip from Faro to Lisbon takes around three hours and costs €38 first class.

Other trains make regular daily departures to the Algarve from the capital. The route runs from the center of Lisbon to the rail junction of Tunes (two-and-a-half hours from Lisbon) and continues on to Albufeira (another 5 minutes) and Faro (another 20 minutes), where you change trains to reach all stations east to Vila Real de Santo António (another hour). For the western route to Silves (another 20 minutes) and Lagos (another 40 minutes), you must change trains at Tunes.

The railroad connects Lagos in the west with Vila Real de Santo António in the east—running close to the N125. Several trains a day run the entire often-scenic route, which takes three to four hours. Tickets are very reasonably priced, and the trip is pleasant. Most trains will have a first-class carriage that is often made up of old-fashioned, individual compartments. Some of the faster trains don't stop at every station, and some of the stations are several miles from the towns they serve, although there's usually a connecting bus. The main train stations generally have someone who speaks some English, but it's easier to get information online or at tourist offices. At the Faro and Lagos offices, timetables are posted. The national rail company is Comboios de Portugal (CP). You can buy tickets online, over the phone, at ticket offices in many stations, at travel agencies, and at ATMs (*multibancos*).

Train Contact CP National Main Office. ⊠ *Calçada do Duque 20, Lisbon* ☏ *707/210220* ⊕ *www.cp.pt.*

RESTAURANTS

Unless otherwise noted, casual dress is acceptable throughout the Algarve. Reservations are not needed off-season, but they're typically required at the better restaurants in summer.

Algarvian cooking makes good use of local seafood. The most unusual regional appetizer—*espadarte fumado* (smoked swordfish)—is sliced thin, served with a salad, and best when accompanied by a dry white wine. Other seafood starters include deep-fried sardines, cold octopus salad, and marinated mackerel fillets. Restaurants generally serve their own version of *sopa de peixe* (fish soup) as well as a variety of succulent shellfish, including *perceves* (barnacles), *santola* (crab), and *gambas* (shrimp). Although main courses often depend on what has been landed that day, there's generally a choice of *robalo* (sea bass), *pargo* (bream), *atum* (tuna), and espadarte.

At simple beach cafés and harbor stalls the unmistakable smell of *sardinhas assadas* (charcoal-grilled sardines) permeates the air. These make a tempting lunch served with fresh bread and a sparkling "green wine" (*vinho verde*), which is indigenous to Portugal. Perhaps the most famous Algarvian dish is *cataplana*—traditionally a stew of clams, pork, onions, tomatoes, and wine, though you can often also find shellfish or mixed fish versions—which takes its name from the lidded utensil used to steam the dish. You have to wait for cataplana to be specially prepared, but once you've tasted it, you won't mind waiting again and again.

Regional desserts are varied and most eateries, right down to the smallest backstreet café, will offer some form of homemade sweet, probably chocolate mousse, caramel flan, doce da casa, or a baked cake. Other traditional Algarvian sweets include rich egg, sugar, and almond custards that reflect the Moorish influence, including *doces de amêndoa* (marzipan cakes in the shapes of animals and flowers), *bolos de Dom Rodrigo* (almond sweets with egg-and-sugar filling), *bolo Algarvio* (cake made of sugar, almonds, eggs, and cinnamon), and *morgado de figos do Algarve* (fig-and-almond paste). You will find these on sale in *pastelarias* (cake shops) and in some cafés. *Prices in the reviews are the average cost of a main course at dinner or, if dinner is not served, at lunch.*

HOTELS

There are busy beachside hotels and secluded retreats in posh country estates. Apartment and villa complexes with luxurious amenities are often built on the most beautiful parts of the coast. They may be 5 km (3 miles) from the nearest town, but most have bars, restaurants, shops, and other facilities. Budget lodgings are also available. In summer, reservations at most places are essential, and rates often rise by as much as 50% above off-peak prices. Since the weather from September through May is still good, you might want to consider a shoulder-season trip to take advantage of the lower rates. *Prices in the reviews are the lowest cost of a standard double room in high season. For expanded hotel reviews, visit www.Fodors.com.*

WHAT IT COSTS IN EUROS			
$	**$$**	**$$$**	**$$$$**
Restaurants	under €16	€16–€20	€21–€25	over €25
Hotels	under €141	€141–€200	€201–€260	over €260

Restaurant prices are per person for a main course at dinner. Hotel prices are for a standard double room, including tax, in high season (off-season rates may be lower).

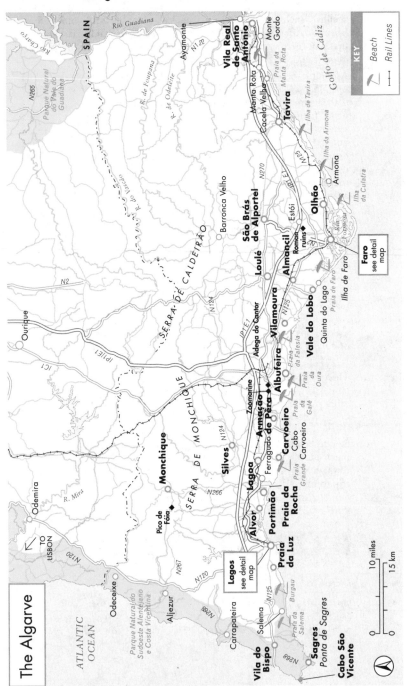

The Algarve

KEY

Beach
Rail Lines

SPAIN

Rio Guadiana

R. do Chança

Parque Natural do Vale do Guadiana

N265

R. de Odeleite

R. de Foupana

Ayamonte

N.22

Vila Real de Santo António

Monte Gordo

Praia da Manta Rota

Manta Rota

Cacela Velha

Tavira

Ilha de Tavira

Golfo de Cádiz

N125

Ilha da Armona

Armona

Ilha da Culatra

Olhão

Estói

Roman ruins

Ria Formosa

Barronca Velho

São Brás de Alportel

N270

Loulé

Almancil

Faro
see detail map

Ouriqué

N2

SERRA DE CALDEIRÃO

N124

Adega do Cantor

IP1/E1

Vilamoura

N125

Vale do Lobo

Quinta do Lago

Praia do Lago

Ilha de Faro

Praia de Faro

IC1

IP1/E1

Zoomarine

Albufeira

Praia da Falesia

Praia da Oura

Armação de Pêra

Ferragudo de Pêra

Carvoeiro

Cabo Carvoeiro

Praia da Galé

SERRA DE MONCHIQUE

N124

Monchique

Silves

N266

Pico de Fóia

R. Mira

Odemira

TO LISBON

N120

Lagoa

Alvor

Portimão

Praia da Rocha

Praia Grande Carvoeiro

Lagos
see detail map

Praia da Luz

N125

Burgau

N267

N120

Odeceixe

Parque Natural do Sudoeste Alentejano e Costa Vicentina

Aljezur

Carrapateira

Salema

Praia da Salema

N268

Sagres

Ponta de Sagres

Cabo São Vicente

Vila do Bispo

N268

ATLANTIC OCEAN

0   10 miles
0   15 km

TOUR OPTIONS

Many companies and individual fishermen along the coast rent out boats for excursions. These range from one-hour tours of local grottoes and rock formations to full-day trips that often involve a stop at a secluded beach for a barbecue lunch. Main centers for coastal excursions are Albufeira, Vilamoura, Portimão, Tavira, Lagos, Sagres, Vila Real, and Armação de Pêra. Consult the tourist offices in these towns for details or simply wander down to the local harbor or along the riverfront, as in Portimão and Lagos, where the prices and times of the next cruise will be posted.

Jeep "safaris," offered by operators like Rotatur, are a unique way to see fascinating inland villages. Riosul Travel, which arranges cruises up the Rio Guadiana, also has half-day overland tours by jeep and full-day cruise-jeep tours that take you off the beaten path to the village of Foz de Odeleite.

Tour Contacts Riosul Travel. ⊠ *Rua Tristão Vaz Teixeira 15C, Monte Gordo* ☎ *281/510200, 962/012112* ⊕ *www.riosultravel.com.* **Rotatur.** ⊠ *Estrada do Aeroporto, Edifício Rotatur, Apartado 2077* ☎ *289/810109* ⊕ *www.rotatur.pt.*

FARO AND NEARBY

Many people fly in to Faro and pass straight through on their way to beaches east and west, which is unfortunate. With its harbor and Cidade Velha (Old Town), Faro deserves a few days of your time. Its many facilities make Faro a fine base for touring the region, too. The city itself may be mostly modern, but the towns and villages that ring it contain their own sights worth seeing, from beaches and markets to churches and ruins. Venture off into the hills and you will find enchanting hamlets like São Brás, where life goes on as it did many, many years ago.

FARO

270 km (168 miles) southeast of Lisbon.

The Algarve's provincial capital combines a smattering of history and ample leisure opportunities in one lively package. It is one of the few places in the region that has a year-round buzz, mainly thanks to the thousands of students who attend universities here. Dotted with historic monuments, Faro is positioned around a small marina where local fishermen and yacht owners keep their vessels. Wander deeper into the city and you will find an attractive shopping street with high-end chains and stores selling local handicrafts, plus a variety of restaurants and bars that remain open in all seasons. Faro is also a great base for exploring the Algarve. It isn't slap-bang in the middle but does offer the best access in terms of public transport and roads to reach both ends of the province.

GETTING HERE AND AROUND

Despite being the region's largest city, most of the main attractions in Faro (as with all Algarvian cities and towns) can pretty much be covered on foot. Nonetheless, urban buses are frequent and taxis are cheap if

Arco da Vila **5**

Doca **4**

Igreja de São
Francisco **8**

Igreja de
São Pedro **2**

Igreja do
Carmo **1**

Museu Marítimo
Almirante
Ramalho
Ortigão **3**

Museu Municipal
de Faro **7**

Sé Catedral
de Faro **6**

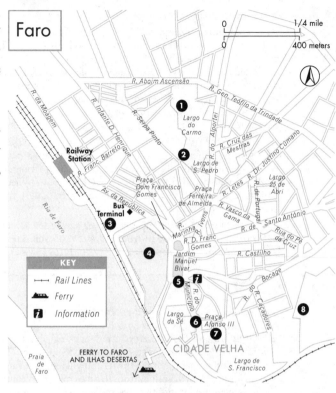

you need to get from one end of town to the other quickly. Faro can be reached by train and bus from anywhere in the Algarve.

ESSENTIALS

Bus Contacts Eva. ✉ *Av. da República 5* ☎ *289/899760* ⊕ *www.eva-bus.com.*

Taxi Contacts Taxis Antral Faro. ✉ *Rua Engenheiro José Campos Coroa 19* ☎ *289/827203, 707/277277* ⊕ *www.antral.pt.*

Train Contacts CP. ✉ *Largo da Estação dos Caminhos de Ferro* ☎ *707/210220* ⊕ *www.cp.pt.*

Visitor Information Faro. ✉ *Faro Airport* ☎ *289/818582* ⊕ *www.visitalgarve.pt* ✉ *Rua da Misericórdia 8–12* ☎ *289/803604* ⊕ *www.visitalgarve.pt.*

EXPLORING
TOP ATTRACTIONS

Arco da Vila. Beyond this 18th-century gate lies Faro's pretty Cidade Velha (Old Town) with its cobbled streets and whitewashed houses. At the top is a niche sheltering a white-marble statue of St. Thomas Aquinas, plus storks that nest here permanently. ✉ *Rua do Município.*

Doca (*dock*). The small dock—flanked by Faro's main square, the Praça Dom Francisco Gomes, and the Manuel Bivar Garden—is filled with small pleasure craft rather than working fishing boats. Come at dusk to enjoy a drink as the sun sets dramatically over the lagoon. ⊠ *Faro.*

Sé Catedral de Faro. This stunning cathedral, flanked by cobblestone streets, whitewashed houses, and fragrant orange trees, is one of Faro's most beautiful monuments. Having survived earthquakes and fires since its construction in 1251, the Sé retains a Gothic tower but is mostly of interest for the 17th- and 18th-century azulejos that fill its interior. On one side of the nave is a red chinoiserie organ, dating to 1751. Best of all, however, is the view from the top of the church tower (up some very steep stairs), looking out over Cidade Velha rooftops and across the lagoon. ⊠ *Largo da Sé* ☎ *289/806632* ✉ *€3.50 for cathedral, tower, and museum.*

WORTH NOTING

Igreja de São Francisco (*Church of St. Francis*). The plain facade of the Igreja de São Francisco gives no hint of the richness of its baroque interior. Inside are glorious 18th-century blue-and-white azulejos and a chapel adorned with gilt work. There aren't any set visiting hours. Ask at the tourist office or push the bell by the church's door; late afternoon is usually the best time to try. ⊠ *Largo de São Francisco* ✉ *Free.*

Igreja de São Pedro (*St. Peter's Church*). This 16th-century sanctuary—perhaps the prettiest of Faro's churches—has an unusual altar set to the left of the main altar. It's entirely carved in gilded chestnut wood and a delicate frieze depicts the Last Supper. ⊠ *Largo de S. Pedro* ☎ *289/805473* ⊕ *www.paroquiasaopedro-faro.org* ✉ *Free.*

Igreja do Carmo (*Carmo Church*). Just north of the city center, this baroque church looks very out of place amid the modern buildings surrounding it. Inside, a door to the right of the altar leads to the Capela dos Ossos (Chapel of the Bones) set in an outside garden area. The tiny chapel's walls are covered with more than 1,000 skulls and bones dug up from the adjacent monks' cemetery—an eerie sight, to say the least, but a fairly common custom in Portugal. ⊠ *Largo do Carmo* ☎ *289/824490* ✉ *€2.*

FAMILY **Museu Maritimo Almirante Ramalho Ortigão.** At this dockside museum, models of local fishing craft are displayed alongside full-size boats of war and exploration. ⊠ *Rua da Comunidade Lusíada (Capitania do Porto de Faro)* ☎ *289/894990* ✉ *€1* ☉ *Closed weekends and national holidays.*

Museu Municipal de Faro (*Municipal Museum*). Housed in a 16th-century convent, this museum—one of the Algarve's oldest—showcases a vast range of artifacts, from mosaics and toys to paintings. ⊠ *Praça Afonso III 14* ☎ *289/870829* ⊕ *cm-faro.pt/349/museu-municipal-de-faro.aspx* ✉ *€2* ☉ *Closed Mon.*

BEACHES

Praia de Faro. The closest beach to town is the long, sandy Praia de Faro, on the Ilha de Faro (Faro Island)—a sandbar 5 km (3 miles) southwest of town. The long main road is flanked by the beach on one side and cafés and restaurants on the other. Activities are limited, and in the height of summer parking can be a struggle. **Amenities:** food and drink; lifeguards; parking (no fee). **Best for:** swimming; walking. ⊠ *Av. Nascente Praia de Faro.*

WHERE TO EAT AND STAY

$ PORTUGUESE 🍴 **Adega Nova.** Popular among locals for celebrations, this down-to-earth *adega* (wine cellar) serves typical Portuguese dishes. The fact that diners are seated on benches around long wooden tables helps keep things lively. You'll find more good cheer, as well as drinks, in the tile-covered bar. It's a good thing, too, as this place is close to the train station in an otherwise dreary area. [$] *Average main: €15* ✉ *Rua Francisco Barreto 24* ☎ *289/813433* 🌐 *www.restauranteadeganova.com* 💳 *No credit cards.*

$ PORTUGUESE 🍴 **Dois Irmãos.** Since 1925 this large, family-run restaurant has attracted a healthy clientele thanks to its regional Algarvian dishes and vast national wine selection. It specializes in seafood dishes; homemade desserts are a bonus. [$] *Average main: €14* ✉ *Praça Ferreira de Almeida 15* ☎ *289/823337* 🌐 *www.restaurantedoisirmaos.com.*

$ PORTUGUESE Fodor's Choice ★ 🍴 **Vila Adentro.** In a lovely square near Faro's main tourist attractions, this charming restaurant in a historic building offers well-prepared Portuguese food with a modern twist. Dine inside surrounded by exposed stone walls, traditional blue-and-white tile, and wood beams, or outside on the spacious patio. The short but enticing menu offers a choice of fish, meat, and vegetable dishes, all just a little bit different than what you'll find at other Portuguese restaurants. Ask to see the catacombs beneath the restaurant for a unique experience. [$] *Average main: €14* ✉ *Praca Dom Afonso III 17* ☎ *289/052173* 🌐 *vilaadentro.pt.*

$$ HOTEL 🏨 **Hotel Eva.** Recently renovated with a cool, contemporary decor, this hotel in the very heart of Faro has a rooftop pool and top-floor restaurant. **Pros:** within walking distance to all amenities and attractions; short taxi, car, or bus ride to airport (5–10 minutes, depending on traffic); good gym. **Cons:** can be rather noisy because a bus terminal is adjacent to the hotel; no nearby beach. [$] *Rooms from: €142* ✉ *Av. da República 1* ☎ *289/001000* 🌐 *hotel-eva-faro.h-rez.com* 🛏 *134 rooms* 🍽 *Breakfast.*

$ HOTEL Fodor's Choice ★ 🏨 **Hotel Sol Algarve.** This renovated 1880s building is one of Faro's nicest budget hotels. **Pros:** private underground garage (€5 per day); two-minute walk from railway station, five-minute walk from main bus terminal; most rooms have a balcony. **Cons:** rooms small; hot water can be inconsistent; dated decor. [$] *Rooms from: €75* ✉ *Rua Infante Dom Henrique 52* ☎ *289/895700* 🌐 *www.hotelsolalgarve.com* 🛏 *38 rooms* 🍽 *Breakfast.*

NIGHTLIFE

Rua do Prior is known for its wide selection of late-closing bars. Friday and Saturday nights are the best time for barhopping.

Chessenta Bar. Open daily till 4 am, this snug, dance-friendly bar is very popular and can fill fast. It offers music for every taste—from karaoke to live folk and blues, and traditional Portuguese tunes. The cocktails are refreshing too. ✉ *Rua do Prior 24* ☎ *931/194314.*

Columbus Cocktail & Wine Bar. In a 600-year-old building in the heart of Faro's historic area, Columbus Cocktail & Wine Bar is popular with the trendy crowd. Outside tables are set in a picturesque cobblestone square, while the historic interior—complete with brick-arch ceilings—is impressive and cool. ✉ *Praça D. Francisco Gomes 13* ☎ *917/776222* 🌐 *www.barcolumbus.pt.*

OLHÃO

8 km (5 miles) east of Faro.

By visiting Olhão's riverfront Mercado dos Pescadores or attending its famous August shellfish festival, you'll see why this town is synonymous with fish. Modern construction has destroyed much of its charm, so Olhão may not be as attractive or touristy as some other towns; however, its fishing port (the Algarve's largest) is still colorful, and its intricate Cidade Velha is appealing. Olhão is also home to the only Algarvian football team in the Portuguese top division, the Primeira Liga.

GETTING HERE AND AROUND

Olhão can be reached by bus or train from anywhere in the Algarve, though those coming from the western end of the region may have to change buses in Albufeira or Faro.

ESSENTIALS

Bus Contact Eva. ⊠ *Rua General Humberto Delgado* ☎ *289/702157* ⊕ *www. eva-bus.com.*

Train Contact CP. ⊠ *Rua da Estação* ☎ *707/210220* ⊕ *www.cp.pt.*

Visitor Information Olhão. ⊠ *Largo Sebastião Martins Mestre 6A* ☎ *289/713936* ⊕ *www.visitalgarve.pt.*

EXPLORING

Olhanense Football Club & José Arcanjo Stadium. Seeing top teams play soccer in the Algarve used to be a rarity until Olhanense gained promotion to the Primeira Liga. Operating on a shoestring budget, the club has many English expat fans. Join them at Estádio José Arcanjo between September and May. ⊠ *Estádio José Arcanjo* ☎ *289/702632* ⊕ *www. scolhanense.com.*

Roman ruins. The ruins at Milreu, about 10 km (6 miles) northwest of Olhão, were first excavated in 1877. The settlement was once known as Roman Ossonoba, and the remains—including a temple (later converted into a Christian basilica) and mosaic fragments adorning some of the 3rd-century baths—date to the 2nd through 6th centuries. A few of the more portable pieces are on display in Faro's archaeological museum. ⊠ *Estói* ☎ *289/997823* ⊕ *monumentosdoalgarve.pt* ☐ *€2 (free 1st Sun. of the month)* ⊙ *Closed Mon. and national holidays.*

Shellfish Festival (Festival do Marisco). The Shellfish Festival or Festival do Marisco is a must for those who are in the Algarve in mid-August. The event, which lasts four to six days, attracts top performers and the food on offer features renowned delicacies from the sea. ⊠ *Olhão* ☎ *289/090287* ⊕ *www.festivaldomarisco.com* ☐ *€5–€8.*

BEACHES

Adding to the allure of area beaches is the fact that this entire section of coastline—including islands and river inlets—has been designated as a nature reserve, due to the great number of migratory birds that flock in while winging south for the winter. To reach beaches on the nearby islands, take a ferry from the jetty at the east end of the municipal gardens. A small kiosk there posts timetables and sells tickets. If it's closed, buy the tickets on board. From June to September, ferries run about every half hour each day; from October through May, there are three or four trips daily. Schedules are available at the tourist office. The fare is about €3.80.

Ilha da Armona. Tiny white vacation villas dot the pedestrian-only Ilha da Armona, a small island 15 minutes from Olhão by boat. About 9 km (5½ miles) long and just under 1 km (½ mile) wide, the island has some fine, isolated stretches of sand, as well as café-bars. It's popular among those who long for a quiet respite from the buzzing throngs of tourists. A wide range of water sports is available for visitors, which is just as well because there's little else to do here except explore sandy dunes by foot. **Amenities:** food and drink; showers; toilets; water sports. **Best for:** surfing; walking. ✉ *15 mins southeast of Olhão by boat.*

Ilha da Culatra. Sandy Ilha da Culatra is crisscrossed with wooden walkways that guide visitors around the island. It has several ramshackle fishing communities, a number of lovely fish restaurants, and, at the southern village of Farol, agreeable beaches. Some stretches are supervised by lifeguards, others are not. The car-free island is 15 minutes by ferry from Olhão, and the boat trip itself is an experience worth having. **Amenities:** food and drink; lifeguards (some). **Best for:** walking. ✉ *15 mins south of Olhão by boat.*

WHERE TO STAY

$$$$ HOTEL Fodor's Choice ★

🏨 **Vila Monte Farm House.** The cool, white, Mediterranean-style buildings, lush grounds, and personalized service here offer a soothing antidote to the big-box properties closer to the Algarvian coast. **Pros:** intimate, boutique feel; chic decor; helpful, efficient service. **Cons:** need a car to travel around the area; no spa, though massages are available; location feels a little remote. [$] *Rooms from: €292* ✉ *Sitio dos Caliços, Moncarapacho* ☎ *289/790790* 🌐 *www.vilamonte.com* 🛏 *55 rooms* 🍴 *Breakfast.*

SHOPPING

FOOD MARKETS

Mercado dos Pescadores. One of the Algarve's best food markets, the Mercado dos Pescadores is held in the riverfront buildings in the town gardens. Feast your eyes on the shellfish for which Olhão is renowned; mussels, in particular, are a local specialty. ✉ *Olhão* ⏲ *Closed Sun.*

SÃO BRÁS DE ALPORTEL

18 km (11 miles) northwest of Olhão.

Peace and tranquillity rule in São Brás, a destination that melds old-fashioned charm with modern amenities. Once the Algarve's largest cork-producing town, it is now more dependent on tourism than trees. A traditional costume museum, a multicultural arts center, and a public picnic area along the sparkling Fonte Férrea springs give visitors a reason to linger.

GETTING HERE AND AROUND

The best way to get to this area is by taxi or bus. Alternatively, you can catch a train to Loulé or Faro, then take a bus or a taxi to São Brás. A taxi from Faro would cost approximately €22 and would take around 20 minutes. A taxi from Loulé would be slightly quicker and cheaper. A bus from Faro takes approximately 45 minutes and costs €4.05. A bus from Loulé costs €3.25 and takes 25 minutes.

ESSENTIALS

Bus Contact **Bus terminal.** ✉ *Rua João Louro* ☎ *289/842286.*

Taxi Contact **Auto Taxis de São Brás.** ✉ *Av. Liberdade 43* ☎ *289/842611.*

Visitor Information **São Brás de Alportel.** ✉ *Largo de S. Sebastião 23* ☎ *289/843165* 🌐 *www.visitalgarve.pt.*

EXPLORING

The Cork Route. Acclaimed internationally for producing unique items made from cork, São Brás now boasts a Cork Route—a guided walking tour tailored for visitors of all ages. Different tours explore a whole new world of sensations that you might not otherwise experience. Feel the bark of the cork oak, smell the countryside in which it grows, learn about the numerous ways in which it can be transformed and the purposes it serves. Walks range from adventures with extreme sports to gentle treks. Prices vary in accordance to tour. ✉ *São Brás de Alportel* ☎ *960/070806* 🌐 *www.rotadacortica.pt.*

6

Museu do Traje (*Costume Museum*). If fashion is your thing you'll love this quaint collection of local costumes from bygone eras. The cultural center and museum are just a short walk from the center of town. Inside you'll find charmingly old-fashioned regional outfits featuring black lacework, bright colors, and the rooster emblem of Portugal. ✉ *Rua Dr. José Dias Sancho 61* ☎ *289/840100* 🌐 *www.museu-sbras.com* 🎫 *€2.*

WHERE TO STAY

$$$ HOTEL 🏨 **Pousada Palácio de Estoi.** Located 8 km (5 miles) from São Brás in the charming neighboring village of Estoi, Pousada Palácio de Estoi provides a comfortable base for exploring the region. **Pros:** a unique, rural Algarve experience; lovely pool area; stunning views. **Cons:** quality of restaurant food could be better; need a car to reach beaches and other restaurants; service can be hit-or-miss. [$] *Rooms from: €215* ✉ *Rua São José, Estói* ☎ *210/407620* 🌐 *www.pousadas.pt* 🛏 *63 rooms* 🍴 *Breakfast.*

LOULÉ

13 km (8 miles) west of São Brás de Alportel.

Positioned north of the N125 and A22 roads, Loulé is more inland than other coastal towns. Castle walls and three stone towers provide visual evidence of its history, while an Arabesque indoor market—complete with pink turrets—offers a true taste of Algarvian culture. In recent years, Loulé's laid-back vibe has also attracted a growing number of artists and artisans, whose works are displayed in shops and galleries.

GETTING HERE AND AROUND

Trains run straight to Loulé from most major cities and towns in the Algarve, and buses run directly from Portimão, Albufeira, and Faro; tickets cost €3–€6. A bus from Portimão would take about two hours to Loulé. The good news is that exploring the city does not require a car and can be covered on foot.

> **ALGARVE MARKET DAYS**
>
> All the main towns and villages have regular food markets, usually open daily from 8 until around 2.
>
> **Albufeira**: first and third Tuesday of the month
>
> **Lagos**: first Saturday of the month
>
> **Loulé**: first and fourth Sunday of the month
>
> **Portimão**: first Monday of the month
>
> **Sagres**: first Friday of the month
>
> **Silves**: third Monday of the month

ESSENTIALS

Bus Contact Eva. ✉ *Rua Nossa Senhora de Fátima* ☎ *289/416655* 🌐 *www.eva-bus.com.*

Train Contact CP. ✉ *Estação dos Caminhos de Ferro de Loulé* ☎ *707/210220* 🌐 *www.cp.pt.*

Visitor Information Loulé. ✉ *Edifício do Castelo, Av. 25 de Abril 9* ☎ *289/463900* 🌐 *www.visitalgarve.pt.*

EXPLORING

Castelo de Loulé (*Loulé Castle*). Once a Moorish stronghold, Loulé has preserved the ruins of the medieval castle, which was enlarged in 1268 after the site had been occupied and fortified since Neolithic times. These days, it houses the archaeology museum. ✉ *Rua Dom Paio Peres Correia 17* ☎ *289/400600* 🌐 *www.cm-loule.pt* 🎫 *€1.62* ⏲ *Closed Sun.*

Igreja de São Clemente, Matriz de Loulé (*Church of São Clemente, Parish Church of Loulé*). This restored 13th-century church has handsome tiles, wood carvings, and an unusual wrought-iron pulpit. ✉ *Largo da Matriz* 🌐 *www.cm-loule.pt.*

WHERE TO STAY

$ HOTEL 🏨 **Loulé Jardim Hotel.** Set in a small square in the old part of town, this lovely hotel has a cozy home-away-from-home feel. **Pros:** attractive, well-kept, sunny exterior and comfortable interior; in the center of Loulé; free private parking garage. **Cons:** extra charge for tea- and coffee-making facilities; extra charge to use the safe in room; the coast is 8 km (5 miles) away. [$] *Rooms from: €109* ✉ *Largo Manuel D'Arriaga* ☎ *289/413095, 968/691167 (mobile), 914/839317 (mobile)* 🌐 *www.loulejardimhotel.com* 🛏 *52 rooms* 🍴 *Breakfast.*

SHOPPING

ART GALLERY

Art Catto. Works by internationally renowned artists are displayed—and sold—at the Art Catto gallery. ✉ *Av. José da Costa Mealha 43* ☎ *289/419447* 🌐 *www.artcatto.com.*

MARKET

Fodor'sChoice **Loulé Municipal Market.** Believed
★ to be one of the oldest municipal
markets in the Algarve, if not the
country, Loulé Municipal Market
is a hive of smells, colors, and
sounds. The century-old, Moor-
ish-styled indoor area has added
a number of "gastro stalls" that
sell ready-to-eat foods, so you
can sample local delicacies as you
browse. But the best time to come
is Saturday morning, when the surrounding outdoor farmers' market
bursts into life. ⊠ *City Center* ☎ *289/400600* ⊕ *www.cm-loule.pt.*

> **LOULÉ'S STREET FESTIVALS**
>
> Loulé is famous for being home
> to one of the oldest and grandest
> carnival parades in the country.
> Held every year around the
> second weekend in February, it
> attracts thousands of visitors to
> the city. *www.cm-loule.pt.*

THE EASTERN ALGARVE

Better known for its distinctive roof tiles than for roof-raising parties,
the eastern Algarve—aka the Sotovento—is quiet and largely underdeveloped, so it's a fine place to visit if you're looking for a slower-paced
holiday. Cities are largely untouched by modernity, and beaches are
vast and flat. Shallow waters mean the sea here can be significantly
warmer than elsewhere in the Algarve. Enjoying a riverside stroll and
bird-watching in the protected Ria Formosa area are the main activities.

TAVIRA

30 km (18 miles) east of Loulé; 28 km (17 miles) east of Faro.

Fodor'sChoice With its castle ruins, riverfront gardens, and old streets, Tavira—at
★ the mouth of the quiet Rio Gilão—is immediately endearing. Many of
the town's white 18th-century houses retain their original doorways
and coats of arms; others are topped with unusual, four-sided "roof
screens," and still others are completely covered in tiles. The town also
has more than 30 churches, most dating to the 17th and 18th centuries.
One of two river crossings—the low bridge adjacent to the arcaded
Praça da República—is of Roman origin, although it was rebuilt in the
17th century and again in recent times after sustaining damage from
floodwaters.

GETTING HERE AND AROUND

Tavira is easily reached by any form of public transport. Once in Tavira
there are several types of local transit—including boats and a tourist
train—that make touring the city entertaining and enjoyable.

ESSENTIALS

Tour Contacts Delgaturis Tourist Train. ☎ *289/389067* ⊕ *www.delgaturis.
com.* **Séqua Boat Tours.** ☎ *960/170789, 918/763020* ⊕ *www.sequatours.com.*
Tavira Tours. ☎ *960/170789, 918/210538* ⊕ *www.taviratours.com.*

Visitor Information Tavira. ⊠ *Praça da República 5* ☎ *281/322511* ⊕ *www.
visitalgarve.pt.*

EXPLORING

Castelo. From the battlemented walls of the ruined 13th-century castle you can look down over Tavira's many church spires and across the river delta to the sea. ⊠ *Stepped street off Rua da Liberdade* ⌷ *Free.*

Igreja da Misericórdia (*Mercy Church*). Widely considered one of the most remarkable examples of the Renaissance movement in the Algarve, this structure has a portal that dates to 1541. On Good Friday at 10 pm, a candlelight procession begins here. ⊠ *West of Praça da República, Travessa da Fonte, Rua da Galeria.*

Santa Maria do Castelo (*St. Mary of the Castle*). One of the town's two major churches, Santa Maria was built on the site of a Moorish mosque in the 13th century. Although it was almost entirely destroyed by the 1755 earthquake, the church retains its original Gothic doorway. ⊠ *Alto de Santa Maria, next to the castelo.*

Torre de Tavira. This old water tower was converted into a camera obscura of the Leonardo da Vinci fashion in 1931. An oversize photographic camera here takes images of the panoramic views it commands of the town. The visit makes a fascinating exploration into the world of photography and a cool, shady afternoon retreat from the sweltering afternoon sunshine. ⊠ *Calçado da Galeria 12* ☎ *281/322527* ⊕ *www.torredetavira.com* ⌷ *€4* ⊙ *Closed Sun.*

> **TAVIRA'S UNIQUE ARCHITECTURE**
>
> Take a moment while you're exploring Tavira to look up and admire the peculiar four-sided roofs which rise like pyramids—locals refer to them as roof screens. These unique architectural elements appeared in the late 19th and early 20th centuries. As the town's prosperity grew, so did the popularity of the screens, which are said to project the house's exterior face. The screens are also deemed important elements in the characterization and individualization of the building.

BEACHES

Fodor's Choice ★ **Ilha de Tavira.** Directly offshore and extending west for some 10 km (6 miles) is the Ilha de Tavira—a long sandbar with several good beaches. It's popular among young people and families in summer, particularly for its above-par camping site (with room for 1,550, this is the main form of accommodation). Ferries run to the island every half hour in July and August and every hour May through June and September through mid-October; the fare is about €2.50 round-trip. In summer, a bus (marked "Quatro Águas") operates between town and the jetty 2 km (1 mile) east. There is a nudist beach on the island, which has been awarded a Blue Flag, indicating quality and cleanliness. Several good restaurants and bars are also on the Ilha. **Amenities:** food and drink; lifeguards; showers; toilets; water sports. **Best for:** partiers; nudists; sunrise; sunset. ⊠ *Directly off Tavira* ⊕ *www.cm-tavira.pt.*

Praia de Manta Rota. About 12 km (7 miles) east of Tavira, Praia de Manta Rota is a small community with a few bars, restaurants, and hotels. But locals say it has "the best 3 km of beach" in the Algarve.

Its warm waters and white sands are a magnet for sun worshippers. One particularly nice strand is the offshore sandbar at the village of Cacela Velha. From Manta Rota to Faro the underwater drop-offs are often steep and you can quickly find yourself in deep water. **Amenities:** lifeguards. **Best for:** walking. ✉ *Rua da Praia da Manta Rota.*

CATCH OF THE DAY

Because Tavira is a tuna-fishing port, you'll find plenty of local color and fresh fish; tuna steaks, often grilled and served with onions, are on restaurant menus all over town at remarkably low prices. In the harbor area, you can sample no-frills dining at its best, alongside the fishermen, at any of the café-restaurants across from the tangle of boats and nets.

WHERE TO EAT AND STAY

$ CAFÉ 🍴 **Pastelaria Veneza.** On the edge of the main square opposite the town hall there are a number of good cafés where you can sit and watch the world go by. Pastelaria Veneza offers light Portuguese appetizers, as well as excellent homemade soups and ice cream. But its specialty is the vast array of freshly baked regional sweets, cakes, and pastries. Don't forget to try a traditional *pastel de nata* (egg-custard tart) or a fig delicacy. Service is prompt, quite a rarity in this part of the world. [$] *Average main: €5* ✉ *Praça da República 11* ☎ *281/370980* 💳 *No credit cards.*

$ PORTUGUESE 🍴 **Ponto de Encontro.** Cross the Roman bridge, bypassing the many Indian and Italian joints, until you reach this typical Portuguese eatery. Here the focus is on fresh fish (the sole in almond sauce is a must-try). The restaurant's interior is traditional, and there is a smattering of outside tables with views to the adjacent square. Despite a central location, prices here remain down-to-earth. [$] *Average main: €11* ✉ *Praça Dr. António Padinha 39* ☎ *281/323730* 🌐 *www.rest-pontoencontro.com* ⏲ *Closed Mon., and last 2 wks of Nov.*

$$$$ HOTEL Fodor's Choice ★ 🏨 **Fazenda Nova.** Explore the beaches and vineyards of the Algarve from a base at your own "home" that's a former private country residence and 25-acre farm featuring a swimming pool, fruit orchards, vegetable and herb plots, olive groves, and flower gardens. **Pros:** amazing service; romantic getaway; lovely location. **Cons:** limited amenities; best visited with a rental car; two-night minimum (five-night minimum in August). [$] *Rooms from: €295* ✉ *Estiramantens, Santo Estevao* ☎ *281/961913* 🌐 *www.fazendanova.eu* 🛏 *10 rooms* 🍽 *Breakfast.*

$$ RESORT 🏨 **Hotel Vila Galé Albacora.** Occupying a converted tuna market, the Vila Galé Albacora is a charming hotel that sits at the confluence of two rivers. **Pros:** lovely location; comprehensive resort with two restaurants, two bars, and a spa; own boat transfer to/from beach. **Cons:** waterfront site attracts insects like mosquitoes; fee for some "extras," like a safe for valuables, beach transport, and parking; shuttle to Tavira town doesn't run every day. [$] *Rooms from: €185* ✉ *Quatro Águas* ☎ *281/380800* 🌐 *www.vilagale.com* 🛏 *162 rooms* 🍽 *Breakfast.*

$ B&B/INN 🏨 **Marés Residencial e Restaurante.** Only a stone's throw from the waterfront (and the summer ferry to the Ilha de Tavira), this tiny hotel sits above a Portuguese restaurant ($$) that shares the same name. **Pros:** best location at a sensible price; free parking a short walk away; free Wi-Fi in public areas. **Cons:** rooms above restaurant can be noisy; no elevator. [$] *Rooms from: €92* ✉ *Rua José Pires Padinha 134/140* ☎ *281/325815* 🌐 *www.residencialmares.com* 🛏 *24 rooms* 🍴 *Breakfast.*

SPORTS AND THE OUTDOORS

GOLF

Fodor's Choice ★ **Quinta de Cima.** This is the sister course to Quinta da Ria and is a stiffer test. Also designed by Rocky Roquemore, water hazards abound, and length as well as accuracy are the premiums. The strength of the challenge is tempered by some wonderful views in a superb setting. Visitors are required to produce a handicap certificate. ✉ *Apartado 161, Vila Nova de Cacela* ☎ *281/950580* 🌐 *www.quintadaria.com* 🎫 *€84* ⛳ *18 holes, 7202 yards, par 72.*

VILA REAL DE SANTO ANTÓNIO

47 km (29 miles) east of Faro.

This community on the Rio Guadiana is the last stop before Spain. Like most border towns, it's a lively place, with lots of bars and restaurants and some traffic-free central streets that encourage evening strolls. If you're interested in a short excursion across the border, visit Ayamonte, the town's Spanish counterpart. Just on the other side of the Guadiana River, Ayamonte can be reached during the day and early evening on a charmingly old-fashioned ferry.

GETTING HERE AND AROUND

Vila Real de Santo António, on the Algarve's eastern end, is easiest reached by train. From Vila Real there's a ferry that carries both vehicles and passengers across the Guardiana River to Ayamonte, in Spain; a one-way crossing should cost about €5 per car and €1.70 per passenger. Ferries operate every 30 minutes in summer; the rest of the year they cross roughly every hour. Alternatively, you can use a toll-free suspension bridge.

ESSENTIALS

Train Contact CP. ✉ *Rua da Estação Velha* ☎ *707/210220* 🌐 *www.cp.pt.*

Visitor Information Monte Gordo. ✉ *Av. Marginal, Monte Gordo* ☎ *281/544495* 🌐 *www.visitalgarve.pt.*

TOURS

Riosul Travel. This company arranges daylong river cruises which include lunch, a swim break, and a final stop in the timeless village of Foz de Odeleite before returning by boat to Vila Real. It also offers jeep safaris, guided walks, and moonlight boat trips. Cruises on the Guadiana River start at €47. Special prices for groups and families are available. ✉ *Rua Tristão Vaz Teixeira 15 C, Monte Gordo* ☎ *281/510200, 281/510202 for reservations* 🌐 *www.riosultravel.com.*

WHERE TO STAY

$ HOTEL 🏨 **Coração da Cidade Hospedaria.** Belonging to the Coração da Cidade group, this city-center inn has basic but spotless rooms—all with private balconies and air-conditioning. **Pros:** great location; kids under three stay free and there are free cots for kids under two; rooftop terrace.

Cons: few facilities; could use an update. $\boxed{S}$ *Rooms from: €65* ⊠ *Rua Dr. Sousa Martins 17* ☎ *281/530470* ⊕ *www.coracaodacidade.com* ↪ *21 rooms* ⦿ *Breakfast.*

$ ⚇ **Hotel Apolo.** Nicely decorated and well kept, this small hotel has a
HOTEL lot to offer. **Pros:** good range of activities available from hotel; free Wi-Fi; private parking. **Cons:** 3-km (3-mile) walk to the nearest beach; additional cost to use safe; no restaurant. $\boxed{S}$ *Rooms from: €89* ⊠ *Av. do Bombeiros Portugueses* ☎ *281/512448* ⊕ *www.apolo-hotel.com* ↪ *56 rooms* ⦿ *Breakfast.*

THE CENTRAL ALGARVE

The central Algarve, between Faro and Portimão to the east, has the heaviest concentration of resorts, but there are also exclusive, secluded hotels and villas. In between built-up areas are quiet bays and amazing rock formations, including arches, sea stacks, caves, and blowholes. Shell-encrusted ocher-and-red cliffs contrast beautifully with the brilliant blues and greens of the sea. With a car it's easy to travel the few miles inland that make all the difference: minor roads lead into the hills and to towns that have resisted the changes wrought upon the coast.

6

ALMANCIL

10 km (6 miles) northwest of Faro.

Easily accessed from both the A22 and the N125, Almancil is near two of the region's biggest draws: the upmarket seaside resort areas of Quinta do Lago, roughly 5 km (3 miles) to the south, and Vale do Lobo, about 5 km (3 miles) to the southwest. Wealthy Europeans love these complexes for their superb hotels and sports facilities. Golf is the thing here, but tennis and horseback riding are also popular.

GETTING HERE AND AROUND

Almancil can be reached by bus or train from anywhere in the Algarve, though those coming from the western end of the region may have to change buses in Albufeira. Once in town, most sights can be visited on foot.

ESSENTIALS

Bus Contact Eva. ☎ *289/899760* ⊕ *www.eva-bus.com.*

Train Contact CP. ⊠ *Estrada Vale Formoso, 1 km (½ mile) north of Amancil* ☎ *707/210220* ⊕ *www.cp.pt.*

EXPLORING

Igreja de São Lourenço (*Church of St. Lawrence*). One of the most important places of worship in the region and Almancil's biggest draw is this church, built in 1730. Note the intricate gilt work and blue-and-white, floor-to-ceiling azulejo panels that depict the story of St. Lawrence. ⊠ *Rua da Igreja* ☎ *289/395451* ⊕ *www.turismo.diocese-algarve.pt* ⊑ *€2* ☽ *Closed Sun.*

WHERE TO EAT AND STAY

$$$$ SEAFOOD FAMILY 🍴 **2 Passos.** Essentially an enormous wooden beach shack on stilts, this seafood restaurant sits in a lovely position overlooking Ancão Beach in Ria Formosa Natural Park, with views of the sea from floor-to-ceiling windows. Inside, the family-friendly atmosphere can be quite boisterous. The fish and seafood is chosen daily from the local markets, although the house specialty, lobster casserole—a whole grilled lobster topped with a creamy sauce—is always on offer. The restaurant is also known for fish prepared Algarvian-style (baked in the oven with potatoes) and seafood cataplana—call a day in advance to put in your order. It's a hugely popular place in summer, so reservations are essential. [$] *Average main: €30* ✉ *Praia do Ancão, Apartado 3404* ☎ *289/396435* 🌐 *www.restaurante2passos.com* 🕓 *Closed Dec. No dinner Sept.–June.*

$$ WINE BAR 🍴 **Simply Tapas & Vinho.** A ranchlike wood exterior—complete with wine barrels flanking the door—make this place look immediately inviting. As the name implies, it offers a great opportunity for you to sample snack-size portions of innovative, international delicacies, all of which can be washed down with a vast range of wines that are also available by the glass. Dining here feels like a fun change of pace. [$] *Average main: €16* ✉ *Estrada Do Vale De Lobo 862* ☎ *289/391145* 🌐 *simplytapasvinho.weebly.com.*

$$$$ HOTEL Fodor's Choice ★ 🏨 **Conrad Algarve Hotel.** Located in the heart of Quinta do Lago, a short walk from the area's upmarket shopping precinct, this luxury Conrad outpost has an on-site spa and numerous restaurants—including the mod, Mediterranean-style Gusto by Heinz Beck ($$$$). **Pros:** luxurious; service second to none; terrific kids' club. **Cons:** prices for drinks on the high side; a short drive to Faro or Almancil; not close to the beach. [$] *Rooms from: €476* ✉ *Estrada da Quinta do Lago* ☎ *289/350700* 🌐 *www.conradalgarve.com* 🛏 *154 rooms* 🍽 *Breakfast.*

$$$$ RESORT 🏨 **Hotel Quinta do Lago.** This deluxe hotel was once the pulse of the Algarve's upmarket Golden Triangle region; now it's like the old grandpa of the group—established, posh, but not cool. **Pros:** impeccable standard of food and service; nearby facilities include first-rate golf courses and restaurants; beach and sandbar accessed via a wooden bridge. **Cons:** seasoned luxury travelers may find the decor a little dated; overpriced. [$] *Rooms from: €455* ✉ *Quinta do Lago* ☎ *289/350350* 🌐 *www.hotelquintadolago.com* 🛏 *141 rooms* 🍽 *Breakfast.*

SPORTS AND THE OUTDOORS

WATER PARK

FAMILY **Aquashow.** Just east of Vilamoura and north of Quarteira, you'll find Aquashow: a large water park which also incorporates theme-park elements like roller coasters and performing critters. There's also an on-site hotel ($$) if you'd like to extend your visit. TIP→ **For €49 you can get up-close-and-personal with sea lions in an interactive experience.** ✉ *Semino E.N. 396, Quarteira* ☎ *289/315129* 🌐 *www.aquashowpark-hotel.com* 🎟 *€29 (€24.65 with online discount)* 🕓 *Closed Oct.–Apr.*

VALE DO LOBO

5 km (3 miles) southwest of Almancil.

Vale do Lobo is a gated luxury villa complex that attracts the superrich and famous from the world over (but yes, it's still open to all). The Dona Filipa Hotel has two prestigious 18-hole golf courses, plus grounds that include extensive and well-tended gardens lined with palms and exotic shrubbery. A private security firm keeps a close eye on things while you make use of the helipad, health spa, indoor riding school, fitness centers, tennis club, yachting club, polo pitches, and a host of restaurants, bars, and cafés. The area is a second home to wealthy Europeans. The local beach is one of the cleanest in the Algarve and remains relatively quiet during peak months. You can access the beach from below the Dona Filipa Hotel, where most of the restaurants are clustered.

GETTING HERE AND AROUND

Due to the wealthy nature of this resort, public transport is hardly used; however, you can take a bus to Almancil followed by a taxi to Vale do Lobo.

ESSENTIALS

Taxi Contact **FaroTaxis.** ☎ *960/204709* 🌐 *www.farotaxi.com.*

WHERE TO STAY

$$$$ HOTEL **Dona Filipa Hotel.** This golf-oriented hotel offers the high standards expected of a luxury property at slightly lower prices and also caters to families with a dedicated kids' club. **Pros:** not as expensive as neighboring resorts; great for golf lovers; family-friendly service and activities. **Cons:** the cheaper rooms in need of an update; no coffee- or tea-making facilities in rooms; no in-house spa or gym (guests referred to nearby spa). [$] *Rooms from: €282* ✉ *Vale do Lobo* ☎ *289/357200* 🌐 *www.donafilipahotel.com* 🛏 *154 rooms* 🍴 *Breakfast.*

SPORTS AND THE OUTDOORS

GOLF

Ocean Course Vale do Lobo. The Ocean Course emerged from an earlier design by Sir Henry Cotton and is a combination of the original "orange" and "green" courses of three 9-hole loops. The undulating fairways are fringed by pine, olive, orange, and eucalyptus trees. Accuracy is the key factor; the course can be challenging and correct club selection is always worth a few shots. Practice facilities include play from mats and from grass. A handicap certificate is required. There's a driving range, a putting green, golf carts, pull carts, and a pro shop, restaurant and bar. ✉ *Vale do Lobo* ☎ *289/353465* 🌐 *valedolobo.com/en/golf* 🎫 *€180* ⛳ *18 holes, 6711 yds, par 73.*

Royal Course Vale do Lobo. A much more difficult challenge than Ocean Course Vale do Lobo (its sister course), the Royal is longer and defended by more water and bunkers. Sir Henry Cotton laid out the original course, but significant changes have been introduced by Rocky Roquemore to make it more up-to-date. The pick of the holes is the famous 16th, which requires a carry of 200 yards over three spectacular cliffs to reach the sanctuary green. A handicap limit of 27 for men and 35 for women is enforced here. ✉ *Vale do Lobo* ☎ *289/353535* 🌐 *valedolobo.com/en/golf* 🎟 *€190* ⛳ *18 holes, 6626 yds, par 72* ✍ *Reservations essential.*

HORSEBACK RIDING

Pinetrees Riding Centre. One of the oldest riding centers in the region, this British-run operation also does noteworthy work with the disabled. Expect lovely treks with experienced guides for riders of all abilities. ✉ *Casa dos Pinheiros, Estrada de Ancão, Almancil* ☎ *289/394369* 🌐 *pinetrees.pt.*

TENNIS

Vale do Lobo Tennis Academy. The Vale do Lobo Tennis Academy has 14 all-weather courts, a bar, a pro shop, a pool, a gym, a steam room, and a restaurant. Court fees start at €32. ✉ *Vale do Lobo* ☎ *289/357850* 🌐 *www.valedolobo.tennis.*

VILAMOURA

10 km (6 miles) west of Almancil.

Glitzy and glamourous Vilamoura is the Algarve's answer to Monaco. Once a prosperous Roman settlement, today it's an upscale resort community with the Algarve's biggest marina—an enormous, self-contained, 1,000-berth complex with apartments, hotels, bars, cafés, restaurants, shops, and sports facilities. The town of Vilamoura and the area surrounding it also have several luxury hotels and golf courses as well as a major tennis center and casino.

GETTING HERE AND AROUND

Besides renting a car, you can reach Vilamoura by train, though the nearest stops are Albufeira in the west and Loulé in the east. Once at these stations, a bus can be caught to Vilamoura. The Aparthotel Aldeia do Mar serves as the town's bus ticket office.

EXPLORING

Museu de Cêrro da Vila. Just off a corner of the marina, the excavations of Roman ruins at the site known as Cêrro da Vila (where Vilamoura was first established), have revealed an elaborate plumbing system as well as several mosaics. The small, well-laid-out Museu de Cêrro da Vila gives access to the site and exhibits pieces found here. ✉ *Av. Cerro do Vila* ☎ *289/312153* 🎟 *€3* ⏲ *Closed Mon. and Tues.*

WHERE TO STAY

$$$ HOTEL 🏨 **Dom Pedro Golf Resort.** Part of a highly successful vacation complex, the Dom Pedro is close to Vilamoura's casino, not far from a splendid beach, and five minutes from the marina. **Pros:** well situated; good for golfers and families; friendly staff. **Cons:** uninspiring dinners; rather dated decor; proximity to popular bars can be a nuisance to some. [$] *Rooms from: €205* ✉ *Rua Atlântico* ☎ *289/300780* 🌐 *www.dompedro.com* ⏲ *Closed early Nov.–late Feb.* 🛏 *266 rooms* 🍴 *Breakfast.*

NIGHTLIFE

Casino Vilamoura. Open weekdays from 3 pm to 3 am and weekends from 4 pm to 4 am, Casino Vilamoura is a big part of Vilamoura's nightlife scene. You'll find two restaurants, a dance club, and the usual selection of games on 13 tables, as well as 500-plus slot machines. For a set price you can see the nightly show and have a free drink; prices vary according to shows. Dress is smart-casual, and you must be 18 to enter. ⊠ *Praça Casino Vilamoura* ☎ *289/310000* ⊕ *www.solverde.pt.*

SPORTS AND THE OUTDOORS

GOLF

Oceanico Millennium Course Vilamoura. Martin Hawtree extended an existing 9-hole layout to create this visitor-friendly course on the vast Vilamoura estate. It shares the umbrella pine tree backdrop common to the other two Vilamoura courses but is a little shorter in length. Tee times can be reserved online, and reservations are advised. ⊠ *Vilamoura, Quarteira* ☎ *289/310188* ⊕ *www.oceanicogolf.com* ✉ *€77, €88, or €95, depending on season* ⅃ *18 holes, 6754 yds, par 72.*

Oceanico Old Course. One of the great golf courses of Europe, this Frank Pennink–designed course is widely regarded as the best of the Vilamoura layouts because of its subtle routing and challenging holes. Umbrella pines line the fairways, and the crack of ball on timber is almost a signature tune on this famous course. The maximum handicap for men is 24 and for women 28. ⊠ *Vilamoura, Quarteira* ☎ *289/310341* ⊕ *www. oceanicogolf.com* ✉ *€117, €129, or €140, depending on season* ⅃ *18 holes, 6839 yds, par 73* ⚓ *Reservations essential.*

SAILING

To rent a sailboat, just walk around Vilamoura Marina and inquire at any of the various kiosks that deal with water sports.

Algarve Seafaris. If you'd like to relax and let someone else do the work, book a sea-caves cruise with Algarve Seafaris, which runs 6-hour, 4½-hour, and 3½-hour outings along the Algarve coastline for €39, €34, and €27, respectively. The company also offers big-game fishing (€52 for those fishing, €32 spectators), along with reef fishing and family-day fishing. ⊠ *Marina de Vilamoura, Cais Q, Escritorio 9/10* ☎ *289/302318 for bookings* ⊕ *www.algarve-seafaris.com.*

ALBUFEIRA

12 km (7 miles) west of Vilamoura.

A long, bar-lined strip lined with enough neon lights to rival Las Vegas makes this a party-revelers' paradise at night. During the day, you can split Albufeira in two: the old town and the newer part. The former has quaint cobblestone streets, traditional restaurants (though it does also have its share of touristy shops and fast-food joints), and its own beach. The latter, up near the strip, is completely geared towards European vacationers and retains no hint of the vintage Algarve, but fans of English breakfasts, Irish pubs, and karaoke bars love it.

Heading east out of Albufeira, you'll come to a slightly quieter, more upmarket part of town (Praia da Falésia–Olhos De Agua), where beautiful beaches are fringed by brand-name hotels.

Centrally located Albufeira is an ideal base for exploring the region. Public transportation is good due to the thousands of tourists who travel in and around the city on any given day. Trains are frequent from most Algarvian communities because they stop here while passing through to other destinations. The biggest bus terminals in the Algarve are found here.

ESSENTIALS
Train Contact CP. ⊠ *Largo da Estação* ☎ *808/210220* ⊕ *www.cp.pt.*

Visitor Information Albufeira. ⊠ *Rua 5 de Outubro* ☎ *289/585279* ⊕ *www. visitalgarve.pt.*

EXPLORING

Adega do Cantor. The "Winery of the Singer," about 10 km (6 miles) west of Albufeira, is now as well known for its wines as it is for its famous owner—British pop legend Sir Cliff Richard (though, as of this writing, the winery is up for sale, but still open to the public). The estate has bottled some seriously strong contenders on the international wine scene, and several of the Adega's Vida Nova wines have gone on to win coveted awards. Tours and tastings are available by appointment only. ⊠ *Quinta do Miradouro, Guia* ☎ *968/776971* ⊕ *www.winesvidanova. com* ⊡ *€7.50 for tour and wine tasting* ⊘ *Closed weekends, and mid-Dec.–early Jan.*

FAMILY **Zoomarine.** Just 6 km (4 miles) northwest of Albufeira, this popular and very pleasant marine park has low-key rides, swimming pools, a 4-D cinema, and shows that feature performing parrots, dolphins, and sea lions. Hotel pickups are available. ■ TIP→ **Visitors willing to part with €169 can sign on for an interactive dolphin experience.** ⊠ *Estrada Nacional 125, Km 65, Guia* ☎ *289/560300* ⊕ *www.zoomarine.com* ⊡ *€29* ⊘ *Closed Nov.–late Mar.*

BEACHES

Praia da Galé. Pretty and popular Praia da Galé, 4 km (2½ miles) west of Albufeira, is surrounded by a rich farming area that is still relatively underdeveloped. It has the classic Algarve rock formations that are characteristic of the region's coastline, plus a smattering of bars and restaurants. Other nice beaches lie on either side of Praia da Gale and can be accessed by foot—the walks from beach to beach are very enjoyable. **Amenities:** food and drink; parking (no fee); water sports. **Best for:** sunset; walking. ⊠ *Estrada da Galé.*

Praia da Oura. This pretty beach, located 2 km (1 mile) east of Albufeira, serves the popular Oura area. Shaped like a bay and surrounded by low-rise hotels and resorts, it's extremely crowded most of the year. It is also relatively small compared to other main beaches belonging to key tourist destinations; nevertheless, it comes equipped with all the summer essentials, like beach beds and water sports. **Amenities:** lifeguards; parking (fee); water sports. **Best for:** partiers. ⊠ *200 meters south of Rua Oliveira Martins.*

Town beach (*Praia dos Pescadores*). In summer, the town beach (reached by tunnel from Rua 5 de Outubro) is so crowded that it can be hard to enjoy its interesting rock formations, caves, and grottoes, not to mention the sand and sea. Yet it offers the latest in water sports and local children love jumping off the pier. Albufeira's old town encases the beach, which is also known as Praia dos Pescadores because fishing boats come in here to supply the local area with their fresh catch. A vast range of eateries and bars are a short stroll away. **Amenities:** lifeguards; water sports. **Best for:** partiers. ⌧ *Rua Bairro dos Pescadores.*

WHERE TO EAT AND STAY

$$$$
SEAFOOD
✕ **A Ruina.** Established in 1971, this large restaurant is built within the rustic remains of an 8th-century castle tower—hence its name. "The Ruins" serves fine renditions of typical Algarvian fare in four separate rooms with balconies overlooking the beach. It's a unique option for a special occasion, but great food in a historic setting comes at a price. $ *Average main: €40* ⌧ *Cais Herculano, Praia dos Pescadores* ☎ *289/512094, 289/586020* ⊕ *www.restaurante-ruina.com* ۞ *Closed early Jan.–early Feb.*

$$$
PORTUGUESE
✕ **Cabaz da Praia.** The name of this long-established restaurant, "Beach Basket," seems fitting given the mixed bag of imaginative Portuguese-French creations on the menu. Top choices include regional fish dishes and mains such as Chateaubriand, steak with Roquefort cheese sauce, and salmon in Pernod sauce. In warmer months, ask for a table on the terrace overlooking the beach. $ *Average main: €22* ⌧ *Praça Miguel Bombarda 7* ☎ *289/512137* ⊕ *www.cabazdapraia.blogspot.pt.*

$$$$
RESORT
FAMILY
Fodor's Choice
★
▦ **Epic Sana Algarve.** The Epic Sana's low-rise architecture beautifully blends into the landscape; the decor is cool, contemporary, and comfortable; and the facilities are first-rate, particularly for active types. **Pros:** beach at your doorstep; dedicated children's pools and kids' club; good selection of on-site restaurants. **Cons:** a drive is needed to get to a town; not the place to go for nightlife. $ *Rooms from: €470* ⌧ *Pinhal do Concelho, Praia da Falésia* ☎ *289/104300* ⊕ *www.algarve.epic. sanahotels.com* ⇝ *229 rooms* ⎮⊚⎮ *Breakfast.*

$$$
RESORT
▦ **Grande Real Santa Eulália.** Grand in style, the clifftop Santa Eulália occupies a privileged, locked-gate position just a stone's throw from shops and bars. **Pros:** direct beach access; four outdoor pools; dedicated kids' club. **Cons:** not within walking distance of Albufeira town center; need to pay extra for sunbeds; lunch and dinner buffets overpriced. $ *Rooms from: €204* ⌧ *Praia de Santa Eulália* ☎ *289/598000* ⊕ *www. granderealsantaeulaliahotel.com* ⇝ *373 rooms* ⎮⊚⎮ *Breakfast.*

$$
HOTEL
▦ **Hotel Vila Galé Cerro Alagoa.** One of Albufeira's most comfortable lodgings is a 10-minute walk from the main square. **Pros:** central to both old and new towns; on-site spa; family friendly. **Cons:** bar drinks expensive; limited entertainment options; extra charge to use the safe. $ *Rooms from: €160* ⌧ *Via Rápida, Rua do Municipio Lt. 26* ☎ *289/583100* ⊕ *www.vilagale.pt* ⇝ *310 rooms* ⎮⊚⎮ *Breakfast.*

$$$$
RESORT
▦ **Pine Cliffs Resort.** Perfect for families, this sprawling Starwood Luxury Collection resort offers all manner of activities from golf to tennis to water sports, along with direct access to a lovely cliff-backed beach. **Pros:** everything guests need for their vacations is within the resort; six swimming pools, so sunbeds always available; beautiful beach in front of resort grounds. **Cons:** atmosphere a bit blandly generic; large size

gives an impersonal feel; extra charge for Wi-Fi in rooms. [$] *Rooms from: €500* ✉ *Praia da Falesia* ☎ *289/500300* 🌐 *www.pinecliffs.com* 🛏 *519 rooms* 🍴 *Breakfast.*

$$$$ HOTEL Fodor's Choice ★ 🏨 **Vila Joya Boutique Resort.** This exclusive German-run jewel is set in lush gardens with no luxury spared. **Pros:** fine dining in an intimate atmosphere; exclusivity at its best, without stuffiness; nice spa. **Cons:** not much in surrounding area—need a car to venture further; concealed location a little difficult to find; high-end luxury travel with prices to match. [$] *Rooms from: €340* ✉ *Praia da Galé* ☎ *289/591795* 🌐 *www.vilajoya.com* 🛏 *20 rooms* 🍴 *Breakfast.*

NIGHTLIFE

Casa do Cerro. Think Morocco in the Algarve, complete with swaths of rich fabric, exotic cocktails, belly dancing, and bubbling Shisha pipes. This breezy, laid-back hilltop venue is a world away from the hustle and bustle of the Algarve in summer. Drink in its exotic smells, sights, and sounds daily from 8 pm to 2 am. ✉ *Cerro da Piedade, Albufeira Jardim I* ☎ *919/596665.*

SHOPPING

Every night in the height of summer, stalls with fairy lights wind their way through the center, selling handicrafts and tourist trinkets. It's fun to browse, and you may pick up the occasional interesting piece. A market selling everything from lightbulbs to cheap clothes (but no produce) is held on the first and third Tuesday of the month at the fairgrounds.

Bookworms. Bookworms, the best little shop of its kind, offers a wide selection of new English-language books, secondhand books, leather and personalized bookmarks, and commercial and handmade cards. ✉ *Rua Manuel Teixeira Gomes Lofa, Lote 2, Areias de São João* ☎ *916/984030.*

ARMAÇÃO DE PÊRA

14 km (8½ miles) west of Albufeira.

Massively overdeveloped with high-rise apartment blocks (the majority of which stand empty for much of the year), Armação de Pêra is probably one of the Algarve's least attractive towns. However, it is saved by its good restaurants, interesting seascapes, and affordable prices. Year-round, local boats can take you on two-hour cruises to caves and grottoes west along the shore, past the Praia Nossa Senhora da Rocha (Beach of Our Lady of the Rocks)—a strand named after the Romanesque chapel above it. To arrange tours, head to Praia Armação de Pêra—a wide sandy beach with a promenade—and speak with the fishermen directly.

GETTING HERE AND AROUND

The town can be reached by stopping at Portimão in the west or Albufeira in the east; a bus from either will shuttle you to this seaside resort.

The Holiday Inn doubles as one of the bus ticket offices.

ESSENTIALS

Bus Contact **Solpraia.** ✉ *Av. General Humberto Delgado 18-r/c* ☎ *282/313334 bus ticket office.*

Visitor Information **Armação de Pêra.** ✉ *Av. Marginal* ☎ *282/312145* 🌐 *www.visitalgarve.pt.*

WHERE TO EAT AND STAY

$ PORTUGUESE 🍴 **Casa de Pasto Zé Leiteiro.** Most *casas de pastos* (loosely translated as "grazing houses") offer big portions of well-cooked regional dishes in no-frills surroundings at shoestring prices. Casa de Pasto Zé Leiteiro is no exception. Enjoy delicious all-you-can-eat fish served with potatoes and salad; the fish keep coming until you tell them to stop. Simple on the outside, basic on the inside, the food and prices do the talking. They don't take reservations, so be prepared to wait for a seat. [$] *Average main: €13* ✉ *Rua Portas do Mar 17* ☎ *282/314551* 💳 *No credit cards* 🕒 *Closed Mon., mid-Dec.–mid. Jan., and last wk in May.*

$ INDIAN 🍴 **Indian Bollywood.** Although it's located directly opposite the fishermen's beach Praia Nossa Senhora da Rocha, Indian Bollywood provides a portal to the Far East. Hot and spicy tandoori dishes are the draw, but mild options are plentiful, as are vegetarian dishes. A take-out service is available. This is one of the Algarve's most popular eateries, so reservations are advisable. [$] *Average main: €13* ✉ *Rua da Praia, Edifício Vista Mar 1* ☎ *282/313755* 🕒 *No lunch Mon.*

$$$$ PORTUGUESE Fodor's Choice ★ 🍴 **Ocean Restaurant.** One of the top dining experiences in the Algarve, Ocean impresses with its innovative tasting menus, fabulous Portuguese wine selection, and wonderful ocean views from the dining room. Choose from two tasting menus of five or eight courses; expect interesting riffs on Portuguese classics using local ingredients and lots of fish and seafood along with all-Portuguese wine pairings. [$] *Average main: €135* ✉ *Vila Vita Parc, Rua Anneliese Pohl, Porches* ☎ *282/310100* 🌐 *www.restauranteocean.com* 🕒 *Closed Mon. and Tues. No lunch.*

$$ HOTEL 🏨 **Holiday Inn.** Although it belongs to an international chain, this well-located hotel boasts personalized, friendly service and a prime beachfront location. **Pros:** the beach is on your doorstep; within walking distance of all attractions and amenities; good on-site Indian restaurant. **Cons:** furniture and fixtures a bit drab; charge for sunbeds on beach. [$] *Rooms from: €150* ✉ *Av. Marginal* ☎ *282/320260* 🌐 *www.holiday-inn.com* 🛏 *186 rooms* 🍽 *Breakfast.*

$$$$ RESORT Fodor's Choice ★ 🏨 **Vila Vita Parc.** Within walking distance of Armação de Pêra, the clifftop Vila Vita Parc is an award-winning resort of impeccable standards. **Pros:** beautiful hotel grounds; spacious rooms; 10 restaurants to choose from. **Cons:** not for couples or singles wanting to experience the Algarve's wilder side; decor a bit old-fashioned; expansive grounds mean using a golf cart to get around or lots of walking. [$] *Rooms from: €545* ✉ *Rua Anneliese Pohl, Porches* ☎ *282/310161* 🌐 *www.vilavitaparc.com* 🛏 *170 rooms* 🍽 *Breakfast.*

SPORTS AND THE OUTDOORS

WATER PARK

Aqualand. The least expensive of the Algarve's three water parks lies just north of town, close to Alcantarilha. It is home to the Banzai Boggan and the Kamikaze (the highest ride in Portugal). ✉ *E.N. 125 Alcantarilha* ☎ *282/320230* 🌐 *www.aqualand.pt* 🎟 *€27* 🕒 *Closed mid-Sept.–June.*

CARVOEIRO

5 km (3 miles) west of Armação de Pêra.

This busy resort town has gone to great lengths to boost tourism but still maintains some of its fishing-village charm. An abundance of good-quality restaurants and pretty clifftop lodgings attracts droves of tourists (parking, as a result, is a problem—particularly in summer, when vehicles are banned from the heart of the village). Location is another of Carvoeiro's assets as it makes a good base for accessing both the east and west coasts. Small beaches lie at the foot of steep, rocky cliffs, and waves have sculpted the distinctive yellow rock into intricate archways and stacks encrusted with fossilized shells.

GETTING HERE AND AROUND

The closest train stations are Silves or Estômbar, with bus services running regularly to this quaint village.

ESSENTIALS

Visitor Information **Carvoeiro.** ✉ *Praia do Carvoeiro* ☎ *282/357728* 🌐 *www.visitalgarve.pt.*

WHERE TO EAT AND STAY

$$ GREEK FUSION 🍴 **Onze Restaurant.** Cool, contemporary Onze offers a unique fusion of Greek-Mediterranean cuisine, as well as one of the best views in the village, right on the cliffside overlooking the beach. Start with the mixed platter of authentic, homemade Greek meze. For mains, the daily risottos are mouthwatering and the meat is top-notch. Onze promises a solid wine selection, tempting desserts, and impeccable service, too. Because it prides itself on being family-friendly, there are no TVs to distract, just the sound of happy chatting in the background. TIP→ **Onze bucks the seasonal trend by being busy year-round, so reservations are recommended.** [$] *Average main: €20* ✉ *Rampa da Sra. da Encarnacao 11* ☎ *282/357427* 🌐 *www.onze-restaurant.com* 🕒 *Closed mid.-Nov.–mid-Dec. and early Jan.–late Feb.*

$$$ HOTEL 🏨 **Tivoli Carvoeiro.** Perched high on a cliff overlooking Carvoeiro's dramatic coastline, the Tivoli Carvoeiro has stunning views and well-kept grounds. **Pros:** excellent location; great on-site dive shop; good for families. **Cons:** rooms and bathrooms could use a makeover (should be improved by renovations); comfortable downhill walk to main town square but the uphill return walk may be challenging for the less able-bodied. [$] *Rooms from: €245* ✉ *Vale do Covo* ☎ *282/351100* 🌐 *www.tivolihotels.com* 🛏 *293 rooms* 🍽 *Breakfast.*

SPORTS AND THE OUTDOORS
GOLF
Vale da Pinta. American course architect Ronald Fream carved the Vale da Pinta layout through an ancient olive grove where some of the trees are more than 700 years old. Fream was the perfect choice for the job, because he is highly regarded for his sensitivity to environmental issues. Five sets of tees on each hole make this an enjoyable course for all levels of ability. There is a chance for ending in style on the par-5 18th for those who can hit the ball long. Booking two weeks in advance is advised for those looking for specific tee times. The greens are large, and there is a feeling of space here. Handicap limits are 27 for men and 35 for women. ⊠ *Apartado 1011* ☎ *282/340900* ⊕ *www. pestanagolf.com* ⊠ *€105 high season, €70 middle season, €115 in Mar. and Oct.* ⚑ *18 holes, 6409 yds, par 71* ☞ *Facilities: driving range, putting green, golf carts, pull carts, rental clubs, pro shop, golf academy/ lessons, restaurant, bar.*

SCUBA DIVING
Algarve Divexperience. This excellent diving school offers many different PADI courses, as well as a variety of beach dives and boat dives. Rates are €75–€100 for two dives, €203–€270 for six, or €300–€400 for 10. The staff speak English. ⊠ *Hotel Tivoli Carvoeiro, Apartado 1299, Praia do Carvoeiro, Vale de Covo* ☎ *282/351194, 963/223892 (mobile)* ⊕ *www.algarve-scuba-diving.com.*

TENNIS
Carvoeiro Clube de Ténis. The Carvoeiro Clube de Ténis has 10 courts and five mini-courts as well as a fitness center, a swimming pool, a mini-golf course, and a restaurant. ⊠ *Mato Serrão* ☎ *282/358236, 961/137201 (mobile)* ⊕ *www.tenniscarvoeiro.com.*

LAGOA

10 km (6 miles) northwest of Armação de Pêra; 15 km (9 miles) northwest of Carvoeiro.

This market town is primarily known for its wine, *vinho Lagoa* (the red is especially good). It is also home to the Algarve's last surviving wine cooperative, a historic structure which also houses a very interesting art gallery.

GETTING HERE AND AROUND
Lagoa has a large bus terminal, which connects with Portimão and Albufeira.

ESSENTIALS
Bus Contact Lagoa Bus Terminal. ⊠ *Rua Jacinto Correia* ☎ *282/341301.*

Visitor Information Armação de Pêra. ⊠ *Av. Marginal, Armação de Pêra* ☎ *282/312145.*

EXPLORING
Cooperativa de Lagoa. The Algarve's last remaining cooperative winery is a piece of living, working history. The Única-Adega Cooperative do Algarve is on the main road just after the Carvoeiro junction, on the

left. Call if you're interested in joining a prearranged group tour and tasting session. At any time during normal working hours you can pop in to the office (at the side of the building) to sample the wine and buy a bottle or two. ■TIP→ **Part of the building has been converted into an art gallery (Lady in Red - Galeria de Arte), featuring national and international artists. The gallery is also open during office hours.** ✉ *N125* ☎ *282/342181* ⊕ *www.vinhosdoalgarve.pt.*

Quinta dos Vales. Although it's one of the more recent players on the regional wine production scene, Quinta dos Vales has earned an impressive reputation. Free wine tasting by the glass is available in the Farm-Shop; there's an extra charge for hour-long guided tastings, which must be booked in advance. Visitors who would like to spend more time exploring the beautiful grounds and open-air sculpture exhibition can book one of the estate's farmhouses, a cottage, a duplex apartment, or a villa; all rent by the week ($$–$$$$). ✉ *Sítio dos Vales, Caixa Postal 112* ☎ *282/431036* ⊕ *www.quintadosvales.eu.*

SPORTS AND THE OUTDOORS

WATER PARK

FAMILY **Slide & Splash.** Water park fans can cool off at Slide & Splash, which promises wild, watery amusements like the Big Wave and Tornado. Bird and reptile shows are also put on. If the smell of doughnuts, chlorine, and sunblock doesn't scream "popular tourist attraction," the rather expensive on-site fast food will. ■TIP→ **It's worth packing a picnic (no glass items).** ✉ *N125, Vale de Deus, Estômbar* ☎ *282/340800* ⊕ *www.slidesplash.com* 🎫 *€27* ☉ *Closed Nov.–Mar.*

SHOPPING

Along the N125 in nearby Porches, you can stop at roadside shops that sell both mass-produced and handmade pottery.

CERAMICS

Olaria Pequena. This pretty little blue-and-white pottery shop embodies the essence of Algarvian ceramics. It is owned and run by a friendly Scot, Ian Fitzpatrick, who has worked in the Algarve for years. He sells handmade pieces at very reasonable prices. ✉ *N125 between Porches and Alcantarilha* ☎ *282/381213* ⊕ *www.olariapequena.com.*

SILVES

7 km (4½ miles) northeast of Lagoa.

Fodor's Choice ★ Silves—once the Moorish capital of the Algarve—is one of the region's most intriguing locales. Small whitewashed villas trickle down from the imposing castle that sits atop town, overlooking the hills beyond. Being inland, Silves is generally warmer than coastal communities, and it has a pretty riverside area where you can enjoy a refreshing stroll or cheap, cheerful meal. In summer, Viking-style canoes run trips down the Arade River to Portimão.

GETTING HERE AND AROUND

The easiest way to get to Silves is by bus, via Lagoa, if you're coming from the eastern Algarve. If you're coming from the western end, the easiest route is via Portimão. The train station is around 7 km (4½ miles) from the city center; a taxi from the station into Silves should cost no more than €10 at peak times (nights, weekends, and national holidays).

ESSENTIALS

Bus Contact Silves Bus Station. ⊠ *Bilheteira Mercado Municipal, Rua Francisco Pablos, Edifício do Mercado* ☎ *282/442338* ⊕ *www.eva-bus.com.*

Taxi Contact Taxi. ⊠ *Rua Castelo Bloco A-Lote 1-c/v-E* ☎ *282/442541.*

Visitor Information Silves. ⊠ *N124, Parque das Merendas* ☎ *282/098927* ⊕ *www.visitalgarve.pt.*

EXPLORING

Fodor'sChoice ★ **Medieval Festival.** The local council goes all out to make the 10-day Silves Medieval Festival feel like a genuine trip back in time. Medieval food merchants and handicraft vendors dressed in traditional garb take over the city in August. (If you want to get in the mood yourself, costumes can be rented for a few euros.) Jousting displays and falconry shows are staged, along with fire-eating, belly dancing, and medieval banquets. Be warned, though: it's not for the claustrophobic. Silves's steep, narrow streets are packed during this event. ⊠ *Silves* ☎ *282/440800* ⊕ *www. cm-silves.pt* 🖼 *€2 (extra charge for special events).*

Museu Arqueológia. With most labels in both Portuguese and English, the items on display at Silves's archaeology museum give interesting insights into the area's history. One primary attraction is an Arab water cistern, preserved in situ, with a 30-foot-deep well. The museum is a few minutes' walk below the cathedral, off Rua da Sé. ⊠ *Rua das Portas de Loulé 14* ☎ *282/440800, 282/444832* ⊕ *www.cm-silves.pt* 🖼 *€2.10; €3.90 combined ticket, includes castle.*

Silves Castle. Sitting imposingly in the middle of Silves, with high red walls that overshadow the little whitewashed houses at the foot of them, is Silves Castle. Built between the 8th and 13th centuries, this polygonal sandstone fortress survived untouched until the Christian sieges. You can walk around inside the remaining walls or clamber about the crenellated battlements, taking in bird's-eye views of Silves and the hills. (Keep an eye open: some places have no guardrails.) Its gardens are watched over by a statue of King Dom Sancho I, and its capacious water cistern is now a gallery space devoted to temporary exhibitions, some of which have nothing to do with the fort. ⊠ *Rua do Castelo* ☎ *282/440837* ⊕ *www.cm-silves.pt* 🖼 *€2.80.*

WHERE TO EAT

$ ECLECTIC **Café Inglês.** Architectural character, great views, and a broad selection of good, affordably priced food combine to make Café Inglês a must-try. In summer make sure you book a table on the rooftop terrace adjacent to the castle. Live entertainment (of the jazzy-arty kind) is staged throughout the year. 🆂 *Average main: €12* ⊠ *Rua do Castelo 11* ☎ *282/442585* ⊕ *www.cafeingles.com.pt* ⊙ *Closed Mon., and Nov.*

$$ SEAFOOD **Rui Marisqueira.** Although there's no atmosphere to speak of, the fish and shellfish are extremely fresh and remarkably good value, which is the main reason why the crowds from the coast come inland to dine here along with in-the-know locals. Grilled sea bream and bass are usually available, along with a good selection of shellfish, including slipper

6

lobster and spider crab. The service is just as good as the food—friendly, knowledgeable, and efficient. [$] *Average main: €18* ✉ *Rua Comendador Vilarinho 27* ☎ *282/442682* 🌐 *www.marisqueirarui.pt* 🕒 *Closed Tues., and 1st 2 wks of Nov.*

SHOPPING

MARKET

Mercado (*produce market*). Silves's mercado, liveliest in the morning, is at the foot of town, close to the medieval bridge. If you arrive at lunchtime, have a delicious meal of spicy grilled chicken, fish, or typical stews like *cozido á Portuguesa* from one of the simple (read: cheap and cheerful) restaurants here. After lunch take a long stroll along the city's riverside area; it's a scenic way to digest your meal. ✉ *Silves* 🕒 *Closed Sun.*

PORTIMÃO

15 km (9 miles) southwest of Silves.

Portimão is a major fishing port, and significant investment has been poured into transforming it into an attractive cruise port as well. The city itself is spacious and has several good shopping streets. There is also a lovely riverside area that just begs to be strolled (lots of the coastal cruises depart from here). Don't leave without stopping for an alfresco lunch at the Doca da Sardinha ("sardine dock") between the old bridge and the railway bridge. You can sit at one of many inexpensive establishments, eating charcoal-grilled sardines (a local specialty) accompanied by chewy fresh bread, simple salads, and local wine.

GETTING HERE AND AROUND

Portimão can be reached by train and bus. The city's impressive Vai e Vem bus service is excellent and enables visitors to zip around at a minimal cost.

ESSENTIALS

Bus Contacts **Eva.** ✉ *Largo do Dique* ☎ *282/418120* 🌐 *www.eva-bus.com.* **Vai e Vem.** ✉ *Rua do Comércio 29/31* ☎ *282/470777* 🌐 *www.vaivem.pt.*

EXPLORING

Quinta da Penina. One of the Algarve's more established wineries, Quinta da Penina is home to the renowned Foral de Portimão wine. Agronomist João Mariano, who mainly uses a blend of certified Portuguese and French grape varieties, has earned international acclaim since launching the company in 2001. Tours and tastings are possible most days of the week by calling in advance; prices vary based on the number of participants. ✉ *Rua da Angola, Lote 2, Loja B+C* ☎ *282/491070, 919/350215 (mobile)* 🌐 *www.vinhosportimao.com.*

Sardine Festival. Portimão stages its renowned Sardine Festival every year at the beginning of August. It's a must for anyone wanting to try the delicious little fish and sample local cuisine while enjoying the sights and sounds of a proper Algarvian party. ✉ *Zona Ribeirinha* ☎ *282/470700* 🌐 *www.festivaldasardinha.pt.*

BEACHES

Praia Grande. There are many reasons to visit Ferragudo, a fishing hamlet across the river from Portimão. It has character, quaint cobblestone streets, quality restaurants, and one of the region's finest beaches—Praia Grande, a long stretch of sand that offers plenty of space for towels even in summer. The 16th-century **Castelo de São João** (St. John's Castle), built to defend Portimão and now privately owned, is right on the beach; and in summer there's live entertainment. Since many boats dock here, the water can have a slight petrol smell, but it is crystal clear and good for snorkeling. When it's time to dry off, sit and watch the cruise liners glide by as they dock in Portimão. **Amenities:** food and drink; lifeguards; parking (no fee); showers; toilets; water sports. **Best for:** snorkeling; sunset; windsurfing. ⊠ *Across the bridge, 5 km (3 miles) east of Portimão, Ferragudo.*

WHERE TO EAT AND STAY

$
SEAFOOD
✕ **Flor da Sardinha Assada.** This is one of several open-air eateries next to Portimão's old bridge, by the fishing harbor, whose staff grills fresh sardines on quayside stoves and serves them to crowds seated at plastic tables. A plateful of these delicious fish, with boiled potatoes (never fries!), and a bottle of the local wine, is one of Portugal's top treats. $ *Average main: €15* ⊠ *Cais da Lota* ☎ *282/424862.*

$
PIZZA
✕ **Nosolo Italia.** Sitting in Portimão's main square, Nosolo Italia (the original location of a Portuguese chain) is as famous for its massive ice-cream sundaes as it is for its privileged location. The menu is made up almost entirely of ice-cream concoctions and simple Italian fare like pizza, pasta, and salad. Thankfully, the long riverside area provides a great opportunity to walk it all off. Open morning till late at night, this place is popular with all ages. $ *Average main: €12* ⊠ *Praça Manuel Teixeira Gomes* ☎ *282/427024* ⊕ *www.nosoloitalia.com* ▭ *No credit cards.*

$$
RESORT
Fodor's Choice
★
▦ **Tivoli Marina Portimão.** This hotel has a simple but stylish 1970s retro interior cleverly laid out around two large swimming pools complete with wooden deck bars and palm gardens. **Pros:** stunning views over river; short walk to Praia da Rocha (main beach, strip of bars, and restaurants) and marina; nice selection at breakfast buffet. **Cons:** Wi-Fi not free in guest rooms; can be noisy from local bars; rooms vary a lot in quality. $ *Rooms from: €170* ⊠ *Marina de Portimão* ☎ *282/460200* ⊕ *www.tivolihotels.com* ⤳ *196 apartments* ⫣ *Breakfast.*

SPORTS AND THE OUTDOORS

BOATING

NoSoloÁgua. At the marina's edge, looking across the river to the pretty village of Ferragudo, this fashionable Indonesian-inspired club has everything you need for a day of indulgence, including sunbeds, a saltwater pool, lovely cocktails, and quality food. An adjacent sister retreat on the beach—NoSoloPraia—holds nightly parties in summer that attract the beautiful people. There's a charge to enter, which includes use of a sunbed for the day. ⊠ *Marina de Portimão* ☎ *282/498180, 910/789991* ⊕ *www.nosoloagua.com.*

SAILING

Santa Bernarda. Take a sailing trip on a twin-masted "pirate ship." Departing from the harbor, the *Santa Bernarda* offers visits to Algarvian caves and barbecues on the beach. ⊠ *Rua Júdice Fialho 11* ☎ *282/422791* ⊕ *www.santa-bernarda.com.*

SHOPPING

Portimão's main shopping street is Rua do Comércio. Shops on Rua de Santa Isabel specialize in crafts, leather goods, ceramics, crystal, and fashion.

Aqua Portimão Shopping Centre. Aqua Portimão has dozens of European high-street retailers under one roof, so it's a great place to splash some cash when the weather is wet. The top floor offers a huge range of eateries, from fast food to sit-down, and there is lots of free covered parking. ⊠ *Rua de São Pedro 72* ☎ *282/413536* ⊕ *www.aquaportimao.pt.*

O Aquario. For ceramics, porcelain, crystal, and handmade copper items, visit O Aquario. ⊠ *Rua Vasco da Gama 42* ☎ *282/426673.*

PRAIA DA ROCHA

3 km (2 miles) southeast of Portimão.

Portimão's crown jewel is a 1-km (½-mile) stretch of sand backed by a curtain of ocher-red cliffs, along the top of which stands a series of striking hotels, restaurants, and bars. In summer it buzzes; in winter the locals promenade along the wooden walkway that runs the entire length of the beach, inhaling the invigorating sea air. Year-round Praia da Rocha is popular among youngsters looking for a place to party (though it's nothing like the scale of Albufeira).

GETTING HERE AND AROUND

Portimão's Vai e Vem shuttle bus serves Praia da Rocha; tickets can be purchased at Hotel Jupiter on Avenida Tomás Cabreira. Portimão station also has regular trains running to Lagos in the west and Faro in the east.

ESSENTIALS

Bus Contact Vai e Vem. ☎ *282/470777* ⊕ *vaivem.portimaourbis.pt.*

Visitor Information Praia da Rocha. ⊠ *Av. Tomás Cabreira* ☎ *282/419132* ⊕ *www.visitalgarve.pt.*

EXPLORING

Fortaleza de Santa Catarina. The eastern end of Praia da Rocha culminates in the 16th-century Fortress of Santa Catarina, which provides wonderful views out to sea and across the Rio Arade to Ferragudo. Directly below it, on the river side, is one of the Algarve's growing number of marinas. On the other side a long concrete jetty extends into the Atlantic. ⊠ *Av. Tomás Cabreira.*

BEACHES

Praia da Rocha. Said to be the country's most photographed beach, Praia da Rocha is definitely one of the most popular, and it draws a constant stream of visitors—from both Portugal and abroad. Dramatic cliffs provide the backdrop for a wide, golden expanse of sand. Many water sports are available, and there's a long pier to stroll on. Several quality bars and restaurants can be found along the beach, all jutting off a wooden boardwalk that stretches down the strand. More can be found further east towards the marina. **Amenities:** food and drink; lifeguards; parking (fee and no fee); showers (at the marina); toilets; water sports. **Best for:** partiers; surfing; swimming; walking. ⊠ *3 km (2 miles) southeast of Portimão.*

WHERE TO EAT AND STAY

$ ✕ **Dolce Vita Pizzeria.** Locals come to Dolce Vita for its fabulous home-
PIZZA made pizzas and pasta, refreshing sangria, and charming wood decor. Meals are served on bench tables with tiled tops that add extra quirkiness to this popular eatery. Be sure to make a reservation in summer. Ⓢ *Average main: €10* ⊠ *Av. Tomas Cabreira* ☎ *282/419444* ⊕ *www. pizzerialadolcevita.pt.*

$$ ✕ **Titanic.** One of Praia da Rocha's oldest and best-known restaurants
FRENCH FUSION offers a ship-shape dining experience off the main strip. It specializes in French cuisine and aims to create a romantic, intimate atmosphere, styled on the original Titanic's interior. Ⓢ *Average main: €20* ⊠ *Rua Eng. Francisco Bivar, Edificio Columbia* ☎ *282/422371, 963/087860* ☾ *Closed Mon.*

$$$$ ⊞ **Hotel Algarve Casino.** The sea vistas from this classy (though a tad
HOTEL dated) hotel are spectacular, so be sure to book a room with a view. **Pros:** great location on Praia da Rocha's main strip; plenty of spots to lounge around the lovely pool; beautiful views from some rooms. **Cons:** dated decor; often overcrowded at breakfast buffet; Wi-Fi can be iffy. Ⓢ *Rooms from: €268* ⊠ *Av. Tomás Cabreira* ☎ *282/423770* ⊕ *hotelalgarvecasino.solverde.pt* ⟳ *208 rooms* ⎟⊙⎟ *Breakfast.*

ALVOR

5 km (3 miles) west of Portimão.

Characterized by a maze of interesting streets, lanes, and alleys, the handsome old port of Alvor is one of the Algarve's best examples of an Arab village. In summer, many vacationers are attracted to its excellent beaches. Alvor also offers appealing nightlife.

GETTING HERE AND AROUND

Alvor is connected by Portimão's Vai e Vem bus service, though taxis are widely used in this popular fishing village.

ESSENTIALS

Bus Contact Vai e Vem. ☎ *282/470777* ⊕ *vaivem.portimaourbis.pt.*

Taxi Contact Taxiarade. ☎ *282/460610* ⊕ *www.taxiarade.com.*

Visitor Information Alvor. ⊠ *Rua Dr. Afonso Costa 51* ☎ *282/457540.*

BEACHES

Praia dos Três Irmãos. The fact that the Portuguese president's official holiday home overlooks this beach reflects its quality. Regular Joes can enjoy the same view by staying at the Pestana Alvor Praia resort. Small and covelike, Praia dos Três Irmãos has lots of little rocks in the water, which means it can either be great for snorkeling or bad for unwitting

6

toes, depending on the tide. ■TIP→ **If it gets too crowded, there's always space to spare on one of the beaches to either side.** **Amenities:** food and drink; lifeguards; parking (no fee); toilets. **Best for:** snorkeling; walking. ✉ *Off the main V3 road, 1½ km (1 mile) from Alvor.*

WHERE TO EAT AND STAY

$$ SEAFOOD
🍴 **Atlântida.** This is a charming restaurant with an absolutely lovely location on the eastern part of a dramatic beach. Specialties here include live shellfish, fresh fish, cataplanas, and flambées, supported by a selection of fine wines. [$] *Average main: €20* ✉ *Praia do Três Irmãos* ☎ *282/459647* ⏲ *Closed Tues.*

$$ RESORT
🏨 **Penina Hotel & Golf Resort.** With three courses within the hotel grounds, the Penina attracts large numbers of golfers. **Pros:** excellent golf course within hotel grounds; good on-site à la carte restaurants; lovely pool area and gardens. **Cons:** rooms in need of a refresh; drinks are expensive; evening entertainment on the thin side. [$] *Rooms from: €192* ✉ *N125, Penina* ☎ *282/420200* 🌐 *www.penina.com* 🛏 *188 rooms* 🍽 *Breakfast.*

$$$$ HOTEL
Fodor's Choice ★
🏨 **Pestana Alvor Praia.** Whether you have a room with a sea or a garden view, this clifftop property looks good from all angles. **Pros:** amazing beach views from sea-view rooms; fresh, clean look in guest rooms and public spaces; free sunbeds on the adjacent beach. **Cons:** strange walk through Hotel Netherlands to reach pool and beach areas; 15- to 20-minute walk to Alvor town and local amenities; expensive food in pool area. [$] *Rooms from: €296* ✉ *Praia dos Três Irmãos* ☎ *282/400900* 🌐 *www.pestana.com* 🛏 *195 rooms* 🍽 *Breakfast.*

SPORTS AND THE OUTDOORS

GOLF

Fodor's Choice ★
Penina. On what was once a flat, uninteresting rice paddy, Sir Henry Cotton worked his design magic and created his most famous course 5 km (3 miles) from Portimão. It is considered the masterpiece among his many layouts because of its difficult challenge and the beautiful setting he created by planting more than 100,000 trees. Sir Henry held court here for years, welcoming the great and good from world golf to the lavish Penina resort. The course that began the Portuguese golf boom in the 1960s has had a face-lift and remains a stern test of golf—the par-3 13th has been ranked among the top 500 holes in the world. Although the course is busy at most times, golfers on different holes seldom come into contact due to the mature trees and wide fairways. Penina Hotel & Golf Resort guests are entitled to special green fee rates. On the championship course, a handicap of 28 is required for men and 36 for women to play. ✉ *N125, Portimão* ☎ *282/420200* 🌐 *www.penina.com/golf/golf-courses* 🎟 *€120 high season, €80 low season* 🏌 *18 holes, 6860 yds, par 73* ✍ *Reservations essential* ☞ *Facilities: driving range, putting green, golf carts, pull carts, rental clubs, pro shop, golf academy/lessons, restaurant, bar.*

SKYDIVING

Skydive Algarve. The Algarve is fast becoming one of the most popular spots in Europe for skydiving. Based at the Alvor airdrome, Skydive Algarve operates jumps with experienced instructors all year, though winter—when the skies remain clear but the temperatures are crisp and cool—is the prime season. Tandem jumps are also available for first-timers. ✉ *Aerodromo Municipal de Portimao* ☎ *914/266832* ⊕ *www. skydivealgarve.com.*

MONCHIQUE

25 km (15 miles) northeast of Alvor; 20 km (12 miles) north of Portimão.

The winding road up to Monchique from Portimão or Silves brings the surprise of lush greenery and an oasis of brightly colored villas surrounded by waterways and fruit groves. Picturesque clusters of whitewashed farms create self-sustained hamlets where life goes on as it always has. Steeped in tradition and folklore, Monchique is home to Fóia, the highest peak in the Algarve, as well as the natural Caldas springs that are said to have healing properties. If you'd prefer to cool off with a standard dip, there's an open-air municipal pool in summer where the public can swim free of charge. In March the town hosts a traditional cured-meats fair to showcase local specialties.

GETTING HERE AND AROUND

Getting to Monchique can be tricky without a car. It's recommended to travel by bus to either Silves or Portimão, or by train to Portimão, and from those cities catch a bus to Monchique. The best way to get to Fóia is by taxi from Monchique town center. ·

ESSENTIALS

Bus Contact Bus ticket office. ✉ *Papelaria Santo António, Rua D. Afonso Henriques 6* ☎ *282/912127* ⊕ *eva-bus.com.*

Taxi Contact Taxi. ☎ *282/912171.*

Visitor Information Monchique. ✉ *Largo de S. Sebastião* ☎ *282/911189* ⊕ *www.visitalgarve.pt.*

EXPLORING

Caldas de Monchique. Monchique's natural springs are renowned for healing waters that bubble out of the ground to create a paradise microclimate where "anything grows." The small chapel of Caldas is where many go for a blessing or to pray in thanks for the health of those who drink its waters. The Thermas de Monchique is just below the chapel and is intrinsic to the area. Visitors come not only for the water's healing properties but for pampering spa treatments. Modern spa facilities complement those for health treatments concerned with digestive, bone, kidney, and respiratory problems. Visitors who really want to immerse themselves in the experience can book into the on-site Villa Termal Das Caldas De Monchique Spa Resort ($). ✉ *Monchique* ☎ *282/910910* ⊕ *www.monchiquetermas.com.*

Feira dos Enchidos Tradicionais. Every year on the first weekend in March, Monchique hosts its annual cured-meats fair. The Feira dos Enchidos Tradicionais is a high point on the locals' calendar and people travel from far and wide to sample typical mountain produce—and not just meats. You will also find jams, dried fruits, liqueurs, and cheeses among the delicacies. It's all rounded off with traditional nightly entertainment. ✉ *Heliporto Municipal* 🌐 *www.cm-monchique.pt.*

Pico de Fóia. A short drive west of Monchique on N266-3 brings you to the highest point in the Serra de Monchique. At 2,959 feet, Pico de Fóia affords panoramic views—weather permitting—over the western Algarve. There's also a café here. ✉ *Monchique* 🌐 *www.cm-monchique.pt.*

WHERE TO EAT AND STAY

$ PORTUGUESE 🍴 **Teresinha.** Just west of Monchique, modest Teresinha has good country cooking, a simple interior, and an outdoor terrace that overlooks a valley as well as the coast. The ham and the grilled chicken are particularly tasty. [$] *Average main: €10* ✉ *N266-3* ☎ *282/912392* ⏲ *No dinner Wed.*

$ B&B/INN 🏨 **Inn Albergeria Bica-Boa.** Inspired by the many springs welling up from the thickly wooded mountainside above Monchique, this small hotel may be on the roadside, but there's very little traffic, and guest rooms face the back. **Pros:** good home-cooked food; lovely, relaxing atmosphere; friendly and attentive service. **Cons:** car is needed to get around; no Wi-Fi in rooms. [$] *Rooms from: €60* ✉ *Estrada da Lisboa 266* ☎ *282/912271* 🛏 *4 rooms* 🍽 *Breakfast.*

$$ RESORT 🏨 **Macdonald Monchique Resort & Spa.** This mountain retreat is 20 minutes from Silves or 25 minutes from Portimão. **Pros:** wonderful views; a vast range of services to enhance well-being; large, modern rooms. **Cons:** car needed to explore further; not much going on in the evenings; suites with kitchens have limited cooking equipment. [$] *Rooms from: €191* ✉ *Lugar do Montinho* ☎ *282/240130* 🌐 *www.macdonaldmonchique.com* 🛏 *190 rooms* 🍽 *Breakfast.*

LAGOS AND THE WESTERN ALGARVE

From the bustling town of Lagos, the rest of the Western Algarve is easily accessible. This is the most unspoiled part of the region, with some genuinely isolated beaches and bays along an often wind-buffeted route that reaches to the southwest and the magnificent Cabo São Vicente. Between Lagos and Sagres a series of quaint villages and hamlets—like Praia da Luz and Burgau—also await.

LAGOS

13 km (8 miles) west of Portimão; 70 km (43 miles) northwest of Faro.

Breezy and cool in every sense of the word, Lagos has an infectious energy and a laid-back feel. However, this bustling fishing port also has a venerable history, and evocative buildings—including the Slave Market, Castelo dos Governadores, Forte Ponta da Bandeira, and Igreja de Santo António—are ocular proof. The town's cobblestone streets have a broad assortment of good restaurants and nighttime hangouts, and pristine beaches with big waves offer outdoor activities nearby.

GETTING HERE AND AROUND

Lagos is 80 km (50 miles) from the Faro airport. You can come from the airport via bus, train, or taxi. The Lagos train and bus station are near each other and the marina, from where most of the city can be explored on foot. Alternatively, you can use the local bus system (Onda), which follows nine routes between 7 am and 8 pm daily in winter and 7 am to 11 pm daily in summer. The tourist train, which departs from the marina, is another great way to see the town; it costs around €3 and runs daily starting at 10 am.

TIMING

Although the main historic sights of the old town are all in close proximity, allow at least two hours for a tour. Be prepared to join lines for museums and, in summer, to negotiate crowds of backpackers, sightseers, and shoppers who throng the many bars, cafés, restaurants, and shops. The Casa da Alfândega alone will probably occupy you for half an hour. Allow plenty of time to explore the Igreja de Santo António: it's striking from the outside and full of surprises inside. The churches between Praça da Republica and Rua do Castelo dos Governadores have unusual architectural styles that make them worth a visit, but photography is discouraged within.

ESSENTIALS

Bus Contacts Eva. ⊠ *Largo Rossío de São João* ☎ *282/762944, 282/422105* ⊕ *www.eva-bus.com.* **Onda.** ☎ *282/768931* ⊕ *aonda.pt.*

Taxi Contact Taxi. ☎ *282/763587.*

Train Contact CP. ⊠ *Estrada de São Roque* ☎ *707/210220* ⊕ *www.cp.pt.*

Visitor Information Lagos. ⊠ *Praça Gil Eanes (Antigos Paços do Concelho)* ☎ *282/763031* ⊕ *www.visitalgarve.pt.*

EXPLORING

Castelo dos Governadores (*Governor's Palace*). It was from the Manueline window of this palace that the young king Dom Sebastião is said to have addressed his troops before setting off on his crusade of 1578. The palace is long gone, though the section of wall with the famous window remains and can be seen in the northwest corner of the Praça do Infante. The crusade was one of Portugal's greatest-ever disasters, with the king and some 8,000 men killed in Morocco at Alcácer-Quibir. (Dom Sebastião is further remembered by a much-maligned, modernistic statue that stands in Praça Gil Eanes.) ⊠ *Praça do Infante.*

Forte Ponta da Bandeira. This 17th-century fort defended the entrance to the harbor in bygone days. From inside you can look out at sweeping ocean views. For an interesting perspective on the rock formations and grottoes of the area's shoreline, take one of the short boat trips offered by the fishermen near the Ponta da Bandeira. Check departure times on the quayside boards. ⊠ *Av. dos Descobrimentos* ☎ *282/761410* €3.

Fodor's Choice ★ **Igreja de Santo António.** This early-18th-century baroque building is Lagos's most extraordinary structure. Its interior is a riot of gilt extravagance made possible by the import of gold from Brazil. Dozens of cherubs and angels clamber over the walls, among fancifully carved woodwork and azulejos. ⊠ *Entrance via Museu Regional, Rua General Alberto Silveira* ☎ *282/762301* €3, *includes entry to Museu Municipal Dr. José Formosinho* ☉ *Closed Mon.*

Castelo dos
Governadores **2**

Forte Ponta
da Bandeira **5**

Igreja de
Santo
António **4**

Mercado de
Escravos **1**

Monte da
Casteleja **6**

Museu
Municipal Dr. José
Formosinho **3**

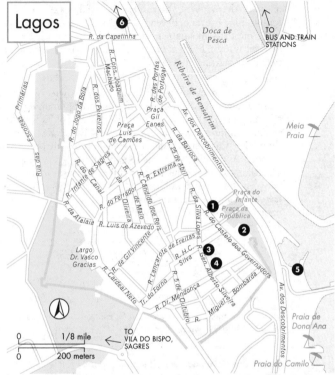

Mercado de Escravos (*Slave Market*). Prince Henry the Navigator brought the first African slaves to Portugal for his personal use in 1441. He later established a slave market in West Africa to cope with increasingly large and barbaric slave auctions; by 1455 around 800 slaves were transported to Portugal each year. The first African slave market in Europe was held under the arches of the old Casa da Alfândega. The building now contains a museum that looks at the history of slavery in the Algarve. ⊠ *Praça do Infante Dom Henrique* ⊕ *www.cm-lagos. pt* ⊠ *€4* ⊗ *Closed Mon.*

Fodor's Choice **Monte da Casteleja.** The motto at this family-run winery—one of the only
★ Algarvian vineyards to produce organic wines—is "think global, drink local." Guided tours and wine-tasting sessions are available by appointment. ⊠ *Monte da Casteleja* ☎ *282/798408* ⊕ *www.montecasteleja. com* ⊠ *€12.50 guided tour with wine tasting, €7.50 wine tasting only* ⊗ *Closed weekends.*

Museu Municipal Dr. José Formosinho. This small regional museum has an amusing jumble of exhibits, including mosaics, archaeological and ethnological items, and a town charter from 1504—all arranged haphazardly. ⊠ *Rua General Alberto Silveira* ☎ *282/762301* ⊠ *€3, includes entry to Igreja de Santo António* ⊗ *Closed Mon.*

BEACHES

Meia Praia. Curving like a crescent moon the entire distance between Lagos and Alvor, Meia Praia is the largest beach near town and one of the best centers for water sports. The golden sand extends for 4 km (2½ miles), and the water is calm and clear. You can walk to it from Lagos city center in less than five minutes by crossing the footbridge; however, if you want to go farther along, you can take a bus from the riverfront Avenida dos Descobrimentos, and in summer there's a ferry service a few hundred yards from Forte Ponta da Bandeira. As this is such a long beach you can normally find a spot to comfortably lay your towel. Certain portions are popular with nudists. **Amenities:** food and drink; lifeguards; parking (no fee); showers. **Best for:** nudists; solitude; swimming; walking; windsurfing. ✉ *2 km (1 mile) east of Lagos city center, off M534.*

Fodor's Choice ★ **Praia de Dona Ana.** This beautiful beach has calm, turquoise waters that are perfect for snorkeling, and cave-riddled cliffs that can be visited on boat tours. You can reach Praia de Dona Ana by car or on an enjoyable 30-minute walk along a clifftop. If you hoof it, pass the fort, turn left at the fire station, and follow the footpaths, which go to the most southerly point. As Praia Dona Ana is a small beach it can get packed, especially when the tide comes in and the sand disappears. Parking is difficult and the steep steps down to the sand can be trying, but it's worth the effort to visit what has been voted one of the most beautiful beaches in the world. **Amenities:** food and drink; lifeguards. **Best for:** snorkeling. ✉ *Between Lagos's eastern lighthouse and Ponta da Piedade, 1 km (½ mile) south of Lagos city center.*

Fodor's Choice ★ **Praia do Camilo.** They say the best things come in small packages, and that's certainly the case here. A short way beyond Praia de Dona Ana, little Praia do Camilo is a hugely popular cove beach. Just beyond it is the Ponta da Piedade, a much-photographed group of rock arches and grottoes. Praia do Camilo is accessed via a long, wooden walkway through picturesque cliffs. At the top of the cliff restaurant O Camilo offers stunning views over the beach. **Amenities:** none. **Best for:** snorkeling. ✉ *To the right of Praia Dona Ana, 1 km (½ mile) south of Lagos city center.*

WHERE TO EAT

$$$ PORTUGUESE 🍴 **MAR — Restaurante & Bar.** In a great location just outside town and overlooking the dramatic Praia da Batata and the Lagos bay, the MAR serves good, modest fare. At tables inside or out you'll find a variety of fresh fish available, along with pasta, meat dishes, and salads. What's more, there's a small public parking area just yards away—a rarity in this busy town. [$] *Average main: €22* ✉ *Av. Descobrimentos* ☎ *282/788006.*

$$ ECLECTIC 🍴 **No Patio.** This cheerful restaurant with an inner patio features menus that incorporate premium local produce, and only the freshest ingredients are used to create interesting dishes with international flair. Eating here is best described as alfresco dining at its finest. In addition to creative fish dishes, standouts include modern takes on lamb and duck. In winter, No Patio has a beautiful open log fire to add warmth and romance. [$] *Average main: €17* ✉ *Rua Lançarote de Freitas 46 r/c*

☎ 282/763777, 912/582636 ⊘ *Closed Sun. and Mon., and last 3 wks of Nov., last wk of Jan., and 1st wk of Feb. No lunch* ⚹ *Reservations essential.*

$$
SEAFOOD
Fodor'sChoice
★

✕ **O Camilo.** For fresh fish by the beach in a modern and trendy setting, you can't do much better than this smart restaurant above beautiful Praia do Camilo. The black-and-white drawings of fish on the dining-room walls tell you all you need to know: any of the daily fish dishes are a good bet. Along with fish, fresh oysters from Ria de Alvor, clams, and slipper lobsters are usually on offer, all local and simply prepared, or you can order the tasty fish cataplana a day ahead. Book a table, especially if you want to sit outdoors on the patio, or be prepared to wait. $ *Average main: €20* ⊠ *Praia do Camilo, Estrada da Ponta da Piedade* ☎ 282/763845 ⊕ *restaurantecamilo.pt* ⊘ *Closed 2 wks in Nov.*

$
PORTUGUESE

✕ **Restaurante Piri-Piri.** On one of the main streets this small, low-key restaurant—done in understated pastels—has an inexpensive but extensive menu. The long list of Portuguese dishes includes a variety of market-fresh fish, but the specialty is the zesty piri-piri chicken that gives the restaurant its name. $ *Average main: €13* ⊠ *Rua Lima Leitão 15* ☎ 282/763803 ⊘ *Closed Sat. in Nov. and Mar.*

WHERE TO STAY

$
B&B/INN
Fodor'sChoice
★

🛏 **Casa da Moura.** It's a little hard to find at first, and you must phone before arriving because the door is locked; but once inside, Casa da Moura feels like your own private retreat. **Pros:** short walk to the beach; loads of character; great breakfast. **Cons:** parking in front of the hotel not always available; reception desk unmanned on occasion; very hard beds. $ *Rooms from: €125* ⊠ *Rua Cardeal Neto 10* ☎ 964/529917 ⇆ *8 apartments* ⦿| *Breakfast.*

$
B&B/INN

🛏 **Surf Experience.** This spacious, central house is open to all who have an interest in surfing, regardless of age. **Pros:** free Wi-Fi; digital entertainment system; cooking facilities. **Cons:** geared for the surf crowd; three-night minimum stay; some rooms have shared baths. $ *Rooms from: €75* ⊠ *Rua dos Ferreiros 21* ☎ 282/086012, 919/830591, 916/137082 ⊕ *www.surf-experience.com* ⇆ *8 rooms, 4 with bath* ⦿| *Breakfast.*

$
HOTEL

🛏 **Tivoli Lagos.** At the eastern edge of the old town, this well-located hotel has an unusual design: it's strung across several levels with gardens, lounges, and patios. **Pros:** centrally located; free beach shuttle; nice pool areas. **Cons:** rooms and public areas in need of a refresh; no tea or coffee facilities in rooms; not always enough sunbeds for guests on beach. $ *Rooms from: €139* ⊠ *Rua António Crisógno dos Santos* ☎ 282/790079 ⊕ *www.tivolihotels.com* ⇆ *324 rooms* ⦿| *Breakfast.*

NIGHTLIFE

Bon Vivant. There are a number of bars at the end of Rua 25 de Abril, most playing music that's brutally loud. Perhaps the most refined of these is Bon Vivant, which has four distinct bar areas and a rooftop terrace way above the din. ⊠ *Rua 25 de Abril 105* ☎ 282/761019.

Fodor'sChoice
★

Mullens. At this excellent bar, the enthusiastic staff help keep things swinging until 2 am; full meals are served, too. ⊠ *Rua Cândido dos Reis 86* ☎ 282/761281, 918/480071 ⊕ *www.mullens-lagos.com.*

Stevie Ray's. Classy Stevie Ray's features a live music lounge dedicated to blues, jazz, Latino, soul, and international music. You can listen while quaffing imported beers and Champagne. ✉ *Rua Senhora da Graça 9* ☎ *914/923885* ☾ *Closed Sun. and Mon.*

SPORTS AND THE OUTDOORS

BOAT TOURS

Seafaris. Dolphin-watching boat tours depart daily from the Lagos Marina. Visitors can also enjoy a fishing trip or motor in to one of the many caves formed by waves crashing into the Algarve's scenic seaside cliffs. Sailing charters, deep-sea fishing excursions, and water-taxi service to Alvor can be arranged as well. ✉ *Loja 5, Marina de Lagos* ☎ *282/798727* ⊕ *www.seafaris.net.*

PRAIA DA LUZ

6 km (4 miles) west of Lagos.

There was formerly an active fishing fleet here, and a favorite pastime was to watch the boats being hauled onto the broad, sandy beach that lends the community its name. Although the boats are gone, this is still an agreeable destination—despite the development that has hit it. At the western edge of town a little church faces an 18th-century fortress that once guarded against pirates and is now a restaurant. Many of the accommodations available in Luz are in private villas and apartments; the tourist office in Lagos may be able to advise you about them.

6

GETTING HERE AND AROUND

Praia da Luz is less than an hour from the Faro airport by car, and driving is the easiest way to get around town. A regular bus service runs from Faro, stopping right outside the picturesque, seaside church. You can also take the train to Lagos, and then catch a taxi or bus to Praia da Luz.

ESSENTIALS

Bus Contacts Bus. ✉ *Terminal Rodoviário de Lagos* ☎ *282/762944.*

Taxi Contacts Taxi. ✉ *Lagos Taxi* ☎ *282/763587.*

BEACHES

Burgau. Four kilometers (2½ miles) west of Praia da Luz is Burgau, a fishing village with narrow, steep streets leading to it. Although the town has partly succumbed to the wave of tourism that has swept over the Algarve, its fine beach remains unchanged. High, sloping hills encase the beach, protecting it from the northern winds. **Amenities:** food and drink; parking (fee and no fee). **Best for:** snorkeling. ✉ *4 km (2½ miles) west of Praia da Luz.*

Salema. This low-key little fishing village, 5 km (3 miles) west of Burgau, is blessed with a 1,970-foot-long beach at the base of green hills. The long, golden strand has cliffs at either end. This area is also popular among hikers for its vast range of hiking trails and breathtaking views. **Amenities:** food and drink; parking (no fee). **Best for:** swimming; walking. ✉ *Travessa do Miramar.*

WHERE TO EAT AND STAY

$$$ INTERNATIONAL
🍴 **Cabanas Beach Restaurant.** If you take the rough road west from Burgau, and then an even rougher one down to the Praia Almadena, you'll be rewarded with this delightful hideaway on a deserted cove. Specialties include the expected seafood and interesting sharing plates. There's live music many nights of the week to accompany your meal. Kids are welcome, too, with a small play area to keep them busy. [$] *Average main: €22* ✉ *Praia Almadena* ☎ *968/871974.*

$$ HOTEL
🏨 **Hotel Belavista da Luz.** This family-owned hilltop hotel's horseshoe configuration gives all the spacious guest quarters a great sea view. **Pros:** child-friendly; helpful service; walking distance to Luz town. **Cons:** no shuttle back from beach, so steep hillside walk; very hard beds; some find the area too quiet. [$] *Rooms from: €155* ✉ *Praia da Luz* ☎ *282/788655* 🌐 *www.belavistadaluz.com* 🛏 *45 rooms* 🍽 *Breakfast.*

$ RESORT
🏨 **Quinta do Mar da Luz.** Set within verdant gardens complete with sculptures, this holiday village west of Praia da Luz offers a calm, peaceful ambience that will soothe the soul. **Pros:** spectacular views along the walk to Burgau; three pools, one for children only; well-stocked breakfast buffet. **Cons:** no restaurant; car necessary to reach Lagos; charge for extra bed for child. [$] *Rooms from: €130* ✉ *Sítio Cama da Vaca* ☎ *282/697323* 🌐 *www.quintamarluz.com* 🛏 *20 rooms, 40 apartments* 🍽 *Breakfast.*

SPORTS AND THE OUTDOORS

DIVING

Blue Ocean Divers. Lessons with PADI-certified scuba instructors, wreck dives, and night dives are available at Blue Ocean Divers. ✉ *Motel Ancora, Estrada de Porto de Mós* ☎ *964/665667* 🌐 *www.blue-ocean-divers.de.*

SAGRES

30 km (18 miles) southwest of Praia da Luz; 3 km (2 miles) southeast of Cabo São Vicente.

Fodor's Choice ★
In the 19th century, this village, amid harsh, barren moorland, was rebuilt over earthquake ruins. Architecturally, there's little of note today apart from a fort. But Sagres does have several golden beaches, and the water at this end of the Algarve is rather more refreshing than at the opposite end—even in the height of summer.

GETTING HERE AND AROUND

Buses are infrequent, so renting a car is recommended for those wishing to travel to the Algarve's westernmost tip. Driving to Sagres takes approximately 1 hour 15 minutes from Portimão and a little over two hours from Faro.

ESSENTIALS

Visitor Information Sagres. ✉ *Rua Comandante Matoso* ☎ *282/624873* 🌐 *www.visitalgarve.pt.*

EXPLORING

FAMILY **Fortaleza de Sagres.** Views from the Sagres Fortress, an enormous run of defensive walls high above the crashing waves, are spectacular. Its massive walls and battlements make it popular with kids. The importance of this area dates to as early as the 4th century BC, when Mediterranean seafarers found it to be the last sheltered port before the wild winds of the Atlantic. In the late 8th century, according to local religious tradition, the mortal remains of the 4th-century martyr of Zaragoza, St. Vincent, washed up here. This led to a Vincentine cult that attracted pilgrims until the destruction of the sanctuary in the mid-12th century. The fortress was rebuilt in the 17th century, and although some historians have claimed that it was the site for Prince Henry's famous navigation school, it's more likely that Henry built his school at Cabo São Vicente. But this doesn't detract from the powerful atmosphere. Certainly the **Venta da Rosa** (Wind Compass, or compass rose) dates to Prince Henry's period. Uncovered only in the 20th century, this large circular construction made of stone and packed earth is in the courtyard just inside the fortress. The simple Graça Chapel is of the same age. ⊠ *Sagres.*

Exhibition Center. A stark, modern building within the fort houses an exhibition center, with revolving exhibits documenting the region's history, flora, fauna, and nautical themes. The tunnel-like entrance to the fortress is about a 15-minute walk from the village; three buses a day run this way on weekdays. ⊠ *Sagres* ☎ *282/620140* 💶 *€3.*

BEACHES

Praia da Baleeira. This small, pretty beach is next to the Baleeira fishing port. Dotted with rocks and rather pebbly, the sand is not the finest; moreover, the beach can get quite windy, meaning this is not the most popular beach for sunbathers. Yet it is the perfect spot to sit and watch the fishing boats sailing in and out of the port. **Amenities:** none. **Best for:** solitude; sunset. ⊠ *Adjacent to the port, ½ km (0.3 mile) east of Sagres.*

Praia do Martinhal. This long, soft stretch of sand runs between the lovely Martinhal Beach Resort & Hotel and the Baleeira fishing harbor. Several professional surfing events are held here, and good wave formations make it very popular among local surf enthusiasts. **Amenities:** lifeguards; parking (no fee). **Best for** : sunrise; sunset; surfing; windsurfing. ⊠ *1 km (0.6 mile) east of Sagres.*

WHERE TO EAT AND STAY

$$ ✕ **O Retiro do Pescador.** This outdoor grill is an incredibly good value and serves a range of meats as well as the most flavorful fresh fish in Sagres. The homemade brandy is worth a try, as are the typical regional desserts prepared by the owner's family. $ *Average main: €20* ⊠ *Vale das Silvas* ☎ *282/624438* ⊕ *www.retiro-do-pescador.com* ⊗ *Closed Mon., and late Oct.–early Mar.*

PORTUGUESE

$$ ✕ **Vila Velha.** Traditional Portuguese cuisine is given a twist of healthy, organic flavor here, and dishes include a range of international vegetarian options. From the terrace grill you can watch the sunset over Cabo São Vicente (Cape St. Vincent). Because this restaurant is so popular with local expats, advance booking is recommended. $ *Average main:*

PORTUGUESE

€20 ✉ *On headland between fishing harbor and Praia da Mareta, Rua Patrão Antonio Faustino* ☎ *282/624788, 917/128402* ⊕ *www. vilavelha-sagres.com* ⊘ *Closed Mon., 2 wks before Christmas, and early Jan.–mid-Feb. No lunch.*

$$$$
RESORT
FAMILY
Fodor's Choice
★

Martinhal Sagres Beach Family Resort Hotel. Martinhal offers up-to-date luxury lodgings in a family-friendly environment with access to a lovely beach. **Pros:** beachside location; along with several types of hotel rooms, family villas are available; excellent facilities for children, babies through teens. **Cons:** not ideal for couples without children; the many hills and cobbled walkways may be difficult for strollers or older guests; expensive prices in the on-site supermarket. Ⓢ *Rooms from: €355* ✉ *Quinta do Martinhal, Apartado 54* ☎ *282/240200* ⊕ *www. martinhal.com* 🛏 *238 rooms* ⦿ *Breakfast.*

$$$
B&B/INN

Pousada Sagres. Occupying a two-story country house across the bay from the Fortaleza de Sagres, Pousada Sagres promises glorious views of the sea and craggy cliffs. **Pros:** loads of atmosphere and charm; pretty pool; good-value three-course dinner menu. **Cons:** not as small or intimate as other pousadas; make sure to ask for a room with panoramic views; some rooms are a bit worn. Ⓢ *Rooms from: €210* ✉ *Ponta da Atalaia, on headland between fishing harbor and Praia da Mareta* ☎ *282/620240* ⊕ *www.pousadas.pt* 🛏 *51 rooms* ⦿ *Breakfast.*

SPORTS AND THE OUTDOORS

The best fishing in Sagres is in winter when seas are rough; *sargo* (big bream bass) and *dourada* (mahimahi) are the main catches. Smaller bream, mullet, mackerel, and bass can be caught during the more settled summer months. **Baleeira** is a small fishing port of Sagres, which houses up to 100 fishing boats, some more than 65 feet in length. You can hire a local fisherman to take you out on a three-hour fishing trip from Salema to Sagres and back, with possible swimming stops at lonely beaches along the way.

CABO SÃO VICENTE

6 km (4 miles) northwest of Sagres; 95 km (59 miles) west of Faro; 30 km (18 miles) southwest of Lagos.

At the southwest tip of Europe, where the land juts starkly into the rough Atlantic, is Cabo São Vicente, called O Fim do Mundo (The End of the World) by early Portuguese mariners. Legends attach themselves easily to this desolate place, which the Romans once considered sacred (they believed it was where the spirits of the light lived because with sunset the light disappeared). It takes its modern name from the martyr St. Vincent, whose relics were brought here in the 8th century; it's said that they were transported to Lisbon 400 years later in a boat guided by ravens. This is not the crowded, overdeveloped Algarve of the south coast. From here you can see the spectacular cliff tops at Murração looking onto seemingly endless deserted beaches. Vast flocks of migratory birds round Cape St. Vincent and the Sagres headlands each year with a navigational precision that would have astounded Columbus. He learned how to navigate at Prince Henry's school after the armed convoy he was traveling with was attacked by pirates off

Cape St. Vincent in 1476. Sixteen years later he set sail from here to discover the Americas.

GETTING HERE AND AROUND

Lack of adequate public transportation means renting a car is the best, if not only, option.

EXPLORING

Fodor'sChoice **Farol de São Vicente** (*St. Vincent Lighthouse*). The keeper of the isolated
★ Farol de São Vicente opens it to visitors at his discretion. That said, views from outside the lighthouse are remarkable, and the beacon is said to have the strongest reflectors in Europe—they cast a beam 96 km (60 miles) out to sea. Turquoise water whips across the base of the rust-color cliffs below, the fortress at Sagres is visible to the east, and in the distance lies the immense Atlantic. There's a small museum and café on-site if you want to linger. ⊠ *Cabo São Vicente.*

VILA DO BISPO

10 km (6 miles) north of Cabo São Vicente.

For a break from the resort buzz, head to this small, quiet town at the crossroads between the west and south coastal roads. The interior of Vila do Bispo's parish church is covered with 18th-century azulejos (to see it, come on a Sunday morning; the church is open only for services at 11:30). What really draws people here, however, is that Vila do Bispo makes a logical base for exploring the Parque Natural Sudoeste Alentejano e Costa Vincentina—a less traveled region of designated parkland that contains some of the Algarve's wildest beaches and draws surfers from all over the world.

GETTING HERE AND AROUND

Like its neighbor to the south, Cabo São Vicente, Vila do Bispo does not have regular public transport; hence a car is required.

BEACHES

Praia do Amado. At almost 13 km (8 miles) in length, Portugal's best surfing beach has enough room for the dozens of surfing camps and schools that have sprung up around it. The water is cool and rocky towards the western tip. The area surrounding the beach is popular for wild camping, but lacks basic facilities (like garbage cans), so sometimes waste is scattered around, spoiling an otherwise beautiful beach. **Amenities:** parking (no fee). **Best for:** surfing, windsurfing. ⊠ *Parque Natural do Sudoeste Alentejano e Costa Vicentina, 6 km (3 miles) from Vila do Bispo.*

WHERE TO EAT

$$$ ✕**A Eira do Mel.** This restaurant excels at mixing local recipes and pro-
ECLECTIC duce with sophisticated international cuisine. The flavors and artful presentation attract a youthful, vibrant crowd of regulars. Ⓢ *Average main: €25 ⊠ Estrada do Castelejo, Mercado Municipal* ☎ *282/639016* ⊘ *Closed Sun. and Mon.*

$ ✕**Café Correia.** Stuffed squid, rabbit cooked with beer and onion
PORTUGUESE sauce, and other Costa Vicentina specialties are favorites at this rustic family-run restaurant in the inland town of Vila do Bispo. The wine

list, presented in a well-worn ledger, contains 180 varieties. $ *Average main: €14* ⊠ *Rua Primeiro de Maio 4* ☎ *282/639127* ⊟ *No credit cards* ⊘ *Closed Sat.*

$$$ ╳ **O Sitio do Forno.** This simple restaurant with gorgeous views overlook-
PORTUGUESE   ing the cliffs is run by a fishing family who catch the menu early in the
morning and cook it without any frills. Charcoal-grilled tiger prawns,
shrimp, *perceves* (gooseneck barnacles), mussels, haddock, and sole
are served with lemon, garlic, or coriander. Bread, local sausage (*chou-
riço*), and potatoes in olive oil, and olives complement the fish. Local
fishermen mingle with curious travelers, lending the place an authentic
atmosphere. $ *Average main: €25* ⊠ *Praia do Amado, Carrapateira*
☎ *282/973914* ⊘ *Closed Mon.*

COIMBRA AND THE BEIRAS

Updated by
Josephine
Quintero

While frequently sidestepped by tourists, this region is arguably the most unspoiled and quintessentially Portuguese part of the country. Even the coastal resorts have, as a whole, retained their intrinsic local character and charm. The Beiras is a diverse area with an abundance of beaches, lagoons, and mountains. The natural beauty of the scenery also serves as a fitting gateway to the drama of the Douro and the Minho farther north.

To the east, Portugal's highest mountains—the Serra da Estrela—rise to nearly 6,600 feet, creating a colorful patchwork of alpine meadows, haunting forests, and wooded hills. High in this range's granite reaches, a clear icy stream begins its tortuous journey to the sea: this is the Rio Mondego, the lifeblood of the Beiras. Praised in song and poetry, it is the longest river within the country and provides vital irrigation to fruit orchards and farms as it flows through the region's heart.

Coimbra—the country's first capital and home to one of Europe's earliest universities—offers an urban counterpoint. A large student population ensures that the city stays lively; however, the past lingers on in the evocative old quarter, its medieval backstreets unchanged for centuries. The university rises magnificently above the river which continues, closer to the sea, under the imposing walls of Montemor Castle. The *rio* (river) then widens to nurture rice fields before merging with the Atlantic at the popular beach resort of Figueira da Foz. Archaeology buffs will also appreciate the region's extraordinary Roman ruins—particularly at Conímbriga, Portugal's largest excavated site.

ORIENTATION AND PLANNING

GETTING ORIENTED

The Beiras region encompasses the provinces of the Beira Litoral (Coastal Beira), the Beira Baixa (Lower Beira), and the Beira Alta (Upper Beira). In total this area covers one-fourth of Portugal's landmass.

The onetime medieval capital and largest city in the region, Coimbra (pronounced "*queembra*"), is a good place to start your exploration. To the west of the city are the seaside resort of Figueira da Foz and the canals and lagoons in and around the delightful old port of Aveiro. Farther inland is the must-see city of Viseu, with its wonderful parks and historic old quarter. The mountain resort of Caramulo and the belle epoque towns of Luso and Curia are some of the country's most popular spas. The region's eastern area includes the Serra da Estrela (Portugal's highest mountains), the renowned Dão wine region, and a chain of ancient fortified towns along the Spanish border.

A BIT OF HISTORY

This region has played an important role in Portugal's development. The Romans built roads, established settlements, and in 27 BC incorporated into their vast empire the remote province known as Lusitania, which encompassed most of what is now central Portugal, including the Beiras. They left many traces of their presence: for proof, witness the well-preserved ruins at Conímbriga, near Coimbra. The Moors swept through the territory in the early 8th century and dominated the region for several hundred years. Many of the elaborate castles and extensive fortifications here show a strong Moorish influence. The towns along the Spanish frontier have been the scene of many fierce battles—from those during the Wars of Christian Reconquest to those during the fledgling Portuguese nation's struggle against invaders from neighboring Castile.

The Beiras also played a part in Portugal's golden Age of Discovery. In 1500 Pedro Álvares Cabral, a nobleman from the town of Belmonte on the eastern flank of the Serra da Estrela, led the first expedition to what is now Brazil. Much of the wealth garnered during this period, when tiny Portugal controlled so much of the world's trade, financed the great architectural and artistic achievements of the Portuguese Renaissance. Throughout the region there are fine examples of the Manueline style, a uniquely Portuguese art form that reflects the nation's nautical heritage. The cathedrals at Guarda and Viseu, the Igreja e Mosteiro de Santa Cruz (Church and Monastery of Santa Cruz) in Coimbra, and the Convento de Jesus (Convent of Jesus) in Aveiro are especially noteworthy.

During the 19th-century Peninsular War, between Napoléon's armies and Wellington's British and Portuguese forces, a decisive battle was fought in the tranquil forest of Buçaco. Later in the same century, this area witnessed a much more peaceful invasion, as people from all corners of Europe came to take the waters at such well-known spas as Luso, Curia, and Caramulo. Around the turn of the 20th century, when the now tourist-packed Algarve was merely a remote backwater, Figueira da Foz was coming into its own as an international beach resort.

Coimbra. Between Lisbon and Porto, the crowning glory of the Beira Litoral, Coimbra is one of Portugal's most intriguing cities, exuding the vibrancy of a student town combined with an evocative sense of history.

The Western Beiras. The coastal region is remarkably unspoiled, with miles of golden sand backed by dunes and forests of pine trees and centered around the only sizable resort: Figueira da Foz.

The Eastern Beiras. The more mountainous eastern region is home to some of the Portugal's most spectacular scenery and is the historic heart of the country, with ancient towns like Viseu, Guarda, and Trancosa set among mountain peaks and verdant valleys.

TOP REASONS TO GO

Foot-tap to the fado. Discover the delights of Coimbra's distinctive style of fado at one of the city's atmospheric fado houses.

Get away from it all. Head for the peaceful beauty of the Buçaco forest, the country's most revered woods and a monastic retreat during the Middle Ages.

Step back in time. Explore ancient mosaics, baths, an aqueduct, and more at Conímbriga, Portugal's finest Roman site.

Enjoy sand between your toes. Take a sunset walk along Figueira's wide 2-km-long (1-mile-long) long sandy beach or grab your surfboard and tackle the waves.

Lace up those hiking boots. Stride out and discover the vast Parque Natural da Sierra da Estrela, with its extensive, well-marked trails and stunning scenery.

PLANNING

WHEN TO GO

Although the Beiras's coastal beaches are popular in summer, the crowds are nothing like those in the Algarve. The water along this shore isn't as warm as it is farther south; as a result, the season is considerably shorter. Plan your beach time here between mid-June and mid-September.

With the exception of the eastern regions, the interior is also considerably cooler than that of the Alentejo or the Algarve, so it's well suited for summertime touring. Aside from occasional showers, the weather is comfortable from early April to mid-November. Winters, especially in the eastern mountain towns, are harsh.

PLANNING YOUR TIME

A week is enough time to experience Coimbra, visit a spa and the coast, and explore the Serra da Estrela. If you have just three days, you can visit Coimbra and the coast, or head straight inland to the mountains. But don't let the distances fool you into being overambitious: mountain roads may not be long, but they take a lot of time to drive.

GETTING HERE AND AROUND

AIR TRAVEL

Coimbra is 197 km (123 miles) north of Lisbon and 116 km (72 miles) south of Porto. Both cities are connected to Coimbra via the A1 (E80) highway. Intercontinental flights usually arrive in Lisbon, but Porto has an increasing number of European connections, including ones operated by several budget airlines.

BUS TRAVEL

Buses of various vintages can take you to almost any destination within the region, and bus depots—unlike train stations, which are often some distance from the town center—are central. Although this is a great way to travel and get close to the local people, it requires considerable time and patience. However, "countdown clocks," introduced at city-center bus stops to specify how long the wait is, do help.

Regional and local bus schedules are posted at terminals, and you can also get information at local tourist offices or online. Rede Expressos provides comfortable bus service between Lisbon, Porto, and Coimbra, and to other parts of the Beiras. International as well as regional services are available at the Rodoviário da Beira Litoral bus station in Coimbra and at the Rodoviário da Beira Interior stations in Castelo Branco and Covilhã.

Bus Contacts Rede Expressos. ⊠ *Av. Fernão de Magalhães, Coimbra* ☎ *239/855270, 707/223344* ⊕ *www.rede-expressos.pt.* **Rodoviário da Beira Interior.** ⊠ *Rua Poe João Roiz, Castelo Branco* ☎ *272/340120* ⊕ *www.rede-expressos.pt* ⊠ *Central de Camionagem, Covilhã* ☎ *275/334914* ⊕ *www.rede-expressos.pt.* **Rodoviário da Beira Litoral.** ⊠ *Av. Fernão de Magalhães, Coimbra* ☎ *275/336700.*

CAR TRAVEL

The Beiras, with their many remote villages, are suited to exploration by car. Distances between major points are short; there are no intimidating cities to negotiate; and except for the coastal strip in July and August, traffic is light. Roads in general are good and destinations well marked; however, parking is a problem in the larger towns.

Allow plenty of time for journeys the moment you are off the main highways. Many of the mountain roads are switchbacks that need to be treated with extreme caution. In addition, you are almost certain to get lost with appalling signposting (usually hidden around the corner or behind a tree) and nightmarish one-way mazes in every town, from the smallest hamlet to the largest city. If you get to your destination without going around the whole town three times, consider yourself lucky. Even the locals admit to getting lost on a regular basis.

Drive defensively at all times; Portugal has one of Europe's highest traffic fatality rates. Among the worst roads in the country for accidents is the IP5 heading inland from Aveiro to the Serra de Estrela.

TRAIN TRAVEL

Although the major destinations in the Beiras are linked by rail, service to most towns, with the exception of Coimbra, is infrequent. Using Coimbra as a hub, there are three main rail lines in the region. Line 110, the Beira Alta line, goes northeast to Luso, Viseu, Celorico da Beira, and Guarda. Line 100 extends south through the Ribatejo to intersect with Line 130, the Beira Baixa line, which runs from Lisbon northeast through Castelo Branco and Fundão to Covilhã, the gateway to the Serra da Estrela. Going north from Coimbra, Line 100 serves Curia, Aveiro, and Ovar and continues north to Porto and Braga.

Coimbra, Luso, Guarda, Ovar, and Aveiro are on the main Lisbon–Porto and Lisbon–Paris lines. Two trains arrive from and depart for Paris daily, and in summer a daily car-train operates between Paris and Lisbon. There are also regular trains linking the principal cities in the Beiras with Madrid, Lisbon, and Porto. Somewhat confusingly, there are two train stations in Coimbra: Coimbra A (Estação Nova), for local routes, is located along the Mondego River, a five-minute walk from the center of town, while Coimbra B (Estação Velha), is located a considerable 5 km (3 miles) west. International trains and trains from

Lisbon and Porto arrive at Coimbra B, where there's a free shuttle to Coimbra A. There are also bus links between stations. Schedules for all trains are posted at both stations.

Train Contact CP (Comboios de Portugal). ☎ 808/208208 ⊕ www.cp.pt.

RESTAURANTS

With the exception of some luxury hotel dining rooms, restaurants are casual in dress and atmosphere, although a bit less casual than in the southern parts of the country. The emphasis is generally more on the food than on the trappings.

At almost any of the ubiquitous beach bar–restaurants, you can't go wrong by ordering the *peixe do dia* (fish of the day). In most cases it will have been caught only hours before and will be prepared outside on a charcoal grill. You'll usually be served the whole fish along with boiled potatoes and a simple salad. Wash it down with a chilled white Dão wine, and you have a tasty, healthful, relatively inexpensive meal. In Figueira da Foz and in the Aveiro region, *enguias* (eels), *lampreia* (lamprey), and *caldeirada* (a fish stew that's a distant cousin of the French bouillabaisse) are popular.

The inland Bairrada region, between Coimbra and Aveiro, is well known for *leitão assado* (roast suckling pig). In Coimbra the dish to try is *chanfana*; this is traditionally made with tender young kid braised in red wine and roasted in an earthenware casserole. In the mountains, fresh *truta* (trout) panfried with bacon and onions is often served, as is *javali* (wild boar). *Bacalhau* (dried salted cod) in one form or another appears on just about every menu in the region. Bacalhau *à brás* (fried in olive oil with eggs, onions, and potatoes) is one of many popular versions of this dish.

The Beiras contain two of Portugal's most notable wine districts: Bairrada and Dão. The reds from these districts generally benefit from a fairly long stay in the bottle. The flowery whites from around here should be drunk much younger. Bairrada is also well-known for its superb sparkling wines. *Prices in the reviews are the average cost of a main course at dinner or, if dinner isn't served, at lunch.*

HOTELS

There are plenty of high-quality accommodations in the western reaches of the Beiras, but the options thin the farther inland you move; make reservations in advance if you plan to travel during the busy summer months. That said, the Beiras has a great variety of lodging choices, ranging from venerable old luxury hotels to gleaming, modern hostelries. The *pousadas* (inns that are members of the Turismo de Habitação organization) here make perfect bases for exploring the entire region. In addition, there are Solares de Portugal lodgings, which are family-owned and -run and can range from mansions to cottages. Most establishments offer substantial off-season discounts. (High season varies by hotel but generally runs July 1–September 15.) *Prices in the reviews are the lowest cost of a standard double room in high season. For expanded hotel reviews, visit www.Fodors.com.*

GREAT ITINERARIES

You can cover Coimbra and the coast in three days. Alternatively, you can veer inland and drive directly to the mountains—just don't underestimate the amount of time it will take to negotiate those winding mountain roads.

IF YOU HAVE 3 DAYS

Spend your first morning in **Coimbra**, with a stroll through the Cidade Velha (Old Town) and the university. In the afternoon visit the Roman ruins at **Conímbriga**. The next day, follow the Rio Mondego to the beach resort of **Figueira da Foz**, head up the coast, and move inland to visit the china factory in **Vista Alegre**. Use the rest of the day and evening to explore **Aveiro**, the famous Ria de Aveiro, and the delightful little coastal villages along the sand spit, such as Costa Nova, south of Aveiro.

WHAT IT COSTS IN EUROS				
	$	**$$**	**$$$**	**$$$$**
Restaurants	under €16	€16–€20	€21–€25	over €25
Hotels	under €141	€141–€200	€201–€260	over €260

Restaurant prices are per person for a main course at dinner. Hotel prices are for a standard double room, including tax, in high season (off-season rates may be lower).

VISITOR INFORMATION

A few companies lead walking tours and organize activities in the mountains, but otherwise the only regularly scheduled guided tours of the Beiras originate either in Lisbon or in Porto.

COIMBRA

197 km (123 miles) northeast of Lisbon.

Coimbra is a fascinating city that combines a tangible sense of history with all of the vibrancy and street life typically associated with a university town. The former is evident in the picturesque medieval quarters, where winding cobblestone streets are flanked by bars, boutiques, and eateries. As for the latter, students are easy to spot as they are traditionally garbed in black capes and carry briefcases adorned with colored ribbons denoting the university they attend. After final exams in May, they burn their ribbons with great exuberance in a ceremony called Queima das Fitas.

The city also has a more cosmopolitan, contemporary side. The riverfront Parque Dr. Manuel Braga is lined with lively clubs and restaurants, while modern shopping malls contrast with idiosyncratic family-owned shops. Providing the sound track for it all is Coimbra's lyrical brand of fado, which you can hear at traditional celebrations, dedicated fado houses, and other venues citywide.

A BIT MORE HISTORY (COIMBRA)

Since its emergence as the Roman settlement of Aeminium, this city on the banks of the Rio Mondego has played an influential and often crucial role in the country's development. In Roman times, it was an important way station, the midway point on the road connecting Lisbon with Braga to the north, and a rival of the city of Conímbriga, across the river to the south. But by the beginning of the 5th century the Roman administration was falling apart, and Aeminium fell under the dominance of Alans, Swabians, and Visigoths in turn. By the middle of the 7th century, under Visigoth rule, its importance was such that it had become the regional capital and center of the bishopric of Conímbriga. Upstart Aeminium had finally gained ascendancy over its rival Conímbriga.

The Moorish occupation of Coimbra is believed to have occurred around the year AD 714, and it heralded an era of economic development: for the next 300 years or so, Coimbra was a frontier post of Muslim culture. North of the city there are no traces of Moorish architecture, but Coimbra has retained fragments of its Muslim past—remains of old walls as well as a small gate, the Arco de Almedina, once an entrance to a medina—and the surrounding country is full of place-names of Moorish origin.

After a number of bloody attempts, the reconquest of Coimbra by Christian forces was finally achieved in 1064 by Ferdinand, king of León, and Coimbra went on to become the capital of a vast territory extending north to the Rio Douro and encompassing much of what are now the Beiras. The city was the birthplace and burial place of Portugal's first king, Dom Afonso Henriques, and was the point from which he launched the attacks against the Moors that were to end in the conquest of Lisbon and the birth of a nation. Coimbra was the capital of Portugal until the late 13th century, when the court was transferred to Lisbon.

The figure who has remained closest to the heart of the city was the Spanish-born wife of King Dinis, Isabel of Aragon. During her life, while her husband and son were away fighting wars, sometimes against each other, Isabel occupied herself with social works, battling prostitution, and fostering education and welfare schemes for Coimbra's young women. She helped found a convent, and had her own tomb placed in it. She bequeathed her jewels to the poor girls of Coimbra to provide them with wedding dowries. When she died on a peacemaking mission to Estremoz in 1336, her body was brought back to Coimbra, and almost immediately the late queen became the object of a local cult. Isabel was beatified in the 16th century, and then canonized in 1625 by Pope Urban VIII after it was determined that her body had remained undecayed in its tomb.

GETTING HERE AND AROUND

There are parking facilities on and around Avenida Fernão Magalhães. Look for the blue "P" sign. Rede Expressos has buses going to/from Lisbon (2½ hours) and Porto (1½ hours) daily, as well as smaller towns, including Braga (2½ hours). Trains also run frequently to/from Lisbon and Porto with similar durations. Local buses are operated by the Serviços Municipais de Transportes de Coimbra (SMTUC). Tickets are valid for one hour and include transfers to other routes. Tickets may be bought individually (€1) or in bundles of three (€2.90) and 10 (€8.50). They are available from ticket shop outlets, as well as automatic machines around town. Bus tickets also cover the *patufinhas* (electric minibuses running between Baixa and Alta Coimbra) and the Elevador do Mercado (an elevator which connects the Sé Nova area and the Municipal Market area).

TIMING

Allow at least two hours for the walk around the old town; double that if you are intending to visit the attractions along the way. If you want to continue across the bridge, you'll probably need a few more hours. The hill is very steep. For this reason, the mapped tour starts at the top of it and works down.

ESSENTIALS

Bus Contacts Coimbra Bus Station. ⊠ *Av. Fernão de Magalhães* ☎ *239/827081* ⊕ *www.rede-expressos.com.* **Serviços Municipais de Transportes de Coimbra** (*SMTUC*). ⊠ *Largo do Mercado* ☎ *239/801100* ⊕ *www.smtuc.pt.*

Train Contacts Coimbra A Train Station (*Estação Nova*). ⊠ *Largo da Ameias* ☎ *707/201280* ⊕ *www.cp.pt.* **Coimbra B Train Station** (*Estação Velha*). ⊠ *Rua do Padrão-Eiras* ☎ *707/201280* ⊕ *www.cp.pt.*

Visitor Information Coimbra tourist office. ⊠ *Praça da Republica* ☎ *939/010084* ⊕ *www.turismodecoimbra.pt.* **Região de Turismo do Centro.** ⊠ *Largo da Portagem* ☎ *239/488120* ⊕ *www.turismo-centro.pt.*

EXPLORING

TOP ATTRACTIONS

Convento de Santa Clara-a-Nova (*New Santa Clara Convent*). This convent on a hill was built in the 17th century to house the Poor Clair nuns who were forced by floods from their old convent. The remains of Queen Isabel were also moved here. The barracks-like exterior protects a sumptuous baroque church and noble cloisters that shouldn't be missed. Queen Isabel's silver shrine is behind the main altar in the church, installed there by Coimbra townspeople in 1696. The queen's original tomb—she ordered it for herself in 1330—stands in the lower choir at the other end of the church. Carved out of a single block of stone, the splendid Gothic sarcophagus is decorated with sculpted polychrome figures of Franciscan friars and nuns. An effigy of the queen dressed in her Poor Clair habit lies on top. During the Peninsular War, the French General Massena used the convent as a hospital for 300 troops wounded during the battle of Buçaco. The carefully hidden

Convento de
Santa
Clara-a-Nova **7**

Convento de
Santa
Clara-a-Velha **8**

Jardim
Botânico **10**

Museu da
Ciência **2**

Museu Machado
de Castro **4**

Pátio da
Inquisição **6**

Quinta das
Lágrimas **9**

Sé Nova ...,.....**3**

Sé Velha **5**

Universidade
Velha **1**

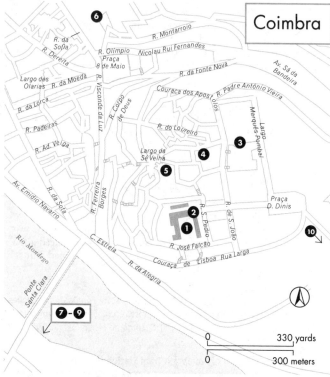

Coimbra

convent treasures escaped the desecration inflicted on so many Portuguese monuments during this period. ✉ *Rua Santa Isabel* ☎ *239/441674* 🖃 *Church €1, cloister €2, cloister and lower choir €3, guided tour (in English) €10* ⊘ *Closed weekends.*

Convento de Santa Clara-a-Velha (*Old Santa Clara Convent*). Restorers have been excavating the interior of this ruined Gothic church, which had been immersed by mud and silt for centuries, since 2000. Founded as a Poor Clair convent in the early 14th century by Queen Isabel, widow of King Dinis and patron saint of Coimbra, the building was beset by periodic flooding and was finally abandoned in 1677. Both the queen and Inês de Castro were originally interred here. Today the well-preserved convent can be visited together with the original chapter house, the refectory, and a cloister. A small museum provides audiovisual information about the convent's history. There is also a café and gift shop on-site. ✉ *Rua das Parreiras* ☎ *239/801160* 🖃 *€6 (free on Sun.)* ⊘ *Closed Mon.*

NEED A BREAK

Café Nicola. Why not succumb to the temptation of the pastry-filled windows of the cafés along the Rua Ferreira Borges? The Café Nicola is a good choice for sampling *arrufada,* Coimbra's most notable contribution to the world's great pastries. This curved confection is said to represent the Rio Mondego's tortuous course. ✉ *Rua Ferreira Borges 35, Baixa.*

FAMILY

Fodor's Choice

★

Museu da Ciência. This superb museum occupies a neoclassical edifice that served as a monastery and, more recently, held the university's chemical laboratory. It houses the most important science collection in Portugal and one of the most important in Europe. There are some 250,000 objects on display, and categories include botany, mineralogy, geology, paleontology, astronomy, and medicine with information provided in both English and Portuguese. There are plenty of family-friendly interactive displays and exhibits. ✉ *Largo Marquês de Pombal* ☎ *239/854350* ⊕ *www.museudaciencia.pt* 🎟 *€4* ⊘ *Closed Mon.*

Sé Nova (*New Cathedral*). The 17th-century Jesuit cathedral was patterned after the baroque church of Il Gesù in Rome, as were many such churches of the day. It took a century to build and shows two distinct styles as fashion changed from classical cleanliness to the florid baroque. The woodwork, from the gilded altarpiece to the blackwood choir stalls, moved across from the Sé Velha (Old Cathedral), are particularly worthwhile. There are a pair of organs, both dating to the 18th century. The church became the local cathedral in 1772, 13 years after the abolition of the Jesuit Order by the Marquis of Pombal. There's also a modest ecclesiastical museum. ✉ *Largo da Sé Nova* 🎟 *Church free, museum €1* ⊘ *Closed Mon.*

Sé Velha (*Old Cathedral*). Made of massive granite blocks and crowned by a ring of battlements, this 12th-century cathedral looks more like a fortress than a house of worship. (Engaged in an ongoing struggle with the Moors, the Portuguese—who were building and reconstructing castles for defense purposes throughout the country—often incorporated fortifications in their churches.) The harsh exterior is softened somewhat by graceful 16th-century Renaissance doorways. The somber interior has a gilded wooden altarpiece: a late-15th-century example of the Flamboyant Gothic style, created by the Flemish masters Olivier of Ghent and Jean d'Ypres. The walls of the Chapel of the Holy Sacrament are lined with touching, lifelike sculptures by Jean de Rouen, whose full-size Christ figure is flanked by finely detailed representations of the apostles and evangelists. The 13th-century cloisters (closed 1–2 pm) are distinguished by a well-executed series of transitional Gothic arches. ✉ *Largo da Sé Velha* ☎ *239/825273* 🎟 *€2* ⊘ *Closed Sun., except during Mass.*

Fodor's Choice

★

Universidade Velha (*Old University*). Coimbra University—one of the oldest academic institutions in Europe—was founded in Lisbon in 1290 and transferred to the Royal Palace of Coimbra in 1537. It's still one of the country's most important universities, and it dominates the city both physically (taking up most of the hill in the center of the old town) and in terms of numbers (having some 20,000 students). Walk to the far end of the courtyard for a view of the Mondego and across it to the Convento de Santa Clara-a-Nova. The double stairway rising from the courtyard leads to the graceful colonnade framing the Via Latina (Latin Way), the scene of colorful student processions at graduation time. Amid much pomp and ceremony, doctoral degrees are presented in the

Ceremonial Hall's **Sala dos Capelos,** which is capped with a fine paneled ceiling and lined with a series of portraits of the kings of Portugal.

The 18th-century **clock-and-bell tower,** rising above the courtyard, is one of Coimbra's most famous landmarks. The bell, which summons students to class and in centuries past signaled a dusk-to-dawn curfew, is derisively called the *cabra* (she-goat; an insulting term common in other parts of Europe, particularly the Mediterranean, and used here to express the students' dismay at being confined to quarters). In the courtyard's southwestern corner is a building with four huge columns framing massive wooden doors: behind them is one of the world's most beautiful libraries, the baroque **Biblioteca Joanina.** Constructed in the early 18th century, it has three dazzling book-lined halls and stunning trompe-l'oeil decorative features. Note that your ticket will specify an entry time to the library as there are restrictions to the number of visitors allowed here at any one time. Although there are modern dormitories and apartments, many of the students, some because of tradition and some for economic reasons, prefer the old *repúblicas* (student cooperatives) scattered around the university quarter. Those who live in these ramshackle houses—with the bare minimum of creature comforts—share costs and chores, allowing themselves the one indulgence of a cook. The dwellings were hotbeds of anti-Salazar activity during the years of the dictatorship, and they historically attract people who lean to the left of the political spectrum. The repúblicas aren't open to the public, but if you can get an invitation to step inside one, don't pass up the opportunity for a glimpse of student life. ■ TIP→ **Get here early to avoid a long line for tickets.** ⊠ *Paço das Escolas* 🎫 *€8 combined ticket, includes Sala dos Capelos, Biblioteca Joanina, and Capela de São Miguel.*

Porta Férrea. Built in 1634 as a triumphal arch, the Porta Férrea marks the entrance to the principal university courtyard and is adorned with the figures of the kings Dinis and João III. The courtyard itself holds a statue of Dom João III; it was during his reign that the university moved permanently to Coimbra. ⊠ *Praça Porta Férrea.*

Capela de São Miguel. Next to the Biblioteca Joanina is the Capela de São Miguel, with a fine 16th-century Manueline portal opening onto the courtyard. Begun in 1517, the chapel's glories are nevertheless from the 18th century. Its baroque organ, mannerist main altar, and rococo side altars are stunning. ⊠ *Largo da Porta Férrea* ☎ *239/859900* 🎫 *€8 combined ticket, includes Biblioteca Joanina and Sala dos Capelos.*

WORTH NOTING

Jardim Botânico (*Botanical Garden*). Find relief from Coimbra's oppressive summer heat in this wonderful shady garden near the university. Designed by British architect William Elsden and two natural history teachers, Domingos Vandelli and Dalla Bella, it was created during the reform of the university in 1772 by the Marquis of Pombal. It's still a place of serious scientific study, with more than 1,200 species of plants on 50 acres. There is also a foliage-filled greenhouse and a small botanical museum. ■ TIP→ **Try to visit on a Saturday morning when there**

is an organic farmers' market here. ✉ *Alameda Dr. Júlio Henriques* ☎ *239/855233* ⊕ *www.uc.pt/jardimbotanico* 🖃 *Free.*

Museu Machado de Castro (*Machado de Castro Museum*). The Museu Machado de Castro is arguably the city's most illustrious museum. The building, itself a work of art, was constructed in the 12th century to house the prelates (bishops) of Coimbra; then extensively modified 400 years later and converted into a museum in 1912. Exhibits include a fine collection of sculpture with works by Jean de Rouen and Master Pero. The Bishop's Chapel, adorned with 18th-century azulejos and silks, is a highlight of the upstairs galleries, which contain a diverse selection of Portuguese paintings and furniture. Don't miss the basement's well-preserved vaulted passageways (the Cryptoporticum), built by the Romans as storerooms for the forum that was once here. Also, be sure to take in the view from the terrace of the Renaissance loggia. As you exit the museum, note the large 18th-century azulejo panel depicting Jerónimo translating the Bible. ✉ *Largo Dr. José Rodrigues* ☎ *239/482469* ⊕ *www.museumachadocastro.pt* 🖃 *€6.*

Pátio da Inquisição (*Patio of the Inquisition*). Buildings around this *pátio*—now housing the Coimbra Visual Arts Centre (CAV), as well as an art gallery and exhibition space—once served as the headquarters of the much-feared Portuguese Inquisition. Former Inquisitors' residences, dungeons, and torture chambers all face onto the deceptively peaceful cloister and garden courtyard. ✉ *Rua Pedro da Rocha* ☎ *239/826178* 🖃 *Free* ⊙ *Closed Mon.*

Café Santa Cruz. Until its conversion to more pedestrian uses in 1923, the Café Santa Cruz was an auxiliary chapel for the monastery. Now its high-vaulted Manueline ceiling, stained-glass windows, and wood paneling make it a great place in which to indulge a favorite Portuguese pastime: sitting in a café with a strong, murky *bica* (Portugal's answer to espresso) and a brandy, reading the day's newspaper. ✉ *Praça 8 de Maio* ☎ *239/833617* ⊕ *www.cafesantacruz.com* ⊙ *Closed Sun.*

Quinta das Lágrimas (*House of Tears*). Popular history has it that Dom Pedro and Inês de Castro lived with their children on this estate. It was here on a black January night in 1355 that Inês was killed by agents of Dom Pedro's father, Afonso IV. The 18th-century manor house on the grounds—which has nothing to do with the Inês tragedy—has been turned into a luxury hotel. You can still visit the gardens and the celebrated Fonte dos Amores (Fountain of Love), whose waters are said to be Dona Inês's tears. ✉ *Estrada das Lages* ☎ *239/802380* 🖃 *€2.*

WHERE TO EAT

✕ **À Capella.** This cheap, cheerful. student-run bar and restaurant is in an atmospheric 14th-century chapel (Capela de Nossa Senhora da Victória) in the Jewish Quarter. Traditional Portuguese fare is prepared using fresh, locally sourced ingredients. If you want to eat dinner here, call in advance to reserve a table. Otherwise, there are drinks and bar food to accompany the live fado music that's performed nightly at 9:30.

CLOSE UP

Fado

The word *fado* means "fate" in Portuguese, and—like the blues—fado songs are full of the fatalism of the poor and deprived, laments of abandoned or rejected lovers, and tales of people oppressed by circumstances they cannot change. The genre, probably an outgrowth of a popular sentimental ballad form called the *modinha,* seems to have emerged in the first half of the 19th century in the poor quarters of Lisbon. Initially, fado was essentially a music of the streets, a bohemian art form born and practiced in the alleys and taverns of Lisbon's Mouraria and Alfama quarters. By the end of the century, though, fado had made its way into the drawing rooms of the upper classes. Portugal's last king, Dom Carlos I, was a fan of the form, and a skilled guitar player to boot.

Strictly an amateur activity in its early years, fado began to turn professional in the 1930s with the advent of radio, recording, and the cinema. The political censorship exercised at the time by Portugal's long-lasting Salazar dictatorship also influenced fado's development. Wary of the social comments *fadistas* might be tempted to make in their lyrics, the authorities leaned on them heavily. Fado became increasingly confined to fado houses, where the singers needed professional licenses and had their repertoires checked by the official censor.

Nowadays, although the tradition of fado sung in taverns and bars by amateurs (called *fado vadio* in Portuguese) is still strong, the place to hear fado is in a professional fado house. Called *casas de fado,* the houses are usually restaurants, too, and some of them mix the pure fado with folk dancing shows. Casas de fado are frequented by the Portuguese, so don't be wary of one being a tourist trap.

There are two basic styles of fado: Coimbra and Lisbon. In both the singer is typically accompanied by three, or sometimes more, guitarists, at least one of whom plays the Portuguese guitar, a pear-shape 12-string descendant of the English guitar introduced into Portugal by the British port-wine community in Porto in the 19th century. It is the Portuguese guitar that gives the musical accompaniment of fado its characteristically plaintive tone, as the musician plays variations on the melody. The other instruments are usually classical Spanish guitars, which the Portuguese call *violas.*

Although the greatest names of Lisbon fado have been women, and the lyrics often deal with racy, down-to-earth themes, Coimbra fado is always sung by men, and the style is more lyrical than that of the capital. The themes tend to be more elevated, too—usually serenades to lovers or laments about the trials of love.

[$] Average main: €9 ✉ Capela Nossa Senhora da Victória, Largo da Vitória–Rua Corpo de Deus ☎ 239/833985 🌐 www.acapella.com.pt ⏰ No lunch ✍ Reservations essential.

$ PORTUGUESE 🍴 **Dom Pedro.** The entrance to this restaurant—just a few steps along the riverfront from the tourist office and next to a car dealer—is hardly impressive, but inside it's a different story. A tasteful blend of arches, tile, and wood makes this just the right place in which to enjoy the excellent chanfana and *açorda de mariscos* (a sort of bread porridge mixed with eggs and mounds of fresh shellfish). There's an extensive list of Portuguese wines, and the service is efficient without being stuffy. $ *Average main: €10* ⊠ *Av. Emídio Navarro 58* ☎ *239/829108.*

$

PORTUGUESE

✕ **Dux Petiscos e Vinhos.** This stylish bar-cum-restaurant specializes in a modern take on Iberian tapas with dishes designed and presented to excite all the senses. The menu changes according to what is fresh in the market that day, but you can expect interesting combinations with plenty of vegetarian options, like chestnut puree topped with grilled shiitake mushrooms, and light bites to share including sweet-potato crisps with garlic mayonnaise—the perfect accompaniment to a glass of hearty local wine. There are two other Dux restaurants in town if you're hooked. $ *Average main: €8* ⊠ *Rua dos Combatentes da Grand Guerra 102* ☎ *239/402818* ⊕ *www.duxrestaurante.com.*

$

PORTUGUESE

✕ **O Trovador.** Seasoned travelers know that the rule of thumb is to avoid restaurants near major sights. But O Trovador—just a step away from the old cathedral—has excellent service, large portions of reliably good regional food, and a soothing traditional setting (picture wood paneling and tile work). There is fado on Friday and Saturday nights, June through September. Reservations are essential for the music. $ *Average main: €12* ⊠ *Largo da Sé Velha 15–17* ☎ *239/825475* ⊕ *www.restaurantetrovador.com* ☻ *Closed Sun.*

$

PORTUGUESE

FAMILY

Fodor'sChoice

★

✕ **Restaurante Zé Manel.** Dating to 1952 but recently updated, this local institution tucked into a narrow, cobbled lane serves up Portuguese classics like octopus and rice or goat stew prepared in red wine. The eldery owner welcomes everyone like an old friend, while family members wait the tables and can advise on the daily specials. $ *Average main: €10* ⊠ *Rua das Azeiteiras 8* ☎ *239/826786* ☻ *Closed Sun.*

$

PORTUGUESE

✕ **Zé Manel dos Ossos.** This back-alley hole-in-the-wall has simple wooden tables and chairs, an open kitchen with a jumble of pots and pans, and walls plastered with an intriguing assortment of scribbled poems and cartoons. The food is great and cheap, so don't pass up the chance for a meal here—if you can get in (it's a favorite with students and, more recently, tourists). For such a small place, it has an amazing choice of dishes, including a wonderful *sopa da pedra* (a rich vegetable soup served with hot stones in the pot to keep it warm). The house wine is pretty good, as well. $ *Average main: €8* ⊠ *Beco do Forno 12* ☎ *239/823790* ⊟ *No credit cards* ☻ *Closed Sun. No dinner Sat.* ⌨ *Reservations not accepted.*

WHERE TO STAY

$

HOTEL

🏠 **Astória.** The domed, triangular Astória faces the Rio Mondego and has been a striking art nouveau landmark since its construction in 1917. **Pros:** an iconic building; excellent service; babysitting service. **Cons:** no restaurant; no Wi-Fi in rooms. $ *Rooms from: €95* ⊠ *Av. Emídio Navarro 21* ☎ *239/853020* ⊕ *www.astoria-coimbra.com* ↻ *62 rooms* ⧓ *Breakfast.*

$

B&B/INN

Fodor'sChoice

★

🏠 **Casa Pombal.** A multilingual Dutch woman runs this charming, laid-back pension in a 100-year old town house on the hill in the heart of the old town. **Pros:** homey atmosphere; great views. **Cons:** rooms are on the small side; no a/c, no elevator; steep stairs. $ *Rooms from: €52* ⊠ *Rua*

7

das Flores 18 ☎ *239/835175* 🌐 *www.casapombal.com* 🛏 *9 rooms (4 with bath)* 🍴 *Breakfast.*

$ HOTEL 🏨 **Dona Inês.** This modern glass-and-marble hotel is on the banks of the Mondego, just a few minutes' walk from the business district and not too far from the historic center. **Pros:** complimentary foreign newspapers; efficient staff. **Cons:** emphasis on business groups; bathrooms on the small side. [$] *Rooms from: €70* ✉ *Rua Abel Dias Urbano 12* ☎ *239/855800* 🌐 *www.hotel-dona-ines.pt* 🛏 *84 rooms, 12 suites* 🍴 *Breakfast; Some meals.*

$$ HOTEL 🏨 **Quinta das Lágrimas.** A former palace, this small Relais & Chateau hotel is on the grounds of the estate where Inês de Castro was supposedly killed at the order of her husband's father, Afonso IV, in 1355. **Pros:** evocative historical surroundings; rates drop by half when booked online. **Cons:** expensive; modern wing may be too minimalist for some. [$] *Rooms from: €160* ✉ *Rua António Augusto Gonçalves* ☎ *239/802380* 🌐 *www.hotelquintadaslagrimas.com* 🛏 *39 rooms* 🍴 *Breakfast; Some meals.*

SPORTS AND THE OUTDOORS

BOATING

O Basófias. O Basófias offers leisurely 45-minute boat trips on the river, Tuesday–Sunday throughout the year. In winter, there are departures at 3, 4, and 5; in summer, they leave at 3, 4, 5, 6, and 7. Boats depart from the pier in Parque Dr. Manuel Braga, just upriver from the Santa Clara Bridge. The cost is €6.50 per person. ✉ *Parque Dr. Manuel Braga* ☎ *969/830664* 🌐 *www.odabarca.com.*

O Pioneiro do Mondego. June through September, the student-run Pioneiro do Mondego conducts kayak trips on the Rio Mondego. You're picked up at 10 am in Coimbra, and taken by minibus to Penacova, a peaceful little river town 25 km (15 miles) north. The descent takes about three hours, but plan on a day for the whole outing. Call the English-speaking staff for information and reservations. Trips cost €22.50 per person, including kayak rental. ✉ *Coimbra* ☎ *239/478385* 🌐 *www.opioneirodomondego.com.*

HIKING/KAYAKING

Trans Serrano. Trans Serrano is an outdoor adventure company based near Lousã Mountain, about 20 km (12 miles) southeast of Coimbra. They will provide transport and English-speaking guides for nature hikes, cultural rambles, and kayaking in the surrounding countryside. There are specific programs for seniors. ✉ *Coimbra* ☎ *235/778938* 🌐 *www.transserrano.com.*

HORSEBACK RIDING

Centro Hípico de Coimbra. You can arrange to horseback ride for an hour or two or take longer equestrian excursions at the Centro Hípico de Coimbra. It's on the right bank of the Rio Mondego, 2 km (1 mile) or so downstream from the Santa Clara Bridge. ✉ *Mata do Choupal* ☎ *239/837695* 🌐 *www.centrohipicodecoimbra.blogspot.com* 🕒 *Closed Aug.*

TENNIS

Clube Tenis de Coimbra. At the Clube Tenis de Coimbra, nonmembers pay an €8-per-hour court fee that covers two to four players. Rackets are available for free, but you'll have to bring your own balls or buy them from the club. Note that court reservations must be made a minimum of 24 hours in advance. ⊠ *Av. Urbano Duarte, Quinta da Estrela* ☎ *239/403469* ⊕ *www.clubeteniscoimbra.com.*

SHOPPING

In addition to the ubiquitous lace and cockerels, numerous stores in the city sell delicate blue-and-white Coimbra ceramics, most of them reproductions of 17th- and 18th-century patterns. This style is very distinct from the jolly earthenware associated with Portugal and can be difficult to find in other regions.

The Baixa district by the river is crowded with shops, selling everything from souvenirs to underwear. Major shopping streets are Rua Ferreira Borges, Praça do Comércio, Rua Eduardo Coelho, Rua Fernão de Magalhães, and Rua Visconde da Luz. The Mercado Municipal (Municipal Market) on Rua Olímpio Nicolau Rui Fernandes has a good collection of fruits and vegetables, but is not particularly charming or photogenic.

MALLS

Dolce Vita. This four-level glass-and-steel commercial center has won several design awards. All the regular chains are here, as well as restaurants and cinemas. ⊠ *Rua General Humberto Delgado* ☎ *239/086302* ⊕ *www.dolcevita.pt* ☉ *Closed Sun.*

Forum Coimbra. If you like mega-size malls, Forum Coimbra is another good bet with 146 shops, a six-screen cinema, and a large food court. ⊠ *Rua da Guarda Inglesa* ☎ *214/136000* ⊕ *www.forum-coimbra.com* ☉ *Closed Sun.*

THE WESTERN BEIRAS

The western Beiras encompass shore and mountain, fishing villages and spa towns, wine country and serene forests. The sights—from castles to cathedrals and monasteries to museums—are similarly diverse, as are the activities, which range from basking in the sun by the Atlantic to sampling the restorative mineral water at one of the unspoiled inland towns.

On the gentle-faced coast, long beaches and sun-baked dunes stretch from Figueira da Foz, on the Mondego River estuary, north toward the great lagoon at Aveiro, where colorful kelp boats bob beyond fine, white-sand beaches. A bit farther inland are the vineyards of the Dão region, the Serra do Caramulo range, the lush forests of Buçaco, and the sedate spa resorts of Curia and Luso.

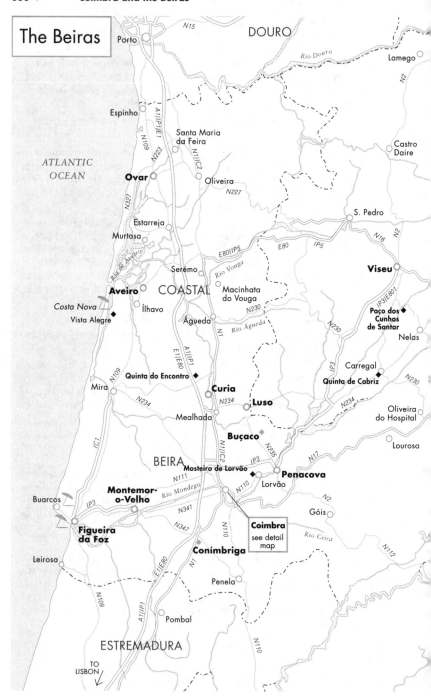

The Beiras

Porto

N15

DOURO

Rio Douro

Lamego

N2

Espinho

Santa Maria
da Feira

Castro
Daire

N109

N223

A1/IP1/E1

N1/IC2

*ATLANTIC
OCEAN*

Ovar

Oliveira

N227

S. Pedro

N16

N2

N327

Estarreja

Murtosa

Ria de Aveiro

Serémo

Rio Vouga

E80/IP5

E80

IP5

Viseu

Aveiro

COASTAL

Macinhata
do Vouga

IP3/E801

Costa Nova

Ílhavo

N230

**Paço dos
Cunhas
de Santar**

Vista Alegre

Águeda

Rio Águeda

Nelas

N1

N230

E1/E80

A1/IP1

Carregal

N230

Quinta do Encontro

N109

Curia

N234

IP3

Quinta de Cabriz

Mira

N234

Luso

Oliveira
do Hospital

IC1

Mealhada

N234

Lourosa

Buçaco

N17

BEIRA

Mosteiro de Lorvão

N11/IC2

IP3

Penacova

Buarcos

N111

Rio Mondego

N110

Lorvão

**Montemor-
o-Velho**

IP3

N341

Góis

N2

**Figueira
da Foz**

N347

N110

Coimbra
see detail
map

Rio Ceira

N112

Leirosa

Conímbriga

E1/E80

N1

Penela

N109

A1/IP1

Pombal

N110

ESTREMADURA

TO
LISBON

CONÍMBRIGA

16 km (10 miles) southwest of Coimbra.

Surrounded by groves of olive trees and rolling hills, Conímbriga is home to one of the Iberian Peninsula's most important archaeological sites. It began as a small settlement in Celtic or possibly pre-Celtic times. In 27 BC, on his second Iberian visit, the emperor Augustus established a Roman province that came to be called Lusitania. It was during this period that, as the Portuguese historian Jorge Alarcão wrote, "Conímbriga was transformed by the Romans from a village where people just existed into a city worth visiting." It still is. There is a café at the on-site museum for refreshments, though you'll find a broader choice of bars and restaurants in the nearby town of Condixa-a-Velha, where archaeologists believe still more Roman remains await excavation.

GETTING HERE AND AROUND

AVIC Joalto runs direct buses from Coimbra to Conímbriga. They depart from Rua João de Ruão 18 in the center of Coimbra at 9 and 9:35 am, and return at 1 and 6 pm. The journey takes approximately 30 minutes.

ESSENTIALS

Bus Contact Transdev. ⊠ *Av. Fernão de Magalhães, Coimbra* ☎ *239/823768* ⊕ *www.transdev.pt.*

EXPLORING

Fodor's Choice
★

Conímbriga. One approaches this extraordinary archeological site via a brick reception pavilion. Pools and gardens surround an artifact-filled museum in which Conímbriga's Iron Age origins, its heyday as a prosperous Roman town, and its decline after the 5th-century barbarian conquests are chronicled.

At the site's entrance is a portion of the original Roman road that connected Olissipo (as Lisbon was then known) and the northern town of Braga. If you look closely, you can make out ridges worn into the stone by cart wheels. The uncovered area represents just a small portion of the Roman city, but within it are some wonderful mosaic floors. The 3rd-century House of the Fountains has a large, macabre mosaic depicting Perseus offering the head of Medusa to a monster from the deep, an example of the amazing Roman craftsmanship of the period.

Across the way is the Casa do Cantaber (House of Cantaber), named for a nobleman whose family was captured by invading barbarians in 465. A tour of the house reveals the comfortable lifestyle of Roman nobility at the time. Private baths included a *tepidarium* (hot pool) and *frigidarium* (cold pool). Remnants of the central heating system that was beneath the floor are also visible. Fresh water was carried 3 km (2 miles) by aqueduct from Alcaibeque; parts of the original aqueduct are still visible. ⊠ *Condeixa-a-Velha* ☎ *239/941177* ⊕ *www.conimbriga.pt* ☑ *€4.50.*

WHERE TO EAT AND STAY

$
PORTUGUESE
FAMILY

✕ **Restaurante do Museu.** You don't need to wander far from the Roman ruins to enjoy a well-prepared and restorative lunch. This on-site restaurant located in the museum offers a reasonable daily menu, which includes a glass of wine and a choice of three meat or fish dishes as a main. Portions are generous and the desserts are delicious; try the chocolate mousse if available. $ *Average main: €8* ✉ *Condeixa-a-Velha* ☎ *239/948218* ۞ *Closed Mon.*

$ ⬚ **Pousada de Condeixa-Coimbra.** A 16th-century palace today houses
HOTEL this elegant pousada in the delightful town of Condeixa-a-Nova. **Pros:** excellent facilities; tranquil location. **Cons:** car essential; popular with tour groups. $ *Rooms from: €100* ✉ *Rua Francisco Lemos, Condeixa-a-Velha* ☎ *239/944025* ⊕ *www.pousadas.pt* ☂ *45 rooms* ❋ *Breakfast.*

MONTEMOR-O-VELHO

20 km (12 miles) west of Coimbra; 16 km (10 miles) northwest of Conímbriga.

The small town of Montemor-o-Velho is most notable for its impressive ruined castle which sits high on a hill, overlooking the surrounding huddle of houses backed by agricultural plains. Within the walls lie the ruins of a palace, a restored church, sweeping lawns, and a pleasant café. On the second and fourth Wednesday of the month, a lively market takes place in town.

GETTING HERE AND AROUND

The most scenic route from Coimbra to the castle, N341, runs along the Rio Mondego's south bank. The route through the village to the castle is extraordinarily complicated; park in the main square and walk up the rest of the way.

EXPLORING

Montemor-o-Velho. On a hill above the fertile Mondego basin between Coimbra and Figueira da Foz, Montemor-o-Velho figures prominently in the region's history and legends. One popular story tells how the castle's besieged defenders cut the throats of their own families to spare them a cruel death at the hands of the Moorish invaders; many died before the attackers were repulsed. The following day the escaping Moors were pursued and thoroughly defeated.

The castle walls and tower are largely intact. But, thanks to damage done during the Napoleonic invasions in 1811, little remains inside the impressive ramparts to suggest this was a noble family's home that once garrisoned 5,000 troops. Archaeological evidence indicates the hill has been fortified for more than 2,000 years. Although the castle played an important role in the long-standing conflict between the Christians and Moors, changing hands many times, the structure seen today is primarily of 14th-century origin. There are threads of the story of Inês de Castro here, for in January 1355 Dom Afonso IV, meeting in the castle with his advisers, made the decision to murder her. The two churches on the hill are also part of the castle complex; the Igreja de Santa Maria de Alcaçova dates to the 11th century and contains some well-preserved Manueline additions. ✉ *Montemor-o-Velho* ☎ *239/680380* ⊡ *Free.*

WHERE TO EAT

$$ PORTUGUESE Fodor's Choice ★ 🍴 **Restaurante a Moagem.** Established in 1987, this restaurant is famed in these parts for its regional cuisine. Dine on specialties like *arroz de tamboril* (monkfish with rice), *bacalhau com natas* (codfish with cream), and *arroz de pata* (rice with duck). Dishes are immaculately presented (not always the case in Portugal!), and the menu changes according to what is fresh and in season. The small dining room is elegant without being stuffy, and the service is exemplary; ask owner Joao to explain the specialties. [$] *Average main: €18* ✉ *Largo Macedo Sotto Mayor–Ponte da Alagoa* ☎ *239/680225* 🕒 *Closed Mon.*

FIGUEIRA DA FOZ

14 km (8½ miles) west of Montemor-o-Velho.

There are various theories as to the origin of the name Figueira da Foz. Locals at this seaside town's busy fishing harbor favor the literal translation: "the fig tree at the mouth of the river." The belief is that when this was just a small settlement, oceangoing fishermen and traders from up the river would arrange to meet at the big fig tree to conduct business. Although there are no fig trees to be seen now, the name has stuck.

Shortly before the turn of the last century, with the improvement of road and rail access, Figueira, with its long, sandy beach and mild climate, developed into a popular resort. Today, although the beach is little changed, a broad four-lane divided boulevard runs along its length. The town side is lined with the usual mélange of apartments, hotels, and restaurants, but the beachfront has been spared from development.

GETTING HERE AND AROUND

Both bus and train services run to Figueira da Foz. Rede Expressos operates three daily buses to/from Lisbon (2¾ hours) and two daily to Leiria (1 hour). Other services include hourly trips to Coimbra (1¼ hours). Trains are operated by Comboios de Portugal (CP), and there are regular services to Coimbra, Leiria, Sintra, and Lisbon. The train and bus stations are located in the same building, around a 20-minute walk east of the center.

ESSENTIALS

Bus Contact **Bus Station.** ✉ *Av. de Saraiva de Carvalho 1530* ☎ *233/402000* 🌐 *www.rede-expressos.pt.*

Train Contact **Train Station.** ✉ *Av. de Saraiva de Carvalho 1530* ☎ *808/208208* 🌐 *www.cp.pt.*

Visitor Information **Figueira da Foz.** ✉ *Av. 25 de Abril* ☎ *233/422610* 🌐 *www.cm-figfoz.pt.*

EXPLORING

Buarcos. Just 2 km (1 mile) north of Figueira, the town of Buarcos has retained some of the character of a Portuguese fishing village in spite of a heavy influx of tourists. Here colorfully painted boats are still pulled up onto the sandy beach, fishermen sit around mending nets, and many of the houses are coated in brightly colored tiles. ✉ *Figueira da Foz.*

NEED A
BREAK

A Plataforma. There are roughly a dozen brightly painted wooden-shack restaurants on the beach. These are wonderful places for fresh grilled fish or just a cold drink. With a large sign proclaiming its name, A Plataforma is one of the best: the fish is so fresh it's almost flopping around. ⊠ *Buarcos.*

> **GREAT VIEWS**
>
> **Farol de Cabo Mondego.** Drive out to the cape where the Cape Mondego Lighthouse stands for a wonderfully uncluttered view of the coastline. The road traces a loop and returns to Buarcos. ⊠ *Figueira da Foz.*

Casa do Paço (*Palace House*). One of Figueira da Foz's more curious sights is the 18th-century Casa do Paço, the interior of which is decorated with about 7,000 Delft tiles. These Dutch tiles were salvaged from a shipwreck at the mouth of the harbor in the late 1600s. ⊠ *Làrgo Prof. Vitor Guerra 4, around corner from main post office* ☎ *233/401320* ⊠ *€1.20* ⊙ *Closed Wed. and Sun.*

Centro de Artes e Espectáculos (CAE). Designed by Luis Marçal Grilo, this impressive arts center sits among the open green spaces of the Parque das Abadias. The interior is flexible enough to host a variety of performance events and also includes exhibition space used for arts, crafts, and photography, plus an art-house cinema and restaurant. ⊠ *Rua Abade Pedro* ☎ *233/407200* ⊕ *www.cae.pt* ⊠ *Exhibitions free.*

Fodor's Choice
★

Museu Municipal Santos Rocha. Just beside the city park, this modern museum may look a tad stark outside, yet it holds one of the province's most diverse and interesting collections. The archaeological section consists mainly of Roman coins sourced from all over the Iberian Peninsula. A second gallery focuses on former Portuguese colonies in Africa, with highlights including some fascinating ritual objects. There is also a gallery dedicated to Portuguese marquetry furniture with exquisite inlaid carvings, plus another devoted to religious items. Exhibits are well displayed with multilingual explanations, and there's a small on-site gift shop. ⊠ *Rua Calouste Gulbenkian* ☎ *233/402840* ⊕ *www.cm-figfoz.pt* ⊠ *€2* ⊙ *Closed Sun. and Mon.*

Praia da Claridade. A major holiday resort, Figuera´s main draw is its magnificent 2-km-long (1-mile-long) beach. Clean and centrally located with generally calm water that offers plenty of shallow areas for paddling tots, it is particularly popular among families. The sandy golden strand is broad (you'll stroll for several minutes just to get your feet wet) and flanked by a promenade that's lined with holiday apartments and sprawling terrace cafés. The Sweet Atlantic Hotel and the Mercure are both excellent choices if you're looking for beachfront lodgings. ■TIP➔ **You can sometimes spot dolphins from the shore. Amenities:** food and drink; lifeguards. **Best for:** sunrise; sunset; swimming. ⊠ *Avenida 25 de Abril.*

WHERE TO EAT

$
SEAFOOD

✕ **Caçarola 1.** Perch on a stool here and enjoy good-value lunch-counter specials served at the bar. Alternatively, grab a table out on the terrace overlooking the pedestrian street and dine on superb seafood like juicy prawns, fish stews, and various rice dishes; everything is wonderfully fresh. This restaurant is very popular with locals, particularly on weekends, so you may have to wait for a table. [$] *Average main: €10* ✉ *Rua Cándido dos Reis 65* ☎ *233/426930* 🌐 *www.cacarola1.com.*

$ PORTUGUESE Fodor's Choice ★ 🍴 **O Peleiro.** In the peaceful, rather than picturesque, village of Paião, 10 km (6 miles) from Figueira, this restaurant—all classic tiles and dark wood—was once a tannery, and that's what the name means. An institution for over 20 years, the menu is heavy on regional specialties, including *sopa da pedra* (vegetable soup). Grilled pork and veal on a spit are also excellent, as is the daily fish or seafood dish. There's a good wine selection, too. Let the charming proprietor advise you. [$] *Average main: €12* ✉ *Largo do Alvideiro 5-7, Paião* ☎ *233/940120* 🕒 *Closed Sun.*

$ PORTUGUESE 🍴 **Olaias.** For a taste of fashionable Figueira, try this cool and contemporary restaurant in the park. The youthful owners have introduced a menu of traditional and international cuisine. Although it changes according to the season, cod steaks with tomato infused rice, seafood risotto, and innovative salads are typical fare. Desserts are stylishly presented and delicious. An outside deck and huge picture windows overlooking the city's main green space maximize the view. TIP→ **There are regular live music sessions in summer, ranging from blues and rock to fado.** [$] *Average main: €10* ✉ *CAE, Rua Abade Pedro* ☎ *968/818033 (mobile)* 🕒 *Closed Sun.*

$ SEAFOOD 🍴 **Teimoso.** Although the menu choices are varied, seafood—sold by weight—is what put this seaside restaurant on the map. Parties of four can opt for the tasty *paella de marisco* (seafood paella). Locals and visitors alike gather in the dining room to order shellfish that comes fresh from huge saltwater tanks. Nonfish aficionados won't go hungry, however, as there are several meat choices, including grilled pork, chicken curry, and roasted duck with an orange sauce. [$] *Average main: €12* ✉ *Av. D. João II, 70, Cabo Mondego, Buarcos* ☎ *233/402720* 🌐 *www.teimoso.com.*

WHERE TO STAY

$ HOTEL FAMILY 🏨 **Hotel Atlantida Sol.** With a sloping concrete exterior designed to maximize on stunning sea views, this large, modern hotel also impresses with modern amenities, updated rooms with balconies, and a beachside location just a mile from the town center. **Pros:** spacious rooms; excellent facilities; sea views. **Cons:** large and impersonal. [$] *Rooms from: €65* ✉ *Av. D. Joã 11, Buarcos* ☎ *308/803399* 🌐 *www.atlantida-sol.com* 🛏 *150 rooms* 🍽 *Some meals.*

$ HOTEL 🏨 **Hotel Aviz.** With a warm ocher exterior and traditional wrought-iron balconies, this charming little guesthouse is a welcoming stop just a few blocks from the beach. **Pros:** near the beach; excellent water pressure. **Cons:** front rooms can be noisy. [$] *Rooms from: €50* ✉ *Rua Dr. A. L. Lopes Guimarães 16* ☎ *233/422635* 🛏 *17 rooms* 🍽 *Breakfast.*

$ HOTEL 🏨 **Sweet Atlantic Hotel.** Although the name makes this place sound like a cute beachside B&B, this modern hotel with its stark blue-and-white exterior soars some 18 floors high. **Pros:** spacious accommodation; good for families; near the beach. **Cons:** no outside pool; sauna costs extra. [$] *Rooms from: €85* ✉ *Av. 25 de Abril 21* ☎ *233/408900* 🌐 *www.sweethotels.pt* 🛏 *68 suites* 🍽 *Breakfast.*

NIGHTLIFE

Casino da Figueira. The 1886 gaming room of the Casino da Figueira has frescoed ceilings, chandeliers, and a variety of table games, including blackjack and American and Continental roulette. Banks of slot machines lie in wait in a separate room. Within the same building there's also a belle époque show room—site of a nightly revue at 11—as well as two cinemas, a piano bar that also has regular fado, and a restaurant. The shows are free, but drinks are expensive. Although dress is casual, jeans and T-shirts aren't permitted. The minimum age to enter is 18; bring your passport. ⊠ *Av. Bernado Lopes* ☎ *233/408400* ⊕ *www. casinofigueira.pt* ✑ *Gaming room free.*

SPORTS AND THE OUTDOORS

Activity centers on the water here. The fishing for sea bream, bass, and mullet is good at Cape Mondego and at the Costa de Lavos and Gala beaches, just south of town. Carp and barbel are caught in the Quiaios Lakes, northeast of Buarcos.

You can rent sailboards and other water-sports gear from most resorts on the shore of either Figueira or Buarcos. The Quiaios Lakes are also popular for windsurfing. Board surfers often find 10- to 12-foot waves at Quiaios Beach (just north of Cape Mondego).

BOATING

Capitão Dureza. Throughout the year, you can take boat and kayak trips on the Mondego River with Capitão Dureza. The company also organizes other activities, including trekking and quad tours. ⊠ *Rua Principal 64C, Telhado, Penacova* ☎ *918/315337* ⊕ *www.capitaodureza.com.*

AVEIRO

60 km (40 miles) north of Coimbra.

Aveiro's traditions are closely tied to the sea and to the Ria de Aveiro, the vast, shallow lagoon that fans out to the north and west of town. Salt is extracted from the sea here, and kelp is harvested for use as fertilizer. Swan-neck *moliceiros* (kelp boats) still glide along canals that run through Aveiro's center, giving rise to its comparison to Venice. In much of the older part of town, sidewalks and squares are paved with *calçada* (traditional Portuguese hand-laid pavement) in intricate nautical patterns. The town's most attractive buildings date from the latter half of the 17th century. Over the last few years, a massive restoration project has transformed the old fishermen's quarter, just off the main canal, into a delightful little area of small bars and restaurants. A central market square hosts live entertainment during the summer months.

GETTING HERE AND AROUND

Rede Expressos buses run to/from Lisbon (3½ hours), Coimbra (2½ hours), Guarda (1½ hours), and Faro (6 hours). There are train services linking Aveiro to Porto, Coimbra, and Lisbon from the train station northeast of the center.

ESSENTIALS

Train Contact Aveiro Train Station. ⊠ *Rua João de Moura* ☎ *707/201280* ⊕ *www.cp.pt.*

Visitor Information Aveiro. ⊠ *Rua João Mendonça 8* ☎ *234/420760* ⊕ *www. rotadaluz.pt.*

EXPLORING

TOP ATTRACTIONS

Convento de Jesus (*Convent of Jesus*). Aveiro isn't just a fishermen's town. A royal presence is what gave impetus to its economic and cultural development. In 1472 Princess Joana, daughter of King Afonso V, retired against her father's wishes to the Convento de Jesus—established by papal bull in 1461—where she spent the last 18 years of her life. The convent was closed in 1874 when the last nun died. It now contains the **Museu de Aveiro**, which encompasses an 18th-century church whose interior is a masterpiece of baroque art. The elaborately gilded wood carvings and ornate ceiling by António Gomes and José Correia from Porto are among Portugal's finest. Blue-and-white azulejo panels have scenes depicting the life of Princess Joana, who was beatified in 1693 and whose tomb is in the lower choir. Her multicolor inlaid-marble sarcophagus is supported at each corner by delicately carved angels. Note also the 16th-century Renaissance cloisters, the splendid refectory lined with camellia-motif tiles, and the chapel of São João Evangelista (St. John the Evangelist). Items on display include sculpture, coaches and carriages, artifacts, and paintings—including a particularly fine 15th-century portrait of Joana by Nuno Gonçalves. ⊠ *Av. de Santa Joana Princesa* ☎ *234/423297* ☞ *€5* ⊘ *Closed Mon.*

Museu Arte Nova. While this museum celebrates the city's rich art nouveau heritage, the main event is the actual building, known as Casa Major Pessoa, a wonderfully flamboyant example of the genre dating to 1909. Notable among the displays are stunning hand-painted tiles decorated with art nouveau motifs, like vivid birds, flowers, and animals. The museum also contains an art gallery, temporary exhibition space, and a fashionable tearoom (Casa de Chá), which morphs into a chic cocktail bar after dark. If you're eager to see more, the museum has a map describing the city's other noteworthy art nouveau edifices. ⊠ *Rua João Mendonça 9-11* ☎ *234/406485* ⊕ *www.cm-aveiro.pt* ☞ *€2* ⊘ *Closed Mon.*

Fodor's Choice ★ **Ria de Aveiro.** This 45-km (28-mile) hydralike delta of the Rio Vouga was formed in 1575, when a violent storm caused shifting sand to block the river's flow into the ocean. Over the next two centuries, as more and more sand piled up, the town's prosperity and population tumbled, recovering only when a canal breached the dunes in 1808. Today the lagoon is a unique combination of fresh and salt water, narrow waterways, and tiny islands. Salt marshes and pine forests border the area, and the ocean side is lined with sandy beaches. In this tranquil setting, colorful moliceiros glide gracefully along, their owners harvesting seaweed. ⊠ *Aveiro.*

FAMILY **Ria de Aveiro boat trips.** Although you can drive through the Ria on back roads, the best way to see the area is by boat. From mid-June to mid-September, boat trips around the lagoon depart throughout the day from the main canal, just in front of the tourism office. The fare is €5 for a 45-minute tour in a moliceiro; reserve via the website or at the tourist office. ✉ *Canal Central* ☎ *234/425563* ⊕ *www.ecoria.pt.*

WORTH NOTING

Estação de Caminhos de Ferro. At Aveiro's northeast edge, the Estação de Caminhos de Ferro (the old train station) displays some lovely azulejo panels depicting regional traditions and customs. ✉ *Av. Dr. Lourenco Peixinho.*

FAMILY **Parque Municipal** (*City Park*). For restless youngsters, the large Parque Municipal, south of Aveiro's center on Avenida Artur Ravara, has a well-equipped playground. ✉ *Aveiro.*

AVEIRO'S CANALS

The best place for viewing Aveiro's boats is along the Canal Central and Canal de São Roque, which is crossed by several attractive bridges. On the banks, to the west of these canals, are checkerboard fields of gleaming, white salt pans. The industry dates back to the 10th century, when salt was used for preserving fish. *Bacalhau* (dried and salted cod) is still a staple of the Portuguese menu.

Praça da República. On the Praça da República, look for the graceful, three-story Câmara Municipal (Town Hall), which has a pointed bell tower. ✉ *Aveiro.*

Igreja da Misericórdia (*Mercy Church*). The plaza's 18th-century Igreja da Misericórdia has an imposing baroque portal; the walls of the otherwise sober interior are resplendent with blue-and-white azulejos. There's a small museum here with vestments and other religious articles. ✉ *Praça da República* ☎ *234/426732* 🎫 *Free* ⊘ *Closed Sun. except during Mass.*

Troncalhada Ecomuseum. This museum is a salt pan, where traditional methods of producing salt are on display. You can try making it yourself using the original equipment and watch workers extracting salt, July through September. ✉ *Cais das Pirâmides* ☎ *234/406485* ⊕ *www.cm-aveiro.pt* 🎫 *€2* ⊘ *Closed weekends.*

WHERE TO EAT

$ ✕ **Mercado do Peixe.** This upscale restaurant is easy to find—just head
SEAFOOD for the city's fish market. Widely considered to be the best place for the freshest seafood in town, its specialties include *caldeirada de enguias* (eel stew) and *arroz de bacalhau e gambas* (rice with cod and prawns). The surroundings are funky industrial chic with plenty of gleaming metal and large picture windows overlooking the canal. $ *Average main: €15* ✉ *Largo da Praça do Peixe 1* ☎ *234/351303* ⊕ *www.mercadodopeixeaveiro.pt* ⊘ *Closed Mon. No dinner Sun.* 🍴 *Reservations essential.*

$$ ✕ **Salpoente.** Two former salt warehouses have been aesthetically
PORTUGUESE restored to create a sophisticated dining space and lounge that's deco-
Fodor'sChoice rated in dark red, gold, and white, with plenty of natural wood. The
★ specialty here is bacalhau: in fact, it's prepared more than seven ways. The *bacalhau contemporâneo* (breaded baked cod with crushed potatoes, roasted peppers, and caramelized shallots) is a highlight. Meat and vegetarian options are also available, and there are several tasting menus (€40–€60). Salpoente also hosts regular art exhibitions and features live music, ranging from sultry jazz to fado, on the weekend. $ *Average main: €18* ✉ *Canal São Roque 82-83* ☎ *234/382674* ⊕ *www.salpoente.pt.*

CLOSE UP

Beaches of the Beira Litoral

There's a virtually continuous stretch of good sandy beach along the entire coastal strip known as the Beira Litoral—from Praia de Leirosa in the south to Praia de Espinho in the north. One word of caution: if your only exposure to Portuguese beaches has been the Algarve's southern coast, be careful: west-coast beaches tend to have heavy surf as well as strong undertows and riptides. If you see a red or yellow flag, do *not* go swimming. Note, too, that the water temperature on the west coast is usually a few degrees cooler than it is on the south coast.

You have your choice of beaches here. There are fully equipped resorts, such as Figueira da Foz and Buarcos; if you prefer sand dunes and solitude, you can spread out your towel at any one of the beaches farther north. Just point your car down one of the unmarked roads between Praia de Mira and Costa Nova and head west. The beaches at Figueira da Foz, Tocha, Mira, and Furadouro (Ovar) are well suited to children; they all have lifeguards and have met the European Union standards for safety and hygiene.

WHERE TO STAY

$ HOTEL **Hotel Aveiro Center.** This small, modern hotel is in an attractive cream-color building (look for the flags) on a quiet backstreet, a few blocks from the main canal. **Pros:** pretty patio; free Wi-Fi. **Cons:** no restaurant; showers only, no tubs. *Rooms from: €65 ✉ Rua da Arrochela 6 ☎ 234/380390 ⊕ www.hotelaveirocenter.com 24 rooms Breakfast.*

$ HOTEL **Hotel Aveiro Palace.** Housed in a sumptuous historic building overlooking the main canal and aesthetically refurbished, this grand hotel offers slick and comfortable accommodations. **Pros:** central location; top-notch facilities; efficient staff. **Cons:** rooms a little bland; small bathrooms. *Rooms from: €70 ✉ Rua Viana do Castelo 4 ☎ 234/421885 ⊕ www.hotelaveiropalace.com 48 rooms Breakfast.*

$ HOTEL Fodor's Choice ★ **Pousada da Ria.** Run by the respected Pestana hotel group, this two-story inn is about a 30-minute drive north of Aveiro, midway down the narrow, pine-covered peninsula that separates the Ria da Aveiro from the sea. **Pros:** prices considerably lower if booked online; tranquil atmosphere. **Cons:** car is essential; not all rooms have views. *Rooms from: €120 ✉ Bico do Muranzel, Torreira ☎ 234/860180 ⊕ www.pousadas.pt 20 rooms Breakfast.*

$ HOTEL **Veneza Hotel.** You'll find the pleasant, well-run Veneza Hotel near the railway station. **Pros:** secure parking; complimentary glass of port. **Cons:** lack of views; 15-minute walk to town center. *Rooms from: €60 ✉ Rua Luis Gomes de Carvalho 23 ☎ 234/404400 ⊕ www.venezahotel.pt 49 rooms Breakfast.*

SPORTS AND THE OUTDOORS

There's no swimming off the lagoon in town, as it's built up with ports, harbors, seafood farms, and salt pans. But within a 20-minute drive you can reach excellent beaches that stretch for miles along the massive sand spit to the north and south of town.

BICYCLING

Near the tourist office on Rua João Mendonça and at other spots around town you'll find racks with bikes that you can use to tour Aveiro and its surroundings. To free a bike, insert a €1 coin as you would a shopping cart. When you return the bike, you get your money back. In case you were wondering, there are tracker devices on the bikes to ensure their return.

HORSEBACK RIDING

Escola Equestre de Aveiro. In addition to riding classes for all levels, Escola Equestre de Aveiro offers guided horseback treks into the wetlands around Aveiro. Hourly prices are €40 per person for groups (up to four) or €45 for an individual; reservations are required. ⊠ *Quinta do Chão d'Agra, 6 km (4 miles) north of Aveiro on N109, Vilarinho* ☎ *234/912108* ⊕ *www.escolaequestreaveiro.com.*

SHOPPING

Armazéms de Aveiro. The Armazéms de Aveiro sells leading Portuguese brands of high-quality ceramics and china, including Vista Alegre and Quinta Nova. The staff will ship purchases as well. ⊠ *Rua Conselheiro Luís de Magalhães 1* ☎ *234/422107.*

Forum Aveiro. The mall Forum Aveiro, beside the main canal in the center of town, has dozens of little shops and restaurants. ⊠ *Rua Batalhão Caçadores 10* ☎ *234/379506* ⊕ *www.forumaveiro.com.*

OVAR

24 km (15 miles) north of Aveiro.

At Ria de Aveiro's northern end, Ovar is a good jumping-off point for the string of beaches and sand dunes to the north. This small town, with its many tiled houses, is a veritable showcase of azulejos.

GETTING HERE AND AROUND

Head north on N109 from Aveiro to Estarreja, then turn west and follow N109-5 through quiet farmlands, and after crossing the bridge over the Ria, continue north on N327 to Ovar.

ESSENTIALS

Visitor Information Ovar. ⊠ *Edifício da Câmara Municipal, Rua Elias Garcia* ☎ *256/572215* ⊕ *www.cm-ovar.pt.*

EXPLORING

Castelo de Santa Maria da Feira (*Castle of Santa Maria da Feira*). The fairy-tale-like Castelo de Santa Maria da Feira is 8 km (5 miles) northeast of Ovar. Its four square towers are crowned with a series of conical turrets in a display of Gothic architecture more common in Germany or Austria than in Portugal. Although the original walls date to the 11th century, the present structure is the result of modifications made

400 years later. From atop the towers you can make out the sprawling outlines of the Ria de Aveiro. ⊠ *Largo do Castelo* ☎ *256/372248* 🎟 *€3* ⊘ *Closed Mon.*

Igreja Matriz (*Parish Church*). The exterior of the late-17th-century Igreja Matriz is completely covered with blue-and-white azulejos. ⊠ *Av. do Bom Reitor and Rua Gomes Freire* ⊘ *Closed Sun. except during Mass.*

Museu de Ovar. Occupying an old house in the town center, the small Museu de Ovar has displays of traditional tiles and regional handicrafts, plus costumes and tableaux re-creating scenes from provincial life in the past. There's also a collection of mementos relating to popular 19th-century novelist Júlio Dinis, a native of Ovar and its most famous son. ⊠ *Rua Heliodoro Salgado 11* ☎ *256/572822* ⊕ *www.museudeovar.pt* 🎟 *€2.*

VISEU

82 km (51 miles) southeast of Ovar; 71 km (44 miles) east of Aveiro.

A thriving provincial capital in the Dão region (one of Portugal's prime wine-growing districts), Viseu has remained a country town in spite of its obvious prosperity. Its newer part is comfortably laid out, with parks and wide boulevards that radiate from a central traffic circle.

GETTING HERE AND AROUND

You can take the scenic but twisting and bone-jarring N227 across the Serra da Gralheira or the smoother, faster, but much less interesting IP1 and IP5. Alternatively there are Rede Expressos buses that run to Viseu from several surrounding towns and cities, including Vila Real (1¼ hours), Coimbra (1¼ hours), and Lisbon (3½ hours). The bus station is located just south of the center.

ESSENTIALS

Bus Contact Viseu Bus Station. ⊠ *Av. Dr António Jose de Almeida* ☎ *232/422822* ⊕ *www.rede-expressos.pt.*

Visitor Information Viseu Tourist Office. ⊠ *Av. Calousste Gulbenkian* ☎ *232/420950* ⊕ *www.turismodocentro.pt.*

EXPLORING
TOP ATTRACTIONS

Adega Cooperativa de Mangualde. This cooperative is a great place to sample locally produced wines. Tours and tastings are available free of charge during the week; on weekends they cost €10 per group, irrespective of the number of people. Sessions generally include three to five wines, plus a 45-minute tour of the wine-making facilities. Call ahead if you'd like to add on local cheeses and cold cuts (€2 per person). ⊠ *Quinta do Melo, Mangualde* ☎ *232/623845* ⊕ *www.acmang.com/enoturismo.htm* ⊘ *Closed Sun.*

Museu Grão Vasco (*Grão Vasco Museum*). Housed in a palatial former seminary beside the cathedral, this lovely museum was originally created to display the works of 16th-century local boy Grão Vasco, who became Portugal's most famous painter. In addition to a wonderful collection of altarpieces by him and his students, the museum has a wide-ranging collection of other art and objects, from Flemish masterpieces to Portuguese faience and Oriental furniture. ⊠ *Paço dos Trê Escalões, Largo da Sé* ☎ *232/422049* ⊕ *www.ipmuseus.pt* ⌖ *€2 (free Sun. until 2)* ⊘ *Closed Mon.*

WORTH NOTING

Largo da Sé. One of Portugal's most impressive squares is bound by three imposing edifices—the cathedral, the palace housing the Museu de Grão Vasco, and the palacelike Igreja da Misericórdia. ⊠ *Viseu.*

Sé. This massive stone structure with twin square bell towers, lends the plaza a solemn air. Construction on this cathedral was started in the 13th century and continued off and on until the 18th century. Inside, massive Gothic pillars support a network of twisted, knotted forms that reach across the high, vaulted roof; a dazzling, gilded, baroque high altar contrasts with the otherwise somber stone. The lines of the 18th-century upper level are harsh when compared with the graceful Italianate arches of the 16th-century lower level. The walls here are adorned with a series of excellent azulejo panels that depict various religious motifs. To the right of the mannerist main portal is a double-tier cloister, which is connected to the cathedral by a well-preserved Gothic-style doorway. The cathedral's Sacred Art Museum has reliquaries from the 12th and 13th centuries. ⊠ *Largo da Sé* ⊕ *www.catedral.diocesedeviseu. pt* ⌖ *Cathedral free, museum €2.50* ⊘ *Museum closed Mon.*

Igreja da Misericórdia (*Church of Mercy*). If the Sé looks like a fortress, the white, rococo Igreja da Misericórdia across from it looks like a residential palace. The fussy ornamentation around the windows and unusual entranceway are more impressive than the interior. ⊠ *Viseu* ⌖ *€1* ⊘ *Closed Mon.*

Paço dos Cunhas de Santar. This historic winery in the pretty village of Santar—an easy 16-km (10-mile) drive southwest of Viseu—centers around a magnificent 16th-century Italian Renaissance–style manor. Signature wines include a spicy Casa de Santar Reserva red and several dessert wines. As well as tastings (four wines, €8), Paço dos Cunhas de Santar offers culinary and wine-appreciation workshops, plus tours of the wine-making facilities. ⊠ *Largo do Paço dos Cunhas de Santar, Santar* ☎ *232/960140* ⊕ *www.daosul.com* ⊘ *Closed Sun.*

Praça da República em Viseu. The tree-lined Praça da República, also known as the Rossío, is framed at one end by a massive azulejo mural depicting scenes of country life. The heroic figure in bronze, standing sword in hand, is Prince Henry the Navigator, the first duke of Viseu. The stately building across from the mural is the **Câmara Municipal.** Step inside to admire the colorful Aveiro tiles and fine woodwork, and be sure to see the courtyard. Just south of the square, a graceful stairway leads to the 18th-century baroque Igreja dos Terceiros de São Francisco (Church of the Brotherhood of St. Francis), behind which is a large, wooded park with paths and ponds. ⊠ *Viseu.*

Praça de Dom Duarte. This square is one of those rare places where just the right combination of rough stone pavement, splendid old houses, wrought-iron balconies, and views of an ancient cathedral (it's just below the Largo da Sé) come together to produce a magical effect.

Try to be here at night, when the romance is further enhanced by the soft glow of the streetlights. There's one restaurant and one café to dip into. ⊠ *Viseu.*

Quinta de Cabriz. Part of the prestigious Dão Sul viticulture company, Quinta de Cabriz is among the best-known wineries in the region. Located 39 km (24 miles) south of town and surrounded by vineyards, it produces red, white, rosé, and sparkling wines. The hearty Cabriz Colheita Seleccina red—which spends six months in French oak and uses primarily local Touriga grape varieties—is one notable award winner. Tastings (four wines, €8) include a 30-minute tour of the wine-making facilities. ⊠ *Carregal do Sal* ☎ *232/960140* ⊕ *www.daosul.com.*

WHERE TO EAT AND STAY

$
PORTUGUESE
 ✕ **Muralha da Sé.** Within confessional distance of the Igreja da Misericórdia, this elegant eatery is housed in a traditional honey-color stone building. The menu has a regional focus, with popular dishes including braised octopus in a red wine jus; desserts are made daily, so save room for the diet-defying chocolate mousse or refreshing mango sorbet. The dining room has moody lighting for an intimate meal, while the terrace provides great people-watching opportunities. $ *Average main: €15* ⊠ *Rua Adro 24* ☎ *232/437777* ⊕ *www.muralhadase.pt* ⊘ *No dinner Sun.*

$
PORTUGUESE
FAMILY
 ✕ **O Hilário.** Expect a warm welcome and no-frills traditional cuisine at this family-run restaurant with a wood-paneled dining room decorated with photos of the famous 19th-century fado star who once lived on this street. The menu changes according to what is fresh in the market that day, but is, unfailingly, unpretentious home-style cooking with huge portions. Desserts are, similarly, a treat not to be missed. $ *Average main: €8* ⊠ *Rua Augusto Hilário 35* ☎ *232/436587* ⊘ *Closed Sun.* ▭ *No credit cards.*

$
B&B/INN
 ▦ **Avenida.** This small town house has the eclectic feel of a bazaar; its deep turquoise and terra-cotta tones evoke a Moroccan market, while African and Chinese antiques (the owners are keen collectors) are liberally scattered across public areas and guest rooms. **Pros:** charming, homey atmosphere; individually decorated rooms. **Cons:** no restaurant; on a busy corner; can be noisy. $ *Rooms from: €50* ⊠ *Av. Alberto Sampaio 1* ☎ *232/423432* ⊕ *www.hotelavenida.com.pt* ⬑ *29 rooms, 2 suites* ❙◯❙ *Breakfast.*

$
HOTEL
 ▦ **Grão Vasco.** Once Viseu's leading hotel, and recently overtaken by newer properties, the Grão Vasco is still a good choice and a great value. **Pros:** surrounded by lovely gardens; free parking. **Cons:** dated decor; Wi-Fi in public areas only. $ *Rooms from: €70* ⊠ *Rua Gaspar Barreiros* ☎ *232/423511* ⊕ *www.hotelgraovasco.pt* ⬑ *109 rooms* ❙◯❙ *Breakfast.*

$
HOTEL
 ▦ **Palácio dos Melos.** Built right into the town walls and dating to the 16th century, this central hotel oozes history; the rooms in the older part of the building are the most atmospheric, with their high ceilings and chandeliers and panoramic views of the town. **Pros:** elegant public rooms; evocative sense of history. **Cons:** can be noisy; hard to drive to with one-way system and narrow streets. $ *Rooms from: €90* ⊠ *Rua Chão Mestre 4* ☎ *232/439290* ⊕ *www.hotelpalaciodosmelos.pt* ⬑ *27 rooms* ❙◯❙ *Breakfast.*

$$ HOTEL Fodor's Choice ★ [$] **Pousada de Viseu.** One of the latest additions to Portugal's government-run pousadas, this handsome neoclassical building dates to 1793 when it was built as the town's hospital. **Pros:** central location; spacious rooms. **Cons:** views are unremarkable. [$] *Rooms from: €145* ✉ *Rua do Hospital* ☎ *232/457320* 🌐 *www.pousadas.pt* 🛏 *84 rooms* 🍴 *Breakfast.*

$ B&B/INN **Quinta da Fata.** At this lovely quinta, about 18 km (10 miles) southeast of Viseu, guests can reserve either modern apartments or antiques-filled rooms in a 19th-century manor house. **Pros:** stunning gardens; free bikes for use of guests. **Cons:** may be too remote for some; rooms vary in size. [$] *Rooms from: €58* ✉ *Vilar Seco, Nelas* ☎ *232/942332* 🌐 *www.quintadafata.com* 🛏 *9 rooms* 🍴 *Breakfast.*

SPORTS AND THE OUTDOORS

GOLF

Montebelo. Although hardly likely to be considered as a venue for the Ryder Cup, this interesting layout near Viseu lies in a picturesque region. It's the only course for many miles and has been built in hilly countryside, almost in the shadow of Portugal's highest mountain, the Serra da Estrela. This is much more informal golf than elsewhere in the country, and a handicap certificate is not required to play here. Walkers may find the hilly terrain a little hard going, but golf carts are available. ✉ *Farminhão* ☎ *232/856464* 🌐 *www.golfemontebelo.pt* 🎫 *9-hole course: €45 weekdays, €60 weekends; 18-hole course: €55 weekdays, €70 weekends* ⛳ *18 holes, 6908 yds, par 72.*

SHOPPING

Narrow Rua Direita, in the old part of town, is lined with shops displaying locally made wood carvings, pottery, and wrought iron. The surrounding rural areas, particularly north toward Castro Daire, are well known for their strong tradition of linen, basketry, and heavy woolen goods.

CURIA

20 km (12 miles) north of Coimbra.

Just 30 minutes by car from the clamor of the summer beach scene, Curia is a quiet retreat with shaded parks and grand belle epoque hotels. The small but popular spa is in the heart of the Bairrada region, an area noted for its fine sparkling wines and roast suckling pig. The waters, with their high calcium and magnesium-sulfate content, are said to help in the treatment of kidney disorders. For the last 100 years, the spring has been contained within an elaborate treatment center that has provided rejuvenating pampering and medical treatment side by side.

GETTING HERE AND AROUND

Trains run roughly half-hourly from Coimbra and Aveiro to Curia (less frequently on weekends). Check the CP website for more details.

ESSENTIALS

Train Contact CP (Comboios de Portugal). ☎ *808/208208* 🌐 *www.cp.pt.*

Visitor Information Curia. ✉ *Largo Dr. Luís Navega* ☎ *231/512248, 231/504442* 🌐 *www.turismodocentro.pt.*

7

EXPLORING

Aliança Underground Museum. Part of the prestigious Aliança wine group, this Aladdin's cave of a museum is located in wine cellars that date back some 50 years. Its exhibits—drawn from the private collection of Portuguese billionaire businessman and art collector, José Barardo—include 18th-century Portuguese ceramics and tile work, African artwork, fossils, semiprecious stones, and assorted archaeological artifacts. Guided tours are offered in English, but advance reservations are necessary. Visitors may also sample two wines on-site—one of them a sparkling variety for which the local wineries are renowned. ✉ *Rua do Comercio 444, Sangalhos* ☎ *234/732045* 🌐 *www.alianca.pt* 🎟 *€3.*

Quinta do Encontro. The eye-popping architecture alone would make this winery, located in a tiny village northwest of Curia, worth visiting. Circular throughout, the building's design is apparently inspired by oak barrels, and the spiral interior walkway is playfully modeled on a corkscrew. Set amidst vineyards and gently rolling hills, Quinta do Encontro offers wine tastings and one-hour tours of its ultramodern wine-making facilities (€10). No advance reservations are necessary. There is also an excellent restaurant on-site ($$$). ✉ *São Lourenço do Bairro* ☎ *231/527155* 🌐 *www.quintadoencontro.pt* 🕒 *Closed Sun.*

Termas da Curia Spa Resort. Located in Curia Park, which centers around a huge lake, this spa has a slightly dated, old-fashioned feel but still offers a range of preventive and regenerative treatments. The calcium salts, sulfur, and magnesium in the waters here are believed to be particularly good for rheumatic and musculoskeletal diseases; programs of varying durations include accommodations at the on-site hotel ($$). The resort as a whole mainly attracts Portuguese who just enjoy wallowing in the therapeutic water; however, nonguests can enjoy the spa on a drop-in basis, with more general treatments including half-hour massages (from €30). ✉ *Tamengos* ☎ *231/519800* 🌐 *www.termasdacuria.com.*

WHERE TO EAT AND STAY

$ PORTUGUESE Fodor's Choice ★ 🍴 **Pedro dos Leitões.** Of the several restaurants specializing in suckling pig, "Suckling Pig Pete" is the most popular. The size of the parking lot is a dead giveaway that this is no intimate bistro, and Pedro's spitted pigs pop out of the huge ovens at an amazing rate (especially in summer)—and in spite of the volume, quality is maintained. The restaurant is about 3 km (2 miles) from Curia. [$] *Average main: €15* ✉ *Rua Alvaro Pedro 1 (N1), Mealhada* ☎ *231/209950* 🌐 *www.pedrodosleitoes.com* 🕒 *Closed 2 wks late June–early July.*

$ HOTEL Fodor's Choice ★ 🏨 **Curia Palace.** The approach down a tree-lined drive is like the beginning of an old movie. **Pros:** palatial surroundings; good for families. **Cons:** can seem a little austere; frequent venue for weddings. [$] *Rooms from: €100* ✉ *Curia* ☎ *231/510300* 🌐 *www.curiapalace.com* 🛏 *114 rooms* 🍽 *Breakfast.*

$ B&B/INN 🏨 **Quinta de São Lourenço.** This delightful 18th-century manor—surrounded by vineyards and pine groves—is in the tiny village of São Lourenço do Bairro. **Pros:** charming owners; spick-and-span rooms. **Cons:** lack of restaurants and shops nearby; decor could be a bit flowery for some. [$] *Rooms from: €80* ✉ *3 km (2 miles) from Curia on N1 to*

Mugofores, São Lourenço do Bairro ☎ *231/528168* 🌐 *www.quinta-de-s-lourenco.pt* 💳 *No credit cards* 🛏 *8 rooms* 🍴 *Breakfast.*

SPORTS AND THE OUTDOORS

GOLF

Curia. Part of the Belver Grande Hotel da Curia complex, this 9-hole course is located just 20 minutes from Coimbra, and the landscaping includes three artificial lakes. ✉ *Rua Platános* ☎ *231/516891* 🌐 *www.portugalgolfe.com* 🎟 *€17.50 weekdays, €25 weekends* ⛳ *9 holes, 2687 yds, par 34.*

LUSO

8 km (5 miles) southeast of Curia; 18 km (11 miles) northeast of Coimbra.

This charming town, built around the European custom of "taking the waters," is on the main Lisbon–Paris train line, in a little valley at the foot of the Buçaco Forest. Like Curia, it has an attractive park with a lake, elegant hotels, and medicinal waters. Slightly radioactive and with a low-sodium and high-silica content, the water—which emerges from the Fonte de São João, a fountain in the center of town—is said to be effective in the treatment of kidney and rheumatic disorders.

GETTING HERE AND AROUND

There are four daily buses on weekdays and two on weekends that run from Coimbra bus station to the center of Luso, near the main spa. There are also a limited number of trains from Coimbra (35 minutes); however, the train station is around a 20-minute hike from the center of town.

ESSENTIALS

Bus Info Luso Bus Station. ✉ *Rua Emidio Navarro 136* ☎ *231/939133.*

Visitor Information Luso. ✉ *Rua Emidio Navarro 136* ☎ *231/939133* 🌐 *www.visitcentrodeportugal.com.pt.*

WHERE TO EAT AND STAY

$ SEAFOOD 🍴 **O Cesteiro.** At the western edge of town, just past the Luso bottling plant, this popular (albeit decidedly dated) local restaurant serves simple fare that includes several types of salt cod, roast kid, and fresh fish. [$] *Average main: €8* ✉ *Rua Dr. Lúcio Abranches* ☎ *231/939360* 🕒 *Closed Wed.*

$ HOTEL Fodor's Choice ★ 🏨 **Grande Hotel de Luso.** This hulking, yellow-stucco complex, constructed in 1945, is a tad bombastic, but the tastefully redone interior is luxurious and serene. **Pros:** stunning public areas; exquisite gardens. **Cons:** staff can seem offhand; buffet breakfast a little scant. [$] *Rooms from: €80* ✉ *Rua Dr. Cid de Oliveira* ☎ *231/937937* 🌐 *www.hoteluso.com* 🛏 *147 rooms* 🍴 *Breakfast.*

$ HOTEL 🏨 **Residencial Imperial.** This neat little hotel has spick-and-span rooms with parquet floors, dark wood furniture, colorful bedding, and small balconies overlooking the street, where there's easy parking. **Pros:** excellent value; pleasantly furnished. **Cons:** the management speak little English;

small rooms. [$] *Rooms from: €42* ✉ *Rua Emídio Navarro* ☎ *231/937570* 🌐 *www.residencialimperial.com* 🛏 *14 rooms* 🍴 *Breakfast.*

BUÇACO

3 km (2 miles) southeast of Luso; 16 km (10 miles) northeast of Coimbra.

In the early 17th century, the head of the Order of Barefoot Carmelites, searching for a suitable location for a monastery, came upon an area of dense virgin forest. A site was selected halfway up the slope of the greenest hill, and by 1630 the simple stone structure was occupied. To preserve their world of isolation and silence, the monks built a wall enclosing the forest. Their only link with the outside was through a door facing toward Coimbra, which one of them watched over. The Coimbra Gate, still in use today, is the most decorative of the eight gates constructed since that time.

Early in the 20th century, much of the original monastery was torn down to construct an opulent royal hunting lodge under the supervision of Italian architect Luigi Manini. Never used by the royal family, the multi-turret extravaganza became a prosperous hotel—now the Palace Hotel do Bussaco—and in the years between the two world wars it was one of Europe's most fashionable vacation addresses.

Today many come to Buçaco just to view this unusual structure, to stroll the shaded paths that wind through the forest, and to climb the hill past the Stations of the Cross to the Alta Cruz (High Cross), their efforts rewarded by a view that extends all the way to the sea.

GETTING HERE AND AROUND

Most (but not all) of the buses that head for Luso have Buçaco as their final destination. However, overall, visitors will find a car invaluable for exploring the national forest.

EXPLORING

Museu Militar de Buçaco (*Buçaco Military Museum*). The small Museu Militar de Buçaco houses uniforms, weapons, and various memorabilia from the Battle of Buçaco. ✉ *On left of N234, just outside forest grounds, Bussaco* ☎ *231/939310* 🌐 *www.cm-mealhada.pt* 🎟 *€2* 🕐 *Closed Mon.*

WHERE TO STAY

$$ HOTEL Fodor's Choice ★ 🏨 **Palace Hotel Do Bussaco** (*Palace Hotel Do Buçaco*). Designed as a royal hunting lodge and set in a 250-acre forest, the Palace is an architectural hodgepodge with elements that run the gamut from neo-Gothic to early Walt Disney. **Pros:** fairy-tale setting; superb restaurant; significant reductions if booked via the website. **Cons:** blatantly ostentatious; often booked by groups. [$] *Rooms from: €160* ✉ *Bussaco* ☎ *231/937970* 🌐 *www.almeidahotels.com* 🛏 *68 rooms* 🍴 *Breakfast; All meals; Some meals.*

PENACOVA

12 km (7 miles) southeast of Buçaco; 12 km (7 miles) northeast of Coimbra.

A little town on a hill at the junction of three low mountain ranges, Penacova affords panoramic views and wonderful hiking opportunities.

GETTING HERE AND AROUND

It's advisable to have your own wheels, as public transportation is sparse in this region. From Buçaco, the most scenic route is N235, through wooded countryside along the foot of the Serra do Buçaco. If you're coming from Coimbra, take N110 along the Rio Mondego.

ESSENTIALS

Visitor Information Penacova. ✉ *Câmara Municipal, Largo Alberto Leitão 5* ☎ *239/470300* 🌐 *www.cm-penacova.pt.*

EXPLORING

Mosteiro de Lorvão. Just outside Penacova, in a small wooded valley, is the village of Lorvão and the Mosteiro de Lorvão. This monastery is worth visiting not just to see what's still standing, but also to feel the vibes of a departed epoch. Its origins are obscure, but there's archaeological evidence of monastic life here dating as far back as the 6th century. In the 13th century Lorvão became a convent for Cistercian nuns and was the custodian of a famed library of 12th-century illuminated manuscripts. The convent was closed down by government order in the 19th century. By that time, the impoverished nuns were partly supporting themselves by making the forerunners of the exquisitely carved willow toothpicks that you can buy in Penacova and in handicrafts shops around the country. (The nuns originally used them to decorate the little cakes they made for sale.) Still standing is a baroque church with beautifully carved choir stalls and an ornate wrought-iron choir grille. The adjacent museum contains archaeological pieces recovered from the site as well as several illuminated manuscripts. ✉ *Off N110, 2 km (1 mile) south of Penacova, Lorvão* ☎ *239/474430* 🎟 *Free.*

7

WHERE TO EAT AND STAY

$ PORTUGUESE 🍴 **O Panorâmico.** It's easy to see how this popular, family-run restaurant got its name: from the spacious dining room there's a wonderful panoramic view of the Rio Mondego as it snakes its way along to Coimbra. Be sure to try the house specialty, *lampreia à mode de Penacova* (lamprey cooked with rice); local game dishes are also a favorite here. [$] *Average main: €10* ✉ *Largo Alberto Leitão 7* ☎ *239/477333.*

$ B&B/INN 🏨 **Casa O Nascer do Sol.** You're guaranteed to get a warm welcome (accompanied by a glass of wine) from Belgian owners Wim and Joke at this homey B&B, about 16 km (10 miles) northwest of town. **Pros:** scenic setting; friendly, informative owners can advise on area activities. **Cons:** in a small village with few amenities; pricey. [$] *Rooms from: €75* ✉ *Largo da Eira Velha 5, Vale da Carvalha* ☎ *239/477366* 🌐 *www.casanascerdosol.net* 🛏 *5 rooms* 🍽 *Breakfast.*

$ HOTEL 🏨 **Pensão Avenida.** Right in the center of town, this simple place has no-fuss, spotless rooms decorated in light pine with traditional wooden shutters; bathrooms vary in size, but most have a double sink. **Pros:**

free parking. **Cons:** can be noisy from street noise. [$] *Rooms from: €39* ✉ *Av. Abel Rodrigues da Costa 20* ☎ *239/477142* 🌐 *www.pensaoavenida.com* 🛏 *19 rooms* 🍴 *Breakfast.*

SPORTS AND THE OUTDOORS

HIKING

Several paths lead over the hills to the monastery in Lorvão or through the vineyards and fields down to the Rio Mondego.

Trans Serrano. Trans Serrano will provide transport and English-speaking guides for nature hikes and kayaking in the surrounding countryside. ✉ *Penacova* ☎ *235/778938* 🌐 *www.transserrano.com.*

KAYAKING

O Pioneiro do Mondego. June through September, there are kayak trips down the Rio Mondego from Penacova to Coimbra. Trips cost €22.50 per person, including kayak rental. For more information, contact the student-run Pioneiro do Mondego or the local tourist office. ✉ *Penacova* ☎ *239/478385* 🌐 *www.opioneirodomondego.com.*

THE EASTERN BEIRAS

It's worth visiting this region to stand atop a centuries-old castle wall and look out on the landscape. The rugged mountains of the Serra da Estrela and the sparse vegetation of the stone-strewn high plateau present a sharp contrast to the sandy beaches, lush valleys, and densely forested peaks along the coast. In this part of the country, where visitors are still something of a curiosity, you'll find perhaps the warmest welcome. With many mellow old buildings uninhabited, this beautiful area is one of Europe's last great undiscovered gems for those wishing to buy a second home away from the madding crowd.

CASTELO BRANCO

150 km (93 miles) southeast of Coimbra.

The provincial capital of Beira Baixa is a modern town with wide boulevards, parks, and gardens. There are some handsome buildings here, as well as a lovely formal garden and a superb museum. The surroundings are noteworthy for their natural beauty. Lying just off the main north–south IP2 highway, Castelo Branco is easily accessible from all parts of the country.

GETTING HERE AND AROUND

There are regular buses to Castelo Branco from several major travel hubs in Portugal, including Coimbra, Lisbon, Guarda, Portalegre, and Faro. The town is also on the Lisbon–Guardia line with six daily trains from Lisbon. Check the Comboios de Portugal's website for more information.

If you are driving from Buçaco, the most scenic route is N235, through wooded countryside along the foot of the Serra do Buçaco. If you're coming from Coimbra, take N110 along the Rio Mondego.

ESSENTIALS

Bus Contact Castelo Branco Bus Station. ✉ *Rua do Saibreiro* ☎ *272/340120* 🌐 *www.rede-expressos.pt.*

Train Contact CP (Comboios de Portugal). ☎ *808/208208* 🌐 *www.cp.pt.*

Visitor Information Castelo Branco. ✉ *Câmara Municipal, Alameda da Liberdade* ☎ *272/330339* 🌐 *www.cm-castelobranco.pt.*

EXPLORING

Castelo Templario (*Templar's Castle*). At the top of the town's hill are the ruins of the 12th-century Castelo Templario. Not much remains of the series of walls and towers that once surrounded the entire community. ✉ *Castelo Branco.*

Fodor's Choice ★ **Jardim do Antigo Paço Episcopal** (*Garden of the Old Episcopal Palace*). These 18th-century gardens are planted with rows of hedges cut in all sorts of bizarre shapes and contain an unusual assemblage of sculpture. Bordering one of the park's five small lakes are a path and stairway lined on both sides with granite statues of the apostles, the evangelists, and the kings of Portugal. The long-standing Portuguese disdain for the Spanish is graphically demonstrated here; the kings who ruled when Portugal was under Spanish domination are carved to a noticeably smaller scale than the "true" Portuguese rulers. Unfortunately, many statues were damaged by Napoléon's troops when the city was ransacked in 1807. ✉ *Rua Bartolomeu da Costa* 🌐 *www.cm-castelobranco.pt* 🎟 €2.

Miradouro de São Gens (*St. Gens Terrace*). Adjoining the Castelo Templario is the flower-covered Miradouro de São Gens, which provides a fine view of the town and surrounding countryside. ✉ *Castelo Branco.*

Museu Francisco Tavares Proença Junior. This small, regional museum is housed in the old Paço Episcopal (Episcopal Palace). In addition to the usual Roman artifacts and odd pieces of furniture, the collection contains some fine examples of the traditional *bordado* (embroidery) for which Castelo Branco is well-known. Adjacent to the museum is a workshop where embroidered bedspreads in traditional patterns are made and sold. ✉ *Largo da Misericórdia* ☎ 272/344277 🌐 *www.ipmuseus.pt* 🎟 €2.

Praça Luís de Camões. You'll find Castelo Branco's best-preserved medieval square—the Praça Luís de Camões—in an older section of town. ✉ *Castelo Branco.*

WHERE TO EAT AND STAY

$ PORTUGUESE 🍴 **Retiro do Cacador.** This restaurant is a carnivore's delight; the theme is clear from the mounted stag's head on the wall to the menu of predominantly meat and game, including deer, wild boar, and venison. Exposed-stone walls, wooden beams, and burgundy paint add to the rustic and cozy feel of the place. Portions are generous and the service attentive, with the waiters going out of their way to explain the more complicated dishes. [$] *Average main: €12* ✉ *Rua Ruivo Godinho 15* ☎ *272/343050* 🌐 *www.restauranteretirocacador.pai.pt.*

$ HOTEL 🏨 **Rainha Dona Amélia.** This graceful, modern, five-story hotel in the center of the town offers good-size guest rooms which are pleasant and airy and decorated with warm earth tones. **Pros:** handsome building; good location. **Cons:** the hotel's size can make it feel impersonal; some rooms lack decent view. $ *Rooms from: €65* ⊠ *Rua de Santiago 15* ☎ *272/348800* ⊕ *www.hotelrainhadamelia.pt* ⇨ *64 rooms* ⦿ *Breakfast; Some meals.*

$ ⊞ **Tryp Colina do Castelo.** Perched atop the hill, this low-rise business-

HOTEL style hotel may lack individuality, but all the conveniences you could ask for are here—along with the added luxuries of a spa, indoor pool, and squash court. **Pros:** friendly, attentive staff; good facilities; exceptional views. **Cons:** it's about a 20-minute walk to and from town; anonymous decor. $ *Rooms from: €65* ⊠ *Rua da Piscina* ☎ *272/349280* ⊕ *www. trypcolinacastelo.com* ⇨ *109 rooms* ⦿ *Breakfast.*

SHOPPING

Tradition in Castelo Branco dictates that a new bride makes an embroidered bedspread for her wedding night. This custom is still followed, and these delicately patterned, hand-embroidered linen-and-silk spreads are among the finest examples of Portuguese craftsmanship. There's a display-and-sales room for these next to the Museu Francisco Tavares Proença Junior.

SORTELHA

150 km west of Coimbra.

Fodor'sChoice If you have time to visit only one fortified town, this should be it.

★ From the moment you walk through Sortelha's massive ancient stone walls, you feel as if you're experiencing a time warp. Except for a few TV antennas, there's little to evoke the 21st century. The streets aren't littered with souvenir stands, nor is there a fast-food outlet in sight. Stone houses are built into the rocky terrain and arranged within the walls roughly in the shape of an amphitheater.

GETTING HERE AND AROUND

If you're traveling from Penamacor, follow N233 north across the high plateau. Regional trains stop at Belmonte-Manteigas station, located around 12 km (7½ miles) away, from where visitors can catch a taxi. There is no regular bus service.

ESSENTIALS

Taxi Contact **Sortelha Taxi.** ☎ *271/388183.*

EXPLORING

FAMILY **Castelo de Sortelha** (*castle*). Above the village are the ruins of a small yet imposing castelo. The present configuration dates back mainly to a late-12th-century reconstruction, done on Moorish foundations; further alterations were made in the 16th century. Note the Manueline coat of arms at the entrance. Wear sturdy shoes so that you can walk along the walls, taking in views of Spain to the east and the Serra da Estrela to the west. The three holes in the balcony projecting over the main entrance were used to pour boiling pitch on intruders. Just to the right of the north gate are two linear indentations in the stone wall. One is exactly a meter (roughly a yard) long, and the shorter of the two is a *côvado*

(66 centimeters or 26 inches). In the Middle Ages, traveling cloth merchants used these markings to ensure an honest measure. ✉ *Sortelha.*

WHERE TO EAT AND STAY

There aren't any hotels or pousadas in this medieval town, but several ancient stone houses offer comfortable, although not luxurious, accommodations at very low rates.

$ PORTUGUESE 🍴 **Restaurante Dom Sancho.** Just inside the gates, this pleasant little restaurant in a restored stone house provides diners with a rustic yet elegant dining experience. It specializes in game dishes like roast wild boar and venison. TIP→ **The wood-beamed bar downstairs attracts plenty of local trade.** [$] *Average main: €10* ✉ *Largo do Corro* ☎ *271/388267* 💳 *No credit cards* 🕒 *Closed Mon. No dinner Sun.*

$ RENTAL 🏨 **Casa da Villa.** A good choice within the walls, Casa da Villa sleeps up to six people and has a small kitchen, laundry facilities, and central heating. **Pros:** perfect for families or small groups; tranquil setting. **Cons:** owner prefers to rent out whole house; very quiet out of season. [$] *Rooms from: €60* ✉ *Rua Direita* ☎ *271/388113* 💳 *No credit cards* 🔑 *3 rooms* 🍽 *No meals.*

$ RENTAL 🏨 **Casas do Campanário.** Just inside the village walls, Casas do Campanário consists of two apartments; one can accommodate two people, the other six. **Pros:** quiet surroundings; central location; the larger apartment has a kitchen. **Cons:** no credit cards; advance reservations essential. [$] *Rooms from: €65* ✉ *Rua da Mesquita* ☎ *271/388198* 💳 *No credit cards* 🔑 *2 apartments* 🍽 *No meals.*

7

BELMONTE

14 km (8½ miles) northwest of Sortelha; 20 km (12 miles) southwest of Guarda.

Three things catch your eye on the approach to Belmonte. The first two, the ancient castle and the church, represent the past; the third, an ugly water tower, symbolizes the new industry of the town, now a major clothing-manufacturing center. Belmonte's importance can be traced back to Roman times, when it was a key outpost on the road between Mérida, the Lusitanian capital, and Guarda. Elements of this road are still visible.

GETTING HERE AND AROUND

If you're driving from Penamacor, follow N233 north across the high plateau. There are daily bus services from Guarda (30 minutes); the stop in Belmonte is around a ½-km (¼-mile) walk from the town center.

ESSENTIALS

Visitor Information **Belmonte.** ✉ *Largo do Brasil, Castelo do Belmonte* ☎ *275/911488* 🌐 *www.cm-belmonte.pt.*

EXPLORING

FAMILY **Castelo de Belmonte** (*Belmonte Castle*). Of the mighty complex of fortifications and dwellings that once made up the castle, only the tower and battlements remain. As you enter, note the scale-model replica of the caravel that carried Cabral to Brazil. On one of the side walls is a coat of arms with two goats, the emblem of the Cabral family (in

Portuguese, *cabra* means "goat"). Don't miss the graceful but oddly incongruous Manueline window incorporated into the heavy fortifications. The castle ruins are on a rocky hill to the north overlooking town. ⊠ *Belmonte* 🔄 *Free.*

Igreja de São Tiago (*Church of St. James*). The 12th-century stone church contains fragments of original frescoes and a fine Pietà carved from a single block of granite. The tomb of Pedro Cabral is also in this church. Actually there are two Pedro Cabral tombs in Portugal, the result of a bizarre dispute with Santarém, where Cabral died. Both towns claim ownership of the explorer's mortal remains, and no one seems to know just who or what is in either tomb. If the church is closed, see if someone at the tourist office can help you gain entrance. ⊠ *Adjacent to Castelo de Belmonte* 🕾 *275/911488* 🔄 *Free.*

Judería (*Jewish Quarter*). Adjacent to the Castelo de Belmonte, a cluster of old houses makes up the Judería. Belmonte had (and, in fact, still has) one of Portugal's largest Jewish communities. Many present-day residents are descendants of the Marranos: Jews forced to convert to Christianity during the Inquisition. For centuries, many kept their faith, pretending to be Christians while practicing their true religion behind closed doors. Such was their fear of repression that Belmonte's secret Jews didn't emerge fully until the end of the 1970s. The community here remained without a synagogue until 1995. A small museum situated within a former 18th-century Catholic church includes a permanent exhibition about the Jewish period; it is also an important center for Jewish studies in Portugal. ⊠ *Rua da Portela* 🕾 *275/088698* ⊕ *www.cm-belmonte.pt* 🔄 *€3* 🕒 *Closed Mon.*

Monument to Cabral. Ask a Portuguese—or better yet a Brazilian—what Belmonte is best known for, and the answer will undoubtedly be Pedro Álvares Cabral. In 1500 this native son "discovered" Brazil and, in doing so, helped make Portugal one of the richest, most powerful nations of that era. The monument, in the town center, is an important stop for Brazilian visitors. ⊠ *Belmonte.*

OFF THE BEATEN PATH

Centum Cellas. A strange archaeological sight on a dirt track signposted off N18 has kept people guessing for years. The massive, solitary, three-story framework of granite blocks is thought to be of Roman origin, but experts are unable to explain its original function convincingly or provide many clues about its original appearance. Some archaeologists believe it was part of a much larger complex, possibly a Roman villa, which was subsequently used as a watchtower. ⊠ *10 km (6 miles) north of Belmonte.*

WHERE TO STAY

$
HOTEL

🏨 **Belsol.** Owner João Pinheiro is an enterprising hotelier who has opted for quality and good service over ostentation. **Pros:** family-friendly; superb service. **Cons:** cut off from town; could be too quiet for some. 🟢 *Rooms from: €55* ⊠ *Quinta do Rio off IP2/N18* 🕾 *275/912206* ⊕ *www.hotelbelsol.com* 🔄 *54 rooms* ⦿ *Breakfast.*

$
B&B/INN

🏨 **Convento de Belmonte.** Just over a kilometer (½ mile) from Belmonte on the slopes of the Serra da Esperança, this sumptuous stone-clad pousada occupies a restored Franciscan monastery. **Pros:** impeccable service; gorgeous architectural detail. **Cons:** small plunge pool; can seem formal. $ *Rooms from: €120* ⊠ *Serra da Esperança* ☎ *275/910300* ⊕ *www.conventodebelmonte.pt* ↝ *25 rooms* ⦿ *Breakfast.*

PARQUE NATURAL DA SERRA DA ESTRELA

123 km (76 miles) northeast of Coimbra.

A region of stunning beauty, this natural park covers approximately 1,011 square km (390 square miles) and is home to the highest mountain in the country: the Torre. It has all kinds of flora and fauna and is particularly popular for outdoor pursuits, ranging from hiking and fishing to skiing.

GETTING HERE AND AROUND

Car travel is the most convenient option here, although drivers should take special care, particularly at high elevations, which can be foggy or icy during the winter months.

ESSENTIALS

Visitor Information Parque Natural de Serra da Estrela. ⊠ *Praça da República 28, Seia* ☎ *238/310440.* **Região de Turismo da Serra da Estrela.** ⊠ *Av. Frei Heitor Pinto, Covilhã* ☎ *275/319560.*

EXPLORING

Fodor'sChoice ★ **Parque Natural da Serra da Estrela.** Until the end of the 19th century, this mountainous region was little known except by shepherds and hunters. The first scientific expedition to the Serra da Estrela was in 1881, and since then it has become one of the country's most popular recreation areas. In summer the high, craggy peaks, alpine meadows, and rushing streams become the domain of hikers, climbers, and trout fishermen. The lower and middle elevations are heavily wooded with deciduous oak, sweet chestnut, and pine. Above the tree line, at about 4,900 feet, is a rocky, subalpine world of scrub vegetation, lakes, and boggy meadows that are transformed in late spring into a vivid, multicolored carpet of wildflowers. The Serra da Estrela Natural Park is home to many species of animals, the largest of which include wild boar, badger, and, in the more remote areas, the occasional wolf. ⊠ *Parque Natural da Serra da Estrela.*

WHERE TO EAT AND STAY

$ PORTUGUESE Fodor'sChoice ★ ✕ **O Borges.** The rustic atmosphere here is accentuated by a decor that includes traditional farming tools, ancient barrels, and dark-wood beams and furniture. Fittingly, the food is hearty farmers' fare: expect generous portions of dishes like roast kid and beef stew with mushrooms. Seafood choices include paella, as well as grilled salmon and squid. The service is exceptional, and waiters go out of their way to accommodate families. $ *Average main: €14* ⊠ *Travessa do Funchal 7, Seia* ☎ *238/313010* ⊕ *www.oborges.com* ☽ *Closed Tues. No dinner Wed.*

$ B&B/INN Fodor'sChoice ★ ⌷ **Pousada de Convento do Desagravo.** In a delightful village with just 400 inhabitants, this gracious pousada began life as a convent in the late 18th century. **Pros:** exudes a tangible sense of history; spacious rooms. **Cons:** expensive; village may be too quiet for some. $ *Rooms from: €140* ⊠ *Vila Pouca da Beira* ☎ *238/670080* ⊕ *www.pousadas.pt* ↝ *37 rooms* ⦿ *Breakfast.*

7

SPORTS AND THE OUTDOORS

CAMPING

There are several official campsites within the park (ask at the tourist office for details) with basic toilet and shower facilities. There are also a number of good commercial campsites in the area.

FISHING

There's excellent trout fishing in the Rio Vouga (Vouga River) and in the rivers and lakes of the Serra da Estrela—particularly the Rio Zêzere, which cuts through one of Europe's deepest glacial valleys—and in the Comprida and Loriga lakes. The Beira Litoral is full of beaches and rocky outcroppings where you can try your luck with a variety of fish, including bass, bream, and sole. Check with the local tourist offices for information about obtaining permits. No permit is required for ocean fishing.

HIKING

This is a hiker's paradise, and there are plenty of well-marked trails. A comprehensive trail guide is available at tourist offices in the region, and although it's in Portuguese, the maps, elevation charts, and pictures are useful. Plenty of other adventure sports are also offered, from hang gliding to climbing.

SKIING

With the coming of winter and the first snows, the area becomes a winter playground, offering many Portuguese their only exposure to winter sports.

It takes about three hours to drive between Torre and Ski Parque, both of which have accommodations. The direct route between them is the highest road in Portugal and offers a thrilling ride above the snow line and into the clouds.

Ski Parque. In Manteigas, on the far side of the mountains, you can ski and snowboard year-round thanks to the synthetic run at the Ski Parque complex. ☒ *Parque Natural da Serra da Estrela* ☎ *275/980090* ⊕ *www.skiparque.pt.*

Torre. Continental Portugal's highest point—Torre, with an elevation of 6,539 feet—is in the south part of the Parque Natural da Serra da Estrela. Although it can't compete with other European ski resorts, it does have five lifts. Facilities include a restaurant and sports-equipment shops that rent gear. Weekday rates for lift passes run from €15 for a half day to €30 for a full day; rates are slightly higher on weekends and at night. Equipment rentals range from €18 for snowboards to €30 for skis. For information, contact the **Ski Station.** ☒ *Parque Natural da Serra da Estrela* ☎ *275/314727.*

GOUVEIA

110 km northwest of Coimbra.

Nestled into the western side of the Mondego Valley, this quiet town of parks and gardens is a popular base from which to explore the Serra da Estrela.

GETTING HERE AND AROUND

At least two daily buses operated by Rede Expressos run to/from Coimbra and Lisbon. The train is less convenient as the town's train station is located 14 km (8½ miles) from the center.

ESSENTIALS

Bus Contacts Bus Station. ✉ *Largo Dr Alípio de Melo* ☎ *238/490180.* **Rede Expressos.** ☎ *707/223344* ⊕ *www.rede-expressos.pt.*

Visitor Information Gouveia. ✉ *Av. 25 de Abril* ☎ *238/490243* ⊕ *www. cm-gouveia.pt.*

EXPLORING

Igreja Matriz de Gouveia (*Parish Church*). The exterior of the baroque Igreja Matriz is covered with blue-and-white tiles, and well-executed azulejos depicting the Stations of the Cross line the inside walls of the small, dimly lighted chapel across the street. ✉ *Praça de São Pedro.*

Museu Municipal de Arte Moderna Abel Manta. Inside this 18th-century manor house you'll see a good collection of paintings by one of the country's most distinguished artists: Abel Manta. He was born in Gouveia in 1888 and died in Lisbon in 1982. Today the exhibition has been expanded with the superb modern paintings by Manta's son João Abel Manta. ✉ *Rua Direita* ☎ *238/490219* ⊕ *www.cm-gouveia.pt* 🎟 *Free.*

WHERE TO STAY

$

HOTEL

🏨 **Hotel Eurosol Gouveia.** This small, modern hotel on one of the main approaches to the Serra da Estrela has comfortable rooms furnished in traditional style; several have small balconies. **Pros:** convenient location; good-size rooms. **Cons:** bland furnishings; perfunctory service. $ *Rooms from: €60* ✉ *Av. 1 de Maio* ☎ *238/491010* ⊕ *www.eurosol. pt* 🛏 *48 rooms, 3 suites* 🍴 *Breakfast.*

GUARDA

150 km northwest of Coimbra.

At an elevation of about 3,300 feet, Portugal's highest city is aptly referred to by the four Fs: *forte, feia, fria, e farta* (strong, ugly, cold, and wealthy). A somber conglomeration of austere granite buildings in a harsh, uncompromising environment, Guarda isn't charming, but it is of historic interest and makes a good base for exploring the mountains and fortified villages along the Spanish border. Winters are cold and gloomy, often cutting into the short springtime.

From pre-Roman times, Guarda has been a strategic bastion on the northeastern flank of the Serra da Estrela, protecting the approaches from Castile. The town is thought to have been a military base for Julius Caesar. After the fall of the Roman Empire, the Visigoths and later the Moors gained control. Guarda was liberated in the late 12th century by Christian forces and, along with a number of towns in the region, enlarged and fortified by Dom Sancho I. The dukes of Bragança were closely related to the kings of Portugal, and with rank came the privilege and aforementioned wealth. For the rather dour and purposeful local mountain residents, Guarda is still a main trading and business center.

GETTING HERE AND AROUND

About three buses run daily to various destinations including to/from Castelo Branco, via Covilhã (1¾ hours), Lisbon (5½ hours), and Porto (3 hours). There are direct fast IC trains from Lisbon (4 hours) and Coimbra (2¾ hours). However, the train station is an inconvenient 5 km (3 miles) northeast of town.

ESSENTIALS

Bus Contact Guarda Bus Station. ⊠ *Rua Dom Nuno Álvares Periera* ☎ *271/222515.*

Visitor Information Guarda. ⊠ *Praça Luís de Camões* ☎ *271/205530* ⊕ *www. turismo.guarda.pt.*

EXPLORING

Museu da Guarda (*Guarda Museum*). This museum, housed in a stately early-17th-century palace-cum-monastery adjacent to the 18th-century **Igreja da Misericórdia** (Church of Mercy), is worth a visit. It documents the region's history with a collection of prehistoric and Roman objects, old paintings, arms, and ecclesiastical art. ⊠ *Rua Frei Pedro Roçadas 30* ☎ *271/213460* ⊕ *museudaguarda.imc-ip.pt* ⌨ €2.

Sé (*Cathedral*). Construction on the fortresslike Sé started in 1390 but wasn't completed until 1540. As a consequence, the imposing Gothic building also shows Renaissance and Manueline influences. Although built on a smaller and less majestic scale, the cathedral shows similarities to the great monastery at Batalha. Inside, a magnificent four-tier relief contains more than 100 carved figures. The work is attributed to the 16th-century sculptor Jean de Rouen. ⊠ *Praça Luís de Camões.*

Torre de Menagem. This castle keep, on a small knoll above the cathedral, and a few segments of wall are all that remain of Guarda's once extensive fortifications. From atop the ruins you get an impressive view across the rock-strewn countryside toward the Castilian plains. ⊠ *Guarda.*

PORTO AND
THE NORTH

Updated by
Benjamin
Kemper

Perched on the steep banks of the River Douro, Porto is Portugal's second-largest city and the heart of Portugal's industrial north. A center for finance, culture, and cuisine, Porto has come into its own as a modern city with plenty to offer beyond its best-known export, port wine. The coast north of Porto is lined with pine forests; inland, the Minho region is equally verdant and harbors Portugal's only national park, Peneda-Gerês. Upriver from Porto, grapes harvested to make port wine are grown in terraced vineyards in the sun-drenched Douro Valley. This is the start of Trás-os-Montes (Beyond the Mountains), a province with harsh but striking landscapes which harbor fascinating folk traditions.

Lining the river that made it a trading hub since pre-Roman times, vibrant and cosmopolitan Porto centers itself some 5 km (3 miles) inland from the Atlantic Ocean. Porto's architecture is more baroque than Lisbon's. Its grandiose granite buildings were financed by the wine trade that made the city wealthy: wine from the upper valley of the Rio Douro (Douro River, or River of Gold) was transported to Porto, from where it was exported. You can follow that trail today by boat or on the scenic Douro rail line, and there are now many wine *quintas* (estates) in the valley, many of which offer overnight stays.

The remote north is as stark as it is breathtaking, in the arid valley of the Rio Douro and in the deep, rural heartland of the Minho, a coastal province north of Porto. The Minho shoreline, home to vast fine-sand beaches and quaint fishing villages, has lush, green landscapes. Some locations have been appropriated by resorts, but there are still plenty of places where you can find solitary dunes or splash in the brisk Atlantic away from crowds. Inland you can lose yourself in villages with country markets and fairs that have hardly changed for hundreds of years. It's worth planning ahead to make sure your visit coincides with a weekly market day (weekends are a sure bet) or one of the many summer festivals that draw locals back home.

Those with a penchant for adventure will find it in the winding mountain roads and far-flung towns and villages of Trás-os-Montes in the northeast. The imposing castle towers and fortress walls of this frontier region are a great attraction, but—as is often the case in rural Europe—it's the journey itself that's Trás-os-Montes's greatest prize: travel past expansive reservoirs, through forested valleys rich in wildlife, across bare crags and moorlands, and finally down to rustic stone villages where TV aerials sit in anachronistic contrast to the medieval-feeling surroundings.

The uncharted uplands of the northern Trás-os-Montes are called the Terra Fria (Cold Land), where you may spot some unusual forms such as Iron Age sculptures of boars with phallic attributes. It's believed these were worshipped as fertility symbols. There are traces of even more ancient civilizations, in the form of what is believed to be the world's largest open-air museum of Paleolithic rock art.

ORIENTATION AND PLANNING

GETTING ORIENTED

The north of Portugal can be divided into four basic regions—Porto and its immediate environs, the Douro Valley, the evergreen Minho, and the somewhat remote and untamed Trás-os-Montes area to the east, a region still slightly short on amenities yet long on spectacular scenery, ancient customs, and superb country cooking. While any trip to the north should include Porto, to get a sense of the variety of landscapes and monuments, it's worth getting out of town to see at least one of these other regions.

Porto. An ancient trading city, Porto has become a sophisticated modern metropolis. At its heart is the Ribeira, best taken in from across the River Douro, where the famous port wine cellars are located. Outside the capital's Old City, myriad art galleries and a vibrant nightlife scene stand out as today's top attractions.

The Coast and the Douro. The coast around Porto is dotted with dunes and resorts, including two casinos within easy reach of town. Meanwhile, on the River Douro, cruise boats glide through one of Europe's most stunning landscapes, where the grapes used in the world-famous port wine are grown.

The Minho and the Costa Verde. The string of beaches between Porto and the Spanish border are not called the "Green Coast" for nothing, as pine forests often provide the backdrop to dunes. Inland, the fertile Minho region is significantly more populous yet somehow serene, with picturesque vineyards neighbored by fruit trees and forest.

Trás-os-Montes. The uplands of this remote province, whose name means "Beyond the Mountains," are among the most difficult landscapes from which to scrape a living, yet they have a certain wild beauty. The hardy natives are fiercely proud of their local traditions, which often date back to pagan times.

PLANNING

WHEN TO GO

It's best to visit the north in summer, when Porto and the Minho region are generally warm, but be prepared for drizzling rain at any time. Coastal temperatures are a few degrees cooler than in the south. Inland, and especially in the northeastern mountains, it can be very hot in summer and cold in winter.

TOP REASONS TO GO

Experiencing the old and the new. Porto may be steeped in history, but it's a country leader in design, gastronomy, and the arts. Beyond Porto, major regional centers, like Guimarães and Braga, juxtapose the old with the new as well, boasting significant historical monuments and a vibrant college-town atmosphere.

Enjoying the outdoors. No trip to the north is complete without a boat trip on the Douro, whose curve after curve of terraced vineyards together form a UNESCO World Heritage Site. The region also harbors the country's only national park, Peneda-Gerês, with its many marked trails, as well as coastal bird sanctuaries and the remote uplands of Trás-os-Montes.

Tasting world-renowned port wines. Porto and the Douro Valley are the world hub for those sweet red wines that take their name from the region's biggest city. Tour port wine bodegas along the river's banks, and learn about the global wine trade that has shaped this country's history.

Shopping for handicrafts. The Minho is famous even in Portugal for its pottery, embroidery, and other handicrafts. They're best viewed at local markets but are also available at shops in Porto and other major centers.

Celebrating at festivals. The biggest party is on the evening of June 23, when Porto residents pour into the streets to celebrate the city's patron saint, St. John, with curbside barbecues, all-night dancing, and curious customs like shaking garlic fronds in the faces of passersby. Countless village festivals across the region are attended by large numbers of emigrants who head home each summer.

PLANNING YOUR TIME

Porto is less than three hours north of Lisbon by highway or express train, so even a short trip to Portugal can include a night or two here. From Porto, it's a two-hour drive up the Minho coastline to reach the Spanish border and another three to four hours east to the less visited Trás-os-Montes and the eastern border with Spain.

It takes only a day or two to experience the more urban pleasures of Porto, such as its wine lodges and nearby coastal resorts. Tack on a few more days to allow excursions to the history-rich towns of Braga and Guimarães or a tour through the lovely Douro Valley. A full week allows you to cover all this territory as well as inland towns and villages along the Lima and Minho Rivers, or you could set off for the remote northeastern Trás-os-Montes and its fascinating towns of Bragança and Chaves.

GETTING HERE AND AROUND

AIR TRAVEL

Porto's Aeroporto Francisco Sá Carneiro, 13 km (8 miles) north of the city, is the gateway to northern Portugal. TAP Portugal runs direct regular flights from Newark, New Jersey, and from Boston, Massachusetts, to Lisbon. There is also direct service from many European cities. The airport is served by the metro system (a 30-minute trip downtown,

€1.85). Taxis and Ubers are also available outside the terminal; the metered fare into town should run €20–€30 with baggage surcharge. Outside the city limits, tariffs are based on kilometers traveled.

Weekday flights from Lisbon to Bragança via Vila Real run twice a day in both directions by Aero Vip, in twin-engine turboprop planes for 18 or 36 passengers.

Airline Contacts Aero Vip. ☎ 21/448–9949 in Porto, 273/313203 in Bragança ⊕ www.aerovip.pt. **TAP.** ☎ 21/843–1100 ⊕ www.flytap.com.

Airports Aeródromo Municipal de Bragança. ☎ 273/304253, 93/255–0351 ⊕ www.cm-branca.pt. **Aeródromo Municipal de Vila Real.** ☎ 259/336620 ⊕ www.cm-vilareal.pt. **Aeroporto Franciso Sá Carneiro (Porto).** ☎ 22/943–2400 ⊕ www.ana.pt.

BUS TRAVEL

Rede Expressos operates frequent bus service to and from Lisbon to major towns in the region, with the ride from the capital to Porto, the main regional hub, taking at least 3½ hours and costing €19 one-way. The journey from Lisbon to Bragança, the remotest city, takes 7½ hours (including breaks) and costs €21.90. Rodonorte links major towns within the northern region, with the trip from Porto to Amarante taking 50 minutes and costing €7.50 and the three-hour ride from Porto to Bragança costing €13.70. Other local operators fill in the gaps. Major terminals are in Porto, Braga, Guimarães, Vila Real, and Chaves; the staff might not speak English, but timetables are easily decipherable with the aid of a dictionary. Within towns, local buses are generally the way to get around; Porto also has a metro system, a funicular, and a few antique trams aimed mainly at the tourist market.

Bus Contacts Rede Expressos. ✉ Rua de Alexandre Herculano 366, Porto ☎ 70/722–3344 ⊕ www.rede-expressos.pt. **Rodonorte.** ✉ Rua do Ateneu Comercial do Porto 19, Porto ☎ 22/200–5637 ⊕ www.rodonorte.pt.

CAR TRAVEL

The densely populated coast around Porto and the Minho region are well served with roads. A half-hour drive on the A3/IP1 toll highway will take you from Porto to Braga (for Guimarães, peel off just beyond halfway on the A7/IC5) before continuing on to Ponte de Lima and Valença on the Spanish border. The IC1 hugs the coast from Porto almost directly north to Viana de Castelo—a drive of just over an hour.

Inland, the A4/E82 toll road connects Porto to Amarante—again, a drive of about an hour. From here the three-lane IP4/E82 passes through Vila Real, Mirandela, and Bragança en route to the Spanish border at Quintanilha—in all, about four hours from Porto. The IP3 comes up from Viseu in the Beiras through Lamego to Peso da Régua and then Vila Real. You can continue north to Chaves on the N2.

Given the nature of the terrain in this hilly region crisscrossed by river valleys, some journeys will never be anything but slow. Examples are the routes Bragança–Chaves–Braga (N103), Vila Real–Chaves (N2), and Bragança–Mirando do Douro (N218). It's best simply to accept the roads' limitations, slow down, and appreciate the scenery. Off the beaten track, always check with local tourist offices to make sure the routes you wish to follow are navigable. Roadwork and winter land-slides can cause detours and delays. In isolated regions, take special care at night, because many roads are unlighted and unpaved.

In city centers, streets are often congested or pedestrianized, and local drivers manic, so leave your car at your hotel. In towns *in this chapter*, you can cover most sights on foot (though be prepared for steep hills in Porto); visit outlying attractions by bus, taxi, or in Porto's case, metro.

TRAIN TRAVEL

Long-distance trains arrive at Porto Campanhã station, east of the center. Note that not all services from Lisbon terminate here; some continue on to Braga. From Campanhã you can take a five-minute connection to the central São Bento station; otherwise, it's a 30-minute scenic walk. The São Bento station is a tourist attraction in its own right, famous for the intricate blue-and-white azulejo tiles that line the walls of the main hall. From Spain, the Vigo–Porto train crosses at Tuy/Valença do Minho and then heads south to Porto, usually stopping at both Campanhã and São Bento. From Porto some of the most scenic rail lines in the country stretch out into the river valleys and mountain ranges to the northeast. Even if you rent a car, try to take a day trip on one. For reservations and schedules, visit São Bento station or the tourist office.

When leaving Porto, be sure to budget plenty of time from São Bento station to make your connection—or take a taxi straight to Campanhã. For the express service to and from Lisbon, reserve your seat at least a few hours in advance. The picturesque Douro Line is served by trains from Campanhã (some with a change at Ermesinde) and pass through Livração, Peso da Régua (Régua), and Tua on the four-hour journey to Pocinho, at the far end of the Alto Douro demarcated grape-growing region. For reservations and current schedules, contact Estação de São Bento or the tourist office in Porto. On summer Saturdays (June–October), a special historic train runs between the Régua and Tua stations, with a stop at Pinhão.

Trains on the main route north along the Costa Verde depart approximately hourly from Campanhã stations and run through Barcelos and Viana do Castelo, as far as Valença do Minho.

Braga and Guimarães are served by Porto suburban services from both São Bento and Campanhã stations. Braga is also served by some long-distance trains through Campanhã.

Train Contacts Estação de Campanhã. ⊠ *Largo da Estação de Campanhã, Porto* ☎ *70/721–0220, 70/721–0746 for disabled services.* **Estação de São Bento.** ⊠ *Praça Almeida Garrett, Porto* ☎ *22/200–2722.*

RESTAURANTS

On the whole, restaurants in Porto and the north offer extremely good value, although the smaller ones often don't accept credit cards. Dress throughout the region is informal, and reservations are usually unnecessary.

The cooking in Porto is rich and heavy. It's typified by the city's favorite dish, *tripas à moda do Porto* (Porto-style tripe), a concoction involving beans, chicken, sausage, vegetables, and spices. *Caldo verde* ("green soup") is also ubiquitous; it's made of potato and shredded kale in a broth and is usually served with a slice or two of *chouriço* sausage. Fresh fish is found all the way up the coast, and every town has a local recipe for *bacalhau* (dried and salted cod); in the Minho it's often *à Gomes de Sá* (cooked with potatoes, onions, and eggs). *Lampreias* (lampreys)—eel-like fish—are found in Minho rivers from February through April and are a specialty of Viana do Castelo and Monção. In the mountains wonderful *truta* (trout) is available in any town or village close to a river.

As is the case throughout Portugal, pork is the meat most often seen on menus, but nearer the border with Spain, wonderfully tender veal and steak can be found in the form of *posta mirandesa* and *barrosã*. Most dishes will be served with *batatas* (potatoes) or *arroz* (rice), both fine examples of staples being raised to an art form. Potatoes here, whether roasted, boiled, or fried, have an irresistibly nutty and sweet flavor. Rice is lightly sautéed with chopped garlic in olive oil before adding water, resulting in a side dish that could easily be devoured as a main course.

The wine available throughout the north is of high quality. The Minho region's vinho verde is a light, young, slightly sparkling red or white wine. The taste is refreshing, fruity, with good acid—qualities that also make it an excellent starting point for distilling *aguardente* (Portuguese brandy). Both reds and whites are served chilled, and vinho verde goes exceptionally well with fish and shellfish. Port enjoys the most renown of the local wines (ask for *vinho do Porto*), but the Douro region, where the grapes are grown for port, also produces some of Portugal's finest table wines. *Prices in the reviews are the average cost of a main course at dinner or, if dinner isn't served, at lunch.*

HOTELS

In Porto, hotel rates rival those in Lisbon, and you should reserve rooms well in advance to avoid disappointment. Lodgings in the Minho and Trás-os-Montes regions are reasonably priced compared with their counterparts elsewhere in the country. The Turismo no Espaço Rural (Rural Tourism) network allows you to spend time at a variety of historic manor houses, country farms, and little village cottages scattered throughout the north. Many of these converted 17th- and 18th-century buildings are found in the lovely rural areas around Ponte de Lima, in the Minho region. *Pousadas* (inns) offer a variety of settings in the north, from a 12th-century monastery in Guimarães to more rustic, hunting-lodge digs in such places as the Marão mountain ridges near

---

FERTILE FIELDS

Little of the green countryside in the Minho is wasted. Vines are trained on poles and in trees high above cultivated fields, forming a natural canopy, for this is *vinho verde* country. This refreshing young "green wine"—light on alcohol but with fine digestive properties—is crisp. There are two types of vinho verde: red and white. Portuguese drink the red more often and export more of the white. Whatever the color, vinho verde is a true taste of the north. The best *aguardente* (Portuguese brandy) is made from distilled vinho verde; when aged, it can rival fine cognacs.

Amarante or a hilltop in Bragança. *Prices in the reviews are the lowest cost of a standard double room in high season. For expanded hotel reviews, visit Fodors.com.*

WHAT IT COSTS IN EUROS			
$	**$$**	**$$$**	**$$$$**
Restaurants €16 or under	€17–€22	€23–€30	over €30
Hotels €140 or under	€141–€200	€201–€260	over €260

Restaurant prices are per person for a main course at dinner, including value-added sales tax. Hotel prices are for a standard double room, including tax, in high season (off-season rates may be lower).

PORTO

Portugal's second-largest city, with a population of roughly 280,000, considers itself the north's capital and, more contentiously, the country's economic center. Locals support this claim with the maxim, "Coimbra sings, Braga prays, Lisbon shows off, and Porto works." Largely unaffected by the great earthquake of 1755, Porto has some fine baroque architecture, but its public buildings are generally sober. Its location on a steep hillside above the Rio Douro, though, affords exhilarating perspectives.

The river has influenced the city's development since pre-Roman times, when the town of Cale on the left bank prospered sufficiently to support a trading port, called Portus, on the site of today's city. The 1703 Methuen agreement with England, giving commercial preference to Portuguese wines, provided Douro Valley vineyards with a new market. It was in Porto that Douro wine was first mixed with brandy to preserve it during the journey and improve it over time. The trade is still big business, based across the river in Vila Nova de Gaia.

Porto is also a cultural hub, thanks to the Serralves Contemporary Art Museum, the cutting-edge galleries along Rua Miguel Bombarda, and to the stunning Casa da Música (House of Music), designed by Dutch architect Rem Koolhaas. Foz do Douro, where the river flows into the Atlantic, is another fashionable spot that some might call "surfer-chic."

GETTING HERE AND AROUND

The city is congested, so leave your car at the hotel. You can walk around most of central Porto, but be prepared for the steep hills, which can prove tiring in the summer heat. To reach the few outlying attractions, you can use the city's good network of buses, trams, and funicular—all run by Sociedade dos Transportes Colectivos do Porto (STCP)—or the metro. Its five lines run from 6 am to 1 am, mostly aboveground as a light-rail service outside the center but converging underground at the Trindade stop. In 2016, the metro began offering 24-hour service on weekends and holidays to select stations, from June to early October. (It remains to be seen if the program will be reinstated

GREAT ITINERARIES

IF YOU HAVE 3 DAYS

Devote the first morning to **Porto**, followed by an afternoon tour of the port wine lodges in Vila Nova de Gaia, across the Rio Douro. Before turning in, spend time enjoying the riverside cafés and restaurants. In the morning, drive north through the sandy coastal towns of **Vila do Conde**, **Póvoa de Varzim**, and **Ofir** and **Esposende**. After taking in the bracing air, seaside shopping, and a lunch consisting of the day's catch, head inland to the ancient city of **Braga**, with its profusion of churches. Overnight here or in the delightfully medieval **Guimarães**, which you should explore on Day 3. Worth a side trip from either town is the fascinating Citânia de Briteiros, the hilltop site of an ancient Iron Age settlement.

Alternatively, you could spend your second two days savoring the pastoral Douro Valley. Follow the winding N108 east from Porto along the river's north bank. Don't miss the view at Entre-os-Rios, where the Douro and Tâmega rivers converge. Then head back up toward **Amarante**, one of the north's most picturesque towns, its halves joined by a narrow 18th-century bridge. It's worth overnighting here. On Day 3, wind your way southeast along the N101, passing through Mesão Frio, to the Douro, where you can follow the river east to **Pêso da Régua**, the heart of port wine country, and tour a wine cellar or two. Across the river and a bit farther south is **Lamego**, with its impressive 18th-century pilgrimage shrine of Nossa Senhora dos Remédios. From either of these towns, it's not far to **Vila Real**, gateway to the remote and beautiful region of Trás-os-Montes. You could spend the night here and head east the next day, or return to Porto.

IF YOU HAVE 5 DAYS

Spend a day and night in **Porto**, then head inland and north. Take two days to explore **Braga**, including the Citânia de Briteiros, and **Guimarães**. On Day 4 go west to **Barcelos**, the folk-art center of the country; try to arrive on a Thursday, when the large weekly market is filled with purveyors of everything from live pigs to hand-painted pottery. Continue north to graceful **Viana do Castelo**, along the Rio Lima. Wander its narrow stone streets and stay the night in the art deco pousada on a hill overlooking town, or drive up along the Costa Verde to Caminha or one of the other partially walled castle towns along the Spanish border: **Vila Nova de Cerveira**, **Valença do Minho**, and Monção.

On Day 5, head to quaint Arcos de Valdevez and rent a rowboat for a couple of hours on the river, then continue on to two nearby towns with beautiful bridges, **Ponte da Barca**, with its 15th-century arched passageway, and **Ponte de Lima**, graced with a long, low Roman footbridge. If you're in Ponte de Lima on the second Monday of the month, you can visit the country's oldest market. From here, return to Porto or Lisbon.

8

in future years.) Bus service is reduced after 9 pm. You can also rent bicycles to pedal out to coastal towns and beaches.

Maps for all routes are available on the STCP website. The tourist office can provide information; they'll also sell you a Porto Card, which is valid for public transportation and admission to 21 city sights (and discounts for others) for 24 hours (€13), 48 hours (€20), or 72 hours (€25). There's also a transport-only Andante Tour card valid for 24 hours (€7) or 72 hours (€15) from the first time it is used, when you must validate it at the yellow box at the entry point.

On buses, you can buy an individual ticket on board (€1.50 one-way), but if you're going to use public transport more than once, save money by first buying a €0.50 rechargeable Andante card from a metro station, STCP kiosk, or affiliated convenience stores (look for the Andante decal), then load it up with cash or trips. For both metro and bus journeys with an Andante card, the cost depends on whether trips are within the city limits (€1.20 one way) or beyond (up to €5). On each trip, tickets and Andante cards must be validated.

In downtown Porto you're never far from a taxi stand, but you can also order a cab by phone or online—the city's main taxi company even has an app for smartphones. Make sure the driver turns on the meter; if you have phoned for the cab, you pay €1 extra. Within the city limits travelers are charged by meter, which starts at €2.50 (rates increase between 9 pm and 6 am, on weekends, and on holidays). Luggage fees are approximately €1.80 per item. Outside the city center (including over the river in Vila Nova de Gaia, where the port wine cellars are), the rate is €1 per km (plus 20% between 9 pm and 6 am, on weekends, and on holidays). Taxis that run outside the city center have a letter "A" on the door. It's considerate, but not obligatory, to tip up to 10%. For a significantly cheaper alternative to city taxis, Uber is a terrific way to get around.

SAFETY AND PRECAUTIONS

Porto is safe compared with many major European cities, even late at night. However, there are parts of the old town below the Sé and certain alleys on the outskirts of the Ribeira district that can become a bit seedy after dark. In general, though, the greatest danger is the odd pickpocket on public transportation—do keep an eye (and preferably a hand) on your belongings. There's a special police station for tourists downtown.

TIMING

You'll need a couple of days to experience Porto and its wine lodges and the nearby coastal resorts. Between *bodega* visits, leave yourself an afternoon or evening free to relax at a riverside bar or restaurant. Art lovers may end up spending hours at the Serralves Contemporary Art Museum, whose extensive gardens will also charm visitors. And to really appreciate the Casa da Música, you should take in a concert.

Several more days here permit a trip out to one of the region's beautiful beaches; up the lovely Douro Valley—rail or boat are options, or rental car, if you want to visit a *quinta* (wine estate); or an excursion to the history-rich towns of Braga, Guimarães, or Amarante.

VISITOR AND TOUR INFORMATION

The main municipal tourist office is next to the city hall at the top of Avenida dos Aliados, but there are branches next to the Sé and down in the Ribeira district. The national tourist office has branches downtown and at the airport. The Vila Nova de Gaia municipality has its own tourist offices (closed Sunday) with information on the local port wine lodges. The organization Rota do Vinho do Porto (Port Wine Route), based upriver in Pêso da Régua, can make reservations for Douro boat and train tours, hotels, and wine tastings at many of the valley's lovely quintas. There's a similar Rota dos Vinhos Verdes promoting visits and stays associated with vinho verde, the young wine produced across the Minho; its office is in Porto. The regional tourism board for the whole of the north (including Porto) is based in Viana do Castelo.

In town, Bluedragon offers walking tours (twice daily Tuesday–Sunday, from €15 for three hours), as well as bicycle and Segway tours (from €15 and €50, respectively, for three hours; reservations required for all tours) and bike rentals. Those on a budget should look no further than Porto Free Walking Tour, which leaves from Praça de Gomes Texeira (better known as Praça dos Leões) Monday through Saturday at 9:20 am (book online in advance). Vieguini, at the bottom of Rua do Infante D. Henrique, rents out mountain bikes (€5 for two hours, €12 for a full day), but you may find their motorized scooters (€20 for a half day, €28 for a full day, €75 for three days) better for tackling the city's hills. TukTour Porto offers tours on eco-friendly tuk-tuk wagons departing from two locations (Porto and across the river in Vila Nova de Gaia) to beaches, nearby fishing villages, and port wine cellars for €15–€25. OportoShare is another local tour company that offers customized tours for small groups or families, by van or Vespa.

Several local companies (and some Lisbon-based ones such as Diana Tours and Cityrama) run bus tours of Porto; these usually last a half day and take in all the main sights, including the port wine lodges in Vila Nova de Gaia. The two City Sightseeing routes run by Douro Acima (one covering downtown and Vila Nova de Gaia, including museums; the other downtown, Foz, and Boavista) depart every half hour, and you may hop on and off as often as you wish. Rival bus operator Living Tours has a minitrain you can pick up outside the Sé. Several companies also operate half- and full-day coach tours to the Douro Valley, the Minho, and the Parque Nacional da Peneda-Gerês.

Some of the same Porto-based companies offer cruises on the Rio Douro, often with free hotel pickup. These range from short trips taking in Porto's bridges and the local fishing villages to one- and two-day cruises that include meals and accommodations. Most of the short cruises depart several times daily from the Cais da Ribeira, at the foot of Porto's old town.

Douro Acima specializes in rides on *rabelos,* centuries-old sailboats traditionally used to transport port wine downriver. The six vessels leave from quays in both Porto's Ribeira district and across the river in Vila Nova de Gaia.

Douro Azul has the widest range of cruises, including trips upriver of up to a week, on air-conditioned hotel boats: the *Invicta* (40 double cabins), *Douro Cruiser* and *Douro Queen* (65 double cabins each, most with private balcony, plus rooftop pool and Jacuzzis), and newer *Viking Torgil* (88 cabins, all outfitted with flat-screen TVs). The company's main Porto office is open weekdays only; the branch in São Bento station is also open Saturday morning.

If you want to get above it all, Helitours offers 12-minute flights over Porto (from €45 per person) and 20-minute flights that take you farther upriver. The three-hour tour (from €325 per person) includes a trip to Mesão Frio, with a stop for lunch. The heliport is in the Massarelos area overlooking the Douro River and next to the Helitours office. Flights are for a minimum of four people.

EXPLORING

DOWNTOWN

TOP ATTRACTIONS

Fodor's Choice ★ **Cais da Ribeira** (*Ribeira Pier*). A string of fish restaurants and *tascas* (taverns) are built into the street-level arcade of timeworn buildings along this pier. In the Praça da Ribeira, people sit and chat at outdoor café tables surrounding a modern, cubelike sculpture; farther on, steps lead to a wide esplanade along the river that's backed by vibrantly hued row houses. The pier also provides the easiest access to the lower level of Porto's most iconic bridge across the Douro, the Ponte Dom Luis I. Those wishing to delve deeper into the Ribeira's 2,000-year past can embark upon informative riverboat tours, leaving from from Cais da Ribeira and across the river in Vila Nova da Gaia, which generally cruise around the city's six bridges and up the river to Peso da Régua and Pinhão. ⊠ *Porto*.

Casa da Música. Home to the National Orchestra of Porto and Portugal's Baroque Orchestra, this soaring postmodern temple to music was designed by legendary Dutch architect Rem Koolhaas ahead of Porto's stint as the European Culture Capital in 2001. Check the website for event listings, but the iconic building deserves a visit even in silence. Guided English tours are given at 10, 11, 4, and 5 daily, and special tourist packages (book in advance) include a backstage pass and a glass of port. ⊠ *Av. da Boavista 604–610* ☎ 22/012–0220 ⊕ *www.casadamusica.com*.

Fodor's Choice ★ **Centro Português de Fotografia** (*Portuguese Centre of Photography*). Housed in a spooky yet stately 18th-century jailhouse, this stellar museum hosts an ever-changing rotation of contemporary and modern 20th-century exhibitions by Portuguese photographers, reflecting their work both at home and abroad. Photography buffs will appreciate the permanent collection of analog cameras housed on the top floor. ⊠ *Edifício da Ex-Cadeia e Tribunal da Relação do Porto, Largo Amor de Perdição, Campo dos Mártires da Pátria* ☎ 22/004–6300 ⊕ *www.cpf.pt* ▭ *Free*.

Estação de São Bento. This train station was built in the early 20th century (King D. Carlos I laid the first brick himself in 1900) and inaugurated in 1915. It sits precisely where the Convent of S. Bento de Avé-Maria was located, and therefore inherited the convent's name—Saint Bento. The atrium, worth a visit even if you don't have a train to catch, is covered with 20,000 azulejos painted by Jorge Colaço (1916) depicting scenes of Portugal's history—from battles to coronations to royal gatherings—as well as ethnographic images. It is one of the city's most magnificent artistic undertakings of the early 20th century. The building was designed by Porto-born architect Marques da Silva. ⊠ *Praça Almeida Garret* ☎ *70/721–0220 for national call center* ⊕ *www.cp.pt.*

Fodor's Choice ★ **Igreja de Santo Ildefonso.** With the most striking exterior of any church in Porto, Ingreja de Santo Ildefonso has a facade covered with some 11,000 blue-and-white azulejo tiles depicting scenes from the Gospels and the life of Saint Ildefonso. The church was completed in the 18th century on the site of a previous chapel from the Middle Ages. While the outside walls are the real attraction, it's worth peeking inside, where you'll find a gilded raised altarpiece by the 18th-century Italian artist Nicolau Nasoni. The church holds a daily mass that's usually packed with locals. ⊠ *Praça da Batalha* ☎ *22/200–4366* ⊕ *www.santoildefonso.org.*

Fodor's Choice ★ **Museu de Arte Contemporânea.** Designed by Álvaro Siza Vieira, a winner of the Pritzker Prize and Portugal's best-known architect, the Contemporary Art Museum is part of the Serralves Foundation and is surrounded by lovely gardens. It has changing international exhibitions, as well as work from Portuguese painters, sculptors, and designers, so be sure to check the website for the latest news. Recharge after your visit with a Chemex-brewed coffee at the Serralves Tea House, whose homemade jams make nice souvenirs. Consider purchasing one of the combination tickets on offer, such as the one to the museum and to the Sea Life aquarium in Foz. ⊠ *Rua D. João de Castro 210* ☎ *22/615–6500, 808/200543* ⊕ *www.serralves.pt* ▣ *€10 museum and garden Tues.–Sat., €5 garden only; free 1st Sun. of the month until 1 pm.*

Sé do Porto (*Cathedral*). Originally constructed in the 12th century by the parents of Dom Afonso Henriques (Portugal's first king), Porto's granite cathedral has been rebuilt twice: first in the late 13th century and again in the 18th century, when the architect of the Torre dos Clérigos, Nicolau Nasoni, was among those commissioned to work on its expansion. Despite the renovations, it remains a fortresslike structure—an uncompromising testament to medieval wealth and power. Notice a low relief on the northern tower, depicting a 14th-century vessel and symbolizing the city's nautical vocation. Size is the only exceptional thing about the interior; when you enter the two-story 14th-century cloisters, however, the building comes to life. Decorated with gleaming azulejos, a staircase added by Nasoni leads to the second level and into a richly furnished chapter house, from which there are fine views through narrow windows. Nasoni also designed the Paço dos Arcebispos (Archbishops' Palace) behind the cathedral; it has been converted to offices, so you can only admire its 197-foot-long facade. ⊠ *Terreiro da Sé* ☎ *22/205–9028* ⊕ *www.diocese-porto.pt* ▣ *Cathedral free, cloisters €3.*

Torre dos Clérigos. Designed by Italian architect Nicolau Nasoni and begun in 1754, the tower of the church Igreja dos Clérigos reaches an impressive height of 249 feet. There are 225 steep stone steps to the belfry, and the considerable effort required to climb them is rewarded by stunning views of the red-roofed Old Town, the river, and beyond to the mouth of the Douro. Binoculars and audio tours are available for an extra charge. The church itself, also built by Nasoni, predates the tower and is an elaborate example of Italianate baroque architecture and is a must-see if only to explore the pathways above and behind the ornate marble chapel. ⊠ *Rua de São Filipe de Nery* ☎ *22/200–1729* ⊕ *www. torredosclerigos.pt* ☒ *Church free, tower €3.*

WORTH NOTING

Casa-Museu de Guerra Junqueiro (*Guerra Junqueiro House and Museum*). This white 18th-century mansion, one of several buildings in Porto attributed by some to a pupil of Nicolau Nasoni and by others to Nicolau himself, was home to the poet Guerra Junqueiro (1850–1923). It's located in the picturesque (if ramshackle) Sé neighborhood, below the cathedral. Furnishings, sculptures, and paintings are labeled in English, but tours are in Portuguese only. ⊠ *Rua de Dom Hugo 32* ☎ *22/200–3689* ☒ *€2.20 (free on weekends)* ⊘ *Closed Mon.*

Igreja de São Francisco (*Church of St. Francis*). During the last days of Porto's siege by the absolutist army (the *miguelistas*) in July 1842, there was gunfire by the nearby São Francisco Convent. These shootings caused a fire that destroyed most parts of the convent, sparing only this church. Today the church is the most prominent Gothic monument in Porto. It's a rather undistinguished, late-14th-century Gothic building on the outside, but inside is an astounding interior: gilded carving—added in the mid-18th century—runs up the pillars, over the altar, and across the ceiling. An adjacent museum (Museu de Arte Sacra) houses furnishings from the Franciscan convent. A guided tour (call the day before) includes a visit to the church, museum, and catacombs. ⊠ *Rua do Infante Dom Henrique 93* ☎ *22/206–2100* ⊕ *www.ordemsaofrancisco.pt* ☒ *Free.*

Museu do Vinho do Porto (*Port Wine Museum*). Not to be confused with the larger, modern port-wine museum upriver in Peso da Régua, this small but worthwhile facility has informative exhibits on the history of the trade that made Porto famous. The setting right on the Douro River makes for a spectacular walk in the late afternoon, or a scenic ride by Bus 500 or electric Tram E1. Displays include implements used in port-wine production—antique glass decanters and textiles, for instance—as well as paintings and engravings depicting the trade. There are occasional tastings as well. ⊠ *Rua de Monchique 98* ☎ *22/207–6300* ⊕ *www.cmp.pt* ☒ *€2.20 (free on weekends).*

Palácio da Bolsa. Formerly Porto's stock exchange, Palácio da Bolsa is one of the city's most breathtaking historical buildings. Guided tours (every half hour) are the only way to see the interior of this masterpiece of 19th-century Portuguese architecture, so if you're only in Porto for one day, it's wise to prebook your tour in the morning for an afternoon time slot. The grand Arab-style ballroom, with its octagonal dome and ornate Moorish arches, is the most memorable chamber. ⊠ *Rua Ferreira Borges* ☎ *22/339–9000* ⊕ *www.palaciodabolsa.com* ⊡ *Tours €8.*

Teleférico de Gaia (*Gaia cable car*). If your feet are tired, skip climbing up Vila Nova de Gaia's steep hills on foot and hop on the cable car, which offers sweeping views of the Douro River and the Ribeira. ⊠ *Calçada da Serra 143, Vila Nova de Gaia* ☎ *22/372–3709* ⊕ *www.gaiacablecar. com* ⊡ *€5 one-way, €8 round-trip.*

Ponte Dom Luís I (*Luís I Bridge*). Designed by Teófilo Seyrig (who apprenticed for Gustave Eiffel), this two-tiered metal bridge leads directly to the city of Vila Nova de Gaia. Its real glory, however, is the magnificent vistas it affords of downtown Porto. A jumble of red-tile roofs on pastel-color buildings mixes with gray-and-white church towers, and all is reflected in the majestic Douro River; if the sun is shining just right, everything appears to be washed in gold. Beside the foot of the bridge on the Porto riverbank is the lower station of the Funicular dos Guindais, the quaintest part of the city's public transportation system, which cranks uphill to the Batalha neighborhood, just east of the cathedral. ⊠ *Porto.*

Vila Nova de Gaia. A city across the Rio Douro from central Porto, Vila Nova de Gaia has been the headquarters of the port-wine trade since the late 17th century, when import bans on French wine led British merchants to look for alternative sources. By the 18th century, the British had established companies and a regulatory association in Porto. The wine was transported from vineyards on the upper Douro to port-wine caves at Vila Nova de Gaia, where it was allowed to mature before being exported. Little has changed in the relationship between Porto and the Douro since those days, as wine is still transported to the city downriver (in temperature-controlled trucks nowadays), and matured and bottled in the warehouses. A couple of the traditional *rabelo* boats are moored at the quayside on the Vila Nova de Gaia side. ⊠ *Vila Nova de Gaia.*

Casa-Museu de Texeira. Vila Nova de Gaia isn't solely devoted to the port-wine trade. Combine a tour of the wine lodges with a visit to the Casa-Museu de Teixeira Lopes, the former home of the sculptor António Teixeira Lopes (1866–1942). It contains some excellent sculpture as well as a varied collection of paintings by Teixeira Lopes's contemporaries. It's worth spending some time perusing the collection of books, coins, and ceramics. ⊠ *Rua Teixeira Lopes 32, Vila Nova de Gaia* ☎ *22/375–1224* ⊡ *Free Tues.–Fri.* ⊙ *Closed Mon.*

OUTSIDE DOWNTOWN

TOP ATTRACTIONS

Casa de Chá da Boa Nova. Architecture buffs intrigued by Álvaro Siza Vieira's work after visiting the Museu de Arte Contemporânea might consider a trip to Matosinhos, north of Foz, to see this modernist "teahouse" wedged between boulders just steps from the sea. One of Siza's earliest projects, completed in 1963, it was designed after careful analysis of the surrounding rock formations, tides, and flora. The approach—a series of platforms, steps, and bifold doors—provides a sense of anticipation and views of the structure and the ocean beyond it. In summer, the enormous windows slide down, creating the impression

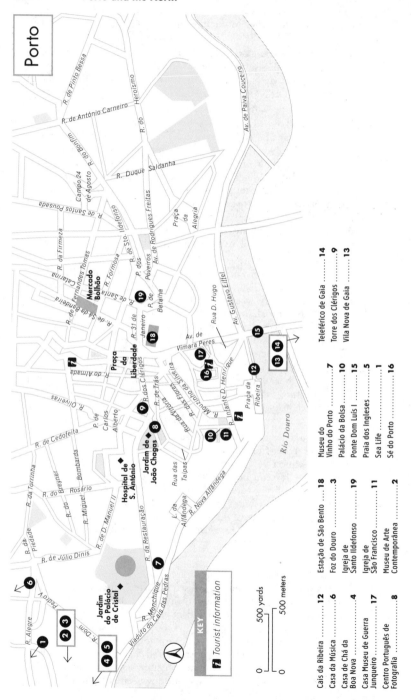

Porto

Cais da Ribeira **12**

Casa da Música **6**

Casa de Chá da
Boa Nova **4**

Casa Museu de Guerra
Junqueiro **17**

Centro Português de
Fotografia **8**

Estação de São Bento **18**

Foz do Douro **3**

Igreja de
Santo Ildefonso **19**

Igreja de
São Francisco **11**

Museu de Arte
Contemporânea **2**

Museu do
Vinho do Porto **7**

Palácio da Bolsa **10**

Ponte Dom Luís I **15**

Praia dos Ingleses **5**

Sea Life **1**

Sé do Porto **16**

Teleférico de Gaia **14**

Torre dos Clérigos **9**

Vila Nova de Gaia **13**

KEY

i *Tourist information*

0 500 yards

0 500 meters

Port Wine

Many of the companies with caves in Vila Nova de Gaia are foreign-owned, and it's been that way for centuries. They include such well-known names as Sandeman, Osborne, Cockburn, Kopke, Ferreira, Calém, Taylor's, Barros, Ramos-Pinto, Real Companhia Velha, Fonseca, Rozès, Burmester, Offley, Noval, and Graham's. All are signposted and within a few minutes' walk of the bridge and each other; their names are also displayed in huge white letters across their roofs. Most bodegas offer free guided tours, which always end with a tasting of one or two wines and an opportunity to buy bottles from the company store. Children are usually welcome and are often fascinated by the huge warehouses and clunky old machinery.

From April through September, the major lodges are generally open daily 9:30–12:30 and 2–6, although some close on weekends; the rest of the year, tours start a little later and end a little earlier. Tours begin regularly, usually when enough visitors are assembled. The tourist office at Vila Nova de Gaia offers a small map of the main lodges and can advise you on hours of the smaller operations. Some lodges also have restaurants with quite sophisticated menus; a prime example is Taylor's **Barão Fladgate** (Rua do Choupelo 250 ☎ 22/374–2800 ⊕ *www.tresseculos. pt*), whose location uphill means its garden and terrace afford magnificent views of Porto.

you can step right out into the sea. Massive renovations in summer 2013 were said to cost €500 million. You can eat here, or order drinks from noon to midnight. ✉ *Rua Boa Nova, Leça da Palmeira, Av. da Liberdade, Leça da Palmeira* ☎ 22/994–0066.

Foz do Douro. Literally "Mouth of the Douro," this prosperous suburb is invariably known here simply as "Foz." You haven't gotten under the skin of Porto if you haven't ventured to this beach community: it's a place where city dwellers flock to kick back beside the sea or go for brisk walks on its magnificent promenades. Grab a bite or coffee at **Praia dos Ingleses** (☎ 22/617–0419), a café perched above a rock-framed beach of the same name, which draws youngsters year-round with well-priced snacks and free Wi-Fi. The area is also one of the city's main nightlife hubs. A fun if slow way to get to Foz is to catch Tram 1; its route hugs the riverbank, starting next to the church of São Francisco in the Ribeira. ✉ *Foz do Douro.*

FAMILY **Sea Life.** Arguably Porto's top kids' attraction since it opened in 2009, this compact aquarium is at the western end of Avenida da Boavista (next to the Castelo do Queijo, a 17th-century coastal fort that's also worth a look). Sharks, jellyfish, and seahorses are among the 5,600 or so animals on display, representing more than 100 species. Other highlights include live turtle feeding and an interactive Finding Dory trail. Joint tickets are available for Sea Life and the Museu de Arte Contemporânea, but if you only plan to visit the aquarium, note that tickets bought online are cheaper. The nearby Parque da Cidade, a large landscaped park dotted with trees and lakes, is a lovely place

8

for a picnic. ✉ *1ª Rua Particular do Castelo do Queijo, Foz do Douro* ☎ *22/619–0400* ⊕ *www.visitsealife.com/porto* ⌫ *€13.*

WHERE TO EAT

$ ✕ **Abadia do Porto.** The cavernous interior, thick tablecloths, and well-heeled clientele tell you this is not just another tasca, but the food at this backstreet abbey is about as down-home as you can get. Although the decor has a monastic theme, meals here are far from austere, so come hungry to make the most of the huge servings of *cabrito assado* (roast kid), *rancho* (mixed grill), *bacalhau à Gomes Sá* (codfish with onions, potato, egg, and olives), and Porto tripas—tripe with beans, chouriço, and vegetables. It's all great value if you share a dish between two or even three people. The chocolate-flavor *pão-de-ló* sponge cake is divine, too. $ *Average main: €14* ✉ *Rua Ateneu Comercial do Porto 22–24* ☎ *22/200–8757* ⊕ *www.abadiadoporto.com* ☾ *Closed Sun.*

PORTUGUESE
Fodor's Choice
★

$ ✕ **Caldeireiros.** These days, embarking on a *petiscos* (Portuguese-style tapas) crawl is the trendiest way to dine in Porto, and there's no better place to sample a smorgasbord of small plates than at Caldeireiros. Cozy and appointed with long, candlelit communal tables, this relative newcomer has already earned a reputation among locals for its refreshing sangria and for comfort-food dishes like *alheira de caça,* a wild-game sausage that's heavy on the garlic. $ *Average main: €13* ✉ *Rua dos Caldeireiros 139* ☎ *22/321–4074* ☾ *Closed Sun.* ▤ *No credit cards.*

PORTUGUESE

$ ✕ **Canelas de Coelho.** There's nothing traditional about this informal little place, which rings the culinary changes with dishes full of interesting combinations of flavors. Start with sweet-and-sour caramelized octopus, and then move on to seared veal steak with mashed chickpeas, or jet-black linguine with scallops and shrimp fumet. Vegetarian dishes are always available, as well as several wines by the glass—and ports to finish, of course. $ *Average main: €14* ✉ *Rua Elísio Melo 29–33* ☎ *22/201–5824* ☾ *Closed Sun. No lunch Sat..*

PORTUGUESE

$$ ✕ **Cantina 32.** This industrial-chic newcomer on Porto's culinary scene could pass as a Williamsburg or Kreuzberg hot spot if it weren't for its predominantly Portuguese cuisine, which runs the gamut from *bacalhau à bras* (a salt-cod-and-shoestring-potato scramble) to a surprisingly delicious amuse-bouche of country bread spread with banana butter. Book your table ahead of time—walk-ins often find themselves out of luck. $ *Average main: €18* ✉ *Rua das Flores 32* ☎ *22/203–9069* ⊕ *www.cantina32.com* ☾ *Closed Sun.*

PORTUGUESE
Fodor's Choice
★

$$$ ✕ **Cantinho do Avillez.** José Avillez, the young, head-turning chef behind the two-Michelin-star restaurant Belcanto in Lisbon, has made a splash on the Porto culinary scene with Cantinho do Avillez, a homey yet modern dining room located just downhill from São Bento railway station. Although the menu rotates according to what's in season, certain items are too good to be taken off—the "Barrosã DOP" hamburger, topped with caramelized onion and foie gras, is a case in point. $ *Average main: €28* ✉ *Rua de Mouzinho da Silveira 166* ☎ *22/322–7879* ⊕ *www.joseavillez.pt.*

PORTUGUESE
Fodor's Choice
★

$$ ✕ **Casa do Aleixo.** Conveniently located steps from Campanhã train station, Casa do Aleixo has built up a strong reputation for its country

PORTUGUESE

fare. A winning meal might start with the *alheira de caça* (a garlicky game sausage) or *polvo com molho verde* (octopus in an herb sauce) and then progress to *filetes de pescada* (haddock fillets) or *vitela assada* (roast veal). There are also daily specials and several wines by the glass. Save room for dessert: the *abade de Priscos* pudding, a port-spiked variation on crème caramel, is a showstopper. $ *Average main: €20* ⊠ *Rua da Estação 216* ☏ *22/537–0462, 91/919–7536* ⊘ *Closed Sun., and last wk in Dec., 1st wk in Jan., and 1st 3 wks in Aug.*

$ ✕ **Casa Guedes.** Without a doubt, one of the most heavenly—and budget-
PORTUGUESE friendly—mouthfuls in Porto is the pulled-pork-and-sheep's-milk-cheese
Fodor's Choice slider from Casa Guedes. Served on a warm country roll and oozing
★ with pungent Serra da Estrela aged in the mountains, it's no wonder there are always lines out the door at this unapologetically lowbrow establishment, which has been in business for 30 years. The perfect pairing? A thirst-quenching bubbly rosé bottled specially for the restaurant. $ *Average main: €5* ⊠ *Praça dos Poveiros 130* ☏ *22/200–2874.*

$$ ✕ **Chez Lapin.** At this Cais da Ribeira restaurant, the service may be slow
PORTUGUESE and the folksy decor a bit overdone, but this is definitely a step up from other touristy spots on the riverfront—the food is consistently good and the location can't be beat. Grab a seat on the attractive outdoor terrace and order generous portions of such traditional Portuguese dishes as bacalhau *à lagareiro* (baked, with potatoes), sardines with rice and beans, and beef medallions with port wine. The restaurant is mainly patronized by foreign visitors, so if you're after authentic Porto cuisine in a less touristy setting, look elsewhere. The family-owned company that owns the restaurant (Douro Acima) offers river excursions on its six traditional boats docked at the quay. $ *Average main: €20* ⊠ *Rua dos Canastreiros 40–42* ☏ *22/200–6418* ⊕ *www.issimo.pt* ⌂ *Reservations essential.*

$$$$ ✕ **DOP.** Chef Rui Paula won national fame with reinventions of Portu-
PORTUGUESE guese classics at his restaurant DOC, upriver on the Douro. Now he's
Fodor's Choice thrilling Porto foodies in this elegant refitted palace with star dishes like
★ *bacalhau com broa* (codfish with corn bread), and stewed *tripas*—if you've tried this Porto dish elsewhere, you'll be amazed by Paula's ultralight version. There are vegetarian options; a wide, eclectic selection of wines by the bottle (from €17) or glass; and desserts featuring typical regional produce such as quince and chestnuts. The €20 three-course tasting menu, served at lunch, is one of the best deals in town. $ *Average main: €70* ⊠ *Palácio das Artes, Largo de São Domingos 18* ☏ *22/201–4313, 91/001–4041* ⊕ *www.ruipaula.com* ⊘ *Closed Sun. No lunch Mon.*

$ ✕ **Essência.** The cuisine of northern Portugal is notoriously meat-heavy,
VEGETARIAN and restaurants in Porto aren't especially sympathetic to vegetarians. That's a shame, since local produce is so excellent that it can easily stand alone as an entrée. Luckily Essência understands this untapped potential, and its menu showcases vegetable-driven dishes that run the gamut from curries to salads to risottos that are objectively delicious, regardless of your dietary preferences. Vegan and gluten-free items are available. $ *Average main: €14* ⊠ *Rua de Pedro Hispano 1196* ☏ *22/830–1813* ⊕ *www.essenciarestaurantevegetariano.com* ⊘ *Closed Sun.*

8

$$$ PORTUGUESE FAMILY 🍴 **O Escondidinho.** In business since 1934, this popular restaurant opened during the first great Portuguese Colonial Exhibition that took place in the Palácio de Cristal. Its long history is evident in the entrance, where hand-painted tiles from the 17th century announce a country-house decor. The menu has French-influenced dishes as well as Douro standbys. Steak is prepared no fewer than six ways (try the smoky version with truffles), and the sole—finished with capers or a port reduction—is always deliciously fresh. The *pudim flan* (egg custard) and *toucinho do céu* (a similar dessert, but with almond and egg yolks) are excellent. [$] *Average main: €25* ✉ *Rua Passos Manuel 142* ☎ *22/200–1079, 93/310–1600* 🌐 *www.escondidinho.com.pt.*

$$$$ CONTEMPORARY 🍴 **Pedro Lemos.** Seemingly a world away from the hustle and bustle of downtown Porto, Pedro Lemos's namesake restaurant occupies a cozy dining room in a stone farmhouse on the Douro's scenic riverbank. Lemos's signature dexterity is in full force here with decadent, expertly prepared dishes that center around the best proteins the region has to offer: blue lobster, milk-fed lamb, and roasted Iberian pork from Alentejo—available in four-, six-, or eight-course tasting menus (€80, €100, and €120, respectively). The rooftop terrace tables are the best seats in the house, weather permitting. [$] *Average main: €80* ✉ *Rua do Padre Luís Cabral 974, Foz do Douro* ☎ *22/011–5986* 🌐 *www.pedrolemos.net* 🕒 *Closed Mon.*

$$$ PORTUGUESE 🍴 **Portucale.** Atop a modern tower block on a hill, the Portucale is known for its excellent food and sweeping views, which take in everything from the Atlantic to the Marão mountains, far inland. Dining here is like stepping back in time: service is genteel and dishes harken back to classic French cuisine (foie gras looms large). Local specialties include tripas and bacalhau *à marinheiro* (with shrimps and clams). The dessert trolley groans across the dining room, laden with Portuguese sweets, which go best with a glass of port. The lunchtime executive menu is an excellent value at €19, including dessert and wine; tasting menus start at €35. A taxi is the best way to reach this place. [$] *Average main: €30* ✉ *Rua da Alegria 598* ☎ *22/537–0717* 🌐 *www.miradouro-portucale.com* ✍ *Reservations essential.*

$ INDIAN 🍴 **Portugandhi.** Many visitors to Porto don't realize that the city is home to a vibrant Indian population, making it one of Europe's top destinations for curry lovers. At Portugandhi, an intimate restaurant always packed with locals just south of Praça do Marquês de Pombal, you can delve your spoon into heady bowls of less-common curries like the Goan-style *xacuti,* thick with coconut cream. Burnished disks of naan, available in several variations, are ideal accompaniments. Prix-fixe weekday lunches are a bargain at €8. [$] *Average main: €15* ✉ *Rua do Bonjardim 1143* ☎ *22/332–2554* 🌐 *www.portugandhi.com* 🕒 *Closed Sun.* 💳 *No credit cards.*

WHERE TO STAY

$ HOTEL 🏨 **Crowne Plaza Porto.** This hotel (formerly the Tiara Park Atlantic) is a modern luxury option with a roster of facilities and bright, comfortable guest rooms. **Pros:** good for Foz and Casa da Música; pet-friendly (€25 per pet); spacious rooms. **Cons:** a little far from the city center.

$ Rooms from: €120 ⊠ Av. Boavista 1466, Boavista ☎ 22/607–2500 ⊕ www.crowneplaza.com/porto ⇆ 190 rooms, 42 suites ⊙ Breakfast Ⓜ Casa da Música or Francos.

$
B&B/INN
FAMILY
▥ **Favorita.** Right on trendy Rua Miguel Bombarda, with its galleries and shops, this small pensão combines contemporary style with a warm welcome. **Pros:** spacious rooms tastefully decorated; large terrace and garden; free Wi-Fi. **Cons:** few facilities; rooms at the front can be noisy. $ Rooms from: €70 ⊠ Rua Miguel Bombarda 267 ☎ 22/013–4157 ⊕ www.pensaofavorita.pt ⇆ 12 rooms ⊙ Breakfast.

$
HOTEL
▥ **Grande Hotel do Porto.** If you enjoy shopping, you can't do better than the stately Grande Hotel do Porto, as it sits on the city's best shopping street. **Pros:** good location; efficient staff; near public transportation. **Cons:** most rooms rather small; restaurant kitchen closes at 10 pm; room safe and Wi-Fi cost extra. $ Rooms from: €116 ⊠ Rua de Santa Catarina 197 ☎ 22/207–6690 ⊕ www.grandehotelporto.com ⇆ 94 rooms ⊙ Breakfast Ⓜ Bolhão.

$
HOTEL
FAMILY
▥ **HF Ipanema Park.** This elegant hotel tower, which is part of the HF hotel collection, is a 15-minute taxi ride from the center of town, but what it lacks in centrality, it makes up for in on-site facilities, including an outdoor swimming pool, kids playroom, bike rentals, and more. **Pros:** lots of amenities; babysitting services available; good breakfast. **Cons:** long walk to the center of town. $ Rooms from: €80 ⊠ Rua de Serralves 124 ☎ 22/532–2100 ⊕ www.hfhotels.com ⇆ 281 rooms ⊙ Breakfast.

$
HOTEL
▥ **Hotel Mercure.** Overlooking one of Porto's central squares, the Praça da Batalha, this upscale chain property is a good choice for location and luxury at a reasonable price. **Pros:** free Wi-Fi; generous breakfast included. **Cons:** outer rooms overlooking the square can be noisy on weekends; scant storage space. $ Rooms from: €105 ⊠ Praca da Batalha 116 ☎ 22/204–3300 ⊕ www.mercure.com ⇆ 145 rooms ⊙ Breakfast.

$$$
HOTEL
Fodor's Choice
★
▥ **InterContinental Porto–Palacio das Cardosas.** The InterContinental Porto–Palacio das Cardosas has got it all: location, luxury, and an intriguing history to boot. **Pros:** central location; outstanding service; complimentary Wi-Fi. **Cons:** only one restaurant in hotel. $ Rooms from: €250 ⊠ Praca da Libertade 25 ☎ 22/003–5600 ⊕ www.ichotelsgroup.com/intercontinental/en/gb/locations/porto ⇆ 105 rooms ⊙ Breakfast Ⓜ São Bento.

$
B&B/INN
▥ **Pão de Açúcar.** Just off Avenida dos Aliados, this simply but elegantly decorated art nouveau pensão offers a lot of amenities for relatively modest rates. **Pros:** free Wi-Fi; prime location. **Cons:** parking a block away; TV-Internet lounge a little small; walls could be thicker. $ Rooms from: €50 ⊠ Rua do Almada 262 ☎ 22/200–2425 ⊕ www.paodeacucarhotel.pt ⇆ 50 rooms, 8 suites ⊙ Breakfast Ⓜ Trindade.

$$$
HOTEL
▥ **Pestana Vintage Porto.** Located in Porto's historic heart, the Pestana Vintage Porto occupies a restored warehouse abutted by a medieval wall that links to several neighboring former houses; as a result, every room is different and some are unusually shaped. **Pros:** charming historic building; well-located for sightseeing in Ribeira and Gaia; new restaurant. **Cons:** few facilities; no on-site parking; bus stop is up a

8

steep hill. $ *Rooms from: €220* ⊠ *Praça da Ribeira 1* ☎ *22/340–2300* ⊕ *www.pestana.com* ⇒ *109 rooms* ❍ *Breakfast.*

$
HOTEL
FAMILY
Fodor's Choice
★

⌂ **Sheraton Porto Hotel & Spa.** Seen by some as the city's top hotel, the Sheraton Porto's declared aim is to blend design and comfort. **Pros:** stunningly stylish; 24-hour luxury spa accessible via VIP lift; international TV channels; free Wi-Fi. **Cons:** a little far from center; only pricier rooms have terraces; spa not included with standard room rate. $ *Rooms from: €140* ⊠ *Rua Tenente Valadim 146, Boavista* ☎ *22/040–4000* ⊕ *www.sheratonporto.com* ⇒ *241 rooms, 25 suites* ❍ *Breakfast; All meals; Some meals* Ⓜ *Francos.*

$
B&B/INN

⌂ **6 Only.** As the name suggests, this friendly modern guesthouse a short walk from the shops of Rua Santa Catarina has six rooms, so book ahead. **Pros:** spacious rooms tastefully decorated; large terrace and garden; attentive owners. **Cons:** no parking; rooms at the front get a bit of street noise; spotty Wi-Fi. $ *Rooms from: €70* ⊠ *Rua Duque de Loulé 97* ☎ *22/201–3971, 92/688–5187* ⊕ *www.6only.pt* ⇒ *6 rooms* ❍ *Breakfast.*

$$$
HOTEL
Fodor's Choice
★

⌂ **The Yeatman.** If you count wine among your passions, a stay at the British-inspired Yeatman Hotel should be on your Portugal itinerary. **Pros:** convenient location; great views; indoor swimming pool and gym. **Cons:** breakfast not included; some might find scale and neoclassical decor over the top. $ *Rooms from: €250* ⊠ *Rua do Choupelo, Santa Marinha, Vila Nova de Gaia* ☎ *22/013–3100* ⊕ *www.theyeatman.com* ⇒ *70 rooms, 12 suites* ❍ *No meals* Ⓜ *General Torres.*

NIGHTLIFE AND PERFORMING ARTS

Noted as a center for modern art, Porto enjoys regular and changing exhibitions at the Museu de Arte Contemporânea, as well as at a variety of galleries, many of which are on Rua Miguel Bombarda. Check local newspapers or with the tourist board for listings of current exhibitions as well as concerts. If you read Portuguese, the monthly magazine *Time Out Porto* and the pocket booklet *Guia da Noite do Porto* (available in cafés, bars, and cultural institutions) are good ways to find out what's on, and what's in.

NIGHTLIFE

BARS

A number of old-style cafés, such as the **Guarany** or **Majestic** (⇨ *see Need a Break? box*), are good places for an early-evening drink but don't represent what locals would term "nightlife." And while the waterfront Ribeira district was once popular with bohemian barhoppers, it's now been left almost exclusively to tourists. But there's been a nightlife renaissance in central Porto in the area just to the north of the Torre dos Clérigos, thanks in part to the vibrant student population. Fashionable bars in this area are open from midafternoon until 3 am (4 am on Friday and Saturday).

Café Candelabro. At this smoky, bohemian bookstore-turned-bar, drinks run cheaper than most other nightspots in the area. It's supposed to close at 2 am, but hours are elastic on weekends. ⊠ *Rua da Conceição 3* ☎ *96/698–4250* ⊕ *www.cafecandelabro.com.*

Clube 3C. By day, this venue is a pleasant if unremarkable restaurant, but at night, the lights go down, the music turns up, and Clube 3C transforms into a petite discotheque. The decor blends the antique and the contemporary, and it's a popular meeting place for fashionable thirtysomethings. ⊠ *Rua Cândido dos Reis 18* ☎ *22/201–8247* ⊕ *www.clube3c.pt.*

DANCE AND MUSIC CLUBS

Hard Club. For live music, head to this club inside a magnificent 18th-century market hall with cast-iron pillars—it's opposite the Palácio da Bolsa. Friday and Saturday (and some Thursdays) you might catch folk, heavy metal, or a nationally known pop group; on other nights there are cinema screenings, theater, and the odd DJ set. There's an airy café-restaurant upstairs with free Wi-Fi. ⊠ *Mercado Ferreira Borges, Rua Infante Dom Henrique 95* ☎ *93/527–4541* ⊕ *www.hard-club.com.*

Hot Five Jazz & Blues Club. With live shows every week (Wednesday–Saturday), Hot Five hosts a range of acts on its stage, from Queen tribute bands to swing ensembles. There's a smoking area on the balcony. Prices vary by event; book a table in advance online. ⊠ *Largo Actor Dias 51* ☎ *93/432–8583* ⊕ *www.hotfive.pt.*

Fodor's Choice ★ **Maus Hábitos.** A meeting place for Porto's leading artists, thinkers, and alternative types, Maus Hábitos (Bad Habits) is a gallery, restaurant, and cultural center—and also the hippest nightlife venue in town. The mixed bag of nightly events range from DJ sets to live concerts to Lindy Hop dance parties. ⊠ *Rua Passos Manuel 178, 4th fl.* ☎ *93/720–2918, 22/208–7268* ⊕ *www.maushabitos.com.*

PERFORMING ARTS

THEATERS AND CONCERT HALLS

Coliseu do Porto. This is one of the biggest showrooms in Portugal, with nearly 3,000 seats. Countless Portuguese and international showbiz legends have appeared here, including Pat Metheny, Diana Krall, Bob Dylan, and Amália Rodrigues. ⊠ *Rua de Passos Manuel 137* ☎ *22/339–4940* ⊕ *www.coliseudoporto.pt.*

Teatro Nacional de São João. Designed in 1978, this theater hosts and produces a good range of classical and contemporary concerts and plays all year round. ⊠ *Praça da Batalha* ☎ *22/340–1900, 800/108675* ⊕ *www.tnsj.pt.*

SPORTS AND THE OUTDOORS

The main sporting obsession in Porto is *futebol* (soccer), and the city has one of the country's best teams, FC Porto, which rivals Lisbon's Benfica for domestic fame and fortune. But soccer isn't Porto's only claim to fame when it comes to sports; surfing is a favorite pastime among locals of all ages, particularly those who live in the city's coastal areas.

Estádio do Dragão (*Dragon Stadium*). Futebol matches are played September through June at this 52,000-seat stadium in the eastern part of the city by the ring road; it is served by four metro lines. ⊠ *Alameda das Antas, off Av. de Fernão de Magalhães* ☎ *22/508–3300* ⊕ *www.fcporto.pt.*

NEED A BREAK?

Many of Porto's old-style coffee-houses—which once rivaled Lisbon's in opulence and literary legend—have disappeared. A few have survived and are perfect places to sit and imbibe both a *cimbalino* (espresso) and the city.

Confeitaria do Bolhão. At the attractively restored Confeitaria do Bolhão, choose from an impressive range of delicious bread, cakes, and pastries. Try a featherlight pão-de-ló sponge cake, served fresh from the oven with the baking paper still around it. ⊠ *Rua Formosa 339* ☎ *22/339–5220* ⊕ *www.confeitari-adobolhao.com.*

Guarany Café. Founded in 1933, the Guarany Café is a superb place

that exudes old-world charm. If you're lucky, you might happen upon a live concert (often fado or Cuban music) or poetry reading. There's also free Wi-Fi. ⊠ *Av. dos Aliados 89/85* ☎ *22/332–1272* ⊕ *www.cafeguarany.com.*

Majestic Café. The ornate, historic Majestic Café—on one of Porto's main shopping drags—should not be missed, despite the inflated coffee prices. The decor takes you back in time, and pastries are among the freshest in town. There's also piano music and rotating art exhibitions. ⊠ *Rua de Santa Catarina 112* ☎ *22/200–3887* ⊕ *www.cafemajestic.com.*

Fodor's Choice ★ **Godzilla Surfcamp.** Downtown Porto may not exude beach-town vibes, but take the blue metro line due west, and you'll arrive at Matosinhos, a seaside enclave on the Atlantic famous for its surf culture. Get in on the action, whether you're a first-timer or a seasoned pro, with the help of Godzilla Surfcamp. Their individual and group lessons are straightforward, professional, and affordable. ⊠ *Rua Mouzinho da Silveira 72* ☎ *92/500–3299* ⊕ *godzillasurfcamp.com.*

SHOPPING

The best shopping streets are those off the Praça da Liberdade, particularly Rua 31 de Janeiro, Rua dos Clérigos, Rua de Santa Catarina, Rua Sá da Bandeira, Rua Cedofeita, and Rua das Flores. Traditionally, Rua das Flores has been the street for silversmiths. Gold-plated filigree is also a regional specialty, found along the same street and along Rua de Santa Catarina. Rua 31 de Janeiro and nearby streets are the center of the shoe trade, and many shops create made-to-measure shoes on request.

You'll see port wine on sale throughout the city, and after sampling a few different types at the caves in Vila Nova de Gaia, you may want to buy a bottle. The more unusual white port, drunk as an aperitif, makes a lovely souvenir as it's not commonly sold in North America or Britain. Try a Portonic, half tonic water and half white port, served in a special glass that you'll see sold in most shops.

CLOTHING AND FOOTWEAR

With Portugal's large textile and apparel industries concentrated in the north, it's no surprise that Porto is home to a number of the country's leading fashion designers. Luís Buchinho was the first to move his store downtown to the Baixa, which has since become the city's most happening district.

Buchinho. The practical, comfortable designs on sale by this Portuguese fashion legend at his flagship store have a strong urban feel to them. The women's wear is particularly stunning. ⊠ *Rua José Falcão 122* ☎ *22/201–0184* ⊕ *www.luisbuchinho.pt.*

Fodor's Choice ★ **The Feeting Room.** This ultramodern boutique specializes in women's shoes, and in accessories for both men and women. Of particular interest are the Maria Maleta leather bags, handmade in Porto since 2013 by two young female entrepreneurs. Wacky flats and platform shoes by Portuguese designer Marita Moreno are also worth seeking out. ⊠ *Largo dos Lóios 89* ☎ *22/011–0463, 93/614–2659 (mobile; available to chat via WhatsApp)* ⊕ *www.thefeetingroom.com.*

Mercado 48. A colorful hodgepodge of Portuguese-made apparel, housewares, and art, Mercado 48 is a lovely place to shop for tasteful gifts and souvenirs. ⊠ *Rua da Conceição 48* ☎ *93/588–1626* ⊕ *www.mercado48.pt* ⊘ *Closed Sun. and Mon.*

CRAFTS AND STATIONERY

A Vida Portuguesa. One of Portugal's most talked-about retailers is this shop, whose Porto branch occupies a magnificent former clothing store. Like the original shop in Lisbon, it carries old Portuguese brands—many with delightful packaging—of products that include soap and other toiletries, stationery, costume jewelry, handicrafts, and period toys. ⊠ *Rua da Galeria de Paris 20* ☎ *22/202–2105* ⊕ *www.avidaportuguesa.com.*

Artesanato dos Clérigos. For a religious-themed handicrafts emporium, try this shop next to Torre dos Clérigos. ⊠ *Rua da Assunção 33–34* ☎ *22/200–0257* ⊕ *www.artesacraporto.com.*

Castelbel. For luxury toiletries, drawer liners, and perfumed paper by a local firm whose products are hard to find abroad, visit this fine store at the Hotel Infante Sagres. ⊠ *Praça D. Filipa de Lencastre 62* ☎ *22/982–6430* ⊕ *www.castelbel.com.*

Fodor's Choice ★ **Livraria Lello e Irmão.** Legend has it that one of J. K. Rowling's chief inspirations for the fantasy world of *Harry Potter* was this turn-of-the-last-century bookstore located in the Vitoria district. Although Rowling hasn't confirmed these rumors, an undeniable fairy-tale-like magic permeates this place, whether you're marveling at its 60,000 books, painted-glass ceiling, neo-Gothic facade, or crimson double-helix staircase. In recent years, the bookstore has become so overrun with tourists that there's now a €3 entry fee, which is redeemable against any purchase in the store. ⊠ *Rua das Carmelitas 144* ☎ *22/200–2880* ⊕ *www.livrarialello.pt.*

Pedro A. Baptista. This is a reputable dealer in antique and modern silver. ⊠ *Rua das Flores 235* ☎ *22/200–2880.*

Prometeu. Downtown, this stylish shop has ceramics, tiles (handmade on-site), and other handicrafts from all over the country. There are three other locations: Rua Mouzinho da Silveira 136, Rua de São João 19, and Rua Alexandre Herculano 355. ⊠ *Rua da Alfândega 7* ☎ *22/201–9295.*

FOOD AND WINE

Bolhão Wine House. Take a break from browsing the colorful Bolhão market and pop into this tiny shop for a port-wine tasting and some delectable canned sardines. It's at the center of the market and offers benches and picnic tables for lounging, as well as wines and ports by the bottle or glass. ⊠ *Mercado do Bolhão, Rua Fernandes Tomás, loja 9* ☎ *91/998–1895* ☉ *Closed Sun.*

Saboriccia. For hard-to-get, authentic delicacies from the countryside east of Porto, stop at this gourmet food shop whose owners have a farm outside of town, where they raise sheep and make many of the products sold here. You'll find local cheeses, jams, sausage, and wine, and there are often free tastings. ⊠ *Rua Senhora da Luz 338–342* ☎ *22/099–6677* ⊕ *www.saboriccia.pt.*

Vinologia. A limited selection of port wines can be had at any supermarket, but to try smaller-production selections that you've never heard of before—plus get expert advice from a French expat—stop by Vinologia, in the Ribeira district. The store organizes tastings of an astonishing selection of 200 ports, accompanied by cheeses and sweets. ⊠ *Rua de São João 28–30* ☎ *91/040–4435* ⊕ *www.vinologia.pt.*

MARKETS AND MALLS

Centro Comercial Bombarda. One of the more intriguing venues on Miguel Bombarda Street (the epicenter of Porto's art scene), CC Bombarda is a sort of postmodern mall—a shopping center filled with one-of-a-kind galleries and storefronts helmed by local artists and entrepreneurs. Stop here for handmade souvenirs and bespoke apparel. ⊠ *Rua Miguel Bombarda 285, Massarelos* ☎ *93/433–7703* ⊕ *www.ccbombarda.blogspot. com.es* ☉ *Closed Sun.*

Galerias Lumière. This posh shopping center boasts some of the most avant-garde boutique stores in Porto and by night it hosts a range of exclusive events. Go for the clothing stores, but stay for a sweet treat; French-inspired **Creperia da Baixa** and **Tête à Croissant** make delectable desserts. ⊠ *Rua José Falcão 157* ☎ *22/203–2499* ☉ *Closed Sun.*

Mercado Bolhão. Though a bit ramshackle these days, this traditional market, with its endless stalls of fruits, vegetables, and meats, is a mustsee for any food lover. Some merchants offer samples of their homemade products, and there are culinary souvenirs to be found in the central part of the market. ⊠ *Edifício Mercado do Bolhão, Rua Fernandes Tomás* ☎ *22/332–6024, 22/209–7200* ☉ *Closed Sun.*

Via Catarina Shopping. This is one of the city's best shopping centers, and unlike most, it's in an old restored building. The top floor is occupied by little restaurants that mimic the Ribeira's architecture with small, medieval-style houses. ⊠ *Rua de Santa Catarina 312–350* ☎ *22/207– 5600* ⊕ *www.viacatarina.pt.*

THE COAST AND THE DOURO

Espinho, south of Porto, and the main resorts to the north—Vila do Conde, Póvoa de Varzim, Ofir, and Esposende—are the best places for water-sports enthusiasts, with equipment-rental establishments often right on the beaches. Inland, the beautiful Douro Valley awaits, with its carefully terraced vineyards dotted with farmhouses stepping down to the river's edge. Drives along the river lead to romantic, ancient towns. This is also the heart of prizewinning wine country, and every town has charming bars where you can pull up a chair, order a bottle and a plate of *petiscos* (mixed appetizers), and watch small-town life go by.

VILA DO CONDE

27 km (17 miles) north of Porto.

Vila do Conde has a long sweep of fine sand, a fishing port, a lace-making school, and a struggling shipbuilding industry that has been making wooden boats since the 15th century. The yards are probably Europe's oldest, and the traditional boat-making skills used in them have changed surprisingly little over the centuries. It was here that the replica of Bartolomeu Dias's caravel was made in 1987 to commemorate his historic voyage around the Cape of Good Hope 500 years earlier. Urban and industrial sprawl mars the outer parts of town, but the center has winding streets and centuries-old buildings.

Vila do Conde has been known for its lace since the 17th century, and it remains the center of a flourishing lace industry. The tourist office can give you information about the Escola de Rendas (Lace-Making School), where you can see how the famed *rendas de bilros* (bone lace) is made. Local artisans also produce excellent sweaters.

GETTING HERE AND AROUND

Although there is no regular aboveground train, Porto's metro (red line) stops at Vila do Conde on its way to Póvoa, every 20 minutes or so. The trip from the Trindade stop in central Porto normally takes over an hour, but there's an hourly express train that takes 40 minutes. There are also frequent daily buses from Porto and from Viana do Castelo, run by local companies AVIC and Autoviação Minho. The tourist office can provide schedules.

ESSENTIALS

Visitor Information Vila do Conde. ✉ *Rua 25 de Abril 103* ☎ *252/248473* ⊕ *www.visitportoandnorth.travel.*

EXPLORING

Convento de Santa Clara. Often called the Santa Clara Monastery or Convent, this impressive structure will reopen as a municipal building by 2017. It sprawls along the north bank of the Rio Ave (Ave River), on which Vila do Conde is situated. Dom Afonso Sanches and his wife, Dona Teresa Martins, established the convent in the 14th century, and it retains its original cloister and the beautiful tombs of its founders. ✉ *Vila do Conde.*

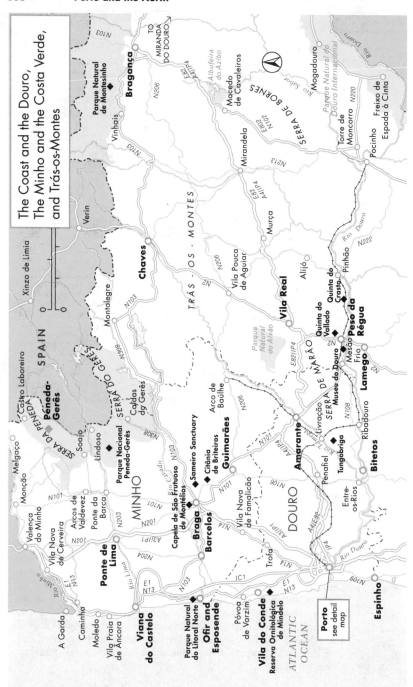

The Coast and the Douro,
The Minho and the Costa Verde,
and Trás-os-Montes

Igreja Matriz. In the center of town near the market, construction on this church began at the end of the 15th century and was completed in the early 16th. It has a superb late-Gothic portal. ✉ *Praça de São João, Av. Doutor Artur Cunha Araújo 46* ☎ *252/640810* 🌐 *www.paroquiadeviladoconde.pt* 🕓 *Closed Mon.*

INTERNATIONAL SHORT FILM FESTIVAL

Festival Internacional de Curtas Metragens. This local film festival, which started in 1993, takes place every July. ✉ *Teatro Municipal, Av. Dr. João Canavarro* ☎ *252/290050* 🌐 *www.curtas.pt.*

Museu das Rendas de Bilros de Vila do Conde (*Museum of Lace Making*). Created in 1919 by António Maria Pereira Júnior, the Escola de Rendas Lace-Making School is attached to the Museu das Rendas de Bilros de Vila do Conde. ✉ *Casa do Vinhal, Rua de S. Bento 70* ☎ *252/248470* 🎟 *€1* 🕓 *Closed Mon.*

Reserva Ornitológica de Mindelo (*Mindelo Ornithological Reserve*). This part of the coast forms part of the Reserva Ornitológica de Mindelo, which in 1957 became Portugal's first protected area. The only semiwild open area in the Porto region, it has 1,500 acres of dunes, fields, and wetlands harboring some 150 bird species. ✉ *10 km south of Vila do Conde, Mindelo.*

BEACHES

Praia de Mindelo. Colorful tents on the clean and coarse sand of the craggy beach Praia de Mindelo create a shield from inconvenient winds. From Vila do Conde, take the EN13 7½ km (4 miles) south to reach the beach's access at the small fishing village of Mindelo. The drive takes about 10 minutes. **Amenities:** food and drink; lifeguards; parking (no fee). **Best for:** walking; windsurfing. ✉ *Mindelo.*

WHERE TO STAY

$ RESORT FAMILY 🏨 **Santana.** This hotel has a lovely landscaped setting on a hill above the River Ave. All rooms face the river and have their own balconies. **Pros:** lovely riverside setting; five minutes on foot to center of Vila do Conde; free facilities include Wi-Fi and tennis courts. **Cons:** little nightlife nearby; spa can get busy in summer. [$] *Rooms from: €80* ✉ *Monte Santana–Azurara* ☎ *252/640460* 🌐 *www.santanahotel.pt* 🛏 *65 rooms, 10 suites* 🍴 *Breakfast; All meals; Some meals.*

OFIR AND ESPOSENDE

27 km (17 miles) north of Vila do Conde; 46 km (29 miles) north of Porto.

Ofir, on the south bank of the Rio Cávado, has a lovely beach with sweeping white sands, dunes, pinewoods, and water sports—a combination that has made it a popular resort. On the opposite bank of the river, Esposende, which also has a beach, retains elements of the small fishing village it once was. You'll have to drive here to appreciate these twin towns: the train line runs inland at this point, passing through Barcelos.

GETTING HERE AND AROUND

Esposende is on the national express bus network of Rede Expressos, which has a local agent in the market square. Bus services to Esposende from Porto and Viana, meanwhile, are run by Autoviação do Minho. Buses between Esposende and Braga are run by Transdev. The Esposende tourist office can provide more details; it's on the first floor of the main municipal building.

ESSENTIALS

Bus Contact Rede Expressos. ⊠ *Marina Bar [local agent], Largo do Mercado, Loja 8, Trav. Vasco da Gama, Esposende* ☎ *213/581472* ⊕ *www.rede-expressos.pt.*

Visitor Information Esposende. ⊠ *Edifício dos Serviços Técnicos Municipais, Rua da Senhora da Saúde 40, Esposende* ☎ *253/960100* ✐ *turismo@ cm-esposende.pt.*

EXPLORING

Parque Natural do Litoral Norte. Extending along 16 km (10 miles) of coast north and south of Esposende is the Parque Natural do Litoral Norte, an important haven for birds and plant life. As well as dune habitats through which you can wander on boardwalks, it includes the river beaches of the River Cávado estuary and pine and oak forest. Guided visits of up to 10 people can be arranged. ⊠ *Office, 1° de Dezembro 65, Esposende* ☎ *253/965830* ⊕ *www.icnf.pt.*

BEACHES

FAMILY **Praia da Apúlia** (*Apúlia Beach*). The old windmills that line Apúlia Beach are no longer in use but have been repurposed as charming rental cottages. Man-made sand dunes protect this notoriously windy beach, making it a perfectly sheltered spot for families. The waters here are famous for their medicinal purposes, because they contain high levels of iodine. You might see locals collecting seaweed, which is used as fertilizer for nearby farms. There are sunshade and boat rentals, and disabled access by a ramp. **Amenities:** food and drink; lifeguards; showers; toilets; water sports. **Best for:** windsurfing. ⊠ *Rua da Colónia, Apúlia.*

FAMILY **Praia de Ofir** (*Ofir Beach*). South of the Cávado river, Ofir's beach is one of the most beautiful stretches along northern Portugal's coast. Huge dunes are bordered by rows of pine trees, which give way to rocks that jut out into the water and are visible at low tide. These rock formations are known locally as "the horses of Fão." Surfers usually hang out on the beach's southern stretch, but there's plenty of room for families farther north. There are also restaurants and beach bars just behind the dunes and huts that rent out sunshades, windsurf boards, and boats. **Amenities:** food and drink; lifeguards; parking (no fee); toilets; water sports. **Best for:** solitude; sunset; windsurfing. ⊠ *Parque Natural do Litoral Norte, Rua do Estaleiro, Ofir.*

ESPINHO

18 km (11 miles) south of Porto.

Frequent trains and the N109 run past a string of quiet family beaches to Espinho, which has become an increasingly fashionable resort over the years. It has plenty of leisure facilities, including a casino, and a good selection of shops. The long, sandy beach is popular in summer, but you can find some space by walking through the pinewoods to less developed areas to the south.

GETTING HERE AND AROUND

Espinho is served by frequently stopping trains from Porto Campanhã to points south; some fast trains from Lisbon also stop here. The N109 highway runs nearby, and the town is also served by a four-lane spur off the A1 toll motorway. There is frequent local service from Porto's main bus station.

ESSENTIALS

Visitor Information **Espinho.** ✉ *Centro Comercial Solverde II, Alameda 8* ☎ *22/490–1316* 🌐 *www.cm-espinho.pt.*

EXPLORING

Casino Espinho. Right by the beach, the casino has 500 slot machines, horse-racing machines, virtual roulette and blackjack, Portuguese dice, and French and American roulette. If these diversions don't do it for you, come for the dining, dancing, and cabaret shows; foreign visitors must present their passports (and be 18 or older), and although there's no formal dress code, smart casual is most appropriate. ✉ *Rua 19, 85* ☎ *22/733–5500* 🌐 *casinoespinho.solverde.pt.*

EN ROUTE

On your way from Espinho or Porto to Amarante, at Freixo—10 km (6 miles) south of Marco de Canaveses on the N211—you can visit the ruins of the Roman town of **Tungobriga,** which harbor the earliest known evidence of a Christian presence in Portugal. As well as traces of a forum, baths, and necropolis, there are colorful mosaics from a paleo-Christian church whose extent shows the place flourished even in late Roman times. The site and **museum** (✉ *Rua António Correia de Vasconcelos* ☎ *255/532099* 🌐 *www.tongobriga.net*) are open for visits every day except Monday, but only in the afternoon on weekends, and from October through March you must book ahead to visit on a Sunday.

8

WHERE TO EAT AND STAY

$$$ SEAFOOD Fodor's Choice ★

🍴 **Aquário Marisqueira de Espinho.** Founded in 1954, this oceanfront restaurant by the casino is one of the most traditional in Espinho. There's an enormous variety of fresh seafood ready to be grilled, boiled, or roasted in the oven, as well as bacalhau and various fish stews and rice dishes. Many are best split between two diners. Customers who want meat can choose between dishes like roast veal or kid—or there's tripe and bean stew, in case you didn't get enough of that in Porto. The wine list is well varied. There are weekend specials, and there's also a late-night beer and snack bar outside. [$] *Average main: €25* ✉ *Rua 4, 540* ☎ *22/733–1000.*

$ RESORT FAMILY

🏨 **Solverde.** Run by the same company as Espinho's casino, this plush resort hotel with extensive grounds is on a hill, and most rooms have ocean views. **Pros:** use of myriad facilities included in room rate; free bicycles available. **Cons:** out of town; far from train and other transport links; dated decor. [$] *Rooms from: €120* ✉ *Av. da Liberdade 212, Praia da Granja* ☎ *22/733–8030* 🌐 *hotelsolverdespa.solverde.pt* 🛏 *169 rooms, 5 suites* 🍽 *Breakfast.*

GOLF

Clube de Golfe de Miramar. This popular club by the sea has a 9-hole, par-4 course. It's located 5 km (3 miles) north of Espinho. You can make it a full round of 18 holes by doubling the course (the greens fee is €70 for 18 holes on weekends, or €50 for 9 holes). ⊠ *Praia de Miramar, Av. Sacadura Cabral, Vila Nova de Gaia* ☎ *22/762-2067* ⊕ *www.cgm.pt* ⅄. *9 holes, 2450 yds, par 36. Greens fee: €50.*

Oporto Golf Club. The 18-hole Oporto Golf Club, founded in 1890 by members of the Port Wine Shippers' Association, is 2 km (1 mile) south of Espinho. On weekends, nonmembers can tee off from 11 to 1 only. ⊠ *Paramos–Espinho* ☎ *22/734-2008* ⊕ *www.oportogolfclub.com* ⅄. *18 holes, 5640 yds, par 71. Greens fee: €75 weekends, €45 weekdays.*

AMARANTE

78 km (48 miles) northeast of Espinho; 60 km (37 miles) northeast of Porto.

Fodor's Choice ★ Small, agreeable Amarante may be overshadowed by its more historic neighbor Guimarães, but the town still deserves an overnight stop. Straddling the Rio Tâmega, its halves are joined by a narrow 18th-century bridge that stretches above tree-shaded banks. Although the river is polluted (which precludes swimming), it's beautiful to look at. Rowboats and paddleboats are for hire at several points along the riverside paths. The riverbank is also the site of the local market, held every Wednesday and Saturday mornings; at these times, the usually peaceful town is disturbed by manic traffic racing along the main street and over the bridge.

GETTING HERE AND AROUND

Regional bus company Rodornorte serves Lamego from Porto and other regional centers such as Guimarães. You can also take the train a good part of the way from Porto Campanhã, getting off at Livração and then catching a local bus to Amarante (about 25 minutes).

ESSENTIALS

Bus Contact Rodonorte. ⊠ *Terminal Rodoviário do Queimado* ☎ *255/422194* ⊕ *www.rodonorte.pt.*

Visitor Information Amarante. ⊠ *Largo Conselheiro António Cândido* ☎ *255/420246* ⊕ *www.amarante.pt.*

EXPLORING

Convento de São Gonçalo (*St. Gonçalo Convent*). This imposing convent, built between the 16th and 20th centuries, is on the north side of the Rio Tâmega. The effigy of the saint, in a room to the left of the altar, is reputed to guarantee marriage to anyone who touches it. His features have almost been worn away over the years as desperate suitors try and, perhaps, try again. ⊠ *Praça da República* ☎ *255/437425* ▣ *Free.*

Fodor's Choice ★ **Museu Amadeo de Souza-Cardoso.** The cloisters and associated buildings of a convent now house the Museu Amadeo de Souza-Cardoso. The museum has an excellent collection of modern Portuguese art, including important works by modernist painter Souza-Cardoso, who pursued variations of fauvism, cubism, futurism, and other avant-garde tendencies. He was born in the area and in 1906 shared an apartment with Amadeo Modigliani in Paris. He returned to Portugal in 1914 and died four years later at the age of 31. The museum also hosts temporary exhibitions and has some interesting archaeological pieces. The star attractions are the *diabos* (devils), a pair of 19th-century carved wooden figures connected with ancient fertility rites. They were venerated on St. Bartholomew's Day (August 24), when the devil was thought to run loose. The originals were destroyed by the French in the Peninsular War. In 1870, the Archbishop of Braga ordered the present two burned because of their pagan function. The São Gonçalo friars didn't go that far, but they did emasculate the male diablo. ✉ *Alameda Teixeira de Pascoaes* ☎ *255/420272, 255/420238* 🎫 *€1* ⏲ *Closed Mon.*

WHERE TO EAT AND STAY

$ PORTUGUESE Fodor's Choice ★

🍴 **Adega Regional Quelha.** The restaurants along or near Rua 31 de Janeiro may have river views, but they don't necessarily serve the best food. This friendly, ham-and-garlic-bedecked place—behind a service station off a square at the end of the main street—has no views, but the regional fare served on its wooden tables is fantastic. Regular dishes include *cozido à portuguesa* (a meat, bean, sausage, and vegetable stew), cabrito assado, and *tripas* (tripe and beans). On weekends there's *arroz de cabidela*: chicken and rice in a rich gravy made from the animal's blood. If you're planning on having dinner, come around 7 pm, because the small space fills up fast. [$] *Average main: €11* ✉ *Rua da Olivença* ☎ *255/425786* 💳 *No credit cards.*

$$ PORTUGUESE

🍴 **Amaranto.** This spacious, well-appointed restaurant next to the Amaranto Hotel is on the river and near the center of town. The views from here are spectacular, and the menu has excellent regional fare. Try the cabrito assado, *arroz de marisco* (seafood rice), or bacalhau *à lagareiro* (baked with olive oil and garlic, and served with tiny baked potatoes). Wash it down with some robust local wine. The place also has a snack bar with lighter and cheaper fare. [$] *Average main: €20* ✉ *Edifício Amaranto, Travessa das Murtas, Rua Acácio Lino 351* ☎ *255/422006.*

$$$$ PORTUGUESE Fodor's Choice ★

🍴 **Largo do Paço.** This internationally renowned, Michelin-starred restaurant in the Casa da Calçada hotel serves innovative Portuguese cuisine and is overseen by talented chef Vítor Matos. Carefully constructed tasting menus are on offer (including one for children and, unusually for Portugal, another for vegetarians), but you may also order à la carte. Note that portions are quite small, so order à la carte for the best value. Dishes available might include bacalhau cooked with parsley and black olives, or braised, deboned oxtail with wild mushrooms. Staff can offer expert help in choosing wine from the lengthy list (which includes the hotel's own vinho verde). [$] *Average main: €50* ✉ *Largo do Paço 6* ☎ *255/410830* 🌐 *www.casadacalcada.com* ✍ *Reservations essential.*

$$$ B&B/INN Fodor's Choice ★

🏨 **Casa da Calçada.** Next to the old bridge and overlooking the river, this carefully restored former nobleman's manor is one of Portugal's finest hotels. **Pros:** charming setting and building; one of Portugal's best restaurants; intimate size and ample facilities give it the feel of a luxury resort. **Cons:** no gym; hotel often hosts private events that may be noisy.

$ *Rooms from: €225* ✉ *Largo do Paço 6* ☎ *255/410830* 🌐 *www.casadacalcada.com* *26 rooms, 4 suites* 🍽 *Breakfast.*

$$ B&B/INN **Pousada de São Gonçalo.** This modern pousada—20 km (12 miles) east of Amarante—is in the dramatic Serra do Marão at an altitude of nearly 3,000 feet. **Pros:** remote yet plenty to do; nice little spa; free Wi-Fi. **Cons:** only reachable by car or taxi; area cold in winter; next to the highway. $ *Rooms from: €150* ✉ *Curva do Lancete, Serra do Marão, Ansiães* ☎ *255/460030* 🌐 *www.pousadas.pt* *14 rooms, 1 suite* 🍽 *Breakfast; Some meals.*

SPORTS AND THE OUTDOORS

GOLF

Golfe de Amarante. This respected course at the property of Quinta da Devesa, 5 km (3 miles) southwest of Amarante, is an 18-hole golf layout with superb mountain views. A handicap certificate is required. ✉ *Quinta da Deveza, Fregim* ☎ *255/446060, 912/356003* 🌐 *www.golfedeamarante.com* *18 holes, 5500 yds, par 68. Greens fee: €75* ☞ *Facilities: driving range, putting green, pitching area, golf carts, caddies, pro shop, golf academy/lessons, restaurant, bar.*

PESO DA RÉGUA

40 km (25 miles) southeast of Amarante; 97 km (60 miles) east of Porto.

This small river port is a working town, and though not as scenic as its smaller neighbor Pinhão, it's the true heart of portwine country, and all the wine from the vineyards of the Upper Douro Valley passes through it on its way to Porto. Local wine lodges offer tours of their cellars, which make a nice contrast to the large-scale operations in Vila Nova de Gaia. The Museu do Douro provides a showcase for the wine-making industry. Many boat tours from Porto end in Régua (the town's shortened name); others pause here before continuing upriver to Pinhão, whose train station is lined with beautiful tile panels. For restaurant accommodations in the wider area, check entries in the Trás-os-Montes section of this chapter for Vila Real, which is 30 km (⇨ *19 miles*) from Régua up the N2.

GETTING HERE AND AROUND

Régua is served by Rodonorte, whose routes cover most of the region. There are also local buses from Vila Real. Most visitors using public transport prefer to take the picturesque Douro line, with regular departures from Porto Campanhã (about two hours). The quickest way by car from Porto is to take the A4 motorway toward Vila Real, turning south on the N2 just outside town. A prettier route is the N103 along the north bank of the Douro.

TOURS

Porto-based Douro Azul does day trips to Régua as well as cruises of up to a week. Land and river trips are also organized by the Rota do Vinho do Porto (Port Wine Route), which also works with local *quintas* (estates) to help wine enthusiasts map out their own tours of the region and book cellar visits and wine tastings. In summer, there's an afternoon historic train tour (with steam or diesel engines) along the Douro from

Régua via Pinhão to Tua; the national train company, Comboios de Portugal (CP), or tourist offices can provide details.

ESSENTIALS

Boat Cruises Douro Azul. ⊠ *Rua de Miragaia 103, Porto* ☎ *22/340–2500* ⊕ *www.douroazul.com.*

Bus Contact Rodonorte. ⊠ *Quiosque Almeida and Almeida, Largo da Estação* ☎ *254/313673* ⊕ *www.rodonorte.pt.*

Historic Train Comboios de Portugal (*CP*). ☎ *707/210220* ⊕ *www.cp.pt.*

Visitor Information Douro. ⊠ *Rua da Ferreirinha* ☎ *254/313846* ⊕ *www.visitdouro.eu.* **Rota do Vinho do Porto.** ⊠ *Associação de Aderentes, Largo da Estação, Apartado 113* ☎ *254/324774* ⊕ *www.ivdp.pt.*

EXPLORING

Fodor's Choice ★ **Museu do Douro.** This stunning museum sits at the center of the Douro Valley, a UNESCO World Heritage Site, underscoring its importance in terms of cultural history and tourism. Housed in the imposing former headquarters of a port-wine company, the institution also has a striking contemporary wing that hosts major exhibitions about the wine-making region, its history, and leading figures connected with it. Those with an appetite can stay for a meal at the riverside restaurant and wine bar overlooking the Douro. The ticket price includes a complimentary glass of port wine. ⊠ *Rua Marquês de Pombal* ☎ *254/310190* ⊕ *www.museudodouro.pt* ⊠ *€6, €20 for guided tour in English.*

Quinta do Crasto. Dating to 1616, this large wine estate on the north bank of Rio Douro, between Régua and Pinhão, was already marked on the first Douro Demarcated Region Map by Baron Forrester. Wines produced here include vintage port, designating wine of exceptional quality made in a single year. It must be bottled between the second and third year after the harvest; it is deep purple in color and full-bodied. It also offers LBV (Late Bottled Vintage) port, wines of a superior quality from a single year which are bottled between the fourth and sixth year after they were made. Reservations must be made to visit this property. ⊠ *Gouvinhas–Ferrão, Sabrosa* ☎ *254/920020, 226/105493* ⊕ *www.quintadocrasto.pt.*

Fodor's Choice ★ **Quinta do Vallado.** One of the oldest quintas in the region, Quinta do Vallado is on the right bank of Rio Corgo near Rio Douro and has stunning views of terraced hillsides along both river gorges. This wine estate has been in the Ferreira family since 1818 and encompasses 158 acres, some with vines more than 70 years old. Make reservations for a visit, which includes a wine tasting. This property holds a museum and a wine store. Like many other quintas throughout the region, it also has rooms for guests, in either a traditional 18th-century manor, or a sleek, modern 21st-century wing. Doubles cost about €140 per night. ⊠ *Vilarinho dos Freires* ☎ *254/323147, 254/318081* ⊕ *www.quintadovallado.com.*

8

EN ROUTE

Boats on Douro cruises of more than a day invariably stop at Pinhão, whose train station is plastered with 25 large azulejo panels depicting scenes from Douro rural life. Part of the building houses **Wine House** (☎ *254/730030* 🌐 *www.quintanova.com; closed Sun. mid-Oct.–mid-Apr.*), whose shop carries books about the region as well as a good selection of wines to buy or taste. It also oversees a small museum in the former railwaymen's quarters, which has interesting displays of traditional equipment used in grape harvesting, wine making, bottling, and coopering. A nearby hotel, the **CS Vintage House** (⇨ *see Where to Eat and Stay*) has a fine restaurant, a well-stocked shop, and a Wine Academy which organizes courses and sessions at which port is matched with gourmet foods like chocolate.

> **WINE TASTING**
>
> **Rota do Vinho do Porto.** To arrange a tasting with lunch or dinner (€30) and/or stays (€90–€180) at one or more quintas, contact the Rota do Vinho do Porto. ✉ *Largo da Estação, Apartado 113* ☎ *254/324774* 🌐 *www.ivdp.pt.*

WHERE TO EAT AND STAY

$$$$ PORTUGUESE Fodor's Choice ★

🍴 **DOC.** This striking modern restaurant 9 km (6 miles) from Régua, on the south bank of the Douro, draws gourmets from far and wide with chef Rui Paula's take on traditional northern cuisine. Only the best ingredients are used in dishes in which bacalhau, *polvo* (octopus), and seafood often loom large, as well as tender *bísaro* pork and *barrosã* veal. The restaurant's wine list and its adept matching of port with food have won it awards. The riverside setting contributes to an unforgettable experience, especially if it's warm enough to dine on the wooden deck that juts out over the river. [$] *Average main: €55* ✉ *Cais da Folgosa, Estrada Nacional 222, Armamar* ☎ *254/858123, 910/014040* 🌐 *www.ruipaula.com* ✍ *Reservations essential.*

$$ PORTUGUESE

🍴 **Gato Preto.** Meaning "black cat," this sleek, family-run restaurant is on Régua's main strip, next to the Museu do Douro. The specialty is traditional Douro cuisine; try the cabrito asado, which locals line up for once the tourists are gone. [$] *Average main: €20* ✉ *Av. João Franco* ☎ *254/313367, 933/251671* 🌐 *www.restaurantegatopreto.webnode.pt.*

$ B&B/INN FAMILY

🏨 **Casa do Visconde de Chanceleiros.** This 18th-century manor house has lovely gardens bursting with flowers, a swimming pool with views of the Douro River valley, plus tennis courts, sauna, and whirlpool. **Pros:** gorgeous rambling gardens; lots of activities for kids. **Cons:** remote and difficult to reach on public transit (a car is the best way to get here). [$] *Rooms from: €135* ✉ *Largo da Fonte, Pinhão* ☎ *254/730190* 🌐 *www.chanceleiros.com* 🛏 *12 rooms* 🍽 *Breakfast; All meals; Some meals.*

$$$ HOTEL Fodor's Choice ★

🏨 **CS Vintage House.** This hotel on the northern bank of the Douro, 32 km (18 miles) east of Régua and set in a beautifully restyled former Tayor port wine warehouse, has unrivaled views. **Pros:** lovely riverside setting; easy to get to by train to the Pinhão station; grape-picking (and stomping) trips can be arranged. **Cons:** remote spot far from larger shops and nightlife; no gym. [$] *Rooms from: €245* ✉ *Lugar da Ponte, Pinhão* ☎ *254/730230, 289/599427* 🌐 *www.cshotelsandresorts.com* 🛏 *36 rooms, 7 suites* 🍽 *Breakfast; All meals; Some meals.*

$$ B&B/INN **Quinta Nova de Nossa Senhora do Carmo.** This hillside estate on the north bank of the Douro is owned by the Amorim family, who dominate Portugal's cork industry, but its "wine hotel" is on an intimate scale. **Pros:** a comfortable place to get away from it all; inside view of wine making. **Cons:** few in-room amenities; isolated unless you have a car. [$] *Rooms from: €152* ✉ *Quinta Nova de Nossa Senhora do Carmo, Covas do Douro* ☎ *254/730430, 96/986–0056* 🌐 *www.quintanova.com* 🛏 *11 rooms* 🍴 *Breakfast; All meals; Some meals.*

LAMEGO

13 km (8 miles) south of Peso da Régua; 110 km (68 miles) southeast of Porto.

A prosperous town set amid a fertile landscape carpeted with vineyards and orchards, Lamego is also rich in baroque churches and mansions. It straddles the River Balsemão, a small tributary of the Douro, and is close to the great river itself. The town is flanked by two hills, one topped by a castle, the other by the Nossa Senhora dos Remédios, a major pilgrimage site. A monumental staircase leads straight up from the town's central avenue to the church steps. The surrounding region has more quintas to visit or stay—plus one of Europe's top spa hotels.

GETTING HERE AND AROUND

Lamego is served by Rodonorte regional buses and fast Rede Expresso buses from Lisbon. Tickets for the latter can be bought at local agent Totolamego. The town is not on the rail network, but it's a short ride on a Transdev bus from Peso da Régua, which is on the picturesque Douro line from Porto.

ESSENTIALS

Bus Contact Rede Expressos. ✉ *Totolamego, Av. Visconde Guedes Teixeira* ☎ *254/656064* 🌐 *www.rede-expressos.pt.*

Visitor Information Douro. ✉ *Delegação de Lamego, Rua dos Bancos, Apartado 36* ☎ *254/615770* 🌐 *www.visitdouro.eu.* **Lamego.** ✉ *Av. Infantaria 9* ☎ *254/099000* 🌐 *www.cm-lamego.pt.*

EXPLORING

Quinta da Pacheca. In the heart of the Douro Valley, the wine estate Quinta da Pacheca has existed since 1551. A 17th-century stone marker bears a Feitoria inscription that indicates that the best-quality wine was made here, the only one that could be exported. The estate mansion has a chapel and a beautiful garden with trees that are hundreds of years old. Wine production is still done the old-fashioned way, with grapes crushed by men in a stone tank, and aging taking place in oak barrels. Reservations must be made if you want to visit this property; tours of the cellars followed by a wine tasting start at €9 per person. You can also take a wine course, cooking workshop, or olive oil lesson. If you want to dally in this lovely setting, the Quinta also has an outsanding restaurant and 15 guest rooms in the €150 range. ✉ *Cambres* ☎ *254/331229* 🌐 *www.quintadapacheca.com.*

8

Fodor's Choice ★ **Santuário de Nossa Senhora dos Remédios** (*Our Lady of Cures Church and Shrine*). The town's most famous monument is the 18th-century Santuário de Nossa Senhora dos Remédios, which is on a hill west of the center of town and in a park of the same name. Leading to the shrine is a marvelous granite staircase of 686 steps decorated with azulejos. Landings along the way have statues and chapels. At the top, you can rest under chestnut trees and enjoy the views. During the Festas de Nossa Senhora dos Remédios, the annual pilgrimage to the shrine, many penitents climb the steps on their knees, just as they do at the shrine of Bom Jesus, near Braga. The main procession is September 8, but the festivities start at the end of August and include concerts, dancing, parades, a fair, and torchlight processions. Pilgrims use the stairs, but you can always reach the top by car. ✉ *Monte de Santo Estevão* ☎ *254/655318* 🎫 *Free.*

WHERE TO STAY

$$$$ RESORT 🏨 **Six Senses Douro Valley.** This luxurious resort 3 km (2 miles) from Lamego has, with its cutting-edge style, helped the region brush up its image as a fashionable destination. **Pros:** stylish and comfortable; stunning setting; spa included in room rate. **Cons:** not reachable by public transport. [$] *Rooms from: €400* ✉ *Quinta do Vale Abrão, Samodães* ☎ *254/660600* 🌐 *www.sixsenses.com* 🛏 *41 rooms, 9 suites, 21 villas* 🍴 *Breakfast.*

BITETOS

50 km east of Porto

The area around Bitetos is thick with Roman ruins and there are even a few crumbling remains in the village itself, as well as small medieval alleys and winding, cobbled lanes. The village itself is navigable, if hilly, by foot, but take care as sidewalks are scarce and the streets are impossibly narrow.

EXPLORING

Convento de Alpendurada. A short drive from Bitetos, this lovely 11th-century Benedictine monastery has been meticulously refurbished and is now a luxury hotel and restaurant. Alpendurada saw several rounds of renovations during the 17th and 18th centuries, but some of the original Romanesque elements remain, like the dramatic medieval kitchen. Predating the foundation of Portuguese nationality by 100 years, the monastery was an important stop for pilgrims traveling to Santiago de Compostela and Rome. It was also the heart of a busy trading center, thanks to its proximity to the Douro. ☎ *255/611371.*

Praia Fluvial Bitetos. The Bitetos Riverside Beach is located just steps from the small marina and tour-boat quay. Weekends can get busy as locals take to the water, either in their own motorboats or in the kayaks that can be rented by the hour. The fine brown sand is litter-free, and trees line the beach, providing plenty of shade. The nearby beach bar offers excellent snacks and refreshment. Be sure to swim within the cordoned area, as the river currents are strong and there can be a lot of boat traffic. **Amenities:** food and drink; lifeguards; toilets; water sports. **Best for:** swimming.

WHERE TO EAT

$

PORTUGUESE

✕ **Bar de Bitetos.** A happening little bar right on the beach, Bar de Bitetos is popular among day-trippers out on the river and beachgoers looking for a break from the sun and sand. The menu is filled with typical Portuguese small plates (think sandwiches, samosas, and croquettes) as well as fun house-made cocktails. No beach bar is complete without the requisite *caipirinha* (cachaça muddled with sugar and lime) and this one is particularly good. Occasionally, visiting guest DJs and live bands keep the party going. $ *Average main: €9* ☎ *917/469–260.*

THE MINHO AND THE COSTA VERDE

The coastline of Minho Province, north of Porto, is a largely unspoiled stretch of small towns and sandy beaches that runs all the way to the border with Spain. The weather in this region is more inclement than elsewhere, a fact hinted at in the coast's name: the Minho is green because it sees a disproportionate amount of rain. It's a land of emerald valleys, endless pine-scented forests, and secluded beaches that are beautiful, but not for fainthearted swimmers. Summers can be cool, and swimming in the Atlantic is bracing at best. "These are real beaches for real people," is the reply when visitors complain about the water temperature.

You can break up your time on the coast with trips inland to medieval towns along the Rio Lima or through the border settlements along the Rio Minho. The remains of ancient civilizations are everywhere; you'll encounter dolmens, Iron Age dwellings, and Celtic and Roman towns. Old traditions are carefully incorporated into modern-day hustle and bustle. Up here, you might happen upon the occasional oxcart loaded with some sort of crop, led by a long-skirted, wooden-shod woman on both highway and country lane.

8

GUIMARÃES

51 km (32 miles) northeast of Porto.

Fodor's Choice

★

Guimarães is a town proud of its past, and this is evident in a series of delightful medieval buildings and streets. The old town's narrow, cobbled thoroughfares pass small bars that open onto sidewalks and pastel houses that overhang little squares and have flowers in their windowsills. In 2001 the historic center of Guimarães was classified as a UNESCO World Heritage Site, and more recently the town has served as the European Capital of Culture (2012) and the European Capital of Sport (2013). These recent designations put Guimarães back on the map, led to vast improvements in tourist infrastructure, and brought the city the attention it deserves.

Many come for the rich history that the town offers. Afonso Henriques was born in 1110 in Guimarães, and Portuguese schoolchildren are taught that *"aqui nasceu Portugal"* (Portugal was born here) with him. Within 20 years he was regarded as king of Portucale (the united Portuguese lands between the Minho and Douro rivers) and had made Guimarães the seat of his power. From this first "Portuguese" capital,

Afonso Henriques drove south, taking Lisbon back from the Moors in 1147.

The volume of tourists in Guimarães is a fraction of what Porto or Lisbon receives, so you'll have many of the city's winding cobblestone streets all to yourself. This truly authentic slice of Portuguese heritage deserves an overnight stay on any trip to the region.

GETTING HERE AND AROUND

Guimarães is served by suburban trains from Porto's São Bento and Campanhã stations, taking about 1 hour 20 minutes and costing €3.10 (or less if you have a €0.50 Andante rechargeable card). Traveling by rail from Braga isn't advisable because you'll have to change, and buses are both quicker and cheaper. The company is Arriva, which also serves Guimarães from Porto. Fast Rede Expresso buses also serve Guimarães from Porto, Lisbon, and beyond.

ESSENTIALS

Bus Contacts Rede Expressos. ⊠ *Rodoviária Entre Douro e Minho, Central de Camionagem* ☎ *253/516229* ⊕ *www.rede-expressos.pt.* **Rodonorte.** ⊠ *Central de Camionagem, Rua Eduardo Almeida 162, 2nd fl.* ☎ *253/423500* ⊕ *www. rodonorte.pt.*

Visitor Information Guimarães. ⊠ *Largo Cónego José Maria Gomes* ☎ *253/421221* ⊕ *www.guimaraesturismo.com.*

EXPLORING

FAMILY **Castelo de Guimarães** (*castle*). This castle was built (or at least reconstructed from earlier remains) in the 11th century by Henry of Burgundy; his son, Afonso Henriques, was born within its great battlements and flanking towers. Standing high on a solid rock base above the town, the castle has been superbly preserved. A path leads down from its walls to the tiny Romanesque Capela de São Miguel, the plain chapel traditionally said to be where Afonso Henriques was baptized—in fact it was built well after his death, although the baptismal font may be older. ⊠ *Rua D. Teresa de Noronha* ☎ *253/412273* 🖃 *€2.*

Fodor's Choice **Citânia de Briteiros.** About 9 km (5½ miles) northwest of Guimarães, ★ you'll find these fascinating remains of a Celtic *citânia* (hill settlement). It dates to around 300 BC and was probably not abandoned until AD 300, making it one of the last Celtic strongholds against the Romans in Portugal, although its residents are now thought to have become gradually romanized. The walls and foundations of 150 huts and a meeting-house have been excavated (two of the huts have been reconstructed to show their original size), and paths are clearly marked between them. Parts of a channeled water system also survive. The site was excavated in the late 19th century by Dr. Martins Sarmento, namesake of a must-see museum in Guimarães, where most of the finds from Briteiros were transferred. You might also visit the smaller Museu da Cultura Castreja, housed in Sarmento's 19th-century family home, in the village of São Salvador de Briteiros, down below the Citânia. It contains finds from several local hill settlements and is open every day except Monday; entry is included in the Citânia ticket. There are several buses daily from downtown Guimaraes, but they stop about 1 km (½ mile) from the Citânia. It's easiest to get here by car. ⊠ *Estrada Nacional (EN) 153, Km 55* ☎ *253/478952* ⊕ *www.csarmento.uminho.pt* ⊠ *€3.*

Igreja de Nossa Senhora da Oliveira (*Church of Our Lady of the Olive Branch*). This church in the delightful square Largo da Oliveira was founded in the 10th century to commemorate one of Guimarães's most enduring legends. Wamba, elected king of the Visigoths in the 7th century, refused the honor and thrust his olive-branch stick into the earth, declaring that only if his stick were to blossom would he accept the crown—whereupon the stick promptly sprouted foliage. In the square in front of the church, an odd 14th-century Gothic canopy sheltering a cross marks the supposed spot. The square is now surrounded by cafés and makes a charming spot for a midmorning coffee and snack. ⊠ *Largo da Oliveira* ☎ *253/423919* ⊠ *Free.*

Igreja de São Francisco (*Church of St. Francis*). The Old Town's streets peter out at the southern end of Guimarães in the Almeida da Liberdade, a swath of gardens whose benches and cafés are often full. Here the stunning Igreja de São Francisco has a chancel decorated with 18th-century azulejos depicting the life of the saint. The church also has a fine Renaissance cloister. The complex now houses a home for the elderly, but both chapels are open to visitors. ⊠ *Largo de São Francisco* ☎ *253/412228.*

Museu da Sociedade Martins Sarmento. At the top of the Largo do Toural is this excellent archaeological museum contained within the cloister and buildings of a church, the Igreja de São Domingos. The museum has rich finds from the Celtic settlement of Citânia de Briteiros (northwest of Guimarães), which makes it a logical stop before or after visiting the Citânia. There are also Lusitanian and Roman stone sarcophagi, a strange miniature bronze chariot, various weapons, and elaborate ornaments. Two finds stand out: the decorative, carved stone slabs known as the *pedras formosas* (beautiful stones)—one of which was found at a funerary monument at Briteiros—and the huge, prehistoric granite Colossus of Pedralva, a figure of brutal power thought to have been used in ancient fertility rites. ⊠ *Rua Paio Galvão 66* ☎ *253/415969* ⊕ *www.csarmento.uminho.pt* ⊠ *€1.50* ⊗ *Closed Mon.*

Museu de Alberto Sampaio. The convent buildings surrounding the Colegiada de Nossa Senhora da Oliveira house this museum, known for its beautiful displays of religious art, medieval statuary, sarcophagi, and coats of arms. The highlight is a 14th-century silver triptych of the Nativity that's full of animation and power. It's said to have been captured from the king of Castile at the Battle of Aljubarrota and presented to the victorious Dom João I, whose tunic, worn at the battle, is preserved in a glass case nearby. In July and August the museum often hosts exhibitions of contemporary art, and opening hours are extended until midnight. ⊠ *Rua Alfredo Guimarães* ☎ *253/423910* ⊕ *www.masampaio.culturanorte.pt* ⊠ *€3 (free 1st Sun. of the month)* ⊗ *Closed Mon.*

8

NEED A BREAK

Clarinhas. Guimarães is an excellent place to sample regional cakes and pastries. One of the most popular spots for this is Clarinhas, which has a range of delicious sweets including traditional *tortas de Guimarães*, pastry rolls with an eggy pumpkin filling. There's also free Wi-Fi. ✉ *Largo do Toural 86/88* ☎ *253/516513.*

Paço dos Duques de Bragança (*Palace of the Dukes of Bragança*). The Paço dos Duques de Bragança, below the castle, is a much-maligned 15th-century palace that once belonged to the dukes of Bragança but which is now the official regional seat of Portugal's president. Critics claim that the restoration during the Salazar regime (1936–59), which turned the building into a state residence, damaged it irrevocably. Certainly the palace's brick chimneys and turrets bear little relation to the original structure, which was an atmospheric ruin for many years. Judge for yourself on an independent or guided tour of the interior, where you'll find much of interest—from tapestries and furniture to porcelain and paintings. You can book guided tours at the main desk. ✉ *Rua Conde D. Henrique* ☎ *253/412273* 🌐 *www.pduques.culturanorte.pt* 🎟 *€6 (free 1st Sun. of the month).*

FAMILY **Teleférico.** If you want to relax and enjoy a view of town, board the Teleférico, a cable car that takes you 440 yards up to the top of Mount Penha in 10 minutes. The journey ends with a nice view from cafés and gardens that overlook the city. The climb is steep, so it's advisable to buy a round-trip ticket. ✉ *Estação Inferior do Teleférico, Rua Aristides Sousa Mendes 37* ☎ *253/515–085* 🌐 *www.turipenha.pt* 🎟 *€3 one-way, €5 round-trip.*

WHERE TO EAT

$$ PORTUGUESE FAMILY

🍴 **Buxa.** This casual restaurant is situated on one of Guimarães's most scenic squares, across from the Museu de Alberto Sampaio, with tables spread indoors and out. Portuguese specialties include bacalhau baked with corn bread, beef *mirandesa* (stewed with garlic and then grilled—a specialty from the northern city of Miranda do Douro), grilled *porco preto* (cured ham), tripa, and an array of local cheeses. The weekday lunch menu is an excellent value, at €12 for three courses with wine. There's a snack bar, too. [$] *Average main: €17* ✉ *Largo da Oliveira 23* ☎ *252/058242.*

$ PORTUGUESE

🍴 **Café Oriental.** This venerable café on one of the city's iconic squares has a restaurant attached that serves tasty regional dishes at equally mouthwatering prices. There's a €12 lunch buffet, but if you opt to order à la carte, the house bacalhau (baked au gratin, with potato slices) and the breaded octopus are fantastic. Or, if on this trip you're not going to make it as far as Miranda do Douro on the Spanish frontier, take the chance to sample *posta à mirandesa*, Portugal's tenderest steak, best washed down with a glass of the house wine. [$] *Average main: €12* ✉ *Largo do Toural 11* ☎ *253/414–048* 🌐 *www.restaurantecafeoriental.com* 🕒 *Closed Sun.*

$ PORTUGUESE

🍴 **Nora Zé da Curva.** This traditional Portuguese restaurant across the street from the Oficina artisans' gallery (questionably) prides itself on cooking bacalhau 1,001 different ways. Behind the traditional exterior you'll find a sleek and modern dining room. There's also a second-floor terrace for alfresco dining. Grilled meats and local wines are the choice of most patrons. $ *Average main: €15* ✉ *Rua da Rainha Doña Maria II 125–129* ☎ *253/554256* ☾ *Closed Mon.*

$$
PORTUGUESE
Fodor's Choice
★

✕ **Quinta de Castelães.** On the road to the Citânia de Briteiros, this charmingly rustic but professionally run restaurant is a good place to sample regional dishes. Among the best are *assado misto de cabrito e vitela* (roast kid and veal), *rolinhos de pescada* (whiting rolls, served with a seafood sauce), and bacalhau dishes served *à broa* (with corn bread) and *com natas* (with cream)—all reasonably priced. Don't forget to try the range of finger-licking starters. The complex includes a small museum with an interesting display of agricultural implements. $ *Average main: €20* ✉ *Rua do Parque Industrial, São João de Ponte* ☎ *253/557002* ☾ *Closed Mon. No dinner Sun.*

WHERE TO STAY

$
B&B/INN

▦ **Casa Dos Pombais.** For an unforgettable overnight experience, stay as a guest of the Visconde Viamonte da Silveira (a modern-day Portuguese count) in his 18th-century manor house on the edge of Guimarães's historic quarter. **Pros:** an antiques lover's dream—feels like you're sleeping in a museum; personal service. **Cons:** no a/c or restaurant; little anonymity; the grounds aren't as manicured as they once were. $ *Rooms from: €65* ✉ *Av. de Londres 100* ☎ *258/931750* ⊕ *www.solaresdeportugal.pt* ⇜ *4 rooms* ◉| *Breakfast.*

$
HOTEL
Fodor's Choice
★

▦ **Hotel da Oliveira.** Town houses that date to the 16th and 17th centuries were remodeled to create this stylish hotel in the historic city center. **Pros:** charming historical building; picturesque central location; free parking and Wi-Fi. **Cons:** no exercise facilities. $ *Rooms from: €125* ✉ *Largo de Oliveira, Rua de Santa Maria* ☎ *253/514157,* ⊕ *www. hoteldaoliveira.com* ⇜ *13 rooms, 7 suites* ◉| *Breakfast.*

$
HOTEL

▦ **Hotel de Guimarães.** This comfortable, no-frills hotel is conveniently located steps from the train station, about 15 minutes from the Old Town. **Pros:** steps away from train station; ample free parking. **Cons:** a bit of a haul uphill from the city center; rooms at front look onto highway flyover. $ *Rooms from: €130* ✉ *Rua Eduardo de Almeida* ☎ *253/424800* ⊕ *www.hotel-guimaraes.com* ⇜ *108 rooms, 8 suites* ◉| *No meals.*

$
HOTEL

▦ **Hotel Ibis.** For a basic, affordable, and modern alternative to Guimarães's historical hotels, it's hard to beat the reasonably priced Ibis. **Pros:** great value; short walk to town; friendly multilingual staff. **Cons:** breakfast costs extra; limited parking (no fee). $ *Rooms from: €45* ✉ *Av. Conde Margaride 12* ☎ *253/424900* ⊕ *www.ibis.com* ⇜ *67 rooms* ◉| *No meals.*

$
HOTEL

▦ **Hotel Mestre de Avis.** This small, family-run hotel has a great mix of historical details and modern amenities, and it couldn't have a better location—on a quiet cobblestone street just around the corner from one of Guimarães's main squares. **Pros:** great location; friendly service; local flavor. **Cons:** no elevator to third-floor rooms; extremely limited on-site parking. $ *Rooms from: €75* ✉ *Rua D. João 40* ☎ *253/422770* ⊕ *www.hotelmestredeavis.pt* ⇜ *16 rooms* ◉| *Breakfast.*

8

$$ HOTEL FAMILY Fodor's Choice ★ **Pousada de Guimarães, Santa Marinha.** This pousada is in a breathtaking 12th-century monastery that was founded by the wife of Dom Afonso Henriques to honor the patron saint of pregnant women. **Pros:** successful blend of historical setting and modern comfort; stunning tile panels alone worth a visit. **Cons:** out of town; limited facilities. *[$] Rooms from: €160 ✉ Largo Domingos Leite de Castro, Lugar da Costa ☎ 253/511249 🌐 www.pousadas.pt 🛏 49 rooms, 2 suites 🍴 Breakfast.*

SHOPPING

Guimarães is a center for the local linen industry. The fabric is handspun and handwoven, then embroidered, all to impressive effect; it's available in local shops or at the weekly Friday market.

A Oficina. Shops owned by artisans themselves offer the best linen buys. Try this cooperative, containing both a showroom and shop and run by local artists and embroidery experts. *✉ Rua de Rainha Dona Maria II 126 ☎ 253/515250 ⏲ Closed Sun. [M] www.aoficina.pt.*

Chafarica. Opened in 2012, this shop offers some of the best local textiles from Guimarães, such as handmade embroidery, and accessories for the bedroom, kitchen, and bath, plus table linens, decorative items, and crafts. *✉ Rua Santa Maria 29 ☎ 253/292912 🌐 www.chafarica.pt.*

BRAGA

25 km (15 miles) northwest of Guimarães; 53 km (33 miles) northeast of Porto.

Braga is one of northern Portugal's outstanding surprises. Founded by the Romans as Bracara Augusta, it prospered in earnest in the 6th century—under the Visigoths—when it became an important bishopric. In the 16th century, the city was beautified with churches, palaces, and fountains, many of which were altered in the 18th century.

Today Braga feels like the religious capital it is. Shops that sell religious items line the pedestrian streets around the cathedral. The Semana Santa (Holy Week) festivities here, including eerie torchlight processions of hooded participants, are impressive. There are also several interesting historical sights—most of them religious in nature—a short distance from the city. You can visit all of them by bus from the center of town; inquire at the tourist office for timetables.

GETTING HERE AND AROUND

Some long-distance trains from Lisbon terminate not in Porto but farther north in Braga, and rail is perhaps the least complicated way to make the trip from the capital. From Porto, suburban trains take 50–70 minutes from downtown São Bento station, costing €3.10 (less if you have a €0.50 Andante card). As for buses, Transdev serves Braga from Viana do Castelo, while regional bus company Rodornorte plies routes from Porto and other regional towns, and Rede Expressos services come from as far as Lisbon.

ESSENTIALS

Bus Contacts Rede Expressos. ☎ *253/209400* ⊕ *www.rede-expressos.pt.* **Rodonorte.** ☎ *253/264693* ⊕ *www.rodonorte.pt.* **Transdev.** ☎ *253/209400,* *253/209401* ⊕ *www.transdev.pt.*

Visitor Information Braga. ✉ *Av. da Liberdade 1* ☎ *253/262550* ⊕ *www.* *cm-braga.pt.*

EXPLORING

Fodor'sChoice
★

Bom Jesus do Monte. Many people come to Braga specifically to see the Bom Jesus do Monte, a pilgrimage shrine atop a 1,312-foot-high, densely wooded hill 5 km (3 miles) east of the city. The stone staircase, a marvel of baroque art that was started in 1723, leads to an 18th-century sanctuary-church, whose terrace commands wonderful views. Many pilgrims climb up on their knees. Fountains placed at various resting places represent the five senses and the virtues, and small chapels display tableaux with life-size figures illustrating the Stations of the Cross. If you don't want to climb up the staircase (which is worth the effort), you can drive up the winding road or take the free funicular. There are restaurants, refreshment stands, and even a couple of hotels beside the sanctuary at the top. Buses run here every half hour from the center of Braga. ✉ *Tenões, Parque do Bom Jesus* ☎ *253/676636* ⊕ *www.bomjesus.pt.*

Capela de São Frutuoso de Montélios. About 4 km (2½ miles) north of town on the EN201, this is one of Portugal's oldest buildings. The original chapel is believed to have been constructed in the 7th century in the form of a Greek cross. It was partially destroyed by the Moors and rebuilt in the 11th century. ✉ *Av. São Frutuoso.*

D. Diogo de Sousa Museum. One of Braga's newest museums, here you'll find artifacts from the old Roman city known as Bracara Augusta (founded 15 BC), from which Braga derives its name. ✉ *Rua dos Bombeiros Voluntários* ☎ *253/273706* ⊕ *www.mdds.culturanorte.pt* 🎟 *€3 (free 1st Sun. of the month)* ☉ *Closed Mon.*

Palácio dos Biscaínhos. The elegant rooms in this baroque mansion, which houses a museum of the same name, are furnished in 18th-century style and display silver and porcelain collections. The ground floor of the palace is flagstone, which allowed carriages to run through the interior to the stables beyond. At the back of the palace is a formal garden with decorative tiles. ✉ *Rua dos Biscaínhos* ☎ *253/204650* 🎟 *€2 (free 1st Sun. of the month).*

NEED A BREAK

Café Vianna. Café Vianna has been in business since 1871 and serves a wide variety of snacks. It's also a good place for breakfast and offers views of the fountain and gardens. ✉ *Praça da República* ☎ *253/262336.*

Santuário Nossa Senhora do Sameiro. On a hilltop 5 km (3 miles) west of Braga on the N309 is this site, which, after Fátima, is the most important Marian shrine (a shrine honoring the Virgin Mary) in Portugal—hundreds of thousands of pilgrims visit annually. The church itself is of little architectural interest. ✉ *Av. Nossa Senhora do Sameiro 44.*

8

Sé Catedral. This huge cathedral was originally Romanesque but is now an impressive blend of styles. The delicate Renaissance stone tracery on the roof is particularly eye-catching. Enter from Rua do Souto through the 18th-century cloister; the cathedral interior is on your left, and there are various interesting chapels. Steps by the entrance to the cathedral lead to the **Museu de Arte Sacra** (Museum of Religious Art), which has a fascinating collection, including a 14th-century crystal cross set in bronze. From the magnificent *coro alto* (upper choir), which you cross as part of the tour, there are views of the great baroque double organ. Across the cloister, you'll see the Capela dos Reis (Kings' Chapel), a 14th-century chapel containing the tombs of Afonso Henriques's parents, Henry of Burgundy and his wife, Teresa. Opt for the €5 entrance fee, which is well worth it for a personal guide in English to the chapels, choir, and museum. ✉ *Rua do Souto 38* ☎ *253/263317* 🌐 *www.se-braga.pt* 🎟 *Cathedral €2, €5 for guided tour.*

WHERE TO EAT AND STAY

$ PORTUGUESE

🍴 **Restaurante Inácio.** Just outside the 18th-century town gate, in a building with a lovely traditional facade, this well-known restaurant serves solid regional fare. Bacalhau is a good bet, as is the roast kid. The place also specializes in *lampreia* (lamprey fish) and *sável* (shad or river herring) when in season. The house wine is on the simple side, but the list is decent, so you have plenty of other options. Service in the stone-clad interior is brisk and efficient. Reservations are essential on weekends. [$] *Average main: €16* ✉ *Campo das Hortas 4* ☎ *253/613235* 🕒 *Closed Tues.* ✍ *Reservations essential.*

$ PORTUGUESE
Fodor's Choice ★

🍴 **Sameiro O Maia.** A meal in this long-established restaurant is worth a climb (or drive) to the top of the hill that's home to the Santuário Nossa Senhora do Sameiro. The traditional dining room is air-conditioned in summer and usually has a roaring fire in the stone fireplace in winter. Views from the spacious, elegantly decorated dining room are superb. The menu is unadulterated northern Portuguese cuisine. If you're brave, start with the *papas de sarrabulho* (a meaty porridge thickened with blood) before moving on to *arroz de vitela com pastelinhos de marisco* (a veal and rice concoction with little seafood pastries) or one of the various bacalhau dishes. The place is renowned for its efficient service. [$] *Average main: €15* ✉ *Rotunda Monte do Sameiro, Espinho* ☎ *253/675114* 🌐 *www.restaurantesameiromaia.pai.pt* 💳 *No credit cards* 🕒 *Closed Mon., and 2 wks in mid-May, and 1st half of Oct.*

$ HOTEL

🏨 **Dona Sofia.** Right downtown, a stone's throw from the cathedral, this pleasant, well-appointed hotel is one of Braga's best bargains. **Pros:** very central; large bathrooms. **Cons:** no gym; cathedral bell sounds from 6:30 am. [$] *Rooms from: €70* ✉ *Largo São João do Souto 131* ☎ *253/263160* 🌐 *www.hoteldonasofia.com* 🛏 *34 rooms* 🍽 *Breakfast.*

$ HOTEL
Fodor's Choice ★

🏨 **Hotel do Elevador.** Many seasoned travelers to the north have made this charming hotel their top choice. **Pros:** fabulous views; tennis courts. **Cons:** no hotel parking; no gym; less luxurious than meets the eye. [$] *Rooms from: €85* ✉ *Bom Jesus do Monte* ☎ *253/603400* 🌐 *www.hoteldoelevadorbraga.com* 🛏 *22 rooms* 🍽 *Breakfast; All meals; Some meals.*

$

HOTEL

FAMILY

Fodor's Choice

★ **Meliá Braga.** This large hotel and spa inaugurated in 2010 is the city's most stylish and luxurious. **Pros:** wide range of facilities; 32-inch LCD TVs in every room. **Cons:** attracts many tour groups; half-hour walk from the center. $ *Rooms from: €110* ⊠ *Av. General Carrilho da Silva Pinto 8* ☎ *253/144000, 800/336–3542 for U.S. reservation line* ⊕ *www.meliabraga.com* ⥵ *161 rooms, 21 suites* ❂ *Breakfast; Some meals.*

NIGHTLIFE

Braga has an active nightlife, not least because it is one of Portugal's most important university towns. The café-bars in the arcaded Praça da República are good places for a drink and are lively at any time of day or night.

BARCELOS

24 km (15 miles) west of Braga; 60 km (38 miles) northeast of Porto.

Barcelos, a bustling market town on the banks of the Rio Cávado with a population of some 18,000, is the center of a flourishing handicrafts industry, particularly ceramics (above all in the form of the famous Barcelos rooster) and wooden toys and models. It's worth coming here if you plan to carry home a host of souvenirs, so if you're traveling the region by public transport, you might make the town your last stop. The best time to visit is during the famous weekly market—Barcelos is an easy day trip from Braga or Viana do Castelo, and there's not so much to do or see on other days, although the Museu de Olaria (Pottery Museum) is always worth visiting.

GETTING HERE AND AROUND

Barcelos is on the main rail line between Porto to Viana, but there are no direct trains from Braga. Rede Expressos buses serve the town from Lisbon as well as Porto; there is no bus station, but the company has a local agent on Avenida Dr. Sidónio País. Regional operator Transdev also runs buses from Braga, but to get from Viana to Barcelos you have to change in Forjães.

ESSENTIALS

Bus Contacts Rede Expressos. ⊠ *Av. Dr. Sidónio Pais 445* ☎ *253/814310* ⊕ *www.rede-expressos.pt.* **Transdev.** ☎ *253/894193* ⊕ *www.transdev.pt.*

Visitor Information Barcelos. ⊠ *Largo Dr. José Novaes 8* ☎ *253/811882* ⊕ *www.cm-barcelos.pt.*

EXPLORING

Centro de Artesanato (*Handicrafts Center*). Ceramic dishes and bowls, often signed by the artist, are a good buy here. Figurines, too, are popular, although none approach the individuality of those made by the late Rosa Ramalho and Mistério, local potters whose work first made Barcelos ceramics famous. ⊠ *Torre Medieval, Largo da Porta Nova* ☎ *253/824261.*

FAMILY **Feira de Barcelos** (*Barcelos Market*). Held every Thursday in the central Campo da República, the Barcelos Market is one of the country's largest. Starting at sunup, vendors cry out their wares, which include almost anything you can think of: traditional Barcelos ceramics (brown pottery with yellow-and-white decoration), workaday earthenware, baskets, rugs, glazed figurines (including the famous Barcelos rooster), decorative copper lanterns, and wooden toys. There are also mounds of vegetables, fruits, cheese, fresh bread and cakes, clothes, shoes, leather, and kitchen equipment—even live poultry. In fall and winter, the scent of roasting chestnuts wafts across the square, promising a snack to tide you over as you browse. ✉ *Campo da República.*

Museu Arqueológico (*Archaeological Museum*). The Rio Cávado, crossed by a medieval bridge, is shaded by overhanging trees and bordered by municipal gardens. High above the river stands the ruin of the medieval Paço dos Condes (Palace of the Counts), where you'll find the Museu Arqueológico. Among the empty sarcophagi and stone crosses is the 14th-century crucifix known as the Cruzeiro do Senhor do Galo (Cross of the Lord of the Rooster). According to local legend, after sentencing an innocent man to death, a judge prepared to dine on a roast fowl. When the condemned man said, "I'll be hanged if that rooster doesn't crow," the rooster flew from the table and the man's life was spared. The Barcelos rooster is on sale in pottery form throughout the town; indeed, it's become something of a national symbol. ✉ *Largo do Município* ☎ *253/809600* 🎟 *Free.*

Museu de Olaria (*Pottery Museum*). This museum reopened in fall 2013 following a four-year closure and €1.2 million in renovations, which have resulted in expanded exhibition galleries, a new cafeteria, and a superb gift shop. If you're not in town on the right day for the weekly market, this is a great place to pick up souvenirs or presents. The museum is a five-minute walk from the medieval bridge and contains more than 7,000 pottery works. Look for selections from current and bygone Portuguese artisans, private donations, and excavation finds from Portugal and all over the world, particularly from Portuguese-speaking countries. It all makes for a fascinating showcase for traditional pottery techniques and styles. ✉ *Rua Cónego Joaquim Gaiolas* ☎ *253/824741* 🌐 *www.museuolaria.pt* 🎟 *Free* 🕒 *Closed Mon.*

WHERE TO EAT AND STAY

$ PORTUGUESE 🍴 **Bagoeira.** Vendors from the town's Thursday market favor this rustic restaurant with its wooden ceiling, black-metal chandeliers, and vases of fresh flowers. *Grelhados* (grilled meats and fish) are prepared in full view of hungry customers on a huge old range that splutters and hisses. Other regional dishes served here include *rojões* (tender fried pork) and *papas de sarrabhulho,* a stew thickened with pig's blood. The restaurant seats hundreds of diners—and often has to on market days. If you get carried away with the house wine, there is a modern hotel attached (the website has more information on both). [$] *Average main: €15* ✉ *Av. Dr. Sidonio Pais 495* ☎ *253/813088* 🌐 *www.bagoeira.com.*

$ B&B/INN FAMILY 🏨 **Quinta de Santa Comba.** Just 5 km (3 miles) from Barcelos on the road to Famalicão, this fine 18th-century manor house—full of wood beams and granite—offers bed and breakfast. **Pros:** lovely garden; hotel has a real family feel. **Cons:** limited in-room amenities; no credit cards accepted. [$] *Rooms from: €65* ✉ *São Bento da Várzea* ☎ *253/832101* 🌐 *www.stacomba.com* 💳 *No credit cards* 🛏 *10 rooms* 🍽 *Breakfast.*

VIANA DO CASTELO

34 km (21 miles) northwest of Barcelos; 71 km (44 miles) north of Porto.

Fodor's Choice ★ At the mouth of the Rio Lima, Viana do Castelo has been a prosperous trading center since it received its town charter in 1258. Many of its finest buildings date to the 16th and 17th centuries, the period of its greatest prosperity. Viana is regarded as the region's folk capital and specializes in producing traditional embroidered costumes. Although these make colorful souvenirs, you'll also find less elaborate crafts, like ceramics, lace, and jewelry. The large Friday market is a good place to shop.

Like many Portuguese towns, it also has its very own sweet, the *torta de Viana*, a cake roll with a yolk-and-sugar filling—it's served in local cafés. Before or after strolling through town, don't miss the excellent local beach, Praia do Cabedelo (reached by ferry from the riverside at the end of the main street). The city's seaside location makes it a popular spot in August for windsurfers as well as families wishing to combine a little culture and history with a beach holiday.

GETTING HERE AND AROUND

Regional trains from Porto Campanhã are fast and regular; if coming from Braga, you must change at Nine. There are fast Rede Expresso buses from Lisbon, while Autoviação do Minho plies the route from Porto, and Transdev regional buses serve Viana from Braga. Viana is a real hub for transport to smaller Minho towns, with frequent services by local companies such as AVIC and Salvador crisscrossing this densely populated area.

ESSENTIALS

Bus Contacts Autoviação do Minho. ☎ *258/800340* ⊕ *www.avminho. pt.* **Central de Camionagem.** ✉ *Av. Capitão Gaspar Castro* ☎ *258/809352, 258/825043* ⊕ *www.rodonorte.pt.* **Rede Expressos.** ✉ *REDM—Central de Camionagem, Av. Capitão Gaspar Castro* ☎ *258/825047* ⊕ *www.rede-expressos.pt.*

Visitor Information Porto e Norte. ✉ *Regional Tourism Authority, Castelo Santiago da Barra* ☎ *258/820270,* ⊕ *www.portoenorte.pt.* **Viana do Castelo.** ✉ *Praça do Eixo Atlântico* ☎ *258/098415, 913/348813* ⊕ *www.cm-viana-castelo.pt.*

EXPLORING

Basílica de Santa Luzia. The Basílica de Santa Luzia is a white granite-domed basilica that overlooks the town from wooded heights. A funicular railway can carry you up there, or you can walk up a narrow footpath, about 2 km (1 mile). The views from the basilica steps are magnificent, and a staircase to the side allows access to the very top of the dome for some extraordinary coastal vistas. This steep climb, up a very narrow staircase to a little platform, is for the agile only. ✉ *Estrada de Santa Luzia* ☎ *258/823173* 🚡 *Funicular €3 round-trip, €2 one-way.*

Castelo de Santiago da Barra. A little ways beyond the Museu Municipal are the great ramparts of this 16th-century fortification that added the words *do castelo* to the town's name and protected Viana against attack from pirates eager to share in its wealth. The castle has since been renovated and given a new function and name: Centro de Congressos Castelo de Santiago da Barra. The congress and meeting center has an auditorium, a translation center, and all the necessary equipment to hold conferences, plus a hotel and tourism school. Outside the castle walls, Viana holds a large market every Friday. ⊠ *Castelo Santiago da Barra* ☎ *258/820270*.

Museu de Artes Decorativas. A 10-minute walk west from the Praça da República across the town's main avenue, the Avenida dos Combatentes da Grande Guerra, takes you to the impressive mansion that houses the municipal musem of Viana do Castelo, recently renamed the Museu de Artes Decorativas. The early-18th-century interior has been carefully preserved, including some lovely tile panels. The collection of 17th-century ceramics and ornate period furniture shows how wealthy many of Viana's merchants were. ⊠ *Largo de São Domingos* ☎ *258/820678* ⊕ *www.cm-viana-castelo.pt* ☜ *€2 (free on weekends)* ☉ *Closed Mon.*

Praça da República. The town's best face is presented in the old streets that radiate from the Praça da República. The most striking building here is the **Casa da Misericórdia**, an 18th-century almshouse, whose two upper stories are supported, unusually, by tall caryatids (carved, draped female figures). The square's stone fountain, also Renaissance in style, harmonizes perfectly with the surrounding buildings, which include the restored town hall and its lofty arcades. ⊠ *Viana do Castelo.*

NEED A BREAK

Zé Natário. This small café right off the main drag of Avenida dos Combatentes da Grande Guerra is a perfect place to soak up the Minho atmosphere. The proprietor makes his own pastries, cakes, and croquettes. Brazilian writer Jorge Amado is rumored to have frequented this place when he was in town. ⊠ *Av. dos Combatentes da Grande Guerra 20* ☎ *258/826856* ⊕ *www.zenatario.com.*

WHERE TO EAT AND STAY

$$
SEAFOOD
✕ **Casa d'Armas.** This cozy, romantic restaurant is in a renovated mansion near the fishing docks. Seafood is the main reason to come here, starting with fish soup and going on with main dishes such as *sapateira recheada* (stuffed crab), *polvo com azeite e alho* (octopus with olive oil and garlic), and *arroz de tamboril* (monkfish rice). But the menu also has several grilled meat dishes as well as *picanha* (tender salted and grilled Brazilian beef) and *arroz de pato* (duck rice). The house bacalhau is rather unusual: it's fried and stuffed with bacon. There's also a comprehensive list of regional wines. $ *Average main: €20* ⊠ *Largo 5 de Outubro 30* ☎ *258/824999* ⊕ *www.casadarmas.com* ☉ *Closed Wed., and 1 wk in Nov.*

$$
PORTUGUESE
Fodor's Choice
★
✕ **Os Três Potes.** The cellarlike dining room, converted from a 16th-century communal bakery and dotted with traditional rural implements, gets busy on summer weekends, when people crowd in for the folk-singing and dancing sessions. There's fado every other Friday. Sitting at tables under stone arches or on the open-air terrace, you can choose from a fine range of regional dishes: start with the *aperitivos regionais*

(a selection of cod pastries and cheeses); move on to the house bacal-hau, the exceedingly tender *polvo na brasa* (charcoal-grilled octopus), or the *cabrito à Serra d'Arga* (roast kid). There's a good wine list and live music on weekends. $ *Average main: €20* ✉ *Beco dos Fornos 7–9, off Praça da República* ☎ *258/829928* 🕑 *Closed Wed.* ⚴ *Reservations essential.*

$$
HOTEL

🏨 **Pousada Santa Luzia do Monte.** A 1920s mansion, perched on a wooded outcrop behind the basilica, houses this pousada. **Pros:** lovely gardens; fine views; nice sports facilities. **Cons:** a little isolated; funicular to hotel from town stops running at 8 pm. $ *Rooms from: €165* ✉ *Monte de Santa Luzia* ☎ *258/800370* ⊕ *www.pousadas.pt* ⌟ *48 rooms, 3 suites* ⦿ *Breakfast.*

NIGHTLIFE

Foz Caffé. A young crowd flocks to this nightspot near the beach. ✉ *Av. do Cabedelo, Darque* ☎ *258/808060, 258/332485* ⊕ *www.fozcaffe. pai.pt.*

PONTE DE LIMA

35 km (22 miles) east of Viana do Castelo on N203.

Ponte de Lima's long, low, graceful bridge is of Roman origin. It's also open only to foot traffic; drivers cross a concrete bridge at the edge of town. The main square by the old bridge has a central fountain and benches and is ringed by little cafés—the perfect places to stop for a leisurely drink. The nearby square tower still stands guard over the town, and beyond, in the narrow streets, there are several fine 16th-century mansions and a busy market. Walking around town, you'll return again and again to the river, which is the real highlight of a visit. A wide beach usually displays lines of drying laundry, and a riverside avenue lined with plane trees leads down to the Renaissance Igreja de Santo António dos Capuchos. The twice-monthly Monday market, held on the riverbank, is the oldest in Portugal, dating to 1125. On market days and during the mid-September Feiras Novas (New Fairs) you'll see the town at its effervescent best.

8

GETTING HERE AND AROUND

Local bus companies such as Cura and Autoviação do Minho serve Ponte de Lima from Viana do Castelo, with buses every half hour at peak times. From Braga the firm that provides fairly frequent services is Esteves e Andreia. Regional bus company Transdev also serves Ponte de Lima, as do fast buses from Lisbon run by Rede Expressos; they share a local agent on Rua Vasco da Gama.

ESSENTIALS

Bus Contact Rede Expressos/Transdev. ✉ *Rua Vasco da Gama* ☎ *258/942870* ⊕ *www.rede-expressos.pt.*

Visitor Information Ponte de Lima. ✉ *Torre da Cadeia Velha, Passeio 25 de Abril* ☎ *258/240208* ⊕ *www.cm-pontedelima.pt.*

WHERE TO EAT

$ ✕ **Cozinha Velha.** It's best to come
PORTUGUESE   hungry to this homey, bright Portuguese restaurant specializing in *orelha de porco* (pig's ear), *favas com fumados* (broad beans with smoked sausage), and cabrito assado (kid roasted in a wood oven). Prices here are a touch higher than other restaurants in the region, and rightfully so, given the quality of ingredients. $ *Average main: €16* ✉ *Caminho da Oliveirinha, Arcozelo* ☎ *258/749664* ⊕ *www.restaurantecozinhavelha.com* ⚑ *Reservations essential.*

$ ✕ **Encanada.** The Encanada is adjacent
PORTUGUESE   to the tree-lined avenue along the riverfront. A terrace provides river views. The menu is limited, but you can count on good local cooking, with dishes that depend on what's available at the market. You might start with the *bolinhos de bacalhau,* fried potato cakes with plenty of cod in them, and then try one of the regional dishes, such as *rojões* (fried pork), accompanied by a vinho verde. Braver souls might go for the *arroz de sarrabulho,* a dish made of rice and pig's blood, for which this restaurant is particularly renowned. $ *Average main: €15* ✉ *Mercado Municipal, Passeio 25 de Abril* ☎ *258/941189.*

> ### BEACHES
>
> The Atlantic is cold, even at the height of summer, and beaches along the Minho are notoriously windswept. More pleasant is a dip in the Rio Lima or Rio Minho, although you should heed local advice about currents and pollution before plunging in. Ponte de Lima has a particularly nice wide, sandy beach. Espinho, south of Porto, and the main resorts to the north (Póvoa de Varzim and Ofir) are the best places for watersports enthusiasts.

PENEDA-GERÊS

90 km northeast of Porto.

The northeastern corner of the Minho is quite unlike most of this densely populated, heavily cultivated region. Here several forested *serras* (mountain ranges) rise up, cut through with deep valleys. A significant part of this area is protected, forming Portugal's only national park, the Parque Nacional de Peneda-Gerês. But there are striking landscapes even outside the park's borders, such as the valley of the River Cavado, which harbors Portugal's first five-star rural resort, and the River Homem, with its Vilarinho das Furnas reservoir. In 1972, the dam here—a precursor to the more actively contested projects of the present day—submerged a village whose traditional way of life is recalled in a small **Museu Etnográfico** (☎ *253/351888* ⊘ *Closed Mon.*) in São João do Campo (Campo do Gerês), in the southern section of the national park. The nearby town of Caldas de Gerês has a popular spa and a cluster of lodging options.

GETTING HERE AND AROUND

In terms of access, the national park itself divides into three main sections. The southern, most easily accessible part is a two-hour drive from Braga: turn off the N103 just after Cerdeirinhas, along the N304. There are up to six buses a day from Braga to Cerdeirinhas and Caldas

RURAL TOURISM

Central Nacional de Turismo no Espaço Rural. The Minho region is well known for its *turismo no espaço rural* (rural tourism). There are some 100 properties in the area, with a particular cluster along the Rio Lima's north bank, each no more than several miles from a town. Facilities are usually minimal; houses may have a communal lounge, tennis, a pool or access to local swimming facilities, fishing, and gardens. Rates include a bed and breakfast, and some places will arrange other meals on request. The Central Nacional de Turismo no Espaço Rural is the central booking agency associated with the rural tourism program; its website includes links to the sites of Solares de Portugal (generally grander old houses), Aldeias de Portugal (village lodgings), and Casas no Campo (more remote rural digs), plus suggestions for themed tour routes. ✉ *Praça da República, Ponte de Lima* ☎ *258/931750* ⊕ *www.center.pt.*

do Gerês, run by local hotel company Empresa Hoteleira do Gerês and by Transdev, both of which have offices in the bus station on Largo de São Francisco in Braga. Buses from Braga also stop in Terras de Bouro, just outside the national park, where there are several restaurants and pensões, but gourmets with wheels should cross the River Homem for Brufe, home to a spectacularly sited restaurant. The Vilarinho das Furnas reservoir is a little farther upstream. The N308 road skirting the national park to the south links up with Montalegre in Trás-os Montes.

The park's central region is accessible by car or bus from Ponte da Barca, from which the N203 heads 30 km (18 miles) east to Lindoso, or from Arcos de Valdevez, from which the minor N202 leads to the village of Soajo. Both towns offer basic accommodations and superb hiking. You can reach Lindoso by Salvador bus from Braga, changing in Ponte da Barca or Arcos de Valdevez.

To see the park's northern reaches, which encompass the Serra da Peneda (Peneda Mountains), it's best to approach from Melgaço, a small town on the Rio Minho, 25 km (15 miles) east of Monção. From Melgaço, it's 27 km (17 miles) on the N202 to the village of Castro Laboreiro, at the park's northernmost point. Salvador buses cover this part.

ESSENTIALS

As well as tourist bureaus and the national park offices in Braga and at the various park gates, an excellent nonofficial source of information on lodgings and organized activities in the region is the not-for-profit group Adere Peneda Gerês in Ponte da Barca.

Bus Contacts Empresa Hoteleira do Gerês. ☎ 253/615896, 253/273434 ⊕ *www.hoteisgeres.com.* **Salvador Transportes.** ☎ 258/521504 ⊕ *www.salvador-transportes.com.* **Transdev.** ☎ 232/319100 ⊕ *www.transdev.pt.*

Visitor Information Adere Peneda Gerês. ✉ *Associação de Desenvolvimento das Regiões do Parque Nacional da Peneda-Gerês, Rua D. Manuel I, Ponte da Barca* ☎ *258/452250, 258/452450* ⊕ *www.adere-pg.pt.*

EXPLORING

Fodor's Choice ★ **Parque Nacional Peneda-Gerês.** The 172,900-acre park, bordered to the north by the frontier with Spain, was created in 1970 to preserve the region's diverse flora and fauna. It remains Portugal's only national park. Even a short trip to the main towns and villages contained within the park shows you wild stretches of land framed by mountains, woods, and lakes. Access is free, and general information is available online, at the park's headquarters in Braga and at its half-dozen entrance gates, all of which keep office hours, at Adere Peneda-Gerês in Ponte da Barca (which can also arrange walking guides), and at tourist offices in Braga, Viana do Castelo, and Caldas do Gerês (often just labeled on maps as Gerês), where you can get a walking map. There are some 30 marked trails. ✉ *Sede do Parque Nacional (headquarters), Av. António Macedo, Braga* ☎ *253/203480* 🌐 *www.adere-pg.pt.*

WHERE TO EAT AND STAY

$$$ PORTUGUESE 🍴 **O Abocanhado.** Worth a trip for its stunning location and prizewinning design alone, this restaurant is also renowned for its regional cuisine. Perched in the Serra Amarela hills, 12 km (7½ miles) from Terras de Bouro, the long building slots into the surrounding slate, its terrace affording panoramic views of the River Homem. Outstanding mains include tender *barrosã* steak and locally raised kid. The dessert menu has family recipes as well as standards such as *pudim abade de priscos* (egg-and-almond pudding) and ricotta with pumpkin jam. From Braga, head north to Vila Verde and then upriver toward the Vilarinho das Furnas reservoir. [$] *Average main: €30* ✉ *Lugar de Brufe, Brufe* ☎ *253/352944, 91/117–3517* 🌐 *www.abocanhado.com* ⏲ *Closed Mon. and Tues. Sept.–June* ✍ *Reservations essential.*

$ B&B/INN FAMILY 🏨 **Hotel Carvalho Araújo.** This family-run pensão in the heart of the national park is one of the best-value lodging options in the area, with doubles at less than €60 most of the year. **Pros:** family-friendly atmosphere; lots of activities on offer; parking garage. **Cons:** limited facilities. [$] *Rooms from: €60* ✉ *Rua de Arnaçó 6, Parque Nacional da Peneda-Gerês* ☎ *253/391185, 96/803–5672* 🌐 *www.hotelcarvalhoaraujo.com* 🛏 *23 rooms* 🍽 *Breakfast.*

TRÁS-OS-MONTES

The name means "Beyond the Mountains," and though roads built in the 1980s have made it easier to get here than in the past, exploring this beautiful region in the extreme northeast still requires a sense of adventure. Great distances separate towns, and twisting roads can test your patience. Medieval villages exist in a landscape that alternates between splendor and harshness, and the population, thinned by emigration, retains rural customs that have all but disappeared elsewhere. Some elderly folk still believe in the evil eye, witches, wolf men, golden-haired spirits living down wells, and even the cult of the dead. During winter festivals, masked men in colorful costumes roam village streets, and the region's Celtic roots are evident in the bagpipes traditionally played here.

GETTING HERE AND AROUND

Having a car is the easiest way to tour the region, but making the trip by car means missing out on some of the finest train journeys in the country. The trip from Porto to Mirandela provides an excellent opportunity to see the changing landscape, and you can take a bus on to Bragança. But it is slow going. Both trains and buses stop at every village, and the journey can take more than nine hours.

The main bus company operating in Trás-os-Montes is Rodonorte, whose terminal in Porto is at Rua da Ateneu Comercial. Bus trips in this region are slow and, on some of the minor routes, uncomfortable.

VILA REAL

98 km (61 miles) east of Porto. By train from Porto, change at Peso da Régua to the Corgo line.

The capital of Trás-os-Montes is superbly situated between two mountain ranges, and much of the city retains a small-town air. Although there's no great wealth of sights, it's worth stopping here to stroll down the central avenue, which ends at a rocky promontory over the gushing Rio Corgo. A path around the church at the head of the promontory provides views of stepped terraces and green slopes. At the avenue's southern end, a few narrow streets are filled with 17th- and 18th-century houses, their entrances decorated with coats of arms.

GETTING HERE AND AROUND

The Corgo Valley line that runs from the banks of the Douro to Vila Real stopped running in 2009, but the city is served by a plethora of local and regional bus companies including Rodonorte and Auto Viação do Tâmega. Rede Expressos long-distance buses also come here from Lisbon, Porto, and other cities across Portugal. Aero Vip also runs near-daily turbo-prop flights from Lisbon to Vila Real's municipal airport.

ESSENTIALS

Airport Aeródromo Municipal de Vila Real. ☎ *259/336620* ⊕ *www.cm-vilareal.pt.*

Airline Contact Aero Vip. ☎ *214/489949, 93/720–5444 in Bragança, 92/751–9893 in Portimão* ⊕ *www.aerovip.pt.*

Bus Contacts Auto Viação do Tâmega. ⊠ *Quinta do Seixo* ☎ *276/332384* ⊕ *www.avtamega.pt.* **Rodonorte.** ⊠ *Rua Dom António Valente da Fonseca 104* ☎ *259/340710* ⊕ *www.rodonorte.pt.*

Visitor Information Douro. ⊠ *Av. Sá Carneiro 326, Bragança* ☎ *273/333590* ⊕ *www.dourovalley.eu.* **Vila Real.** ⊠ *Av. Carvalho Araújo 94* ☎ *259/322819* ⊕ *www.cm-vilareal.pt.*

EXPLORING

Fodor'sChoice ★ **Casa de Mateus** (*Mateus Palace*). An exceptional baroque mansion believed to have been designed by Nicolau Nasoni (architect of Porto's Clérigos Tower), the Casa de Mateus is 4 km (2½ miles) east of Vila Real. Its U-shape facade—with high, decorated finials at each corner—is pictured on the Mateus Rosé wine label (though that is the full extent of the association, as the winemaker is not based here). Set behind the main house is the chapel, with an even more extravagant facade. The elegant interior is open to the public, as are the formal gardens, which are enhanced by a "tunnel" of cypress trees that shade the path. Be forewarned: admission and parking are overpriced by most standards, and some of the gardens seem a bit unloved as of late. ✉ *N322 (road to Sabrosa), Mateus* ☎ *259/323121* 🌐 *www.casadamateus.com* 🎟 *€11 house, gardens, and tour; €8 gardens only; parking €8.*

Igreja dos Clérigos (*Church of the Clergy*). The finest baroque work in Vila Real, this curious fan-shape building is also called the Capela Nova (New Chapel). Its facade is dominated by two heavy columns. Built in the 18th century and dedicated to Saint Peter, it's believed by some to have been designed by Nicolau Nasoni, architect of Porto's emblematic Torre dos Clérigos. ✉ *Rua dos Combatentes da Grande Guerra 74* 🎟 *Free.*

WHERE TO EAT AND STAY

$ PORTUGUESE 🍴 **Cêpa Torta.** The "Twisted Vine," next to the cooperative winery in Alijó, is a sophisticated yet homey restaurant run by locals. Starters include bacalhau *línguas* (tongue—the tenderest part of the fish) and a range of cured and smoked sausages. Meat predominates among the main dishes, among them *perdiz com queneles de batata* (partridge with potato dumplings) and cabrito assado. It's all an excellent value, as are the wines on a long list that reaches past the Douro to Trás-os-Montes, and beyond. [$] *Average main: €15* ✉ *Rua Doutor José Bulas da Cruz, Alijó* ☎ *259/950177* 🌐 *www.douro-gourmet.com* 🕒 *Closed Mon. Dec.–Mar. No dinner Sun.*

$ PORTUGUESE FAMILY Fodor's Choice ★ 🍴 **Terra de Montanha.** Not only is this an excellent restaurant, but it has a memorable design, too, with tables in the two spacious dining rooms nestled inside oversize wine barrels. Most of the upper portions are cut away, giving you a view of the room, but some barrels are more enclosed for a sense of privacy. There's a wide range of dishes drawing on top-quality meats and other local ingredients, and an excellent bacalhau *com presunto e broa no forno* (baked with smoked ham and corn bread). Feeling adventurous? Opt for *orelheira estufada* (stewed pig's ear). There's even a vegetarian menu. Service is friendly, and prices are reasonable. They serve dinner until late here—almost midnight on weekends. [$] *Average main: €12* ✉ *Rua 31 de Janeiro 16–18* ☎ *259/372075* 🌐 *www.terrademontanhasite.xpg.uol.com.br* 🕒 *No dinner Sun.*

$ HOTEL 🏨 **Miracorgo.** The reception area is handsome, the guest rooms are bright, and the service is good—all of which more than make up for the rather unattractive exterior of this midrange hotel. **Pros:** great views; TV with 90 channels; breakfast included in room rate. **Cons:** inelegant building; no gym. [$] *Rooms from: €95* ✉ *Av. 1 de Maio 76–78* ☎ *259/325001* 🌐 *www.hotelmiracorgo.com* 🛏 *164 rooms, 2 suites* 🍽 *Breakfast.*

$$ HOTEL 🏨 **Pousada do Barão de Forrester.** Time fades away as you sit reading by the fire in the lounge, glass of port at your side, at this pousada in Alijó, some 30 km (18 miles) southeast of Vila Real. **Pros:** peaceful setting; excellent restaurant and terrace. **Cons:** no gym; beginning to show its age. [$] *Rooms from: €160* ✉ *Rua Comendador José Rufino, Alijó* ☎ *259/959467* 🌐 *www.pousadas.pt* 🛏 *21 rooms* 🍽 *Breakfast.*

BRAGANÇA

116 km (72 miles) northeast of Vila Real; 212 km (131 miles) northeast of Porto.

This ancient town in the northeastern corner of Portugal has been inhabited since Celtic times (since about 600 BC). The town lent its name to the noble family of Bragança (or Braganza), whose most famous member, Catherine, married Charles II of England—the New York City borough of Queens is named after her. Descendants of the family ruled Portugal until 1910; their tombs are contained within the church of São Vicente de Fora in Lisbon. Unfortunately, since improved roads have encouraged development, the approaches to Bragança have been spoiled by many ugly new buildings.

Just past the town's modern outskirts rises the magnificent 15th-century Castelo (Castle), found within the ring of battlemented walls that surround the Cidadela (Citadel), the country's best-preserved medieval village and one of the most thrilling sights in Trás-os-Montes. Bragança has locally made ceramics, and there's a good crafts shop within the walls of the Citadel. Baskets, copper objects, pottery, woven fabrics, and leather goods are all well made here.

GETTING HERE AND AROUND

Trains to Bragança were discontinued some years ago, much to locals' frustration, but bus company Rodonorte serves the town from major regional centers. There are also Rede Expressos fast services from Lisbon; the company's local agent is in Avenida João da Cruz. Aero Vip also runs near-daily turbo-prop flights from Lisbon to Bragança's municipal airport.

ESSENTIALS

Airport Aeródromo Municipal de Bragança. ☎ *273/304253*
⊕ *www.cm-braganca.pt.*

Airline Contact Aero Vip. ☎ *214/489949 in Portimão, 93/720–5444*
⊕ *www.aerovip.pt.*

Bus Contacts Rede Expressos. ✉ *Sanvitur, Av. João da Cruz 38* ☎ *273/331826*
⊕ *www.rede-expressos.pt.* **Rodonorte.** ✉ *Rua Vale D'Alvaro* ☎ *273/300183*
⊕ *www.rodonorte.pt.*

Visitor Information Bragança. ✉ *Av. Cidade de Zamora* ☎ *273/381273*
⊕ *www.cm-braganca.pt.*

EXPLORING

FAMILY
Fodor'sChoice
★

Cidadela (*Citadel*). Within the walls of the Cidadela, you'll find the Castelo and the **Domus Municipalis** (City Hall), a rare Romanesque civic building dating to the 12th century. It's always open, but you may need to get a key from one of the local cottages for the Igreja de Santa Maria (Church of St. Mary), a building with Romanesque origins that has a superb 18th-century painted ceiling. A prehistoric granite boar, with a tall medieval stone pillory sprouting from its back, stands below the castle keep. The Torre de Menagem now contains the **Museu Militar**, which displays armaments from the 12th century through World War I. The most exciting aspect of the museum is the 108-foot-high Gothic

8

tower with its dungeons, drawbridge, turrets, battlements, and vertiginous outside staircase. ⊠ *Bragança* ☎ *273/322378* ☜ *Free.*

Igreja de São Bento. Outside the walls of the Citadel is this Renaissance church, with fine Mudejar (Moorish-style) vaulted ceiling and a gilded retable. Founded in the 16th century to serve the attached monastery, it also has some 18th-century additions. The church does not have regular opening hours, but is usually open around 5 pm for about two hours. ⊠ *Rua de São Francisco* ☜ *Free.*

Museu Ibérico da Máscara e do Traje. If you can't make your visit to the region coincide with one of the winter festivals in which local lads wearing wooden masks roam the streets, scaring children and young women, the Iberian Mask and Costume Museum is definitely worth a visit. A joint Portuguese-Spanish initiative, it has displays on midwinter celebrations in villages across Trás-os-Montes, on similar events over the border in Zamora, and on Carnival traditions in both. The many costumes on show are riotously colorful and the masks strikingly carved. Information in English is available, but for guided visits, you must book a week in advance. The museum's website has a handy festival schedule. ⊠ *Rua D. Fernando O Bravo 24–26* ☎ *273/381008* ⊕ *museudamascara.cm-braganca.pt* ☜ *€1* ⊘ *Closed Mon.*

Parque Natural de Montesinho. A swath of hilly land north of Bragança forms a 185,000-acre protected area where some fine walks are marked out. Information can be found online, at the park headquarters in Bragança—where you can also book visits to ethnographic museums in the villages of Babe, Caravela, and Palácios—or at the Vinhais park entrance. Local wildlife includes a growing population of Iberian wolves, which shun contact with humans but are a focus for safari tours. In the villages that dot the park, some ancient traditions survive. **Rio de Onor,** right on the Spanish border in Portugal's far northeastern corner, is officially a separate village from its Spanish twin, but some land is still used communally by residents from both. There are protected parks on the Spanish side of the frontier, too. This is one of the most remote, least developed swaths of either country. In traditional dwellings of Rio de Onor and other nearby hamlets, livestock inhabit the ground floor and humans live one story up, warmed by the animals' body heat in cold winter months. ⊠ *Associação de Defesa & Promoção do Parque Natural de Montesinho, Apartado 108* ☎ *93/833–1942* ⊕ *www.montesinhovivo.pt.*

OFF THE
BEATEN
PATH
Miranda do Douro, some 80 km (50 miles) southeast of Bragança, is a curiosity: the only city in Portugal to have its own officially recognized language. More closely related to Latin than to Portuguese, Mirandês was always spoken by elders and is now taught in local schools. The old traditions are just as vibrant, with spectacular folk dances taking place during the Festas de Santa Bárbara in mid-August. The town has a hulking ruin of a castle, a museum showcasing local customs, a 16th-century cathedral with lovely decorative elements, and several imposing palaces. The **Turismo** (⊠ *Largo do Menino Jesus da Cartolina* ☎ *273/431132*) has information on daily boat trips on the Douro, where eagles may be spotted nesting on the river cliffs. The valley here

forms part of **Parque Natural do Douro Internacional** (⊕ *www.icnf.pt/ portal*); its headquarters is farther south in Mogadouro, but it has a branch in Miranda (☎ *273/431457 or 273/432833*).

WHERE TO EAT AND STAY

$ ✕**Lá Em Casa.** This low-key but attractive restaurant, with its slate
PORTUGUESE walls and fireplace, is midway between the castle and the cathedral. As you might expect this far inland, seafood dishes are considerably more expensive than the excellent regional meat dishes, which include veal and lamb. They also have an unusual recipe for *arroz de pato* (baked duck rice) which features beer. For a snack or starter, there are excellent ham and cheese platters, grilled chouriço and *alheira* (cured garlic sausage) and a wine list whose quality matches that of the food. Chestnuts feature not only in several meaty main dishes but in desserts, too. Ⓢ *Average main: €12* ✉ *Rua Marquês de Pombal 7* ☎ *273/322111* ⌦ *Reservations essential.*

$ ✕**Restaurante Típico Dom Roberto.** The wooden balcony and signage out-
PORTUGUESE side may remind Americans of the old American West, but this delight-
Fodor'sChoice fully rustic house in Gimonde, 8 km (5 miles) east of Bragança, is rich in
★ regional dishes. There's pork from native *bísaro* pigs, game specialties (hare, wild boar, pheasants), and smoked sausages. For dessert, try the creamy rice pudding or local cheese with homemade compote. The stone-walled, red-tiled dining room is cozy, and the service helpful and gracious. The owners also preside over six rentable rural houses within the Parque Natural de Montesinho, a protected area. Ⓢ *Average main: €15* ✉ *Rua Coronel Álvaro Cepeda 1, Gimonde* ☎ *273/302510* ⊕ *www. amontesinho.pt* ⌦ *Reservations essential.*

$$$ ✕**Solar Bragancano.** This traditional, family-run restaurant is housed in
PORTUGUESE an old manor house overlooking Bragança's historic plaza. Start your
Fodor'sChoice visit with a complimentary glass of port in the wood-paneled recep-
★ tion area, lined with antique bookshelves. The whole place is imbued with old-world elegance, from the ornate silver candlesticks to the fine crystal and lace tablecloths. The menu features regional delicacies like pheasant, *jabalí* (wild boar), and cabrito assado—plus a few vegetarian options. There's a leafy terrace with tables outside for summer evenings. Reservations are a good idea on weekends, especially in summer. Ⓢ *Average main: €25* ✉ *Praça de Sae 34* ☎ *273/323875.*

$ ⌂**Pousada de São Bartolomeu.** On a hill just west of the town center,
RESORT Bragança's modern pousada offers comfort and terrific views. **Pros:** all
FAMILY rooms have citadel views; pools for both adults and children. **Cons:** could use a renovation; removed from the center of town. Ⓢ *Rooms from: €125* ✉ *Estrada do Turismo* ☎ *273/331493* ⊕ *www.pousadas.pt* ⬎ *27 rooms, 1 suite* ⧉ *Breakfast.*

CHAVES

96 km (60 miles) west of Bragança.

Chaves was known to the Romans as Aquae Flaviae (Flavian's Waters). They established a military base here and popularized the town's ther-mal springs. The impressive 16-arch Roman bridge across the Rio Tâmega, at the southern end of town, dates from the 1st century AD and displays two original Roman milestones. Today Chaves is characterized most by a series of fortifications built during the late Middle Ages, when the city was prone to attack from all sides. The town lies 12 km (7 miles) from the Spanish border. Its name means "keys"—whoever controlled Chaves held the keys to the north of the country.

GETTING HERE AND AROUND

Chaves is served by bus company Rodonorte, which has routes to major towns in the region. Rede Expressos also serves the town from Lisbon and other towns around Portugal and has a local ticket agent.

ESSENTIALS

Bus Contacts **Rede Expressos.** ✉ *Auto Viação do Tâmega, Largo da Estação* ☎ *276/332352* 🌐 *www.rede-expressos.pt.* **Rodonorte.** ✉ *Av. de Santo Amaro, Edifício Parque dos Príncipes, Bloco B, Loja 1* ☎ *276/318143* 🌐 *www.rodonorte.pt.*

Visitor Information **Chaves.** ✉ *Terreiro de Cavalaria* ☎ *276/348180* 🌐 *www.chaves.pt.*

EXPLORING

Igreja da Misericórdia (*Mercy Church*). This late-17th-century church next door to the Torre de Menagem is lined with huge panels of blue-and-white azulejos depicting scenes from the New Testament. ✉ *Praça de Camões* ☎ *276/321384.*

Torre de Menagem. The most obvious landmark is this great, blunt, 14th-century fortress overlooking the river. It houses the **Museu da Região Flaviense** (Flaviense Regional Museum), which is made up of the **Museu Militar** (Military Museum); the **Museu Arqueológico** , a hodgepodge of local archaeological finds and relics that tell the town's history; and the **Museu de Arte Sacra** (Sacred Art Museum). Its grounds offer grand views of the town. The tower is surrounded by narrow, winding streets filled with elegant houses, most of which have carved wood balconies on their top floors. ✉ *Praça de Camões* ☎ *276/340500.*

WHERE TO STAY

$ HOTEL FAMILY Fodor's Choice ★ 🏨 **Forte de São Francisco.** The ruins of a 17th-century Franciscan monastery have been transformed to create this remarkable hotel. **Pros:** delightfully renovated historic building; well-stocked games room; kids' programs and babysitting available. **Cons:** spotty Wi-Fi; gym is tiny. [$] *Rooms from: €100* ✉ *Forte de São Francisco, Rua do Terreiro da Cavalaria* ☎ *276/333700* 🌐 *www.fortesaofrancisco.com* 🛏 *54 rooms, 4 suites* 🍴 *Breakfast.*

$ HOTEL FAMILY 🏨 **Hotel Aquae Flaviae.** The facade of this old-fashioned, midrange hotel has an art deco touch—it looks more like an enormous movie house than a hotel—and the interior achieves an old-world feel with its smooth lines and polished surfaces. **Pros:** wide range of indoor and outdoor activities; exclusive access to thermal baths. **Cons:** 1980s decor; not enough outlets. [$] *Rooms from: €80* ✉ *Praça do Brasil* ☎ *276/309000* 🌐 *www.hoteispremium.com* 🛏 *159 rooms, 6 suites* 🍴 *Breakfast.*

PORTUGUESE VOCABULARY

If you have reading knowledge of Spanish and/or French, you will find Portuguese easy to read. Portuguese pronunciation, however, can be somewhat tricky. Despite obvious similarities in Spanish and Portuguese spelling and syntax, the Portuguese sounds are a far cry—almost literally so—from their ostensible Spanish equivalents. Some of the main peculiarities of Portuguese phonetics are the following.

Nasalized vowels: If you have some idea of French pronunciation, these shouldn't give you too much trouble. The closest approach is that of the French *accent du Midi,* as spoken by people in Marseille and Provence, or perhaps an American Midwest twang will help. Try pronouncing *an, am, en, em, in, om, un,* etc., with a sustained *ng* sound (e.g., *bom = bong,* etc.).

Another aspect of Portuguese phonetics is the vowels and diphthongs written with the tilde: *ã, ão, ães.* The Portuguese word for wool, *lã,* sounds roughly like the French word *lin,* with the *-in* resembling the *an* in the English word "any," but nasalized. The suffix "-tion" on such English words as "information" becomes in Portuguese spelling *-ção,* pronounced *-sa-on,* with the *-on* nasalized: *Informação,* for example. These words form their plurals by changing the suffix to *-çoes,* which sounds like "*-son-ech*" (the *ch* here resembling a cross between the English *sh* and the German *ch:* hence *informações*).

The cedilla occurring under the "c" serves exactly the same purpose as in French: It transforms the "c" into a *ss* sound in front of the three so-called "hard" vowels ("a," "o," and "u"): e.g., *graça, Açores, açúcar.* The letter "c" occurring without a cedilla in front of these three vowels automatically has the sound of "k": *pico, mercado, curto.* The letter "c" followed by "e" or "i" is always *ss,* and hence needs no cedilla: *nacional, Graciosa, Terceira.*

The letter "j" sounds like the "s" in the English word "pleasure." So does "g" except when the latter is followed by one of the "hard" vowels: hence, *generoso, gigantesco, Jerónimo, azulejos, Jorge,* etc.

The spelling *nh* is rendered like the *ny* in "canyon": e.g., *senhora.*

The spelling *lh* is somewhere in between the *l* and the *y* sounds in "million": e.g., *Batalha.*

In the matter of syllabic stress, Portuguese obeys the two basic Spanish principles: (1) in words ending in a vowel, or in "n" or "s," the tonic accent falls on the next-to-the-last syllable: *fado, mercado, azulejos;* (2) in words ending in consonants other than "n" or "s," the stress falls on the last syllable: *favor, nacional.* Words in which the syllabic stress does not conform to the two above rules must be written with an acute accent to indicate the proper pronunciation: *sábado, república, politécnico.*

Numbers

1	um, uma
2	dois, duas
3	três
4	quatro
5	cinco
6	seis
7	sete
8	oito
9	nove
10	dez
11	onze
12	doze
13	treze
14	catorze
15	quinze
16	dezaseis
17	dezasete
18	dezoito
19	dezanove
20	vinte
21	vinte e um
22	vinte e dois
30	trinta
40	quarenta
50	cinquenta
60	sessenta
70	setenta
80	oitenta
90	noventa
100	cem
110	cento e dez
200	duzentos
1,000	mil
1,500	mil e quinhentos

Days of the Week

Monday	Segunda-feira
Tuesday	Terça-feira
Wednesday	Quarta-feira

Thursday	Quinta-feira
Friday	Sexta-feira
Saturday	Sábado
Sunday	Domingo

Months

January	Janeiro
February	Fevereiro
March	Março
April	Abril
May	Maio
June	Junho
July	Julho
August	Agosto
September	Setembro
October	Outubro
November	Novembro
December	Dezembro

Useful Phrases

Do you speak English?	Fala Inglês?
Yes	Sim
No	Não
Please	Por favor
Thank you	Obrigado/a
Thank you very much	Muito obrigado/a
Excuse me, sorry	Desculpe, Com licença
I'm sorry	Desculpe-me
Good morning or good day	Bom dia
Good afternoon	Boa tarde
Good evening or good night	Boa noite
Goodbye	Adeus
How are you?	Como está?
How do you say in Portuguese?	Como se diz em Português?
Tourist Office	Turismo
Fine	Optimo
Very good	Muito bem (muito bom)
It's all right	Está bem
Good luck	Felicidades (boa sorte)
Hello	Olá
Come back soon	Até breve

Where is the hotel?	Onde é o hotel?
How much does this cost?	Quanto custa?
How do you feel?	Como se sente?
How goes it?	Que tal?
Pleased to meet you	Muito prazer em o (a) conhecer
The pleasure is mine	O prazer é meu
I have the pleasure of introducing Mr., Miss, Mrs., or Ms. . . .	Tenho o prazer de lhe apresentar o senhor, a senhora . . .
I like it very much	Gosto muito
I don't like it	Não gosto
Don't mention it	De nada
Pardon me	Perdão
Are you ready?	Está pronto?
I am ready	Estou pronto
Welcome	Seja benvindo
What time is it?	Que horas são?
I am glad to see you	Muito prazer em o (a) ver
I don't understand	Não entendo
Please speak slowly	Fale lentamente por favor
I understand (or) It is clear	Compreendo (or) Está claro
Whenever you please	Quando quizer
Please wait	Faça favor de esperar
Toilet	Casa de banho
I will be a little late	Chegarei um pouco atrasado
I don't know	Não sei
Is this seat free?	Está vago este lugar?
Would you please direct me to . . . ?	Por favor indique-me . . . ?
Where is the station, museum . . . ?	Onde fica a estação, museu . . . ?
I am American, British	Eu sou Americano, Inglês
It's very kind of you	É muito amavel
Please sit down	Por favor sente-se

Sundries

cigar, cigarette	charuto, cigarro
matches	fosforos
dictionary	dicionário
key	chave
razor blades	laminas de barbear
shaving cream	creme de barbear

soap	sobonete
map	mapa
tampons	tampões
sanitary pads	pensos higiénicos
newspaper	jornal
magazine	revista
telephone	telefone
envelopes	envelopes
writing paper	papel de carta
airmail writing paper	papel de carta de avião
postcard	postal
stamps	selos

Merchants

bakery	padaria
bookshop	livraria
butcher's	talho
delicatessen	charutaria
dry cleaner's	limpeza a seco
grocery	mercearia
hairdresser, barber	cabeleireiro, barbeiro
laundry	lavandaria
shoemaker	sapateiro
supermarket	supermercado

Emergencies/Medical

ill, sick	doente
I am ill	Estou doente
I have a fever	Tenho febre
My wife/husband/child is ill	Minha mulher/marido/criança está doente
doctor	doutor/médico
nurse	enfermeira/o
prescription	receita
pharmacist/chemist	farmacia
Please fetch/call a doctor	Por favor, chame o doutor/medico
accident	acidente
road accident	acidente na estrada
Where is the nearest hospital?	Onde é o hospital mais proximo?
Where is the American/British Hospital?	Onde é o hospital Americano/Britanico?

dentist	dentista
X-ray	Raios-X
aspirin	aspirina
painkiller	analgésico
bandage	ligadura
ointment for bites/stings	pomada para picadas
cough mixture	xarope para a tosse
laxative	laxativo
thermometer	termómetro

On the Move

plane	avião
train	comboio
boat	barco
taxi	taxi
car	carro/automovel
bus	autocarro
seat	assento/lugar
reservation	reserva
smoking/no-smoking compartment	compartimento para fumadores/ não fumadores
rail station	estação caminho de ferro
subway station	estação do Metropolitano
airport	aeroporto
harbor	estação mártima
town terminal	estação/terminal
shuttle bus/train	autocarro/comboio com ligação constante
sleeper	cama
couchette	beliche
porter	bagageiro
baggage/luggage	bagagem
baggage trolley	carrinho de bagagem
single ticket	bilhete de ida
return ticket	bilhete de ida e volta
first class	primeira classe
second class	segunda classe
When does the train leave?	A que horas sai o comboio?
What time does the train arrive at . . . ?	A que horas chega o comboio a . . . ?

TRAVEL SMART
PORTUGAL

GETTING HERE AND AROUND

▌ AIR TRAVEL

The flying time to Lisbon is 6½ hours from New York on a direct flight; it's 10 hours from Chicago and 15 hours from Los Angeles on indirect flights. The flight from London to Lisbon is just under 3 hours.

Note that some budget airlines, such as Irish low-cost airline Ryanair, only allocate seats for an extra fee. Also, Ryanair and U.K.-based easyJet generally don't serve meals but do sell (overpriced) sandwiches, drinks, and other items. If you're on a special diet, pack appropriate snacks in your carry-on bag.

When traveling with most European low-cost airlines you'll have to pay to check in a suitcase (32 kilograms or 70½ pounds max), but one carry-on case per person is free as long as it complies with the airline's specific cabin measurements and weight.

TRAVEL TIMES FROM LISBON TO:	BY AIR	BY BUS
Faro (Algarve)	40 mins	2 hrs 40 mins
Porto	55 mins	3 hrs
Funchal (Madeira)	1 hr 50 mins	N/A
Ponta Delgada Island, Azores	2 hrs 15 mins	N/A
Coímbra	N/A	2 hrs 15 mins
Fátima	N/A	1 hr 30 mins

AIRPORTS

The major gateway to Portugal is Lisbon's Aeroporto Portela (LIS), approximately 8 km (5 miles) northeast of the center of the city. The underground Lisbon Metro runs from Terminal 1. Arrivals to the city center are about every 6–9 minutes from 6:30 am to 1 am (16 minutes, €1.40). An AeroBus also departs from outside Arrivals and goes to the city center (45 minutes, €3.15) roughly every 20 minutes from 7 am to 11 pm.

Porto's Aeroporto Francisco Sá Carneiro (OPO) also handles international flights and, like Lisbon, operates an AeroBus to the city center (25 minutes, €4) from 7:30 am to 8 pm. The Aeroporto de Faro (FAO) handles the largest number of charter flights because of its location in the popular tourist destination of the Algarve. Several buses run into town (15 minutes, €1.95), while a taxi will cost approximately €12.

The organization that oversees Portugal's airports, Aeroportos de Portugal (ANA), has a handy website with information in English.

Airport Information Aeroporto de Faro. ☏ 289/800800 for flight info. **Aeroporto Francisco Sá Carneiro.** ☏ 229/432400. **Aeroporto Portela.** ☏ 21/841–3500. **ANA.** ⊕ www.ana.pt.

FLIGHTS

Domestic air travel can be a good value between major cities, such as Porto and Lisbon or Lisbon and Faro, though prices tend to increase during the busy summer months.

TAP Air Portugal has daily nonstop flights from New York (Newark Liberty International Airport) to Lisbon and Porto with connections to Faro and Madeira. United's daily nonstop flights between Newark Liberty International Airport and Lisbon are scheduled to provide convenient connections from destinations elsewhere in the eastern and southern United States.

British Airways, TAP, Ryanair, and easyJet have regular nonstop flights from United Kingdom to several destinations in Portugal. From Spain, TAP, Iberia, and easyJet have daily Madrid–Lisbon flights; TAP, Vueling, and Iberia fly daily nonstop from Barcelona to Lisbon. From the Netherlands, KLM, TAP, easyJet, and Transavia have frequent nonstop flights from Amsterdam to several Portuguese cities.

Consider flying to London first and picking up an onward no-frills budget airline or charter flight: you might save money *and* have a wider choice of destinations in Portugal. There are often good deals to Faro in particular, because the Algarve is popular with British vacationers. In summer, last-minute, round-trip flights have cost as little as $150.

Airline Contacts British Airways. ⊕ *www. ba.com.* **easyJet.** ⊕ *www.easyjet.com.* **Iberia.** ⊕ *www.iberia.com.* **KLM.** ⊕ *www.klm.com.* **Ryanair.** ⊕ *www.ryanair.com.* **TAP Air Portugal.** ⊕ *www.flytap.com.* **Transavia.** ⊕ *www. transavia.com.* **United.** ⊕ *www.united.com.* **Vueling.** ⊕ *www.vueling.com.*

▌ BOAT TRAVEL

CRUISES

Portugal is a port of call for many cruise liners. Most stop at Lisbon, while a few include Madeira in their itinerary. There are also companies that offer more localized cruising opportunities, including River Cruise Tours, which offers luxury boat trips along the Douro River from Porto to the Spanish border.

Local Cruise Line River Cruise Tours. ☎ *888/942–3301* ⊕ *www.rivercruisetours.com.*

▌ BUS TRAVEL

Bus service within Portugal is comprehensive, punctual, and comfortable. Some luxury coaches even have TVs and food service, and all have a strict no-smoking policy. All that said, bus travel can be slow, though it's also a relatively inexpensive way to get around the country.

For major bus lines, you can buy a ticket online before you depart. For smaller rural lines, look for the schedules at the local tourist offices; if there isn't a ticket booth at the bus stop, you can usually buy a ticket at the closest café. It's always wise to reserve a ticket at least a day ahead, particularly in summer for destinations in the Algarve.

An under-30 card (⊕ *www.cartaojovem. pt*) for young adults and students should get you a discount of 10%–20% on the long-distance services. You can buy a card for €10 at post offices or youth hostels with a photo ID.

BUS CLASSES

There are three classes of bus service: *expressos* are comfortable, fast, direct buses between major cities; *rápidas* are fast regional buses; and *carreiras* stop at every crossroad. Expressos are generally the best cheap way to get around (particularly for long trips, where per-kilometer costs are lowest).

BUS LINES

Three of the largest bus companies are Rede Expressos, which serves much of the country; Rodo Norte, which serves the north; and Eva Transportes, which covers the Algarve and also has service to and from major cities, like Évora.

Bus Contacts Eva Transportes. ⊕ *www. eva-bus.com.* **Rede Expressos.** ⊕ *www.rede-expressos.pt.* **Rodo Norte.** ⊕ *www.rodonorte.pt.*

▌ CAR TRAVEL

In general, Portugal's roads are in good condition. When driving through the country, you'll often have the roads to yourself, though traffic can be busy in and around urban centers. On the downside, tolls here can add up quickly. ▌TIP➔ **The local driving may be faster and less forgiving than you're used to; drive carefully.**

Red tape–wise, your driver's license from home is recognized in Portugal. However, you should learn the international road-sign system (charts are available to members of most automobile associations).

GASOLINE

Gas stations are plentiful, and many are self-service. Fuel tends to cost more on motorways. At this writing, gasoline costs €1.52 per liter (approximately ¼ gallon) for 98 and 95 octane *sem chumbo* (unleaded) and €1.34 for diesel. Credit cards are frequently accepted at gas stations. If you require a receipt, request *um recibo*.

ROUTES

Commercially operated *autoestradas* (toll roads with two or more lanes in either direction identified with an "A" and a number) link the principal cities, including Porto, with Lisbon, circumventing congested urban centers. The autoestrada runs from Lisbon to Faro, and a toll road (E90) links Lisbon with Portugal's eastern border with Spain at Badajoz (from which the highway leads to Madrid).

Many main national highways (labeled "N" with a number) have been upgraded to toll-free, two-lane roads, identified with "IP" (Itinerario Principal) and a number; highways of mainly regional importance have been upgraded to IC (Itinerario Complementar). Roads labeled with "E" and a number are routes that connect with the Spanish network.

■TIP➔ **Because of all this road upgrading, one road might have several designations—A, N, IP, E, etc.—on maps and signs.**

Autoestrada tolls are steep, costing, for example, €22.55 between Lisbon and Porto, but time saved by traveling these roads usually makes them worthwhile. Minor roads are often poor and winding, with unpredictable surfaces.

In the north the IP5 shortens the drive from Aveiro to the border with Spain, near Guarda. Take extra care on this route, however. It's popular with trucks (you may get stuck behind a convoy), *and* it has curves and hills.

The IP4 connects Porto through Vila Real to Bragança. Pick up the IP2 just southwest of Bragança and continue to Ourique in the Alentejo, where it connects to the IP1 down to Albufeira on the southern coast. This same IP1 is an autoestrada from Albufeira and runs east across the Algarve to the Spanish border near Ayamonte, 1½ hours east of Seville.

Heading out of Lisbon, there's good, fast access to Setúbal and to Évora and other Alentejo towns, although rush-hour traffic on the Ponte 25 de Abril across the Rio Tejo (Tagus River) can be frustrating. An alternative is taking the 17-km-long (11-mile-long) Ponte Vasco da Gama (Europe's second-longest water crossing after the Channel Tunnel and Europe's longest bridge) across the Tejo estuary to Montijo; you can then link up with southbound and eastbound roads.

Signposting on these fast roads isn't always adequate, so keep your eyes peeled for exits and turnoffs.

TOLLS

Some highways in Portugal now use electronic tolls only, with no method of payment accepted on the roads themselves. To avoid getting fined for not paying the tolls, if you rent a car in Portugal, make sure the rental car company installs an electronic device that adds the costs of the tolls to your final bill. Otherwise, you have several options. You can: buy a three-day unlimited-use toll pass online, once you know your license plate number; associate a credit card with your license plate number, from which the tolls will automatically be deducted; or buy a preloaded toll card activated by SMS from your mobile phone. Sign up for any of these services online or in person at various pick-up points within Portugal.

Tolls Information Portugal Tolls. ⊕ *www. portugaltolls.com.*

ROADSIDE EMERGENCIES

If you are unfortunate enough to be involved in a mild accident, you will be required to fill out a *Declaração amigável* (European Accident Statement), which will be used by the respective insurance companies (including those relating to rental cars) to exchange information.

All large garages in and around towns have breakdown services, and you'll see orange emergency (SOS) phones along turnpikes and highways. The national automobile organization, Automóvel Clube de Portugal, provides reciprocal membership with AAA and other European automobile associations.

Car theft is common with rental cars. Never leave anything visible in an unattended car, and contact the rental agency immediately, as well as the local police, if your car is stolen.

Emergency Services Automóvel Clube de Portugal. ☎ 70/750–9510 for emergency help (24 hrs) ⊕ www.acp.pt.

RULES OF THE ROAD

Driving is on the right. The speed limit on the autoestrada is 120 kph (74 mph); on other roads, it's 90 kph (56 mph), and in built-up areas, 50 kph (30 mph).

At the junction of two roads of equal size, traffic coming from the right has priority. Vehicles already in a traffic circle have priority over those entering it from any point. The use of seat belts is obligatory. Horns shouldn't be used in built-up areas, and you should always carry your driver's license, proof of car insurance, a reflective red warning triangle, and EU-approved reflective jacket for use in a breakdown.

Children under 12 years old *must* ride in the backseat in age-appropriate restraining devices (facing backwards for children under 18 months). Motorcyclists and their passengers must wear helmets, and motorcycles must have their headlights on day and night.

Billboards warning you not to drink and drive dot the countryside, and punishable alcohol levels are just 0.5g/L—equivalent to approximately three small glasses of beer.

CAR RENTALS

To rent a car in Portugal you must be a minimum of 21 years old (with at least one year's driving experience) and a maximum of 75 years old and have held your driving license for over a year. Some car-rental companies may require you to have an International Driving Permit (IDP), which can be used only in conjunction with a valid driver's license and which translates your license into 10 languages. Check the AAA website for more info as well as for IDPs ($20) themselves.

In general, it's a good idea to reserve your car two weeks in advance (a month in advance if possible) for car rentals in the Algarve between May and September. Among the most common car makes are Citroën, Opel, Nissan, Toyota, Volkswagen, Peugeot, and Ford. Four-wheel-drive vehicles are only available from the larger international agencies, such as Avis and Hertz.

CAR-RENTAL RATES

Rates in Lisbon begin at around $70 per day, with three-day rates starting at around $120 and weeklong rates starting at about $210 for a standard economy car with unlimited mileage. The value-added tax (V.A.T.) on car rentals is 23% and is included in the rate. Algarve rates can be considerably higher due to the increase in demand.

Automatic cars are more expensive and harder to find than standard ones. The good news is that most rental cars have air-conditioning and, increasingly, use diesel fuel, which equals a lot more mileage. There's generally a surcharge of around $8 per day for each additional driver, and most agencies charge a small surcharge of around $11–$13 per day for children's car seats, which must be reserved at the time of booking.

CAR-RENTAL INSURANCE

If you own a car, your personal auto insurance may cover a rental to some degree, though not all policies protect you abroad; always read your policy's fine print. If you don't have auto insurance, then seriously consider buying the collision- or loss-damage waiver (CDW or LDW) from the car-rental company, which eliminates your liability for damage to the car.

Some credit cards offer CDW coverage, but it's usually supplemental to your own insurance and rarely covers SUVs, minivans, luxury models, and the like. If your coverage is secondary, you may still be liable for loss-of-use costs from the car-rental company. But no credit-card insurance is valid unless you use that card for *all* transactions, from reserving to paying the final bill. All companies exclude car rental in some countries, so be sure to find out about the destination to which you are traveling. In Portugal CDW will cost around $25 per day depending on the type of car and will reduce your liability to a few hundred euros. For an additional fee, you can take out a Super CDW where you will be completely covered.

▌ TRAIN TRAVEL

Portugal's train network, Comboios de Portugal (CP), covers most of the country, though it's thin in the Alentejo region. The cities of Lisbon, Coimbra, Aveiro, Porto, Braga, and Faro are linked by the fast, extremely comfortable Alfa Pendular services.

Most other major towns and cities are connected by Intercidade trains, which are reliable, though slower and less luxurious than the Alfa trains. The regional services that connect smaller towns and villages tend to be infrequent and slow, with stops at every station along the line.
▐TIP→ Ask the local tourist board about hotel and local transportation packages that include tickets to major museum exhibits or other special events.

TRAIN CLASSES

There are three main classes of long-distance train travel: *regional* trains, which stop at every town and village; reasonably fast *interregional* trains; and express trains appropriately known as *rápido*. The Alfa Pendular is a deluxe, marginally faster train that runs between Lisbon and Porto as well as other major cities. There's also a network of suburban *(suburbano)* train lines.

The standards of comfort vary from Alfa Pendular train luxury—with air-conditioning, free Wi-Fi, food service, and airline-type seats at which you can plug in your laptop—to the often spartan conditions on regional lines.

Most Intercidade trains have bar and restaurant facilities, but the food is famously unappealing. Smoking is not allowed on any Portuguese trains.

A first-class ticket will cost you 40% more than second class and will buy you extra leg- and elbow room but not a great deal more on Alfa and Intercidade trains. The extra cost is definitely worth it on most regional services, however.

BOOKING

Advance booking is mandatory on long-distance trains and is recommended in the case of popular services like the Alfa. Reservations are also advisable for other trains if you want to avoid long lines in front of the ticket window on the day the train leaves. You can avoid a trip to the station to make the reservation by booking it online.

SPAIN−PORTUGAL ROUTE

A direct, nightly train connects Spain and Portugal. The train departs from Madrid's Chamartín station at 9:27 pm and arrives at Lisbon's Santa Apolónia station at 8:10 the following morning; for the reverse trip, the train leaves Lisbon at 9:34 pm, arriving in Madrid at 8:40 am the next day. Passengers can also connect to the train to and from Porto by switching at the Coimbra station; trains depart Porto at 9:55 pm daily on their way to Madrid, while trains from Madrid arrive in Porto at 6:50 am each day.

RAIL PASSES

Eurail passes provide unlimited first-class rail travel in all participating countries for the duration of the pass. If you plan to rack up the miles, get a standard pass. These are available in units from three days to three months. In addition to a standard Eurail pass, ask about special rail-pass plans. Among these are the Eurail Youthpass (in second class for those under age 26), the Eurail Saverpass (which gives a discount for two to five people traveling together), a Eurail Flexipass (which allows 10 or 15 travel days within a two-month period), and the Eurail Select Pass n Drive (which combine travel by train and rental car). It's best to purchase your pass before you leave for Europe.

■ TIP→ **Be aware that if you don't plan to cover many miles, you may come out ahead by buying individual tickets instead of rail passes.**

Seat reservations are required on some European trains, particularly high-speed trains, and are a good idea on trains that may be crowded—particularly in summer on popular routes. You will definitely need a reservation if you purchase sleeping accommodations.

Train Information CP. ☎ *707/210220* ⊕ *www.cp.pt.* **Rail Europe.** ☎ *800/622–8600* ⊕ *www.raileurope.com.*

ESSENTIALS

■ ACCOMMODATIONS

There are many different types of lodging options in Portugal. Many who travel to the Algarve region book themselves into luxurious resorts and never step outside them, thanks to amenities such as golf courses, tennis courts, and entertainment.

Although there are many international chain hotels in Portugal, *residências* and *pensões* (simple accommodations with private bathrooms, and breakfast as the only meal served) in former private homes are also popular and very affordable. They can be found in cities and rural towns as well.

Pousadas (inns) are within historic structures, often former castles or palaces, and are usually decorated with local crafts or antique reproductions. They still offer modern amenities, such as television.

APARTMENT AND HOUSE RENTALS

The rental properties in the Algarve are in high demand. Most apartments and villas are privately owned, with a local management company overseeing the advertising, maintenance, and rent collection. Two reliable Algarve-based agencies are Villas & Vacations and Resort Rentals Algarve.

For lists of rental properties and reputable agents elsewhere in Portugal, contact tourist offices. Avoid time-share touts on the street; they'll try to lure you in to view a property with the promise of free vacations and cash. These are often sophisticated (and costly) scams.

Rental Agencies Resort Rentals Algarve. ☎ 282/771132 ⊕ resortrentalsalgarve.com. **Villas & Vacations.** ☎ 289/390500 ⊕ www. villas-vacations.com.

COUNTRY HOUSES

Throughout the country, though particularly in the north, many *solares* (manors) and *casas no campo* (farm- or country houses) have been remodeled to receive small numbers of guests in a venture called Turismo de Habitação (TURIHAB). These guesthouses are in bucolic settings, near parks or monuments or in historic *aldeias* (villages). If they are larger properties, such as farmhouses, guests stay in self-contained cottages on the grounds. Breakfast is always included in the price.

The Central Nacional do Turismo no Espaço Rural (National Center for Rural Tourism) serves as a clearinghouse for information from several organizations involved in this endeavor.

Information Central Nacional do Turismo no Espaço Rural. ☎ 258/931750 ⊕ www. center.pt. **TURIHAB.** ☎ 258/741672 ⊕ www. turihab.pt.

HOME EXCHANGES

With a direct home exchange, you stay in someone else's home while they stay in yours. Some outfits also deal with vacation homes, so you're not actually staying in someone's full-time residence, just their vacant weekend place. In Portugal most home-exchange properties are in Lisbon, though there are a few elsewhere, and a handful in the Algarve.

Although home-exchange is not common practice in Portugal, it could be a viable option for experienced home-swappers, particularly in summer, when peak rates apply in hotels, and especially in key regions like Lisbon and the Algarve.

Exchange Clubs Home Exchange.com. ☎ 800/877–8723 ⊕ www.homeexchange. com. **HomeLink International.** ☎ 800/638–3841 ⊕ www.homelink.org. **Intervac U.S.** ☎ 866/884–7567 ⊕ www.intervac-homeexchange.com.

HOTELS

Portugal has many excellent and reasonably priced hotels, though good properties can be hard to come by in remote inland areas. The government officially grades accommodations with one to five stars or with a category rating. Ratings, which are assigned based on the level of comfort and the number of facilities offered, can be misleading, because quality is difficult to grade. In general, though, the system works.

Most hotel rooms have such basic amenities as a private bathroom and a telephone; those with two or more stars may also have air-conditioning, cable or satellite TV, a minibar, and room service. (Note that all hotels listed *in this guide* have private bath unless otherwise indicated, although most hotels up to three stars will have a shower, rather than bathtub.)

High season means not only the summer months, but also the Christmas and New Year's holiday period on Madeira, Easter week throughout the country, and any time a town is holding a festival. In the off-season (generally November through March), however, many hotels reduce their rates by as much as 20%.

The websites of the Portuguese National Tourist Office and Mais Turismo have search engines for accommodations throughout the country.

Information Mais Turismo. ⊕ *www.maisturismo.pt.* **Portuguese National Tourist Office.** ⊕ *www.visitportugal.com.*

POUSADAS

The term *pousada* is derived from the Portuguese verb *pousar* (to rest). Portugal has a network of about 35 of these hotels, formerly state run but now managed by the Pestana Group, which are in restored castles, palaces, monasteries, convents, and other charming buildings. Each pousada is in a particularly scenic and tranquil part of the country and is tastefully furnished with regional crafts, antiques, and artwork. All have restaurants that serve local specialties; you can stop for a meal or a drink without spending the night.

Rates are reasonable, considering that most pousadas are four- or five-star hotels and a stay in one can be the highlight of a visit. They're extremely popular with foreigners and Portuguese alike, and some have 10 or fewer rooms; make reservations well in advance, especially for stays in summer. Also check for seasonal and senior-citizen discounts, which can be as high as 40%.

Information Pousadas de Portugal. ☏ *218/442001 for reservations, 888/441–4421 in the U.S. (toll-free)* ⊕ *www.pousadas.pt.*

SPAS

Concentrated mostly in the northern half of the country is a profusion of *termas* (thermal springs), whose waters reputedly can cure whatever ails you. In the smaller spas, hotels are rather simple; in the more famous ones, they're first-class. Most are open from May through October.

Information Associação das Termas de Portugal. ☏ *21/794–0574, 21/794–0602* ⊕ *www.termasdeportugal.pt.*

▌ COMMUNICATIONS

PHONES

The country code for Portugal is 351. When dialing a Portuguese number from abroad, dial the nine-digit number after the country code.

CALLING WITHIN PORTUGAL

All phone numbers have nine digits. Numbers in the area in and around Lisbon and Porto begin with a two-digit area code; phone numbers anywhere else in the country begin with a three-digit area code. All fixed-phone area codes begin with 2; mobile numbers, which also have nine digits, begin with 9. For general information, dial ☏ *118* (operators often speak English).

Information Portugal Telecom. ⊕ *www.telecom.pt.* **Yellow Pages.** ⊕ *www.pai.pt.*

CALLING OUTSIDE PORTUGAL

Calling abroad is expensive from hotels, which often add a considerable surcharge. The best way to make an international call is through Skype on your computer or smartphone, if you have access to Wi-Fi.

CALLING CARDS

Purchasing a *cartão telefônico* (calling card) from a post office, newsagent, or tobacconist can save you money and the aggravation of finding enough change for a pay phone. Cards come in denominations of €5 and €10, sometimes more, and can be used from both private and public phones for national and international calls.

MOBILE PHONES

If you have an unlocked smartphone, the least expensive option for using it within Portugal is to buy a prepaid SIM card. For about €5–€15, you'll receive a Portuguese phone number and credit for domestic calls and texts. (International calls cost more; check with the mobile-phone provider for special rates.) SIM cards are available at Vodafone, MEO, and NOS stores, with locations within most Portuguese airports and cities. You can also often rent a cell phone from these same vendors, but the expenses are usually much higher than simply using a SIM card with your current phone.

▮ EATING OUT

The Portuguese love to sit down for a meal, whether it's a traditional little restaurant that offers office workers home cooking at a modest price or a fancy white-tablecloth place with modern takes on old classics.

Although Portugal's plush, luxury restaurants can be very good, they don't always measure up to their counterparts in other European countries. The best food by far tends be found in the moderately priced and less-expensive spots. Don't expect much in the way of decor, and if you have trouble squeezing in, remember the rule of thumb: if it's packed, it's probably good.

Restaurants featuring charcoal-grilled meats and fish, called *churrasqueiras,* are also popular (and often economical) options, and the Brazilian *rodízio*-type restaurant, where you are regaled with an endless offering of spit-roasted

meats, is entrenched in Lisbon, Porto, and the Algarve.

Shellfish restaurants, called *marisqueiras,* are numerous along the coast; note that lobsters, mollusks, and the like are fresh and good but pricey. Restaurant prices fall appreciably when you leave the Lisbon, Porto, and Algarve areas, and portion sizes increase the farther north you go.

▮TIP➜ **While you ponder the menu, you may be served an impressive array of appetizers. If you eat any of these, you'll probably be charged a small amount called a coberto or couvert. If you don't want these appetizers, you're perfectly within your rights to send them back. However, you should do this right away.**

Portuguese restaurants serve an *ementa* (or *prato*) *do dia,* or set menu of three courses. This can be a real bargain—usually 80% of the cost of three courses ordered separately.

Vegetarians can have a tough time in Portugal, although *sopa de legumes* (vegetable soup) is often included as a starter, together with the inevitable *salada* (salad). In general, the only other option (for vegetarians) are omelets. The larger cities and the Algarve have a few vegetarian restaurants, and Chinese, Italian, and Indian restaurants are increasingly common and always have plenty of vegetarian (and vegan) options.

MEALS AND MEALTIMES

Breakfast (*pequeno almoço*) is the lightest meal, usually consisting of nothing more than a croissant or pastry washed down with coffee; lunch (*almoço*), the main meal of the day, is served between noon and 3 pm, although nowadays, office workers in cities often grab a quick sandwich in a bar instead of stopping for a big meal. Some cafés and snack bars serve light meals throughout the afternoon.

Around 5 pm, there's a break for coffee or tea and a pastry; dinner (*jantar*) is eaten around 8 pm, and restaurants generally serve from 7 pm to 10 pm. Monday is a common day for restaurants to close, although this does vary and is noted in the restaurant listings *in this guide.*

Unless otherwise noted, the restaurants listed *in this guide* are open daily for lunch and dinner.

PAYING

Major credit cards are accepted in better restaurants and those geared to tourists, particularly on the Algarve. Humbler establishments generally only accept cash. Always check first, or you may end the evening washing dishes.

⇨ *For guidelines on tipping, see Tipping below.*

RESERVATIONS AND DRESS

Regardless of where you are, it's a good idea to make a reservation if you can. In some places (Lisbon, for example), it's expected. We only mention them specifically when reservations are essential (there's no other way you'll ever get a table) or when they are not accepted.

For popular restaurants, book as far ahead as you can (often 30 days), and reconfirm as soon as you arrive. (Large parties should always call ahead to check the reservations policy.) We mention dress only when men are required to wear a jacket or a jacket and tie.

WINES, BEER, AND SPIRITS

Portuguese wines are inexpensive and, in general, good. Even the *vinho da casa* (house wine) is perfectly drinkable in most restaurants. Among the most popular are the reds from the Dão and Douro regions, Bairrada from the Coimbra/Aveiro region, and Ribatejo and Liziria from the Ribatejo region. The light, sparkling *vinhos verdes* ("green wines," named not for their color but for the fact that they're

drunk early and don't improve with age) are also popular.

The Instituto dos Vinhos do Douro e Porto (Douro and Port Wine Institute), the Comissão de Viticultura da Região dos Vinhos Verdes (Vinho Verde Region Viticulture Commission), and Vinhos de Portugal (Wines of Portugal) have fascinating websites—with information in several languages, including English—that will help you learn more about Portuguese wines.

The leading brands of Portuguese beer—including Super Bock, Cristal, Sagres, and Imperial—are available on tap and in bottles or cans. They're made with fewer chemicals than the average American beers, and are on the strong side with a good, clean flavor. Local brandy—namely Macieira and Constantino—is cheap, as is domestic gin, although it's marginally weaker than its international counterparts.

You have to be 16 or older to drink and buy beer and wine and 18 or older to drink and buy spirits at shops, supermarkets, bars, and restaurants. Note that having brandy with your morning coffee will mark you as a local.

Wine Information Comissão de Viticultura da Região dos Vinhos Verdes. ⊕ www.vinhoverde. pt. Instituto dos Vinhos do Douro e Porto. ⊕ www.ivdp.pt. Vinhos de Portugal (Wines of Portugal). ⊕ www.winesofportugal.info.

▌ELECTRICITY

The electrical current in Portugal is 220 volts, 50 cycles alternating current (AC); wall outlets take plugs with two round prongs.

Consider making a small investment in a universal adapter, which has several types of plugs in one lightweight, compact unit. Most laptops and mobile phone chargers are dual voltage (i.e., they operate equally well on 110 and 220 volts), so require only an adapter. These days the same is true of small appliances such as hair dryers. Always check labels and manufacturer instructions to be sure. Don't use 110-volt outlets marked "for shavers only" for high-wattage appliances such as hair dryers.

▮ EMERGENCIES

The national number for emergencies is ☏ *112*, which is the universal emergency number within the European Union. The ambulance service in Portugal is run by volunteers and free. Contact details of English-speaking doctors can be obtained from American consular offices. Pharmacies *(farmácias)* will have a notice posted on the door with directions to the nearest 24-hour pharmacy.

▮ HEALTH

Sunburn and sunstroke are common problems in summer in mainland Portugal and virtually year-round on Madeira. On a hot, sunny day, even people not normally bothered by strong rays should cover up. Sunscreen can be found in pharmacies and supermarkets, and some U.S. brands are available. The sun protection factor (SPF) is always noted.

Carry sunscreen for nose, ears, and other sensitive areas; be sure to drink enough liquids; and above all, limit your sun exposure for the first few days until you become accustomed to the heat. Mosquitoes are found throughout Portugal and, while they don't carry malaria, they can cause irritation, so pack or buy a local insect repellent.

SHOTS AND MEDICATIONS

No special shots are required before visiting Portugal, Madeira, or the Azores, unless you have come from or recently traveled through an infected area. You might consider a tetanus-diphtheria booster if you haven't had one recently.

▮ HOURS OF OPERATION

Lunchtime is taken very seriously throughout Portugal. Many businesses, particularly outside urban areas, close between 1 and 3 and then reopen for business until 6 or 7. Government offices are typically open 9–noon and 2–5. It's worth noting religious and public holidays, as most businesses grind to a halt, and even the local transport service may be reduced. Also, if the holiday falls on a weekend, then typically a Friday or Monday will also be a holiday.

Banks are open weekdays 8:30–3, with some branches open Saturday. Money exchange booths at airports and train stations are usually open all day (24 hours at Portela Airport in Lisbon).

Most gas stations on main highways are open 24 hours. In more rural areas, stations are open 7 am–10 pm. Note that gas stations can seem few and far between away from the towns and cities, so if you are planning to explore in the hinterland, always start out with a full tank of gas.

Museums and palaces generally open at 10 and close at 5 or 6, though some stay open into the evening; a few still close for lunch from 12:30 to 2. The 23 sites of the nationwide Directorate General for Cultural Heritage (DGPC) are closed Easter Sunday, May 1, December 24 and 25, January 1, and municipal holidays.

Pharmacies are usually open weekdays 9–1 and 3–7, and sometimes Saturday 9–1; 24-hour pharmacies operate in shifts; timetables of 24-hour pharmacies will be posted on the door.

Most shops are open weekdays 9–1 and 3–7, and Saturday 9–1. In December, Saturday hours are the same as weekdays. Shops often close Sunday. *Hipermercados* (giant supermarkets), *supermercados* (regular supermarkets), and shopping centers are typically open seven days a week from 10 am to midnight. In the seaside resorts of the Algarve, many shops, including souvenir shops and supermarkets, open all day between May and September.

HOLIDAYS

New Year's Day (January 1); Mardi Gras (better known as Carnaval, held during the last few days before Lent); Good Friday; Easter Sunday; Liberty Day (April 25); Labor Day (May 1); Corpo de Deus (varies late May–early June); Camões Day (June 10); Assumption (August 15); Republic Day (October 5); All Saints' Day (November 1); Independence Day (December 1); Immaculate Conception (December 8); Christmas Day (December 25).

If a national holiday falls on a Tuesday or Thursday, many businesses also close on the Monday or Friday in between, for a long weekend called a *ponte* (bridge). There are also local holidays when entire towns, cities, and regions grind to a standstill. Check the nearest tourist office for dates.

▌ MAIL

Expect a letter or postcard to take 7–10 days to reach the United States. Postcards mailed internationally cost €1.85; letters the same for up to 20 grams. All post is sent airmail unless otherwise specified.

The Portuguese postal service—the CTT—has a website in English and Portuguese with information such as how to trace mail and the location and hours of countrywide post offices.

You can buy *selos* (stamps) at *correios* (post offices) or at kiosks and shops displaying a red "correios–selos" sign. Stamp-vending machines are scattered about Lisbon.

Information CTT. ⊕ *www.ctt.pt.*

▌ MONEY

Lisbon isn't as expensive as most other international capitals, but it's not the extraordinary bargain it used to be. The coastal resort areas from Cascais and Estoril down to the Algarve can be expensive, though there are lower-priced hotels and restaurants catering mainly to the package-tour trade. If you head off the beaten track, you'll find substantially cheaper food and lodging.

Transportation is still cheap in Portugal when compared with the rest of Europe. Gas prices are controlled by the government, and train and bus travel are inexpensive. Highway tolls are steep but may be worth the cost if you want to bypass the small towns and villages. Flights within the country can be a good bargain if you use the low-cost airlines.

Museums that are part of the Directorate General for Cultural Heritage (DGPC) are free the first Sunday of the month. Lisbon and Porto sell cost-saving passes that cover city transport and entry to museums and other sights; their respective tourist offices can fill you in. You can often also save as much as 50% on accommodations if you visit Portugal out of season.

If you're undeterred by potentially wet weather, consider traveling November to March, when many hotels discount their rates by up to 20%. In Lisbon and Porto, check with the tourist office about discount cards offering travel deals on public transport, reduced or free entrance to certain museums, and discounts in some shops and restaurants.

Prices throughout *this guide* are given for adults. Substantially reduced fees are almost always available for children, students, and senior citizens.

▌TIP➔ **Banks never have every foreign currency on hand, and it may take as long as a week to order. If you're planning to exchange funds before leaving home, don't wait until the last minute.**

ATMS AND BANKS

ATMs are ubiquitous. The Multibanco, or MB, system is state-of-the-art and reliable. The cards most frequently accepted are Visa, MasterCard, American Express, Eurocheque, Eurocard, Cirrus, and Electron. You need a four-digit PIN to use ATMs in Portugal.

Always be sure, when using an ATM machine, that nobody is looking over your shoulder. Similarly, if the machine appears tampered with, stay away. There is a scam throughout Europe whereupon a dummy cover is placed over the machine and/or a tiny camera notes your PIN number. There is usually a limit of €200 per withdrawal.

CREDIT CARDS

It's a good idea to inform your credit-card company before you travel, especially if you're going abroad and don't travel internationally very often. Otherwise, the credit-card company might put a hold on your card owing to unusual activity—not a good thing halfway through your trip.

Although it's usually cheaper (and safer) to use a credit card abroad for large purchases (so you can cancel payments or be reimbursed if there's a problem), note that some credit-card companies *and* the banks that issue them add substantial percentages to all foreign transactions, whether they're in a foreign currency or not. Check on these fees before leaving home, so there won't be any surprises when you get the bill.

■TIP➜ Before you charge something, ask the merchant whether he or she plans to do a dynamic currency conversion (DCC). In such a transaction the credit-card *processor* (shop, restaurant, or hotel, not Visa or MasterCard) converts the currency and charges you in dollars. In most cases you'll pay the merchant a 3% fee for this service in addition to any credit-card-company and issuing-bank foreign-transaction surcharges.

Merchants who participate in dynamic currency conversion programs are supposed to ask whether you want to be charged in dollars or the local currency, but they don't always do so. And even if they do offer you a choice, they may well avoid mentioning the additional surcharges. The good news is that you *do* have a choice—always opt to pay in the local currency. And if this practice really gets your goat, you can avoid it entirely

thanks to American Express; with its cards, DCC simply isn't an option.

CURRENCY AND EXCHANGE

Portugal is one of the 28 European Union countries, and it's also one of the 19 eurozone countries to use a single currency—the euro (€). Coins are issued in denominations of 1, 2, 5, 10, 20, and 50 euro cents, as well as in denominations of €1 and €2. Notes are issued in denominations of €5, 10, 20, 50, 100, 200, and 500. At this writing, the exchange rate was US$1 to €0.89.

■TIP➜ Even if a currency-exchange booth has a sign promising no commission, rest assured that there's some kind of huge, hidden fee. (Oh ... that's right: the sign didn't say "no fee.") And as for rates, you're almost always better off getting foreign currency at an ATM or exchanging money at a bank.

▌ PACKING

Older generations of Portuguese citizens tend to dress up more than their counterparts in the United States or the United Kingdom. That said, attitudes toward clothes have become more relaxed in recent years among the younger generations.

Jeans, however, are generally still paired with a collared shirt and, if necessary, a sweater or jacket. Dressier outfits are needed for more expensive restaurants, nightclubs, and fado houses, though, and people still frown on shorts in churches.

Sightseeing calls for casual, comfortable clothing (well-broken-in low-heel shoes, for example). Away from beaches, wearing bathing suits on the street or in restaurants and shops is not considered good taste.

Summer can be brutally hot; spring and fall, mild to chilly; and winter, cold and rainy. Sunscreen and sunglasses are a good idea any time of the year, since the sun in Portugal is very bright.

PASSPORTS AND VISAS

Citizens of the United States need a valid passport to enter Portugal for stays of up to 90 days; passports must be valid for six months beyond the period of stay. Visas are required for longer stays and, in some instances, for visits to other countries in addition to Portugal.

RESTROOMS

Restaurants, cinemas, theaters, libraries, and service stations are required to have public toilets. Restrooms can range from marble-clad opulence to little better than primitive, but in most cases they're reasonably clean and have toilet paper, although it's always useful to carry a small packet of tissues just in case! Few are adapted for travelers with disabilities. Restrooms are occasionally looked after by an attendant who customarily receives a tip of €0.50. Train stations are likely to have pay toilets.

SAFETY

Be cautious in crowded areas and in the poorer areas of large cities. Be wary of anyone stopping you on the street and even in car parks to ask for directions, the time, or where you're from—particularly if there's more than one person and if you have recently visited the bank or an ATM.

There's enough of a police presence in Portugal that women traveling solo are relatively safe. Take normal precautions, though, and avoid dark, empty streets at night. Ask your hotel staff to recommend a reliable cab company, and whenever possible, call for a taxi instead of hailing one on the street at night. Avoid eye contact with unsavory individuals. If such a person approaches you, discourage him politely but firmly by saying, "*Por favor, me dê licença*" (Excuse me, please) and then walk away with resolve.

Shopkeepers, restaurateurs, and other business owners are generally honest, and credit card receipts are rarely subject to copying. There have been occasional incidents of highway robbery, where the thief slashes the victim's tires during a stop at a gas station and then follows the victim, offering to "help" when the tire goes completely flat. In other cases, the thief takes advantage of an unwary traveler who has left car keys in the ignition or money or a handbag on the seat while stopped at a gas station by telling the driver(s) that they have a puncture in a back tire and urging them to get out of the car to inspect.

TAXES

Value-added tax (IVA, pronounced *ee-vah*) is 6% for hotels (5% in Madeira and 5% in the Azores). By law prices must be posted at the reception desk and should indicate whether tax is included. Restaurants are also required to charge 23% IVA (22% in Madeira and 18% in the Azores). Menus generally state at the bottom whether tax is included (*IVA incluido*) or not (*mais 23% IVA*). When in doubt about whether tax is included in a price, ask, "*Está incluido o IVA?*"

The sales tax is 23% on shop goods (22% in Madeira and 18% in the Azores). A number of Portuguese stores, particularly large ones and those in resorts, will refund this amount on single items worth more than €60.

When making a purchase, ask for a V.A.T. refund form and find out whether the merchant gives refunds—not all stores do, nor are they required to. Have the form stamped like any customs form by customs officials when you leave the country or, if you're visiting several European Union countries, when you leave the EU.

After you're through passport control, take the form to a refund-service counter for an on-the-spot refund (which is usually the quickest and easiest option), or mail it to the address on the form (or the envelope with it) after you arrive home. You receive the total refund stated on the form, but the processing time can be long, especially if you request a credit-card adjustment.

Global Blue is a Europe-wide service with more than 275,000 affiliated stores and more than 700 refund counters at major airports and border crossings. Its refund form, called a Tax Free Form, is the most common across the European continent. The service issues refunds in the form of cash or credit-card adjustment.

V.A.T. Refunds Global Blue.
☎ *800/32111111 from Portugal, landline with enabled international calling only, 232/111111 from Portugal, mobile or landline with enabled international calling, 866/706–6090 from U.S.* ⊕ *www.globalblue.com.*

▋ TIME

Portugal sets its clocks according to Greenwich Mean Time, five hours ahead of the U.S. East Coast. Portuguese summer time (GMT plus one hour) requires an additional adjustment from late March to late October.

▋ TIPPING

Service is not always included in café, restaurant, and hotel bills. Waiters and other service people are sometimes poorly paid, and leaving a tip of around 5%–10% will be appreciated (though locals often don't tip at all). If, however, you received bad service, never feel obligated (or intimidated) to leave a tip. Also, if you have something small, such as a sandwich or *petiscos* (appetizers) at a bar, you can leave just enough to round out the bill to the nearest €1.

TIPPING GUIDELINES FOR PORTUGAL	
Bartender	€1 per drink
Bellhop	€1 per bag
Hotel Concierge	€5 or more, if he or she performs a service for you
Hotel Doorman	€1–€2 if he helps you get a cab
Hotel Maid	€1–€3 per day (either daily or at the end of your stay, in cash)
Hotel Room-Service Waiter	€1–€2 per delivery, even if a service charge has been added
Porter at Airport or Train Station	€1 per bag
Skycap at Airport	€1–€3 per bag checked
Taxi Driver	Round up the fare to the next dollar amount
Tour Guide	€5
Valet Parking Attendant	€1–€2, but only when you get your car
Waiter	5%–10%, nothing additional if a service charge is added to the bill

▋ TRIP INSURANCE

Comprehensive trip insurance is valuable if you're booking a very expensive or complicated trip (particularly to an isolated region) or if you're booking far in advance. Comprehensive policies typically cover trip cancellation and interruption, letting you cancel or cut your trip short because of illness, or, in some cases, acts of terrorism in your destination. Such policies might also cover evacuation and medical care. Some also cover you for trip delays because of bad weather or mechanical problems as well as for lost or delayed luggage.

Another type of coverage to consider is financial default—that is, when your trip is disrupted because a tour operator, airline, or cruise line goes out of business.

Generally you must buy this when you book your trip or shortly thereafter, and it's available to you only if your operator isn't on a list of excluded companies.

Always read the fine print of your policy to make sure that you're covered for the risks that most concern you. Compare several policies to be sure you're getting the best price and range of coverage available.

Insurance Comparison Info **Insure My Trip.** ☎ 800/487–4722, 401/773–9300 ⊕ www. insuremytrip.com. **Squaremouth.** ☎ 800/240–0369 ⊕ www.squaremouth.com.

Comprehensive Insurers **AIG Travel Guard.** ☎ 800/826–4919 ⊕ www.travelguard.com. **Allianz Travel Insurance.** ☎ 866/884–3556, ⊕ www.allianztravelinsurance.com. **CSA Travel Protection.** ☎ 800/348–9505 ⊕ www.csatravelprotection.com. **Travel Insured International.** ☎ 800/243–3174 ⊕ www.travelinsured.com. **Travelex Insurance.** ☎ 800/228–9792 ⊕ www.travelexinsurance.com.

∎ VISITOR INFORMATION

Portuguese National Tourist Offices **Portuguese National Tourist Office.** ⊕ www.visitportugal.com. **Portuguese National Tourist Office—United States.** ✉ 590 5th Ave., 4th fl., New York ☎ 646/354–4403.

INDEX

A

À Capella ✕, 325–326
A Casa de Luis ✕, 143
A Nova Casa de Ramiro ✕, 175
A Vida Portuguesa (shop), 113
Abadia do Porto ✕, 376
Abrantes, 201–203
Accommodations, 11, 432–433. ⇨ See also Lodging
Adega Cooperative de Mangualde, 342
Adega do Cantor, 288
Adega do Isaias (Estremoz) ✕, 238
Adega do Isaias (Évora) ✕, 223
Adega Regional Quelha ✕, 391
Air travel and airports, 16, 426–427
Algarve, 266–267
Coimbra and the Beiras, 316
Estremadura and the Ribatejo, 160
Évora and the Alentejo, 214
Lisbon, 51–52
Porto and the North, 362–363
Albufeira, 278, 287–290
Alcácer do Sal, 260–262
Alcântara (Lisbon), 50, 73–77, 92–93
Alcobaça, 185–188
Alentejo. ⇨ See Évora and the Alentejo
Alfama (Lisbon), 50, 56, 58–62, 81, 84, 94, 103–104, 110–111
Algarve, The, 14, 264–312
Aliança Underground Museum, 346
AlmaLusa ☑, 94
Almancil, 283–284
Almeirim, 196–198
Alto Alentejo, 213, 229–248
Alvito, 249, 251
Alvor, 299–301
Amarante, 390–392
Apartment and house rentals, 432
Aquário Marisqueira de Espinho ✕, 389
Aquariums, 79–80, 375–376
Aqueduto (Serpa), 255
Aqueduto da Agua da Prata, 227–228

Aqueduto da Amoreira, 240
Aqueduto das Aguas Livres, 68–69
Aqueduto dos Pegões, 203
Aqui Há Peixe ✕, 85
Archaeological sites
Algarve, 275
Coimbra and the Beiras, 332, 354
Évora and the Alentejo, 222, 228, 261
Lisbon, 60–61, 64–65
Porto and the North, 389, 398–399
Architecture, 30, 280
Arco da Rua Augusta, 63
Arco da Vila, 272
Areis do Seixo ☑, 170
Armação de Pêra, 290–292
Arte da Terra (shop), 111
Arts. ⇨ See Nightlife and the arts
As Janelas Verdes ☑, 100
ATMs, 437–438
Aveiro, 337–341
Avenida da Liberdade (Lisbon), 68
Azoia, 143–144
Azulejos, 30, 59, 235

B

Bairro Alto (Lisbon), 50, 65–67, 85–89, 95, 98, 104–106, 112–114
Bairro Alto Hotel ☑, 95
Baiuca (club), 103
Baixa (Lisbon), 50, 62–65, 84–85, 94–95, 104, 111–112
Baixo Alentejo, 213, 249–262
Banks, 437–438
Barcelos, 405–406
Barragem do Alqueva, 231
Basilica da Estrela, 72–73
Basilica de Nossa Senhora de Fátima, 206
Basilica de Santa Luzia, 407
Basilica de Santissima Trindade, 206
Batalha, 188–191
Battle of Aljubarrota Interpretation Center174
Beaches
Algarve, 273, 275–276, 280–281, 288–289, 297, 298–300, 305, 307, 309, 311

Coimbra and the Beiras, 335, 340
Estremadura and the Ribatejo, 165–166, 169, 172, 181, 185, 186, 192
Évora and the Alentejo, 259
Lisbon environs, 134, 146
Porto and the North, 387, 388, 396, 410
Beiras. ⇨ See Coimbra and the Beiras
Beja, 251–254
Belcanto ✕, 85–86
Belém (Lisbon), 50, 73–77
Belmonte, 353–355
Benavente, 193–196
Berlengas, 171
Bicycling, 226, 341
Bitetos, 396–397
Boat and ferry travel, 427
Lisbon, 52
Lisbon environs, 120
Boating and sailing
Algarve, 282, 287, 297, 307
Coimbra and the Beiras, 328, 337, 338–339
Lisbon environs, 151
Porto and the North, 392–393, 396
Boca do Inferno, 129–134
Bom Jesus do Monte, 403
Braga, 402–405
Bragança, 415–417
Buarcos, 334
Buçaco, 348
Buddha Eden, 175
Bus travel, 16, 427
Algarve, 267
Coimbra and the Beiras, 316–317
Estremadura and the Ribatejo, 160–161
Évora and the Alentejo, 214
Lisbon, 52
Lisbon environs, 120–121
Porto and the North, 363
Business hours, 436–437

C

Cable cars, 373, 400
Cabo da Roca, 143–144
Cabo Espichel, 154–155
Cabo São Vicente, 310–311
Café Filipe ✕, 155
Cais da Ribeira (Porto), 370

Cais do Sondré (Lisbon), *50, 92, 101, 106–107*
Caldas da Rainha, *180–183*
Caldas de Monchique, *301*
Camping, *356*
Cantar de Grilo ⌧, *256*
Cantina *32* ✕, *376*
Cantinho do Avillez ✕, *376*
Capela das Aparições, *206–207*
Capela de São Frutuoso de Montélios, *403*
Car rentals, *429–430*
Car travel, *16, 427–430*
Algarve, *267–268*
Coimbra and the Beiras, *317*
Estremadura and the Ribatejo, *161, 171*
Évora and the Alentejo, *214–215*
Lisbon, *52*
Lisbon environs, *121*
Porto and the North, *363–364*
Carvoeiro, *292–293*
Casa Amarela ⌧, *248*
Casa Cadaval, *196*
Casa da Baía ✕, *150*
Casa da Calçada ⌧, *391–392*
Casa da Misericórdia, *408*
Casa da Moura ⌧, *306*
Casa da Música, *370*
Casa da Tia Amália ⌧, *258*
Casa de Chá da Boa Nova, *373, 375*
Casa de Mateus, *413–414*
Casa de Serpa ⌧, *256*
Casa do Paço, *335*
Casa dos Bicos, *60*
Casa dos Patudos, *198*
Casa Guedes ✕, *377*
Casa Miradouro ⌧, *141*
Casa-Museu de Guerra Junqueiro, *372*
Casa-Museu de Texeira, *373*
Casa-Museu José Regio, *243*
Casa-Museu Medeiros e Almeida, *69*
Casa Pinto ⌧, *232–233*
Casa Pombal ⌧, *327–328*
Casas dos Pastorinhos, *207*
Cascais, *129–134*
Casino Espinho, *389*
Casinos
Algarve, *286–287*
Coimbra and the Beiras, *337*
Lisbon, *107*
Lisbon environs, *126*
Porto and the North, *389*
Castelo (Castelo de Vide), *247*

Castelo (Tavira), *280*
Castelo Branco, *350–352*
Castelo de Abrantes, *202*
Castelo de Almourol, *22, 200–201*
Castelo de Beja, *251–252*
Castelo de Belmonte, *353–354*
Castelo de Belver, *202–203*
Castelo de Elvas, *240*
Castelo de Guimarães, *398*
Castelo de Leiria, *191*
Castelo de Loulé, *278*
Castelo de Marvão, *22, 245*
Castelo de Mértola, *257*
Castelo de Montmor-o-Novo, *228–229*
Castelo de Óbidos, *175*
Castelo de Portalegre, *242*
Castelo de Santa Maria da Feira, *341–342*
Castelo de Santiago da Barra, *407–408*
Castelo de São Jorge, *22, 59*
Castelo de Serpa, *255*
Castelo de Sesimbra, *155*
Castelo de Sortelha, *352–353*
Castelo de Torres Vedras, *169*
Castelo de Vide, *246–248*
Castelo dos Governadores, *303*
Castelo dos Mouros, *137–138*
Castelo Templario, *351*
Castles, *22*
Algarve, *278, 280, 295*
Coimbra and the Beiras, *333, 341–342, 351, 352–354*
Estremadura and the Ribatejo, *169, 175, 191, 200–201, 202–203*
Évora and the Alentejo, *228–229, 240, 242, 245, 247, 251–252, 257*
Lisbon, *22, 59*
Lisbon environs, *137–138, 155*
Porto and the North, *398, 407–408*
Caves, *207–208*
Central Algarve, *265, 283–286*
Centro de Artes e Espectáculos (CAE), *335*
Centro de Artesanato, *405*
Centro de Interpretação da Batalha de Aljubarrota, *189*
Centro Potrugues de Fotografia, *370*
Centum Cellas, *354*
Champlimaud Centre for the Unknown, *75*
Chaves, *417–418*

Chiado (Lisbon), *50, 65–67, 85–89, 95, 98, 104–106, 112–114*
Chico Elias ✕, *205*
Churches, convents, and monasteries
Algarve, *273, 280, 283, 303*
Coimbra and the Beiras, *321–322, 323, 324, 338, 339, 342, 349, 354, 357, 358*
Estremadura and the Ribatejo, *172, 175, 186, 189–190, 199, 204, 206–207*
Évora and the Alentejo, *218–219, 221–222, 229, 243, 252, 257*
Lisbon, *60, 66, 72–73, 74*
Lisbon environs, *139, 149*
Porto and the North, *371, 372, 385, 387, 390, 396, 399, 403–404, 407, 414, 415–416, 418*
Cidadela, *415–416*
Citânia de Briteiros, *398–399*
Climate, *17*
Clube de Golfe do Estoril, *128*
Coimbra and the Beiras, *14, 314–358*
Communications, *433–434*
Conímbriga, *332–333*
Conrad Algarve Hotel ⌧, *284*
Conserveira de Lisboa (shop), *111*
Constância, *200–201*
Convent of St. João de Deus, *229*
Convento de Alpendurada, *396*
Convento de Arrábida, *149*
Convento de Cristo, *204*
Convento de Jesus (Aveiro), *338*
Convento de Nossa Senhora da Conceição, *252*
Convento de Santa Clara (Vila do Conde), *385*
Convento de Santa Clara-a-Nova, *321–322*
Convento de Santa Clara-a-Velha, *322*
Convento de São Francisco, *257*
Convento de São Gonçalo, *390*
Convento do Carmo, *66*
Convento dos Capuchos, *139*
Convents. ⇨ See Churches, convents, and monasteries
Cooking and Nature-Emotional Hotel ⌧, *190*

Cooperativa de Lagoa, 293–294
Cork Route, The, 277
Costa da Caparica, 146
Costa Verde, 361, 397–412
Coudelaria de Alter, 242–243
Country houses, 432
Credit cards, 11, 438
Cripta Arqueológica do Castelo, 261
Cromlech and the Menhir of Almedres, 228
CS Vintage House ⚑ , 394
Cuisine, 17, 21, 26–27, 281
Curia, 345–347
Currency, 438

D

D. Diogo de Sousa Museum, 403
Delfina ✕ , 84–85
Dining, 11, 434–435
Algarve, 268–269, 274, 281, 284, 289, 291, 292, 295–296, 297, 299, 300, 302, 305–306, 308, 309–310, 311–312
Coimbra and the Beiras, 318, 322–323, 325–327, 332–333, 334, 335–336, 339, 344, 346, 347, 349, 351, 353, 355
Estremadura and the Ribatejo, 161–162, 166–167, 169–170, 175, 177, 181–182, 184, 186–187, 192–193, 194, 197, 199–200, 202, 205, 208–209
Évora and the Alentejo, 215, 221, 223–224, 229, 232, 238, 241, 243, 244, 248, 249, 251, 252–254, 256, 259–260, 261
Lisbon, 63, 67, 74, 80–93
Lisbon environs, 122, 126, 130–131, 134–135, 139–141, 143–144, 146, 148, 150–151, 153, 155
Porto and the North, 364–365, 375, 376–378, 382, 389, 391, 394, 397, 400–401, 403, 404, 406, 408–409, 410, 412, 414, 417
prices, 81, 123, 162, 215, 269, 319, 366
DOC ✕ , 394
Doca (Faro), 272–273
Dolmen of Zambujeiro, 228
Dom Gonçalo Hotel & Spa ⚑ , 209

DOP ✕ , 377
Douro, 361, 385–397

E

Eastern Algarve, The, 265, 279–283
Eastern Beiras, 315, 350–358
El Corte Inglés (shop), 115
Electricity, 435–436
Elevador da Glória, 66
Elevador de Santa Justa, 62
Elvas, 239–241
Emergencies, 428–429, 436
Encosta da Quinta, 180
Epic Sana Algarve ⚑ , 289
Ericeira, 165–167
Espaço Memória dos Exilios, 126
Espinho, 388–390
Esposende, 387–388
Estação de Caminhos de Ferro, 339
Estação de São Bento, 370–371
Estádio da Luz, 109
Estórias na Casa da Comida ✕ , 89
Estoril, 124–129
Estoril Casino, 126
Estoril Coast, 118, 124–135
Estrela (Lisbon), 50, 71–73, 91
Estremadura and the Ribatejo, 14, 158–209
Estremoz, 236–239
Évora and the Alentejo, 14, 212–262
Exhibition Center, 309

F

Fábrica Sant'Anna (shop), 112
Fado music, 21, 103–104, 106, 326
Faro and environs, 265, 271–279
Faro de São Vicente, 311
Farol de Cabo Mondego, 335
Fátima, 206–209
Fazenda Nova ⚑ , 281
Feeting Room, The (shop), 383
Feira de Barcelos, 405–406
Feira da Ladra (market), 111
Feira do Artesanato (fair), 129
Feira dos Enchida Tradicional, 301–302
Feira Nacional do Cavalo, 198
Ferias, 20
Ferry and boat travel, 427
Lisbon, 52
Lisbon environs, 120

Festival de Chocolate, 176
Festival Internacional de Curtas Metragens, 387
Festival Internacional Literário de Óbidos, 176
Festival Nacional de Gastronomia, 199
Festivals and seasonal events, 17, 20, 39–44
Algarve, 275, 279, 295, 296, 301–302
Estremadura and the Ribatejo, 176, 198, 199
Lisbon environs, 129, 142
Porto and the North, 387
Figueira da Foz, 334–337
Film, 108, 387
Fishing
Algarve, 310
Coimbra and the Beiras, 356
Estremadura and the Ribatejo, 173
Évora and the Alentejo, 226
Lisbon environs, 133, 156
Fly London (shop), 115
Fnac (shop), 114
Fort de Santa Luzia, 240
Fortaleza da Santa Catarina (Praia da Rocha), 298
Fortaleza de Peniche, 171–172
Fortaleza de Sagres, 309
Fortaleza do Guincho ⚑ , 135
Forte de São Francisco ⚑ , 418
Forte Ponta da Bendeira, 303
Forts
Algarve, 298, 303, 309
Estremadura and the Ribatejo, 171–172
Évora and the Alentejo, 240, 261
Porto and the North, 418
Four Seasons Hotel Ritz Lisbon ⚑ , 99
Foz do Douro, 375
Fundação Arpad Szenes-Viera da Silva, 69

G

Gadanha ✕ , 238
Galeria Cristina Guerra, 73
Galeria Filomena Soares, 59
Galeria 111, 69
Galleries
Algarve, 278
Coimbra and the Beiras, 335
Évora and the Alentejo, 226
Lisbon, 59, 69, 73, 112
Porto and the North, 405

Gardens
Coimbra and the Beiras,
324–325, 351
Estremadura and the Ribatejo,
175
Évora, 219, 222
Lisbon, 60, 75
Lisbon environs, 153
Garrafeira Alfaia (bar), *105*
Gay and lesbian clubs,
105–106
GN Cellar (shop), *111*
Godzilla Surfcamp, *382*
Go-karts, *179*
Golegã, *198*
Golf, *31*
Algarve, 282, 285–286, 287,
293, 300
Coimbra and the Beiras, 345,
347
Estremadura and the Ribatejo,
179, 195
Lisbon environs, 128, 133, 142,
145, 152
Porto and the North, 390, 392
Gouveia, *356–357*
Grande Hotel de Luso ▦ , *347*
Grutas da Moeda (Coin
Caves), *207–208*
Guadalupe, *227–228*
Guarda, *357–358*
Guimarães, *397–402*
Guincho, *134–135*

H

Health and fitness, *109*
Health concerns, *436*
Henry the Navigator, Prince,
78
Herdade da Barrosinha ▦ ,
262
Herdade do Esporão, *231–232*
Hiking, *328, 350, 356*
History, *57, 221, 315, 320*
Holidays, *437*
Home exchanges, *432*
Horseback riding
Algarve, 286
Coimbra and the Beiras, 328,
341
Estremadura and the Ribatejo,
195–196
Évora and the Alentejo, 226
Horta da Moura ▦ , *233*
Hospitals. ⇨ *See* Emergencies
Hotel Bejense ▦ , *254*
Hotel Britânia ▦ , *99*
Hotel Cascais Miragem ▦ , *132*
Hotel do Elevador ▦ , *404*

Hotel M'AR De AR Aqueduto
▦ , *225*
Hotel São Joã de Deus ▦ , *241*
Hotel Sol Algarve ▦ , *274*
Hotels, *11, 432–433.* ⇨ *See*
also Lodging
House rentals, *432*

I

Igreja da Graça, *199*
Igreja da Misericórdia (Aveiro),
339
Igreja da Misericórdia
(Chaves), *418*
Igreja da Misericórdia (Tavira),
280
Igreja da Misericórdia (Viseu),
343
Igreja da Nossa Senhora da
Assunção, *240*
Igreja de Jesus, *149*
Igreja de Misericórdia (Évora),
222
Igreja de Nossa Senhora da
Oliveira, *399*
Igreja de Santa Maria (Beja),
252
Igreja de Santa Maria (Óbi-
dos), *175*
Igreja de Santa Maria do
Olival, *204*
Igreja de Santo António, *303*
Igreja de Santo Ildefonso, *371*
Igreja de São Bento, *416*
Igreja de São Clemente, Matriz
de Loulé, *278*
Igreja de São Francisco
(Évora), *218–219*
Igreja de São Francisco (Faro),
273
Igreja de São Francisco (Gui-
marães), *399*
Igreja de São Francisco
(Porto), *372*
Igreja de São Leonardo, *172*
Igreja de São Lourenço, *283*
Igreja de São Pedro, *273*
Igreja de São Tiago, *354*
Igreja do Carmo, *273*
Igreja dos Clérigos, *414*
Igreja dos Lóios, *219*
Igreja e Museu de São Roque,
66
Igreja Matriz (Gouveia), *357*
Igreja Matriz (Mértola), *257*
Igreja Matriz (Ovar), *342*
Igreja Matriz (Vila do Conde),
387
Ilha de Tavira, *280*

Incomúm by Luis Santos ✕ ,
140
Insurance, *440–441*
for car rentals, 429–430
InterContinental Porto-Palacio
das Cardosas ▦ , *379*
International Design Hotel
▦ , *95*
International Short Film Festi-
val, *387*
Irmas Flores Artesano, *237*
Itineraries, *32–38*
Coimbra and the Beiras, 319
Estremadura and the Ribatejo,
163
Évora and the Alentejo, 217
Lisbon environs, 125
Porto and the North, 367

J

Jardim Botânico (Coimbra),
324–325
Jardim Botânico da Ajuda, *75*
Jardim de Diana, *222*
Jardim do Antigo Paço Episco-
pal, *351*
Jardim Muicipal (Évora), *219*
Jardim Zoológico, *69*
Jeep tours, *226*
José Maria da Fonseca Com-
pany, *153*
Juderia (Belmonte), *354*

K

Kayaking, *328, 350*
Kite surfing, *135*

L

Lagoa, *293–294*
Lagos, *265, 278, 302–307*
Lamego, *395–396*
Language, *419–424*
Lapa (Lisbon), *50, 71–73, 91,*
100–101, 106
Largo ✕ , *88*
Largo da Praça de Touros, *197*
Largo da Sé (Viseu), *343*
Largo das Portas de Moura
(Évora), *222*
Largo do Paço ✕ , *391*
Largo Luis de Camoes, *257*
Lawrence's Hotel ▦ , *141*
Leiria, *191–193*
Lighthouses
Algarve, 311
Coimbra and the Beiras, 335
Lisbon environs, 154–155
Lisboa Carmo Hotel ▦ , *98*

Lisboa Story Centre, *63*
Lisbon, *14, 46–116*
Lisbon Cathedral (Sé de Lisboa), *60*
Lisbon environs, *14, 118–156*
Literary Man Óbidos Hotel ⬚ , *178*
Living Science Museum (Centro Ciencia Viva), *237*
Livraria Lello e Irmáo (shop), *383*
Lodging, *11, 432–433*
   Algarve, *269, 274, 276, 277, 278, 281–283, 284, 285, 286, 289–290, 291, 292, 297, 300, 302, 306, 308, 310*
   Coimbra and the Beiras, *318, 327–328, 333, 336, 340, 344–345, 346–348, 349–350, 351–352, 353, 354–356, 357*
   Estremadura and the Ribatejo, *162, 166, 170, 177–179, 182, 184–185, 187–188, 190, 193, 194, 197–198, 200, 201, 202, 205, 209*
   Évora and the Alentejo, *215, 224–225, 232–233, 236, 239, 241, 244, 248, 251, 254, 256, 258, 260, 262*
   Lisbon, *93–102*
   Lisbon environs, *122–123, 127–128, 132, 135, 141, 144–145, 146, 148, 152, 155–156*
   Porto and the North, *365–366, 387, 389, 391–392, 394–395, 396, 401–402, 404–405, 406, 409, 412, 414, 417, 418*
   prices, *93, 123, 162, 215, 269, 319, 366*
Loulé, *277–279*
Loulé Municipal Market, *279*
Lounge, *106*
Luso, *347–348*
Luvaria Ulisses (shop), *113*
Lx Boutique ⬚ , **101**
LX Factory, **75**

M

Mail, *437*
Malhão Beach, *259*
Marble Museum, *234*
Martinhal Sagres Beach Family Resort Hotel ⬚ , *310*
Marvão, *245–246*
Maus Hábitos (club), *381*
Medeia Monumental, *108*
Medieval Festival, *295*
Mélia Braga ⬚ , *405*

Memmo Alfama Wine Bar and Terrace ✕ , *81*
Menhir of Almedres, *228*
Menhir of Outeiro, *232*
Mercado de Escravos, *304*
Mercado Franco, *247*
Mercado Medieval, *176*
Mértola, *256–258*
Mesa de Frades (club), *104*
Minho and the Costa Verde, *361, 397–412*
Miradouro de Santa Luzia, *60*
Miradouro de São Gens, *351*
Miranda do Douro, *416–417*
Misericordia Church, *229*
Modern City (Lisbon), *50, 67–71, 89–90, 98–100, 106, 114–115*
Molhó Bico ✕ , *256*
Monasteries. ⇨ *See* Churches, convents, and monasteries
Monchique, *301–302*
Money matters, *11, 16, 437–438*
Monsaraz, *231–233*
Monserrate Park and Palace, *138*
Monte da Casteleja (vineyard), *304*
Monte Mar ✕ , *131*
Montemor-o-Novo, *228–229*
Montemor-o-Velho, *333–334*
Monument to Cabral, *354*
Mosteiro da Batalha, *189–190*
Mosteiro de Alcobaça, *186*
Mosteiro de Lorvão, *349*
Mosteiro de S. Bernardo, *243*
Mosteiro de São Vicente, *60*
Mosteiro dos Jerónimos, *74*
Mullens (bar), *306*
Museu Alberto Sampaio, *399*
Museu Amadeo de Souza-Cardoso, *390–391*
Museu Arqueológia (Silves), *295*
Museu Arqueológico (Barcelos), *406*
Museu Arqueológico (Chaves), *418*
Museu Arqueológico (Serpa), *255*
Museu Arqueológico de Carmo, *66*
Museu Arqueológico de São Miguel de Odrinhas, *139*
Museu Arte Nova, *338*
Museu Berardo, *75–76*
Museu Calouste Gulbenkian, *67–68*

Museu da Cerâmica, *181*
Museu da Ciència, *323*
Museu da Farmácia, *66*
Museu da Guarda, *358*
Museu da Marioneta, *73*
Museu da Região Flaviense, *418*
Museu da Sociedade Martins Sarmento, *399*
Museu das Rendas de Bilros (Peniche), *172*
Museu das Rendas de Bilros de Vila do Conde, *387*
Museu de Arte Antiga (Lisbon), *72*
Museu de Arte Contemporânea (Porto), *371*
Museu de Arte Contemporanea de Elvas (MACE), *240*
Museu de Arte Sacra (Braga), *404*
Museu de Arte Sacra (Chaves), *418*
Museu de Arte Sacra (Estremoz), *237*
Museu de Arte Sacra da Sé, *222*
Museu de Artes Decorativas, *408*
Museu de Cera, *208*
Museu de Cêrro da Vila, *286*
Museu de Évora, *219*
Museu de Leiria, *191*
Museu de Marinha, *76*
Museu de Olaria, *406*
Museu de Ovar, *342*
Museu de Relógio, *255*
Museu de Setúbal, *149*
Museu de Tapeçaria Guy Fino, *243*
Museu do Douro, *393*
Museu do Mar (Cascais), *130*
Museu do Oriente (Lisbon), *76–77*
Museu do Teatro Romano, *60–61*
Museu do Traje, *277*
Museu do Vidro, *192*
Museu do Vinho do Porto, *372*
Museu dos Coches (Vila Viçosa), *234*
Museu dos Condes Castro Guimarães, *130*
Museu-Escola de Artes Decorativas, *59*
Museu Etnográfico (Peneda-Gerês), *410*
Museu Etnográfico (Serpa), *255*
Museu Fotografia, *240–241*

Museu Francisco Tavares Proença Junior, *351*
Museu Grão Vasco, *342–343*
Museu Ibérico da Máscara e Traje, *416*
Museu José Malhoa, *181*
Museu Lusa-Hebraico Abraham Zacuto-Sinagoga, *204*
Museu Machado de Castro, *325*
Museu Maritimo Almirante Ramalho Ortigáo, *273*
Museu Militar (Bragança), *415–416*
Museu Militar (Chaves), *418*
Museu Militar (Lisbon), *61*
Museu Militar de Buçaco, *348*
Museu Monsaraz, *232*
Museu Municipal de Arte Moderna Abel Manta, *357*
Museu Municipal de Estremoz, *237*
Museu Municipal de Faro, *273*
Museu Municipal de Portalegre, *243*
Museu Municipal Dr. José Formosinho, *304*
Museu Municipal Leonel Trindade, *169*
Museu Municipal Santos Rocha, *335*
Museu Nacional de Arte Antiga, *72*
Museu Nacional de Arte Contemporânea, *66–67*
Museu Nacional do Azulejo, *59*
Museu Nacional do Vinho, *186*
Museu Nacional dos Coches (Lisbon), *77*
Museu Visigótico, *253*
Museums
Algarve, *273, 277, 286, 295, 304*
Coimbra and the Beiras, *323, 325, 335, 338, 339, 342–343, 346, 348, 351, 357, 358*
Estremadura and the Ribatejo, *169, 171–172, 181, 186, 189, 191–192, 204, 207, 208*
Évora and the Alentejo, *219, 222, 232, 234, 237, 240–241, 243, 253, 255, 257–258*
Lisbon, *59, 60–61, 63, 66–68, 69, 72, 73, 75–77*
Lisbon environs, *126, 130, 139, 149*
Porto and the North, *370, 371, 372, 373, 387, 389,* *390–391, 393, 394, 398–399, 403, 404, 406, 408, 410, 415–416*
Museus de Mértola, *257–258*
MusicBox (club), *107*
Myriad by SANA Hotels ☲ , *102*

N

Nature reserves
Estremadura and the Ribatejo, *194*
Évora and the Alentejo, *243–244, 261*
Porto and the North, *387, 388, 416*
Nazaré, *183–185*
Nightlife and the arts
Algarve, *274, 286–287, 290, 306–307*
Coimbra and the Beiras, *337*
Évora and the Alentejo, *225–226*
Lisbon, *102–109*
Lisbon environs, *128, 132*
Porto and the North, *380–381, 405, 409*
The North. ⇨ *See* Porto and the North
Núcleo Arqueologico da Rua dos Correeiros, *64–65*

O

O Borges ✕ , *355*
O Camilo ✕ , *306*
O Casarão ✕ , *192*
O Escondidinho ✕ , *244*
O Fialho ✕ , *224*
O Milagre de Fátima - Museu Interativo, *208*
O Peleiro ✕ , *336*
O Pereira ✕ , *131*
O Pescador ✕ , *131*
O Toucinho ✕ , *197*
Óbidos, *174–180*
Óbidos Vila Natal, *176*
Ocean Restaurant ✕ , *291*
Oceanário de Lisboa, *79–80*
Ofir, *387–388*
Oitavos Dunes (golf course), *133*
Olhanense Football Club & José Arcanjo Stadium, *275*
Olhão, *275–276*
Olissippo Lapa Palace ☲ , *101*
100 Maneiras ✕ , *84*
Opera, *108*
Os Três Potes ✕ , *408–409*

Outdoor activities and sports.
⇨ *See* Specific sports
Ovar, *341–342*

P

Packing, *438*
Paço dos Cunhas de Santar, *343*
Paço dos Duques de Bragança, *400*
Paço Ducal, *234*
Padrão dos Descobrimentos, *77*
Palace Hotel Do Bussaco ☲ , *348*
Palaces
Algarve, *303*
Estremadura and the Ribatejo, *168*
Évora and the Alentejo, *222–223, 234, 237*
Lisbon, *68, 77*
Lisbon environs, *138–139, 144*
Porto and the North, *372–373, 403, 413–414*
Palácio da Ajuda, *77*
Palácio da Bolsa, *372–373*
Palácio da Pena, *22, 138*
Palácio de Dom Manuel, *222–223*
Palácio de Monserrate, *138*
Palácio dos Biscainhos, *403*
Palácio dos Marqueses da Fronteira, *68*
Palácio Estoril Golf & Spa Hotel ☲ , *128*
Palácio Nacional de Mafra, *168*
Palácio Nacional de Queluz, *144*
Palácio Nacional de Sintra, *138–139*
Palmela, *147–148*
Panteão de Santa Engrácia, *61*
Pap'açorda ✕ , *92*
Parks
Coimbra and the Beiras, *339, 355–356*
Estremadura and the Ribatejo, *190–191, 194, 199*
Évora and the Alentejo, *222, 243–244*
Lisbon, *71, 79–80*
Lisbon environs, *130, 138, 150*
Porto and the North, *387, 388, 412, 416*
Parque das Nações (Lisbon), *50, 79–80, 93, 102, 107*

Parque do Marechal Carmona, 130
Parque Eduardo VII, 71
Parque Municipal, 339
Parque Nacional da Peneda-Gerês, 412
Parque Natural da Serra da Estrela, 355–356
Parque Natural da Serra de São Mamede, 243–244
Parque Natural das Serras de Aire e Candeeiros, 190–191
Parque Natural de Montesinho, 416
Parque Natural do Litoral Norte, 388
Parreirinha d'Alfama (club), 104
Passports and visas, 439
Pastelarias, 20
Pátio da Inquisição, 325
Pavilhão Chinês (bar), 105
Pedro and Inês, 187
Pedro dos Letões ✕ , 346
Penacova, 349–350
Peneda-Gerês, 410–412
Peneda-Gerês National Park, 412
Penha Longa Golf Course, 142
Penha Longa Resort ☑ , 141
Peniche, 170–174
Penina (golf course), 300
Peninsula de Tróia, 151–152
Pensão Amor (bar), 106–107
Pensão Policarpo ☑ , 225
Pérgola House ☑ , 132
Peso da Régua, 392–395
Pestana Alvar Praia ☑ , 300
Pestana Palace ☑ , 101
Ponte de Lima, 409–410
Ponte Dom Luis, 373
Ponte 25 de Abril, 77–78
Portalegre, 241–244
Portas do Sol, 199
Portimão, 278, 296–298
Portinho da Arrábida, 150
Porto and the North, 14, 360–418
Portuguese vocabulary, 419–424
Pousada Castelo de Óbidos ☑ , 178–179
Pousada Castelo Palmela ☑ , 148
Pousada da Rainha Santa Isabel ☑ , 22, 239
Pousada da Ria ☑ , 340
Pousada de Convento do Desagravo ☑ , 355

Pousada de D. João IV ☑ , 236
Pousada de Dom Alfonso II ☑ , 262
Pousada de Guimarães, Santa Marinha ☑ , 402
Pousada de Viseu ☑ , 345
Pousada do Castelo de Alvito ☑ , 251
Pousadas, 433
Praça da República (Aveiro), 339
Praça da República (Beja), 253
Praça da República (Viana do Castelo), 408
Praça da República em Viseu, 343
Praça de Dom Duarte (Viseu), 343–344
Praça de Touros de Campo Pequeno, 69
Praça do Comércio (Lisbon), 63
Praça do Giraldo (Évora), 219
Praça Dom Pedro V (Castelo de Vide), 247
Praça dos Restauradores (Lisbon), 71
Praça Luís de Camões (Castelo Branco), 351
Praça Marquês de Pombal (Lisbon), 71
Praia da Claridade, 335
Praia da Luz, 307–308
Praia da Rocha, 298–299
Praia de Dona Ana, 305
Praia d'El Ray Marriott Golf & Beach Resort ☑ , 179
Praia do Camilo, 305
Praia do Guincho, 134
Praia Fluvial Bitetos, 396
Praia Mar ✕ , 155
Prices, 11, 16
dining, 81, 123, 162, 215, 269, 319, 366
lodging, 93, 123, 162, 215, 269, 319, 366
Prince Henry the Navigator, 78
Public transportation, 52–53
Purex (gay club), 106

Q

Queluz, 119, 135–136, 144–145
Quinta da Alorna, 196
Quinta da Bacalhoa, 153
Quinta da Dourada ☑ , 244
Quinta da Foz ☑ , 182
Quinta da Pacheca, 395
Quinta da Penina, 296
Quinta da Regaleira, 139

Quinta das Lágrimas, 325
Quinta de Cabriz, 344
Quinta de Castelães ✕ , 401
Quinta de Cima, 282
Quinta do Casal Branco, 196–197
Quinta do Crasto, 393
Quinta do Encontro, 346
Quinta do Miguel ☑ , 155
Quinta do Sanguinhal, 175
Quinta do Vallado, 393
Quinta dos Vales, 294

R

Reserva Natural do Estuário do Tejo, 194
Reserva Natural do Sado, 261
Reserva Ornitológico de Mindelo, 387
Residencial Florescente ☑ , 95
Restaurante a Moagem ✕ , 334
Restaurante D. Pedro V ✕ , 248
Restaurante Tipico Dom Roberto ✕ , 417
Restrooms, 439
Ribatejo, The, 14, 158–163, 193–209
Rio de Aveiro boat trips, 338–339
Rio de Onor, 416
Rio do Prado ☑ , 179
Rio Maravilha (bar), 107
Roda do Mouchão, 205
Roman ruins
Algarve, 275
Coimbra and the Beiras, 332, 354
Évora and the Alentejo, 222
Lisbon, 60–61, 64–65
Porto and the North, 389
Rossío (Lisbon), 63–64
Rossío (Estremoz), 237
Rota do Vinho do Porto, 394
Royal Palace (Estremoz), 237
Rua 5 de Outubro (Évora), 221
Rural tourism, 411

S

Sabores d'Italia ✕ , 182
Safety, 439
Lisbon environs, 136, 145
Porto and the North, 368
Sagres, 278, 308–310
Sailing. ⇨ See Boating and sailing
Salpoente ✕ , 339
Sameiro O Maia ✕ , 404
Santa Maria do Castelo, 280

Santarém, *198–200*
Santo António das Areias, *246*
Santos (Lisbon), *50, 92, 101, 106–107*
Santuário de Nossa Senhora dos Remédios, *396*
Santuário Nossa Senhora do Sameiro, *403*
São Bento (Lisbon), *50, 115*
São Brás de Alportel, *276–277*
São Martinho do Porto, *186*
São Pedro do Corval, *233*
São Rosas ✕, *238*
Sardine Festival, *296*
Scuba diving
Algarve, *293, 308*
Lisbon environs, *133, 156*
Sé (Évora), *221–222*
Sé (Guarda), *358*
Sé (Lisbon), *60*
Sé (Viseu), *343*
Sé Catedral (Braga), *404*
Sé Catedral de Faro, *273*
Sé de Portalegre, *243*
Sé do Porto, *371*
Sé Nova (Coimbra), *323*
Sé Velha (Coimbra), *323*
Sea Life, *375–376*
Semana Internacional de Piano de Óbidos, *176*
Senhor Vinho (fado club), *106*
Serpa, *254–256*
Serra da Arrábida, *150*
Sesimbra, *154–156*
Setúbal, *148–151*
Setúbal Peninsula, *119, 145–156*
Shellfish Festival, *275*
Sheraton Porto Hotel & Spa ▦, *380*
Shopping
Algarve, *276, 278–279, 290, 294, 296, 298*
Coimbra and the Beiras, *329, 341, 345, 352*
Estremadura and the Ribatejo, *179–180, 181, 183, 185, 188*
Évora and the Alentejo, *223, 226–227, 233, 237, 247*
Lisbon, *110–116*
Lisbon environs, *129, 133–134, 142, 148, 153–154*
Porto and the North, *382–384, 394, 402, 405–406*
Silves, *278, 294–296*
Silves Castle, *295*
Sinagoga, *247–248*
Sintra, *119, 135–142*
Sítio de Nazaré, *184*

Skiing, *356*
Skydiving, *300–301*
Soccer, *109, 381*
Sociedade Circulo Montemo-rense ✕, *229*
Solar Bragancano ✕, *417*
Solar das Avencas ▦, *244*
Solar do Castelo ▦, *94*
Solar do Vinho do Porto (bar), *105*
Sortelha, *352–353*
Spas, *433*
Algarve, *301*
Coimbra and the Beiras, *346*
Estremadura and the Ribatejo, *185, 188*
Sports. ⇨ *See* Specific sports
Storytailors (shop), *113*
Surfing, *135, 382*
Symbols, *11*
Synagogues, *204, 247–248*

T

Taberna do Arrufa ✕, *249, 251*
Tasca do Celso ✕, *260*
Tasca do Joel ✕, *173*
Tavira, *279–282*
Taxes, *439–440*
Taxis
Algarve, *268*
Lisbon, *53–54*
Lisbon environs, *121*
Teatro Nacional de São Carlos, *108*
Teleférico (Guimarães), *400*
Teleférico de Gaia, *373*
Telephones, *433–434*
Templo Romano, *222*
Tennis
Algarve, *286, 293*
Coimbra and the Beiras, *329*
Termas da Curia Spa Resort, *346*
Terra de Montanha ✕, *414*
Theater, *109, 381*
Thermal waters, *301, 346*
Time, *440*
Timing the visit, *17*
Algarve, *265–266*
Coimbra and the Beiras, *316*
Estremadura and the Ribatejo, *160*
Évora and the Alentejo, *213–214*
Lisbon, *51*
Lisbon environs, *119–120*
Porto and the North, *361–362*
Tipping, *440*

Tivoli Hotel Palácio de Seteais ▦, *141*
Tomar, *203–205*
Torre de Belém, *74*
Torre de Menagem (Beja), *251–252*
Torre de Menagem (Chaves), *418*
Torre de Menagem (Guarda), *358*
Torre de Tavira, *280*
Torre dos Clérigos, *372*
Torres Vedras, *167, 169–170*
Tours and packages
Algarve, *271, 282, 307*
Coimbra and the Beiras, *338–339*
Estremadura and the Ribatejo, *162–163, 201*
Évora and the Alentejo, *226*
Lisbon, *54–55*
Lisbon environs, *123–124, 137, 151*
Porto and the North, *369–370, 392–393*
Train travel, *16, 430–431*
Algarve, *268*
Coimbra and the Beiras, *317–318*
Estremadura and the Ribatejo, *161*
Évora and the Alentejo, *215*
Lisbon, *54*
Lisbon environs, *121–122*
Porto and the North, *364*
Transportation, *16, 426–431*
Trás-os-Montes, *361, 412–418*
Trip insurance, *440–441*
Tromba Rija ✕, *192–193*
Troncalhada Ecomuseum, *339*
Trumps (gay club), *106*
Tungobriga, *389*

U

Universidade de Évora, *223*
Universidade Velha, *323–324*

V

Vale do Lobo, *285–286*
Venta da Rosa, *309*
Vertigem Azul (boat tours), *151*
Viana do Castelo, *407–409*
Vila Adentro ✕, *274*
Vila do Bispo, *311–312*
Vila do Conde, *385, 387*
Vila Joya Boutique Resort ▦, *290*
Vila Maria ▦, *248*

Vila Monte Farm House ⌶,
276
Vila Nogueira de Azeitão,
152–154
Vila Nova de Gaia, 373
Vila Nova de Milfontes,
258–260
Vila Real, 413–414
Vila Real de Santo António,
282–283
Vila Viçosa, 233–234, 236
Vila Vita Parc ⌶, 291
Vilamoura, 286–287
Visas and passports, 439
Viseu, 342–345
Visitor information, 441
Coimbra and the Beiras, 319
Évora and the Alentejo, 215
Lisbon, 55–56
Lisbon environs, 123–124
Porto and the North, 369–370,
411
Viúva Lamego (shop), 114
Vocabulary, 419–424

W

W.A. Sarmento (shop), 112
Walking tours, 55
Water parks
Algarve, 284, 288, 292, 294
Estremadura and the Ribatejo,
173

Water sports, 174, 182
Weather, 17
Western Algarve, 265,
302–312
Western Beiras, 315, 329–350
Windsurfing, 135
Wine and wineries, 28–29, 435
Algarve, 293–294, 296, 304
Coimbra and the Beiras, 342,
343, 344, 346
Estremadura and the Ribatejo,
153, 175, 180, 196–197
Évora and the Alentejo,
231–232
Porto and the North, 365, 375,
393, 394, 395
Wine House, 394

Y

Yeatman, The ⌶, 380

Z

Zoomarine, 288
Zoos, 69

PHOTO CREDITS

Front cover: Mauricio Abreu / AWL Images [Description: Houses in the historic village of Sintra, Portugal]. 1, Manuela Ferreira I Dreamstime.com. 2, Karola i Marek/Shutterstock. 4, Robertovell I Dreamstime.com. 5 (top), Wessel Cirkel I Dreamstime.com. 5 (bottom), Martin Lehmann I Dreamstime.com. 6 (top left), Dmitriy Yakovlev I Dreamstime.com. 6 (top right), SeanPavonePhoto/iStockphoto. 6 (bottom left), PHB.cz (Richard Semik)/Shutterstock. 6 (bottom right), inacio pires/Shutterstock. 7 (top), Carlos Caetano/Shutterstock. 7 (bottom), Devy I Dreamstime.com. 8 (top left), Gustavo Fernandes I Dreamstime.com. 8 (top right), Studio Barcelona/Shutterstock. 8 (bottom), inacio pires/Shutterstock. **Chapter 1: Experience Portugal:** 13, inacio pires/Shutterstock. 20, Anitasstudio I Dreamstime.com. 21, Paulovilela I Dreamstime.com. **Chapter 2: Lisbon:** 45, Emi Cristea/Shutterstock. **Chapter 3: Lisbon Environs:** 117, Carlos Caetano/Shutterstock. **Chapter 4: Estremadura and the Ribatejo:** 157, inacio pires/Shutterstock. **Chapter 5: Évora and the Alentejo:** 211, Inacio Pires I Dreamstime.com. **Chapter 6: The Algarve:** 263, aniad/Shutterstock. **Chapter 7: Coimbra and the Beiras:** 313, Olga Meffista/Shutterstock. **Chapter 8: Porto and the North:** 359, Mapics/Shutterstock. **Back cover, from left to right:** Myrtilleshop/Shutterstock; StevanZZ/Shutterstock; Carlos Caetano/Shutterstock. Spine: inacio pires/shutterstock.

NOTES

NOTES

NOTES

Fodor's ESSENTIAL PORTUGAL

Design: Tina Malaney, *Associate Art Director*; Erica Cuoco, *Production Designer*

Photography: Jennifer Arnow, *Senior Photo Editor*

Maps: Rebecca Baer, *Senior Map Editor*; Mark Stroud (Moon Street Cartography), David Lindroth, *Cartographers*

Production: Angela L. McLean, *Senior Production Manager*; Jennifer DePrima, *Editorial Production Manager*

Sales: Jacqueline Lebow, *Sales Director*

Business & Operations: Chuck Hoover, *Chief Marketing Officer*; Joy Lai, *Vice President and General Manager*; Stephen Horowitz, *Head of Business Development and Partnerships*

Writers: Lucy Bryson, Lauren Frayer, Liz Humphreys, Benjamin Kemper, Josephine Quintero, Alison Roberts

Editors: Teddy Minford, Jacinta O'Halloran, Douglas Stallings

Production Editor: Jennifer DePrima

1st Edition

ISBN 978-0-1-4754668-5

ISSN 2472–565X

SPECIAL SALES

This book is available at special discounts for bulk purchases for sales promotions or premiums. For more information, e-mail specialmarkets@penguinrandomhouse.com.

PRINTED IN THE UNITED STATES OF AMERICA

10 9 8 7 6 5 4 3 2 1

ABOUT OUR WRITERS

Lucy Bryson is a British freelance writer who moved to Portugal in 2015 after nine years living and working in Rio de Janeiro, Brazil. She has written extensively on Portugal, Brazil, and South America for a wide range of print and online publications, including Fodor's, *USA Today* 10Best, *Vice, Porthole Cruise Magazine,* Matador Network, Horizon Travel Press, and Rough Guides. She lives with her British-Brazilian daughter in a fishing village near Lisbon, where she enjoys the beaches, the seafood restaurants, and long runs in the Serra da Arrabida hills. For this edition she updated the Experience Portugal, Lisbon, and Side Trips from Lisbon chapters.

Lauren Frayer is the Madrid correspondent for NPR and the *Los Angeles Times*. Before moving to Europe, she spent nearly 10 years reporting for the Associated Press based in Washington, Jerusalem, Cairo, and Baghdad. Lauren updated the Évora and the Alentejo chapter.

Liz Humphreys has lived in Europe since 2012, after relocating from New York City, where she spent a decade in editorial positions for media companies including Conde Nast, Time Inc., and *USA Today*. Liz has an advanced certificate in wine studies from WSET (Wine & Spirit Education Trust), and Por is her favorite destination to indu her love of food and wine, whic chronicles on her blog (⊕ *www.wilust.com*). Liz updated the Algarv Travel Smart chapters.

Benjamin Kemper followed the siren song of Ibérico ham from Brooklyn to Madrid, where he writes about the places that make him hungriest. Keep up with his food adventures on Instagram (@Eating-España). Benjamin updated the Porto and the North chapter.

Journalist and travel writer **Josephine Quintero** is from England and has worked in California, the Middle East, and, since 1990, in southern Spain, where she makes frequent trips into neighboring Portugal. Josephine writes for many magazines and travel publications, mainly covering the Iberian peninsula. Josephine updated the Coimbra and the Beiras chapter.

Alison Roberts is a freelance journalist, writer and translator based in Lisbon who has worked for international broadcasters as well as newspapers and magazines. Born in London, she has also lived in Canada, India, and Germany but now spends as much time as possible exploring Portugal. Her interests include travel, languages, and culture. Alison updated the Estremadura and the Ribatejo chapter.